Engineering Graphics
with AutoCAD
Release 13

Second Edition

James D. Bethune
Boston University

Prentice Hall

Upper Saddle River, New Jersey   Columbus, Ohio

To Mom, David, Maria, Randy, and Hannah

Library of Congress Cataloging-in-Publication Data

Bethune, James, D.
  Engineering graphics with AutoCAD release 13 / James D. Bethune. —
 2nd ed
  p. cm.
  Rev. ed. of: Engineering graphics with AutoCAD. c1995
   Includes index.
   ISBN 0-13-567892-7
   1. Engineering graphics. 2. AutoCAD (Computer file) I. Bethune,
 James D., 1941- Engineering graphics with AutoCAD. II Title.
 T357.B48 1997   96-22491
 604.2'0285'5369—dc20   CIP

Editor: Stephen Helba
Production Editor: Patricia S. Kelly
Design Coordinator: Jill E. Bonar
Cover Designer: Brian Deep
Production Manager: Pamela D. Bennett
Marketing Manager: Danny Hoyt
Illustrations: James D. Bethune

This book was set in Times and Helvetica by James D. Bethune and
was printed and bound by Von Hoffmann Press, Inc. The cover was
printed by Von Hoffmann Press, Inc.

© 1997 by Prentice-Hall, Inc.
Simon & Schuster/A Viacom Company
Upper Saddle River, New Jersey 07458

Earlier edition, entitled Engineering Graphics with AutoCAD, þ
1995 by Prentice-Hall.

Printed in the United States of America

10 9 8 7 6 5 4 3 2 1

ISBN: 0-13-567892-7

Prentice-Hall International (UK) Limited, London
Prentice-Hall of Australia Pty. Limited, Sydney
Prentice-Hall of Canada, Inc., Toronto
Prentice-Hall Hispanoamericana, S. A., Mexico
Prentice-Hall of India Private Limited, New Delhi
Prentice-Hall of Japan, Inc., Tokyo
Simon & Schuster Asia Pte. Ltd., Singapore
Editora Prentice-Hall do Brasil, Ltda., Rio de Janeiro

Preface

This book is a revision of Engineering Graphics with AutoCAD Release 12, for Release 13. There are three important changes in the revision. The errors, unfortunately associated with many first editions, have been corrected. Many of the line type drawings have been replaced by "screen captures". Screen captures are illustrations generated by capturing the actual AutoCAD screen electronically, and then reproducing it as an illustration. There are approximately 200 more illustrations in this revision than were in the first edition.

The third significant change deals with the design aspects of the book. Most of the chapters include both sample design problems, as well as design exercise problems. These problems are located at the end of the chapters. Design problems start with simple shape revisions and advance to open ended problems that have many possible solutions.

The book was written to include both WINDOWS and DOS versions. Great care was taken to write so that a reader with either version could easily follow the text. All appropriate dialog boxes are shown as screen captures, so the reader will see an illustration that will look exactly like the AutoCAD screen.

This book teaches technical drawing and uses AutoCAD as its drawing instrument. It follows the general format of many technical drawing texts and presents much of the same material about drawing conventions and prac-

tices, with emphasis on creating accurate, clear drawings. For example, the book shows how to locate dimensions on a drawing so that they completely define the object in accordance with current national standards, but the presentation centers on the DIMENSIONING command and its associated commands and parameters. The standards are presented and their applications are shown using AutoCAD. This integrated teaching concept is followed throughout the book.

Chapters 1 through 3 cover AutoCAD's DRAW and EDIT commands. Descriptions of both DOS and Windows versions are included. The text starts with simple LINE commands and proceeds through geometric constructions. The last section of Chapter 3 describes how to bisect a line, and how to draw a hyperbola, a parabola, a helix, and an ogee curve. These constructions are included in most on-the-board technical drawing books because they help the students develop accuracy and an understanding of how to use their equipment. The same type of learning experience also occurs when the constructions are done using AutoCAD. Redrawing many of the classic geometric shapes will help students learn how to use the DRAW and EDIT commands, along with other associated commands, with accuracy and creativity.

Chapter 4 presents freehand sketching. Simply stated, there is still an important place for sketching in technical drawing. Many design ideas start as freehand sketches and then are developed on the computer.

Chapter 5 presents orthographic views. Students are shown how to draw three views of an object using AutoCAD. The discussion includes projection theory, hidden lines, compound lines, oblique surfaces, rounded surfaces, holes, irregular surfaces, castings, and thin-walled objects. The chapter ends with several intersection problems. These problems serve as a good way to pull together orthographic views and projection theory.

Chapter 6 presents sectional views and introduces the HATCH command. The chapter includes multiple, broken-out, partial sectional views and how to draw an S-break for a hollow cylinder.

Chapter 7 covers auxiliary views and shows how to use the SNAP, ROTATE commands to create axes aligned with slanted surfaces. Secondary auxiliary views are also discussed. The Advanced Model Extension, as well as other solid modeler packages, greatly simplifies how to determine the true shape of a line or plane, but a few examples of secondary auxiliary views help the students refine their understanding of orthographic views and eventually the application of UCSs.

Chapter 8 shows how to dimension both two-dimensional shapes and orthographic views. The DIM command and its associated commands are demonstrated including the EDIT MTEXT options The commands are presented as needed to create required dimensions. The conventions demonstrated are in compliance with ANSI Y32.

Chapter 9 introduces tolerances. First, the chapter shows how to draw dimensions and tolerances using the DIMENSIONING and TOLERANCE commands, among others. The chapter ends with an explanation of fits and shows how to use the tables included in the appendix to determine the maximum and minimum tolerances for matching holes and shafts.

Chapter 10 discusses the meaning of geometric tolerances and explains how Release 13 can be used to create geometric tolerance symbols directly from dialog boxes. This is a new AutoCAD feature. Both profile and positional tolerances are explained. The overall intent of the chapter is to teach students how to make parts fit together. Fixed and floating fastener applications are discussed and design examples are given for both conditions.

Chapter 11 covers how to draw and design using standard fasteners, including bolts, nuts, machine screws, washers, hexagon heads, square heads, set screws, rivets, and springs. Students are shown how to create WBLOCKS of the individual thread representations and how to use them for different size requirements.

Chapter 12 discusses assembly drawings, detail drawings, and parts lists. Instructions for drawing title blocks, tolerance blocks, release blocks, and revision blocks, and drawing notes are also included to give stu-

dents better preparation for industrial practices.

Chapter 13 presents gears, cams, and bearings. The intent of the chapter is to teach how to design based on gears selected from a manufacturer's catalog. The chapter shows how to select bearings to support gear shafts and how to tolerance holes in support plates to maintain the desired center distances of meshing gears. The chapter also shows how to create a displacement diagram and then draw the appropriate cam profile.

Chapter 14 introduces AutoCAD's 3D capabilities. This chapter is intended to teach students about AutoCAD's 3D commands and coordinate system definition before introducing surface and solid models. Both WCS and UCS are explained and demonstrated along with SETTINGS and VIEW commands. 3D primitives are introduced and used to create simple shapes. The chapter concludes by showing how to create orthographic views from the drawn 3D shapes.

Chapter 15 continues the discussions of Chapter 14 to cover surface modeling. The basic geometric shapes of the 3D SURFCAES command are presented as well as the REVSURF, TABSURF, RULESURF, 3D FACE, and MESH commands. All the surface commands are demonstrated and used to create 3D shapes.

Chapter 16 introduces solid modeling. Solid PRIMITIVES are demonstrated and used with the SOLUNION and SOLSUB commands to create 3D shapes. Orthographic views are then created from the solid shapes. More complex shapes are created using the SOLEXT command 3D edit commands, such as SOLCHAM and SOLMOVE. The chapter concludes with several sample problems that demonstrate a solid modeling approach to intersection problems as originally introduced at the end of Chapter 5. The chapter also demostrates the LIST and MASSPROP commands.

Chapter 17 presents a solid modeling approach to Descriptive Geometry. For example, a plane is drawn as a solid that is 0.00001 thick. AutoCAD's solid modeling and other commands can then be used to manipulate the plane. The true lengths of lines and shapes of planes, point and plane locations, and properties between lines and planes are discussed. Piercing points and line visibility are also covered.

Thanks to Steve Helba, a great editor; Marianne L'Abbate, the copyeditor who again polished a rough manuscript into an acceptable form; Patty Kelly, the production editor who pulled it all together; and Mom, David, Maria, Randy, and Hannah for their continued support.

James D. Bethune
Boston University
Boston, Massachusetts

Contents

Chapter 10 — Geometric Tolerances 411

Chapter 11 — Threads and Fasteners 453

Chapter 12 — Working Drawings 489

Chapter 13 — Gears, Bearings, and Cams 521

Chapter 14 — Fundamentals of 3D Drawing 555

Chapter 15 — Surface Modeling 583

Chapter 16 — Solid Modeling 625

Chapter 17 — Descriptive Geometry 685

Appendix 725

Getting Started

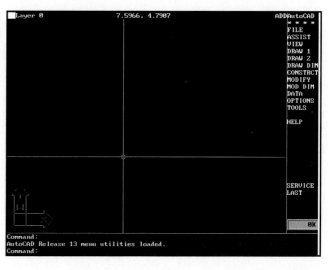

WINDOWS SCREEN

DOS SCREEN

Pull down menu headings

Drawing file name

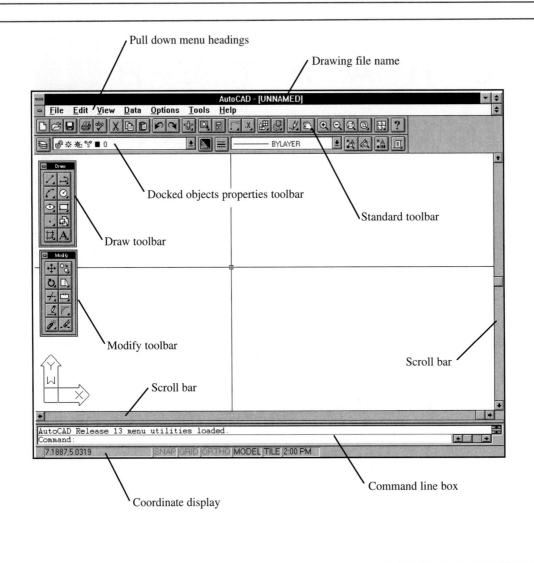

Docked objects properties toolbar

Standard toolbar

Draw toolbar

Modify toolbar

Scroll bar

Scroll bar

Command line box

Coordinate display

Figure 1-1

1-1 INTRODUCTION

This chapter explains and demonstrates some AutoCAD fundamentals needed to start a drawing. The first sections of the chapter present an introduction to the Windows version, followed by an introduction to the DOS version. The commands NEW, SAVE, SAVE AS, UNITS, LIMITS, GRID, and SNAP are used to help set up and save a new drawing file. The chapter ends by introducing the ERASE, UNDO, REDO, ZOOM, and REDRAW commands and shows how they are applied using sample problems.

1-2 INTRODUCTION — WINDOWS

This section explains the various aspects of AutoCAD's Windows drawing screen and shows how they can be manipulated. Figure 1-1 shows the initial AutoCAD windows screen. Your screen may look slightly different because of your selected screen resolution values.

The topmost line on the screen

AutoCAD-[UNNAMED]

displays the name of the current drawing. Because no drawing has been named, the line reads "unnamed". Once a drawing name has been defined, it will appear at the top of the screen.

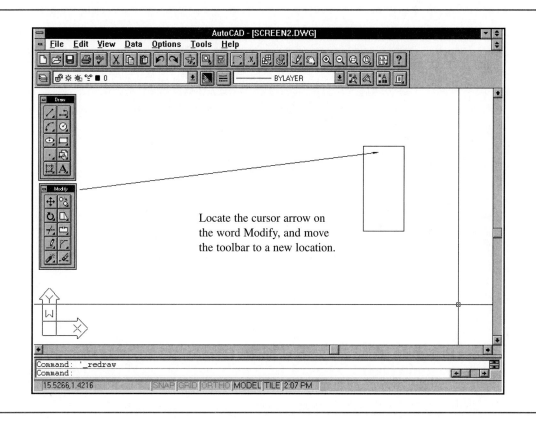

Figure 1-2

The top line also displays the standard window's icons for exiting a program and changing a program. It is assumed that the reader is familiar with basic Window operations.

The second line from the top is the standard toolbar and contains a group of the most commonly used commands.

The third line contains some command icons and an area that shows the current or docked object properties that are active.

The bottom left corner of the screen shows the coordinate display position of the horizontal and vertical crosshairs in terms of an x,y coordinate value, whose origin is the lower left corner of the drawing screen.

The commands listed on the bottom line are displayed in light gray when they are off and black when they are on.

The horizontal and vertical scroll bars can be used to move around the drawing screen and function as they do with other Windows applications.

The large open area in the center of the screen is called the drawing screen or drawing editor.

The two rectangular boxes, located along the left edge of the drawing screen contain command icons and are the Draw and Modify toolbars.

1-3 TOOLBARS

An AutoCAD toolbar is a group of command icons located under a common heading. The initial AutoCAD screen contains three toolbars; the Standard, Draw, and Modify. There are 13 additional predefined toolbars, and you can create your own user specific toolbars as needed.

To move a toolbar

See Figure 1-2.

1. Locate the cursor arrow on the heading Modify.
2. Press and hold down the left mouse button.

A light gray broken line box will appear around the edge of the toolbox.

3. Still holding the left mouse button down, move the gray outline box to a new location on the screen.

4. Release the left button.

The toolbox will apppear in the new location.

To change the shape of a toolbar.

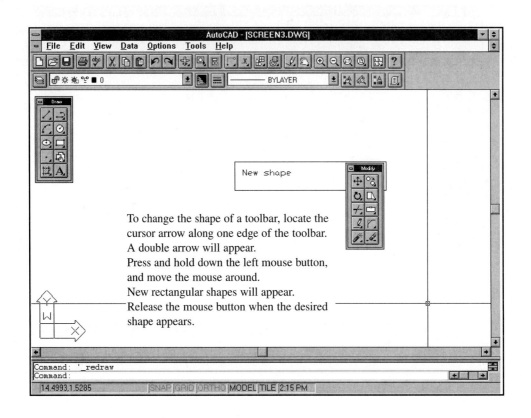

Figure 1-3

See Figure 1-3.

1. Locate the cursor arrow along the right edge of the Modify toolbox.

A double opposing arrowhead will appear.

2. Press and hold the left mouse button.

A light gray broken line box will appear around the outside of the toolbox.

3. Still holding the left mouse button down, move the mouse around and watch how the gray box changes shape.

4. When the gray toolbox shape is a long vertical rectangle, release the left mouse button.

A newly shaped toolbox will appear.

To return the toolbar to its original location and shape.

1. Locate the cursor arrow along the bottom or edge lines of the toolbox and return the toolbox to its

original shape using the procedure outlined in Figure 1-3.

2. Move the reshaped toolbox back to its original location along the left side of the drawing screen using the procedure outlined in Figure 1-2.

To add a new toolbar to the screen.

See Figures 1-4 and 1-5.

1. Locate the cursor arrow on the Tools pulldown menu heading and press the left mouse button.

2. Select (locate the cursor arrow on the word Toolbar and press the left mouse button) the item Toolbars.

A second pulldown will appear. This is a list of available toolbars. See Figure 1-4.

3. Select Dimensioning.

The Dimensioning toolbar will appear. See Figure 1-5. Any toolbar can be moved or have its shape changed as described in Figures 1-2 and 1-3.

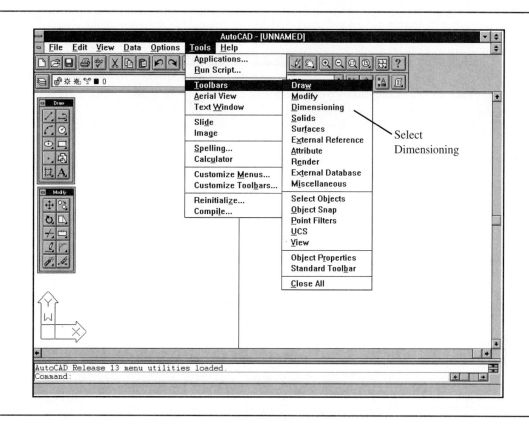

Figure 1-4

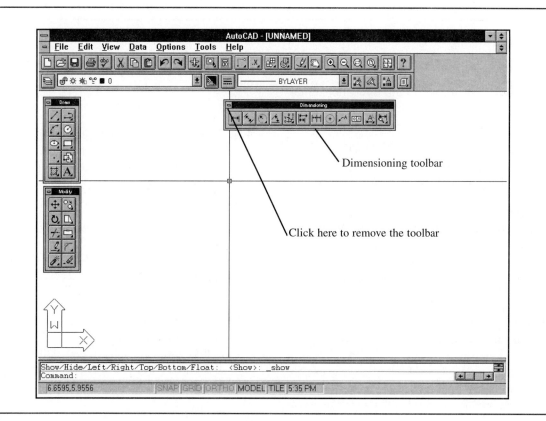

Figure 1-5

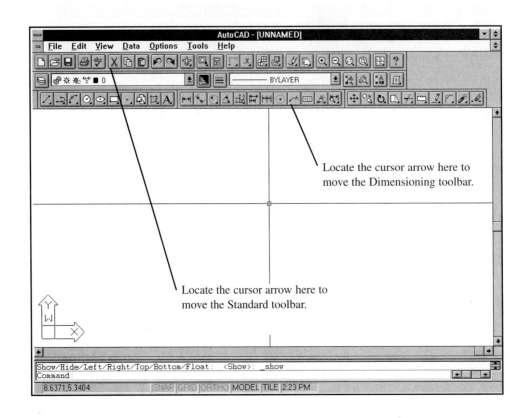

Locate the cursor arrow here to move the Dimensioning toolbar.

Locate the cursor arrow here to move the Standard toolbar.

Figure 1-6

To remove a toolbar from the screen

1. Locate the cursor arrow on the short horizontal line, located in the upper right corner of the toolbar, and press the left mouse button.

Figure 1-6 shows the Draw and Modify toolbars docked horizontally at the top of the drawing screen. The Dimensions toolbar has been located between them. To relocate the toolbars from the positions shown, locate the cursor arrow above the icons but still below the horizontal line that defines the toolbar area, and press and hold down the left mouse button. A gray box will appear around the toolbars that will move with the cursor arrow.

Note:

The standard toolbar may be moved and reshaped using the same procedure described above to undock the Draw and Modify toolbars.

Figure 1-7 shows the Draw, Modify, and Dimension toolbars docked on the right side of the drawing screen. Note that the toolbars are arranged with three columns of icons and not two columns as they were on the initail screen.

1-4 THE COMMAND LINE BOX

The size of the command window, located at the bottom of the screen, may be changed to display more or fewer command lines. It is recommend that at least two command lines be visible at all times.

To move and resize the Command line box

See Figure 1-8.

1. Locate the cursor arrow along the far left edge of the command line box and press and hold down the left mouse button.
2. Still holding the left mouse button down, move the cursor arrow to a new location on the drawing screen.

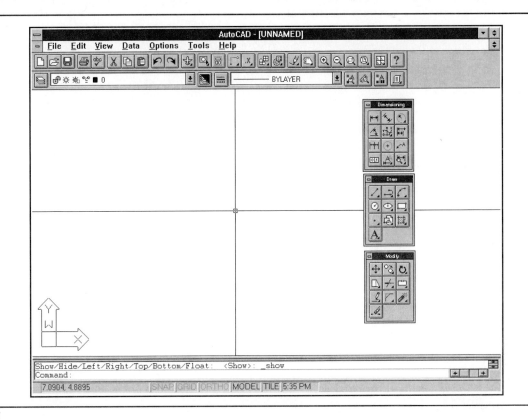

Figure 1-7

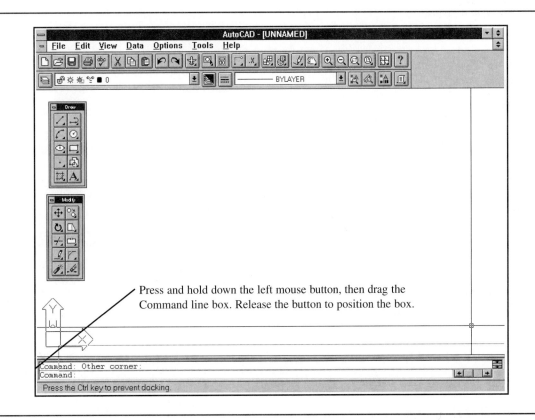

Press and hold down the left mouse button, then drag the
Command line box. Release the button to position the box.

Figure 1-8

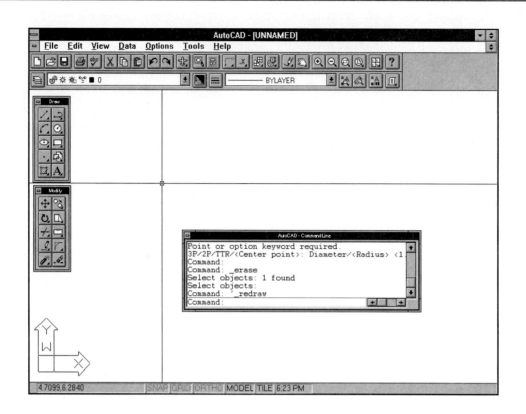

Figure 1-9

A gray, broken line box moves with the cursor arrow and serves to display the new command line box location and shape.

3. Release the left mouse button to relocate the Command line box.

The Command line box may now be moved and reshaped just as a toolbar is moved. Figure 1-9 shows the Command line box shortened and moved to the right side of the drawing screen.

1-5 COMMAND ICONS

An icon is a picture that represents an AutoCAD command. Most commands have equivalent icons.

To determine the command an icon represents

See Figure 1-10.

1. Locate the cursor arrow on the selected icon.

In the example shown, the CIRCLE CENTER RADIUS command icon within the Draw toolbar was selected.

2. Hold the arrow still without pressing any mouse button.

The icon command name will appear below the icon. A small solid right triangle in the lower right corner of an icon means that there are other related icons under the icons shown.

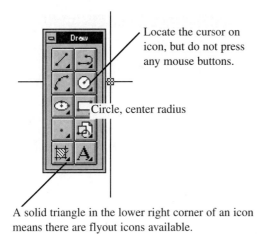

Locate the cursor on icon, but do not press any mouse buttons.

Circle, center radius

A solid triangle in the lower right corner of an icon means there are flyout icons available.

Figure 1-10

Toolbar flyout icons

Figure 1-11

To activate and select an icon's subcommands (flyouts)

See Figures 1-11, 1-12, and 1-13.

1. Locate the cursor arrow on an icon and press and hold down the left mouse button.

Additional icons will fly out. See Figure 1-11. In the example shown, the CIRCLE CENTER RADIUS command icon within the Draw toolbar was selected. Figure 1-12 shows the ARC command flyout icons.

2. Still holding the left button down, move the cursor arrow to the desired icon (DONUT) and release the button.

The new command will be activated and the selected icon will replace the previous icon in the toolbar. In the example shown, the DONUT command was selected and replaced the original circle icon. See Figure 1-13.

The CIRCLE CENTER RADIUS icon can be returned to the Draw toolbar by using the same procedure.

ARC flyout icons

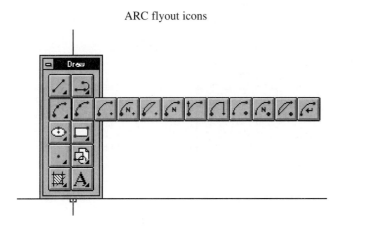

Figure 1-12

DONUT icon replaced CIRCLE, Center, Radius icon.

Figure 1-13

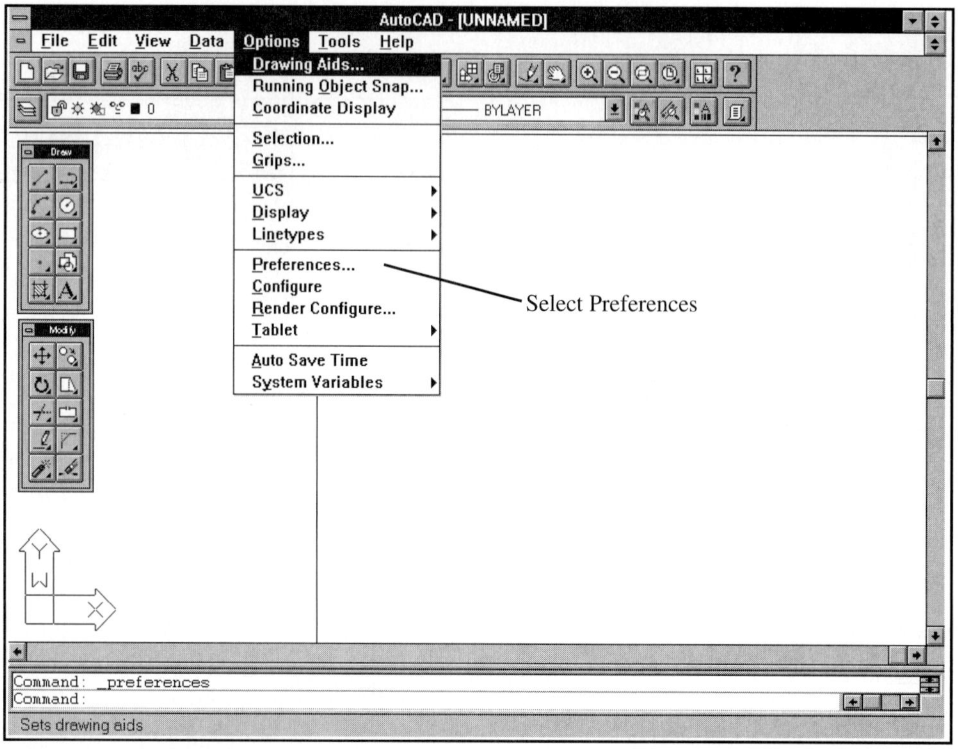

Figure 1-14

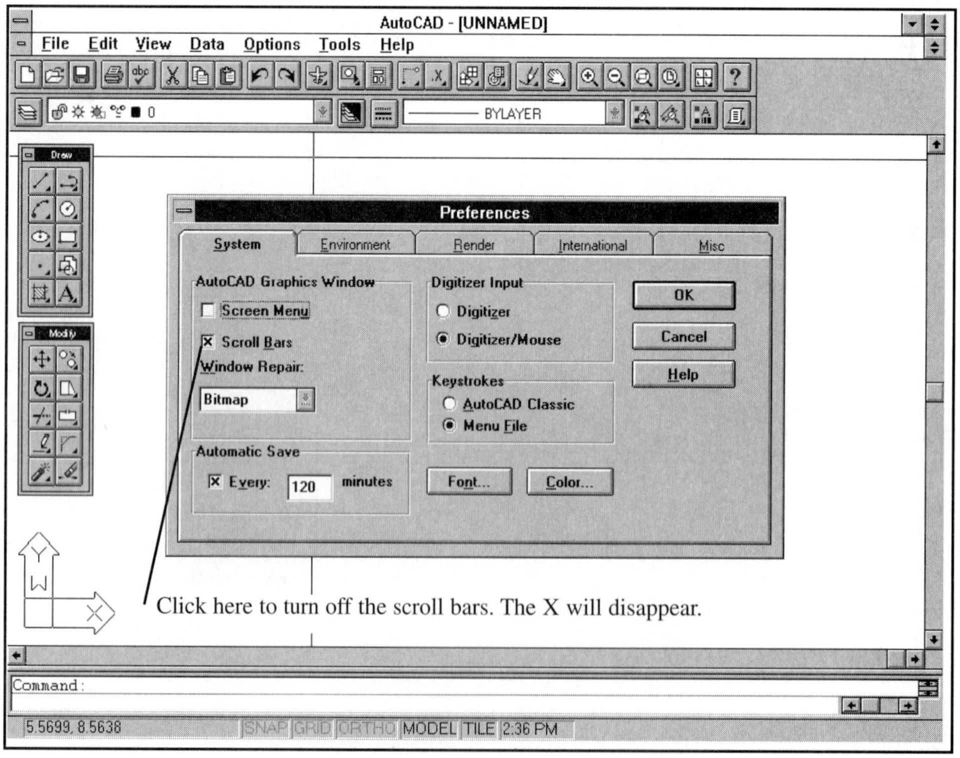

Figure 1-15

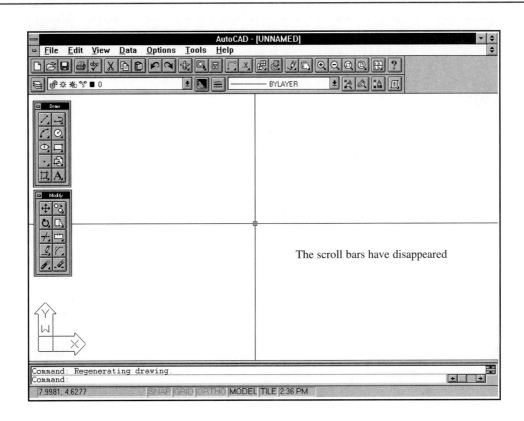

The scroll bars have disappeared

Figure 1-16

1-6 SCROLL BARS

The horizontal and vertical scroll bars can be removed from the screen. See Figures 1-14, 1-15, and 1-16.

1. Select the Options pulldown menu.
2. Select Toolbars.

See Figure 1-14. The Preferences dialog box will appear. See Figure 1-15.

AutoCAD's dialog boxes are visual listings of parameters associated with a certain function. In this example, the scroll bar prefence box is located on the left side of the dialog box. The black X within the box indicates that the preference is on.

3. Locate the cursor arrow within the box to the left of the word Scroll, and press the left mouse button.

The X will disapear, indicating the function is turned off.

4. Select the OK box.

The Preference dialog box will disappear, and the screen will appear without the scroll bars. See Figure 1-16.

1-7 SCREEN MENUS

If you are used to working with AutoCAD's DOS versions or are just not comfortable with the command icons, you can activate screen menus. You may then select commands from the menu rather than use the icons.

To activate the screen menus

1. Select the Options pulldown mene; then select Preferences.

See Figure 1-14. The Preferences dialog box will appear.

2. Click the box to the left of the words Screen Menu

An X will appear in the box, meaning that the screen menus are on. See Figure 1-17. In this example, the scroll bars were left on.

3. Select OK.

The drawing screen will appear with screen menus on the right side of the drawing screen. See Figure 1-18.

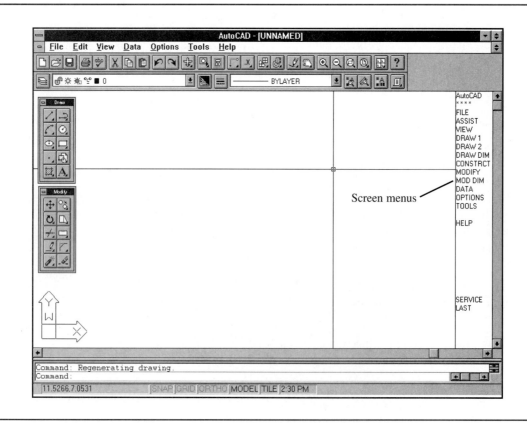

Figure 1-17

Figure 1-18

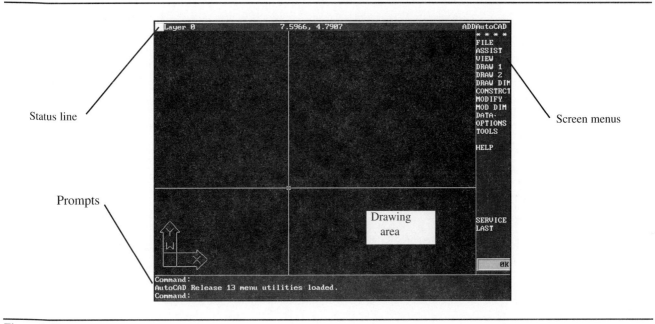

Status line

Screen menus

Prompts

Drawing
area

Figure 1-19

1-8 INTRODUCTION — DOS

Figure 1-19 shows an empty drawing screen for the DOS version. It should be the first screen that appears after you activate AutoCAD Release 13 DOS version. The screen has four regions; menus, prompts, drawing area, and status line. Commands are listed in alphabetical order in the menu region. Information needed to complete the commands is specified in the prompts region.

AutoCAD has pulldown command menus that are activated by moving the cursor crosshairs into the status line region. See Figure 1-20. Pulldown menus contain the com-

mands most often used and allow for slightly faster access to the commands and dialog boxes than does access through the menu region. A triangular arrowhead next to a command in a pulldown menu means there is a submenu for that command. Figure 1-21 on page 14 shows the CIR-CLE submenu.

Commands may be accessed in one of three ways: from the menus or icon box, from the pulldown menus, or by typing the name of the command in response to a Command: prompt.

Many of AutoCAD's commands are accompanied by a dialog box. Figure 1-22 shows the DRAWING AIDS dialog box. Dialog boxes present a group of related settings

Pulldown menu

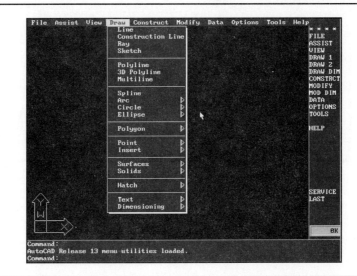

Triangles after a heading means
that there are submenus

Figure 1-20

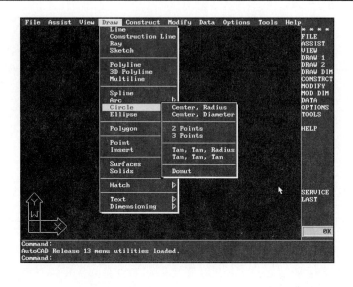

The CIRCLE submenus

Figure 1-21

and can be used to easily change the given settings. To turn a command ON or OFF, select the square next to the command and press the left mouse button. An X will appear in a box that has been activated.

Radio buttons in dialog boxes are used to restrict settings. For example, in Figure 1-22, only a Left, Top, or Right Isometric plane may be active. No two may be activated simultaneously.

An underlined letter in a dialog box means that the command may be activated by typing that letter from the keyboard. The ORTHO command may be activated by typing O.

An X in a box indicates that a function is ON.

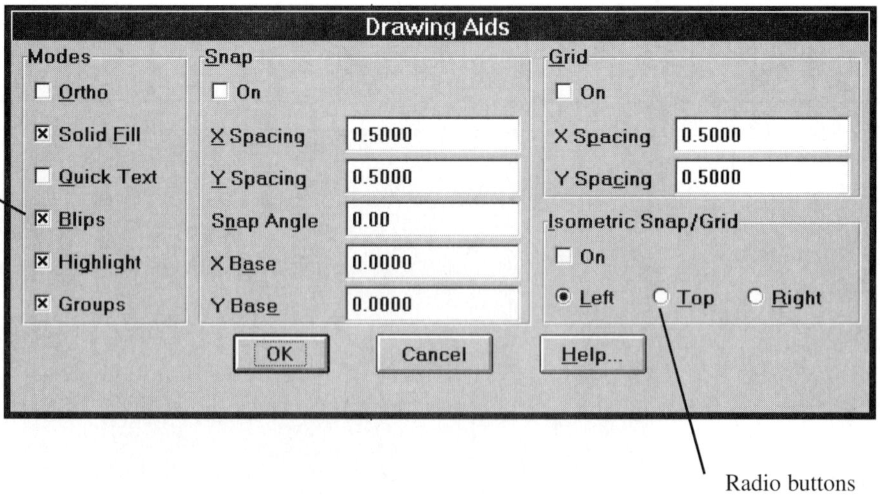

Radio buttons

Figure 1-22

1-9 READING THIS BOOK (NOTATIONS)

The word *select* or *pick* will be used throughout the book to mean selecting either a command word or icon by first moving the crosshairs over the word or icon and then pressing the left mouse button. See Figure 1-23. The right mouse button operates the same as the ENTER key. The middle button, if available, will activate the OSNAP settings commands. OSNAP commands are discussed in Chapter 3.

The term *default* refers to a preassigned value or drawing specification that AutoCAD will use unless another value is entered. Default values are enclosed within greater than and less than symbols (< >) in command prompts. For example, when using the CIRCLE command, the following prompt line will appear.

Command:_circle 3P/2P/TTR/<Center point>:

Center point is the default specification. This means that the next input will be the location of the circle's center point. If the circle location is to be defined by three point locations rather than the default center point location, the 3P response should be entered.

All AutoCAD commands referenced in this book will be presented using all capital letters, even though they may not appear on the screen in only capital letters. The command DRAW is listed in all capital letters on the main menu, but only the D is capitalized in the pulldown menu. Expressing commands in all capital letters will help distin-

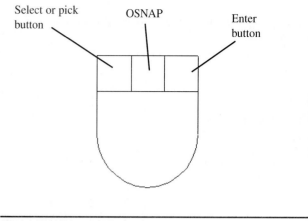

Figure 1-23

guish between commands and prompts or other input information.

1-10 HELP

The HELP command, found in the pulldown menu, will generate the HELP dialog box. See Figure 1-24. The Contents option will generate an index of the available HELP options. The Search option will generate a list of all AutoCAD's commands. If you select HELP for a specific command, a detailed illustrated explanation will appear on the screen.

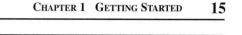

Figure 1-24

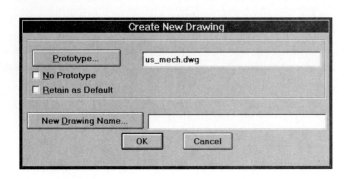

Type name of new drawing here

Figure 1-25

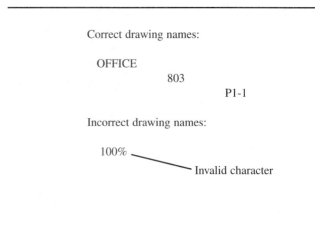

Correct drawing names:

OFFICE

803

P1-1

Incorrect drawing names:

100% ——————

Invalid character

Figure 1-26

1-11 STARTING A DRAWING

Figure 1-1 shows an empty drawing screen. It is in fact an untitled blank drawing. A drawing can be created on the screen, but it cannot be saved until it is titled. It is good practice to name a drawing before you start drawing in order to help prevent accidently losing the drawing.

To name a drawing

DOS:

1A. Select FILE (pulldown)
1B. Select NEW...

WINDOWS:

1. Select the New icon from the Standard Toolbar..

See Figure 1-1. The Create New Drawing dialog box will appear on the screen. See Figure 1-25.

2. Select New Drawing Name... box
3. Type in the drawing name
4. Select the OK box

Drawing names may contain up to eight alphabetical characters or numbers, or the symbols $, -, and _ (under-score). No spaces may be used. It is recommended that drawings from this book be assigned their referenced numbers. Sample Problem one is referenced as SP1-1. This designation could also be used as a drawing name. Figure 1-26 shows some sample drawing names.

AutoCAD automatically assigns a file extension of .dwg. There is no need to enter .dwg when naming the drawing. Other extensions may be used, but AutoCAD is set up to work with the .dwg extension, so it is best to accept the default setting.

A drawing may be saved directly to a floppy disk by specifying the drive letter of the floppy disk. If drawing P1-1 is to be saved on a floppy disk located in the A drive, type A:P1-1 as the drawing name. For further information about saving a drawing, see Section 1-25, SAVE.

1-12 TO OPEN AN EXISTING DRAWING

DOS:

1A. Select File (pulldown)
1B. Select Open...

WINDOWS:

1. Select the OPEN DRAWING icon on the Standard toolbar.

See Figure 1-1. The Select Drawing dialog box will appear. See Figure 1-27.

2. Select the drawing from the Files: list.

The file name should appear in the File: box.

3. Select the OK box

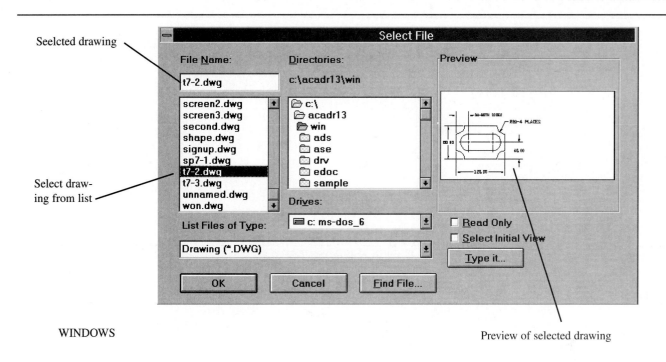

Seelcted drawing

Select drawing from list

WINDOWS

Preview of selected drawing

Figure 1-27

To open a drawing located on a floppy disk in the A: drive

DOS:

1A. Select File (pulldown)
1B. Select Open...
1C. Scroll down the file list and select A:

See Figure 1-28.

WINDOWS:

1A. Select the Open Drawing icon from the Standard toolbar

The Select Drawing dialog box will appear.

1B. Select the arrow on the right of the Drives: box and select the A: drive

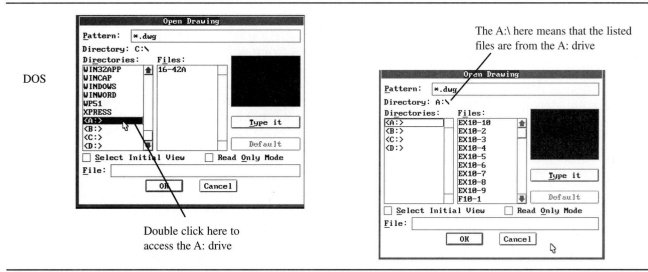

DOS

Double click here to access the A: drive

The A:\ here means that the listed files are from the A: drive

Figure 1-28

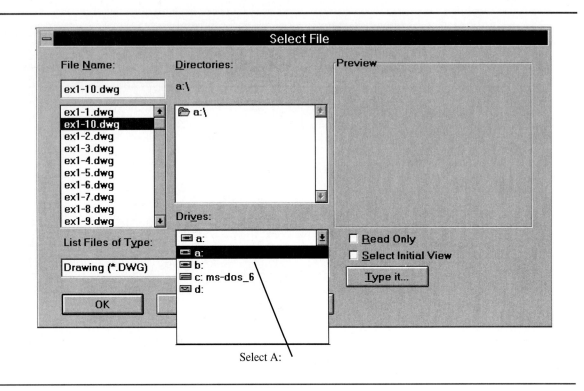

Figure 1-29

See Figure 1-29.

2. Select the drawing from the new File Name or Files list

A preview of the drawing will appear in the Preview box.

3. Select OK

If you forget which file name has been assigned to which drawing, use the Browse/Search option to visually search the file directory.

To browse and search the drawing files

1. Select the Find File... box on the Select files dialog box

The Browse/Search dialog box will appear. See Figure 1-30. Previews of all existing drawings will appear in the preview box. Use the scroll bar located at the bottom of the box to advance the files.

2. Select a drawing by clicking its picture twice

The drawing name will appear in the File Name box.

3. Select the Open box

You can browse different directories by using the Drives: box, or you can browse different drawing file extensions by using the List Files of Type: box.

To search for a file

The search option allows you to be more specific in looking for an existing file. For example, you can specify the date the drawing was created, and the search option will locate and present a preview of all drawings created on that date. Note in Figure 1-30 the words "Browse" and "Search" are located on what appears to be the tabs of file folders. This means that there two different dialog boxes within the dialog box.

1. Locate the cursor on the heading Search on what looks like a file folder tab near the top of the Browse/Search dialog box.
2. Define the type of search to be performed.
3. Select the Open box, or select the Browse heading to return to the Browse option box.

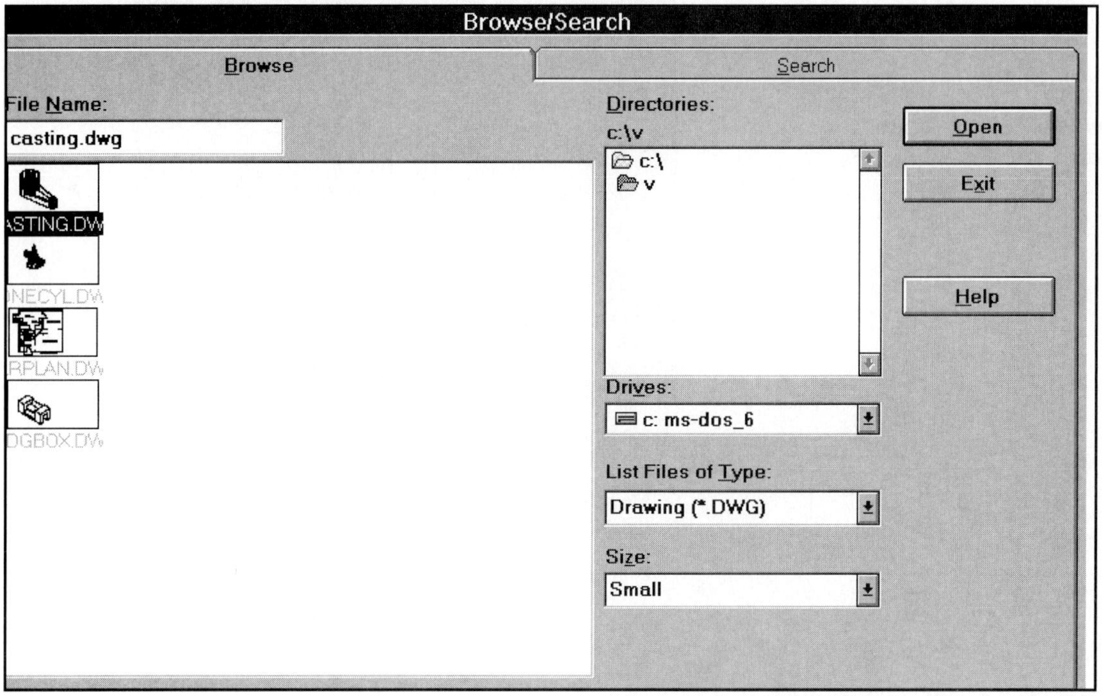

Figure 1-30

1-13 UNITS

AutoCAD is capable of working in any one of five different units as listed in the Units Control dialog box. See Figure 1-31.

To access the Units Control dialog box

1. Select DATA (pull down)

2. Select Units...

The Unit Control dialog box will appear. See Figure 1-30. Decimal Units are the default setting. Decimal Units may be used for either inch or millimeter values. Most technical drawings use Decimal Degrees, which is the default value. Four other angular units are available.

The Precision box of the Units Control dialog box is used to set the number of decimal places to the right of the decimal point when using decimal units. The default value is four places, or 0.0000.

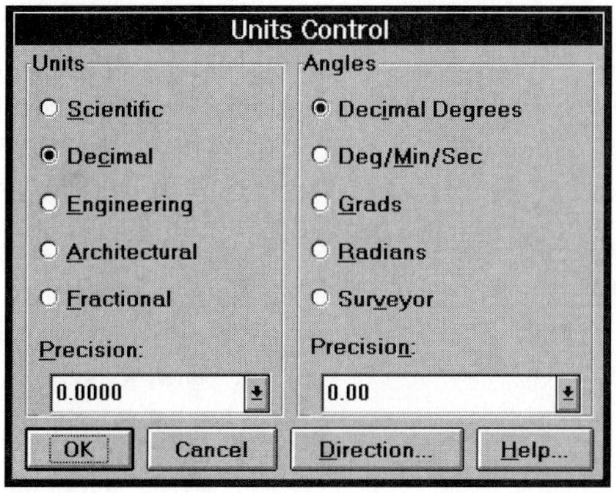

Figure 1-31

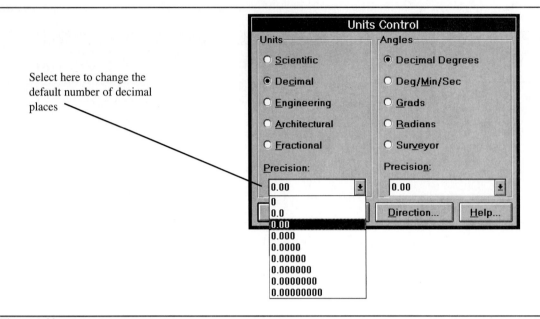

Select here to change the default number of decimal places

Figure 1-32

To change the number of decimal places to two

1. Select the Precision box on the Units Control dialog box
2. Select 0.00

   See Figure 1-32.

3. Select OK

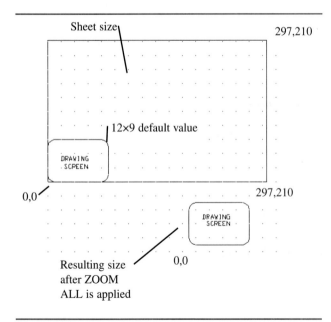

Sheet size

297,210

12×9 default value

DRAWING SCREEN

0,0

297,210

DRAWING SCREEN

0,0

Resulting size after ZOOM ALL is applied

Figure 1-33

1-14 LIMITS

The LIMITS command is used to set the size of the drawing boundaries. The ZOOM command is then used to fit the drawing boundaries within the viewing screen. To help understand this concept, consider two pieces of drawing paper: one that measures 12″ × 9″ and another that measures 297mm × 210mm. These two sheets are approximately the same size, but their unit values are very different. The 12 × 9 limits are the default values, meaning the screen size will automatically be calibrated to these values. If the limits are set to 297 × 210, there will be no visual change on the drawing screen. AutoCAD has interpreted these values based on the current limits of 12 × 9. The 297 × 210 boundaries are far beyond the edges of the viewing screen. See Figure 1-33.

The ZOOM ALL command is then applied and acts to fit whatever boundaries have been defined to the screen size. The default settings fit a distance of 12 units to the width of the screen. After the new limits are entered and ZOOM ALL has been applied, the distance across the screen is 297 units. A horizontal line 6 units long would appear half the distance across the screen if the screen limits were 9 × 12, but would appear only about 2% of the distance across a screen set with 297 × 210 limits.

Drawings limits should always be set to match standard drawing sheet sizes. Using standard drawing sheet sizes helps ensure that the drawing will always match standard printer and plotter paper sizes. When setting the LIMITS for standard sheet sizes, the longest dimension is usually defined as the X value. Figure 1-34 lists standard drawing sheet sizes (drawing limits) for both inches and millimeters. First estimate the approximate size of your drawing and then choose a drawing sheet size that will accept the drawing. Set the screen drawing LIMITS to match the drawing sheet size.

The default values of 12 × 9 are acceptable for most of the drawings with inch units in the first three chapters of this book. Limits of 297 × 210 are acceptable for most of the drawings that use millimeter units.

To create a sheet size (A4) for a drawing using millimeters

1. Select DATA (pulldown)
2. Select Drawing Limits

Reset Model space limits:
ON/OFF/...,0.0000:

3. Type ENTER

Upper right limit:

4. Type 297,210 ENTER
5. Select VIEW (pulldown)
6. Select ZOOM or Zoom All icon
7. Select ZOOM ALL

To verify that the new drawing limits are in place, move the cursor around the screen and watch the scrolling cursor coordinate values change. Near the upper right corner of the drawing, they should read approximately 297,210.

If larger drawing sheet sizes are necessary, the following procedure may be used.

To create a B (11 × 17) size drawing sheet

1. Select DATA (pulldown)
2. Select Drawing Limits

Respond to the prompts as follows.

Reset Model space limits:
ON/OFF<Lower left corner><0.0000,0.0000>:

3. Type ENTER

This accepts the 0,0 default value and assigns the lower left corner of the drawing screen as the 0,0 value.

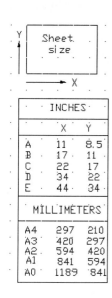

INCHES		
	X	Y
A	11	8.5
B	17	11
C	22	17
D	34	22
E	44	34

MILLIMETERS		
A4	297	210
A3	420	297
A2	594	420
A1	841	594
A0	1189	841

Figure 1-34

Upper right corner <12.0000,9.0000>:

4. Type 17,11 ENTER

These values redefine the upper right corner of the drawing sheet, creating a drawing sheet that is 17 in the horizontal direction and 11 in the vertical direction. Any sheet size values can be entered.

5. Select VIEW (pulldown)
6. Select ZOOM or the Zoom All icon
7. Select ZOOM ALL

1-15 GRID

The GRID command creates a dotted grid background on the drawing screen. See Figure 1-35. It is analogous to the gridded board covers used when creating pencil drawings. Grids serve as visual references when creating drawings and are helpful in judging a drawing's proportional values.

To create a grid with dot spacing equal to 0.5

1. Select Options (pulldown)
2. Select DRAWING AIDS...

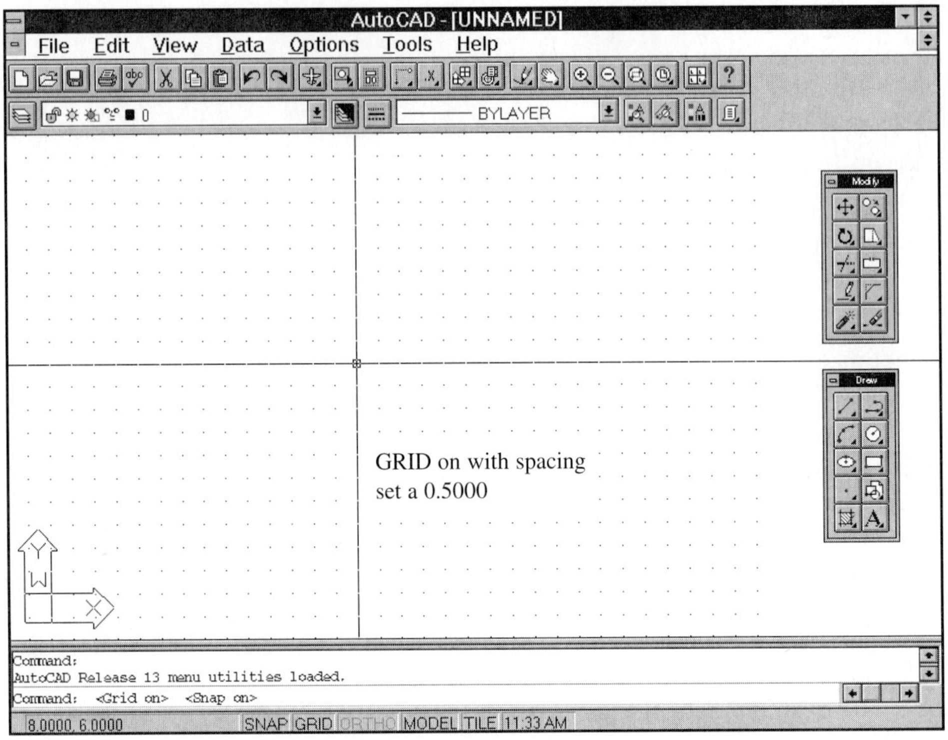

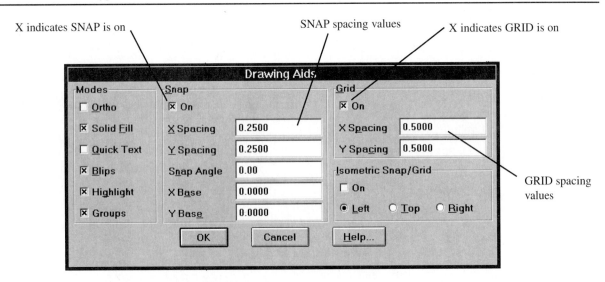

Figure 1-35

The Drawing Aids box will appear on the screen. See Figure 1-36.

3. Select the GRID ON box.
4. Select the X-Spacing box.

Place the cursor to the right of 0.0000, backspace out the current value, and then type in the new value (0.5000).

5. Type ENTER

This will make the Y Spacing equal to the X Spacing.

6. Select the OK box.

X indicates SNAP is on

SNAP spacing values

X indicates GRID is on

GRID spacing values

Figure 1-36

1-16 SNAP

The SNAP command limits the crosshairs to a specific spacing on the drawing screen. The SNAP spacing is usually made equal to or a fractional part of the GRID spacing. If both GRID and SNAP are set to 0.5000, then the crosshairs will move only from grid dot to grid dot. If the GRID spacing is set to 0.5000 and the SNAP spacing is set at 0.2500, then the crosshairs will move from a grid dot to a location halfway between it an another dot.

To set a SNAP spacing of 0.2500

1. Select Options (pulldown)
2. Select DRAWING AIDS...

The Drawing Aids box will appear on the screen. See Figure 1-36.

3. Select the SNAP ON box
4. Select the X-Spacing box

Locate the cursor to the right of the 1.0000, backspace out the current value, and type in the new value.

5. Type ENTER

This will make the Y Spacing equal to the X Spacing.

6. Select the OK box.

1-17 TOGGLE KEYS

AutoCAD uses many of the F keys on the keyboard as toggle switches, that is, to turn functions on and off. See Figure 1-37. The background GRID is toggled using the F7 key, the SNAP using F9, and the cursor status reading at the top of the screen using F6. Other toggle references are also shown.

The F1 key toggles between the drawing screen and the text screen. It is sometimes helpful to refer to the text screen to check on input values. Many of the help and status outputs are shown on the screen using the text screen. To return from the text screen to the drawing screen, press the F1 key when the Command: prompt appears.

1-18 LINE COMMAND

There are four ways to draw straight lines using AutoCAD: randomly select the line's endpoint using the select button, select grid points by aligning the SNAP spacing with the GRID spacing, enter the coordinate values of the start and end points of the line, or enter the line's starting point and use polar coordinates to define the length and angle of the line. The LINE command can also be used to draw construction and ray lines. The LINE command will be discussed further in Chapter 2.

How AutoCAD uses the F keys on the keyboard

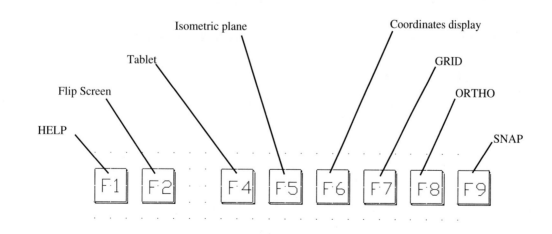

Figure 1-37

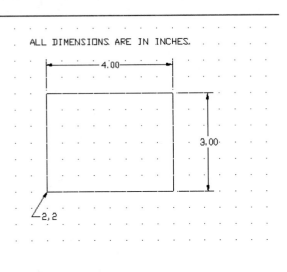

ALL DIMENSIONS ARE IN INCHES.

Figure 1-38

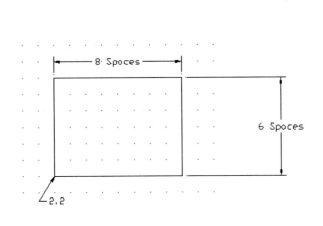

Figure 1-39

The following three examples demonstrate three different techniques for drawing the rectangle show in Figure 1-38.

To draw lines using GRID and SNAP

See Figure 1-39.

1. Select DATA (pulldown)
2. Select DRAWING AIDS...
3. Select the GRID ON box
4. Select the X Spacing box

Locate the cursor to the right of 0.0000 and backspace out the current value.

5. Type in 0.5000
6. Type ENTER
7. Select the SNAP ON box
8. Select the X Spacing box

Locate the cursor to the right of 1.0000 and backspace out the current value.

9. Type in 0.5000
10. Type ENTER
11. Select the OK box

DOS

12A. Select DRAW (pulldown)
12B. Select LINE
12C. Select Segments

WINDOWS

12. Select the LINE icon from the Draw toolbar

Follow the Command prompts as follows.

Command:_line From point:

Make sure the cursor coordinate values at the top of the screen are toggled ON (F6). Move the crosshairs until the coordinate values read 2.0000,2.0000.

13. Select the point 2.0000,2.0000

Move the crosshairs to the right 8 spaces, or 4 inches. The coordinate values should read 6.0000,2.0000.

To point:

14. Select point 6.0000,2.0000

To point:

15. Select point 6.0000,5.0000

To point:

16. Select point 2.0000,5.0000

To point:

17. Select CLOSE or type C in response to a Command prompt

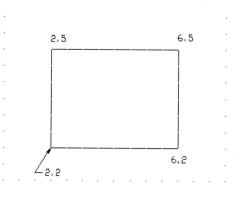

Figure 1-40

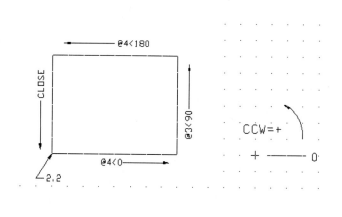

Figure 1-41

The CLOSE command (located on the menu list) connects the last point drawn to the first point drawn.

To draw lines using coordinate values

See Figure 1-40.

DOS

1A. Select DRAW (pulldown)
1B. Select LINE
1C. Select SEGMENTS

WINDOWS

1. Select the LINE icon from the Draw toolbar

Respond to the prompts as follows.

Command:_line From point:

2. Type 2,2 ENTER

To point:

3. Type 6,2 ENTER

To point:

4. Type 6,5 ENTER

To point:

5. Type 2,5 ENTER

To point:

6. Type C ENTER

Polar coordinates draw lines by specifying a distance and an angle. A horizontal line to the right is defined as 0 degrees, and counterclockwise is the positive direction. Negative values can be entered for both distances and angles. The @ symbol (shift 2) is used to tell AutoCAD that the next input is in terms of polar coordinates.

To draw lines using polar coordinate values

See Figure 1-41.

DOS

1A. Select DRAW (pulldown)
1B. Select LINE
1C. Select SEGMENTS

WINDOWS

1. Select the LINE icon from the Draw toolbar

Respond to the prompts as follows.

Command:_line From point: 2,2 ENTER
To point:

2. Type @4<0 ENTER

To point:

3. Type @3<90 ENTER

To point:

4. Type @4<180 ENTER

To point:

5. Type C ENTER

1-19 SAMPLE PROBLEM SP1-1

Figure 1-42 shows a dimensioned object. All dimensions are in inches. Redraw the object first using the coordinate point values and using polar coordinate values.

To draw Figure 1-42 using coordinate values

See Figure 1-43. All dimensions are in inches, so the default values for LIMITS and Decimal Units are acceptable. Set up a GRID and SNAP if desired.

Create a NEW drawing—SP1-1a

1. Select the LINE command

A starting point of 3,2 was arbitrarily chosen. Use the given dimension to determine the coordinate values of each corner point. The horizontal line to the right of the starting point is 4.00 inches long. This means that the X value of the line's endpoint is 4 units greater than the starting point's, or 3 + 4 = 7. The line is horizontal, so the Y value is unchanged. It remains 2.

The slanted line from the right end of the horizontal line has an X distance of 1.50 and a Y value of 1.50. This means that its endpoint has an X coordinate value of 3 + 4 + 1.50 = 8.5 and a Y coordinate value of 2 + 1.50 = 3.50.

The remaining coordinate points were determined in the same manner.

The commands and prompts are as follows

Command:_line From point:

2. Type 3,2 ENTER

To point:

3. Type 7,2 ENTER

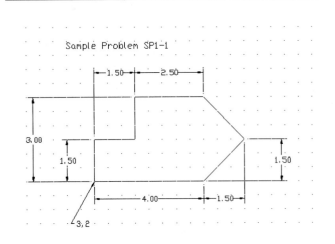

Figure 1-42

To point:

4. Type 8.5,3.5 ENTER

To point:

5. Type 7,5 ENTER

To point:

6. Type 4.5,5 ENTER

To point:

7. Type 4.5,3.5 ENTER

To point:

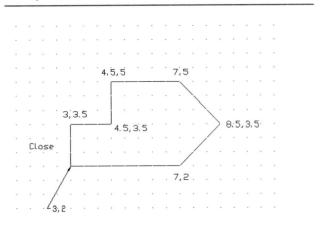

Figure 1-43

8. Type 3,3.5 ENTER

To point:

9. Type C ENTER

To draw Figure 1-42 using polar coordinate values

See Figure 1-44. All dimensions are in inches, so the default values for LIMITS and Decimal Units are acceptable. Set up a GRID and SNAP if desired.

Create a NEW drawing—SP1-1B

1. Select LINE command

Polar coordinates require a distance and an angle input to draw a line. The 4-inch horizontal line to the right of the 3,2 starting point is created with an input of @4<0, where 4 is the distance and 0 is the angle. (Horizontal to the right is by definition 0 degrees.) The slanted line at the end of the 4-inch line has an X value of 1.50 and a Y value of 1.50, or 45 degrees. The length of the line can be calculated using trigonometry as 2.1213. The input to create the slanted line is @2.1213<45.

The command and prompt sequence is as follows.

Command:_line From point:

2. Type 3,2 ENTER

To point:

3. Type @4<0

To point:

4. Type @2.1213<45

To point:

5. Type @2.1213<135

To point:

6. Type @2.50<180

To point:

7. Type @1.50<−90

To point:

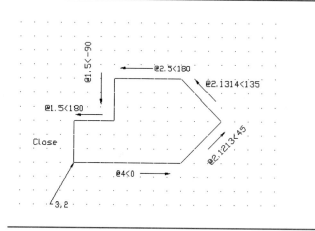

Figure 1-44

8. Type @1.50<180

To point:

9. Type C ENTER

1-20 ERASE

The ERASE command is used to erase lines or other objects from the screen. The ERASE commands may be used to erase lines individually or in groups using the Windows option.

To erase an individual line

DOS

1A. Select Modify (pulldown)
1B. Select ERASE

WINDOWS

1. Select the ERASE icon from the Modify toolbar

The crosshairs will change to a rectangle. This is a select box.

2. Locate the select box over the object to be erased and press the select mouse button
3. Press the right mouse button to complete the command sequence.

If the right button is press again (double clicked), the command sequence will start over.

To define an erase window

DOS

1A. Select MODIFY (pulldown)
1B. Select ERASE

WINDOWS

1. Select the ERASE icon from the Modify toolbar

Locate the cursor above and to the right of the objects to be erased. Move the cursor down and across the objects. Horizontal and vertical lines will follow the cursor movement, defining a window. Do not hold the select button down as you move the cursor. Once the size of the window is acceptable, press the mouse select button.

Only entities located completely within the erase window will be erased. In Figure 1-45 the rectangle is completely enclosed in the erase window and will be erased. The line A-B is not completely enclosed and will remain in the drawing screen.

If the wrong object is accidentally erased, select the OOPS command from the menu list and the object will be returned to the screen. OOPS works only if used immediately after the erase command. If another command has been entered, OOPS will not function. Objects can always be restored using the UNDO command.

1-21 UNDO

The UNDO command is used to step back through the command sequence used to create a drawing. It is similar to ERASE because it removes parts of a drawing, but different because the objects to be removed are not selected from the screen.

AutoCAD creates and saves a drawing as a list of commands. Part of the command list may be seen by pressing the F1 key. The F1 key will toggle between the drawing screen and the text screen mode. Some of AutoCAD's operating sequences will automatically switch into the text screen mode. If this happens, press F1 when the Command: prompt appears and the drawing screen will reappear. If, as a drawing is being created, errors are made, the errors can be removed by undoing the drawing (working backward through the command list) to the point were the drawing is error free. Commands must be undone in reverse sequence to their entry, so you may have to UNDO correct commands as well as incorrect commands to clean up the drawing.

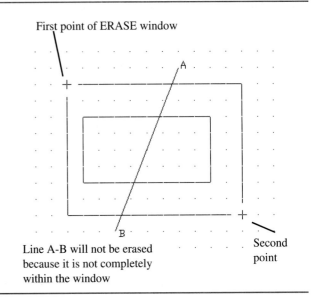

First point of ERASE window

A

B

Line A-B will not be erased because it is not completely within the window

Second point

Figure 1-45

To use the UNDO command

DOS

1A. Select ASSIST (pulldown)
1B. Select UNDO

WINDOWS

1. Select the UNDO icon from the Standard toolbar

The following prompt will appear.

Command:Auto/Back/End/Group/Mark/ <number>:

2. Type 3 ENTER

The number 3 means to undo the last three commands entered. If it is not clear how many commands to undo, enter 1, check the drawing on the screen, then press ENTER again to start the UNDO sequence over. Enter 1 again and continue to repeat the process until the desired place in the drawing sequence is reached.

1-22 REDO

REDO erases UNDO commands. It acts as AutoCAD's failsafe system; that is, it prevents you from undoing too many commands. If you UNDO too many commands, use REDO, found directly under the UNDO command in the ASSIST pulldown menu.

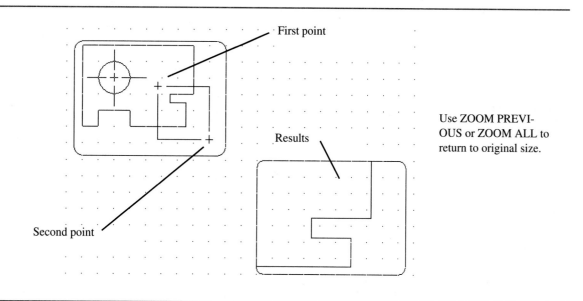

First point

Results

Use ZOOM PREVI-
OUS or ZOOM ALL to
return to original size.

Second point

Figure 1-46

1-23 ZOOM

The ZOOM command allows you to enlarge specific areas of the drawing. There are 6 different ZOOM subcommands. Four will be explained here: Window, Dynamic, Previous, and All.

To use ZOOM Window

See Figure 1-46.

DOS

1A. Select VIEW (pulldown)
1B. Select ZOOM
1C. Select Window

WINDOWS

1. Select the Zoom Window icon from the Standard toolbar

The prompts will appear as follows.

Command:_'zoom
All/Center/Dynamic/Extents/Left/Previous/
Vmax/Window/<Scale(X/XP)>:W
First corner:

2. Select a point above and to the left of the area to be zoomed.

Other corner:

3. Move the cursor across the area to be enlarged and select another point below and to the right of the area. Do not hold the mouse button down as you move the cursor across the area.

To return the drawing to its original size

1. Select VIEW (pull down)
2. Select ZOOM
3. Select Previous

Zoomed areas can be zoomed again and again as needed. Each ZOOM can be offset by a ZOOM Previous or ZOOM All. Zoom All returns the drawing to its original screen size as defined by the LIMITS commmand.

The ZOOM DYNAMIC command is used to first define a zoom window area and then move that window over the area of the drawing to be zoomed.

To use Zoom Dynamic

See Figure 1-47.

1. Select VIEW (pulldown)
2. Select ZOOM
3. Select DYNAMIC

Two rectangular windows will appear on the screen, one made from dashed lines and one made from thin, solid (continuous) lines. The dashed lined rectangle shows the current zoom dynamic area. The solid rectangle will be

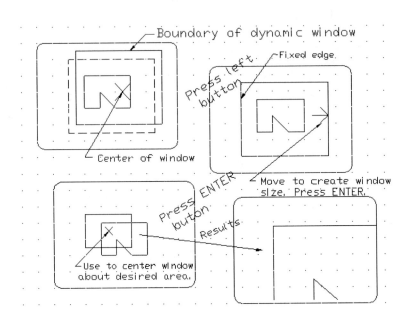

Figure 1-47

exactly the same size as the dashed rectangle but can be moved about the screen. The solid lined window is the dynamic window.

The size of the window is changed by first pressing the left mouse button. The left edge of the window will remained fixed, but an arrow will appear on the right edge. The window will change size as the mouse is moved about. When the desired window size is created, press the ENTER button and the window size will be fixed. Now moving the mouse will move the window. An X marks the center of the window. Locate the window over the portion of the drawing to be enlarged and press the ENTER button. ZOOM PREVIOUS is used to return the drawing to its original size.

A drawing can be zoomed using a scale factor. A scale factor of 2 would create a drawing twice as big as the original, and a scale factor of .5 would create a drawing half as big as the original.

To use ZOOM scale factors

1. Select VIEW (menus)
2. Select ZOOM

Respond to the prompts as follows.

Command:_'Zoom
All/Center/Dynamic/Extents/Left/Previous/Vmax/
Window/<X/XP>:

3. Type 4 ENTER

This creates a drawing 4 times bigger then the original. ZOOM ALL or a zoom scale factor of .25 is used to return the drawing to its original size.

1-24 REDRAW

As a drawing is created, small marks will appear on the screen. These are called blips and occur when you select a point on the screen. Redraw allows you to remove all blips from the screen.

To use REDRAW

1. Select VIEW (pulldown)
2. Select REDRAW

1-25 SAVE

The SAVE command is used to save a drawing to a disk. If no disk drive is specified, AutoCAD will automatically SAVE the drawing on the same disk as the AutoCAD program, usually the C: drive or other hard drive.

To SAVE a drawing

DOS

1A. Select FILE (pulldown)
1B. Select SAVE...

WINDOWS

1. Select the SAVE icon from the Standard toolbar
   The command prompt will read

Command:_qsave

The drawing will be saved using the original drawing name. If no drive specification was given, the drawing will automatically be saved on the hard drive with a .dwg root. If a drive specification was included in the original drawing name (A:P1-1:), then the drawing will be saved to the specified drive (A:).

1-26 SAVE AS

The SAVE AS... command allows either a different drive or different file name to be specified for the drawing. A drawing started as C:TEST could be SAVED AS A:TEST or A:NEW.

Sometimes two drawings are so similar that the second may be created by simply modifyng the first. First create one of the drawings and save it. Then make the modifiaction and use SAVE AS to save the drawing as the second drawing.

To SAVE a drawing on the A: drive

1. Select File (pulldown) or the SAVE AS icon from the Standard toolbar
2. Select SAVE AS...

The Save Drawing As dialog box will appear. Figure 1-48 shows the Windows dialog box.

3. Type the new name of the drawing file in the File Name: box near the top of the dialog box.
4. Select the arrow to the right of the Drives: box and select Drive A

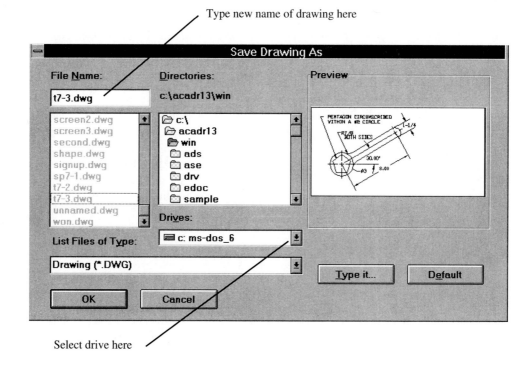

Figure 1-48

The references under the Directories: box will change to reflect the files listed on the disk in the A: drive.

5. Select OK

The Type it box allows you to type the drawing name, including the drive specification, directly from the keyboard.

1-27 TEXT

Words and numbers are added to a drawing using the TEXT command. There are three subcommands within the TEXT command: MTEXT, DYNAMIC TEXT, and SINGLE LINE TEXT.

To add dynamic text to a drawing

DOS

1A. Select DRAW (pulldown)
1B. Select TEXT
1C. Select DYNAMIC

WINDOWS

1. Select the DYNAMIC TEXT icon from the Draw toolbar

The DYNAMIC TEXT command may also be activated by typing DTEXT in response to a Command: prompt. AutoCAD uses the word dynamic to mean that things appear on the screen as you work. Dynamic text means the text will appear on the screen as it is typed. The prompts will be as follows (See Figure 1-49):

Command:_dtext/Justify/Style/<Start point>:

The default settings will create text from left to right from a selected starting point.

2. Select a starting point

Height <0.2000>:

3. Type .25 ENTER

Rotation angle <0>:

4. Type ENTER

Text:

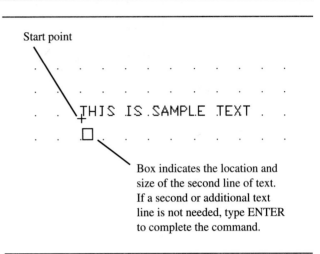

Box indicates the location and size of the second line of text. If a second or additional text line is not needed, type ENTER to complete the command.

Figure 1-49

5. Type All dimensions are in inches ENTER

Text:

6. Type unless otherwise stated. ENTER

Text:

7. Type ENTER

AutoCAD will always ask for another line of text, indicated by the rectangular text box appearance on the screen and a text: prompt line. The second line of text or the second text entry need not be located directly below the previous entry. The dynamic text box may be relocated by simply moving the crosshairs to a new location and pressing the left mouse button.

Press the ENTER key to clear the system and return to a Command prompt when you have completed all your text entries. This is refered to as a null entry.

Text can also be created that is positioned to the left of a given selected starting point, centered about a selected point, or justified between two selected points. See Figure 1-50.

To create text to the left of a selected point

DOS

1A. Select DRAW (pulldown)
1B. Select TEXT
1C. Select DYNAMIC

WINDOW

1. Select the DYNAMIC TEXT icon from the Draw toolbar

Respond to the prompts as follows:

Command:_dtext/Justify/Style/<Start point>:

2. Type J ENTER

*Align/Fit/Center/Middle/Right/TL/TC/TR/ML/MC/
MR/BL/BC/BR:*

3. Type R ENTER
4. Select a starting point. The right end of the text
will be aligned with this point. The text will first
appear to go from left to right, but will be aligned
to the starting point after typing the text is complete and the ENTER key is pressed.

Text:

5. Type This text will be aligned ENTER

Text:

6. Type to a point on the right. ENTER

Text:

7. Type ENTER

Figure 1-51 shows some examples of the other justification features of the TEXT command. Both the Align
and Fit commands place text between two specified points,
but the Align command scales the letter sizes so that the

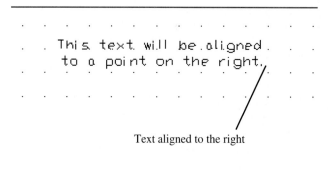

Text aligned to the right

Figure 1-50

proportions of the letters are maintained. The heights of the
letters will be changed accordingly. The FIT command will
distort the letters' proportions without changing their
height.

TL, TC, TR align the text using the tops of the letters; ML, MC, MR use the middle of the letters; and BL,
BC, BR use the bottoms of the letters.

The style of the letters used in TEXT can be
changed. It should be noted that technical drawings tradi-
tionally use only one text style. Drafters were trained to
create the same style letters, either upright or slanted, in
order to give drawings a uniform appearance. Ideally the
drawing reader could not tell if more than one person
worked on the drawing. It is recommended that you choose
one of the simple style letters (the Gothic styles are generally considered too stylistic for technical drawings) and do
all your drawings in that style.

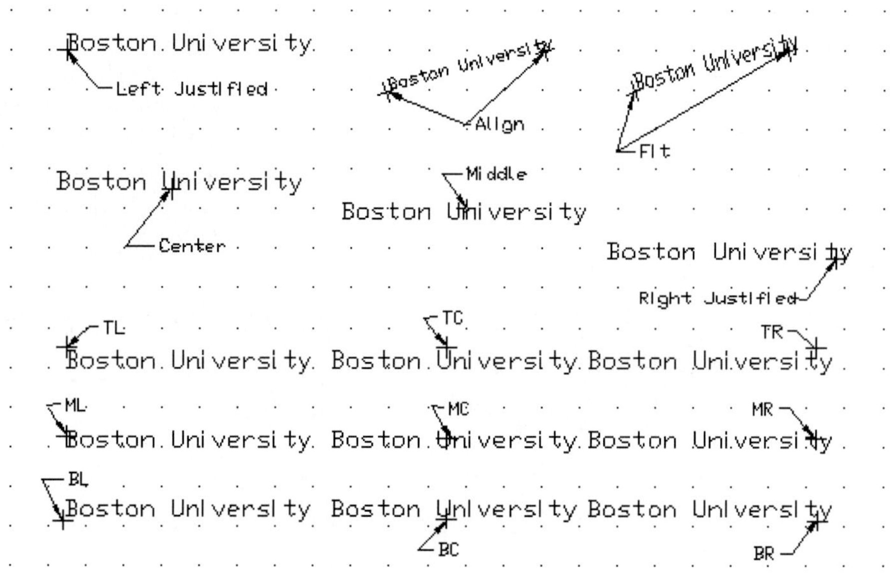

Figure 1-51

To use MTEXT

The MTEXT command is used to enter large amounts of text. MTEXT first defines an area on the screen in which the text is to be entered. See Figure 1-52. The WINDOWS version will then access the Edit MTEXT dialog box. See Figure 1-53. The DOS version will access a completely new drawing screen. See Figure 1-54. Text is typed into the open area just as with word processing programs, then transfered back to the drawing screen.

DOS

1A. Select DRAW (pulldown)
1B. Select TEXT, TEXT
1C. Type the required text or define a text window as shown in Figure 1-52, then type the text

WINDOWS

1A. Select the MTEXT icon from the Draw toolbar

Attach/Rotate/Style/Height/Direction?<Insert point>:

1B. Select a point

The area defined is for the entire text entry. If you are not sure about the size of the area needed, select an area much larger than you think you will need. The excess area can be written or drawn over.

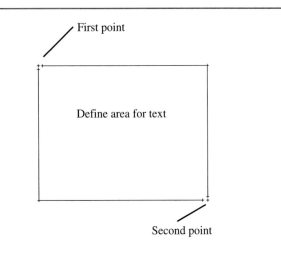

Figure 1-52

Attach/Rotate/Style/Height/Direction/Width/2 Points/<Other corner>:

1C. Define the other corner of the text area

The Edit MTEXT dialog box will appear. A flashing cursor will appear in an open area of the box, indicating that text can be typed in that area. The area will be equivalent to the area originally defined on the drawing screen.

1D. Type the required text

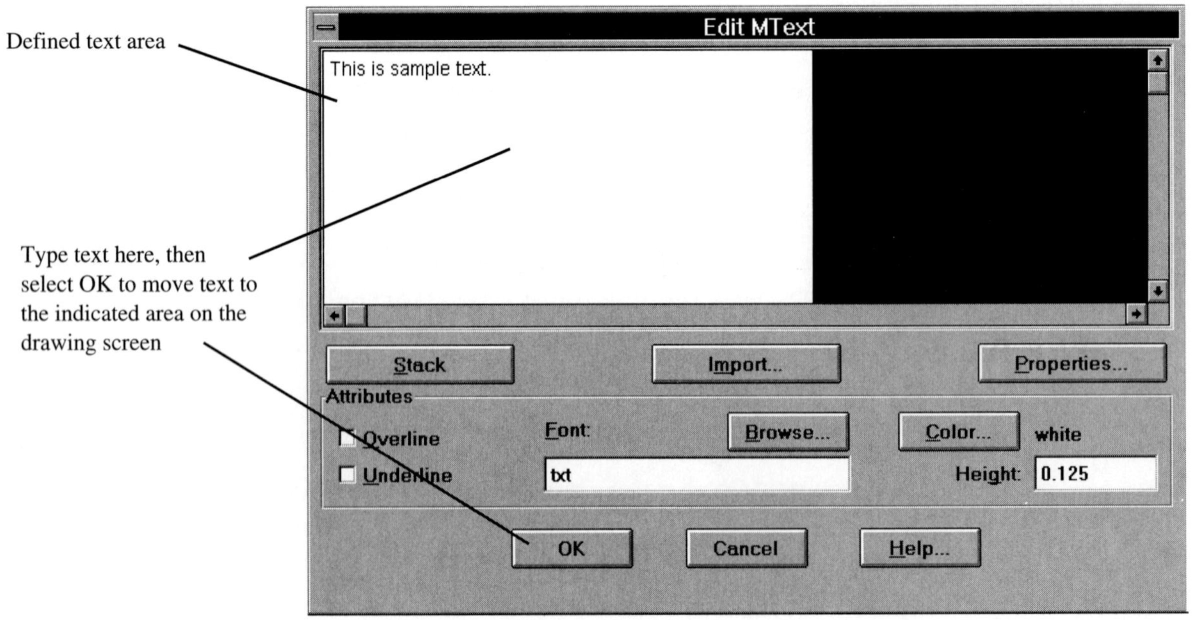

Defined text area

Type text here, then select OK to move text to the indicated area on the drawing screen

Edit MText

This is sample text.

Stack   Import...   Properties...

Attributes

☐ Overline   Font: Browse...   Color...   white
☐ Underline   txt   Height: 0.125

OK   Cancel   Help...

Figure 1-53

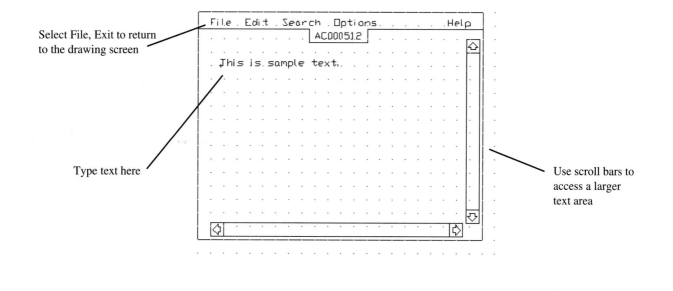

Select File, Exit to return to the drawing screen

Type text here

Use scroll bars to access a larger text area

Figure 1-54

To exit MTEXT and return to the drawing screen

DOS

1A. Select the File (pulldown), then Exit

A box will appear asking if you want to save the text.

1B. Type Y ENTER

WINDOWS

1. Select the OK box

The drawing screen will reappear with the text. If the text is not located properly, use the MOVE command to reposition the text.

1-28 SAMPLE PROBLEM SP1-2

Redraw the object shown in Figure 1-55.

1. Select FILE or the NEW icon from the Standard toolbar
2. Select NEW...
3. Type in New Drawing Name SP1-2
4. Select OK
5. Select SETTINGS (pulldown)
6. Select DRAWING AIDS...

7. Turn on GRID and set the spacing for 0.50
8. Turn on SNAP and set the spacing for 0.50

GRID and SNAP are optional.

9. Select DRAW or the LINE icon from the Draw toolbar
10. Select LINE
11. Select SEGMENT

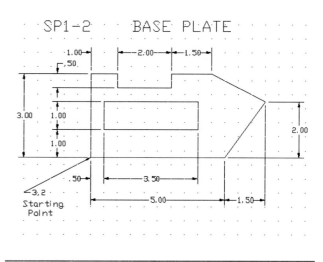

Figure 1-55

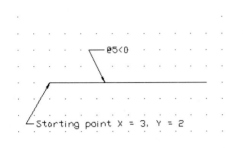

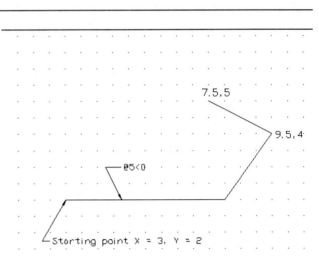

Figure 1-56

Figure 1-57

Respond to the prompts as follows. See Figure 1-56.

Command:_line From point:

12. Type 3,2 ENTER

To point:

13. Type @5<0 ENTER

The next two endpoints are entered using coordinate values. The X value for the first point is 3(starting point)+5+1.5=9.5. The Y for the first point is 2(starting point)+2=4. The second point coordinate value is derived in a similar manner. See Figure 1-57.

To point:

14. Type 9.5,4 ENTER

To point:

15. Type 7.5,5 ENTER

To point:

16. Type @1.5<180 ENTER

To point:

17. Type @.5<–90 ENTER

To point:

18. Type @2<180 ENTER

To point:

19. Type @.5<90 ENTER

To point:

20. Type @1<180 ENTER

To point:

21. Select Close

See Figure 1-58. Press ENTER to clear the LINE command, then press ENTER again to start it over and draw the inside rectangle. See Figure 1-59.

Determine the starting point for the inside rectangle by using the given starting point and the dimensions. The X coordinate value is 3+.5=3.5. The Y value is 2+1=3. Respond to the prompts as follows.

Command:_line From point:

22. Type .5,3 ENTER

To point:

23. Type @3.5<0 ENTER

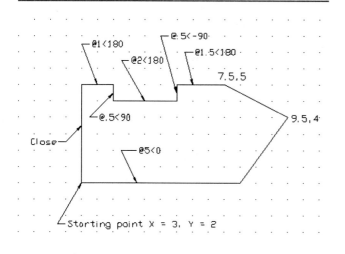

Figure 1-58

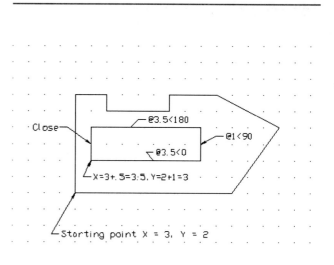

Figure 1-59

To point:

24. Type @1<90 ENTER

To point:

25. Type @3.5<180 ENTER

To point:

26. Select Close
27. Select FILE (pulldown) or the SAVE icon from the Standard toolbar

28. Select SAVE

If you want to save the drawing on a disk or under a name different than SP1-2, select SAVE AS and enter the new name.

If you are done with AutoCAD

1. Select FILE
2. Select Exit AutoCAD

DOS AND WINDOWS

1-29 EXERCISE PROBLEMS

WINDOWS

EX1-1

How many subcommands (flyouts) are located under the Snap From icon?

EX1-2

How many icons are there in the Object Snap toolbar?

EX1-3

How many icons are there in the Surface toolbar?

EX1-4

How many subcommnads (flyouts) are located under the Radius Dimension icon?

EX1-5

Create a screen with the Draw and Modify toolbars located at the top of the drawing screen and the scroll bars removed.

EX1-6

Create a screen as shown below.

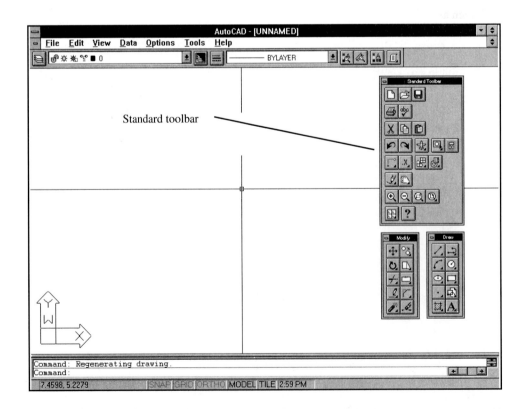

EX1-7

Create a screen as shown below.

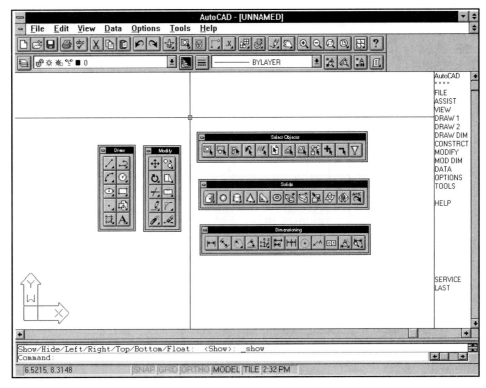

EX1-8

Create a screen as shown below.

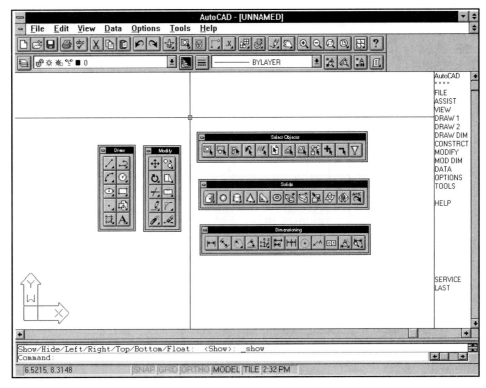

EX1-19 INCHES

Redraw the following shape

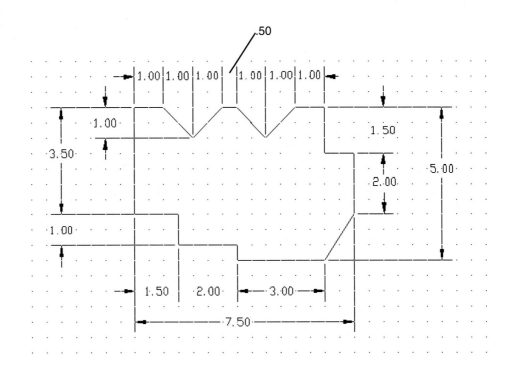

EX1-7

Create a screen as shown below.

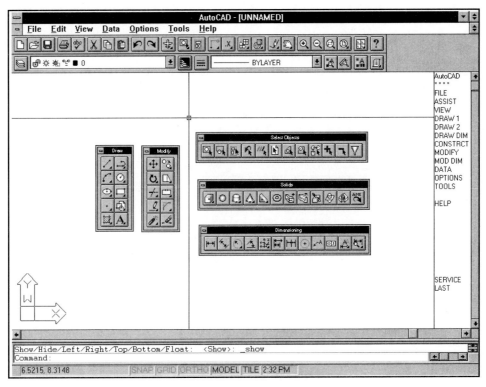

EX1-8

Create a screen as shown below.

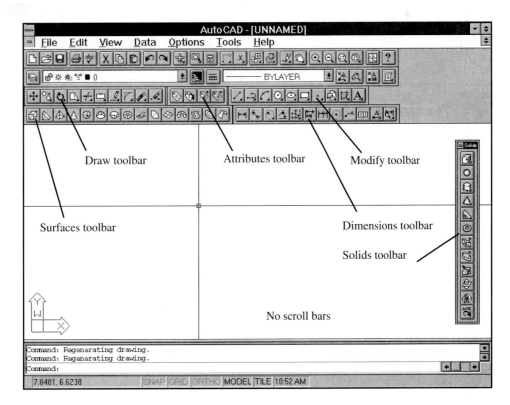

Draw toolbar

Attributes toolbar

Modify toolbar

Surfaces toolbar

Dimensions toolbar

Solids toolbar

No scroll bars

DOS AND WINDOWS

EX1-9 INCHES

Draw the given lettering. All dimension are in inches.

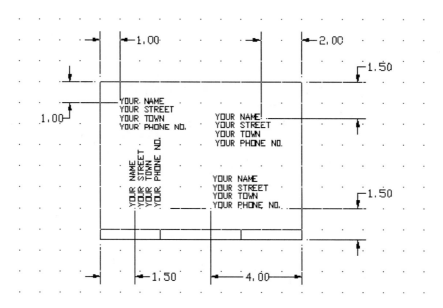

EX1-10 MILLIMETERS

Draw the given lettering. All dimensions are in millimeters.

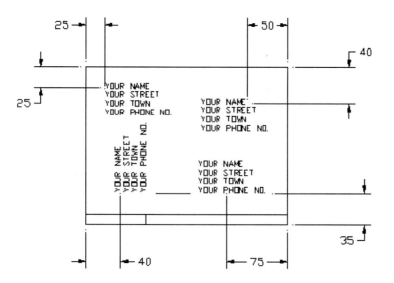

EX1-11 INCHES

Redraw the given figure. All dimensions are in inches. Use the appropriate drawing format.

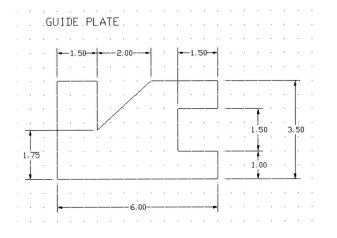

EX1-13 INCHES

Redraw the given figure. All dimension are in inches. Use the correct drawing format.

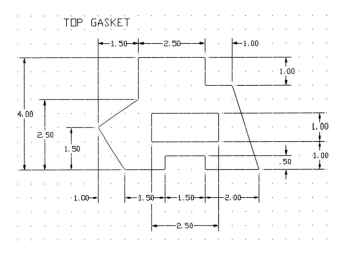

EX1-12 MILLIMETERS

Redraw the given figure. All dimensions are in millimeters. Use the appropriate drawing format.

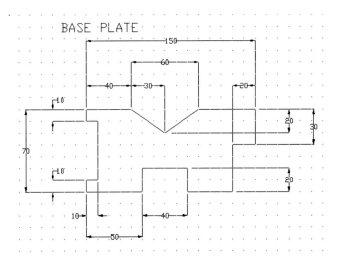

EX1-14 MILLIMETERS

Redraw the given figure. All dimensions are in millimeters. Use the appropriate drawing format.

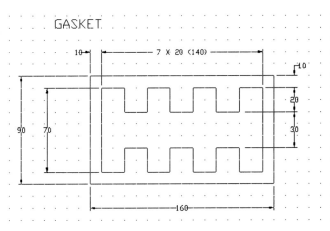

EX1-15 INCHES

Redraw the given figure using the following line distances and angles. All dimensions are in inches. Use the appropriate drawing format. Label each corner point.

    A-B = 5.0000
    B-C = 1.9526
    C-D = 2.3049
    D-E = 1.8039
    E-F = 3.2500
    F-G = 4.1003

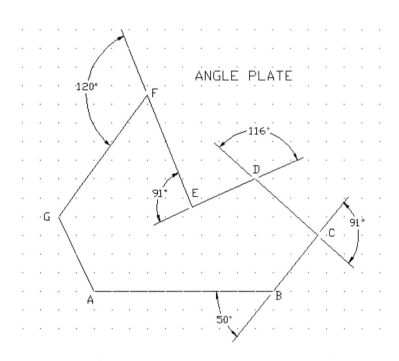

EX1-16 MILLIMETERS

Redraw the given figure using the following line distances and angles. All dimensions are in millimeters. Use the appropriate drawing format. Label each corner point.

    A-B = 67.0820
    B-C = 50.0000
    C-D = 64.0312
    D-E = 50.0000
    E-F = 42.4264
    F-G = 64.0312
    G-H = 76.1577

EX1-17 INCHES

Draw the following DRAWING LAYOUTS and save them as drawing files D1 and D2.

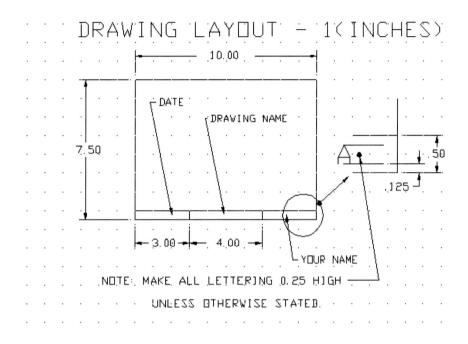

EX1-18 MILLIMETERS

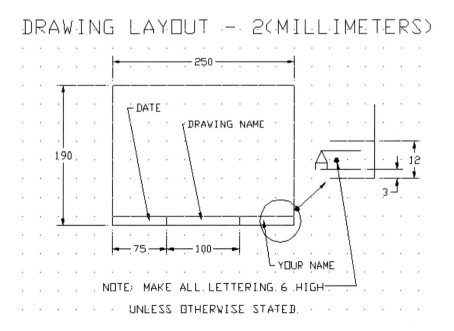

EX1-19 INCHES

Redraw the following shape

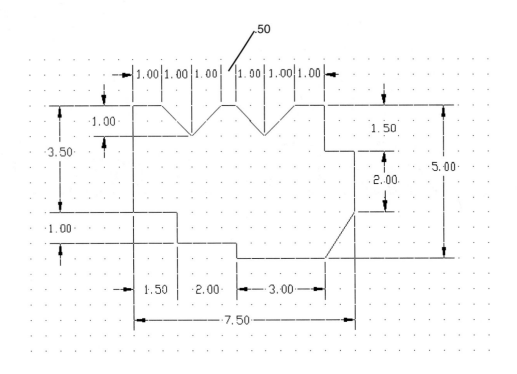

Fundamentals of 2D Construction

Draw and Modify
toolbars

Screen menu

A sample WINDOWS screen

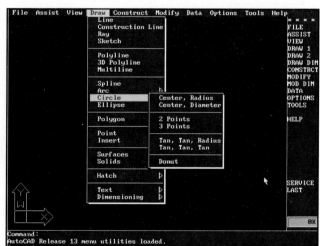

A sample DOS screen with the DRAW
pulldown menu activated

Figure 2-1

2-1 INTRODUCTION

This chapter introduces the DRAW, MODIFY, and CONSTRUCT commands. DRAW commands are used to create shapes, such as lines, circles, polygons, and arcs. MODIFY commands, such as TRIM and BREAK, are used to modify the drawn shapes. CONSTRUCT commands, such as ARRAY and MIRROR, are used to augment the DRAW commands.

The DOS version accesses the DRAW commands via the DRAW pulldown menu, or the DRAW 1 and DRAW 2 commands in the screen menu. The WINDOWS version accesses the DRAW commands via the DRAW toolbar. See Figure 2-1.

The DOS version accesses the MODIFY and CON-STRUCT commands via the pulldown menus or the screen menus. The WINDOWS version accesses both the MODI-FY and CONSTRUCTION commands via the Modify toolbar. There is no Construction toolbar.

2-2 LINE

There are three basic line commands: point-to-point, which was demonstrated in Chapter 1; construction lines; and ray. Figure 2-2 shows the flyout icons for the commands, and Figure 2-1 shows the command access locations under the DRAW pulldown menu.

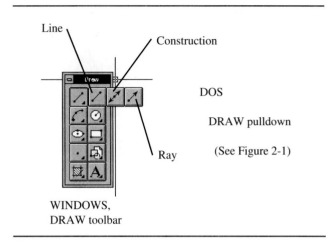

Figure 2-2

To use the LINE point-to-point command

See Figure 2-3.

1. Select the POINT-TO-POINT icon on the Draw toolbar or the LINE command from the DRAW pulldown or screen menu.

Command: Line From point:

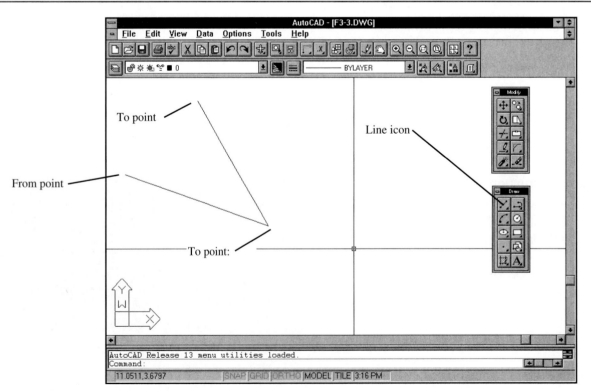

Figure 2-3

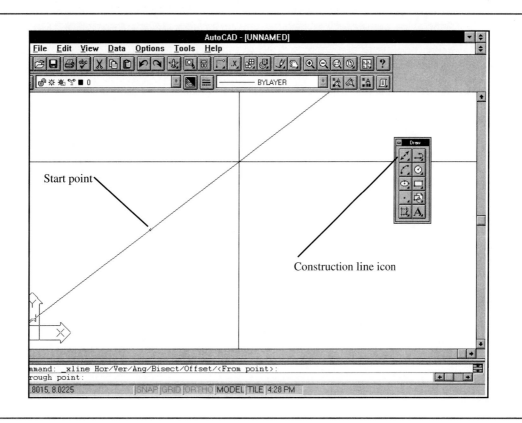

Figure 2-4

2. Select a start point

To point:

3. Select the endpoint of the line

To point:

4. Type ENTER

The ENTER command ends the drawing sequence.

To use the construction line command

The CONSTRUCTION LINE command is used to draw lines of infinite length. Construction lines are very helpful during the initial layout of a drawing. They can be trimmed during the creation of the drawing as needed.

1. Select the CONSTRUCTION LINE icon from the draw toolbar or CONSTRUCTION LINE from the DRAW pulldown menu.

   Command:_ xline/Hor/Ver/Ang/Bisect/Offset/ <From point >:

   The From point: command is the default setting.

2. Select a starting point

Through point:

A line will pivot about the designated starting point and extend at infinite length in a direction through the crosshairs. You can position the direction of the line by moving the crosshairs. See Figure 2-4.

3. Select a through point

An infinite length line will be drawn through the two designated points.

Note:

AutoCAD often presents a listing of options in association with a command. For example, the command line generated when the construction LINE command is activated is

Command: _xline/Hor/Ver/Ang/Bisect?Offset/ <From point>:

These options may be activated by typing the capital letters in their headings. Typing a response of h will activate the Hor (horizontal) command.

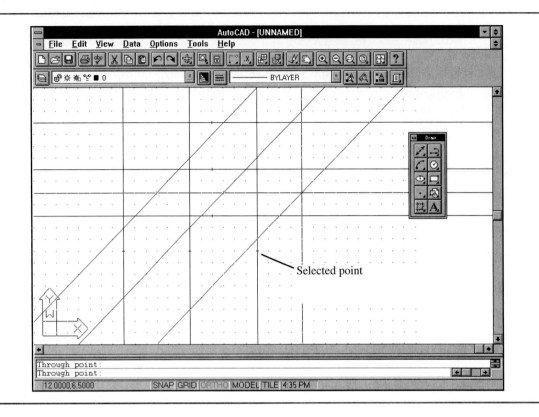

Figure 2-5

Through point:

Another infinite line will appear through the starting point and through the crosshairs.

4. Type ENTER

This will end the construction line command sequence. The sequence may be reactivated, another construction line may be drawn, by pressing the ENTER key a second time.

Other Construction line commands — Hor/Ver/Ang

The lines shown in Figure 2-5 were created using the Hor (horizontal), Ver (vertical), and Ang (angular) options. A grid was created and the snap option was turned on so that the lines could be drawn through known points. Figure 2-5 was created as follows.

1. Set up the drawing screen with grid and snap spacing of .5
2. Select the CONSTRUCTION LINE command

Command:_ xline/Hor/Ver/Ang/Bisect/Offset/ <From point>:

3. Type h ENTER

A horizontal line will appear through the crosshairs.

Through point:

4. Select a point on the drawing screen

A horizontal line will appear through the point. As you move the mouse, another horizontal line will appear through the crosshairs.

Through point:

5. Select a second point

Through point:

6. Select a third point

Through point:

7. Double click the enter key

Command:_ xline/Hor/Ver/Ang/Bisect/Offset/ <From point>:

8. Type v ENTER

Through point:

9. Draw three vertical lines; then double click the ENTER key

Command:_ xline/Hor/Ver/Ang/Bisect/Offset/ <From point>:

10. Type A ENTER

Reference/<enter angle(0.0000)>:

11. Type 45 ENTER

Trough point:

An infinite line at 45 degrees will appear through the crosshairs.

12. Draw three 45 degree lines

Through point:

13. Type ENTER

Your drawing should look approximately like Figure 2-5.

Other construction line commands — offset

The offset option allows you to draw a line parallel to an existing line, regardless of the line's orientation, at a predefined distance. See Figure 2-6.

1. Select the CONSTRUCTION LINE command

Command:_ xline/Hor/Ver/Ang/Bisect/Offset/ <From point>:

2. Draw a line approximately 15 degrees to the vertical (see Figure 2-6)

Through point:

3. Double click the ENTER key to restart the construction line command sequence

Command:_ xline/Hor/Ver/Ang/Bisect/Offset/ <From point>:

4. Type O ENTER

Offset distance or through <Through>:

5. Type .5 ENTER

Select a line object:

6. Select the line

Side to offset:

7. Select the right side of the line

Select a line object:

8. Select the line just created by the offset option

Side to offset:

9. Again select the right side of the selected line

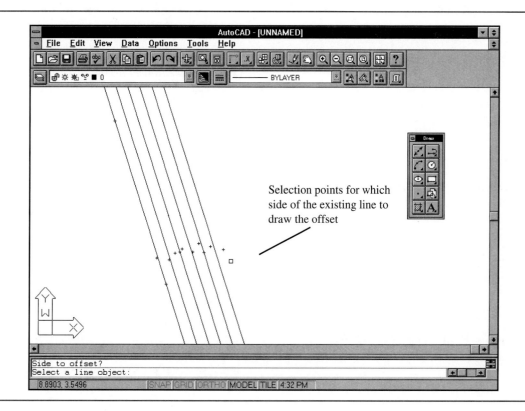

Selection points for which side of the existing line to draw the offset

Figure 2-6

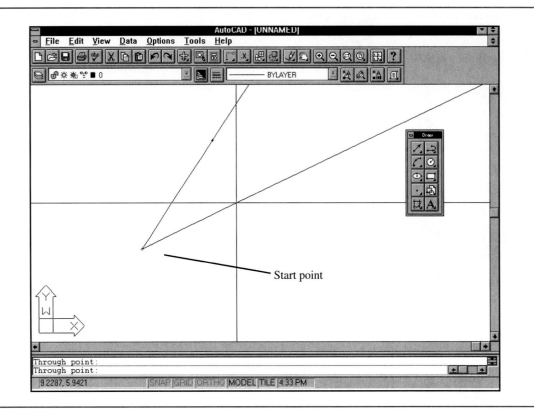

Figure 2-7

Select a line object:

10 Draw several more lines

Select a line object:

11. Press the right mouse button

This will end the offset command sequence and return a command prompt to the command prompt line.

To use the ray command

The RAY command creates a line from a defined point of infinite length, but unlike the construction line command, the line will extend only in the direction of the crosshairs. See Figure 2-7.

1. Select the RAY icon from the Draw toolbar or select the RAY command from the Draw pull-down menu.

   Command:_ray From point:

2. Select the starting point for the ray line

   Through point:

3. Select a point

Another line will appear from the starting point through the crosshairs.

Through point:

4. Select another point

Through point:

5. Type ENTER

This will end the ray command sequence and return you to a command prompt.

2-3 CIRCLES

The CIRCLE command is accessed via the DRAW menu or the CIRCLE icons on the Draw toolbar. See Figure 2-8. The CIRCLE subcommand shows that there are six different ways to draw a circle using AutoCAD. Center points or other required locating points can be entered by selecting points on the screen or by entering the point's XY coordinate value. The radius values and diameter values can be entered by first using the DRAG mode to visually select a value or by entering a numerical value.

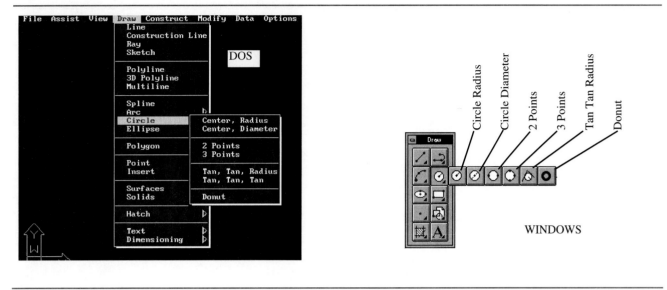

Figure 2-8

To draw a 2.00″ diameter circle

1. Set up GRID and SNAP with Spacing = 0.5
2. Select DRAW (pulldown menu), then CIRCLE DIAMETER, or select the CIRCLE, DIAMETER icon from the DRAW toolbar

Respond to the Command: prompts as follows.

Command:_circle 3P/2P/TTR/<Center point>:

3. Select a grid point

If you move the crosshairs, you will see a circle increase in diameter as you move the crosshairs away from the selected center point. This dynamic circle motion appears because AutoCAD is operating in the DRAG mode. The circle drags along with the crosshairs. DRAG modes are present in many of AutoCAD's commands and are very helpful in designing because they give a visual preview of the shape before exact values are entered.

Radius/<Diameter>:

4. Type 2 ENTER

See Figure 2-9.
NOTE: Press the ENTER button again to restart the command sequence.

To draw a circle with a 1.25″ radius

1. Select DRAW (pulldown menu) then CIRCLE RADIUS, or select the CIRCLE, RADIUS icon from the Draw toolbar

Command:_circle 3P/2P/TTR/<Center point>:

2. Select a point

Diameter<Radius>:

3. Type 1.25 ENTER

See Figure 2-10.

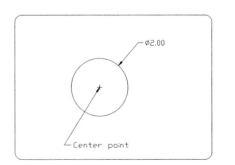

Figure 2-9

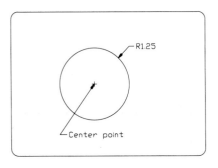

Figure 2-10

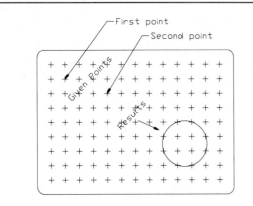

Figure 2-11

To draw a circle given two points

1. Select DRAW (pulldown menu), then CIRCLE, 2 POINTS, or select the CIRCLE, 2 POINTS icon from the Draw toolbar

   Command:_circle 3P/ 2P/ TTR/ <Center point>:_2P
   First point on diameter:

2. Select first point

   Second point on diameter:DRAG

3. Select second point

See Figure 2-11. The word DRAG in the command prompt indicates that AutoCAD is operating in the DRAG mode. A dynamic circle will appear as you move the crosshairs.

To draw a circle given three points

1. Select DRAW (pulldown menu), then CIRCLE, 3 POINTS, or select the CIRCLE, 3 POINTS icon from the Draw toolbar

   Command:_circle 3P/ 2P/ TTR/ <Center point>:_3P
   First point:

2. Select point 1

   Second point:

3. Select point 2

   Third point: DRAG

4. Select point 3

See Figure 2-12.

To draw a 2.00″ diameter circle tangent to 2 given circles

1. Select DRAW (pulldown menu), CIRCLE, TAN TAN RADIUS or the TAN TAN RADIUS icon from the DRAW toolbar

   Command:_circle 3P/2P/TTR/<Center point>:T
   Enter Tangent spec:

2. Select one of the given circles

   Enter second Tangent spec:

3. Select the other circle

   Radius<0.0000>:

4. Type 1.00 ENTER

   See Figure 2-13.

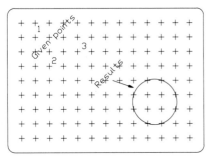

Figure 2-12

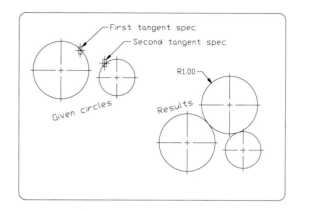

Figure 2-13

To draw a circle tangent to three existing circles

1. Select the DRAW (pulldown) or the DRAW 1 screen menu, then TAN TAN TAN or the 3 POINTS

   Command:_circle 3P/ 2P/ TTR/ <Center point>:_3p First point:_ tan to

2. Select one of the existing circles

   Second point:_ tan to

3. Select another circle

   Third point:_ tan to

4. Select the third circle

   See Figure 2-14. Note that the TAN TAN TAN command is quadrant sensitive. The resulting circle will depend on the quadrants selected on the existing circle.

2-4 CENTER LINES

It is good practice to start to draw a circle by first drawing the circle's center point. Most holes are manufactured by a drill or hole punch. Both processes require an accurate definition of the hole's centerpoint location.

Center lines use a long-short, broken-line pattern as shown in Figure 2-15. If possible, two short line segments should cross at the center point. Solid, unbroken lines are called continuous lines by AutoCAD. Much of the drafting literature refers to solid unbroken lines as object lines.

AutoCAD can create center lines by changing existing continuous lines into center lines using the EDIT command or by adding center lines to an existing circle using the SETVAR command.

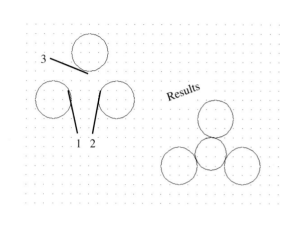

Figure 2-14

To CHANGE existing continuous lines to center lines

1. Select MODIFY (pulldown menu or screen menus), CHANGE, or the POINT icon on the MODIFY toolbar

   Select objects:

2. Select one of the lines

   Select objects: 1 selected, 1 found
   Select objects:

3. Select the other line ENTER
4. Type ENTER

   Change what property/<Change point>:

5. Type P ENTER

   Change what property? (color / Elev / Layer / Ltype / Thickness)?:

6. Type LT ENTER

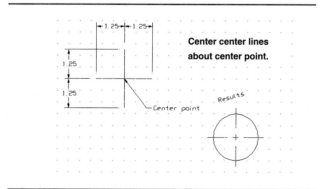

Figure 2-15

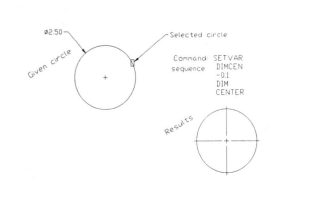

Figure 2-16

New line type <BYLAYER>:

7. Type or select CENTER ENTER

Change what property? (color / Elev / Layer / Ltype / Thickness)?:

8. Select Color

New color:

9. Select Red
10. Type ENTER

This repeated command may at first seem confusing because you have just responded to change line types. AutoCAD is asking if you want to change any other property of the line such as color. Technical drawings done by hand used different line thicknesses for different line types; object (continuous) lines were drawn thick, center lines were drawn thin. The intent was to create a visual distinction between the lines so the reader could more easily read the drawing.

Only the most expensive printers and plotters can create different line thicknesses, but with the advent of color the required visual distinction can be created by changing colors for different line types.

Any color may be used for center lines. The only rule is to be consistent. All center lines should use the same color. In the example in this book, all center lines are red. If black center lines are acceptable, press the ENTER button to enter a null change and return to a command prompt.

Draw a circle about the center point created by the two intersecting lines. See Figure 2-15.

To draw center lines for an existing circle

See Figure 2-16.

1. Draw a 2.00″ diameter circle anywhere on the screen.

Command:

2. Type SETVAR ENTER

Variable name or?:

3. Type DIMCEN ENTER

New value for DIMCEN<0.0900>:

4. Type –0.1 ENTER (use –3.0 for metric scales)

Be sure to type –0.1. The minus sign is critical.

Command:

5. Select DIM (menu listing)

Command: Dim:

6. Type CENTER ENTER

Select arc or circle:

7. Select any point on the circle.

The CHANGE command can now be used to change the center lines to a different color. Color and line type changes can also be made using the LAYER command.

The centerline pattern spacing is determined by a mathmatical input that is based on the default screen size and UNITS. If you use a metric size of 297,210, the center lines will change color but will still appear as solid lines. The default sizing is too small to be visible. (This can be confirmed by extensive zooming of the line.)

The LTSCALE command is used to alter the centerline pattern so that it can be seen on a metric drawing. See Figure 2-17.

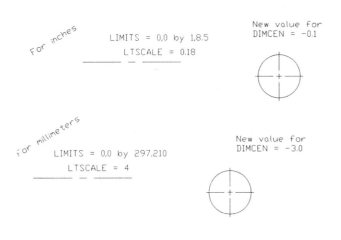

Figure 2-17

To create center lines for metric drawings

1. Set up the drawing

   LIMITS lower left = 0,0
   LIMITS upper right = 297,210
   ZOOM ALL
   GRID = 10
   SNAP = 10

2. DRAW a LINE anywhere on the screen
3. Select MODIFY (pulldown)
4. Select CHANGE

   Command:_ CHANGE
   Select objects:

5. Select the line

   Select objects:

6. Type ENTER

   Change what property<Change point>:

7. Select LType

   New linetype<BYLAYER>:

8. Select Center

   Change what property?(Color / Elev / LAyer / LType / Thickness)?:

9. Select Color

   New Color:

10. Select red

The line should change color but still appear solid. Use LTSCALE to change the centerline spacing parameters.

11. Select SETTINGS (pulldown menu)
12. Select NEXT
13. Select LTSCALE

    Command:LTSCALE
    New scale factor<.18>

14. Type 4 ENTER

The line should change to a red center line. Different numerical values may be used to create the best looking center lines for a given circle, but remember that all center lines on the drawing will be changed, so what looks good on one circle may not on another. The SETVAR, DIMCEN commands yield the most constant results.

DOS MODIFY pulldown menu

Trim icon

Figure 2-18

2-5 TRIM

The TRIM command is used to erase part of a line. The TRIM command is accessed using the MODIFY pulldown menu, or the TRIM icon on the MODIFY toolbar. See Figure 2-18.

The TRIM command first requires you to define a cutting edge. Think of a cutting edge as a knife that is used to cut the line. After the cutting edge is defined, then the lines to be cut are selected.

Draw two lines and a circle as shown in Figure 2-19.

To TRIM lines

1. Select MODIFY (pulldown menu), then TRIM, or the TRIM icon from the MODIFY toolbar

   Command:_trim Select cutting edge(s)...
   Select objects:

2. Select the circle

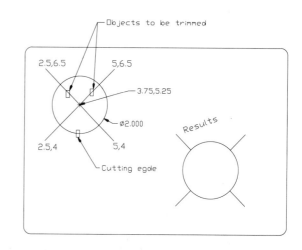

Figure 2-19

Select objects:

3. Type ENTER

The ENTER response tells AutoCAD you are through selecting cutting edges and are now ready to select lines to trim.

Select object to trim:

4. Select a line inside the circle

Select object to trim:

5. Select the other line

Select object to trim:

6. Type ENTER

The ENTER response tells AutoCAD you are finished trimming and are ready for a new command prompt.

2-6 SAMPLE PROBLEM SP2-1

Redraw the figure shown in Figure 2-20.

1. Start a New Drawing called SP2-1
2. Set up the drawing with GRID and SNAP spacing = 0.50
3. Use the DRAW,LINE commands to create a 5 X 3.5 rectangle, as shown in Figure 2-14
4. Add the four 2.00″ diameter circles to the corners of the rectangle
5. Select the TRIM command

Respond to the prompts as follows. Turn off the SNAP command by pressing the F9 key. Snap off should appear next to the command prompt.

Command:_trim Select cutting edges...
Select objects:

6. Select the four lines.

The lines will change from solid black to a broken gray pattern when selected.

Select objects:

7. Type ENTER

Select objects to trim:

8. Select the outside edge of each circle

Select objects to trim:

9. Type ENTER

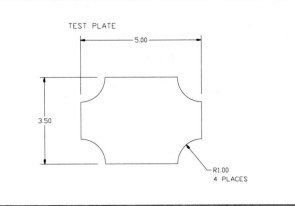

Figure 2-20

10. Type ENTER

The first ENTER tells AutoCAD you are done trimming and the second ENTER restarts the TRIM command sequence. Pressing ENTER twice at the end of any command will restart the command. See Figure 2-21.

Command:_trim Select cutting edge(s).
Select objects:

11. Select the four lines

Select objects:

12. Type ENTER

Select objects to trim:

13. Select the outside edges of the four circles

Select object to trim:

14. Type ENTER

SAVE the drawing if desired.

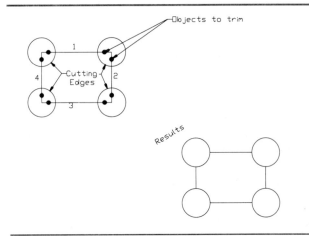

Figure 2-21

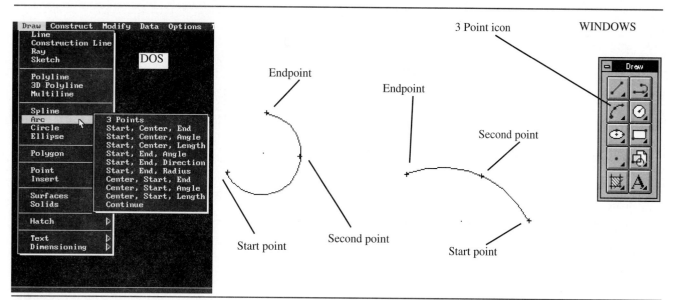

Figure 2-22

2-7 ARC

The ARC command is accessed using the DRAW pulldown menu or the ARC icon on the DRAW toolbar. The arc command has 11 submenus.

To draw an arc — 3 points

See Figure 2-22.

1. Select the ARC 3 POINT command

   Command:_ arc Center/<Start point>:

2. Select a start point

   Center/End/<Second point>:

3. Select a second point

   End point:

Move the cursor around and note how the arc changes.

4. Select a third point

   Command:

Figure 2-22 also shows a second arc created using the 3 point option.

To draw an arc — Arc Start Center End

See Figure 2-23.

1. Select the ARC START CENTER END command

   Command:_ arc Center/<Start point>:

2. Select a start point

   Center/End/<Second point>: _c Center:

Notice the similarity between this prompt line and the prompt line generated after step 2 for 3 point arcs. The _c Center means that for this sequence the center point input has been automatically selected. It is now the default prompt.

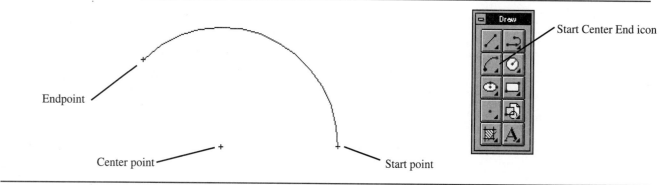

Figure 2-23

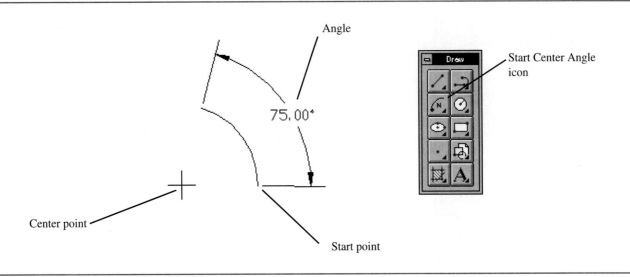

Figure 2-24

3. Select a center point:

   Angle/Length of chord/<End point>:

4. Select an end point

To draw an arc — Arc Start Center Angle

   See Figure 2-24.

1. Select the ARC START CENTER ANGLE command

   Command:_arc Center/<Start point>:

2. Select a start point

   Center/End/<Second point>: _c Center:

3. Select a center point

   Angle/Length of chord/<End point>:_a Included angle:

4. Type 75 ENTER

To draw an arc — Arc Start Center Length

   See Figure 2-25.

1. Select the ARC START CENTER LENGTH command

   Command:_ arc Center/<Start point>:

2. Select a start point

   Center/End/<Second point>: _c Center:

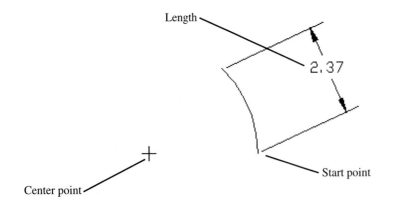

Figure 2-25

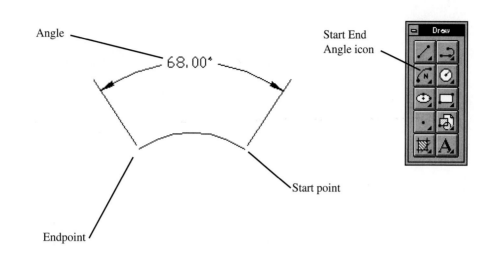

Figure 2-26

Center/End/<Second point>:_c Center:

3. Select a center point

Angle/Length of chord/<End point>: _l length of chord:

4. Type 2.37 ENTER

To draw an arc — Arc Start End Angle

See Figure 2-26.

1. Select the ARC START END ANGLE command

Command:_arc Center/<Start point>:

2. Select a start point

Endpoint:

3. Select an endpoint

Angle/Direction/Radius/<Center point>: _a included angle:

4. Type 68 ENTER

The size of the included angle is directly related to the radius of the arc.

To draw an arc — Arc Start End Direction

See Figure 2-27.

1. Select the ARC START END DIRECTION command

Command:_ arc Center/<Start point>:

2. Select a start point

Endpoint:

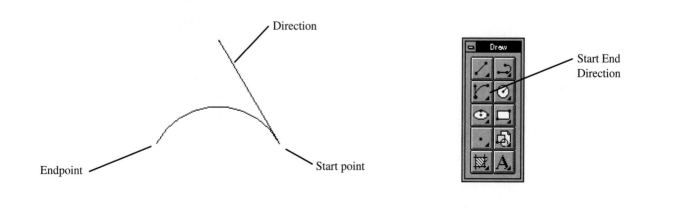

Figure 2-27

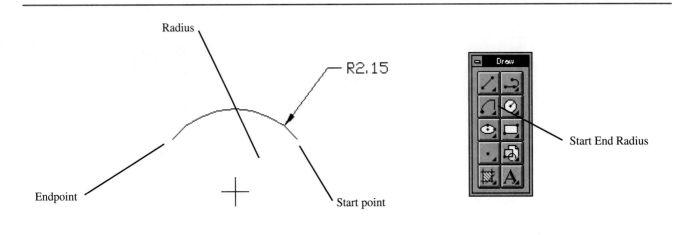

Figure 2-28

3. Select an endpoint

Angle/Direction/Radius/<Center point>: _d direction from start point:

4. Select a direction above the start and end points

To draw an arc — Arc Start End Radius

See Figure 2-28.

1. Select the ARC START END RADIUS command

Command:_arc Center/<Start point>:

2. Select a start point

Endpoint:

3. Select an endpoint

Angle/Direction/Radius/<Center point>: _r Radius:

4. Type 2.15 ENTER

To draw an arc — Arc Center Start End

See Figure 2-29.

1. Select the ARC CENTER START END command

Command: -arc Center/<Start point>: _c Center:

2. Select a center point

Start point:

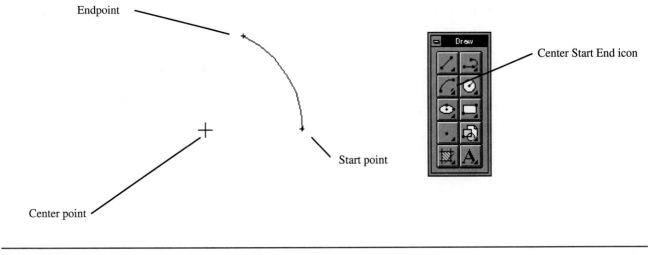

Figure 2-29

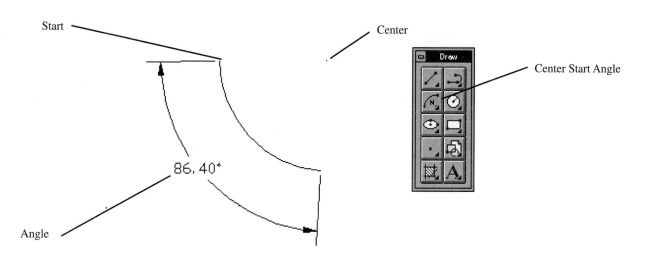

Figure 2-30

3. Select a start point

Angle/Length of chord/<Endpoint>:

4. Select an endpoint

To draw an arc — Arc Center Start Angle

See Figure 2-30.

1. Select the ARC CENTER START ANGLE command

Command: -arc Center/<Start point>: _c Center:

2. Select a start point

Start point:

3. Select a start point

Angle/Length of chord/<endpoint>: _a Included angle:

4. Type 86.4 ENTER

AutoCAD draws arcs with counterclockwise as the positive direction. This is why the arc is drawn down from the start point, as opposed to the Start Center End option that drew the arc upward. See Figure 2-30.

To draw an arc — Arc Center Start Length

See Figure 2-31.

1. Select the ARC CENTER START LENGTH command

Command: -arc Center/<Start point>: _c Center:

2. Select a center point

Start point:

3. Select a start point

Angle/Length of chord/<endpoint>: _ l Length of chord:

4. Select a chord length

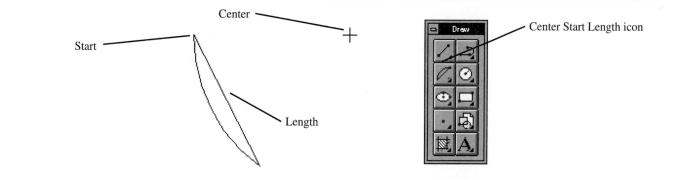

Figure 2-31

2-8 RECTANGLES AND POLYGONS

A polygon is any enclosed figure made from straight lines: triangles, squares, pentagons, hexagons, etc. If all sides of a polygon are of equal length, it is said to be a regular polygon. AutoCAD's POLYGON command can draw only regular polygons. Irregular polygons are created using either the LINE or POLYLINE commands.

The RECTANGLE and POLYGON commands are accessed via the DRAW pulldown menu, followed by the POLYGON command, or by using the RECTANGLE icon and its associated flyout icons. See Figure 2-32.

To draw a rectangle

See Figure 2-33.

1. Select the RECTANGLE command

   Command: rectang
   First corner:

2. Select a point

   Other corner:

3. Select a point

The distance between the two points is the diagonal distance across the rectangle's corners.

A rectangle drawn using the RECTANGLE command is considered to be a single entity, not four individual lines. It must be EXPLODED before its individual elements can be manipulated.

Figure 2-34 shows three hexagons (six-sided polygons) drawn using different inputs. The hexagons labeled "inscribed" and "circumscribed" were created from a defined center point and radius value. The hexagon label

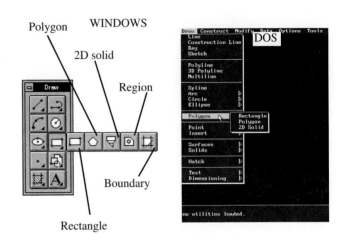

Figure 2-32

edge distance was created by defining a location and the length of one of the hexagon's edges.

To draw a polygon using a center point

1. Select the POLYGON command

   Command:_ polygon Number of sides<4>:

2. Type 6 ENTER

   Edge/<Center of polygon>:

3. Select a center point

   Inscribe in circle/Circumscribe about a circle(I/C)<I>:

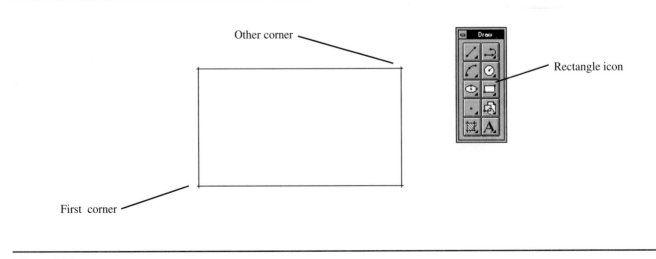

Figure 2-33

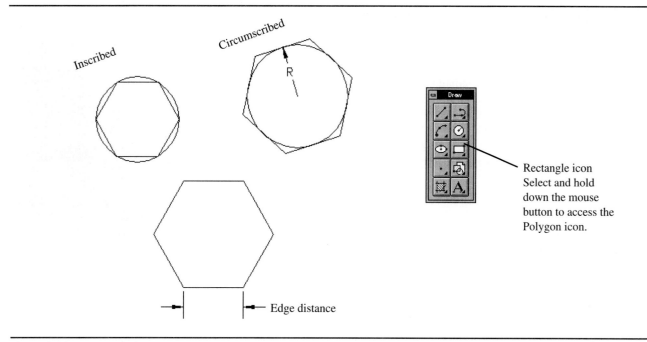

Figure 2-34

If a hexagon is inscribed about a circle, the radius value used will be equal to half the distance across the hexagon's corners. If a hexagon is circumscribed about a circle, the radius value used will equal half the distance across the hexagon's flats. See Figure 2-35.

4. Type ENTER

Radius of circle:

5. Type 1.25 ENTER

To draw a polyline using an edge distance

1. Select the POLYGON command

Command:_polygon Number of sides <6>

2. Type ENTER (if default value is 6)

Edge/<Center of polygon>:

3. Type E ENTER

First endpoint of edge:

4. Select a start point for the edge

First endpoint of edge: Second endpoint of edge:

5. Select a point

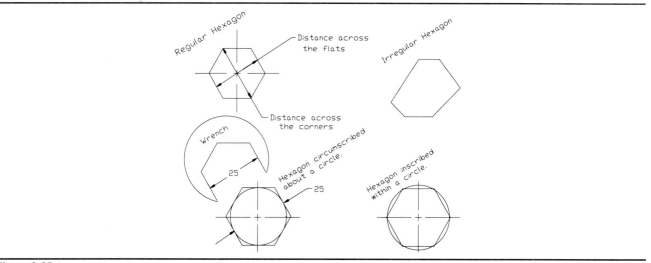

Figure 2-35

2-9 EXPLODE

Polygons drawn using the POLYGON command are individual, whole entities to AutoCAD. Hexagons are not six individual line segments but one continuous line. If you try to erase part of a polygon, the entire polygon will be erased.

The EXPLODE command is used to break down a polygon into its individual line segments. The EXPLODE command is located on the MODIFY pulldown menus or on the MODIFY toolbar.

To explode a given hexagon

1. Select the EXPLODE command

   Respond to the prompts as follows. See Figure 2-36.

   Command:_explode
   Select object:

2. Select the object
3. Type ENTER

There will be no visible change in the hexagon. To verify that it has been exploded, use the ERASE command and erase one of the hexagon's line segments. Use OOPS to restore the line.

2-10 MOVE

The MOVE command is used to relocate an object within the drawing. The MOVE command is accessed via

DOS
MODIFY pulldown menu

Figure 2-36

the MODIFY pulldown menu or the MODIFY toolbar. See Figure 2-37.

To move an object

1. Select the MOVE command

   Command:_move
   Select Objects:

2. Window the entire object, including the center lines.

Any element not entirely within the window will not be selected for the MOVE. Elements of the object may be selected individually using the select button. The window

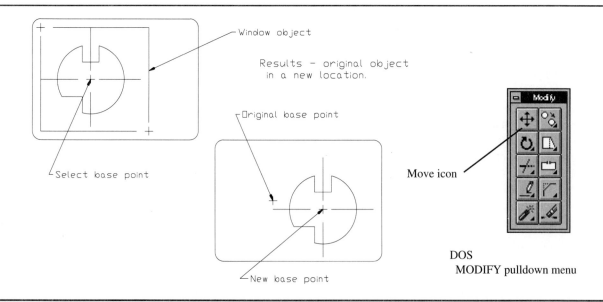

Figure 2-37

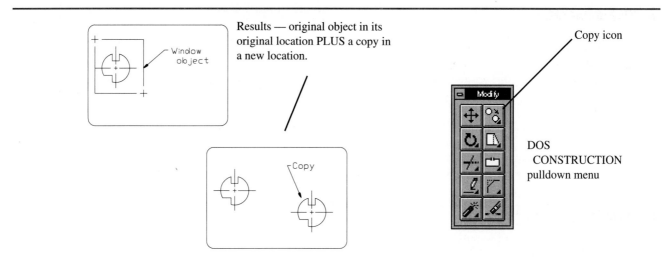

Results — original object in its original location PLUS a copy in a new location.

Copy icon

DOS CONSTRUCTION pulldown menu

Figure 2-38

function is activated by locating the crosshairs in an open area of the drawing and pressing the select button. The window size can then be defined by dragging the cursor across the desired area and then again pressing the select button. The select button need not be held down as the window is created. Create a window

Base point or displacement:

3. Select the object's center point

Any point on the drawing can be selected as a base point. The point does not necessarily have to be on or part of the object. The base point may also be entered using its coordinate values (X,Y).

Second point of displacement:

4. Select the new base point location

2-11 COPY

The COPY command is used to create new objects in addition to the original object copied. COPY is different than MOVE because the original object remains in its original location and the copy is moved to a new location. The COPY command is accessed via the CONSTRUCTION pulldown menu or the COPY icon on the MODIFY toolbar.

To copy an object

See Figure 2-38.

1. Select the COPY command

Command:_copy
Select objects:

2. Window the object

<Base point or displacement>/Multiple:

3. Select the object's center point

Second point of displacement:

4. Select the new base point location

To make more than one copy

See Figure 2-39.

1. Select the COPY command

Command:_copy
Select objects:

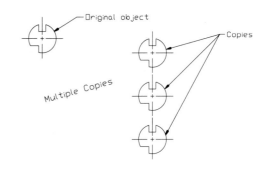

Figure 2-39

1. Window the objects

   <Base point or displacement>/Multiple:

2. Select Multiple (menu)

   _Multiple Base point:

3. Select base point

   Second base point:

4. Select new base point

   Second base point:

The object can be copied as many times as needed. Move the copied object to a new location and press the select button. Another copy is instantly available by again moving the object to a new location and pressing the select button. Press the ENTER button when you have completed all the copies.

It is possible to create a copy directly on top of the original object and then use the ROTATE command to relocate the copy. See Sample Problem SP2-2.

2-12 ROTATE

The ROTATE command is used to rotate an object about a specified base point. The base point need not be part of the object. The angle of rotation can be defined using either positive or negative numbers. See Figure 2-40.

The ROTATE command is accessed via the MODIFY pulldown menu or the ROTATE icon on the MODIFY toolbar.

To ROTATE an object

1. Select ROTATE command

   Command:_rotate
   Select objects:

2. Window the objects

As with the COPY and MOVE commands, a selection window is created by locating the cursor in an open area of the drawing and pressing the select button. The size of the window is defined by dragging the cursor across the area to be selected and pressing the select button again. An object must be entirely within the window to be selected.

   Base point:

3. Select the center point

   <Rotation angle>/Reference:

4. Type 90 ENTER

In Figure 2-40 the object was rotated about its own center point. Figure 2-41 shows an object that was rotated –60 degrees about a point located outside the object. Any point on the drawing may be used as a base point.

DOS
MODIFY pulldown menu

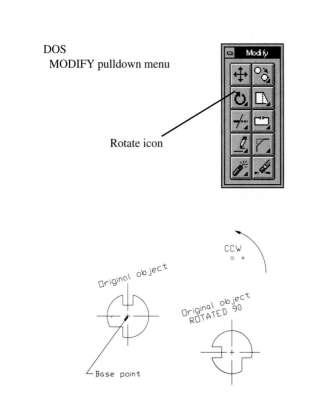

Rotate icon

Figure 2-40

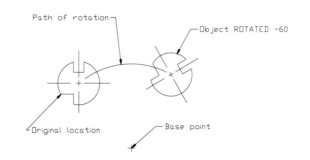

Figure 2-41

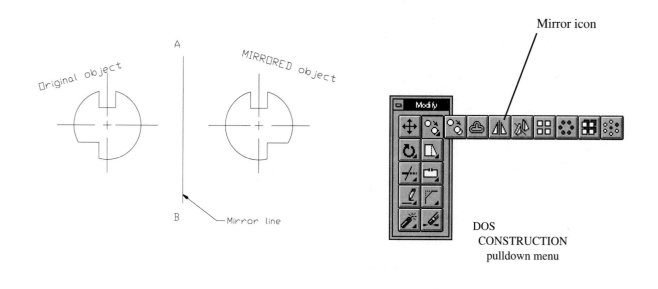

Figure 2-42

2-13 MIRROR

The MIRROR command is used to create mirror images of an object. A mirror image is different than a copy of an object rotated 180 degrees. See Figure 2-42. Objects are mirrored about a mirror line. Mirror lines can be a line within the object or a seperate line located anywhere on the drawing.

The MIRROR command is accessed via the CONSTRUCTION pulldown pulldown menu or the MIRROR icon on the MODIFY toolbar.

To MIRROR an object.

1. Select the MIRROR command

   Command:_mirror
   Select objects:

2. Window the objects

   First point on the mirror line:

3. Select point A

   Second point:

4. Select point B

   Delete old objects?<N>

5. Type ENTER

If a Y response in entered to the Delete old objects prompt, the original object will be erased and only its mirror image will remain.

The MIRROR command is very helpful when drawing symmetrical objects. Only half the object needs to be drawn. The other half can be created using MIRROR. See Figure 2-43.

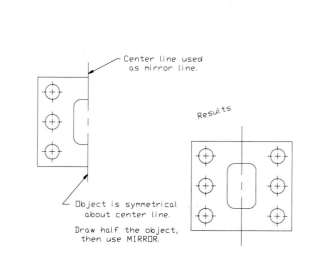

Figure 2-43

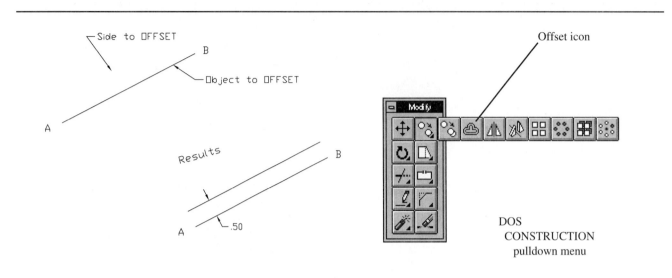

Figure 2-44

2-14 OFFSET

The OFFSET command is used to draw parallel lines. See Figure 2-44. The OFFSET command is accessed via the CONSTRUCTION pulldown menu, or the OFFSET icon on the MODIFY toolbar.

To OFFSET a line .5 inches from a given line

1. Select OFFSET command

   Command:_offset
   Offset distance or through<Through>:

2. Type .5 ENTER

   Select object to offset:

3. Select line A-B

   Side to offset?:

4. Select any point on the drawing above line A-B
5. Type ENTER

The OFFSET command can be used to draw a series of parallel line by repeating the sequence defined above. See Figure 2-45. Press ENTER twice after the first parallel line is completed, then select the new line. The through distance will now be the default distance, so press ENTER to accept the distance. Select the side to offset and press ENTER. Press ENTER again to repeat the OFFSET sequence.

2-15 FILLET

The FILLET command is used to draw round corners. Corners that are convex are called rounds and corners that are concave are called fillets. The FILLET command is accessed via the CONSTRUCTION pulldown menu, or the FILLET icon on the MODIFY toolbar. See Figure 2-46.

To draw FILLETS of radius .375

1. Select FILLET command

   Command:_fillet Polyline/Radius/<Select first

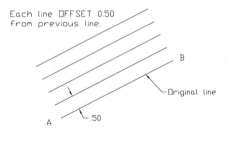

Figure 2-45

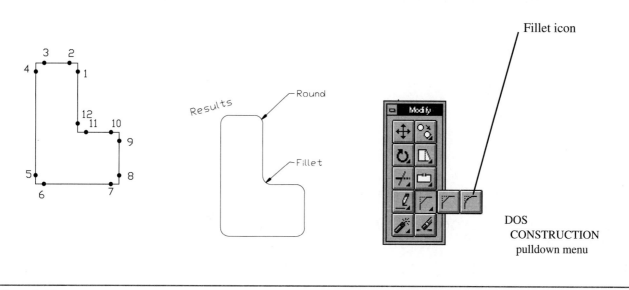

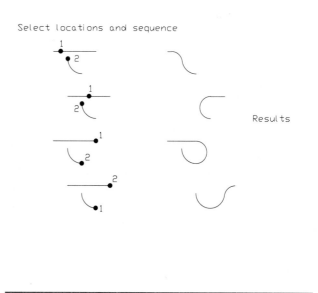

Figure 2-46

2. Select Radius (menu)

   Enter fillet radius <0.0000>:

3. Type .375 ENTER

   FILLET Polyline/Radius/<Select first object>:

4. Select line labeled 1

   Select second object:

5. Select line labeled 2
6. Type ENTER
7. Type ENTER

The second ENTER command will start the FILLET command sequence over again. The radius has now been defined and entered as the default value, so only the first and second lines of the fillet need to be selected. For the object shown in Figure 2-46, the selected points were 3 and 4, 5 and 6, 7 and 8, 9 and 10, and 11 and 12. If another size radius were specified, respond to the Select first object prompt with Radius and enter the new radius value.

The FILLET command can also be used to create different types of combinations of arcs depending on the selection sequence and selection point location used. Figure 2-47 shows four possibilities. Each shape begins with a horizontal line and an arc located below the line. The line is chosen first in three of the examples and the arc

in the other example. The select point also varies from on the line to the left of the arc, on the line above the arc to on the line to the right of the arc. Note carefully where on the line and arc the select point was chosen and the resulting shape created.

Figure 2-47

2-16 SAMPLE PROBLEM SP2-2

Draw the object shown in Figure 2-48. The dimensions will be given throughout the problem.

1. Select FILE, NEW
2. Name the new drawing SP2-4

> Drawing Setup
> GRID = .5
> SNAP = .25
> LIMITS = default values

3. Select the LINE command and draw the center lines shown in Figure 2-49.
4. Use the CIRCLE, POLYGON, and OFFSET commands to create the drawing shown in Figure 2-50.
5. Use the ARC command to create the rounded handle end as shown in Figure 2-51. Use TRIM to remove excess lines.
6. Use the FILLET command to add the fillets shown in Figure 2-52.
7. Use the COPY command and create a copy of the handle directly on top of the original handle. The handle includes the two FILLETs, two OFFSET lines, the ARC, and the center line. Use ROTATE to move the top copy 120 degrees (150 degrees from the horizontal). See Figure 2-53.
8. Repeat the copy process and ROTATE the new copy −120 degrees. The figure should now look like Figure 2-48.

SAVE the object if desired.

The idea of placing a copy of an object directly over the original object is sometimes counterintuitive. How can two objects occupy the same space at the same time? AutoCAD can stack objects directly on top of each other and will operate on the objects in reverse order of their creation. For example, if a line is drawn directly on top of another line and then the ERASE command is used to select the line, the second line will be erased but not the first. In the above example, the copy was rotated, but the original remained in its original location.

2-17 ARRAY

The ARRAY command is used to create multiple images of an object in a predetermined pattern. Both polar and rectangular arrays can be created. The ARRAY command is accessed via the CONSTRUCTION pulldown menu or the MODIFY toolbar. See Figure 2-54.

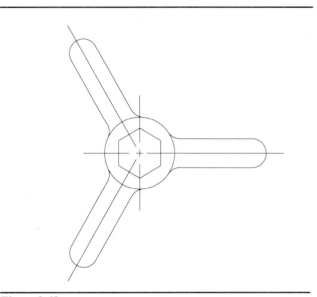

Figure 2-48

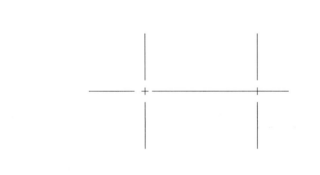

Figure 2-49

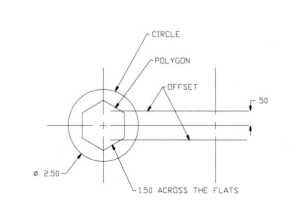

Figure 2-50

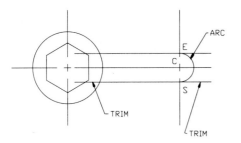

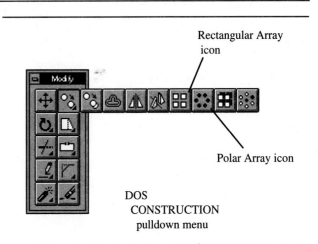

DOS
CONSTRUCTION
pulldown menu

Figure 2-51

Figure 2-54

To create a polar array

See Figure 2-55.

1. Select the POLAR ARRAY command

   Command:_array
   Select object:

2. Select the object

   Rectangular or Polar (R/P):
   Center point of array:

3. Select the center point

   Number of items:

4. Type 8 ENTER

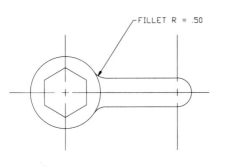

Figure 2-52

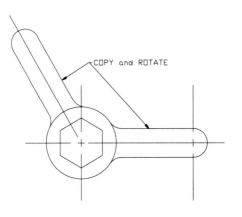

Figure 2-53

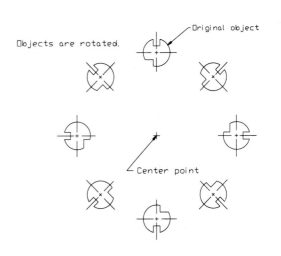

Figure 2-55

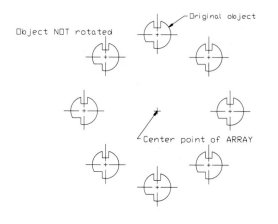

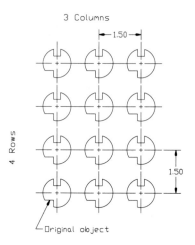

Figure 2-56

Figure 2-57

The original item is counted as part of the final number of items. In this example, 7 new objects were created, plus the original object, for a total of 8 objects.

Angle to fill(+=ccw)<360>:

5. Type ENTER

Rotate objects as they are copied?<Y>:

6. Type N ENTER

Figure 2-56 shows the same object arrayed using a polar array but with the objects rotated. Note the difference between Figures 2-55 and 2-56.

To create a rectangular array

See Figure 2-57.

1. Select the ARRAY command

Command:_array
Select object:

2. Window the object

Rectangular or Polar array (R/P):

3. Type R ENTER

Number of rows(- - -)<1>:

4. Type 4 ENTER

Number of columns(lll)<1>:

5. Type 3 ENTER

Distance between rows(- - -):

6. Type 1.50 ENTER

Distance between columns(lll)<1>:

7. Type 1.50 ENTER

2-18 CHAMFER

The CHAMFER command is used to create straight lined bevels between two given lines. Chamfers are defined in AutoCAD using two distances from a corner. See Figures 2-58 and 2-59. Most chamfers are 45 degrees, so the two defining distances are equal. AutoCAD will automatically set the second distance equal to the first. The set distance will appear as the default value for the second distance. The CHAMFER command is accessed via the CONSTRUCTION pulldown menu, or the CHAMFER icon on the MODIFY toolbar.

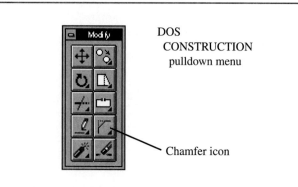

DOS
CONSTRUCTION
pulldown menu

Chamfer icon

Figure 2-58

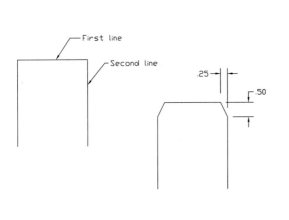

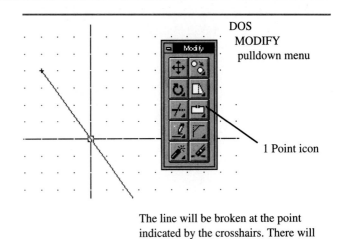

The line will be broken at the point
indicated by the crosshairs. There will
be no visible change in the line.

Figure 2-59

Figure 2-60

To create a chamfer

1. Select the CHAMFER command

   Command:_chamfer
   Chamfer Polyline/Distance/<Select first line>:

2. Type D ENTER

   Enter first chamfer distance<0.0000>:

3. Type .25 ENTER

   Enter second chamfer distance<0.2500>:

4. Type .50 ENTER

   Command:
   CHAMFER Polyline/Distance/<select first line>:

5. Select horizontal line

   Select second line:

6. Select the vertical line
7. Type ENTER

If ENTER is pressed a second time, the CHAMFER
sequence will start again using the distance values defined
as default values.

2-19 BREAK

The BREAK command is used to divide a line or
other entity into two parts. The POINT 1 and POINT 1
SELECT commands simply divide the line. There will be
no visible change to the line, but the original line will

become two individual lines. The 2 POINT and 2-POINT
SELECT commands create a visible gap between the two
lines created from a single original line.

The BREAK command is accessed using the MODI-
FY pulldown menu or the BREAK icons on the MODIFY
toolbar.

To use the BREAK 1 POINT command

See Figure 2-60.

1. Select the BREAK 1 command

   Select object:

2. Select a point on the object

The line will be divided into two parts at the selected
point.

To use BREAK 1 POINT SELECT

See Figure 2-61.

1. Select the 1 POINT SELECT command

   Select object
   Command:_break Select object:

2. Select the object

   Enter second point (or F for first point):-f
   Enter first point:

3. Select the break point

The difference between the BREAK 1 POINT and

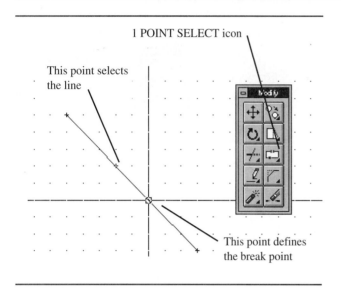

1 POINT SELECT icon

This point selects the line

This point defines the break point

Figure 2-61

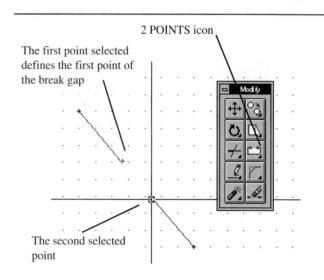

2 POINTS icon

The first point selected defines the first point of the break gap

The second selected point

Figure 2-62

BREAK 1 POINT SELECT commands is that the 1 POINT uses the selection point as the break point, whereas the 1 POINT SELECT command uses the first selected point as a way to identify the object, and the second select point as the break point.

To use the BREAK 2 POINTS

See Figure 2-62.

1. Select the BREAK 2 POINT command

   Command:_break Select object:

2. Select a point on the object

   This selection point not only selects the object, but also the first break point of a gap opening.

   Enter the second point (or F for first point):

3. Select the second point

   This selection point will define the length of the gap between the two parts of the broken object.

To use BREAK 2 POINTS SELECT

See Figure 2-63.

1. Select the 2 POINTS SELECT command

   Select object:

2. Select a point on the object

   This selection point only identifies the object; it will not affect the size or location of the gap.

   Enter second point (or F for first point):_f
   Enter first point:

3. Select the first point of the gap

   Enter second point:

4. Select the second point of the gap

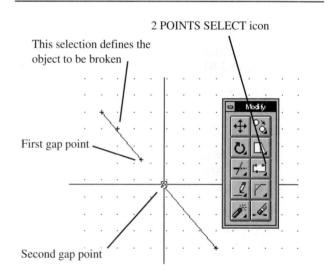

2 POINTS SELECT icon

This selection defines the object to be broken

First gap point

Second gap point

Figure 2-63

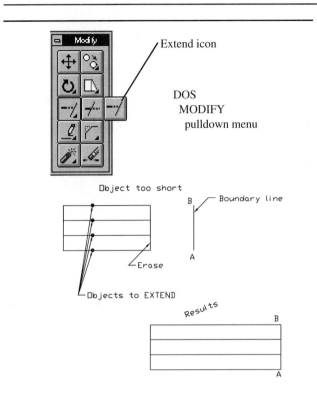

Figure 2-64

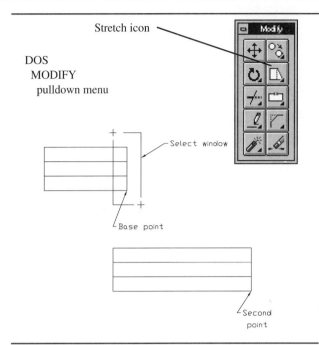

Figure 2-65

2-20 EXTEND

EXTEND is used to extend existing lines to a new length. It is helpful when designing and you find that you want to increase the length of an object.

The EXTEND command is accessed via the Modify pulldown menu or the EXTEND icon on the MODIFY toolbar. See Figure 2-64.

To extend lines

1. Select EXTEND command

Command:_extend
Select boundary edge(s)...
Select objects:

2. Select line A-B

<Select objects to extend>/Undo:

3. Select each horizontal line
4. Type ENTER

Boundary edges do not have to be lines. Arcs, circles, polygons, etc., can also be used.

2-21 STRETCH

The STRETCH command is used to extend groups of lines to a new length. It is similar to EXTEND but is capable of affecting more than one line at a time.

The STRETCH command is accessed via the MODI-FY pulldown menu or the STRETCH icon on the MODI-FY toolbar. See Figure 2-65.

To STRETCH a group of lines

1. Select the STRETCH command

Select objects to stretch by window or poly-gon...
Select objects:

2. Select the first window corner

Other corner:

3. Select the other window corner

Select objects:

4. Type ENTER

Base point of displacement:

5. Select point 1

Second point or displacement:

6. Select the second point of displacement
7. Type ENTER

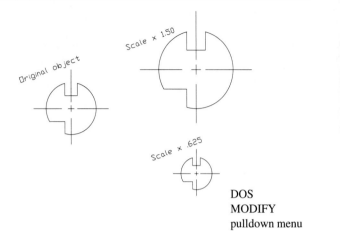

Figure 2-66

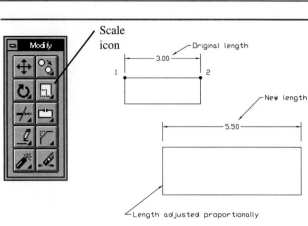

Figure 2-67

2-22 SCALE

The SCALE command is used to change the size of an object after it is drawn. See Figure 2-66.

The SCALE command is accessed via the MODIFY pull down menu or the SCALE icon on the MODIFY toolbar.

1. Select the SCALE command

   Command:_scale
   Select objects:

2. Select the object

   Base point:

3. Select a point on the object

In the example shown, the center point of the object was selected.

   <Scale factor>/Reference:

4. Enter the numerical value of the scale factor
5. Type ENTER

To scale an object by changing one of its lengths

See Figure 2-67.

1. Select the SCALE command

   Command:_scale
   Select objects:

2. Select the object

   Base point:

3. Select point 1 (see Figure 2-67)

   <Scale factor>/Reference:

4. Type R ENTER

   Reference length <1>:

5. Type 3 ENTER

   New Length:

6. Type 5.5 ENTER

2-23 POLYLINE

Polylines are lines made of a series of connected line segments that act as a single entity. Polylines are used to generate curves and splines and can be used in three-dimensional applications to produce solid objects.

There are four subcommands associated with the POLYLINE command: POLYLINE, 3D POLYLINE, SPLINE, and MULTILINE. The commands are accessed via the DRAW pulldown menu or the icons on the DRAW toolbar. See Figure 2-68.

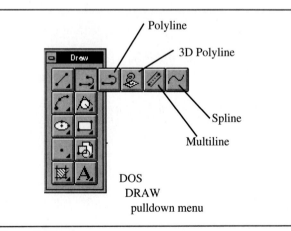

Figure 2-68

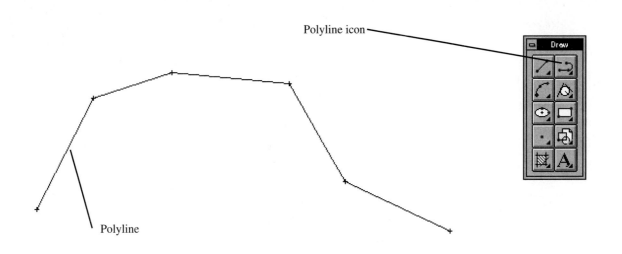

Polyline icon

Polyline

Figure 2-69

To draw a polyline

See Figure 2-69.

1. Select the POLYLINE command

Command: _pline
From point:

2. Select a start point

Arc/Close/Halfwidth/Length/Undo/Width/<Endpoint of line>:

3. Select a second point

Arc/Close/Halfwidth/Length/Undo/Width/<Endpoint of line>:

4. Select several more points

Arc/Close/Halfwidth/Length/Undo/Width/<Endpoint of line>:

5. Type Enter

To verify that a polyline is a single entity

1. Select the ERASE icon from the MODIFY toolbar or type the word ERASE

Select objects:

2. Select any one of the line segments in the polyline

Select objects:

The entire polyline, not just the individual line segment, will be selected. This is because, to AutoCAD, the polyline is one line.

3. Type ENTER

The entire polyline will disappear.

4. Select the UNDO icon from the standard toolbar

The object will reappear.

To draw a polyline — Arc

See Figure 2-70.

1. Select the POLYLINE command

From point:

2. Select a start point

Arc/Close/Halfwidth/Length/Undo/Width/<Endpoint of line>:

3. Type A ENTER

Angle/CEnter/CLose/Direction/Halfwidth/Line/Radius/Second pt/Undo/Width/<Endpoint of arc>:

4. Select a second point

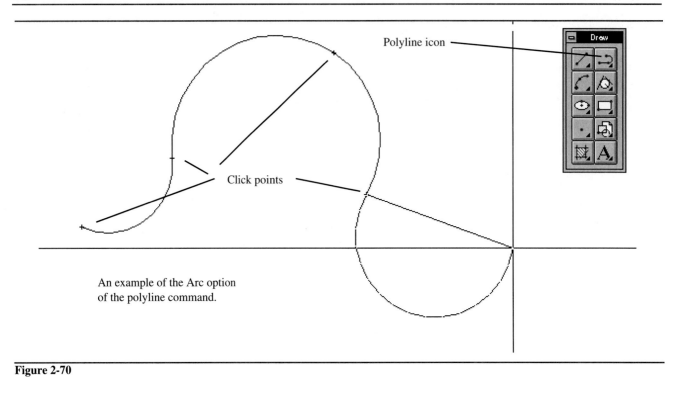

Polyline icon

Click points

An example of the Arc option
of the polyline command.

Figure 2-70

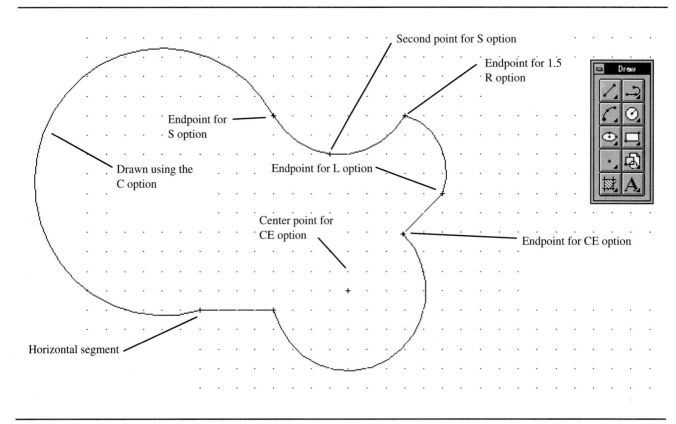

Second point for S option

Endpoint for 1.5
R option

Endpoint for
S option

Drawn using the
C option

Endpoint for L option

Center point for
CE option

Endpoint for CE option

Horizontal segment

Figure 2-71

To use other options associated with Polyline, arc

See Figure 2-71. The example shown includes a background grid with .5 spacing.

1. Select the POLYLINE command

Command: _pline
From point:

2. Select a start point

Arc/Close/Halfwidth/Length/Undo/Width/<Endpoint of line>:

3. Draw a short horizontal line segment

Arc/Close/Halfwidth/Length/Undo/Width/<Endpoint of line>:

4. Type A ENTER

Angle/CEnter/CLose/Direction/Halfwidth/Line/Radius/Second pt/Undo/Width/<Endpoint of arc>:

5. Type CE ENTER

CE activates the center option. You can now define an arc that will be part of the polyline by defining the arc's center point and its angle, chord length, or endpoint.

Center point:

6. Select a center point

Angle/Length/<Endpoint>:

7. Select an endpoint

Angle/CEnter/CLose/Direction/Halfwidth/Line/Radius/Second pt/Undo/Width/<Endpoint of arc>:

8. Type L ENTER

The Line option is used to draw straight line segments

Arc/Close/Halfway/Length/Undo/Width/<Endpoint>:

9. Select an endpoint

Arc/Close/Halfway/Length/Undo/Width/<Endpoint>:

10. Type A ENTER

Angle/CEnter/CLose/Direction/Halfwidth/Line/Radius/Second pt/Undo/Width/<Endpoint of arc>:

11. Type R ENTER

Radius

12. Type 1.5 ENTER

Angle/<Endpoint>:

13. Select an endpoint

Angle/CEnter/CLose/Direction/Halfwidth/Line/Radius/Second pt/Undo/Width/<Endpoint of arc>:

14. Type S ENTER

Second point:

15. Select a point

Endpoint:

16. Select an endpoint

Angle/CEnter/CLose/Direction/Halfwidth/Line/Radius/Second pt/Undo/Width/<Endpoint of arc>:

17. Type CL ENTER

The CLose option will join the last point drawn to the first point of the polyline using an arc.

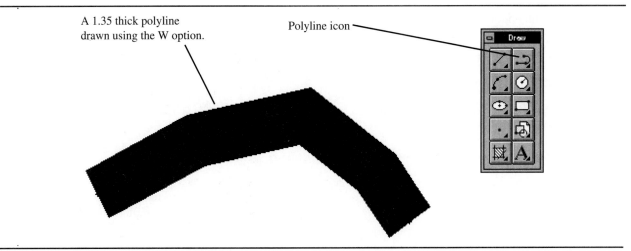

A 1.35 thick polyline drawn using the W option.

Polyline icon

Draw

Figure 2-72

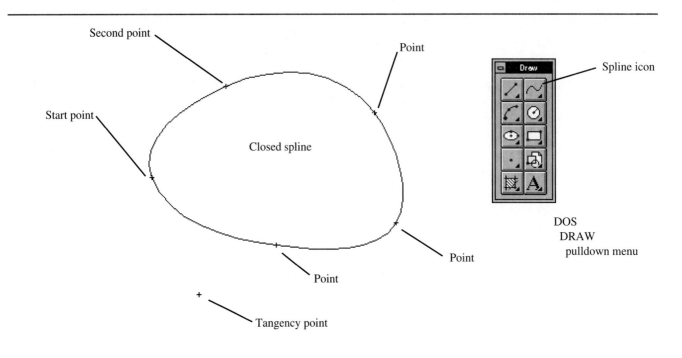

Figure 2-73

To draw different line thicknesses

See Figure 2-72.

1. Select the POLYLINE command

   From point:

2. Select a start point

   Angle/CEnter/CLose/Direction/Halfwidth/Line/ Radius/Second pt/Undo/Width/<Endpoint of arc>:

3. Type W ENTER

   The Width option is used to define the width of a line. The halfwidth option is used to define half the width of a line.

   Starting width <0.0000>:

4. Type 1.35 ENTER

   Ending width <1.3500>:

5. Type ENTER

   Arc/Close/Halfwidth/Length/Undo/Width/<End- point of line>:

6. Draw several line segments

To draw a SPLINE

A spline is a curved line. If the curve forms an enclosed area, it is called a closed spline. Curved lines are called open splines. See Figure 2-73.

1. Select the SPLINE command

   Command: _spline
   Object/<Enter first point>:

2. Select a start point

   Enter point:

3. Select a second point

   Close/Fit tolerance/<Enter point>:

4. Select three more points

   Close/Fit tolerance/<Enter point>:

5. Type C ENTER

   Enter tangent

6. Select a point

   Note how, as you move the cursor to locate the tangent point, the shape of the spline changes. These changes are based on your selection of a tangency point, which, in turn, affects the mathematical calculations used to create the curve.

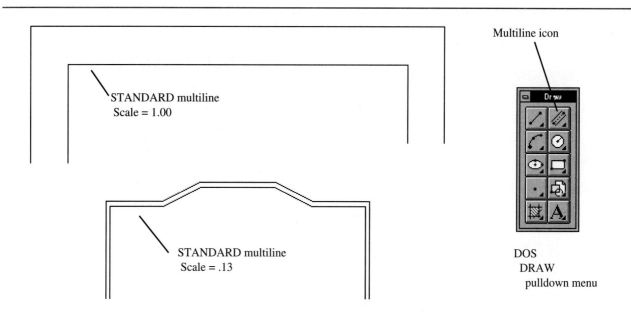

Figure 2-74

To draw a multiline

A multiline is a group of parallel lines that can be drawn together as if they were a single line. The default setting is two parallel lines located at a unit scale of 1.00 apart. See Figure 2-74.

1. Select the MULTILINE command

Justification = Top, Scale = 1.00, Style = STANDARD
    Justification/Scale/STyle/<Front point>:

2. Select a start point

To point:

3. Select a second point

Undo<to point>:

4. Select another point

Close/Undo<to point>:

5. Type ENTER

The close option will draw a line across the end of the two parallel lines. The jusitication line allows you to use either the top, bottom, or an imaginary line (zero) between the two parallel lines to define the multilines location. See Figure 2-75.

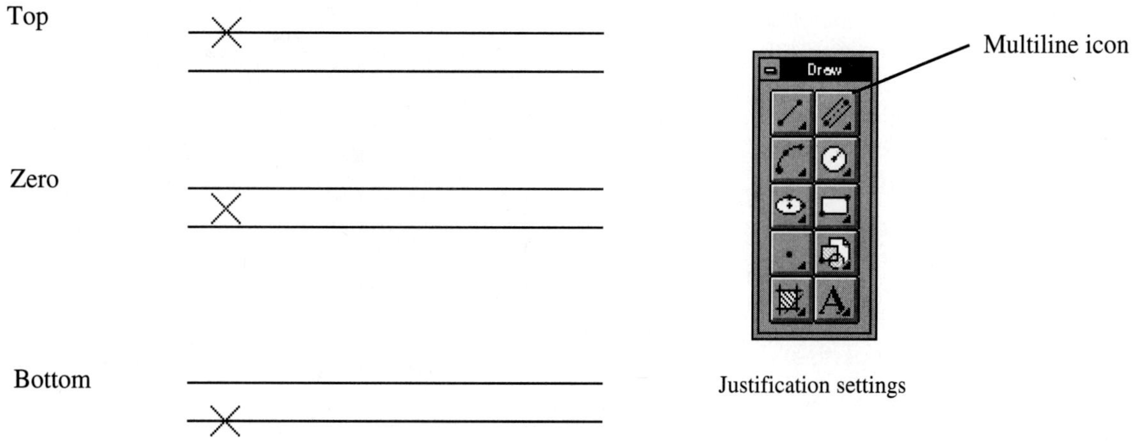

Top

Zero

Bottom

Justification settings

Multiline icon

Figure 2-75

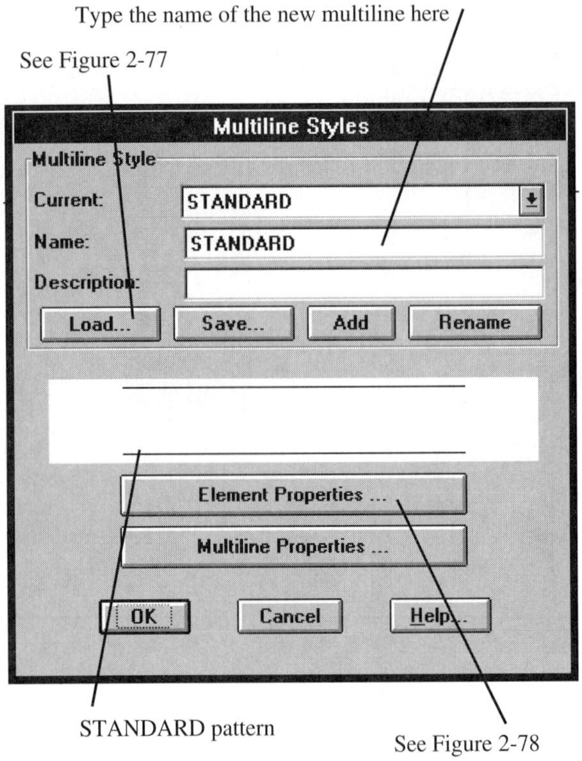

Type the name of the new multiline here

See Figure 2-77

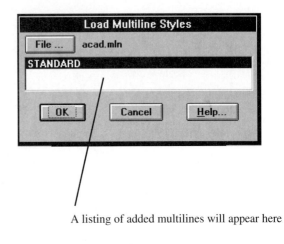

STANDARD pattern

See Figure 2-78

Figure 2-76

To create a new style of a multiple line

Different parallel line patterns may be created and saved for future use.

Command:

1. Type mlstyle ENTER

The Multiline Styles dialog box will appear. See Figure 2-76. The Load... option is used to load all existing multilines saved. Multilines have a file extension of .mln.

2. Select the Load... box

The Load Multiline dialog box will appear. See Figure 2-77. No other multilines exist at this time, so return to the Multiline dialog box.

3. Select the OK box

The Multiline dialog box will appear and will be used to create a new multiline style MLINE1.

4. Select the Elementary Properties... box

The Elementary Properties dialog box will appear. See Figure 2-78. This dialog box is used to define the new multiline.

A listing of added multilines will appear here

Figure 2-77

5. Select the Add box

A new setting will appear in the Elements box

0.0

The 0.0 number means that the new line will be drawn between the existing lines. It will have a 0.0 offset from the center line of the pattern. The Offset box can be used to change this value.

6. Select the Color... box to set the color of the new line and the Linetype... to change the line's pattern.

0.0 will appar here

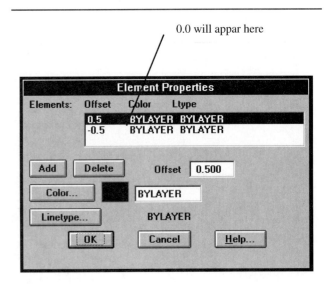

Figure 2-78

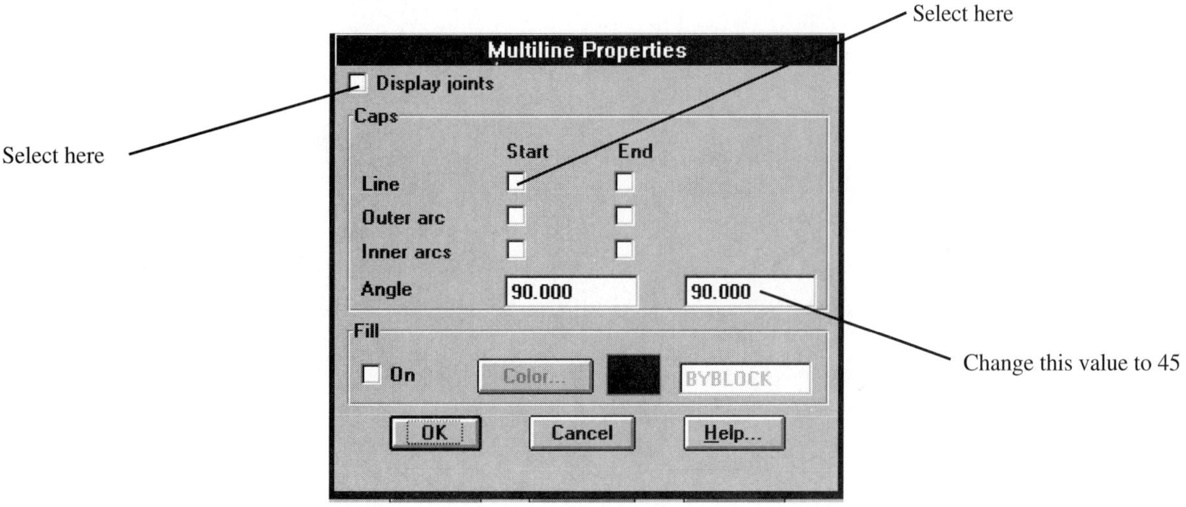

Select here

Select here

Change this value to 45

Figure 2-79

7. Select the OK box

The Multiline Styles box will reappear.

8. Select the Multiline Properties... box

The Multiline Properties dialog box will appear. See Figure 2-79. This box is used to set the joints, end lines and angles, and fill pattern for the line.

9. Select the Display joints box (an X will appear in the box when it is on) and the Start Line box, and change the End angle from 90 to 45.
10. Select the OK box

The Save multiline styles dialog box will reappear.

See Figure 2-80.

11. Type MLINE1 in the Name: box
12. Select the OK box

A Save As dialog box will appear. Multiline formats are saved using .mln extensions.

13. Select the Add box

The Current: box should display MLINE1.

14. Select the OK box and draw a multiline.

Figures 2-81 and 2-82 show examples of multiline MLINE 1 with various options.

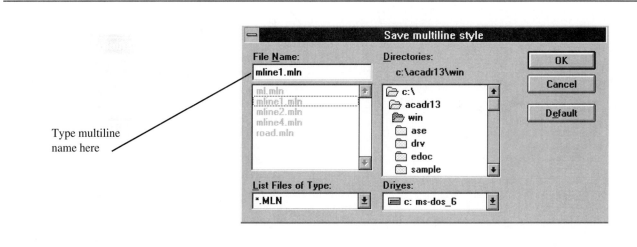

Type multiline name here

Figure 2-80

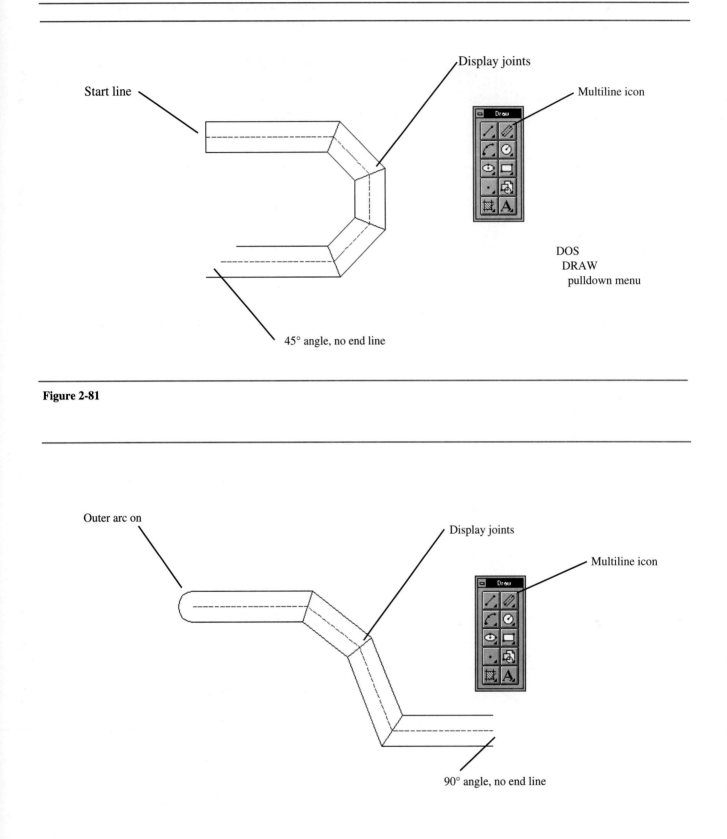

Figure 2-81

Figure 2-82

2-24 ELLIPSE

There are three submenus associated with the ELLIPSE command. See Figure 2-83. These three options allow you to define an ellipse using the lengths of its major and minor axes, an angle of rotation about the major axis, and an included angle.

The ELLIPSE commands are accessed via the DRAW pulldown menu or the DRAW toolbar.

To draw an ellipse — ellipse axis end

See the upper left figure in Figure 2-84.

1. Select the ELLIPSE AXIS END command

    Arc/Center/Isocircle/<Axis endpoint 1>:

2. Select a start point for one of the axes

    Axis endpoint 2:

3. Select an endpoint that defines the length of the axis

    <Other axis distance,/Rotation:

4. Select a point that defines half the length of the other axis

This distance is the radius of the axis. In the example shown, points 1 and 2 were used to define the major axis, and point 3 defines the minor axis.

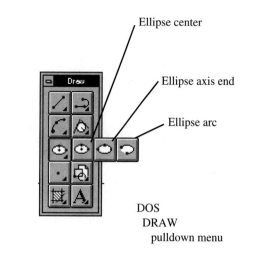

Ellipse center

Ellipse axis end

Ellipse arc

DOS
DRAW
pulldown menu

Figure 2-83

To draw an ellipse — ellipse center

See the upper right figure in Figure 2-84.

An ellipse may also be defined in terms of its angle of rotation about the major axis. See Figure 2-85. An ellipse with 0 degrees of rotation is a circle: an ellipse of constant radius. An ellipse with 90 degrees of rotation is a straight line: an end view of an ellipse.

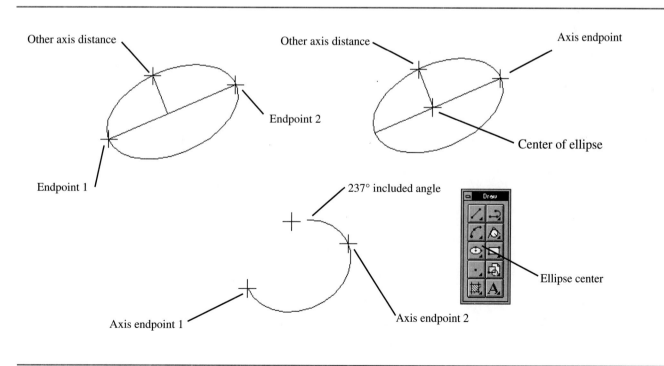

Figure 2-84

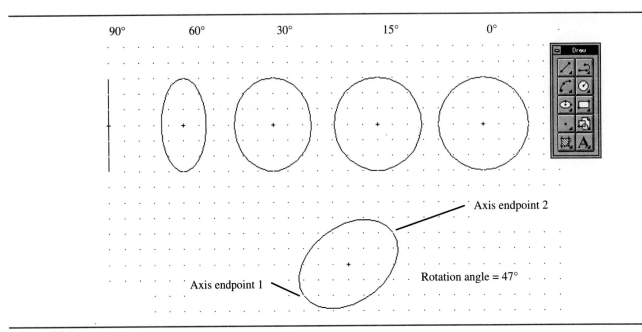

Figure 2-85

To draw an ellipse by defining its angle of rotation about the major axis

See Figure 2-85.

1. Select the ELLIPSE AXIS ENDPOINT command

   Arc/Center/<Axis endpoint 1>:

2. Select an endpoint of the major axis

   Axis endpoint 2:

3. Select the other endpoint of the major axis

   <Other axis distance>:Rotation:

4. Type r ENTER

   Rotation about major axis:

5. Type 47 ENTER

2-25 EXERCISE PROBLEMS

Redraw the figures in exercise problems EX2-1 through EX2-39. Do not include dimensions.

EX2-1 INCHES

CENTER DUCT

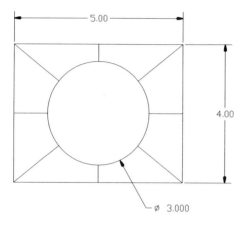

EX2-3 INCHES

SIDE BRACKET

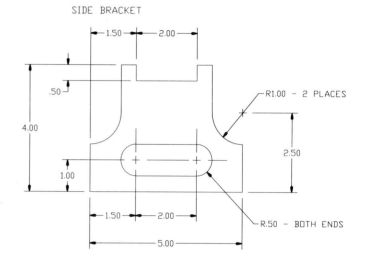

EX2-2 MILLIMETERS

CENTER COVER

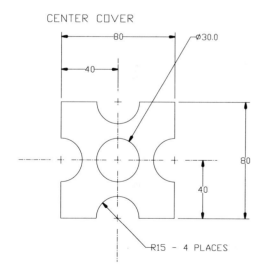

EX2-4 MILLIMETERS

CIRCLE PLATE

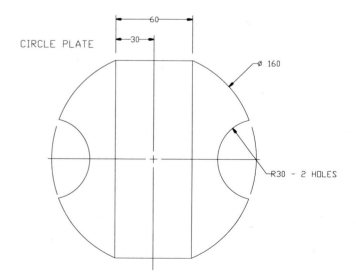

EX2-36 INCHES

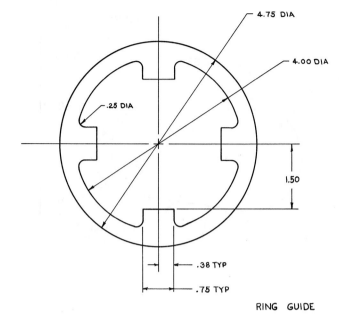

4.75 DIA
4.00 DIA
.25 DIA
1.50
.38 TYP
.75 TYP

RING GUIDE

EX2-38 MILLIMETERS

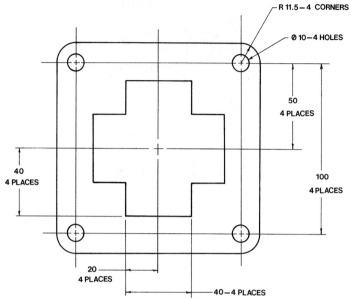

R 11.5 — 4 CORNERS
Ø 10 — 4 HOLES
50
4 PLACES
40
4 PLACES
100
4 PLACES
20
4 PLACES
40 — 4 PLACES

EX2-37 INCHES

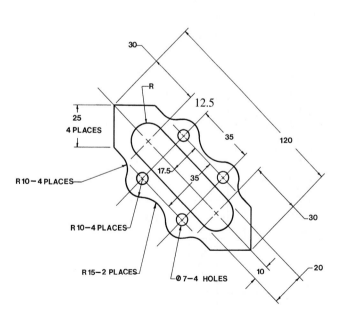

30
R
12.5
35
120
25
4 PLACES
17.5
35
R 10 — 4 PLACES
30
R 10 — 4 PLACES
R 15 — 2 PLACES
Ø 7 — 4 HOLES
10
20

EX2-39 MILLIMETERS

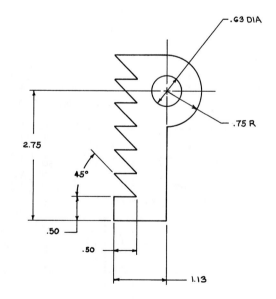

.63 DIA
.75 R
2.75
45°
.50
.50
1.13

2-25 EXERCISE PROBLEMS

Redraw the figures in exercise problems EX2-1 through EX2-39. Do not include dimensions.

EX2-1 INCHES

CENTER DUCT

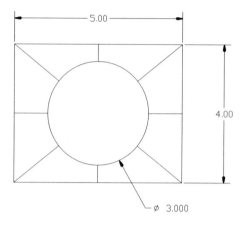

EX2-3 INCHES

SIDE BRACKET

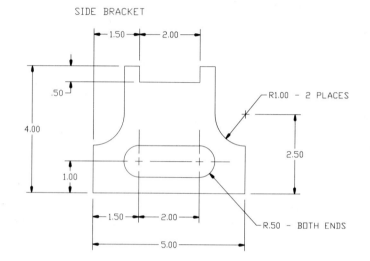

EX2-2 MILLIMETERS

CENTER COVER

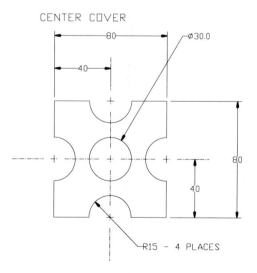

EX2-4 MILLIMETERS

CIRCLE PLATE

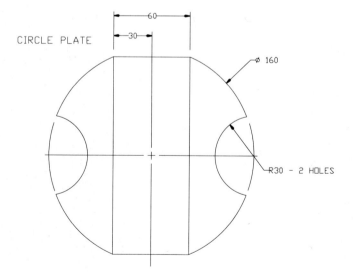

EX2-5 MILLIMETERS

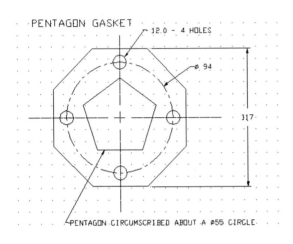

PENTAGON GASKET
12.0 - 4 HOLES
ø 94
117
PENTAGON CIRCUMSCRIBED ABOUT A ø55 CIRCLE

EX2-7 INCHES

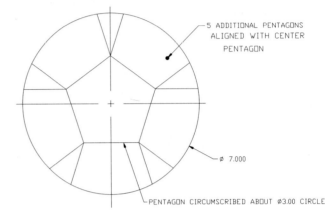

5 ADDITIONAL PENTAGONS ALIGNED WITH CENTER PENTAGON
ø 7.000
PENTAGON CIRCUMSCRIBED ABOUT ø3.00 CIRCLE

EX2-6 MILLIMETERS

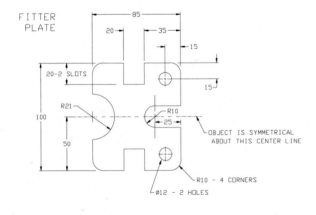

FITTER PLATE
85
20
35
15
20-2 SLOTS
15
100
R21
R10
50
25
OBJECT IS SYMMETRICAL ABOUT THIS CENTER LINE
R10 - 4 CORNERS
ø12 - 2 HOLES

EX2-8 INCHES

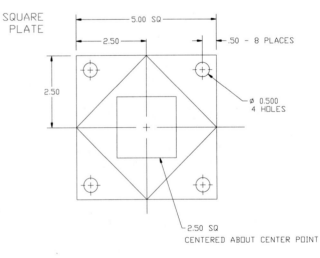

SQUARE PLATE
5.00 SQ
2.50
.50 - 8 PLACES
2.50
ø 0.500 4 HOLES
2.50 SQ CENTERED ABOUT CENTER POINT

EX2-9 INCHES

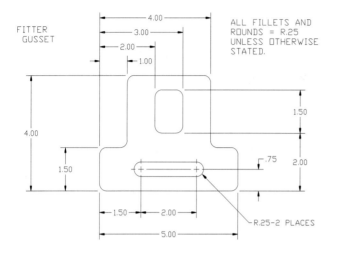

EX2-11 MILLIMETERS

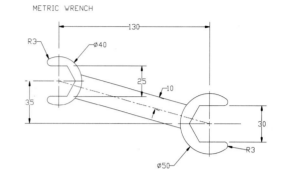

EX2-10 MILLIMETERS

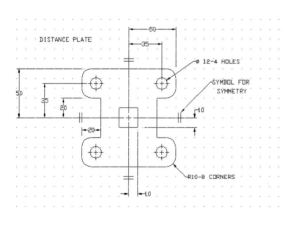

EX2-12 INCHES

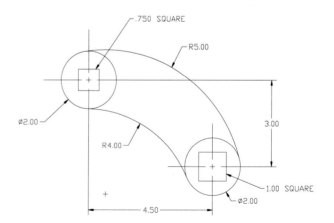

EX2-13 INCHES

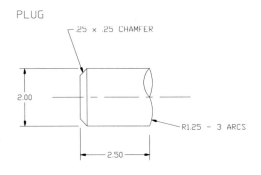

PLUG

.25 × .25 CHAMFER

2.00

R1.25 – 3 ARCS

2.50

EX2-15 MILLIMETERS

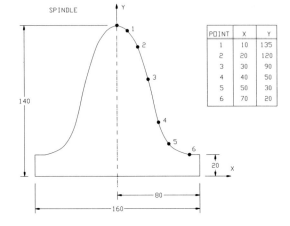

SPINDLE

Y

140

80

160

20

X

POINT	X	Y
1	10	135
2	20	120
3	30	90
4	40	50
5	50	30
6	70	20

EX2-14 MILLIMETERS

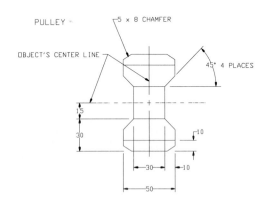

PULLEY

5 × 8 CHAMFER

OBJECT'S CENTER LINE

45° 4 PLACES

15

30

10

30   10

50

EX2-16 MILLIMETERS

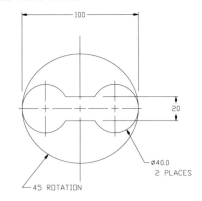

ELLIPTICAL GASKET

100

20

Ø40.0
2 PLACES

45 ROTATION

EX2-17 MILLIMETERS

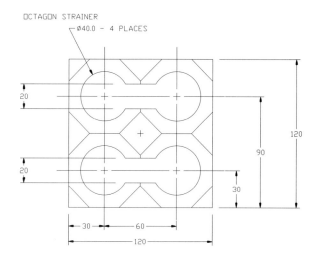

EX2-19 MILLIMETERS

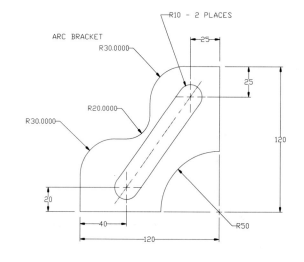

EX2-18 INCHES

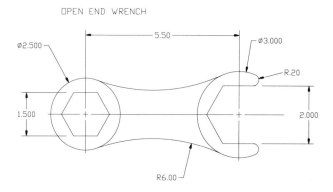

EX2-20 MILLIMETERS

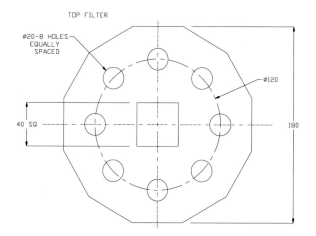

EX2-21 INCHES

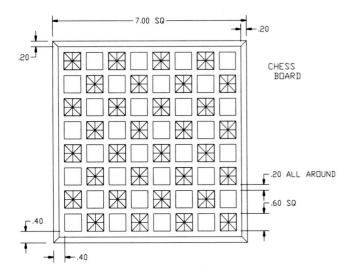

EX2-23 INCHES

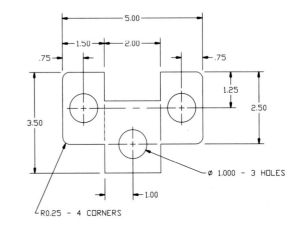

EX2-22 MILLIMETERS

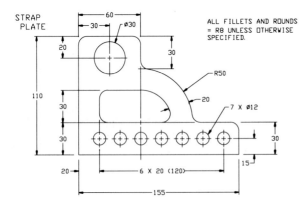

EX2-24 MILLIMETERS

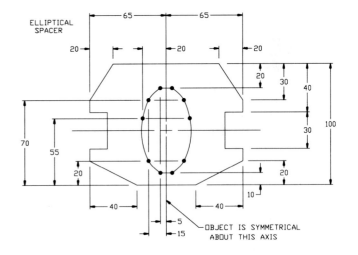

EX2-25 MILLIMETERS

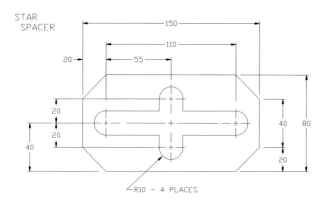

EX2-27 MILLIMETERS

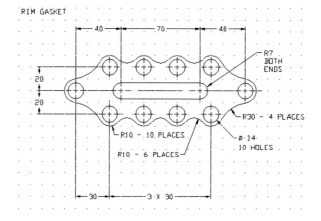

EX2-26 INCHES

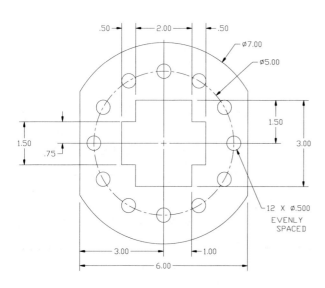

EX2-28 MILLIMETERS

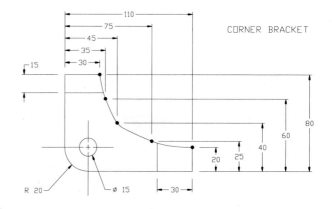

EX2-29 MILLIMETERS

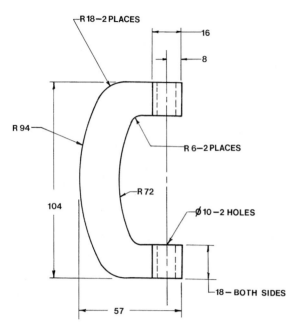

EX2-31 MILLIMETERS

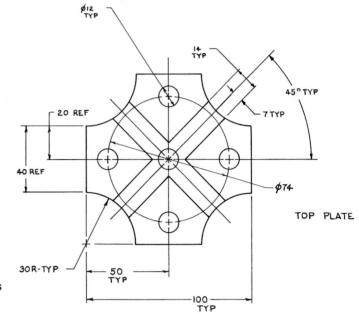

TOP PLATE

EX2-30 MILLIMETERS

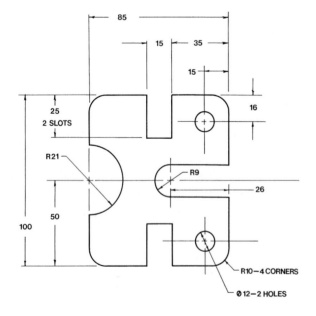

NOTE: OBJECT IS SYMMETRICAL ABOUT THE HORIZONTAL CENTER LINE

EX2-32 INCHES

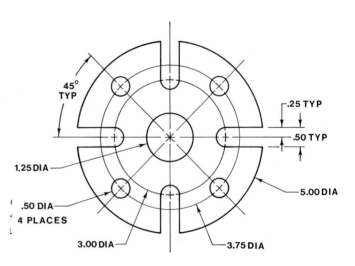

MATL .25 STEEL

EX2-33 INCHES

EX2-35 INCHES

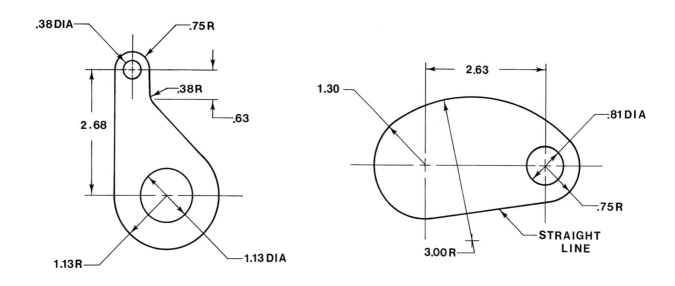

EX2-34 INCHES

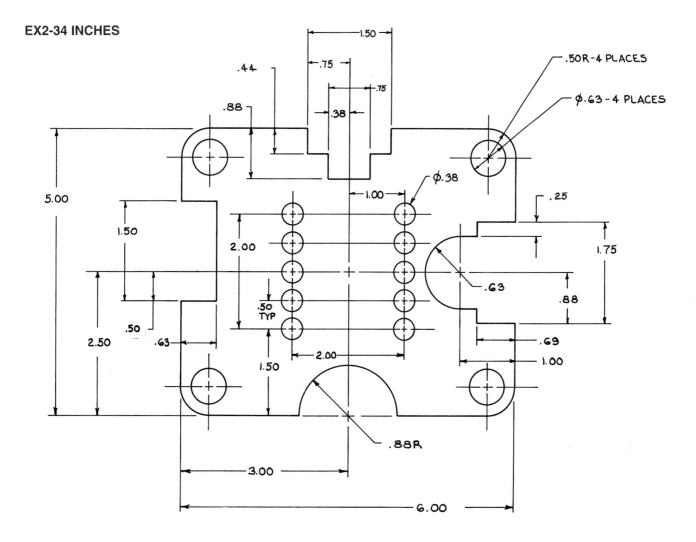

EX2-36 INCHES

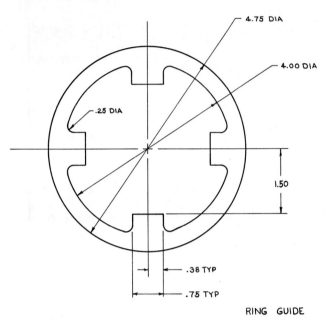

RING GUIDE

EX2-38 MILLIMETERS

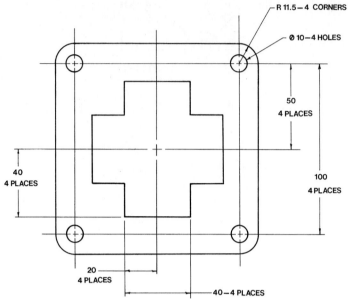

EX2-37 INCHES

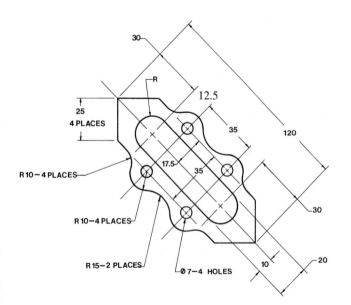

EX2-39 MILLIMETERS

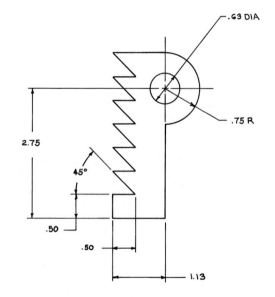

C H A P T E R 3

Drawing and Design

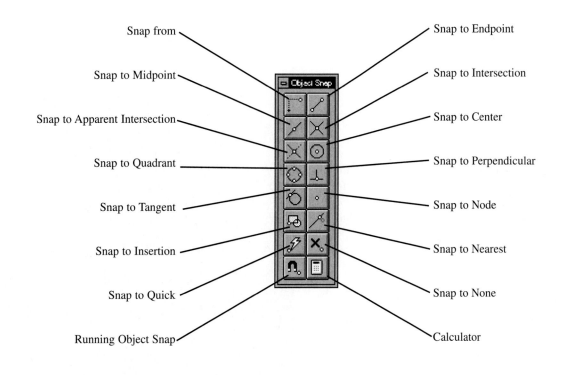

Snap from

Snap to Midpoint

Snap to Apparent Intersection

Snap to Quadrant

Snap to Tangent

Snap to Insertion

Snap to Quick

Running Object Snap

Snap to Endpoint

Snap to Intersection

Snap to Center

Snap to Perpendicular

Snap to Node

Snap to Nearest

Snap to None

Calculator

Figure 3-1

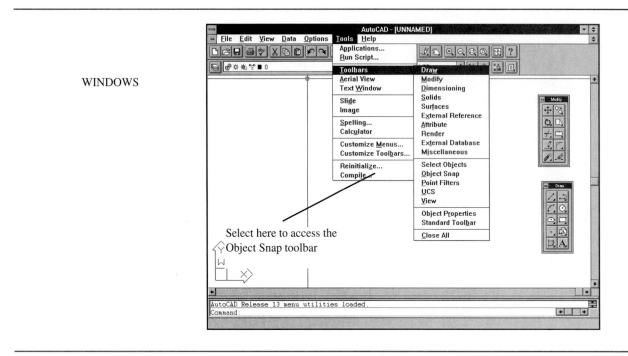

WINDOWS

Select here to access the
Object Snap toolbar

Figure 3-2

3-1 INTRODUCTION

This chapter introduces the more advanced techniques used to create drawings including the OSNAP, GRIPS, LAYERS, and ATTRIBUTES commands. Many classical geometric constructions are presented to help you develop the ability to use many different commands accurately and efficiently. The chapter concludes with an introduction to shape design based on a set of given parameters.

3-2 OSNAP

Figure 3-1 shows the Object Snap toolbar used in the WINDOWS version to access the OSNAP commands. There are no flyout icons associated with the Object Snap toolbar. Figure 3-2 shows how to access the Object Snap toolbar. Figure 3-3 shows how to access the OSNAP commands in the DOS version using the ASSIST pulldown menu. The QUICK, INSERT, and CALCULATOR commands will not be included in this chapter.

To access the Object Snap commands using the keyboard and mouse

The Object Snap command options may be accessed in conjunction with other commands by pressing the shift key and the right mouse button simultaneously. The OSNAP commands will appear as a column of commands. See Figure 3-4.

3-3 ENDPOINT

The endpoint option is used to snap to the endpoint of an existing entity. Figure 3-5 shows an existing line.

1. Select the OSNAP, ENDPOINT command

Command: _line From point:

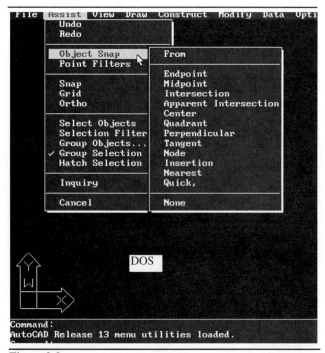

Figure 3-3

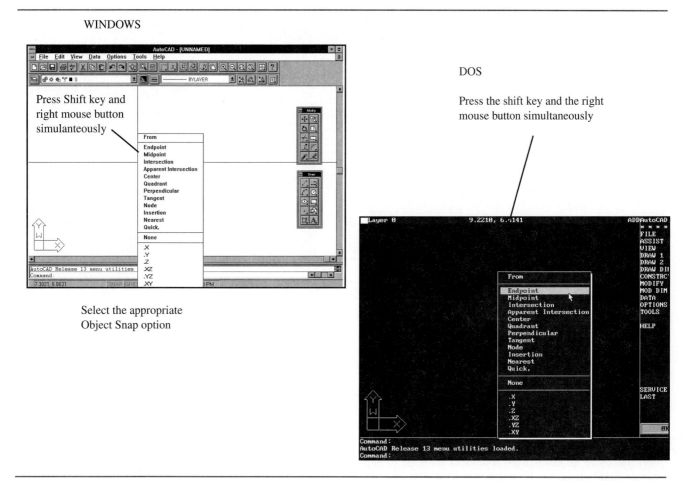

WINDOWS

Press Shift key and right mouse button simulanteously

Select the appropriate Object Snap option

DOS

Press the shift key and the right mouse button simultaneously

Figure 3-4

The OSNAP cursor will appear, indicating that the OSNAP command is ready for use. The OSNAP options do not work independently but in conjunction with other commands. In this example, the Line command had to be activated first, then the OSNAP command. Note that the cursor changes shape, from crosshairs to crosshairs with a rectangle. Locate the cursor rectangle over the end of the line and press the left mouse button. The starting point of the line will be at the endpoint of the existing line. The Endpoint command also works with arcs, mlines, and 3D applications.

3-4 RUNNING OBJECT SNAP

The RUNNING OBJECT SNAP option is accessed via the OPTIONS pulldown menu or the RUNNING OBJECT SNAP icon on the OSNAP toolbar. See Figure 3-6. The Running Object Snap dialog box can be used to turn an Object Snap option on permanently; that is, the

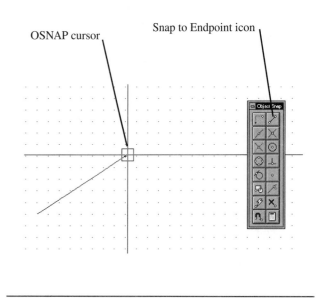

OSNAP cursor

Snap to Endpoint icon

Figure 3-5

WINDOWS

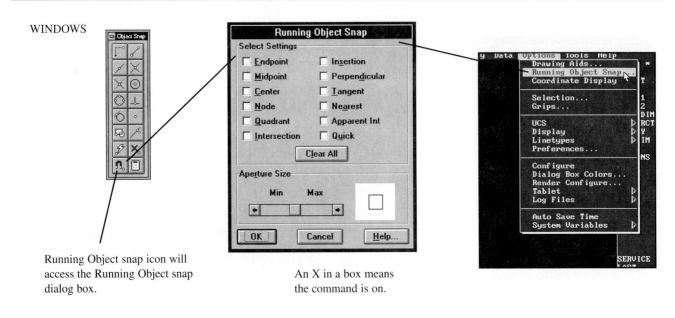

Running Object snap icon will access the Running Object snap dialog box.

An X in a box means the command is on.

Figure 3-6

option will remain on until you turn it off. If the ENDPOINT option were turned on, the cursor would snap to the nearest endpoint every time a point selection is made. Turning an Object Snap option on is very helpful when you know you are going to select a number of a certain type of point. However, in most cases, it is more practical to activate an Object Snap option as needed and the Object Snap menu using the shift key/ right mouse button option.

To turn on an Object Snap command option

1. Select the RUNNING OBJECT SNAP command

The Running Object Snap dialog box will appear

2. Select the OBJECT SNAP command option by clicking the box to the left of the command name

If the ENDPOINT box were clicked, an X would appear in the box, indicating the command is on. When you return to the drawing screen, the cursor will include a rectangle and will automatically snap to the endpoint of any entity selected.

If an OSNAP command is on, you do not have to use the OSNAP icons or the shift/right button option to activate the commands. However, if a command is on and you wish to use another command (the ENDPOINT command is on and you want to use INTERSECTION), you will have to turn the ENDPOINT command off, then activate the other command.

To turn off an Object Snap command

There are two methods that can be used to turn an OBJECT SNAP command off.

1. Select the RUNNING OBJECT SNAP command and click the activated option

The X will disappear from the box, indicating the command is off.

2. Select the NONE option on any of the OSNAP options menus.

All OSNAP commands will be turned off

To change the size of the Object Snap aperture box

The Running Object Snap dialog box also contains an aperture size option. This option allows you to change the size of the rectangular box on the cursor. A larger box makes it easier to grab objects, but too large a box may grab more than one object or the wrong object.

3-5 MIDPOINT

The MIDPOINT option is used to snap to the midpoint of an existing entity. In the example presented, a circle is to be drawn with its center point at the midpoint of an existing line. See Figure 3-7.

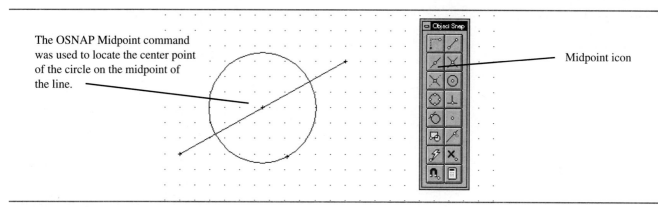

The OSNAP Midpoint command was used to locate the center point of the circle on the midpoint of the line.

Midpoint icon

Figure 3-7

To draw a center about the midpoint of a line

1. Select the CIRCLE command

   Command: _circle 3P/2P/TTR/<Center point>:

2. Select the OSNAP MIDPOINT option

   Command: _circle 3P/2P/TTR/<Center point>: _mid of

3. Select the line

   Command: _circle 3P/2P/TTR/<Center point>: _mid of: <snap off> Diameter/<Radius>:

4. Select a radius value

3-6 INTERSECTION

The INTERSECTION option is used to snap to the intersection of two or more entities. Figure 3-8 shows a set of projection lines that are to be used to define an ellipse.

To use the Osnap Intersection command to define an ellipse

1. Select the ELLIPSE CENTER command

   Center of ellipse:

2. Select the OSNAP INTERSECTION option

   Center of ellipse: _appoint of

3. Select the center point for the ellipse

   Axis endpoint

4. Select the OSNAP INTERSECTION option, then select the intersection that defines the length of one of the axes from the ellipse center point.

   <Other axis distance>/Rotation: int of

5. Select the OSNAP INTERSECTION option, then select the intersection that defines the other axis length.

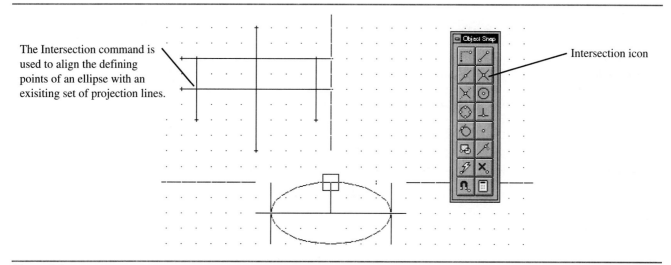

The Intersection command is used to align the defining points of an ellipse with an exisiting set of projection lines.

Intersection icon

Figure 3-8

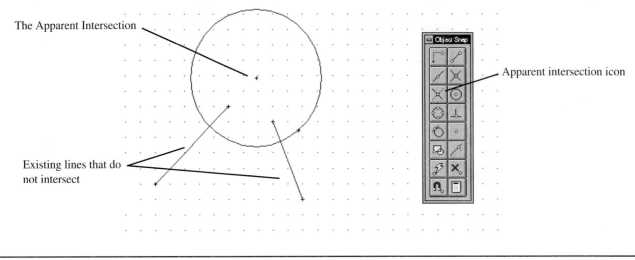

Figure 3-9

3-7 APPARENT INTERSECTION

The APPARENT INTERSECTION option is used to snap to an intersection that would be created if the two entities were extended to create an intersection. Figure 3-9 shows two lines that do not intersect, but if continued, would intersect.

To draw a circle centered about an apparent intersection

1. Select the CIRCLE command

   Command: _circle 3P/2P/ TTR/ <Center point>:

2. Select the OSNAP APPARENT INTERSECTION option

   Command: _circle 3P/2P/ TTR/ <Center point>: _appint of

3. Select one of the lines

   Command: _circle 3P/2P/ TTR/ <Center point>: _appint of and

4. Select the other line

   <Snap off> Diameter/:<Radius>:

5. Select a radius value for the circle

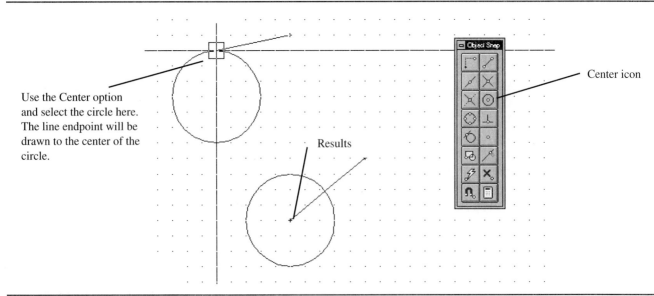

Figure 3-10

3-8 CENTER

The CENTER option is used to draw a line from a given point directly to the center point of a circle. See Figure 3-10.

To draw a line to the center point of a circle

1. Select the LINE command

   Command: _line From point:

2. Select the start point for the line.

   To point:

3. Select the OSNAP CENTER option

   To point: _cen of

4. Select any point on the circle.

Do not try to select the center point directly. Select any point on the edge of the circle or arc, and the center point will be calculated automatically.

3-9 QUADRANT

The QUADRANT option is used to snap directly to one of the quadrant points of an arc or circle. Figure 3-11 shows the quadrant points for an arc and a circle.

To draw a line to one of a circle's quadrant points

See Figure 3-12.

1. Select the LINE command

   Command: _line From point:

2. Select a start point for the line

   To point:

3. Select the OSNAP QUADRANT option

   To point: _qua of

4. Select a point on the circle near the desired quadrant point

Quadrant points

Quadrant icon

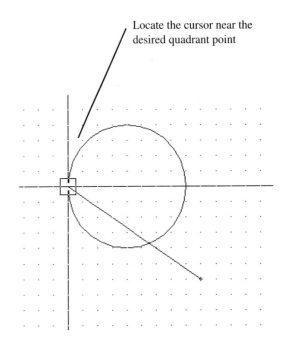

Locate the cursor near the desired quadrant point

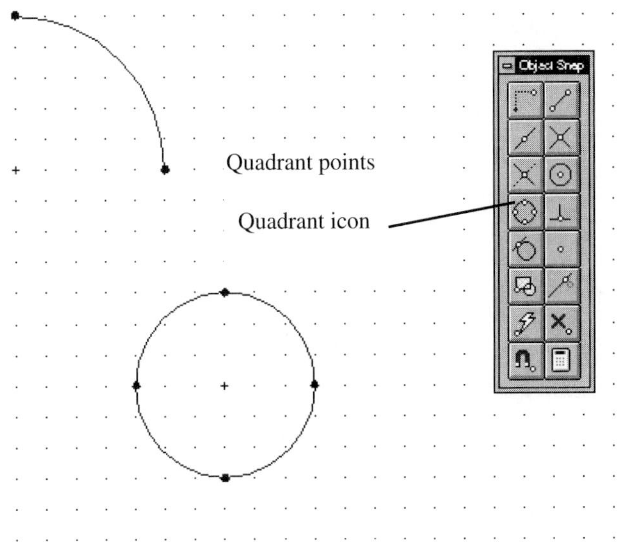

Figure 3-11

Figure 3-12

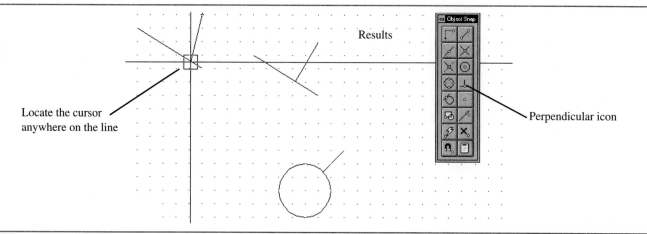

Figure 3-13

3-10 PERPENDICULAR

The PERPENDICULAR option is used to draw a line perpendicular to an existing entity. See Figure 3-13.

To draw a line perpendicular to a line

1. Select the LINE command

   Command: _line From point:

2. Select a start point for the line

   To point:

3. Select the OSNAP PERPENDICULAR option

   To point: _per to

4. Select the line that will be perpendicular to the drawn line

   Figure 3-13 also shows a line drawn perpendicular to a circle.

3-11 TANGENT

The TANGENT option is used to draw lines tangent to existing circles and arcs. See Figure 3-14.

To draw a line tangent to a circle

1. Select the LINE command

   Command: _line From point:

2. Select the start point for the line

   To point:

3. Select the OSNAP TANGENT option

   To point: _tan to

4. Select the circle

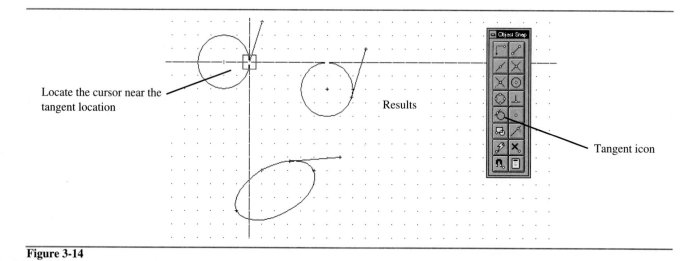

Figure 3-14

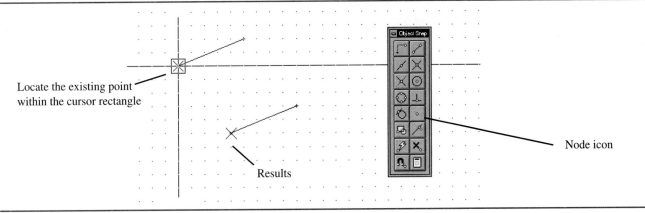

Locate the existing point within the cursor rectangle

Results

Node icon

Figure 3-15

3-12 NODE

The NODE option is used to draw a line to an existing point. The point must have been defined previously as a point. The node option will not snap to a random point within an existing entity, for example, a point on a line. See Figure 3-15.

To draw a line to an existing point

1. Select the LINE command

   Command: _line From point:

2. Select a start point for the line

   To point:

3. Select the OSNAP NODE option

   To point: _ nod of

4. Select the existing point

3-13 NEAREST

The NEAREST option is used to snap to the nearest available point on an existing entity. See Figure 3-16.

To draw a line from a point to the nearest selected point on an existing line

1. Select the LINE command

   Command: _line From point

2. Select a start point for the line

   To point:

3. Select the OSNAP NEAREST option

   To point: _nea to

4. Select the existing line

The existing line need only be within the rectangular box on the cursor. The line endpoint will be snapped to the nearest available point on the line.

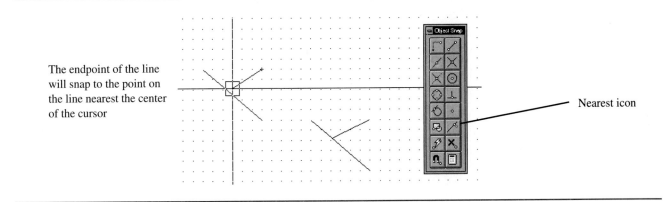

The endpoint of the line will snap to the point on the line nearest the center of the cursor

Nearest icon

Figure 3-16

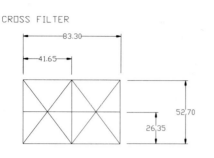

Figure 3-17

3-14 SAMPLE PROBLEM SP3-1

Redraw the object shown in Figure 3-17. Do not include dimensions.

1. NEW drawing called SP3-1
2. Drawing setup

    LIMITS: Lower left = <0.0000,0.0000>
    LIMITS: Upper right = 297,210
    ZOOM ALL
    GRID = 10
    SNAP = 5

3. Draw a 83.3 x 52.7 rectangle starting at point 40,40. Use relative coordinate values to draw the rectangle's edge lines (@Distance<Angle). See Figure 3-18.
4. Draw line A-B-C. Point A is a GRID SNAP point, so it may be selected directly. Point B is selected using OSNAP MIDPOINT and Point C is selected using OSNAP ENDPOINT (or INTERSECTION). See Figure 3-19.

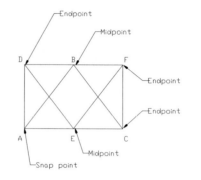

Figure 3-19

5. Draw line D-E-F using ENDPOINT, MIDPOINT, and ENDPOINT, respectively
6. Draw line B-E using INTERSECTION. See Figure 3-20.
7. Draw line G-H using MIDPOINT
8. SAVE the drawing if desired

3-15 SAMPLE PROBLEM SP3-2

Redraw the object shown in Figure 3-21. Do not include dimensions.

1. NEW drawing called SP3-2
2. Drawing setup

    LIMITS: accept the default values
    GRID = .50
    SNAP = .25

3. Draw lines A-B, C-D, A-C, and C-B. The endpoint of each of these lines is located on a GRID SNAP point so the points can be selected. 4. x

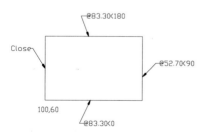

Figure 3-18

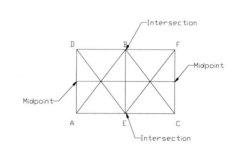

Figure 3-20

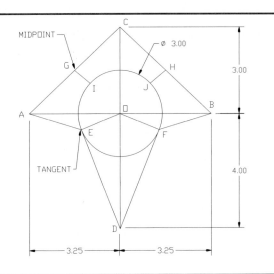

Figure 3-21

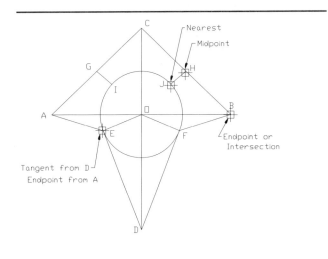

Figure 3-23

4. Draw circle O. Respond to the center point prompt by selecting INTERSECTION from the OSNAP pop-up menu. See Figure 3-22.
5. Draw lines G-I and H-J using MIDPOINT and NEAREST
6. Draw lines D-E and D-F using TANGENT. Draw lines A-E and A-F using ENDPOINT. Points A, B, and D are GRID SNAP points and are also endpoints. See Figure 3-23.
7. SAVE the drawing if desired

3-16 GRIPS

The GRIPS function is used to quickly identify and lock onto convenient points on an entity such as the endpoints of lines or the center point of a circle. Figure 3-24 shows some examples of grip points.

GRIPS is helpful when using some EDIT commands. For example, if a line is to be ROTATED about its center point, GRIPS can be used to first identify the line's center point (pickbox) and then lock on to it as the center point (base point) for the rotation. The center point of a circle could be used to MOVE the circle to a new location.

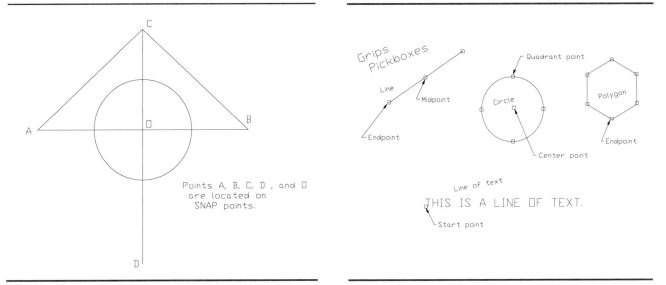

Figure 3-22

Figure 3-24

WINDOWS and DOS

Options (pulldown menu)

Grips...

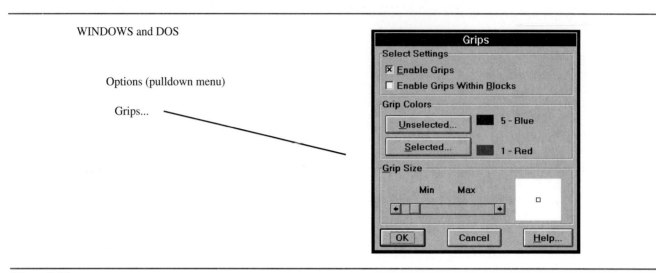

Figure 3-25

The GRIP command is located under the OPTIONS pulldown menu. The GRIP dialog box is shown in Figure 3-25. The dialog box can be used to set the size of the pick-box, size of the grip boxes on the screen, and the colors of the identifying pickboxes and the basepoint boxes.

By default, the GRIP command is automatically on. The GRIP submenu contains five functions: STRETCH, MOVE, ROTATE, SCALE, MIRROR. These functions operate as explained in Chapter 2, but can be accessed and used more quickly with GRIP.

GRIP pickboxes are activated by locating the cursor on an entity and pressing the select button. The prompt line must display a Command: prompt, meaning no command is presently active. The base point is gripped by locating the cursor on one of the pickboxes and again pressing the select button. See Figure 3-24.

3-17 STRETCH (GRIPS)

To extend the length of a line

See Figure 3-26. Given line A-B, extend it 1.25 inches.

1. Select CIRCLE, CENTER, RADIUS command and draw a circle of radius 1.25 using point B as the circle's center point. Use OSNAP, END-POINT to snap onto point B.
2. Select the word AutoCAD from the top of the menu or press the ENTER key to ensure a Command: prompt
3. Select line A-B

Blue pickboxes should appear at the two endpoints and at the midpoint.

4. Select point B

The blue pickbox should change to a solid red square box.

5. Select STRETCH from the menu or use the ENTER key to toggle through the GRIP options, which will appear on the command line

<Stretch to point>/Base point/Copy/Undo/eXit:

Stretch point B to the edge of the 1.25 circle by first pressing the middle mouse button and selecting NEAREST from the pop-up menu, then pressing the left mouse button.

6. Erase the circle

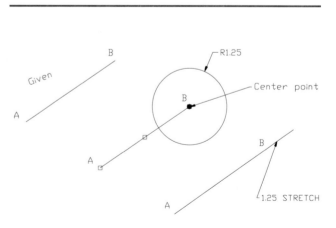

Figure 3-26

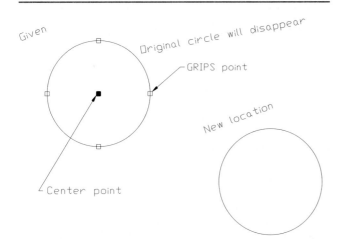

Figure 3-27

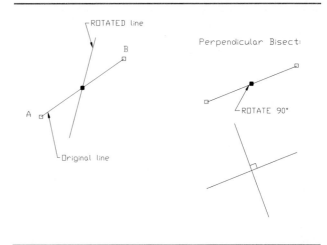

Figure 3-28

3-18 MOVE (GRIPS)

To move an object using GRIPS

See Figure 3-27. Given Circle O, move it to a new location on the drawing.

1. Select the word AutoCAD from the top of the menu or press the ENTER key to ensure a Command: prompt
2. Select any point on the circumference of circle O

Blue pickboxes should appear at circle O's center point and each of the quadrant points.

3. Select the center point (or any other pickbox)

The centerpoint pickbox should change to a red solid square box.

4. Select MOVE from the menu or use the ENTER key to toggle through the GRIP options, which will appear on the command line

MOVE
   <Move to point>/Base point/Copy/Undo/eXit:

5. Move the circle to a new location and press the left mouse button

3-19 ROTATE (GRIPS)

To rotate an object using GRIPS

See Figure 3-28. Given line A-B, rotate it 35 degrees about its midpoint.

1. Select the word AutoCAD from the top of the menu or press the ENTER key to ensure a Command: prompt
2. Select line A-B

Blue pickboxes should appear at the line's two endpoints and its midpoint, point C.

3. Select point C

The blue pickbox at point C should change to a solid red square box.

4. Select ROTATE from the menu or use the ENTER key to toggle through the GRIP options, which will appear on the command line

ROTATE
   <Rotation angle> / Base point /Copy /Undo / Reference / eXit:

5. Type 35 ENTER

3-20 SCALE (GRIPS)

To change the scale of an object

See Figure 3-29. Given line A-B, reduce it to half its original length.

1. Select the word AutoCAD from the top of the menu or press the ENTER key to ensure a Command: prompt
2. Select line A-B

Blue pickboxes should appear at the line's two endpoints and its midpoint, point C.

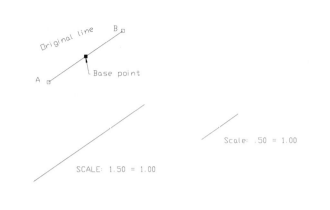

Figure 3-29

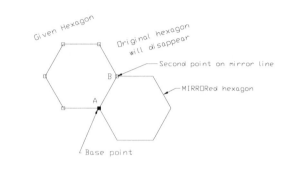

Figure 3-30

3. Select any one of the pickboxes

The selected pickbox should change to a red solid square box.

4. Select SCALE from the menu or use the ENTER key to toggle through the GRIP options, which will appear on the command line

SCALE
<Scale>/Base point/Copy/Undo/Reference/eXit:

5. Type .5 ENTER

3-21 MIRROR (GRIPS)

To mirror an object

See Figure 3-30. Given a hexagon, draw another hexagon aligned with edge A-B.

1. Select the word AutoCAD from the top of the menu or press the ENTER key to ensure a Command: prompt
2. Select any point on the edge of the hexagon

Blue pickboxes should appear at each corner intersection of the hexagon.

3. Select the pickbox at point A

The selected pickbox should change to a red solid square box.

4. Select MIRROR from the menu or use the ENTER key to toggle through the GRIP options, which will appear on the command line

MIRROR
<Second point>/Base point/Copy/Undo/eXit:

5. Select point B

The hexagon will be mirrored about line A-B.

3-22 BLOCKS

Blocks are groups of entities saved as a single unit. Blocks are used to save shapes, and groups of shapes, that are used frequently when creating drawings. Once created, blocks can be inserted into drawings, thereby saving drawing time. The BLOCK commands are accessed using the BLOCK icon on Draw toolbar.

Predrawn blocks

AutoCAD offers "PartSpec" as part of its "AutoDESK Mechanical Library." PartSpec contains over 200,000 drawn BLOCKs of standard manufacturers' parts and material specifications presented on 2 CD-RAMs. These blocks can be inserted directly into a drawing. PartSpec saves time when designing because it acts as a manufacturer's catalog and because the listed parts are already saved as drawings.

To create a BLOCK — WINDOWS

Figure 3-31 shows an object. A BLOCK can be made from this existing drawing as follows.

1. Select the BLOCK icon from the DRAW toolbar

   Command: _block Block name (or ?):

2. Type SHAPE ENTER

   BLOCK names may contain up to 31 characters.

   Insertion base point:

3. Select the object's center point

   Select objects:

4. Window the entire object

   Select objects:

5. Type ENTER

The object will disappear from the screen. It will be saved as part of the existing drawing.

To insert a BLOCK — WINDOWS

1. Select the INSERT BLOCK icon from the DRAW toolbar or type the word INSERT in response to a Command: prompt.

   The Insert dialog box will appear. See Figure 3-32.

2. Select the Block... box

The Defined Blocks dialog box will appear. See Figure 3-35 on page 113.

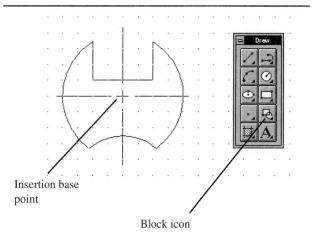

Insertion base point

Block icon

Figure 3-31

3. Select SHAPE

   The word SHAPE will appear in the Selection box.

4. Select OK

   The Insert dialog box will reappear with the word SHAPE in the box next to the Block... box.

5. Select OK

The SHAPE BLOCK will appear on the screen with its insertion point aligned with the crosshairs. The SHAPE will move as you move the crosshairs.

Command: _ddinsert
Insertion point:

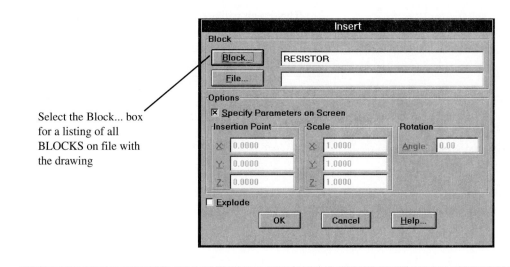

Select the Block... box for a listing of all BLOCKS on file with the drawing

Figure 3-32

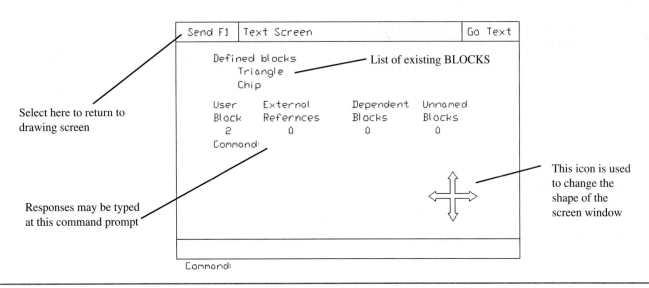

Select here to return to drawing screen

List of existing BLOCKS

This icon is used to change the shape of the screen window

Responses may be typed at this command prompt

Figure 3-33

To create a BLOCK — DOS

This procedure assumes that the shape shown in Figure 3-31 is presently on the drawing screen and that it is to be made into a BLOCK named SHAPE.

1. Select the CONSTRUCTION pulldown menu, then BLOCK

   Command:_ block Block name (or ?):

2. Type SHAPE ENTER

   Insertion base point

3. Select the object's center point

   Select objects:

4. Window the entire object

   Select objects:

5. Type Enter

For a listing of existing BLOCKS — DOS

1. Select the CONSTRUCTION pulldown menu, then BLOCK

   Command:_ block Block name (or?):

2. Type ? ENTER

   Block(s) to list <>:*

3. Type ENTER

The screen will appear as shown in Figure 3-33.

4. Select the Send F1 box to return to the drawing screen

To insert a BLOCK — DOS

1. Type INSERT in response to a command prompt

   Block name or (?):

2. If you know the name of the BLOCK, type it; if not, type ? enter

   Block(s) to list <>:*

3. Type ENTER

The screen will appear as shown in Figure 3-34.

4. Type insert in response to a command prompt:
5. Type the name of the BLOCK

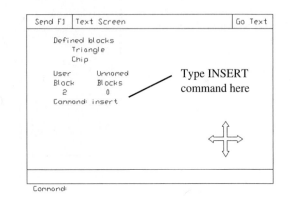

Type INSERT command here

FIgure 3-34

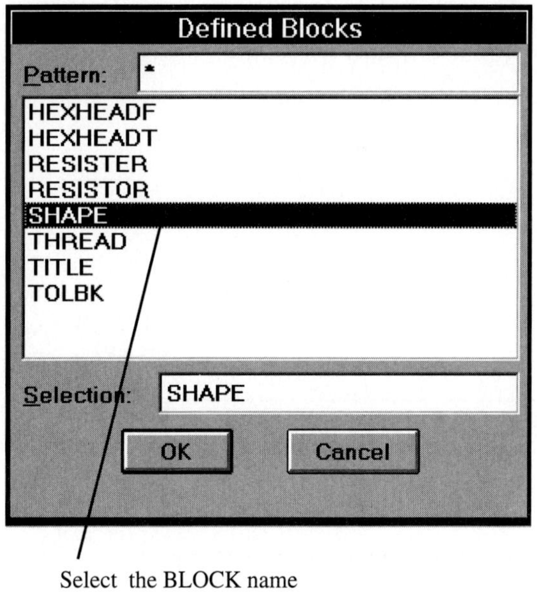

Select the BLOCK name

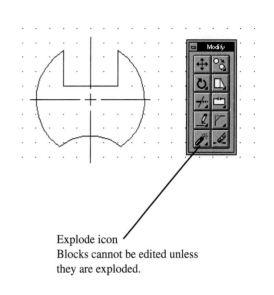

Explode icon
Blocks cannot be edited unless
they are exploded.

Figure 3-35

Figure 3-36

The following commands are common to both WINDOWS and DOS

6. Select an insertion point for the SHAPE

Insertion point: X scale factor <1>/ Corner/ XYZ:

The default scale factor is 1. This means that if you accept the default value by typing ENTER, the SHAPE will be redrawn at its original size. The shape of the object may be changed by moving the crosshairs. Verify that the shape can be changed dynamically by moving the crosshairs around the drawing and observing how the SHAPE changes.

7. Type ENTER

Y scale factor (default =X):

The SHAPE will temporarily disappear from the screen. The Y scale factor will automatically be made equal to the X scale factor unless a different value is defined.

8. Type ENTER

Rotation angle <0.00>:

9. Type ENTER

The BLOCK is now part of the drawing. However, the BLOCK in its present form may not be edited. BLOCKS are treated as single entities, and not as individual lines. You can verify this by trying to erase any one of the lines in the BLOCK. The entire object will be erased. The object can be returned to the screen by selecting the UNDO command.

A BLOCK must first be exploded before it can be edited.

To EXPLODE a BLOCK

See Figure 3-36.

1. Select the EXPLODE command

Command: _explode
Select objects:

2. Window the entire object

Select objects:

3. Type ENTER

The object is now exploded and can be edited. There is no visible change in the screen, but there will be a short blink after the EXPLODE command is executed.

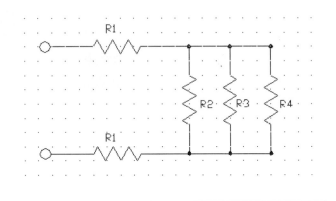

Figure 3-37

3-23 WORKING WITH BLOCKS

Figure 3-37 shows a resistor circuit. It was created from an existing BLOCK called RESISTOR. The drawing uses Decimal units with a GRID set to .5 and a SNAP set to .25. The default Drawing Limits were accepted. The procedure is as follows.

To insert blocks at different angles

1. Select or type the INSERT BLOCK command

The Defined Blocks dialog box will appear (WINDOWS only)

2. Select or type the name of the Block...

The Insert dialog box will appear. See the previous section if you cannot remember the BLOCK name while using the DOS version.

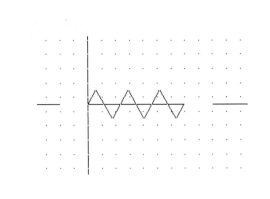

Figure 3-39

3. Select the BLOCK called RESISTOR

See Figure 3-38.

4. Select OK, OK to return to the drawing screen

The RESISTOR BLOCK will appear attached to the crosshairs. The BLOCK will attach to the crosshairs at the predefined insert point. See Figure 3-39.

The RESISTOR is too large for the drawing, so a reduced scale will be used to generate the appropriate size.

Insertion point:

5. Select an insertion point

Insertion point: X scale factor <1> /Corner/XYZ:

6. Type .50 ENTER

Y scale factor (default=X):

7. Type ENTER

Rotation angle <0.00>:

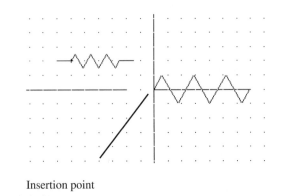

Insertion point

Figure 3-38

Figure 3-40

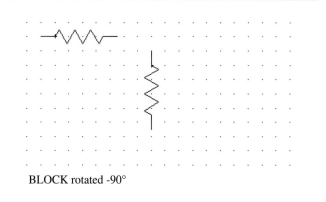

BLOCK rotated -90°

Figure 3-41

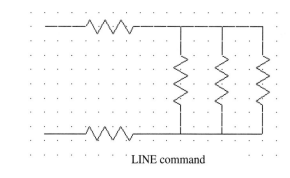

LINE command

Figure 3-43

8. Type ENTER

This will set the RESISTOR in place.

9. Type ENTER

This will reactivate the INSERT BLOCK command. The Insert dialog box will appear on the screen with the word RESISTOR in the box next to the Block... button.

10. Select OK

A second RESISTOR will appear on the screen.

11. Select an insertion point as shown in Figure 3-40.

Insertion point: X scale factor <1> /Corner/XYZ:

12. Type .50 ENTER

Y scale factor (default=X):

13. Type ENTER

Rotation angle <0.00>:

14. Type -90 ENTER

Your screen should look like Figure 3-41.

15. Use the COPY command to add the additional required resistors.

See Figure 3-42.

16. Use the LINE command to draw the required lines.

See Figure 3-43.

17. Use the DONUT command to draw the circular shapes at the connection points

*Command: _donut
Inside diameter <0.5000>:*

18. Type 0.0 ENTER

Outside diameter <1.0000>:

19. Type .125 ENTER

Center of doughnut:

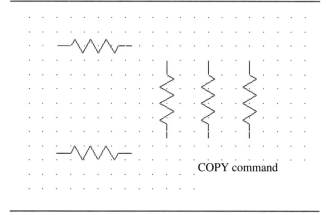

COPY command

Figure 3-42

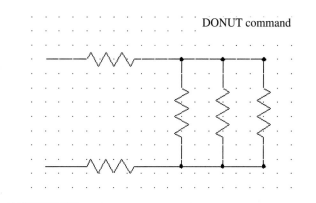

DONUT command

Figure 3-44

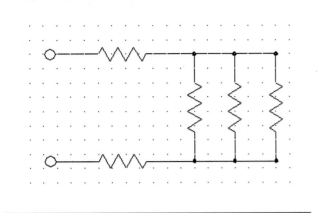

Figure 3-45

20. Locate the solid donuts on the connection points

    See Figure 3-44.

21. Select the CIRCLE command and draw a circle of diameter .375
22. Use the COPY command to create a second circle
23. Use the EXTEND command to draw the lines that touch the edges of the two open circles

    See Figure 3-45.

24. Use the DTEXT command to add the appropriate text

To insert BLOCKS with different scale factors

Figure 3-46 shows four different size threads, all created from the same BLOCK. The BLOCK labeled A used the default scale factor of 1, so it is exactly the same size as the original drawing used to create the BLOCK. The BLOCK labeled B was created with an X scale factor equal to 1, and a Y scale factor equal to 2. The procedure is as follows.

1. Select the INSERT BLOCK command
2. Select the THREAD BLOCK

The THREAD BLOCK is not an AutoCAD creation. THREAD was created specifically for this example.

Insertion point:

3. Select an insertion point

    Insertion point: X scale factor <1> /Corner/XYZ:

4. Type ENTER

    Y scale factor (default=X):

5. Type 2

    Rotation angle <0.00>:

6. Type ENTER

The THREAD labeled C has an X scale factor of .75 and a Y scale factor of 1.25. The THREAD labeled D has an X scale factor of .5, a Y scale factor of .75, and a rotation angle of 180.

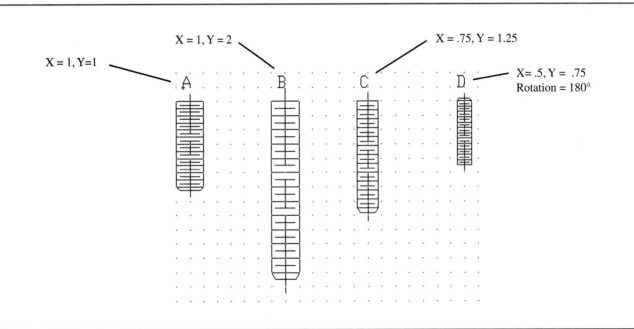

Figure 3-46

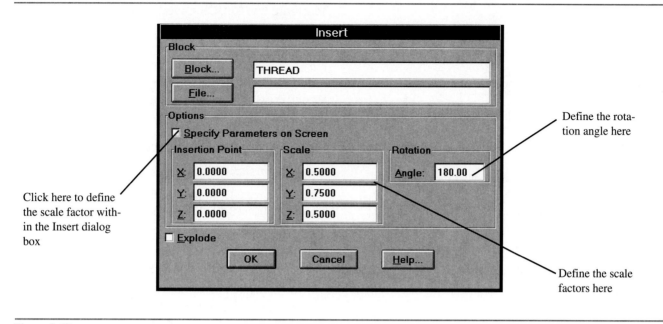

Click here to define the scale factor within the Insert dialog box

Define the rotation angle here

Define the scale factors here

Figure 3-47

To use the Insert dialog box to change the shape of a BLOCK

The D THREAD scale factors and rotation angle were defined using the Insert dialog box. The procedure is as follows.

1. Select or type the INSERT BLOCK command

The Insert dialog box will appear. See Figure 3-47 (WINDOWS only).

2. Click the box to the left of the words "Specify Parameters on Screen"

The click should remove the X in the box, indicating that the option has been turned off. When the X is removed, the options labeled Insertion point, Scale, and Rotation should change from gray to black in the dialog box.

3. Locate the cursor arrow within the X Scale box, backspace out the existing value, and type .50
4. Change the Y scale factor to .75
5. Change the Angle to 180

See Figure 3-47. The insertion point could also have been defined using the Insert dialog box. In this example, the THREAD will appear on the screen with its insertion point at the 0.0000,0.0000 point. The THREAD could then be moved using the MOVE command. When the prompt

Base point or displacement:

appears while you are using the MOVE command, respond with 0,0 ENTER and then locate the THREAD by moving the crosshairs and selecting a point.

To combine BLOCKS

Figure 3-48 shows a hex head screw that was created from two BLOCKS. The threaded portion of the screw was created first, then the head portion was added. Note in Figure 3-48 that the original proportions of the head were changed. When the head block was created, the insertion point was deliberately selected so that it could easily be aligned with the center line and top surface of the THREAD block.

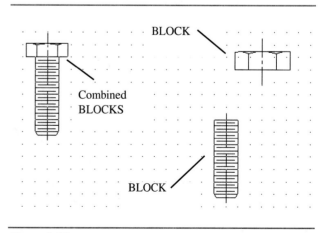

BLOCK

Combined BLOCKS

BLOCK

Figure 3-48

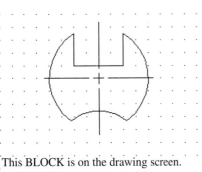

This BLOCK is on the drawing screen.
A WBLOCK must be created from an
existing BLOCK

Figure 3-49

3-24 WBLOCKS

WBLOCKS are BLOCKS that can be entered into
any drawing. When a BLOCK is created, it is unique to the
drawing on which it was defined. This means that if you
create a BLOCK on a drawing, then SAVE and EXIT the
drawing, the BLOCK is saved with that drawing but cannot be used on another drawing. If you start a NEW drawing, the saved BLOCKS will not be available.

Any BLOCK can be defined and saved as a
WBLOCK. WBLOCKS are saved as individual drawing
files and can be inserted into any drawing.

To create a WBLOCK saved on a disk in the A: drive

Figure 3-49 shows the BLOCK SHAPE inserted into
a drawing screen. WBLOCKS can be created only from
existing BLOCKS. In this example, the BLOCK SHAPE
already exists (see previous sections).

Command:

1. At a command prompt, type WBLOCK ENTER

   Command: WBLOCK

The Create Drawing File dialog box will appear. See
Figures 3-50 and 3-51. There is no WBLOCK icon.

2. Select the A: drive
3. Locate the cursor in the File Name: box, backspace out the current drawing name, and type in
   the WBLOCK name

In this example the WBLOCK was given the same
name, SHAPE, as the existing BLOCK. A different
BLOCK name could be assigned.

4. Select OK

The original drawing will appear with the following
prompt.

Command: _wblock
Block name:

5. Type SHAPE ENTER

WINDOWS

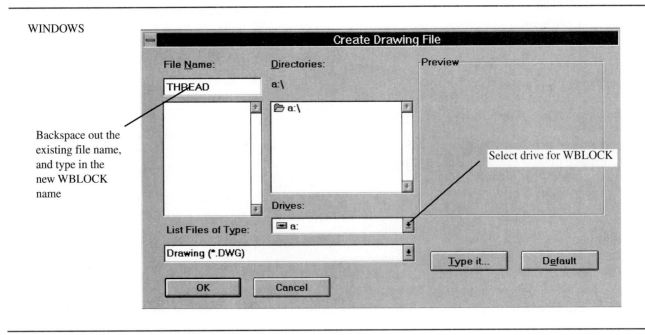

Figure 3-50

The drive letter specification will change to A:\ after selection

DOS

Double click here to select the A: drive

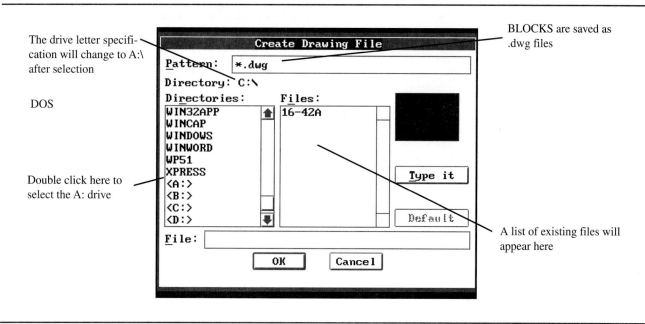

BLOCKS are saved as .dwg files

Type it

Default

A list of existing files will appear here

Figure 3-51

The WBLOCK must be created from an existing BLOCK. In this example the BLOCK and WBLOCK used the same name, but different names may be used.

The original drawing will return.

Figure 3-52

To verify that a WBLOCK has been created

1. Select OPEN FILE icon from the Standard toolbar

   The Save Changes? box will appear. See Figure 3-52.

2. Select the appropriate response

   The Select file dialog box will appear.

3. Select the A: drive from the Drivers: box

   A listing of all drawings on the A: drive will appear under the File Name: box. This list will include all WBLOCKS. Note in Figure 3-53 that the WBLOCK SHAPE is listed.

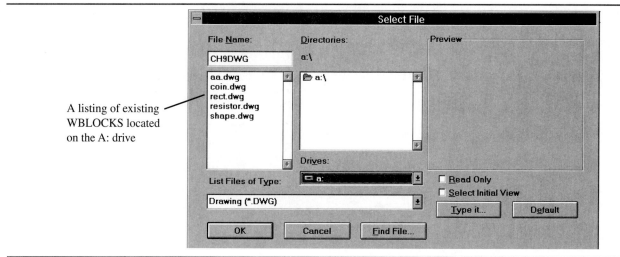

A listing of existing WBLOCKS located on the A: drive

Figure 3-53

To insert a WBLOCK into a drawing

This example assumes that you have started a new drawing or are working on a drawing other than the one on which the original BLOCK was created.

1. Select the OPEN file command

The Select File dialog box will appear.

2. Select the A: drive from the Drivers: box

A listing of all the drawings, including the WBLOCKS, will appear.

3. Select the SHAPE WBLOCK file

SHAPE.dwg will appear in the File name box.

4. Select OK

The WBLOCK will appear on the drawing screen. If the WBLOCK appears at an awkward location or appears only partially on the screen, use the MOVE or PAN commands to position the WBLOCK to an appropriate location.

3-25 ATTRIBUTES

Attributes are sections of text added to BLOCK that prompt the designer to add information to the drawing. For example, a title block could have an ATTRIBUTE that prompts the designer to add the date to the title block as it is inserted into a drawing. ATTRIBUTES have their own toolbar.

To access the ATTRIBUTES toolbar — WINDOWS

1. Select the Tools pulldown menu, then TOOL-BARS, then ATTRIBUTES

Figures 3-54 and 3-55 show the ATTRIBUTE toolbar.

To access the ATTRIBUTES toolbar — DOS

1. Select the CONSTRUCTION pulldown menu, then ATTRIBUTES

The Attribute Definition dialog box will appear.

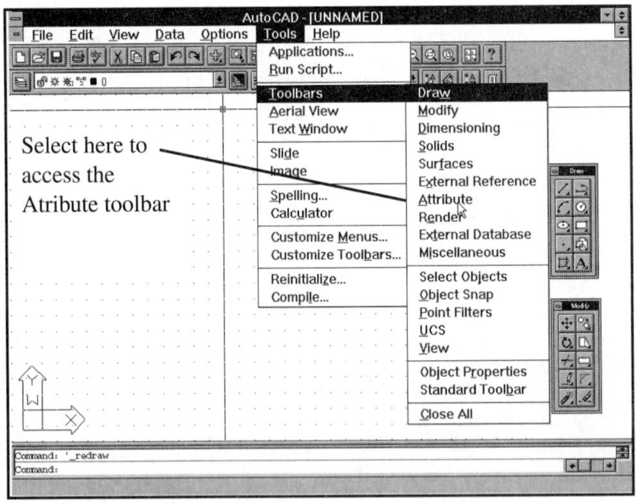

WINDOWS

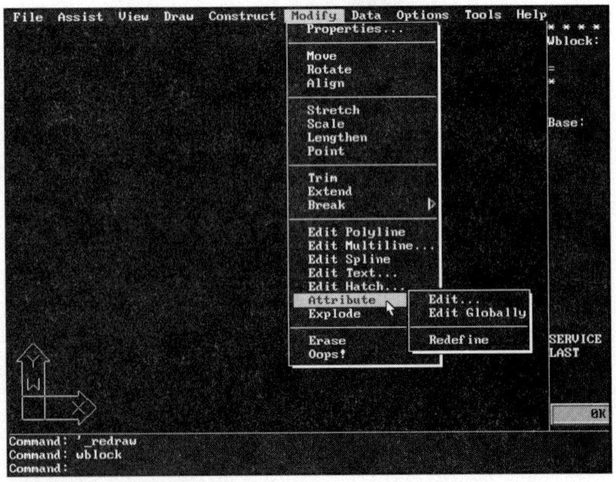

DOS

Figure 3-54

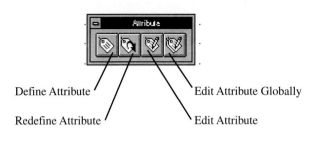

Define Attribute

Redefine Attribute

Edit Attribute Globally

Edit Attribute

Figure 3-55

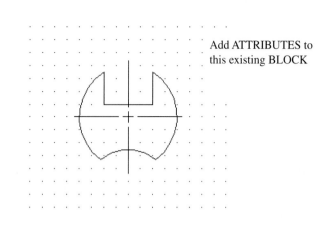

Add ATTRIBUTES to this existing BLOCK

Figure 3-56

To add an ATTRIBUTE to a block

Figure 3-56 shows a BLOCK. This example will add attributes that request information about the parts part number, material, quantity, and finish.

1. Select the DEFINE ATTRIBUTE icon from the Attributes toolbar or the CONSTRUCT, ATTRIBUTE pulldown commands

The Attribute Definition dialog box will appear. See Figure 3-57.

2. Select the Tag: box and type NUMBER

A tag is the name of an attribute and is used for filing and reference purposes. Tag names must be one word with no spaces.

3. Select the Prompt: box and type Define a part number

The prompt line will eventually appear at the bottom of the screen when a BLOCK containing an attribute is inserted into a drawing. If you do not define a Prompt, the TAG name will be used as a prompt.

4. Leave the Value box empty

Attribute Definition

Mode
- ☐ Invisible
- ☐ Constant
- ☐ Verify
- ☐ Preset

Attribute

Tag: NUMBER

Prompt: Define the part number

Value: None

Type ATTRIBUTE information here.

Insertion Point

Pick Point <

X: 0.0000

Y: 0.0000

Z: 0.0000

Text Options

Justification: Left

Text Style: STANDARD

Height < 0.1250

Rotation < 0.00

☐ Align below previous attribute

OK   Cancel   Help...

Figure 3-57

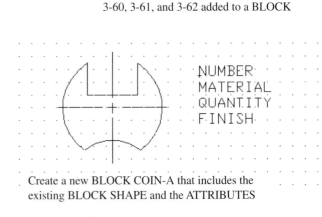

Figure 3-58

The coordinate values of the selected start point for the ATTRIBUTE

The Value box entry will be the default value if none is entered when the prompt appears. Based on the defined Prompt and Value inputs, the following prompt line will appear when the ATTRIBUTE is combined with a BLOCK

Define a part number <>:

5. Select Pick Point<

The drawing will appear with crosshairs. Select a location for the ATTRIBUTE tag by moving the crosshairs, then pressing the left mouse button.

The Attribute Definition dialog box will reappear with the X,Y coordinate values of the selected point listed in the Insertion Point box. See Figure 3-58.

6. Select OK

Figure 3-59 shows the ATTRIBUTE tag applied to a drawing. Figures 3-60, 3-61, and 3-62 (next page) show three more Attribute Definition dialog boxes. Note that the Align below previous attribute box has an X, indicating it has been turned on. The option is turned on by clicking the box. Figure 3-63 shows the resulting drawing.

The ATTRIBUTE tag from Figure 3-58 applied to a BLOCK

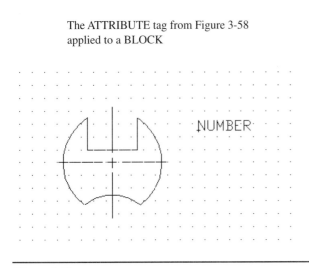

Figure 3-59

The ATTRIBUTES created in Figures 3-60, 3-61, and 3-62 added to a BLOCK

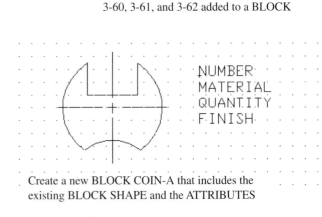

Create a new BLOCK COIN-A that includes the existing BLOCK SHAPE and the ATTRIBUTES

Figure 3-63

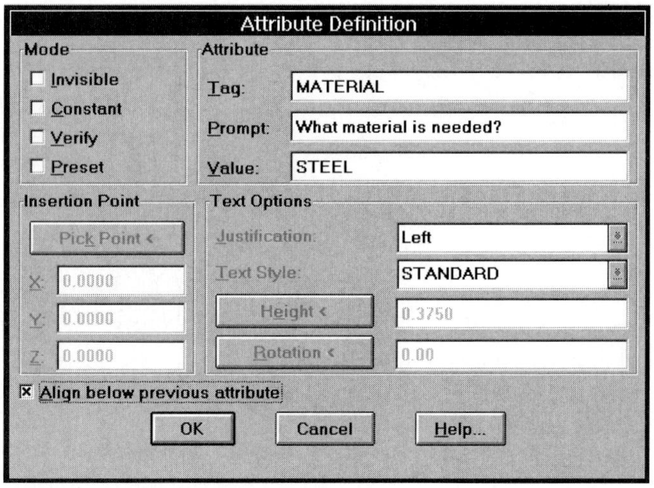

Figure 3-60

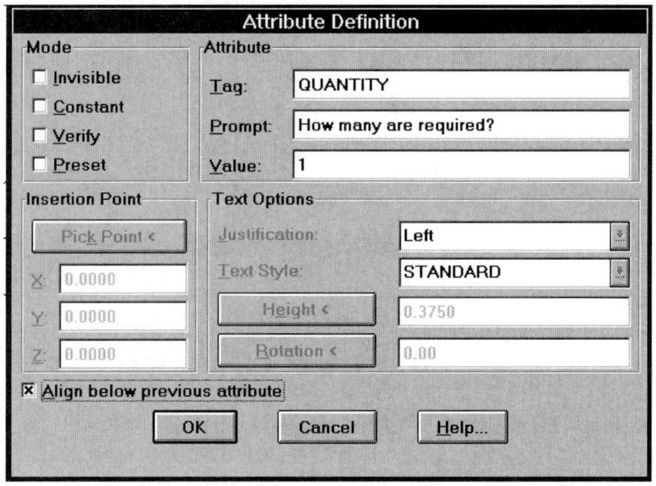

Figure 3-61

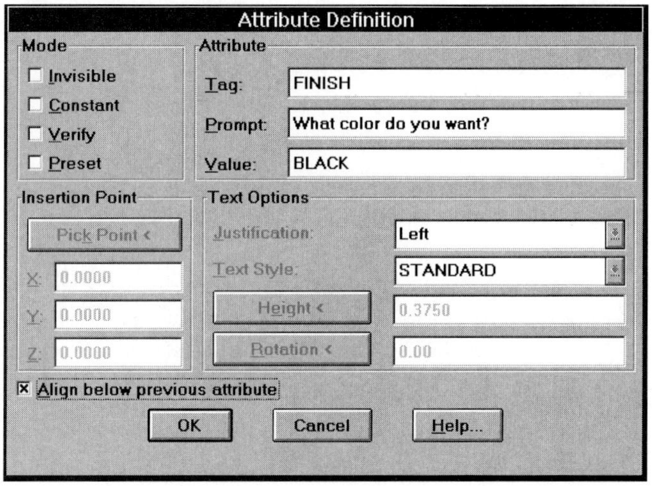

Figure 3-62

**To create a new BLOCK that includes
ATTRIBUTES**

1. Select the BLOCK command

   Command: _block Block name (or?):

2. Type Coin-A ENTER

   Insertion base point:

3. Select a base point.

   Select objects:

4. Window the BLOCK and all the ATTRIBUTE tags shown in Figure 3-63.

   Select objects:

5. Type ENTER

   The new BLOCK will disappear from the screen.

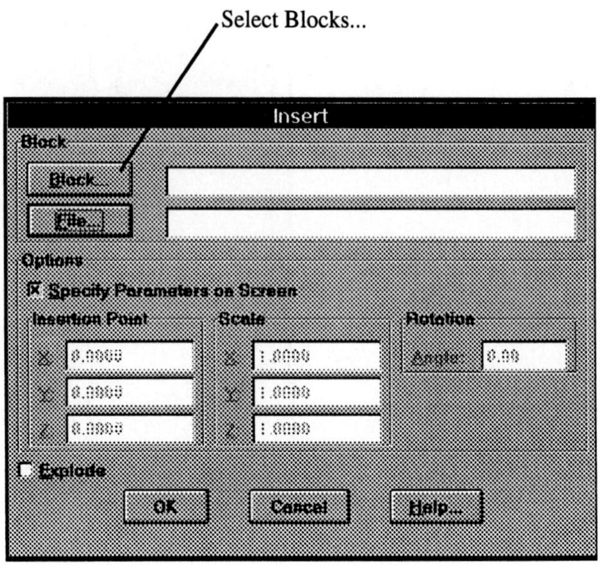

To insert a BLOCK with ATTRIBUTES

1. Select the INSERT BLOCK command

   For WINDOWS the Insert dialog box will appear. See Figure 3-64. For DOS request a BLOCK listing by responding with a ? and * to the two prompts See Figure 3-34 and the accompanying text.

2. Select Block...

   For WINDOWS the Defined Blocks dialog box will appear. See Figure 3-65.

3. Select COIN-A, OK, OK or type the name COIN-A in response to the insert prompt

   Insertion point:

4. Select an insertion point

   Insertion point: X scale factor <1> / Corner / XYZ:

5. Type ENTER

   Y scale factor (default=X):

6. Type ENTER

   Rotation angle <0.00>:

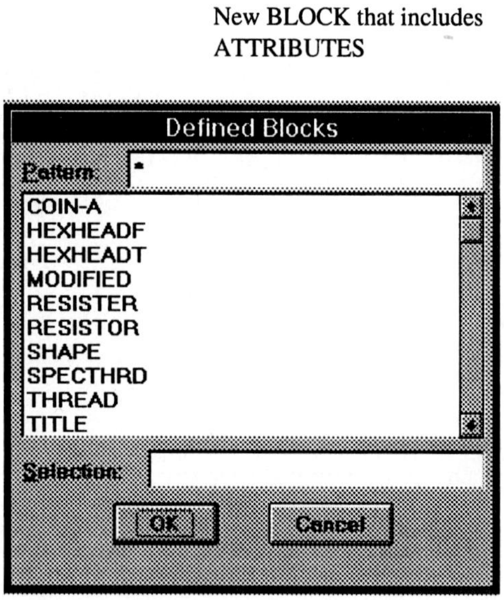

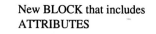

Select Blocks...

Figure 3-64

New BLOCK that includes
ATTRIBUTES

Figure 3-65

How many are required? <1>: 4

What material is required <STEEL>:

0.0000, 1.5000   SNAP GRID ORTHO MODEL TILE

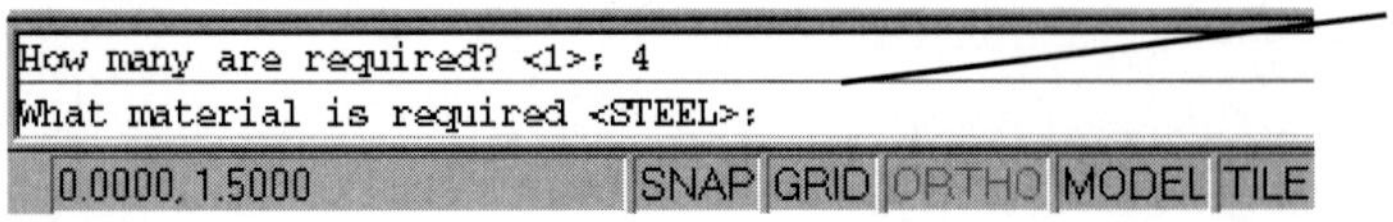

The words entered in the Attribute Definition dialog box Prompt box will appear on the prompt line when the BLOCK is inserted. The Value input will be the default value.

Figure 3-66

The BLOCK will appear on the screen and the ATTRIBUTE prompt values you assigned will appear at the bottom of the screen in the prompt line. See Figure 3-66.

What color do you want? <BLACK>:

7. Accept the default value BLACK by typing ENTER

How many are required<1>:

8. Type 4 ENTER

What material is required <STEEL>:

9. Type ALUMINUM

Define the part number <None>:

10. Type BU-96S ENTER

Figure 3-67 shows the resulting drawing.

To edit an existing ATTRIBUTE

Once a BLOCK has been created that includes ATTRIBUTES, it may be edited using the EDIT ATTRIBUTE command. The procedure is as follows. The BLOCK to be edited must be on the drawing screen.

1. Select the EDIT ATTRIBUTE icon from the Attributes toolbar or select the MODIFY pull-down menu, then ATTRIBUTE, then EDIT

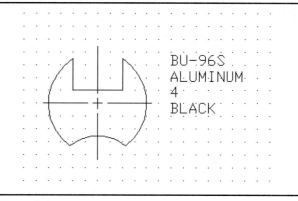

Figure 3-67

Command: _ddate
Select block:

2. Select the BLOCK

The Edit Attributes dialog box will appear. See Figure 3-68. In this example, the color will be changed from BLACK to GREEN. Note that the attribute prompt lines originally entered in the Attribute Definition dialog box are listed on the left side of the Edit attributes dialog box.

3. Locate the cursor to the right of the word BLACK, backspace out BLACK, and type in GREEN.

Figure 3-69 shows the resulting changes.

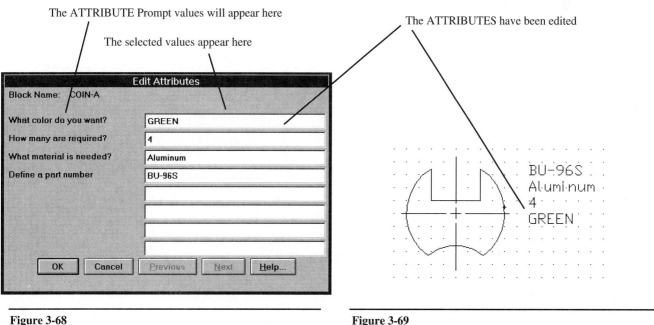

Figure 3-68

Figure 3-69

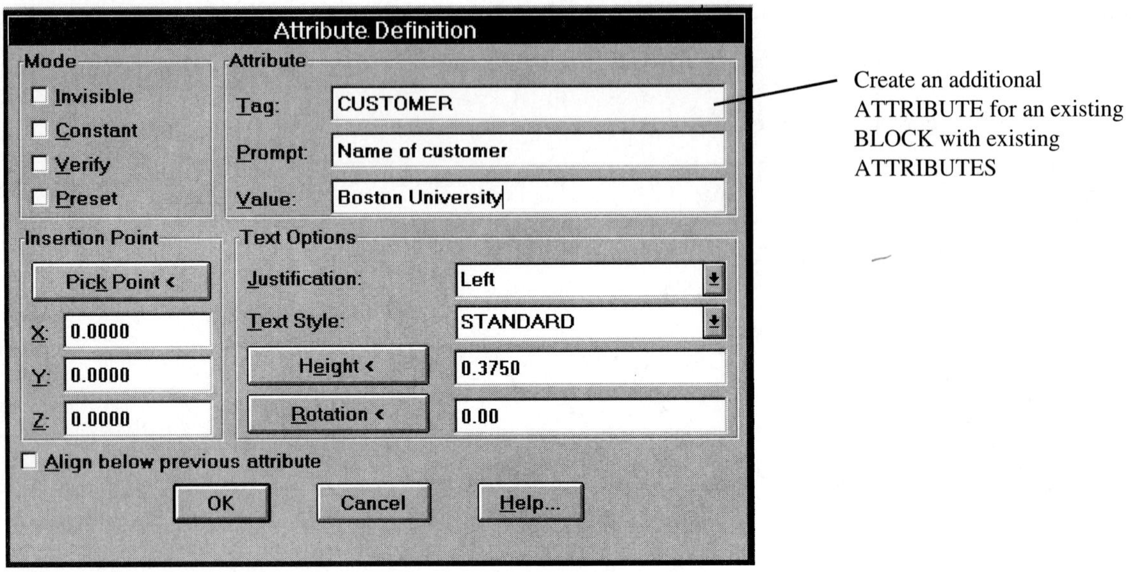

Attribute Definition

Mode
- ☐ Invisible
- ☐ Constant
- ☐ Verify
- ☐ Preset

Attribute
- Tag: `CUSTOMER`
- Prompt: `Name of customer`
- Value: `Boston University`

Insertion Point
- Pick Point <
- X: `0.0000`
- Y: `0.0000`
- Z: `0.0000`

Text Options
- Justification: `Left`
- Text Style: `STANDARD`
- Height < `0.3750`
- Rotation < `0.00`

☐ Align below previous attribute

[OK] [Cancel] [Help...]

Create an additional ATTRIBUTE for an existing BLOCK with existing ATTRIBUTES

Figure 3-70

To use the REDEFINE ATTRIBUTE command

The REDEFINE ATTRIBUTE command is used to add additional attributes to an existing BLOCK with ATTRIBUTES. The REDEFINE ATTRIBUTES command is accessed using the REDEFINE ATTRIBUTES icon on the ATTRIBUTES toolbar or by selecting the MODIFY pull-down menu, then ATTRIBUTES, then REDEFINE.

1. Select the REDEFINE ATTRIBUTES command

   The Attributes Definition dialog box will appear.

2. Create an additional attribute tag as shown in Figure 3-70.
3. Select Pick Point<

   Start point:

   The Attribute Definition dialog box will reappear with the coordinate values of the selected start point listed in the Insertion Point box.

4. Select OK

   The new attribute tag will appear on the screen as shown in Figure 3-71.

5. Select the REDEFINE ATTRIBUTES icon from the Attributes toolbar

   Command: _attredef
   Name of Block you wish to redefine:

6. Type COIN-A ENTER

Select objects for new Block...
Select objects:

7. Window the existing BLOCK and the new ATTRIBUTE tag

   Select objects:

8. Type ENTER

   Insertion base point of new Block:

9. Select a point

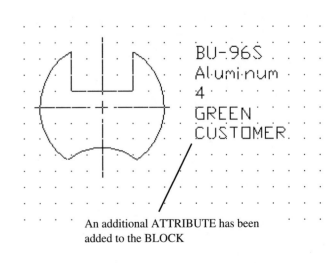

An additional ATTRIBUTE has been added to the BLOCK

Figure 3-71

To use the EDIT ATTRIBUTE GLOBALLY command

The EDIT ATTRIBUTE GLOBALLY command is used to change information in a BLOCK independently of the BLOCK's definitions. The BLOCK to be edited must be on the screen. The EDIT ATTRIBUTE GLOBALLY command is accessed via the EDIT ATTRIBUTE GLOBALLY icon on the ATTRIBUTES toolbar or by selecting the MODIFY pulldown menu, then ATTRIBUTE, then EDIT GLOBALLY.

1. Select the EDIT ATTRIBUTE GLOBALLY command

   Command: _attedit
   Edit attributes one at a time? <Y>:

2. Type ENTER

   Block name specification<>:*

3. Type COIN-A ENTER

   Attribute tag specification:

4. Type QUANTITY ENTER

   Attribute value specification:

5. Type 4 ENTER

   Select Attributes:

6. Select the number 4 associated with the COIN-A BLOCK on the screen

   Value/Position/Height/Angle/Style/Layer/Color/
   Next <N>:

   The value 4 will disappear from the screen and a large X will appear on the screen. See Figure 3-72.

7. Type V ENTER

   Change or replace? <R>:

   The change option is used to modify a few characters of the existing value. The replace option is used to create an entirely new value. The replace option is the default option.

8. Type ENTER

   New attribute value:

9. Type 12 ENTER

   Value/Position/Height/Angle/Style/Layer/Color/
   Next <N>:

10. Type ENTER

    The new value will replace the former value. See Figure 3-73.

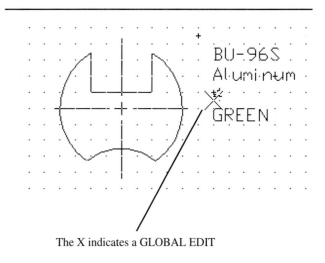

The X indicates a GLOBAL EDIT

Figure 3-72

NOTE:

It is possible to create a BLOCK that contains only ATTRIBUTES. A drawing is not required. Use the DEFINE ATTRIBUTES command and define as many tags as desired, locate the tags on the drawing screen, then SAVE them as a BLOCK.

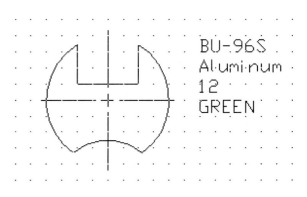

The ATTRIBUTE has been edited

Figure 3-73

3-26 TITLE BLOCKS WITH ATTRIBUTES

Figure 3-74 shows a title block that has been saved as a BLOCK. It would be helpful to add attributes to the BLOCK so that when it is called up to a drawing, the designer will be prompted to enter the required information.

Figures 3-75 through 3-79 show the five Attribute Definition dialog boxes used to define the title block attributes. Note that the text height in Figures 3-77 and 3-78 was changed to 0.250. Also note that no Attribute values were assigned. This means that the space on the drawing will be left blank if no prompt value is entered. Figure 3-80 shows the resulting title block with the attribute tags in place.

The new BLOCK with ATTRIBUTES was saved using the BLOCK command as TITLE-A. It could now be saved as a WBLOCK and used on future drawings. Figure 3-81 shows the BLOCK generated prompt lines with responses, and Figure 3-82 shows a possible title block created from the TITLE-A BLOCK.

BOSTON UNIVERSITY
110 CUMMINGTON ST.
BOSTON, MA 02215

TITLE

DWG NO.   REV

SCALE: DATE

Add ATTRIBUTES to this existing BLOCK

Figure 3-74

Figure 3-75

Figure 3-76

Figure 3-77

Figure 3-78

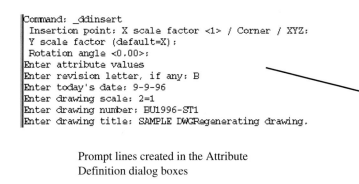

Figure 3-79

Title BLOCK with ATTRIBUTES tags in place

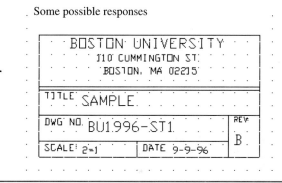

Figure 3-80

```
Command: _ddinsert
 Insertion point: X scale factor <1> / Corner / XYZ:
 Y scale factor (default=X):
 Rotation angle <0.00>:
Enter attribute values
Enter revision letter, if any: B
Enter today's date: 9-9-96
Enter drawing scale: 2=1
Enter drawing number: BU1996-ST1
Enter drawing title: SAMPLE DWGRegenerating drawing.
```

Prompt lines created in the Attribute
Definition dialog boxes

Figure 3-81

Some possible responses

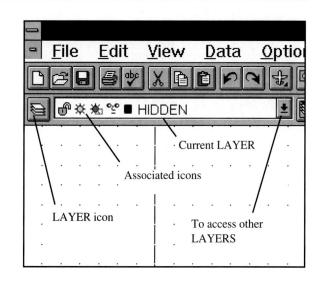

Figure 3-82

3-27 LAYERS

A layer is like a clear piece of paper you can lay directly over the drawing. You can draw on the layer and see through it to the original drawing. A layer can be made invisible and information can be transferred between layers.

In the example shown, a series of layers will be created, then a group of lines will be moved from the initial 0 layer to the other layers.

For WINDOWS the LAYER icon is located just below the Standard toolbar and includes 6 associated icons and headings. See Figure 3-83. The associated icons are not command icons but indicators of the status of the LAYER options. For example, the open padlock shown indicates that the LAYER is not locked. If it were locked, the padlock icon would change to the closed position.

For DOS select the DATA pulldown menu, then LAYERS.

Figure 3-83

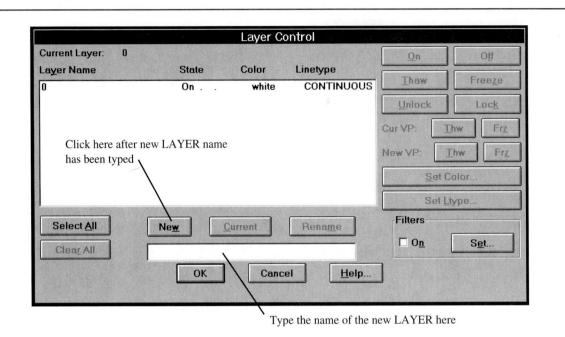

Figure 3-84

To create new LAYERS

This exercise will create two new LAYERS: HIDDEN and CENTER.

1. Select the LAYER icon located on the left of the screen just below the standard toolbar or the DATA pulldown menu, then LAYERS

The Layer Control dialog box will appear. See Figure 3-84. A flashing cursor will appear in the box under the NEW box.

2. Type HIDDEN, then click the New box.

The name HIDDEN should appear under the 0 layer heading in the Layer Name box. See Figure 3-85.

3. Type CENTER, then click the New box

The name CENTER will appear in the Layer Name box. There are now three LAYERS associated with the drawing. The 0 layer is the current layer as indicated by the 0 to the right of the Current Layer heading

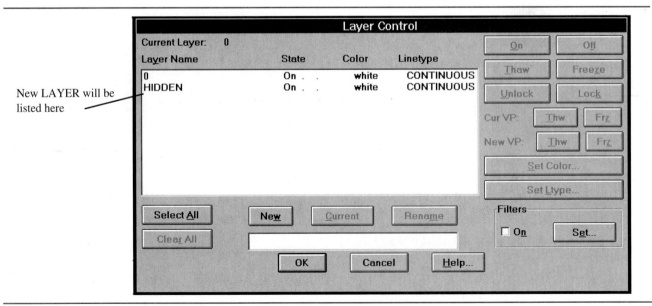

Figure 3-85

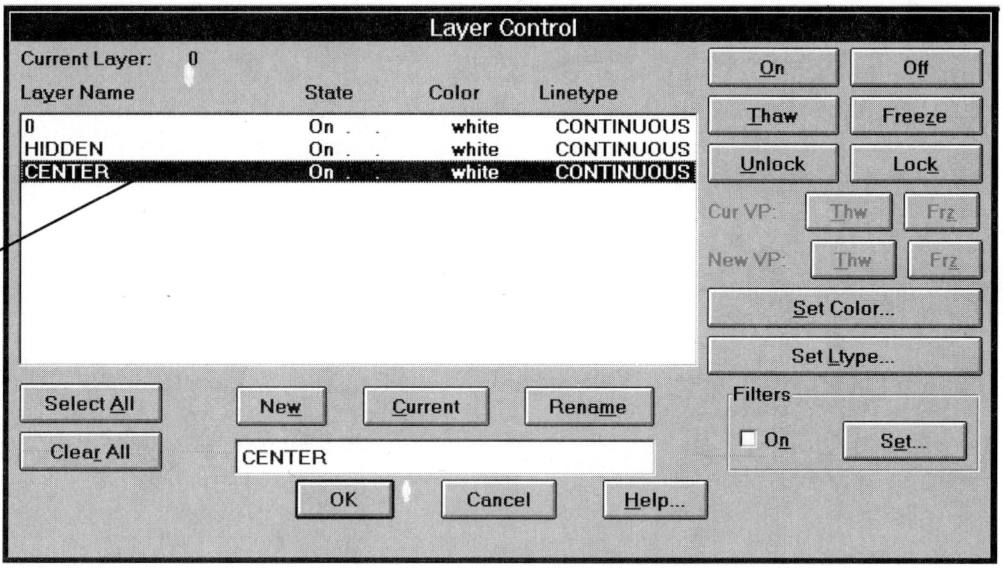

Figure 3-86

To change the color and line type of a LAYER

1. Move the arrow cursor to the CENTER LAYER line and press the left mouse button

The line will be highlighted as shown in Figure 3-86.

2. Select the Set Color... box

The Select Color dialog box will appear. See Figure 3-87.

3. Select the red color patch at the top of the dialog box.

The word "red" should appear in the Color box along with a red patch.

4. Select OK

The Layer Control dialog box will reappear. The word "red" will appear on the CENTER line in the color column.

5. Select the Set Ltype... box

The Select Linetype dialog box will appear. See Figure 3-88.

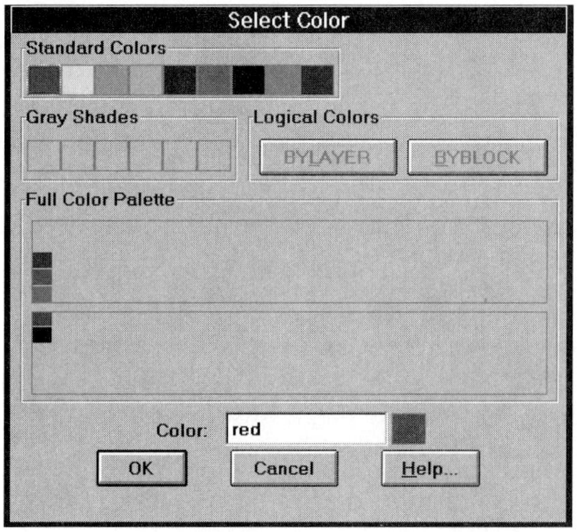

Figure 3-87

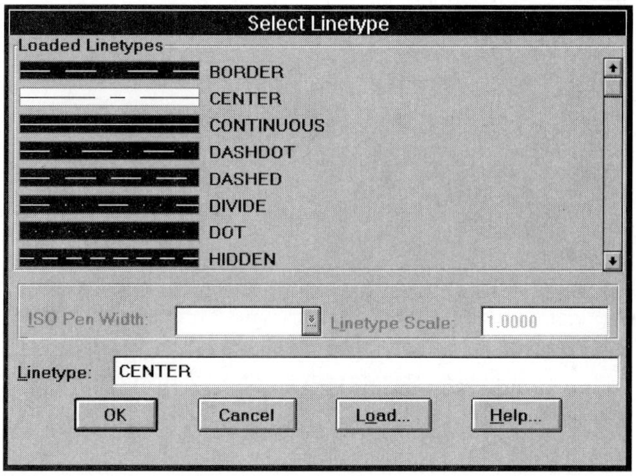

Figure 3-88

Layer Control

Current Layer:	0		
Layer Name	State	Color	Linetype
0	On . .	white	CONTINUOUS
HIDDEN	On . .	blue	HIDDEN
CENTER	On . .	red	CENTER

On Off
Thaw Freeze
Unlock Lock

Cur VP: Thw Frz
New VP: Thw Frz

Set Color...
Set Ltype...

Select All   New   Current   Rename

Filters
☐ On   Set...

Clear All   HIDDEN

OK   Cancel   Help...

Figure 3-88

6. Select the centerline pattern by clicking the pattern preview to the left of the word CENTER in the Loaded Linetypes box

The word CENTER should appear in the Linetype box.

7. Select OK

The Layer Control dialog box will reappear and the word CENTER should be listed in the CENTER line under the Linetype heading.

8. Select the HIDDEN line

The line will be highlighted.

9. Select the CENTER line

The existing highlight should disappear, indicating the LAYER is not active.

10. Repeat the above procedure for the HIDDEN LAYER and change the color to blue, and the linetype to HIDDEN

Your Layer Control dialog box should look like Figure 3-88.

To use the screen LAYER CONTROL — WINDOWS only

It is not necessary to use the LAYERS icon to access the Layer Control dialog box in order to make changes to the LAYERS. The LAYER CONTROL box (see Figure 3-89) can be used to access the LAYERS and their options directly.

1. Select the arrow box on the right side of the LAYER CONTROL box

A listing of defined LAYERS will cascade down. See Figure 3-90. The icons shown on the same line as the LAYER name can be used to change the LAYER's options. The icons are toggle switches that allow you to turn the various options on or off.

2. Select the open lock icon on the 0 LAYER line

The icon will change to a closed lock. The LAYER is now locked.

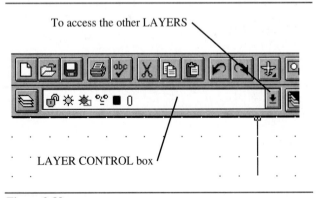
To access the other LAYERS

LAYER CONTROL box

Figure 3-89

3. Select the sun icon on the CENTER LAYER line

The sun icon will be replaced with a snowflake, and the word CENTER will become lighter, indicating the LAYER is now frozen.

4. Select the face on the HIDDEN LAYER line

The eyes of the icon will close, indicating that the LAYER is off.

5. Click all the changed icons again, returning them to their original settings
6. Click the cursor anywhere on the open drawing screen to return to a complete drawing screen.

To draw in different layers

The default LAYER is the 0 LAYER. This is indicated on the screen by the 0 in the LAYER CONTROL box or a 0 in the upper left coner of the screen.

1. Select the LINE command and draw a line on the screen

See Figure 3-91. This line is on the 0 LAYER. You can draw only on the current LAYER. You can see other LAYERS, but you can work only on the current LAYER.

2. Change LAYERS to the CENTER LAYER using the LAYER CONTROL dialog box

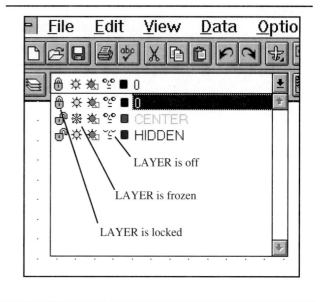

Figure 3-90

The current LAYER is now the CENTER LAYER. The color patch in the LAYER CONTROL indicator will be red and the word CENTER will be next to the red color patch.

3. Select CIRCLE from the Draw toolbar and draw a circle on the screen

Figure 3-91

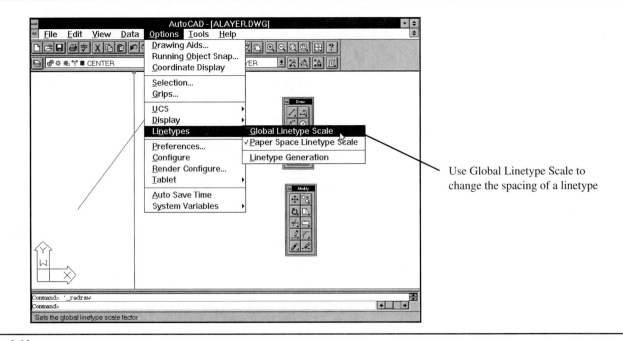

Figure 3-92

See Figure 3-92. The circle will appear red and will use the centerline pattern.

To change the scale of a linetype

The circle in Figure 3-92 is drawn using the centerline pattern. The spacing of the centerline pattern is based on default values, which may not be acceptable for all drawings. If the scale factor is not changed for drawings calibrated for millimeter units, the line will change colors, but will not appear to be drawn using the centerline pattern. The pattern has been changed, but the spaces are so small that they are not visible.

Figure 3-93

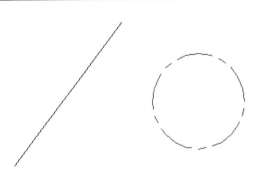

Note the difference in the spacing of
the centerline pattern

Figure 3-94

1. Select the OPTIONS pulldown menu
2. Select LINETYPES
3. Select GLOBAL LINE TYPE SCALE

See Figure 3-93.

Command: _ltscale New scale factor <0.2500>:

4. Type 1 ENTER

See Figure 3-94. Note the difference between the centerline patterns shown in Figures 3-92 and 3-94.

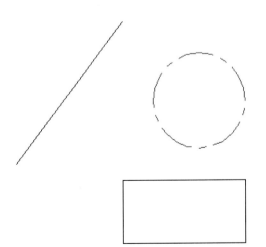

The rectangle is first drawn on the 0 LAYER, then
transferred to the HIDDEN LAYER

Figure 3-95

To change LAYERS

An object may be drawn on one LAYER then moved to another LAYER. This feature is helpful when designing because an original layout can be created in a single layer, then lines can be transferred to different LAYERS as needed. As a line changes LAYERS, it assumes the color and linetype of the new LAYER.

1. Return to LAYER 0 and draw a rectangle

See Figure 3-95.

2. Select the EDIT or MODIFY pulldown menu
3. Select PROPERTIES...

Command: _(ai_propchk)
Select objects:

4. Select the rectangle

Select objects:

5. Type ENTER

The Modify Polyline dialog box will appear. See Figure 3-96. Note that this dialog box can also be used to change color and Linetype Scale.

6. Select the LAYER box

The Select Layer dialog box will appear. See Figure 3-97.

7. Select the HIDDEN LAYER

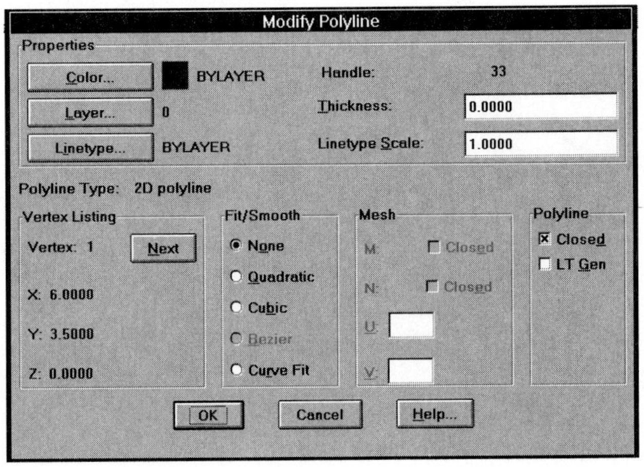

Figure 3-96

```
┌─────────────────────────────────────────────────────────┐
│                      Select Layer                        │
│ Current Layer:      0                                    │
│ Layer Name                    State      Color   Linetype │
│ ┌─────────────────────────────────────────────────────┐ │
│ │0                              On . . . . white  CONTINUOUS│
│ │CENTER                         On . . . . red    CENTER  │
│ │HIDDEN                         On . . . . blue   HIDDEN  │
│ │                                                       │ │
│ │                                                       │ │
│ └─────────────────────────────────────────────────────┘ │
│ Set Layer Name:   │HIDDEN                              │ │
│              ┌────────┐      ┌────────┐                  │
│              │   OK   │      │ Cancel │                  │
│              └────────┘      └────────┘                  │
└─────────────────────────────────────────────────────────┘
```

Select the HIDDEN LAYER. The rectangle will be transferred to the HIDDEN LAYER.

Figure 3-97

The highlighted line will switch from the 0 LAYER to the HIDDEN LAYER.

8. Select OK, OK to return to the original drawing.

The rectangle will now be drawn using the hidden line pattern and will be blue. See Figure 3-98.

To work with LAYERS

When preparing a drawing, it is sometimes desirable not to see a LAYER, or to see a LAYER but not be able to accidently edit it. For example, you want to work in the

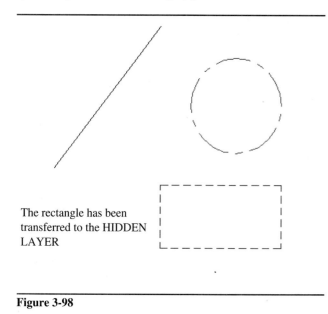

The rectangle has been transferred to the HIDDEN LAYER

Figure 3-98

CENTER LAYER but not see either the 0 or HIDDEN LAYERS. You need to make the CENTER LAYER the current LAYER, and turn off the other LAYERS.

The following procedures for working with LAYERS are only for the WINDOWS version. The same manipulations are done in the DOS version using the LAYER CONTROL dialog box. See Figure 3-88.

To turn LAYERS off — WINDOWS only

1. Select the LAYER CONTROL icon

A listing of current LAYERS will cascade down.

2. Select the word CENTER

The CENTER LAYER is now the current LAYER.

3. Select the LAYER CONTROL icon again
4. Select the face icon for both the 0 and HIDDEN LAYERS

The eyes on the icons will close, indicating that the LAYER is off. See Figure 3-99. The resulting drawing will show only the circle. The line and the rectangle are still part of the drawing, but because their LAYERS are turned off, they are not visible.

Other LAYER options

The Lock/Unlock option allows you to lock a LAYER. A locked LAYER cannot be edited, but you can add shapes to a locked LAYER.

The Freeze/Thaw option makes LAYERS invisible. Frozen LAYERS will not appear in a plot of the drawing.

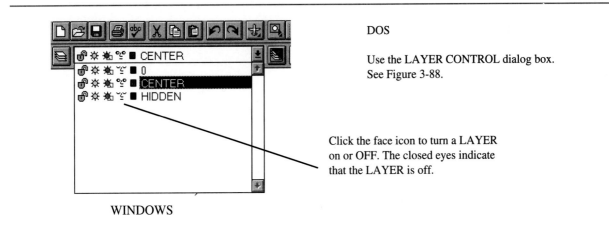

WINDOWS

DOS

Use the LAYER CONTROL dialog box.
See Figure 3-88.

Click the face icon to turn a LAYER
on or OFF. The closed eyes indicate
that the LAYER is off.

Figure 3-99

3-28 CONSTRUCTING A HEXAGON INSCRIBED WITHIN A CIRCLE

See Figure 3-100. Given a circle O of diameter 2.00, inscribe a hexagon within it.

1. Select the DRAW, CIRCLE, CEN, DIA commands

Draw circles 2.00 in diameter at the intersections of circle O's vertical center line as shown. Use OSNAP, INTERSECTION to ensure that the circles' centerpoints are located exactly on the intersection of circle O and its vertical center line.

2. Draw the hexagon as shown. Use the DRAW, LINE along with OSNAP, INTERSECTION commands to ensure accuracy.

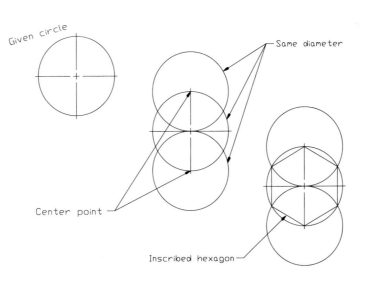

Given circle

Same diameter

Center point

Inscribed hexagon

Figure 3-100

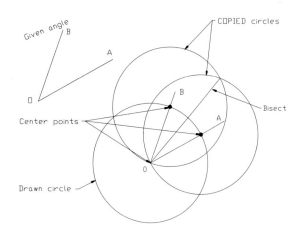

Figure 3-101

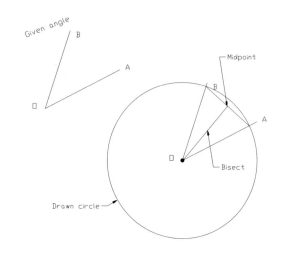

Figure 3-102

3-29 CONSTRUCTING THE BISECT OF AN ANGLE — METHOD I

See Figure 3-101.

Given angle A-O-B, bisect it

1. Select the DRAW, CIRCLE, CEN, RAD commands
2. Draw a circle with a center point located at point O. The circle may be of any radius. This is an excellent place to take advantage of AutoCAD's DRAG mode. Move the cursor until the circle appears approximately the same size as that shown
3. Select COPY, MULTIPLE to draw two more circles equal in radius to the one drawn in step 1. Locate the circles' center points on intersections of the first circle and angle A-O-B. Use OSNAP, INTERSECTION to ensure accuracy
4. Draw a line from point O to intersection C as shown. Use OSNAP, INTERSECTION to ensure accuracy

3-30 CONSTRUCTING THE BISECT OF AN ANGLE — METHOD II

See Figure 3-102.

Given angle A-O-B, bisect it

1. Draw a circle with a center point located at point O. The circle may be of any radius. This is an excellent place to take advantage of AutoCAD's DRAG mode. Move the cursor until the circle appears approximately the same size as that shown
2. Draw a line between the intersection point created by the circle and angle A-O-B. Use OSNAP, INTERSECTION to ensure accuracy
3. DRAW a LINE between point O and the midpoint of the line. Use OSNAP, MIDPOINT to ensure accuracy

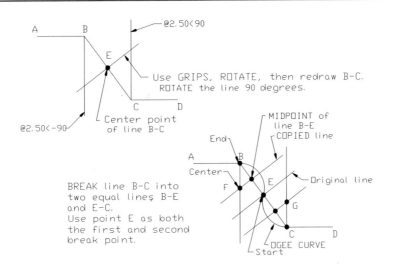

Figure 3-103

3-31 CONSTRUCTING AN OGEE CURVE (S-CURVE) WITH EQUAL ARCS

See Figure 3-103.

Given points B and C, construct an ogee curve between them

1. DRAW a straight LINE between points B and C. Use OSNAP, ENDPOINT to ensure accuracy
2. DRAW LINEs perpendicular to lines A-B and C-D as shown

Use OSNAP, ENDPOINT to accurately start the lines on points B and C, respectively. Use relative coordinates to draw the lines. The lines may be of any length greater than the perpendicular distance between lines A-B and C-D.

3. Construct a perpendicular bisect of line B-C. See Section 3-18.
4. Define the intersections of the perpendicular lines drawn in step 2 with the perpendicular bisect of B-C as points F and G
5. Draw an ARC using S, C, and E and let point E be the starting point, point F be the center point, and point B be the endpoint
6. Draw an ARC using S, C, and E and let point E be the starting point, point G be the center point, and point C be the endpoint

The two arcs of steps 5 and 6 define an ogee curve using equal arcs.

Figure 3-104 shows the construction of an ogee curve with unequal arcs. The construction techniques are similar to those presented above.

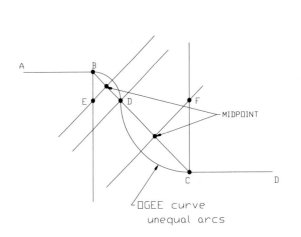

Figure 3-104

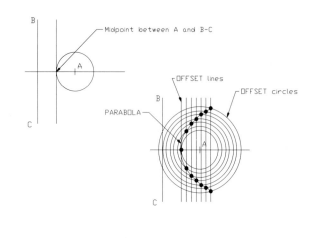

Figure 3-105

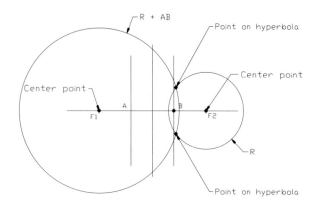

Figure 3-106

3-32 CONSTRUCTING A PARABOLA

A parabola is the locii of points such that the distance between a fixed point, the focus, and a fixed line, the directrix, are always equal.

See Figures 3-105 and 3-106. Given a focus point A and a directrix B-C, construct a parabola.

1. DRAW a LINE parallel to B-C so that it intersects the midpoint between line B-C and point A. Use OFFSET
2. DRAW a CIRCLE centered about point A, whose radius is equal to half the distance between line B-C and point A
3. OFFSET lines and a circle 0.2 inches from the parallel line and the circle created in steps 1 and 2
4. Identify the intersections of the lines and circles created in step 3. In this example, a DONUT was created with a 0.00 inside radius and a small outside radius. The donuts were located accurately using OSNAP, INTERSECTION
5. DRAW a PLINE connecting all the intersection points
6. Use PEDIT, CURVE FIT to change the PLINE to a parabolic curve

3-33 CONSTRUCTING A HYPERBOLA

A hyperbola is the locii of points equidistant between two fixed foci points.

See Figures 3-107, 3-108, and 3-109. Given focus points F1 and F2 equidistant from a vertical line and two other vertical lines drawn through points A and B, draw a hyperbola.

1. Draw a circle of arbitrary radius using point F2 as the center. If possible, set up the drawing so that both points F1 and F2 are on SNAP points. If this is not possible, draw vertical lines through point F2 so that OSNAP, INTERSECTION may be used to locate the center accurately
2. Draw a circle centered about F2 of radius equal to the radius of the circle drawn in step 1, plus the distance between points A and B. See Figure 3-107

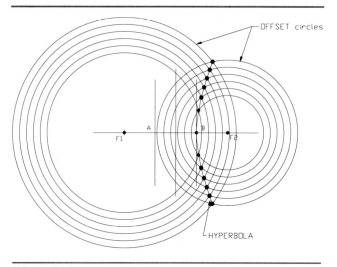

Figure 3-107

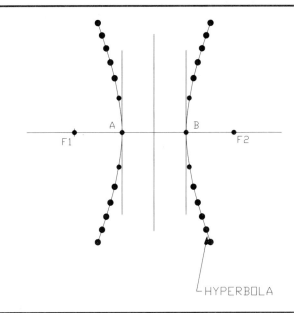

HYPERBOLA

Figure 3-108

Figure 3-109

3. DRAW concentric circles about the circles centered about F1 and F2. The distance between all the circles should be equal. Use OFFSET

4. Mark the intersections between the smaller and larger circles as shown in Figure 3-107. Use DONUT with a 0.00 inside radius and a small outside radius, and use OSNAP INTERSECTION to ensure location accuracy

5. DRAW a PLINE connecting point 10 through point 11

6. Use PEDIT and CURVE FIT to draw the hyperbola

7. Use MIRROR to create the opposing hyperbola. See Figure 3-108

3-34 CONSTRUCTING A SPIRAL

See Figure 3-109.

Construct a spiral of Archimedes

1. DRAW a set of perpendicular center lines as shown

2. DRAW 12 concentric circles about centerpoint O. Use OFFSET to draw circles

3. DRAW 12 equally spaced ray lines as shown. ARRAY either the horizontal or vertical line using polar ARRAY. Use point O as the center of rotation

4. DRAW a PLINE starting a point O. The second point is the intersection of the 30-degree ray with the first circle. Point 2 is the intersection of the 60-degree ray and the second circle. Continue through all 12 rays and circles

5. Use PLINE and CURVE FIT to change the PLINE to a spiral

3-35 CONSTRUCTING A HELIX

See Figure 3-110.

Construct a helix that advances 1.875 inches every 360 degrees

1. DRAW a vertical line 1.875 inches long and a horizontal line as shown

2. DRAW a horizontal line that can easily be divided into 12 equal spaces. The length of the horizontal line is arbitrary. Set up a GRID so that the 12 equal spaces can easily be identified

3. Draw a circle as shown. Use ARRAY and divide the circle using 12 equally spaced rays. Use polar ARRAY with the circle's center point as the center of rotation

4. DRAW line A-B as shown. Draw 12 vertical, equally spaced lines between the horizontal line and line A-B

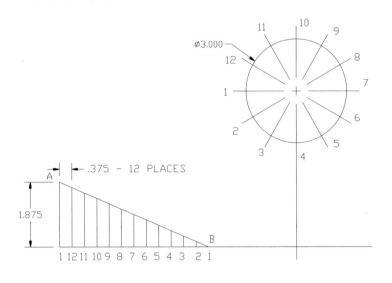

Figure 3-110

5. Label both the circle and horizontal line as shown. The number of divisions must be the same for both the circle and the horizontal line
6. Draw vertical lines from the intersections of the 12 equally spaced rays and the circle's circumference as shown in Figure 3-111. Use OSNAP, INTERSECTION to ensure accuracy
7. Draw horizontal lines from the intersections on

line A-B so that they intersect the vertical lines from step 5. Use OSNAP, INTERSECTION to ensure accuracy
8. Mark the intersections of the lines from steps 5 and 6 as shown
9. Use PLINE to connect the horizontal and vertical intersections as shown
10. Use PEDIT and CURVE FIT to draw the helix

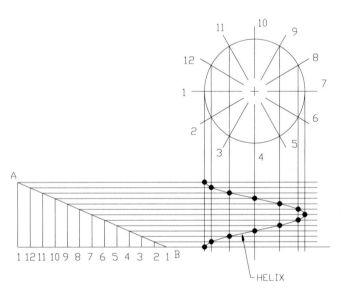

Figure 3-111

Given hole locations

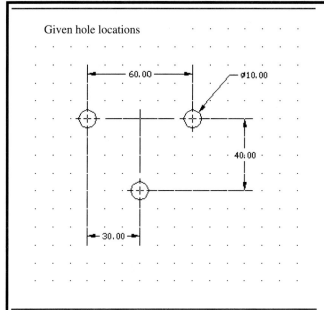

Figure 3-112

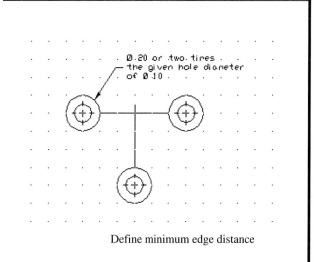

Define minimum edge distance

Figure 3-113

3-36 DESIGNING USING SHAPE PARAMETERS

An elementary design problem often faced by beginning designers is to create a shape based on a given set of paramenters. This section will present two examples of this type of design problem.

Design Problem DP3-1

Design a shape that will support the hole pattern shown in Figure 3-112 subject to the following parameters. Design for the minimum amount of material. All dimensions are in millimeters.

1. The edge of the material may be no closer to the center of a hole than a distance equivalent to the diameter of the hole.
2. The minimum distance from any cutout to the edge of the part may not be less than the smallest distance calculated in step 1.
3. The minimum inside radius for a cutout is R=5 millimeters.

The solution is as follows.

1. Calculate the minimum edge distances for the holes

Add tangent lines

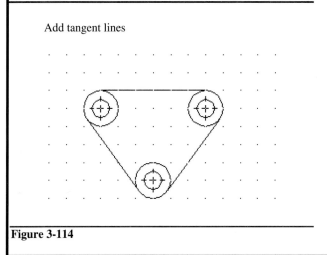

Figure 3-114

Use the minimum edge distance
to defne internal cutout

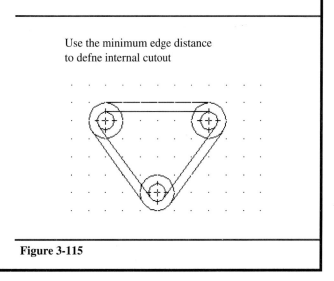

Figure 3-115

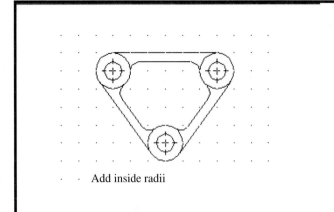

Add inside radii

Figure 3-116

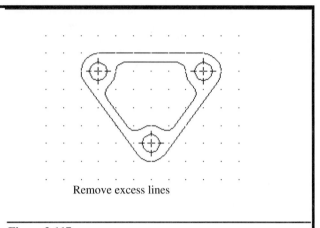

Remove excess lines

Figure 3-117

In this problem the three holes are all the same diameter: 10 millimeters. Given the parameter that an edge may be no closer to the center of a hole than a distance equivalent to the size of the hole's diameter, the distance from the outside edge of the hole to the edge of the part must equal 5 millimeters, or a circular shape of diameter 20 millimeters.

2. Draw Ø 20 circles using the existing circle's center points, as shown in Figure 3-113
3. Draw outside tangent lines as shown in Figure 3-114
4. The second parameter limits the minimum edge distance to the minimum edge distance calculated in step 1. In this example that distance is 5 millimeters, so use OFFSET to draw lines 5 millimeters from the outside tangent lines, as shown in Figure 3-115, to define the internal cutout

5. Use the inside radius parameter of 5 millimeters and add fillets as shown in Figure 3-116.
6. Erase any excess lines.

Figure 3-117 shows the final shape.

Design problem DP3-2

Design a shape that will support the hole pattern shown in Figure 3-118. Support the center hole with four perpendicular webs. All dimensions are in inches.

This problem is similar to DP3-1 but has a large, centrally located hole that must be supported. The design parameters are as follows.

1. The edge of the material may be no closer to the center of a hole than a distance equivalent to the diameter of the hole.
2. The minimum distance from any cutout to the edge of the part may not be less than the smallest distance calculated in step 1.
3. The minimum inside radius for a cutout is R=.125 inches.
4. Support the central hole on four sides.

The solution is as follows.

1. Calculate the minimum edge distances for the holes based on the given parameters

In this example, twice the hole diameters are 2.00 and 3.00 inches.

2. Add circles about the existing center points based on the first parameter, as shown in Figure 3-119

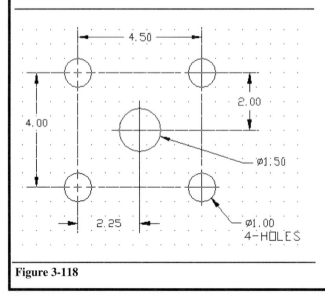

Figure 3-118

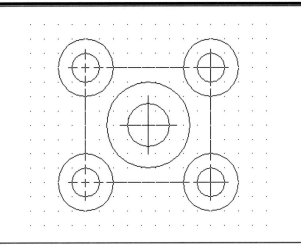

Figure 3-119

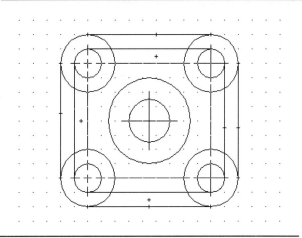

Figure 3-120

The minimum edge distance based on the Ø1.00 of the smallest hole equals 0.50 inches.

3. Use the minumum calculated edge distance and define the inside edges of the cutouts as shown in Figure 3-120
4. Use the minimum edge distance to define the four supporting webs for the center hole, as shown in Figure 3-121.
5. Add the inside radii; See Figure 3-122

The inside radii were added using the FILLET command. This causes a portion of the internal edge line to disappear. Use OFFSET again to draw another line to define the internal edge for the other cutout area.

6. Remove all excess lines

Figure 3-123 shows the final design shape.

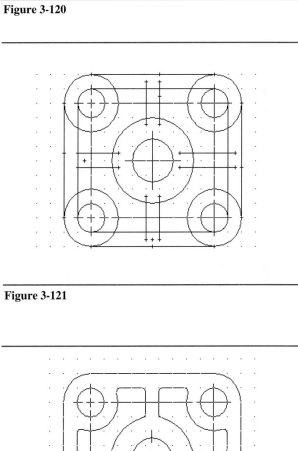

Figure 3-121

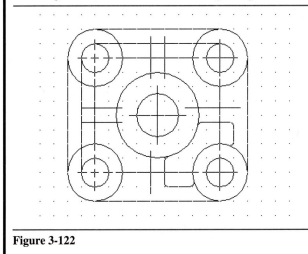

Figure 3-122

Figure 3-123

3-37 EXERCISE PROBLEMS

Redraw the shapes in exercise problems EX3-1 to EX3-4.

EX3-1 INCHES

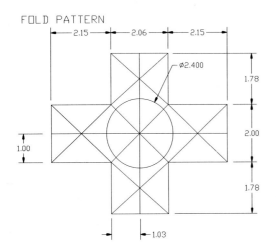

EX3-3 MILLIMETERS

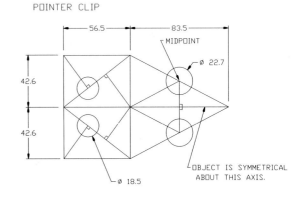

EX3-2 MILLIMETERS

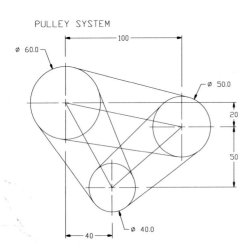

EX3-4 MILLIMETERS

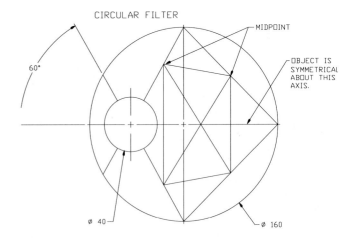

EX3-5

Draw a 54-degree angle; construct the bisect.

EX3-6

Draw an 89.33-degree angle; construct the bisect.

EX3-7 INCHES

Given points A and B as shown, construct an ogee curve of equal arcs.

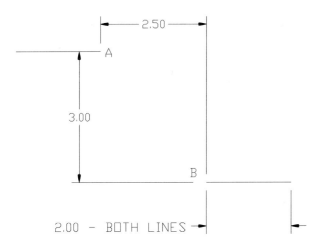

EX3-8 MILLIMETERS

Given points A, B, and C as shown, construct an ogee curve that starts at point A, passes through point C, and ends at point B.

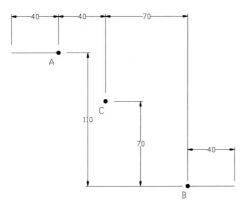

EX3-9

Construct a hexagon inscribed within a 3.63² diameter circle.

EX3-10

Construct a hexagon inscribed within a 120mm diameter circle.

EX3-11 INCHES

Given point A and directrix B-C as shown, construct a parabola.

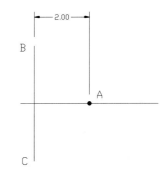

EX3-12 MILLIMETERS

Given point A and directrix B-C as shown, construct a parabola.

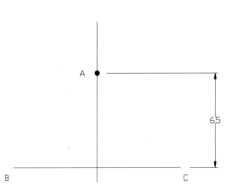

EX3-13 INCHES

Given foci F1 and F2 as shown, draw a hyperbola.

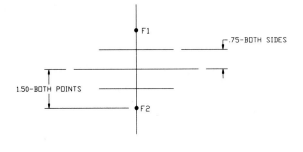

EX3-14 MILLIMETERS

Given foci F1 and F2 as shown, draw a hyperbola.

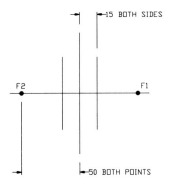

EX3-15 INCHES

Given the concentric circles and rays shown, construct a spiral.

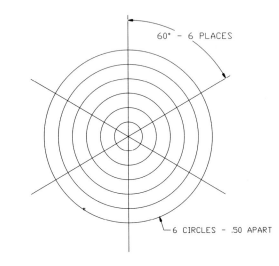

EX3-16 MILLIMETERS

Given the concentric circles and rays shown, construct a spiral.

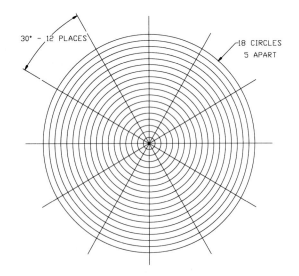

EX3-17 INCHES

Given the setup shown, construct a helix.

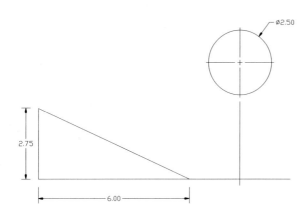

Redraw the objects in exercise problems EX3-19 to EX3-42 based on the given dimensions.

EX3-19 MILLIMETERS

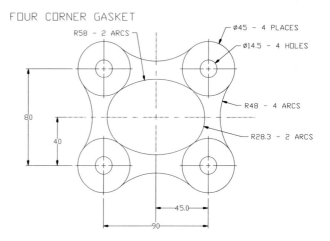

EX3-18 MILLIMETERS

Given the setup shown, construct a helix.

EX3-20 MILLIMETERS

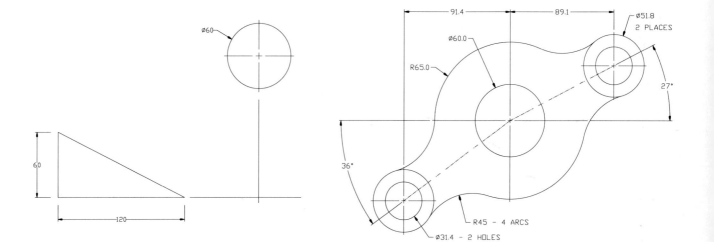

EX3-21 INCHES

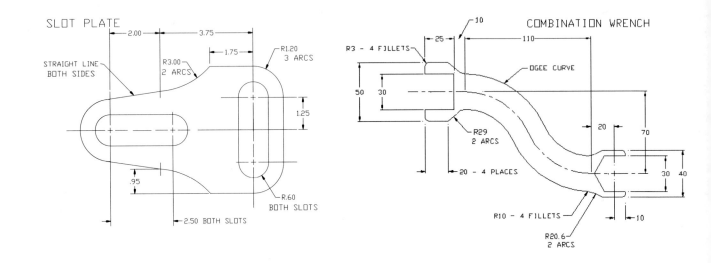

SLOT PLATE

EX3-23 MILLIMETERS

COMBINATION WRENCH

EX3-22 INCHES

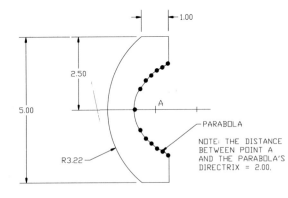

EX3-24 MILLIMETERS

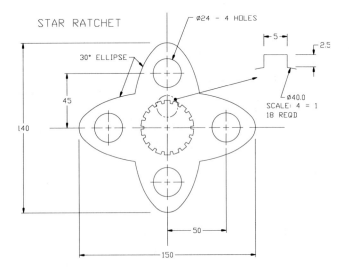

STAR RATCHET

EX3-25 MILLIMETERS

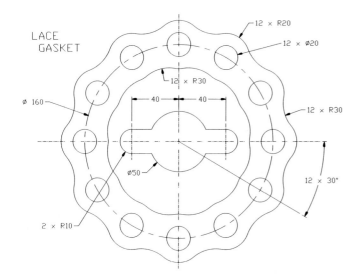

EX3-27 INCHES

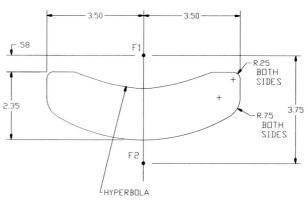

EX3-26 MILLIMETERS

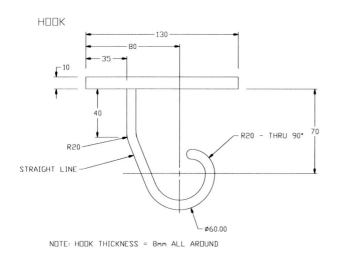

EX3-28 MILLIMETERS

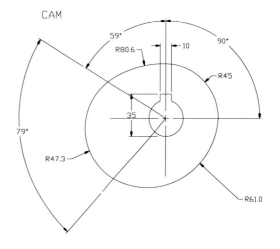

EX3-29 MILLIMETERS

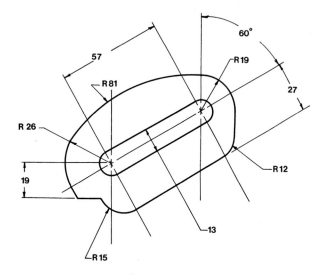

EX3-31 MILLIMETERS

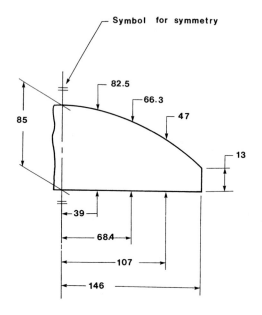

EX3-30 INCHES

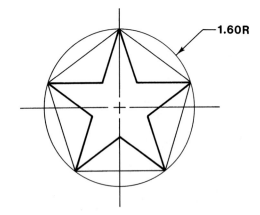

EX3-32 MILLIMETERS

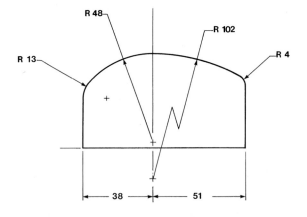

EX3-33 MILLIMETERS

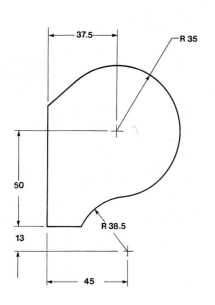

EX3-35 INCHES

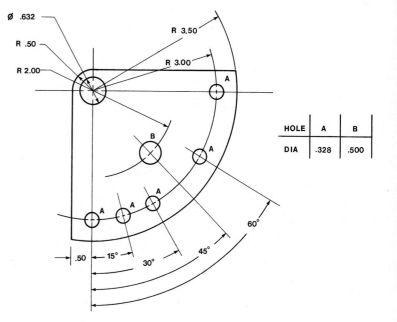

HOLE	A	B
DIA	.328	.500

EX3-34 MILLIMETERS

EX3-36 INCHES

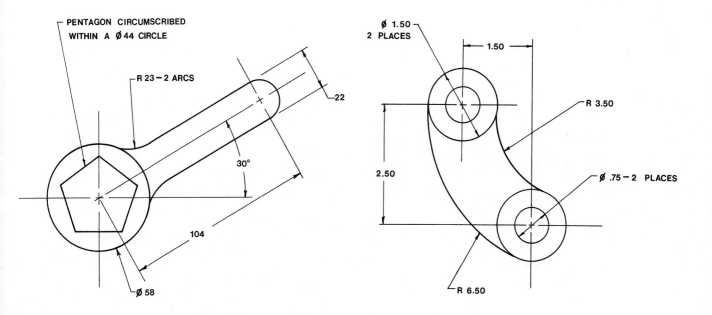

EX3-37 INCHES

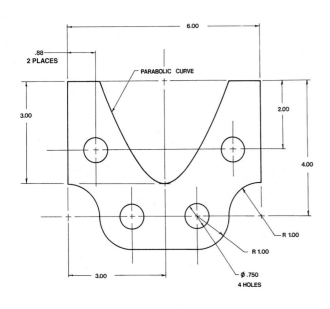

EX3-39 MILLIMETERS

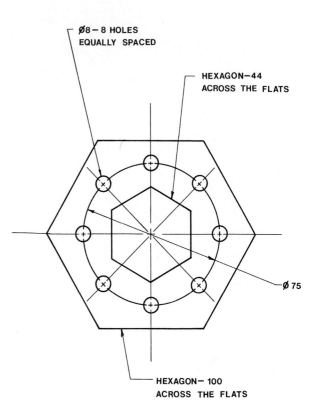

EX3-38 MILLIMETERS

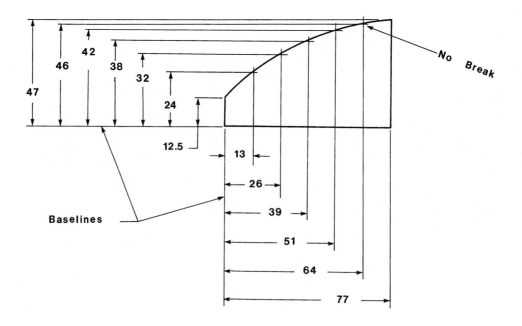

EX3-40 CENTIMETERS

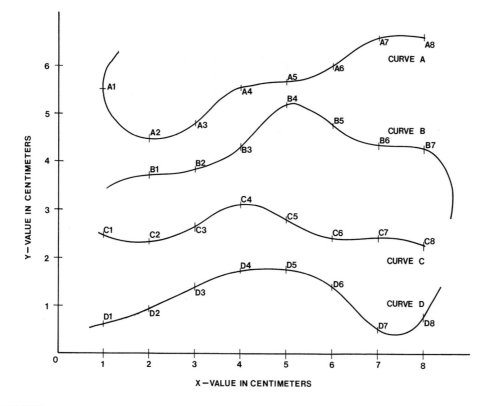

EX3-41 INCHES

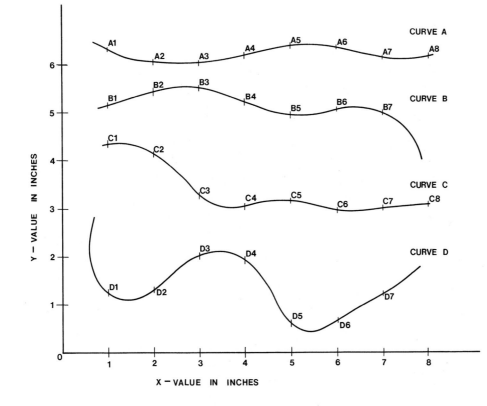

EX3-42 MILLIMETERS

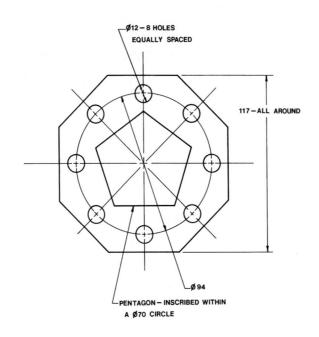

Ø12 − 8 HOLES
EQUALLY SPACED

117 − ALL AROUND

Ø 94

PENTAGON − INSCRIBED WITHIN
A Ø70 CIRCLE

EX3-43

Draw a circle, mark off 24 equally spaced points, then connect each point with every other point using only straight lines. Erase the circle.

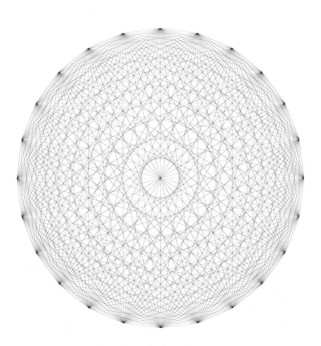

Redraw the following imaginary objects. Determine the dimensions by measuring the given drawings.

Just for fun

EX3-44

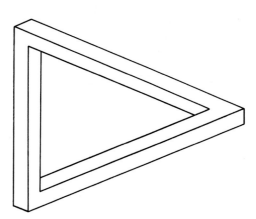

EX3-45

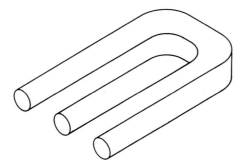

EX3-46

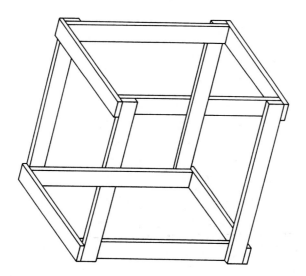

EX3-47 MILLIMETERS

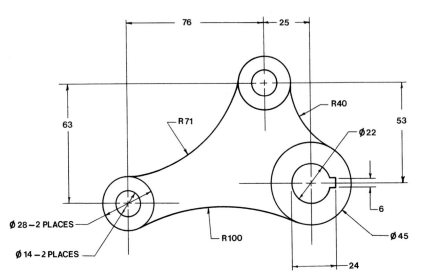

EX3-48 MILLIMETERS

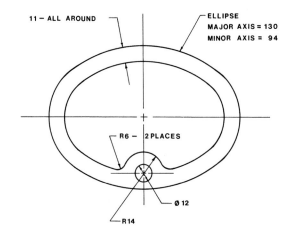

EX3-49 MILLIMETERS

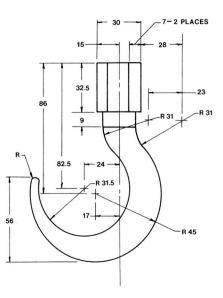

EX3-50

A. Create a title BLOCK based on the following drawing layout.
B. Add and align the following ATTRIBUTES.
Tag = DATE
Prompt = Enter today's date
Value = leave blank

Tag = DRAWING
Prompt = Enter the drawing number
Value = leave blank

Tag = NAME
Prompt = Enter your name
Value = leave blank

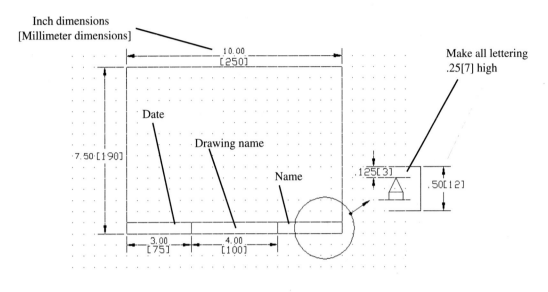

EX3-51

A. Redraw or create your own title BLOCK based on the sample shown below.

B. Create and align ATTRIBUTES for the BLOCK. The blank boxes may be used for your name, drawing sheet number (SHT 1 OF 2), or sheet size (A, etc.).

DESIGN

EX3-52 INCHES

Design a shape that will support the hole pattern shown. Design for a minimum amount of material and to satisfy the following parameters.

1. The edge of the material may be no closer to the center of a hole than twice the diameter of the hole.

2. The minumum edge distance from any cutout to the edge of the part may be no less than the smallest distance calculated in step 1.

3. The minimum inside radius for a cutout is R=.250

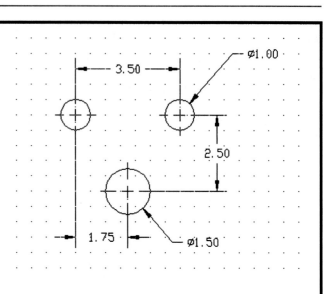

EX3-53 MILLIMETERS

Design a shape that will support the hole pattern shown. Design for a minimum amount of material and to satisfy the following parameters.

1. The edge of the material may be no closer to the center of a hole than twice the diameter of the hole.

2. The minumum edge distance from any cutout to the edge of the part may be no less than the smallest distance calculated in step 1.

3. The minimum inside radius for a cutout is R = 4.

4. The center hole must be supported using diagonally located webs centered about lines drawn from the center points of the corner holes and the central hole.

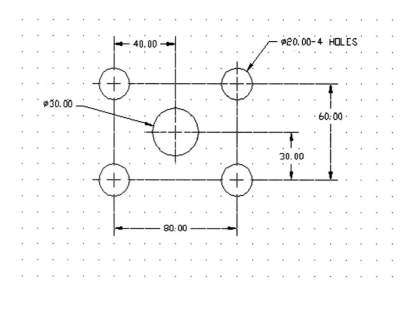

EX3-54 MILLIMETERS

Design a shape that will support the hole pattern shown. Design for a minimum amount of material and to satisfy the following parameters.

1. The edge of the material may be no closer to the center of a hole than twice the diameter of the hole.

2. The minumum edge distance from any cutout to the edge of the part may be no less than the smallest distance calculated in step 1.

3. The minimum inside radius for a cutout is R = 4.

4. The central hole must be supported by 3 webs, located 120° apart.

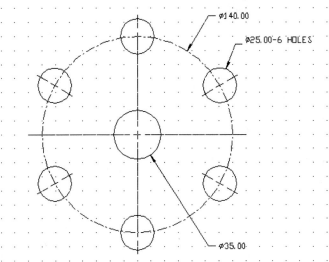

EX3-55 MILLIMETERS

Design a shape that will support the hole pattern shown. Design for a minimum amount of material and to satisfy the following parameters.

1. The edge of the material may be no closer to the center of a hole than twice the diameter of the hole.

2. The minumum edge distance from any cutout to the edge of the part may be no less than the smallest distance calculated in step 1.

3. The minimum inside radius for a cutout is R = 4.

4. Support the center slot with two horizontal and two vertical webs.

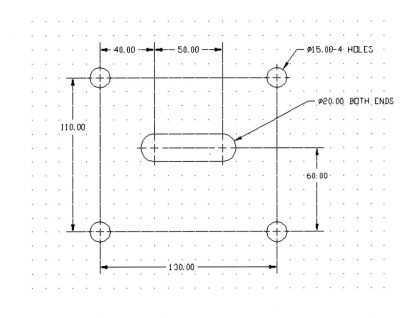

EX3-56 INCHES

Design a shape that will support the hole pattern shown. Design for a minimum amount of material and to satisfy the following parameters.

1. The edge of the material may be no closer to the center of a hole than twice the diameter of the hole.

2. The minumum edge distance from any cutout to the edge of the part may be no less than the smallest distance calculated in step 1.

3. The minimum inside radius for a cutout is R = .125.

4. Support the center hole with two horizontal and two vertical webs.

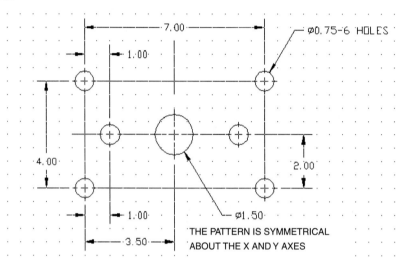

THE PATTERN IS SYMMETRICAL
ABOUT THE X AND Y AXES

EX3-57 MILLIMETERS

Design a shape that will support the hole pattern shown. Design for a minimum amount of material and to satisfy the following parameters.

1. The edge of the material may be no closer to the center of a hole than twice the diameter of the hole.

2. The minumum edge distance from any cutout to the edge of the part may be no less than the smallest distance calculated in step 1.

3. The minimum inside radius for a cutout is R = 4.

4. Support the centers with four webs located to minimize the overall weight of the object.

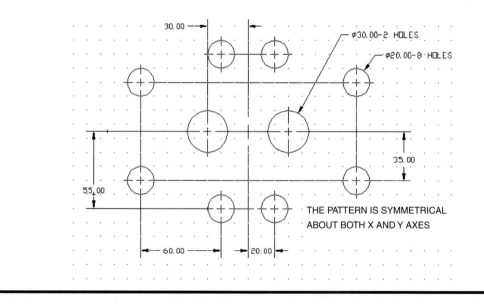

THE PATTERN IS SYMMETRICAL
ABOUT BOTH X AND Y AXES

C H A P T E R

Sketching

4-1 INTRODUCTION

The ability to create freehand sketches is an important skill for engineers and designers to acquire. The old joke about engineers and designers not being able to talk without a pencil in their hands is not far from the truth. Many design concepts and ideas are very difficult to express verbally, so they must be expressed visually. Sketches can be created quickly and used as powerful aids for communicating technical ideas.

This chapter presents the fundamentals of freehand sketching applied to technical situations. It includes both two-dimensional and three-dimensional sketching. Like any skill, freehand sketching is best learned by lots and lots of practice.

4-2 ESTABLISH YOUR OWN STYLE

As you learn and practice how to sketch, you will find that you develop your own way of doing things: your own style. This is very acceptable as there is no absolutely correct method for sketching; there are only recommendations.

The most important aspect of freehand sketching is that you be comfortable. As you practice and experiment, you will find you may prefer a certain pencil lead hardness, a certain angle for your paper, and a certain way to make your lines, both straight and curved. You may find that you prefer to use oblique sketches rather than isometric sketches when sketching three-dimensional objects. Eventually you will develop a style that is comfortable for you and that you can consistently use to create good quality sketches.

It is recommended that all types of sketches presented in the chapter be tried. Only after you have tried and practiced all the different types will you be able to settle on a technique and style that work best for you.

4-3 GRAPH PAPER

Graph paper is very helpful when preparing freehand sketches. It helps you sketch straight lines, allows you to set up guide points for curved lines, and can be used to establish proportions. It is recommended that you start by doing all two-dimensional sketches on graph paper. As your sketching becomes more proficient, you may sketch on plain paper. Because most technical sketching requires some attention to correct proportions, grid paper will always be helpful.

Graph paper is available in many different scales

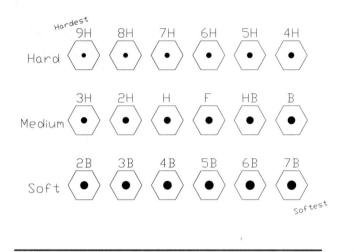

Figure 4-1

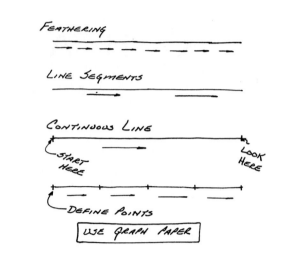

Figure 4-2

and in both inch and metric units. Some graph paper is printed using light blue lines because many copying machines cannot easily reproduce blue lines. This means that copies of the sketches done on light blue guidelines will appear to have been drawn on plain paper and will include only the sketch.

4-4 PENCILS

Pencils are made with a wide variety of lead hardnesses. See Figure 4-1. Hard leads can produce thin, light lines and are well suited for the accuracy requirements of on-the-board type drawings, but are usually too light for sketching. The soft leads produce broad, dark lines but tend to smudge easily if handled too much.

The choice of lead hardness is a personal one. Some designers use 3H leads very successfully, others use HB leads with equal results. You are probably used to a 2H lead because this is the most commonly available. Start sketching with a 2H lead and if the lines are too light, try a softer lead. If they are too dark, try a harder lead until you are satisfied with your work. Pencils with different lead hardnesses are available at most stationery and art supply stores.

Most sketching is done in pencil because it can easily be erased and modified. If you want the very dark lines that inked lines produce, it is recommended that you first prepare the drawing in pencil, then use a pen to trace over the lines you want to emphasize.

4-5 LINES

Straight lines are sketched using one of two methods: a series of short lines, called "feathering," or by a series of line segments. The line segments should be about 1 to 2 inches or 25 to 50 millimeters long. It is very difficult to keep the line segments reasonably straight if they are much longer. As you practice you will develop a comfortable line segment distance. See Figure 4-2.

Lines may also be sketched with a long continuous line. First locate the pencil at the line's starting point, then look at the endpoint as you sketch. This will help develop straighter long lines. Continuous lines are best sketched on graph paper because the graph lines will serve as an additional guide for keeping the lines straight.

Long lines can be created by a series of shorter lines, and very long lines can be sketched by first defining a series of points, then using short segments to connect the points.

It is usually more comfortable to turn the paper slightly when sketching, as shown in Figure 4-3. Righthanders turn the paper counterclockwise and lefthanders clockwise.

It is also easier to sketch all lines in the same direction, that is, with your hand motion always the same. Rather than change your hand position for lines of different angles, simply change the position of the paper and sketch the lines as before. Horizontal and vertical lines are sketched using exactly the same motion, the paper is just positioned 90 degrees differently. Straight lines of any angle can be sketched in the same manner.

Don't squeeze the pencil too hard. Lines should be

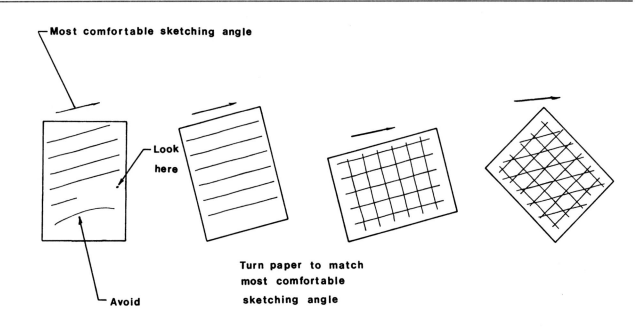

Most comfortable sketching angle

Look here

Avoid

Turn paper to match most comfortable sketching angle

Figure 4-3

sketched with more of an arm motion than a wrist motion. If too much wrist motion is used, the lines will tend to curve down at the ends and look more like arcs than straight lines.

4-6 PROPORTIONS

Sketches should be proportional. A square should look like a square and a rectangle like a rectangle. Graph paper is very helpful in sketching proportionally, but it is still sometimes difficult to be accurate even with graph paper. Start by first sketching very lightly and then check the proportionality of the work. See Figure 4-4. Go back over the lines, making corrections if necessary, then darken the lines. The technique of first sketching lightly, checking the proportions, making corrections, and then going over the lines is useful, regardless of the type of paper used.

It is often helpful to sketch a light grid background based on the unit values of the object being sketched. This is true even if you are working on graph paper as it helps emphasis the unit values you need. See Figure 4-5.

The exact proportions of an object are not always known. A simple technique to approximately measure an

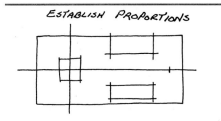

ESTABLISH PROPORTIONS

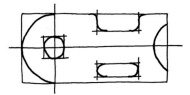

ADD DETAIL

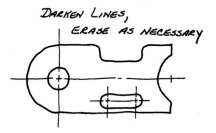

DARKEN LINES, ERASE AS NECESSARY

Figure 4-4

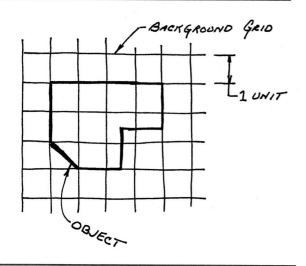

Figure 4-5

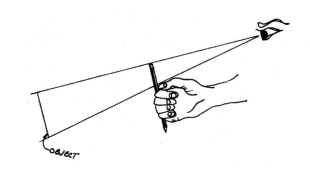

Figure 4-6

object is to use the sketching pencil. See Figure 4-6. Hold the pencil at arm's length and sight the object. Move your thumb up the pencil so that the distance between the end of the pencil and your thumb represents a distance on the object. Transfer the distance to the sketch. Continue taking measurements and transferring them to the sketch until reasonable proportions have been created.

4-7 EXERCISE PROBLEMS

Sketch the shapes in exercise problems EX4-1 to EX4-6. Measure the shapes to determine their dimensions.

EX4-1

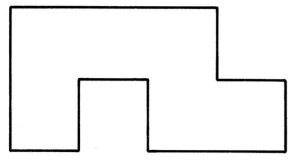

EX4-2

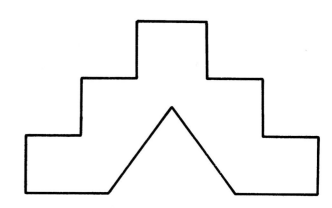

EX4-3

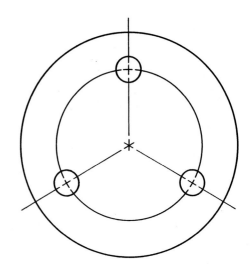

EX4- 4

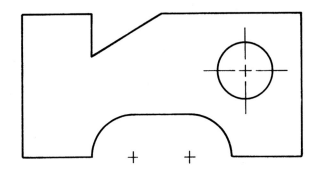

EX4-5

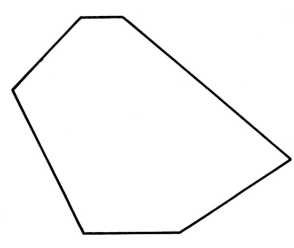

EX4-6

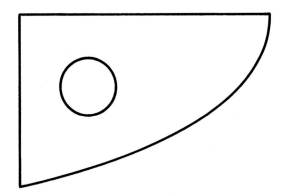

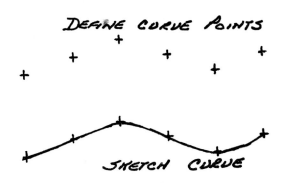

Figure 4-7

4-8 CURVES

Sketching curved shapes is best done by first defining points along the curve, then lightly sketching the curve between the points. See Figure 4-7. Evaluate the accuracy and smoothness of the curve, make any corrections necessary, then darken the curve.

Circles can be sketched by sketching perpendicular centerlines and marking off four points equally spaced from the centerpoint along the centerlines. The distance between the centerpoint and the points on the centerlines should be approximately equal to the circle's radius. See Figure 4-8.

Draw a second set of perpendicular centerlines approximately 45 degrees to the first. Again mark four points approximately equal to the radius of the circle. Sketch a light curve between the 8 points. Check the curve

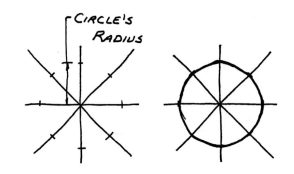

Figure 4-8

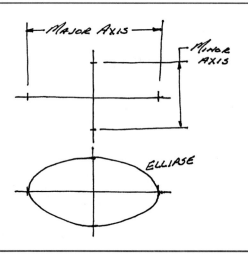

Figure 4-9

for accuracy and smoothness. Make any corrections necessary and darken the circle.

An ellipse can be sketched by first sketching a perpendicular axis, then locating four marks on the center lines that are approximately equal to major and minor axis distances. Sketch a light curve, make any corrections necessary, and darken the elliptical shape. See Figure 4-9.

Figure 4-10 shows how to sketch a slot. To sketch the slot, center lines for the two end semicircles are located and sketched. Two additional radius points are added, then the overall shape of the slot is lightly sketched. Corrections are made and the final lines are darkened.

The triangular object is first sketched as a triangle. Guidelines and an axis are added for the curved sections and the final shape of the object is sketched.

4-9 SAMPLE PROBLEM SP4-1

Sketch the object shown in Figure 4-11.

1. Sketch the overall rectangular shape of the object. See Figure 4-12.
2. Add proportional guidelines for the outside shape

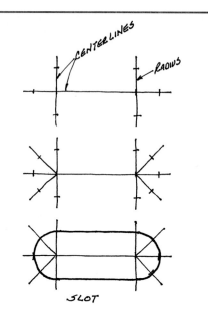

Figure 4-10

of the object and lightly sketch the outside shape.
3. Locate and sketch guidelines and axis lines for the other features.
4. Lightly sketch the object and make any corrections necessary.
5. Darken the final lines.

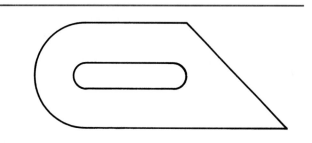

Figure 4-11

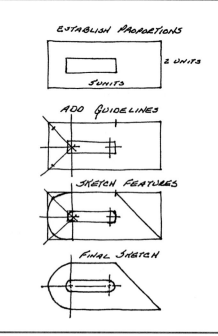

Figure 4-12

4-10 ISOMETRIC SKETCHING

Isometric sketches are based on an isometric axis that contains three lines 120 degrees apart. See Figure 4-13. The isometric axis can also be drawn in a modified form that contains a vertical line and two 30-degree lines. The modified axis is more convenient for sketching and is the more commonly used form. See Figure 4-14.

The receding lines of an isometric sketch are parallel. This is not visually correct as the human eye naturally sees objects farther away as smaller than those closer. Railroad tracks appear to converge. However, it is easier to draw objects with parallel receding lines and, if the object is not too big, the slight visual distortion is acceptable. See Section 4-15 for an explanation of perspective drawings whose receding lines are not parallel but convergent.

The three planes of an isometric axis are defined as the left, right, and top planes. See Figure 4-14. When creating isometric sketches, it is best to start with the three planes drawn as if the object were a rectangular prism or cube. Think of creating the sketch from these planes as working from a piece of wood and trimming away the unnecessary areas. Figure 4-15 shows an example of an isometric sketch. In the example, the overall proportions of the object were used to define the boundaries of the object, then other surfaces were added as necessary.

Isometric sketches may be sketched in different orientations. Figure 4-16 shows 6 possible orientations. Note how orientation 1 makes the object look like it is below you, and orientation 6 looks like it is above you. Orientation can also serve to show features that would otherwise be hidden from view. The small cutout in the rear of the object is visible in only four of the orientations. Always try to orientate the isometric sketch so that it shows as many of the object's features as possible.

Figure 4-17 shows an isometric drawing of a cube

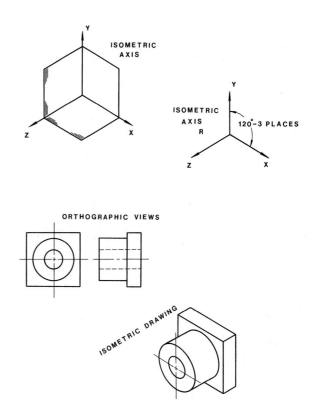

Figure 4-13

that has a hole in the top plane. The hole must be sketched as an ellipse to appear visually correct in the isometric drawing. The axis lines for the ellipse are parallel to the edge lines of the plane. The proportions of the ellipse are defined by four points equidistant from the ellipse centerpoint along the axis lines. The ellipse is then sketched lightly, checked for accuracy, then darkened.

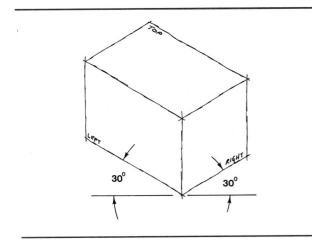

Figure 4-14

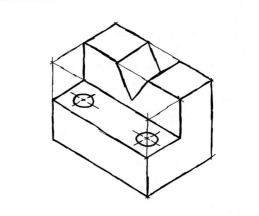

Figure 4-15

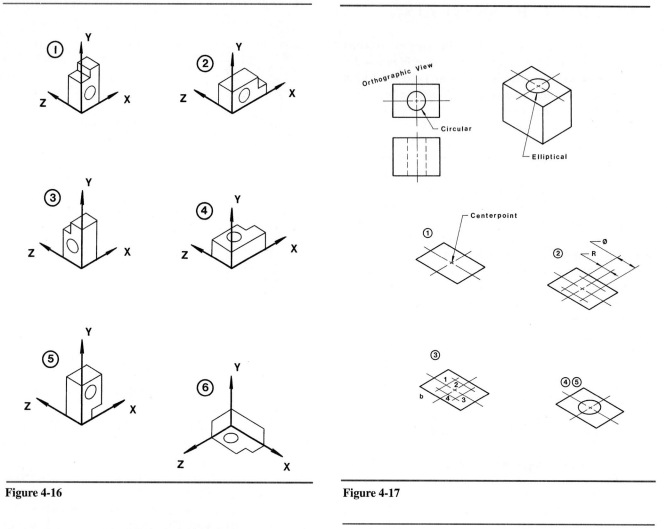

Figure 4-16

Figure 4-17

4-11 SAMPLE PROBLEM SP4-2

Sketch the object shown in Figure 4-18. Do not include dimensions but keep the object proportional.

1. Use the overall dimensions of the object to sketch a rectangular prism of the correct proportions. This is a critical step. If the first attempt is not proportionally correct, erase it and sketch again until a satisfactory result is achieved. See Figure 4-19.
2. Sketch the cutout.
3. Sketch the rounded surfaces. Note how axis lines are sketched and the elliptical shape is added. Tangent lines are added and visually incorrect lines are erased.
4. Sketch the holes by locating their centerlines and then sketching the required ellipses.

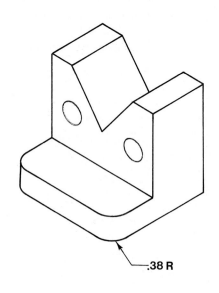

Figure 4-18

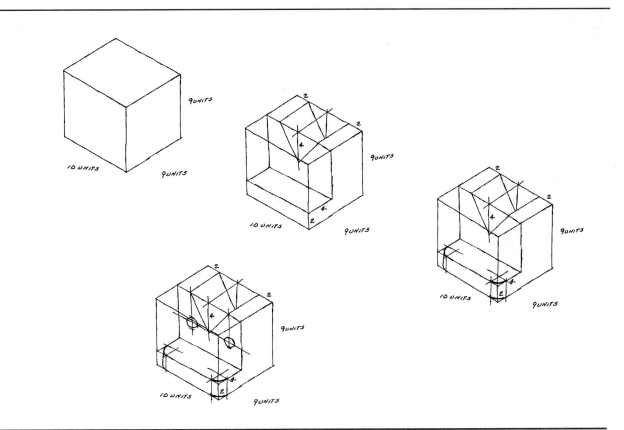

Figure 4-19

4-12 EXERCISE PROBLEMS

Prepare isometric sketches of the objects shown in exercise problems EX4-7 to Ex4-12. Measure the objects for their dimensions.

EX4-7

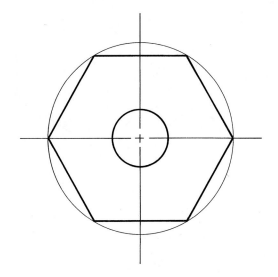

EX4-8

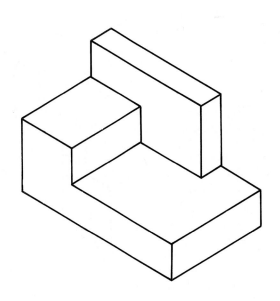

EX4-9

EX4-11

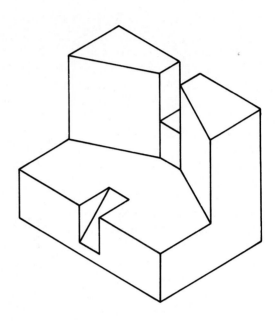

EX4-10

EX4-12

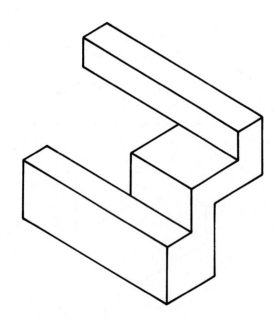

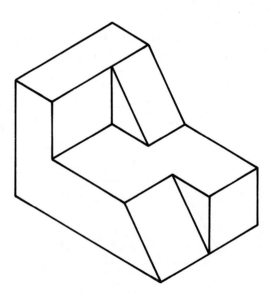

4-13 OBLIQUE SKETCHES

Oblique sketches are based on an axis system that contains one perpendicular set of axis lines and one receding line. See Figure 4-20. The front plane of an oblique axis is perpendicular so the front face of a cube will appear as a square and the front face of a cylinder as a circle. The receding lines can be at any angle, but 30 degrees is most common.

The receding lines of oblique sketches are parallel. As with isometric sketches, this causes some visual distortions, but unless the object is very large, these distortions are acceptable.

Holes in the front plane of an isometric sketch may be sketched as circles, but holes in the other two planes are sketched as ellipses. See Figure 4-21. The axis lines for the ellipse are parallel to the edge lines of the plane. The proportions of the ellipses are determined by points equidistant from the centerpoint along the axis.

Figure 4-22 shows an example of a circular object sketched as an oblique sketch. Oblique sketches are particularly useful in sketching circular objects because they

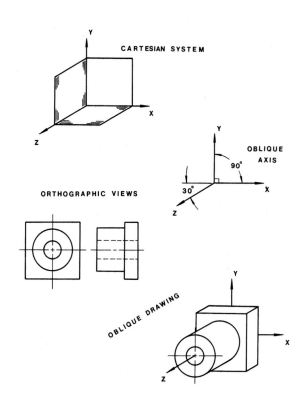

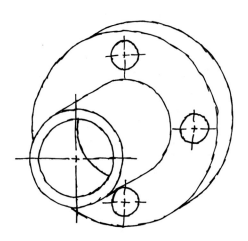

Figure 4-20

allow circles in the frontal planes to be sketched as circles rather than the elliptical shapes required by isometric sketches.

Figure 4-23 shows an object. Figure 4-24 shows how an oblique sketch of the object was developed.

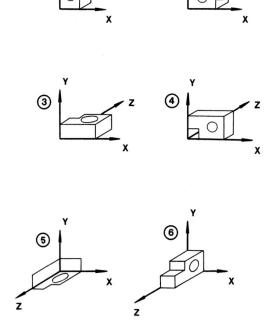

Figure 4-21

Figure 4-22

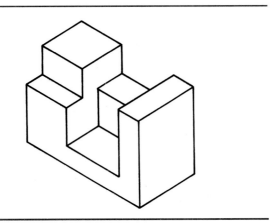

Figure 4-23

4-14 EXERCISE PROBLEMS

Prepare oblique sketches of the objects shown in exercise problems EX4-13 to EX4-18. Measure the objects to determine their dimensions.

EX4-13

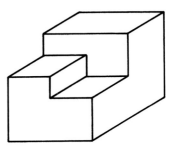

EX4-14

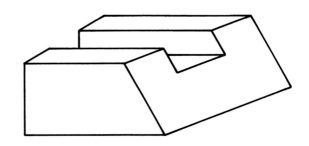

EX4-15

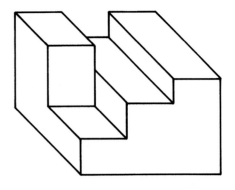

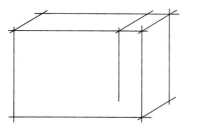

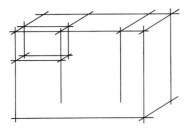

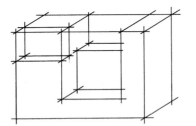

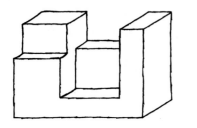

Figure 4-24

EX4-16

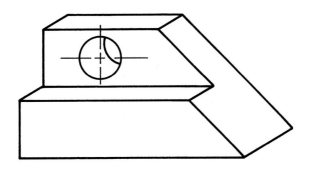

EX4-17

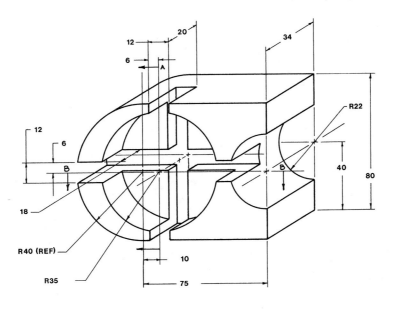

EX4-18

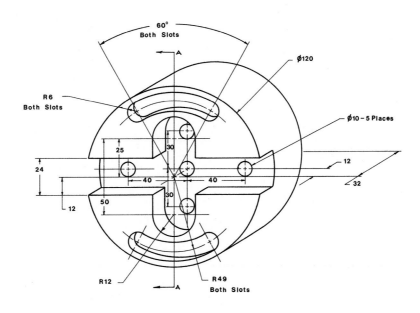

4-15 PERSPECTIVE SKETCHES

Perspective sketches are sketches whose receding lines converge to a vanishing point. Perspective sketches are visually accurate in that they look like what we see; objects farther away appear smaller than those that are closer.

Figure 4-25 shows a comparison between the axis systems used for oblique, isometric, and two-point perspective drawings The receding lines of the perspective drawing converge to vanishing points that are located on a theoretical horizon. The horizon line is always located at eye level. Objects above the horizon line appear to be above and objects below the horizon appear to be below.

Perspective drawings are often referred to as pictorial drawings. Figure 4-26 shows an object drawn twice: once as an isometric drawing and again as a pictorial or two-point perspective. Note how much more lifelike the pictorial drawing looks in comparison to the isometric drawing.

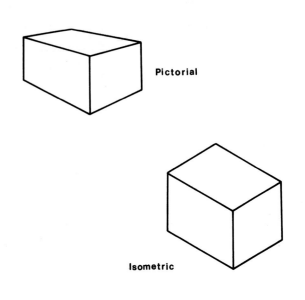

Figure 4-26

Figure 4-27 shows a perspective sketch based on only one vanishing point. One-point perspective sketches are similar to oblique sketches. The front surface plane is sketched using a 90-degree axis and then receding lines are sketched from the front plane to a vanishing point. Eventually as you practice sketching you will not need to include a vanishing point but will imply its location.

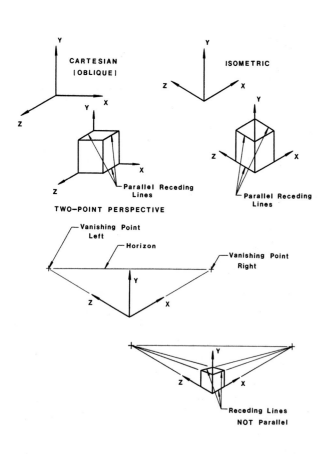

Figure 4-25

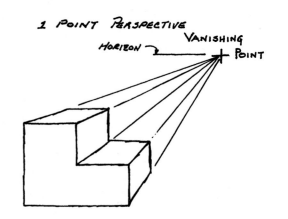

Figure 4-27

Figure 4-28 shows how to sketch circular shapes in both one- and two-point perspective sketches. In each style the axis lines are either vertical lines or lines that align with the receding edge lines. Circular shapes in perspective sketches are not elliptical but are irregular splines. Each surface will require a slightly different shape to produce a visually accurate shape.

4-16 LETTERING

Lettering on freehand sketches is very individualistic: everyone does it differently. The one rule is that the lettering be easy to understand. If lettering is very stylistic and very beautiful but difficult to read, it is not acceptable.

Drafters that worked on drawing boards were trained to letter using the same style letters. This meant that if two or more persons worked on the same drawing the lettering would be consistent and look uniform. Two styles, vertical and slanted, were used. Figures 4-29, 4-30, and 4-31 show the two styles for both letters and numbers. It is recommended that you try working in both styles following the indicated pattern strokes until you find which is the more comfortable for you. Either style will help you develop clear, easy-to-read lettering on your freehand sketches.

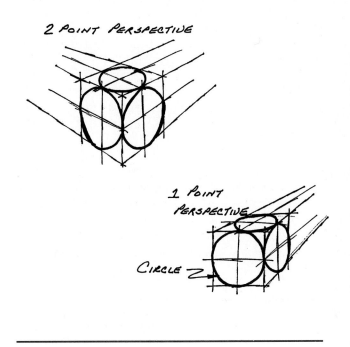

Figure 4-28

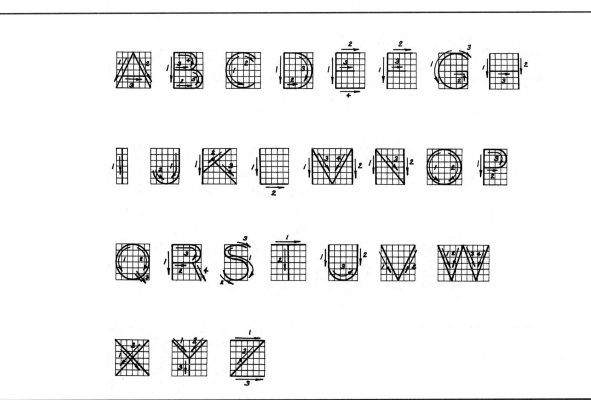

Figure 4-29

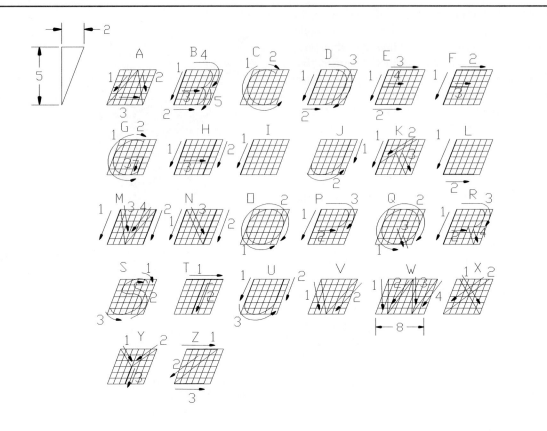

Figure 4-30

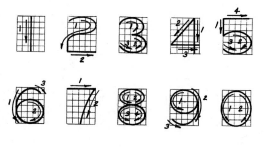

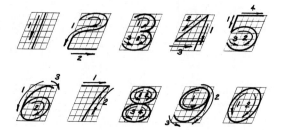

Figure 4-31

4-17 EXERCISE PROBLEMS

Sketch the shapes and figures in exercise problems EX4-19 to EX4-33. The figures are presented as isometric drawings but may be sketched as either isometric, oblique, one-point or two-point presepectives.

It is suggested that one figure be sketched using all four styles and the results compared.

EX4-19

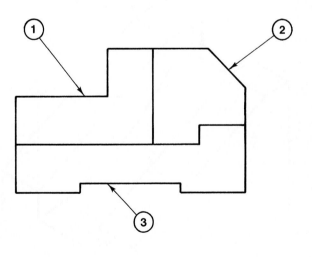

EX4-20

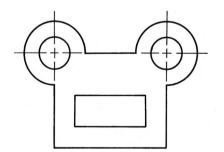

SCALE: $\frac{1}{2}$ = 1

EX4-21

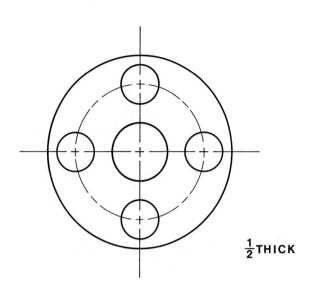

$\frac{1}{2}$THICK

EX4-22

EX4-23

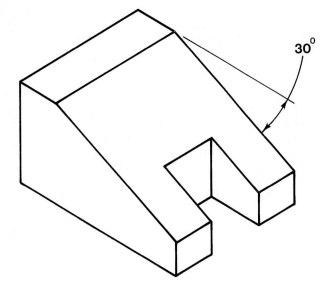

EX4-25

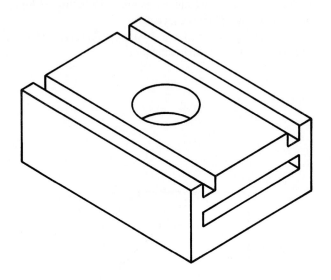

EX4-24

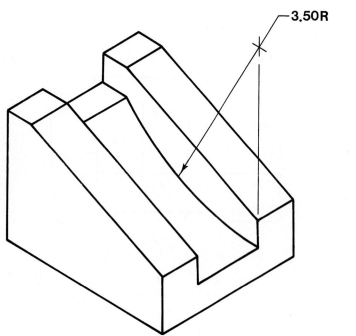

EX4-26

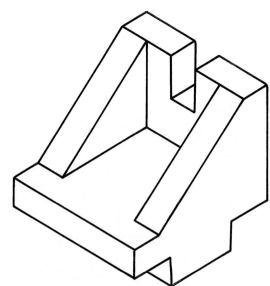

EX4-27

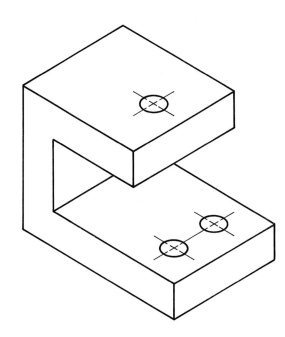

EX4-29

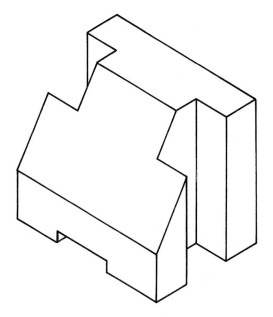

EX4-28

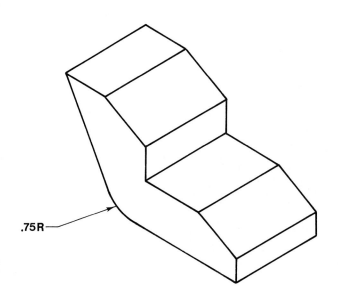

.75R

EX4-30

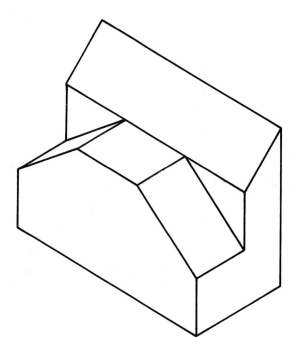

EX4-31 INCHES

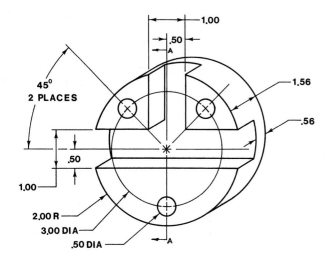

EX4-33 MILLIMETERS

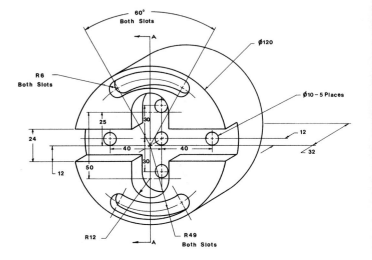

EX4-32 MILLIMETERS

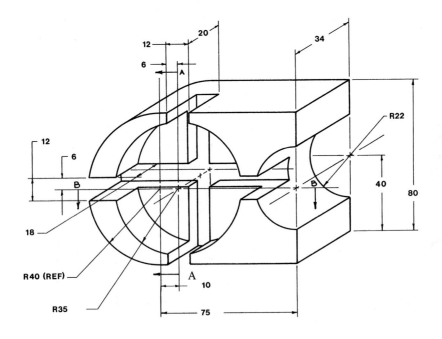

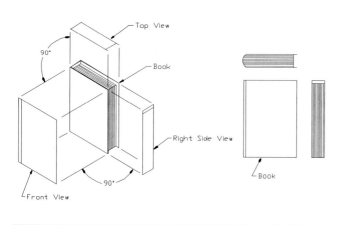

Figure 5-5

this text under the file name F5-6. The orthographic views shown in Figure 5-6 may be verified by opening the F5-6 drawing file and rotating the object into the appropriate orthographic planes.

To verify the orthographic views shown in Figure 5-6

1. Select FILE pulldown menu, OPEN, A: F5-6

This step assumes that the drawing disk is in the A: drive. If it is not, be sure to specify the correct drive.

2. Select VIEW pulldown menu, 3D DYNAMIC VIEW

Select objects:

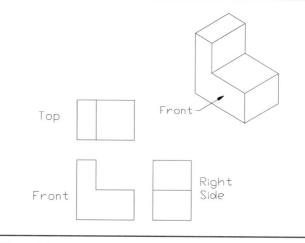

Figure 5-6

3. Window the entire object.

CAmera/TArget/Distance/POints/PAn/Zoom/ TWist/CLip/Hide/Off/Undo/<eXit>:

4. Type CA ENTER

The object will now rotate as the cursor is moved. Move the cursor until the object looks like the front view shown in Figure 5-6. To see the right-side view, move the cursor to the left, and to see the top view, move the cursor toward the bottom of the screen.

Figures 5-7 and 5-8 also show objects and three views of that object. Each object is also included on the drawing disk under the file names F5-7 and F5-8, respectively. Open each file and use the procedure given for F5-6 to verify the orthographic views.

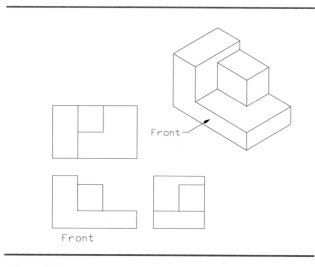

Figure 5-7

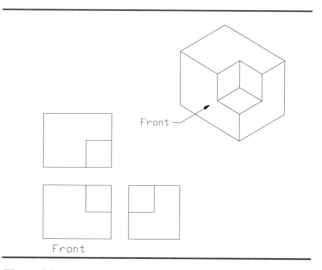

Figure 5-8

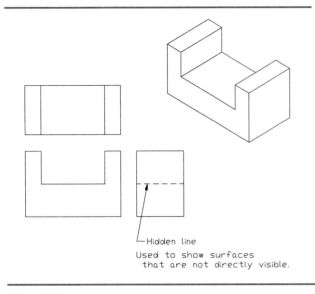

Figure 5-9

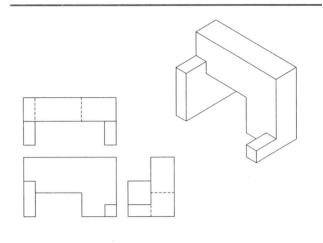

Figure 5-10

5-4 HIDDEN LINES

Hidden lines are used to represent surfaces that are not directly visible in an orthographic view. Figure 5-9 shows an object that contains surface A-B-C-D that is not directly visible in the side view. A hidden line is used to represent the end view of plane A-B-C-D in the side view.

Figure 5-10 shows an object and three views of the object. The top and side views of the object contain hidden lines.

Figure 5-11 shows an object that contains edge line A-B. In the top view of the object, line A-B is partially hidden and partially visible. When the line is directly visible through the square hole, it is drawn as a continuous line; when it is not directly visible, it is drawn as a hidden line.

5-5 HIDDEN LINE CONVENTIONS

Figure 5-12 shows several conventions associated with drawing hidden lines. Whenever possible show intersections of hidden lines as touching lines, not as open gaps. Corners should also be shown as touching lines.

The LTSCALE command on the SETTINGS submenu (not pulldown menu) can be used to change the spacing of hidden lines. However, all lines will be changed to whatever parameter is specified, so always check the entire drawing for visual accuracy whenever LTSCALE is used.

Figure 5-13 shows two hidden lines and a continuous line that are aligned. A small gap should be included between the two types of lines to prevent confusion as to where one type of line ends and the other begins. A visual

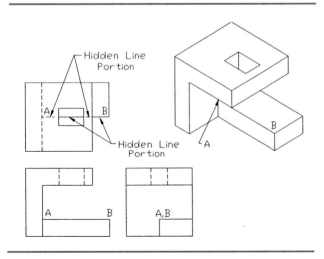

Figure 5-11

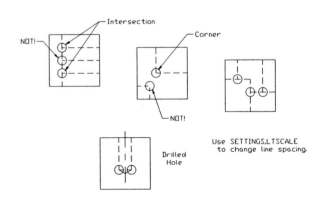

Figure 5-12

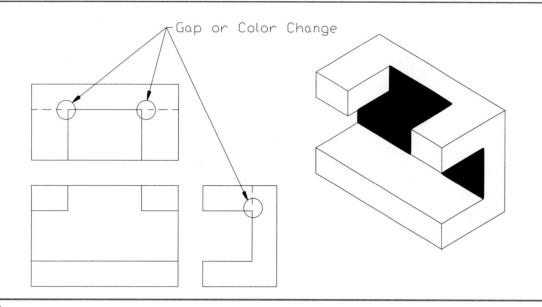

Figure 5-13

distinction can also be created by selecting a different color for hidden lines. If continuous and hidden lines are drawn using different colors, then gaps are not necessary.

5-6 DRAWING HIDDEN LINES

There are two methods for drawing hidden lines: CHANGE the line from a continuous line to a hidden line, or transfer the continuous line to a special LAYER created specifically for hidden lines.

To CHANGE a continuous line to a hidden line

See Figure 5-14.

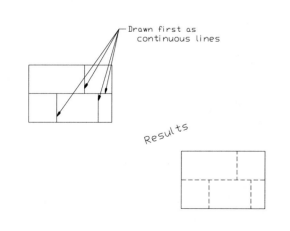

Figure 5-14

1. Select the EDIT (WINDOWS), or MODIFY (DOS) pulldown menu, then PROPERTIES (there is a PROPERTIES icon located on the STANDARD toolbar on the WINDOWS version)

Select objects:

2. Select the lines, then ENTER

The MODIFY LINE dialog box will appear. See Figure 5-15.

3. Select the LINETYPE... box

The SELECT LINETYPE dialog box will appear. See Figure 5-16a.

4. Select HIDDEN, OK

If a complete list of linetypes does not appear in the dialog box, load the linetype file using the LOAD box located near the bottom of the SELECT LINETYPE box.

The MODIFY LINE dialog box will reappear. This allows you to select other options such as COLOR. Hidden lines are usually drawn using a different color than continuous lines.

5. Select the COLOR... box

The SELECT COLOR dialog box will appear. See Figure 5-16b.

WINDOWS
PROPERTIES icon located
on the STANDARD toolbar

DOS

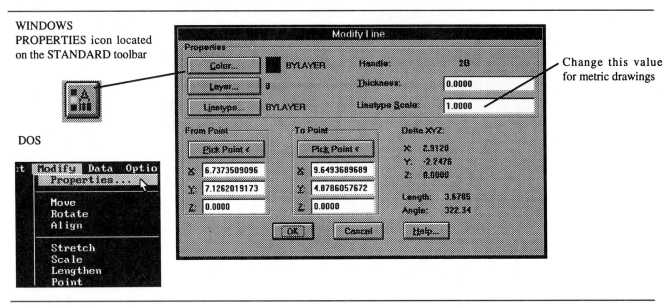

Change this value
for metric drawings

Figure 5-15

6. Select GREEN (optional choice), OK

The MODIFY LINE dialog box will again reappear.

7. Select OK

The lines will now appear using the hidden line pattern and will be green. If the lines change color but still appear to be continuous, return to the MODIFY LINE dialog box and change the LINETYPE SCALE value. For drawings done using millimeter dimensions with drawing limits of 297 × 210, values between 10 and 18 are recommended.

To use LAYER to create a hidden line

This procedure may seem a bit lengthy when compared to the CHANGE procedure outline above, but it is very efficient for large drawings where there are many lines to change.

A hidden line layer may also be included as part of a prototype drawing, meaning it will be automatically set up every time the prototype drawing is used. It is suggested that a HIDDEN line layer be added to both PROMET and ACAD prototype drawings.

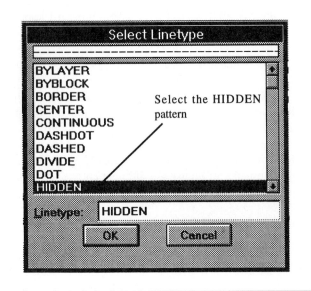

Figure 5-16a

Figure 5-16b

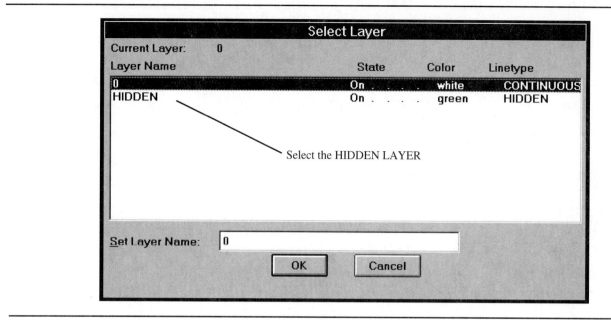

Figure 5-16c

1. Create a HIDDEN LAYER that includes both the hidden line pattern and color

See Section 3-27 for instructions on creating a new LAYER.

2. Select the EDIT or MODIFY pulldown menus, then PROPERTIES to access the MODIFY LINE dialog box
3. Select the LAYER... box

The CHANGE LAYER dialog box will appear. See Figure 5-16c.

4. Select the HIDDEN LAYER, OK

The MODIFY LAYER dialog box will reappear.

5. Select OK

The lines will appear green using the hidden line pattern. If the lines do not appear, check to see if the HIDDEN LAYER is ON.

Figures 5-17 and 5-18 show examples of drawings that include hidden lines.

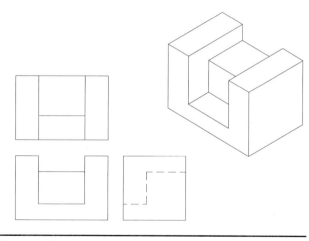

Figure 5-17

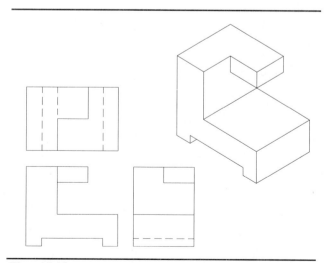

Figure 5-18

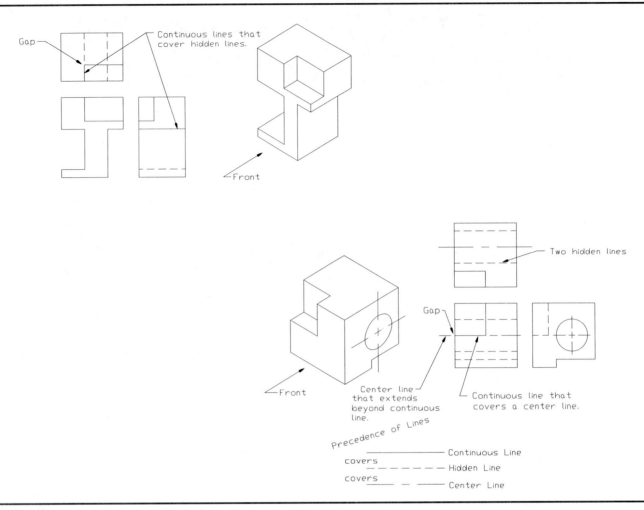

Figure 5-19

5-7 PRECEDENCE OF LINES

When preparing orthographic views, it is not unusual for one type of line to be drawn over another type: a continuous line over a center line. See Figure 5-19. Drawing convention has established a precedence of lines. A continuous line takes precedence over a hidden line and a hidden line takes precedence over a center line.

If different line types are of different lengths, include a gap where the line changes from continuous to either hidden or center to create a visual distinction between the lines. Color changes may also be used to create visual distinctions between lines.

5-8 SLANTED SURFACES

Slanted surfaces are surfaces that are not parallel to either the horizontal or vertical axis. Figure 5-20 shows a

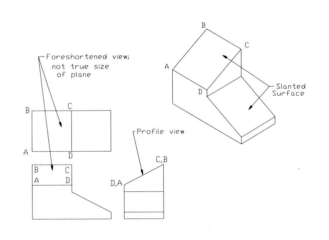

Figure 5-20

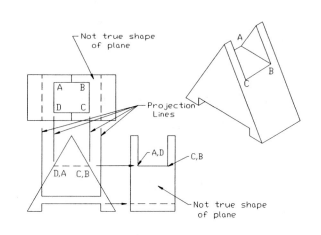

Figure 5-21

slanted surface A-B-C-D. Slanted surface A-B-C-D appears as a straight line in the side view and as a plane in both the front and top views. It is important to note that neither the front nor top views of surface A-B-C-D are true representations of the surface. Both orthographic views are actually smaller than the actual surface. Lines B-C and A-D in the top view are true length, but lines A-B and C-D are shorter than the actual edge lengths. The same is true for the front view of the surface. The side view shows the true length of lines A-B and D-C. True lengths of lines and true shapes of planes are discussed again in Chapter 7, Auxiliary Views.

Figure 5-21 shows another object that contains slanted surfaces. Note how projection lines are used between the views. As objects become more complex, the shape of a

surface or the location of an edge line will not always be obvious, so projecting information between views, and therefore exact, correct relative view location, becomes critical. Information can be projected only between views that are correctly positioned and accurately drawn.

Both the objects shown in Figures 5-20 and 5-21 are also on the drawing disk under the file names F5-20 and F5-21. Use the method outlined in Section 5-3 to call up these drawings and to verify the shapes of the given orthographic views.

5-9 PROJECTION BETWEEN VIEWS

Information is projected between the front and side views using horizontal lines and between the front and top views using vertical lines. Information can be projected between the top and side views using a combination of horizontal and vertical lines that intersect a 45-degree miter line. See Figure 5-22.

A 45-degree miter line is constructed between the top and side views. This line allows the projection lines to change direction, turn a corner, change from horizontal to vertical lines. To go from the top view to the side view, construct horizontal projection lines from the top view so that they intersect the miter line. Construct vertical lines from the intersection points on the miter line into the side view. The reverse process is used to go from the side view to the top view.

The following sample problem shows how projection lines can be used to create orthographic views using AutoCAD.

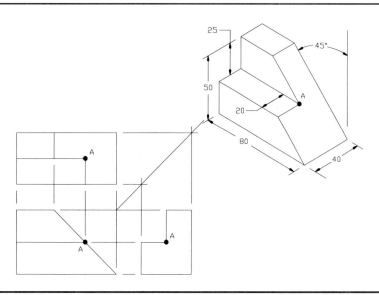

Figure 5-22

5-10 SAMPLE PROBLEM SP5-1

Draw the front, top, and right-side orthographic views of the object shown in Figure 5-22.

1. Set up the drawing as follows. These specifications are the same as those recommended for the creation of prototype drawing PROMET as explained in Section 1-19 and modified to include a HIDDEN line layer as recommended in Section 5-7.

$$LIMITS = 297 \times 210$$
$$GRID = 10$$
$$SNAP = 5$$
$$ORTHO = ON \ (F8)$$
$$LAYER = HIDDEN \ (LType = HIDDEN, \ Color = Green)$$

2. Use the overall dimensions (length = 80, height = 50, and depth = 40) to define the overall size requirements of the three orthographic views. See Figure 5-23. The 20 spacing between the views is arbitrary. The distance between the front and top views does not have to equal the distance between the front and side views. In this example the two distances are equal.

3. Draw a 45-degree miter line starting from the upper right corner of the front view. This step is possible only if the distance between the views is equal. If the distances are not equal, draw the front and top views, add the miter line, and project the overall size of the side view from the front and top views.

3a. (Optional) TRIM away the excess lines to clearly define the areas of the front, top, and side views.

3b. (Optional) LAYERS may be used to create a layer for construction lines and another layer for final drawing lines. The lines for the final drawing may then be transfered to the final drawing layer and the construction layer turned OFF. This method eliminates the need for extensive ERASEing or TRIMing.

4. Draw the 45-degree slanted surface in the front view as shown in Figure 5-23. Project the intersection of the slanted surface and the top edge of the front view into the top view. Add a horizontal line across the front and right-side views 25 from the bottom edge line. The 25 value comes from the given dimension. Label the

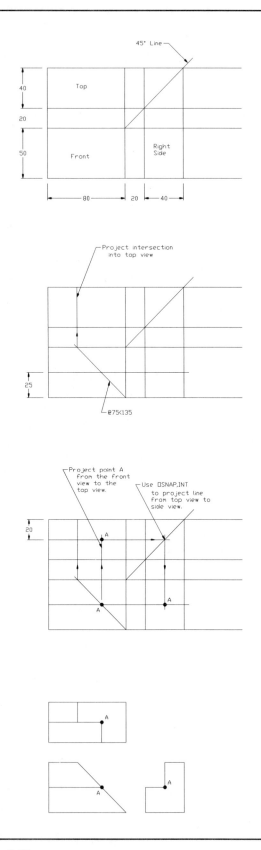

Figure 5-23

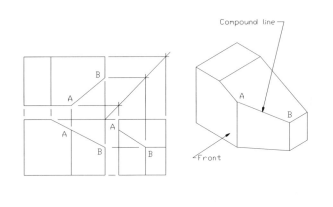

Figure 5-24

intersection of the slanted line and the horizontal line as point A.

5. Draw a horizontal line in the top view 20mm from the top edge as shown in Figure 5-23. Continue the line so that it intersects the miter line. Project the line into the side view. Use OSNAP, INTersection with ORTHO On to ensure an accurate projection. Label point A in the side view.

6. Project point A in the front view into the top view (vertical line). Label the intersection of the projection line and the horizontal line in the top view as point A.

7. Use ERASE and TRIM to remove the excess lines.

8. Save the drawing if desired.

5-11 COMPOUND LINES

A compound line is formed when two slanted surfaces intersect. See Figure 5-24. The true length of a compound line is not shown in either the front, top, or side views.

Figure 5-25 showns another object that contains compound lines. The three orthographic views of a compound line are sometimes difficult to visualize, making it more important to be able to project information accurately between views. Usually part of an object can be visualized and part of the orthographic views created. The remainder of the drawing can be added by projecting from the known information.

Both Figures 5-24 and 5-25 are included on the drawing disk under the file names F5-24 and F5-25. Call them up and rotate them to verify the orthographic views using the procedure outlined in Section 5-3.

5-12 SAMPLE PROBLEM SP5-2

Figure 5-26 shows how the front, top, and side views of the object shown in Figure 5-25 were created by projecting information. The procedure is as follows.

1. Set the drawing up as follows. These drawing specifications will be used for many of the sample problems in the book that use inch dimensions. It is suggested that a prototype drawing be created or the default ACAD prototype be modified to include GRID and SNAP commands.

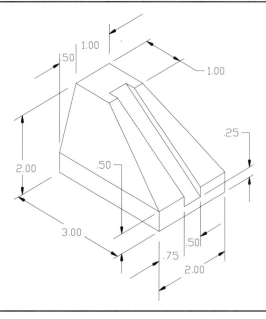

Figure 5-25

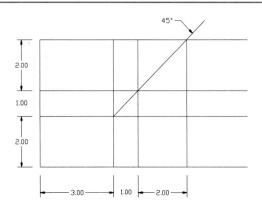

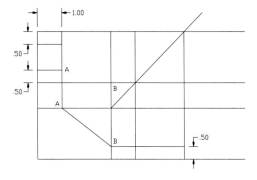

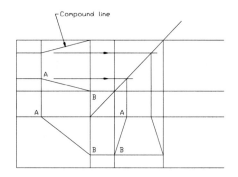

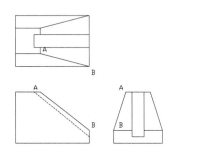

Figure 5-26

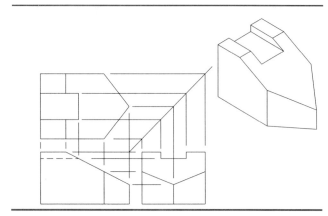

Figure 5-27

> LIMITS = Default
> GRID = .5
> SNAP = .25

2. Use the overall dimensions to define the space and location requirements for the views. Draw the 45-degree miter line.
3. Use the given dimensions to define the starting and end points on the compound lines in the top and front views. One of the lines has been labeled A-B.
4. Draw the compound line in the top view and then project it into the side view using information from both the top and front views.
5. Add the dovetailed shape using the given dimensions. Draw the appropriate hidden lines for the dovetail.
6. ERASE and TRIM the excess lines.
7. SAVE the drawing if desired.

Figure 5-27 shows the three views and pictorial view of another example of an object that includes compound lines. Some of the projection lines have also been included.

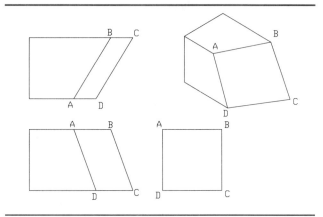

Figure 5-28

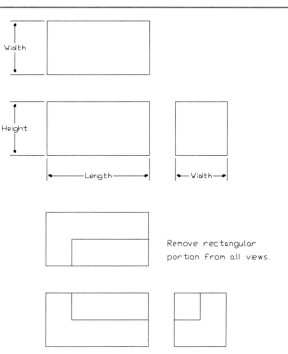

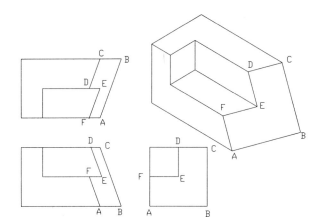

Figure 5-29

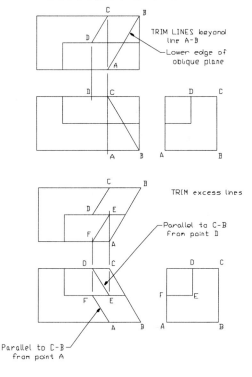

5-13 OBLIQUE SURFACES

Oblique surfaces are surfaces that do not appear correctly shaped in either the front, top, or side views. Figure 5-28 shows an object that contains oblique surface A-B-C-D. Figure 5-28 also shows three views of just surface A-B-C-D. Oblique surfaces are projected by first projecting their corner points and then joining the points with straight lines. The orthographic views of oblique surfaces are sometimes visually abstract. This makes the development of their orthographic views more dependent on projection than other types of surfaces.

Figure 5-29 shows another object that contains an oblique surface. Figure 5-30 shows how the three orthographic views were developed. The oblique surface is defined using only two angles, but this is sufficient to create the three views because the surface is flat. The edge lines are parallel. Lines A-B, C-D, and E-F are parallel to each other and lines C-B, D-E, and F-A are also parallel to each other. Figure 5-30 also shows three views of just the oblique surface along with the appropriate projection lines.

Figure 5-30

5-14 SAMPLE PROBLEM SP5-3

The three views of the object shown in Figure 5-31a may be drawn as follows. The given dimensions are in millimeters.

1. Use LINE, OFFSET and the given overall dimensions to set up the size and locations of the three views, Use OSNAP, INTERSECTION to draw the projection lines. See Figure 5-31b.
2. Draw an oblique surface based on the given dimensions. The edge lines of the oblique surface are parallel.
3. Draw the slanted surface in the side view and project the surface into the other views. Use the intersection between the slanted surface and the flat sections on the top and side of the object to determine the shape of the oblique surface.
4. Use ERASE and TRIM to remove any excess lines. SAVE the drawing if desired.

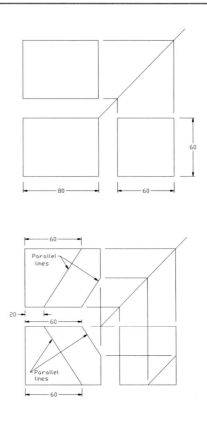

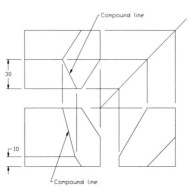

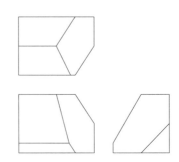

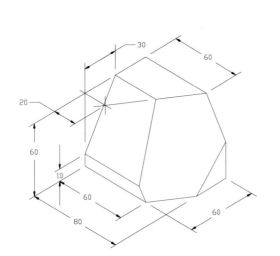

Figure 5-31a

Figure 5-31b

5-15 ROUNDED SURFACES

Rounded surfaces are surfaces that have constant radii such as arcs or circles. Surfaces that do not have constant radii are classified as irregular surfaces. See Section 5-27.

Figure 5-32 shows an object with rounded surfaces. Surface A-B-C-D is tangent to both the top and side surfaces of the object so no edge line is drawn. This means that the top and side orthographic views of the object are ambiguous. If only the top and side views are considered, then other interpretations of the views are possible. Figure 5-32 shows another object that generates the same top and side orthographic views but does not include rounded surface A-B-C-D. The front view is needed to define the rounded surfaces and limit the views to only one interpretation.

Surfaces perpendicular to an orthographic view always produce lines in that orthographic view. The vertical surface shown in the front view of object A in Figure 5-33 requires an edge line in the top view. The vertical line in the front view is perpendicular to the top views. Object B in Figure 5-33 has no lines perpendicular to the top view, so no lines are drawn in the top view. Object C in Figure 5-33 shows two rounded surfaces that intersect at points tangent to their center lines. The intersection point is considered sufficient to require an edge line in the top view.

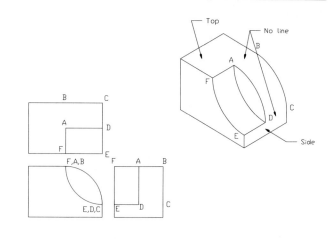

Figure 5-32

No line would actually be visible on the actual object, but drawing convention prescribes that a line be drawn.

Figure 5-34 shows an object that contains two semicircular surfaces. Note how lines representing the widest and deepest point of the surfaces generate lines in the top view. No line would actually appear on the object.

Figure 5-35 shows additional examples of rounded surfaces.

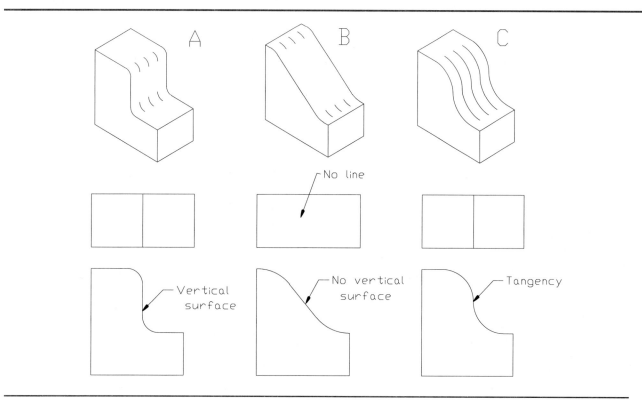

Figure 5-33

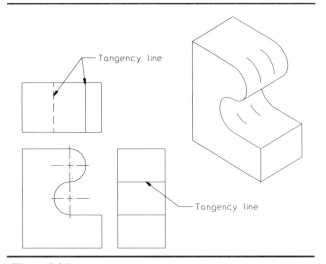

Figure 5-34

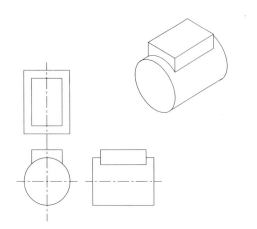

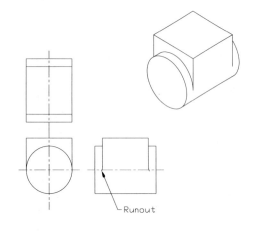

Figure 5-35

5-16 SAMPLE PROBLEM SP5-4

Figure 5-36 shows an object that includes rounded surfaces and Figure 5-37 shows how the three views of the object were developed. The procedure is as follows.

1. Use the given overall dimensions to lay out the size and location of the three views.
2. DRAW in the external details, the cutout, and the circular extension in all three views.
3. Add the appropriate hidden lines. Use either EDIT or CHANGE, or create a HIDDEN line LAYER.
4. ERASE and TRIM any excess lines and SAVE the drawing if desired.

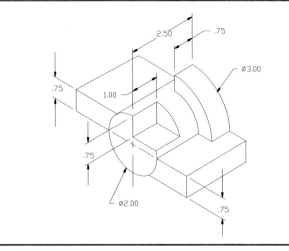

Figure 5-36

5-17 HOLES

Holes are represented in orthographic views by circles and parallel hidden lines. All views of a hole always include center lines. See Figure 5-38. It is suggested that a layer entitled CENTER be added to any prototype drawings being used. Specify a linetype center and a color red.

Holes that go completely through an object are dimensioned using only a diameter. The notation THRU may be added to the diameter specification for clarity.

Holes that do not go completely through an object include a depth specification in their dimension. The depth specification is interpreted as shown in Figure 5-38. Holes that do not go completely through an object must include a conical point. The conical point is not included in the depth specification. Conical points must be included because most holes are produced using a twist drill with conically shaped cutting edges.

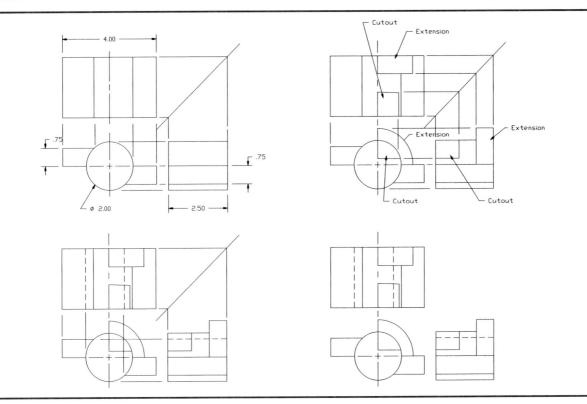

Figure 5-37

The cutting angles of twist drills vary, but they are always represented by a 30-degree angle as shown.

Figure 5-39 shows an object that contains two through holes and one hole with a depth specification. Note how these holes are represented in the orthographic views and how center lines are used in the different views.

Figure 5-40 is another example of an object that includes a hole. The hole is centered about the edge line between the two normal surfaces. Figure 5-41 shows the same object with the hole's center point offset from the edge line between the two normal surfaces. Compare the differences between Figures 5-40 and 5-41.

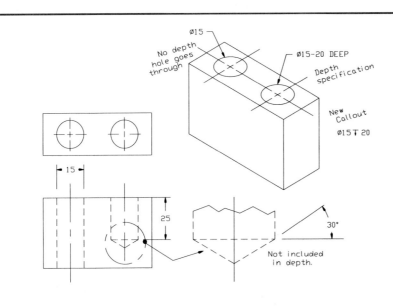

Figure 5-38

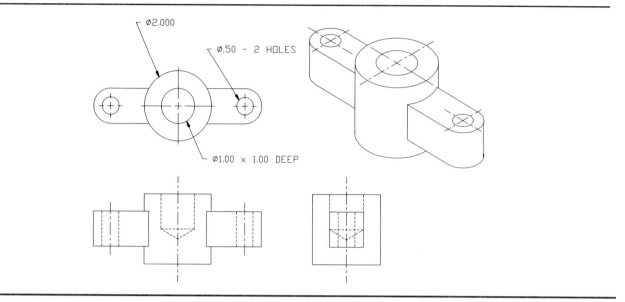

Figure 5-39

5-18 HOLES IN
SLANTED SURFACES

Figure 5-42 shows a hole that penetrates a slanted surface. The hole is perpendicular to the bottom surface of the object. The top view of the hole appears as a circle because we are looking straight down into it. The side view shows a distorted view of the circle and is represented using an ellipse.

The shape of the ellipse in the side view is defined by projecting information from the front and top views.

Points 1 and 2 are known to be on the vertical center line so their location can be projected from the front view to the side view using horizontal lines. Points 3 and 4 are located on the horizontal center line, so their location can be projected from the top view into the side view using the 45-degree miter line.

The elliptical view of the hole in the side view is drawn connecting the projected points using the ELLIPSE command. Sample Problem SP5-7 shows how to draw an ellipse projected onto a slanted surface.

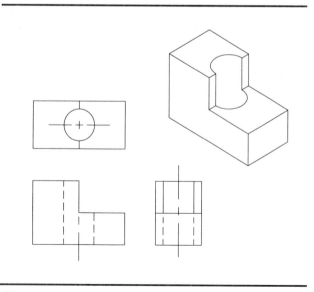

Figure 5-40

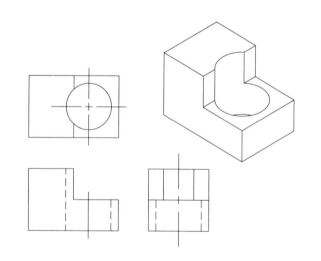

Figure 5-41

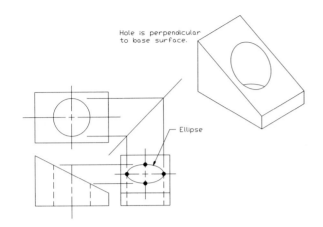

Figure 5-42

To draw an ellipse representing a projected hole

See Figure 5-43.

1. Define the FIRST POINT as one of the points where the major axis intersects one of the center lines.
2. Define the SECOND POINT as the other point on the major axis that intersects the same center line.
3. Define the THIRD POINT as one of the points on the minor axis that intersects the center line perpendicular to the center line used in steps 1 and 2.

To draw three views of a hole in a slanted surface

Figure 5-44 shows an object that includes a hole drilled perpendicular to the slanted surface. The hole is 1.00 in diameter. The hidden lines in the front view that represent the edges of the hole are drawn parallel to the center line at a distance of 0.50. The horizontal and vertical center lines of the hole are located in the top and right views. The intersection of the hole edges with the slanted surface shown in the front view are projected into the top and side views as shown.

The slanted surface shown in Figure 5-44 appears as a straight line in the front view. This means that the hole representations in the top and side views are rotated about only one axis. This in turn means that the hole representation is foreshortened in only one direction. The other direction, the other axis length, remains at the original diameter distance on 1.00. The four points needed to define the projected elliptical shape can be defined by the projection lines and the measured 1.00 distance.

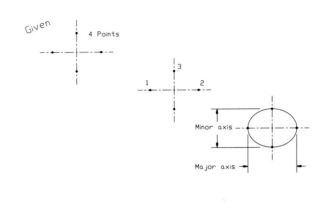

Figure 5-43

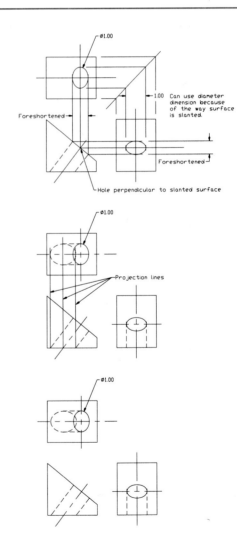

Figure 5-44

The hole also penetrates the bottom surface, forming a different size ellipse. The hole's penetration can be shown in the side view by hidden lines parallel to the given center line. The elliptical shape in the top view is defined by drawing horizontal parallel lines from the intersection of the hole's projected shape with the vertical center line, and by projection lines from the front view that define the hole's length.

To draw three views of a hole through an oblique surface

Figure 5-45 shows a hole drilled horizontally through the exact center of an oblique surface of an object. The oblique surface means that both axes in the top and front views will be foreshortened. The procedure used to created the hole's projection in the front and top views is as follows. See Figure 5-45a.

1. DRAW the hole in the side view. The hole will appear as a circle because it is drilled horizontally.
2. DRAW the hole's center lines in the front and top views. The hole is located exactly in the center of the oblique surface so lines parallel to the surface's edge lines located midway across the surface may be drawn.
3. Project the intersection of the hole and the horizontal center line into the top view, and project the intersection of the hole with the vertical center line into the front view.
4. Project the intersections created in step 3 with the horizontal center line, represented by the slanted center line, onto the horizontal center line in the front view. Likewise project the intersection points created in step 3 on the horizontal center line in the front to the slanted center line in the top view.
5. DRAW the ellipses as required, add the appropriate hidden lines, and ERASE and TRIM any excess lines. SAVE the drawing if desired.

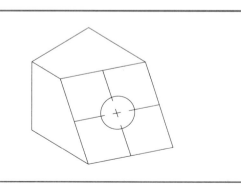

Figure 5-45

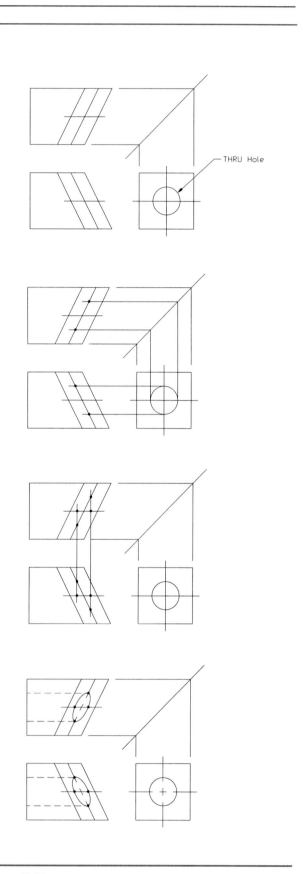

THRU Hole

Figure 5-45a

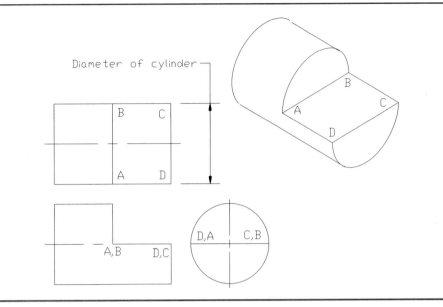

Figure 5-46

5-19 CYLINDER

Figure 5-46 shows three views of a cylinder that is cut along the center line by surface A-B-C-D. Note that each of the three views includes center lines. The front and top views of a cylinder are called the rectangular views and the side view (end view) is called the circular view. The width of the top view is equal to the diameter of the cylinder.

Figure 5-47 shows a cylinder that has a second surface E-F-G-H located above the center line in the front view. The top view of the cylinder shows the flat surface and the rounded portion of the cylinder. Both the flat surface and the two rounded surfaces appear as rectangles.

Figure 5-48 shows a cylinder with a surface J-K-L-M that is located below the center line in the front view. The top view of this surface does not include any rounded surfaces because they have been cut away.

5-20 SAMPLE PROBLEM SP5-5

Figure 5-49 shows a cylindrically shaped object that has three surface cuts: one above the center line, one below the center line, and one directly on the center line. Figure 5-50 shows how the three views of the object were developed. The procedure is as follows.

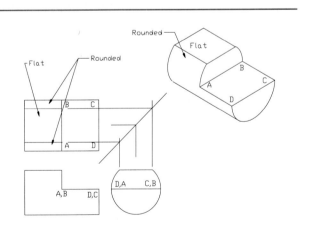

Figure 5-47

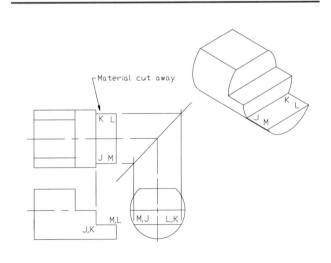

Figure 5-48

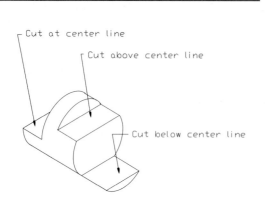

Cut at center line

Cut above center line

Cut below center line

Figure 5-49

1. Use the given overall length of the cylinder and its diameter to create the two rectangular top and front views and the circular end views.
2. DRAW horizontal lines in the side view that define the end views of the three surfaces. Project the size and location of the surfaces into the front and top views. Use OSNAP, INTersection, with ORTHO on for accurate projection.
3. ERASE and TRIM the excess lines.
4. SAVE the drawing if desired.

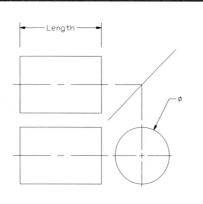

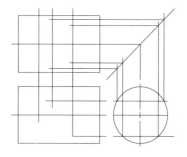

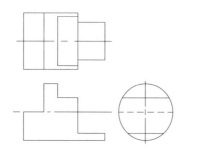

Figure 5-50

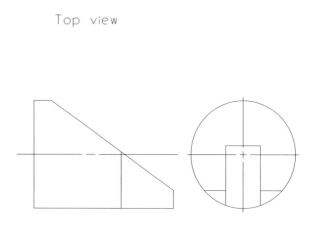

Top view

Figure 5-51

5-21 CYLINDERS WITH SLANTED AND ROUNDED SURFACES

Figure 5-51 shows a front and top view of a cylindrical object that includes a slanted surface. Slanted surfaces are projected by defining points along their edges in known orthographic views and then projecting the edge points. At least two known views are needed for accurate projection. Sample Problem SP5-6 shows how to define and project a slanted cylindrical surface into the top view given the front and side views.

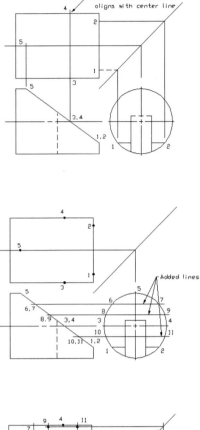

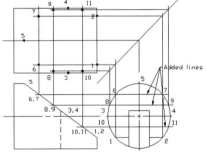

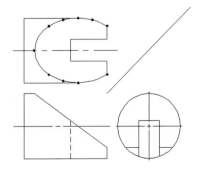

5-22 SAMPLE PROBLEM SP5-6

See Figure 5-52.

1. DRAW the rectangular shape of the top view by projecting the length from the front view and the width from the side view. Project the center lines.
2. Label points 1, 2, and 3 in the front and side views. The locations of these points are known from the given information.
3. Draw three horizontal lines across the front and side views. The location of the lines is arbitrary. Label the intersections of the horizontal lines with the edge of the slanted surface as shown.
4. The three horizontal lines serve to define point locations along the surface's edge.

A line contains an infinite number of points, so any six can be used.

5. Draw vertical projection lines (OSNAP, INTersection) from the six point locations in the front view into the area of the top view.
6. Project the six point locations from the side view into the area of the top view. Use the 45-degree miter line to make the turn between the two views. The intersection of the vertical projection lines of step 2 and the projection lines from the side view defines the location of the points in the top view. Label the six points.
7. Use DRAW, PLINE, PEDIT, FIT CURVE to create a smooth line between the six projected points.
8. Remove any excess lines and SAVE the drawing if desired.

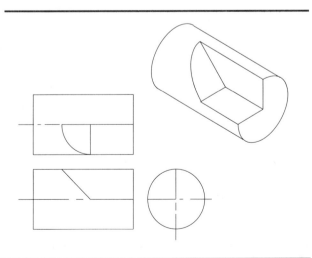

Figure 5-52

Figure 5-53

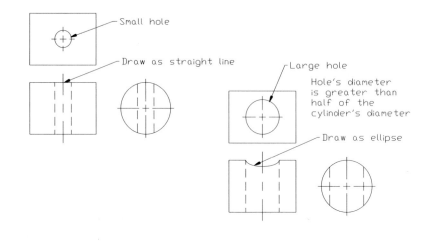

Figure 5-54

Figure 5-53 shows another cylindrical object that contains a slanted surface along with some of the projection lines. Both the objects shown in Figures 5-51 and 5-53 are included on the drawing disk. Call up the objects and use the procedure outlined in Section 5-3 to verify the orthographic views.

5-23 DRAWING CONVENTIONS AND CYLINDERS

A hole drilled into a cylinder will produce an ellipti-

cally shaped edge line in a profile view of the hole. See Figure 5-54. Drawing convention allows a straight line to be drawn in place of the elliptical shape for small holes. The elliptical shape should be drawn for large holes in cylinders. A large hole is one whose diameter is greater than half the diameter of the cylinder.

Drawing convention also permits straight lines to be drawn for the profile view of a keyway cut into a cylinder. See Figure 5-55. As with holes, if a keyway is large relative to a cylinder, the correct offset shape should be drawn. A keyway is considered large if its width is greater than half the diameter of the cylinder.

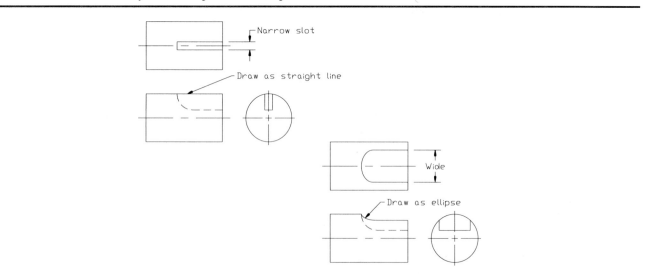

Figure 5-55

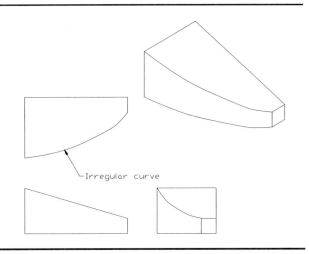

Figure 5-56

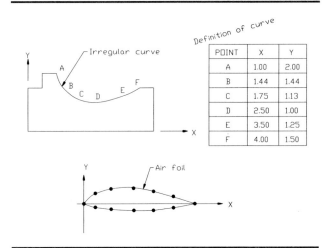

POINT	X	Y
A	1.00	2.00
B	1.44	1.44
C	1.75	1.13
D	2.50	1.00
E	3.50	1.25
F	4.00	1.50

Figure 5-57

5-24 IRREGULAR SURFACES

Irregular surfaces are curved surfaces that do not have constant radii. See Figures 5-56 and 5-57. Irregular surfaces are defined using the XY coordinates of points located on the edge of the surface. The points may be dimensioned directly on the view but are often presented in chart form as shown in Figure 5-57. Figure 5-57 also shows a wing surface defined relative to a given XY coordinate system.

Irregular surfaces are projected by defining points along their edges and then projecting the points. At least two known views are needed for accurate projection. The more points used to define the curve, the more accurate the final curve shape will be.

5-25 SAMPLE PROBLEM SP5-7

Figure 5-58 shows an object that includes an irregular surface. The irregular surface is defined by points referenced to an XY coordinate system. The point values are listed in a chart. Draw three views of the object shown in Figure 5-58. See Figure 5-59.

1. DRAW the front and top views using the given dimensions and chart values. DRAW the outline of the side view using the given dimensions.
2. Project the points that define the irregular curve in the top view into the front view. Label the points.
3. Project the points for the curve from both the top and front views into the side view. Label the intersection points.

4. Use PLINE, PEDIT, and FIT CURVE to create a curve that represents the side view of the irregular surface.
5. ERASE and TRIM any excess lines. SAVE the drawing if desired.

Remember it is possible to use LAYER to create a layer for construction lines and for the final drawing. After the initial drawing is layed out, the final drawing lines may be copied onto another layer and the constrution layer turned OFF. This method eliminates the need for extensive erasing and trimming.

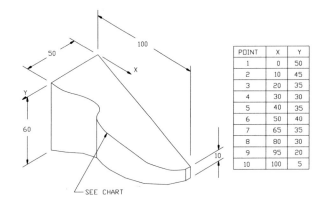

POINT	X	Y
1	0	50
2	10	45
3	20	35
4	30	30
5	40	35
6	50	40
7	65	35
8	80	30
9	95	20
10	100	5

Figure 5-58

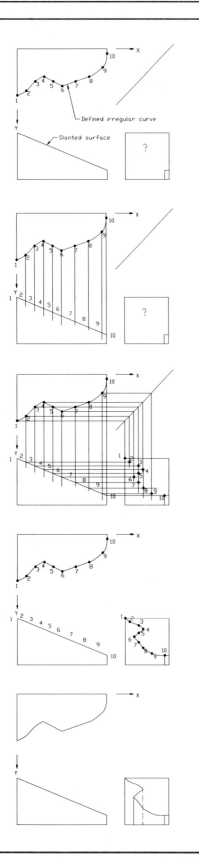

Figure 5-59

5-26 HOLE CALLOUTS

There are four hole-shaped manufacturing processes that are used so often that they are defined using a standardized drawing callout: ream, counterbore, countersink, and spotface. See Figure 5-60.

A ream is a process that smooths out the inside of a drilled hole. Holes created using twist drills have spiral shaped machine marks on their surfaces. Reaming is used to remove the spiral machine marks and to increase the roundness of the hole. Ream callouts generally include a much tighter tolerance than do drill diameter callouts.

A counterbore is two holes drilled along the same center line. Counterbores are used to allow fasteners or other objects to be recessed, thus keeping the top surface uniform in height.

A counterbore drawing callout specifies the diameter of the small hole, the diameter of the large hole, and the depth of the large hole. The information is given in this sequence because it is also the sequence of the manufacturer. Note that the hidden lines used in the front view of the counterbored hole clearly show the intersection between the two holes.

Figure 5-60 also shows a new type of drawing callout defined by ISO standards (see Chapter 8) that is intended to remove language from drawings. As parts are often designed in one country and manufactured in another, it is important that drawing callouts be universally understandable.

A countersink is a conical-shaped hole used primarily for flat head fasteners. The drawing callout specifies the diameter of the hole, the included angle of the countersink, and the diameter of the countersink as measured on the surface of the object. Almost all countersinks are 82 degrees, but some are drawn at 45 degrees.

To draw a countersunk hole

See Figure 5-61.

1. DRAW a 0.50 diameter hole (CIRCLE,CEN,DIA) in the top view. Project the hole's diameter into the front view.
2. DRAW a 1.00 diameter hole in the top view and project its diameter into the front view. In the front view DRAW 45-degree LINEs from the intersection on the 1.00 diameter hole and the top surface of the front view so that the lines intersect the 0.50 diameter hole's projection lines. Use OSNAP, INTersection to ensure accuracy.
3. DRAW a horizontal line through the intersections created in step 2. Again use OSNAP, INTersection.

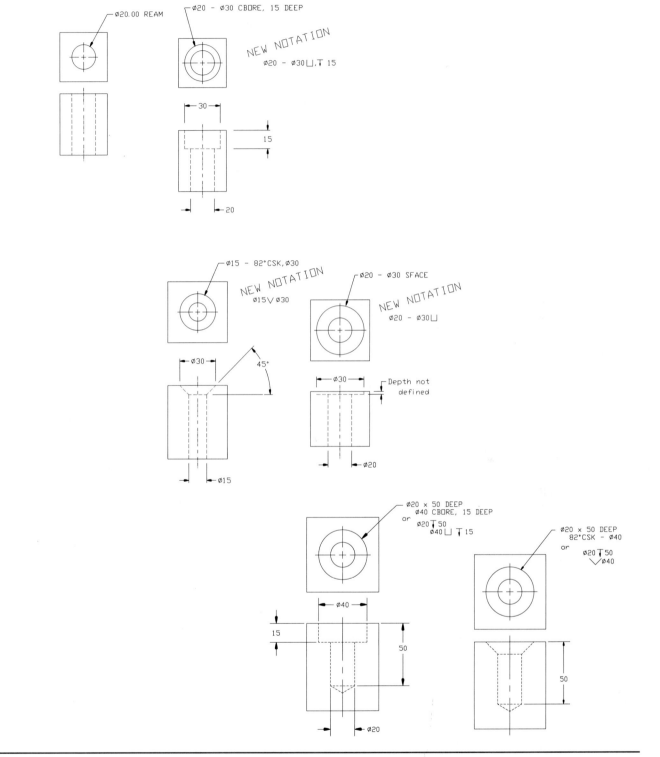

Figure 5-60

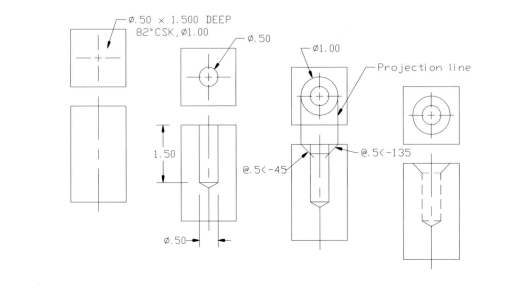

Figure 5-61

4. ERASE and TRIM the excess lines.

A spotface is a very shallow counterbored hole generally used on cast surfaces. Cast surfaces are more porous than machine surfaces. Rather than machine an entire surface flat, a spotface is cheaper to manufacture because it machines only a small portion of the surface. Spotfaces are usually used for bearing surfaces of fasteners.

A spotface callout defines the diameter of the hole and the diameter of the spotface. A depth need not be given. When machining was done more by hand, the machinist would make the spotface just deep enough to produce a shiny surface (most cast surfaces are more gray in color) so no depth was needed. Automated machines require a spotface depth specification. Usually the depth is very shallow.

5-27 CASTINGS

Casting is one of the oldest manufacturing processes. Metal is heated to liquid form, then poured into molds and allowed to cool. The resulting shapes usually include many rounded edges and surface tangencies because it is very difficult to cast square edges. Concave edges are called rounds and convex edges are called fillets. See Figure 5-62. A runout is used to indicate that two rounded surfaces have become tangent to one another. A runout is a short arc of arbitrary radius, arbitrary as long as the runout is visually clear.

Cast objects are often partially machined to produce flatter surfaces than can be produced by the casting process. Machined surfaces are defined using machine marks (check marks) as shown in Figure 5-62. The numbers within the machine marks specify the flatness requirements in terms of microinches or micrometers. Machine marks are explained in greater detail in Section 9-28.

A boss is a turretlike shape that is often included on castings to localize and minimize machining. A boss is defined by its diameter and its height. The sides of a boss are rounded and defined by a radius usually equal to the height of the boss. See Figure 5-63.

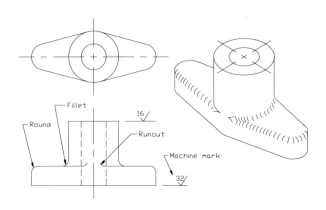

Figure 5-62

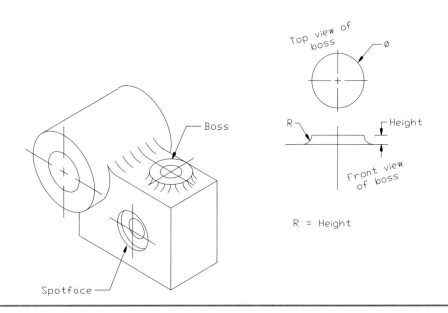

Figure 5-63

Spotfacing is a machine process often associated with castings. As with bosses, spotfaces help localize and minimize machining requirements. Spotfaces were defined in Section 5-30.

The direction of runouts is determined by the shape of the two surfaces involved. Flat surfaces intersecting rounded surfaces generate runouts that turn out. Rounded surfaces that intersect rounded surfaces generate runouts that turn in. See Figure 5-64.

The same convention is followed for flat and rounded surfaces that intersect flat surfaces.

The location of a runout is determined by the location of the tangent it represents. See Figure 5-65. The loca-

tion of a tangency point can be determined by first drawing the top view of the tangency line using OSNAP, TANgency. A line can then be drawn from the center point of the circular top view to the end of the tangency line using OSNAP, ENDpoint. The point of tangency can then be projected from the top view to the front view using OSNAP, INTersection with ORTHO on.

Use ARC to draw runouts. Any convenient radius may be used, providing the runout is clearly visible and visually distinct from the straight line.

Figure 5-66 shows some additional examples of cast surfaces that include runouts.

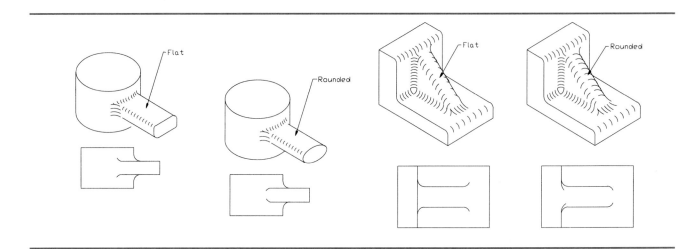

Figure 5-64

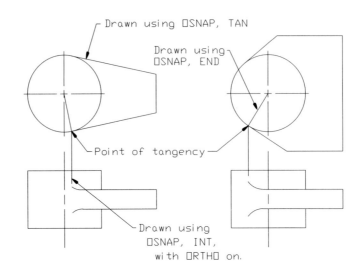

Figure 5-65

5-28 SAMPLE PROBLEM SP5-8

Draw three views of the object shown in Figure 5-67. The solution was drawn as follows. See Figure 5-68.

1. Use the given overall dimensions and draw the outline of the front, top, and side views.
2. CHANGE the appropriate lines to hidden lines. Draw the fillets and rounds. The FILLET command may erase needed lines. This cannot

always be avoided, so simply redraw the needed lines after the fillet or round is complete.
3. Draw the spotface and boss in each of the views. The hole in the boss is .500 deep. Clearly show the bottom of the hole, including the conical point. Draw the hole in the front view and use MODIFY, COPY to copy the hole into the side view.
4. Use DRAW, CIRCLE to draw the 1.00 diameter hole in the front view. DRAW the appropiate hidden and center LINES in the other views.
5. SAVE the drawing if desired.

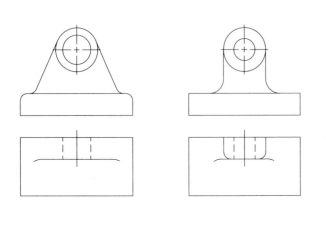

Figure 5-66

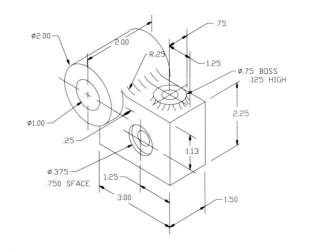

Figure 5-67

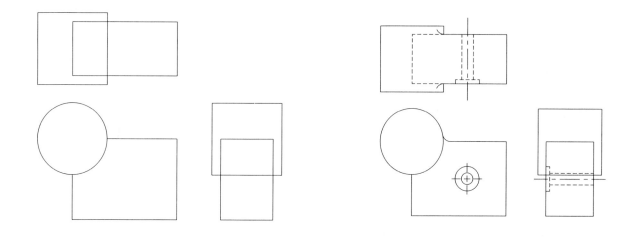

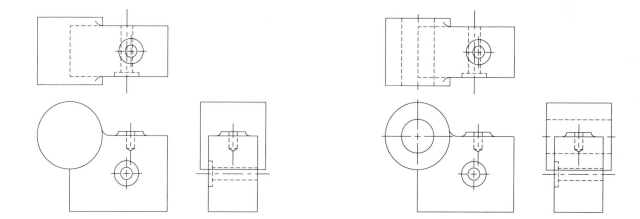

Figure 5-68

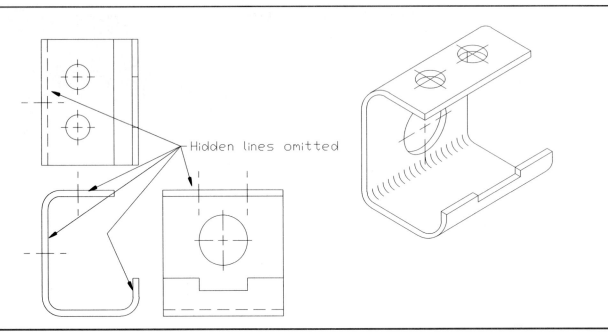

Figure 5-69

5-29 THIN-WALLED OBJECTS

Thin-walled objects such as parts made from sheet metal or tubing present some unique drawing problems. For example, the distance between surfaces is usually so small that hidden lines can be used to define holes. There isn't enough distance to draw a broken line pattern. See Figure 5-69.

Hidden lines may be applied to thin-walled objects in one of three ways: draw the lines as continuous lines but use a different color than the actual continuous lines, use an enlarged detail of the area including the hidden lines, or omit the hidden lines and include only a center line. Each

of these techniques is shown in Figure 5-69. All holes must include a center line.

Companies often have a drawing manual that states their policy on drawing hidden lines in thin-walled objects. The most important goal is to be consistent in the representation.

Many sheet metal parts are manufactured by bending. Bending produces an inside bend radius and an outside bend radius. The inside bend radius plus the material thickness should equal the outside bend radius. See Figure 5-70. The same radius should not be used for both the inside and outside bend.

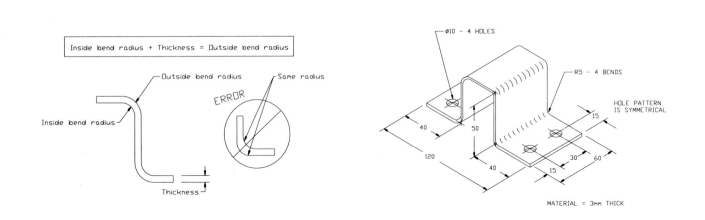

Figure 5-70

Figure 5-71

5-30 SAMPLE PROBLEM SP5-9

Draw three views of the object shown in Figure 5-71. Figure 5-72 shows how the three views were developed.

1. Use the given overall dimensions to DRAW the outline of the three views. Draw the object as if all bends were 90 degrees.
2. Use OFFSET set to a distance of 3mm to draw the thickness of the object. Use EXTEND and TRIM to add or remove lines as needed. The thickness could also be drawn by setting the SNAP spacing equal to the material thickness.

Change the appropriate lines to hidden lines.

3. Draw FILLETS using a radius of 5mm for the inside bend radii and 8mm for the outside bend radii.
4. Use DRAW, CIRCLE to draw the holes in the appropriate view and add center lines as shown.
5. SAVE the drawing if desired.

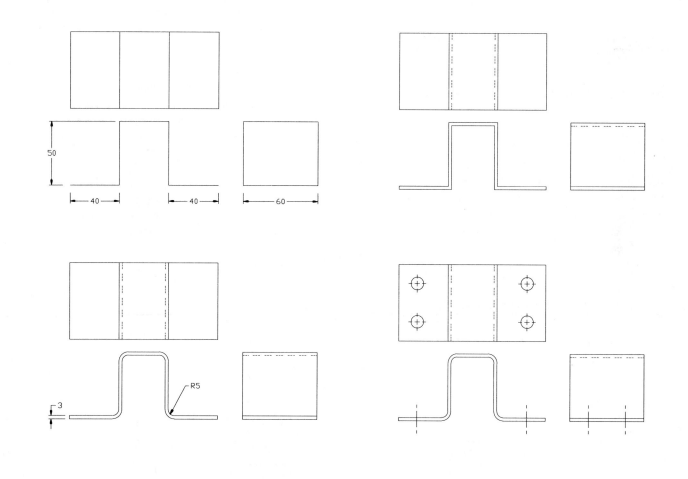

Figure 5-72

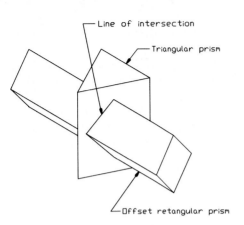

Figure 5-73

5-31 INTERSECTIONS

Intersection drawings are drawings that show the intersection of two objects. Figure 5-73 shows the intersection between two offset squares. A discussion of intersections has been included at this point in the book because they rely heavily on projection of information between views. They require not only a knowledge of the principles of projection but also an understanding about what the various lines represent. Intersections will be discussed again in Chapter 16, Solid Modeling.

Three intersection problems are presented in the following three sample problems.

5-32 SAMPLE PROBLEM SP5-10

Given the side and top views of a smaller circle intersecting a larger circle as shown in Figure 5-74, draw the front view. All dimensions are in inches. Because the object is symmetrical, the intersection for one side will be developed and then MIRRORED.

1. DRAW the outline of the front view by projecting lines from the given top and front views. See Figure 5-75.
2. Define points on the edge of the smaller circle. In this example, 17 points were defined.
3. EXTEND the horizontal center line of the smaller circle in the side view into the area of the front view. Use DRAW, OFFSET and add six lines parallel to the horizontal center line in the side view. Label the intersection of the horizontal lines with the edge of the smaller circle as shown.
4. Project points 5, 6, 7, 8, 9, and 10 into the top view. Use DRAW, LINE along with OSNAP, INTersection to draw vertical lines from the side view so that they intersect the 45-degree miter line. Then project the intersections on the miter line into the top view using horizontal lines. Label the points as shown.
5. Project points 5, 6, 7, 8, 9, and 10 from the top view into the area of the front view so they intersect the horizontal lines from the side view. Label the points as shown. Use DRAW, PLINE, EDIT, PEDIT, and FIT CURV to draw the curve that represents the intersection.
6. Add the lines needed to complete the front view, remove all excess lines, and save the drawing if desired.

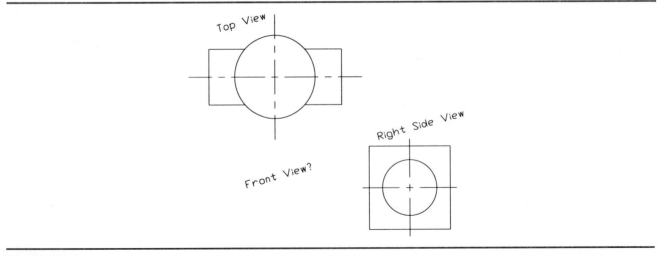

Figure 5-74

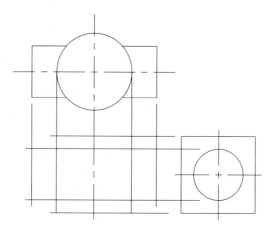

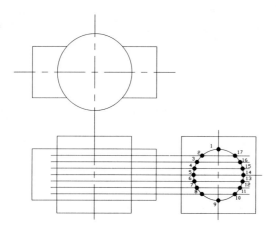

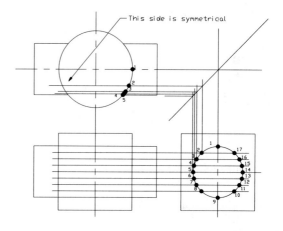

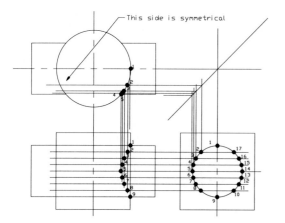

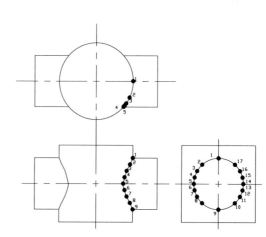

Figure 5-75

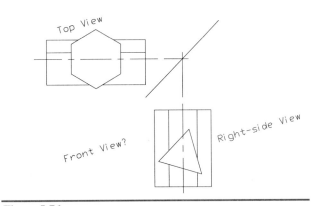

Figure 5-76

5-33 SAMPLE PROBLEM SP5-11

Figure 5-76 shows the top and front view of a triangular-shaped piece intersecting a hexagon-shaped piece. What is the shape of the front view?

Figure 5-77 shows the solution obtained by projecting lines from the two given views into the front view. Figure 5-77 also shows an enlargement of the intersecting surfaces. Use a straight edge and verify the location of each labeled point by projecting horizontal lines from the front view and vertical lines from the top view into the front view.

5-34 SAMPLE PROBLEM SP5-12

Given the side and top views of a circle intersecting a cone as shown in Figure 5-78, draw the front view.

As in the previous sample problems, the problem is solved by defining intersection points in the given two views and then projecting them into the front view. The cone, however, presents a unique problem because it is both round and tapered. There are few edge lines to work with.

The solution requires that there be a more precise definition of the cone's surface than is presented by the circle and center lines in the top view and the profile front view.

1. Figure 5-79, step 1, shows how points 1 and 3 are projected from the side view to the front view and then to the top view. Points 1 and 3 are located on the vertical center line of the cylinder. The vertical center line is aligned with the right-side profile line of the cone so that it can be used for projection.

This is not true for points 2 and 4, located on the horizontal center line in the side view. Currently the location of points 2 and 4 is unknown in both the front and top views, so projection lines cannot be drawn. The location of points 2 and 4 can be determined in the front and top views.

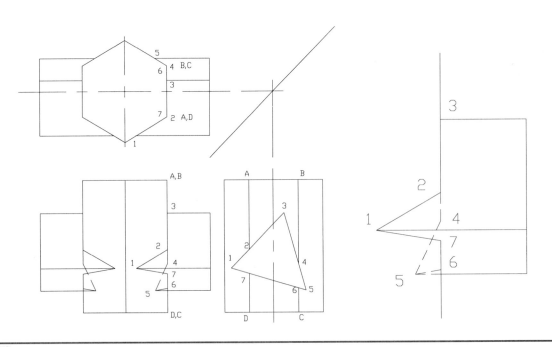

Figure 5-77

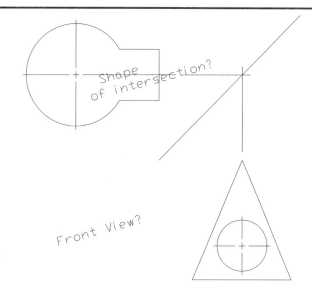

Figure 5-78

2. EXTEND the horizontal center line in the side view so that it intersects the edge lines of the cone. Use OSNAP, INTersection, with ORTHO on and project the intersection of the extended horizontal center line and the cone's edge line so that it intersects the vertical center line in the top view. Draw a circle in the top view using the distance between the intersection with the vertical center line and the projection line and the center point of the cone as the radius.

The circle in the top view represents a slice of the cone located at exactly the same height as points 2 and 4. Points 2 and 4 must be located somewhere in the slice.

3. Project points 2 and 4 into the top view from the side view so that the projection line intersects the circular slice drawn in step 2. Label the intersections 2 and 4.
4. Project the locations of points 2 and 4 in the top view into the front view using a vertical line. Project the points' location from the side view into the front view using a horizontal line. The intersection of the vertical and horizontal projection lines defines the location of points 2 and 4 in the front view.

5. The procedure explained in steps 2 and 3 is expanded by drawing a series of horizontal projection lines between the front and side views as shown. DRAW was used for the first line and OFFSET for the other lines. The location of these additional lines is random.

OSNAP, INTersection with ORTHO on was used to project the intersections of the horizontal lines with the cone's edge lines in the top view.

6. Circles are drawn using the distance between the cone's center point and the projection lines' intersection with the vertical center line as radii. OSNAP, INTersection was used to locate the circles' center point and radii distances.
7. DRAW, PLINE, PEDIT, and FIT CURV are used to draw the required curves in the top and front views. Use OSNAP, INTersection to ensure accurate curve point locations. The command FIT VERT located on the PEDIT submenu can be used to MOVE vertex points on the curves to make them appear smoother and more continuous.
8. TRIM and ERASE all excess lines and SAVE the drawing if desired.

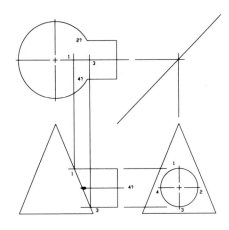

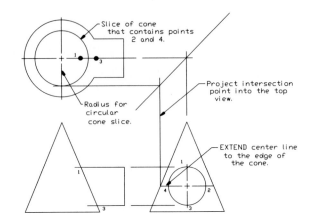

Slice of cone
that contains points
2 and 4.

Project intersection
point into the top
view.

Radius for
circular
cone slice.

EXTEND center line
to the edge of
the cone.

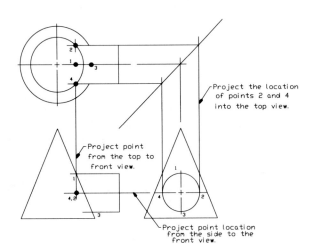

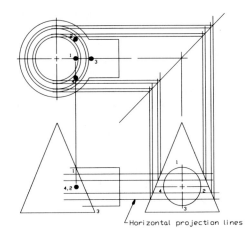

Project the location
of points 2 and 4
into the top view.

Project point
from the top to
front view.

Project point location
from the side to the
front view.

Horizontal projection lines

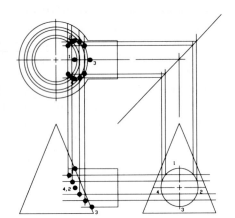

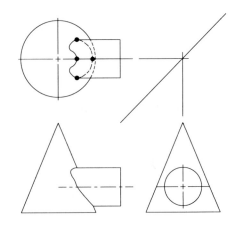

Figure 5-79

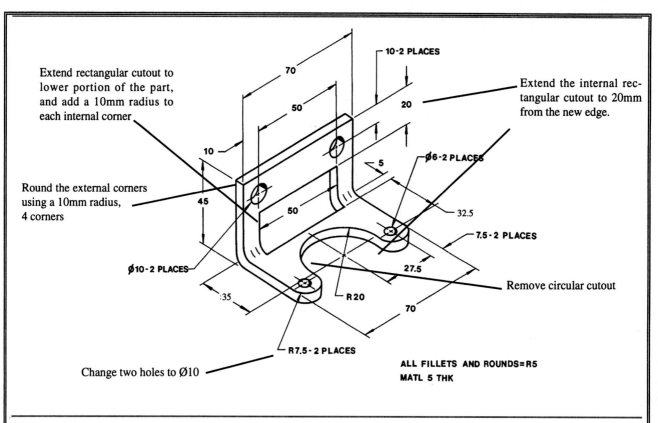

Figure 5-80

5-35 DESIGNING BY MODIFYING AN EXISTING PART

Many beginning design assignments require that an existing part be modified to meet a new set of requirements. Figure 5-80 shows a dimensioned part and Figure

5-81 shows the three orthographic views of the part. The part is to be redesigned as follows.

1. Replace the two Ø7.5 holes with Ø10 holes.
2. Remove the R20 cutout.
3. Modify the horizontal portion of the part so it is

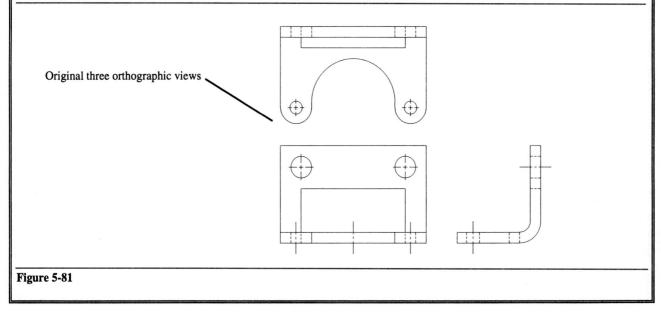

Figure 5-81

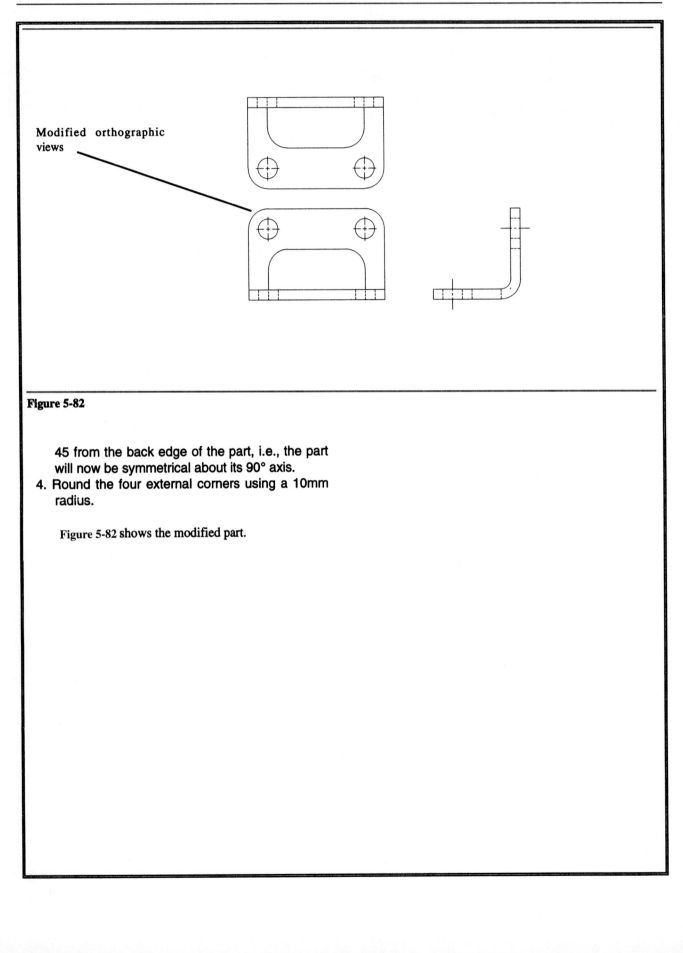

Modified orthographic views

Figure 5-82

45 from the back edge of the part, i.e., the part will now be symmetrical about its 90° axis.
4. Round the four external corners using a 10mm radius.

Figure 5-82 shows the modified part.

5-36 EXERCISE PROBLEMS

Draw a front, top, and right-side orthographic view of each of the objects in exercises problems EX5-1 to EX 5-94. Do not include dimensions.

EX5-1 INCHES

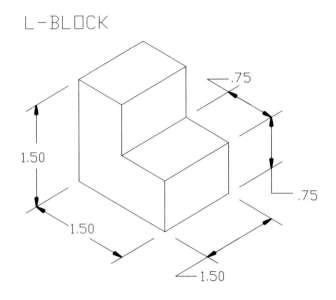

EX5-3 MILLIMETERS

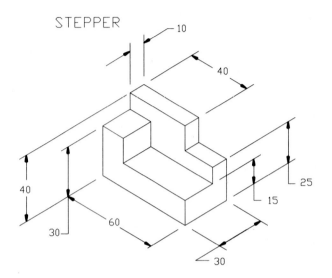

EX5-2 MILLIMETERS

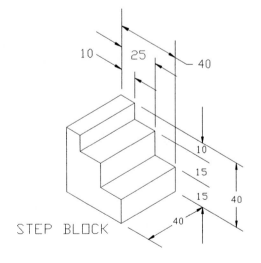

EX5-4 MILLIMETERS

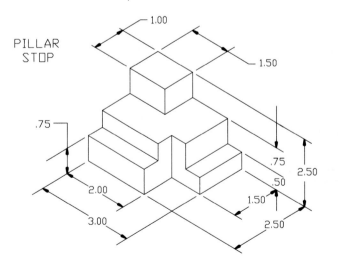

EX5-5 MILLIMETERS

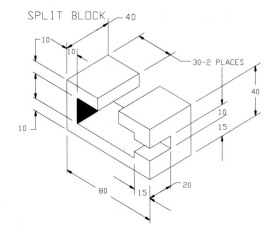

EX5-7 MILLIMETERS

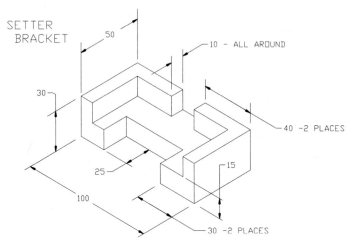

EX5-6 MILLIMETERS

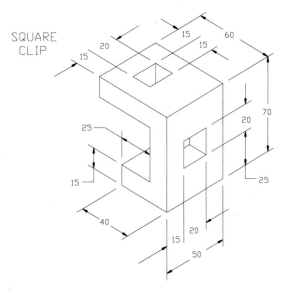

EX5-8 MILLIMETERS

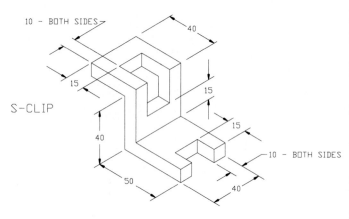

EX5-9 INCHES

EX5-11 MILLIMETERS

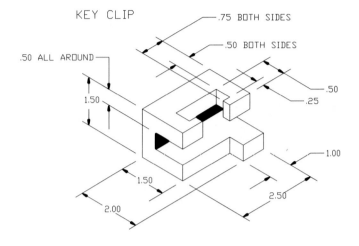

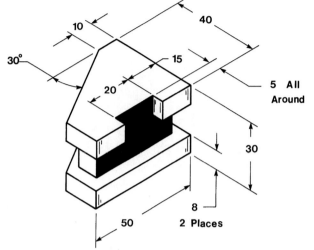

EX5-10 MILLIMETERS

EX5-12 INCHES

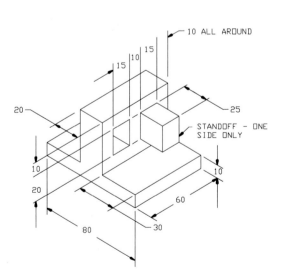

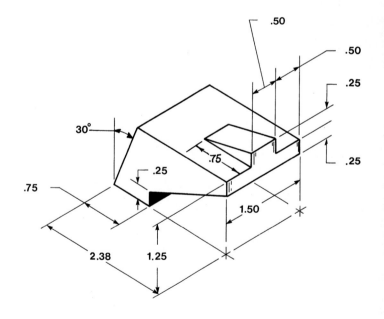

EX5-13 MILLIMETERS

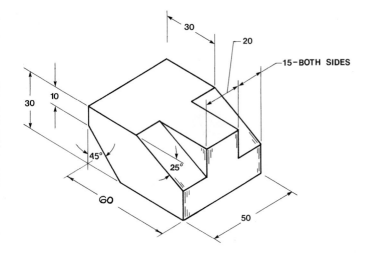

EX5-15 INCHES

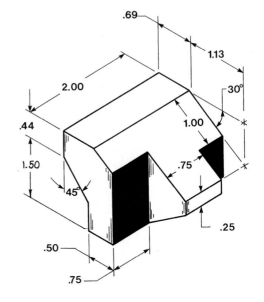

EX5-14 MILLIMETERS

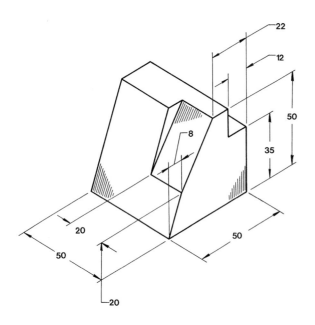

EX5-16 INCHES

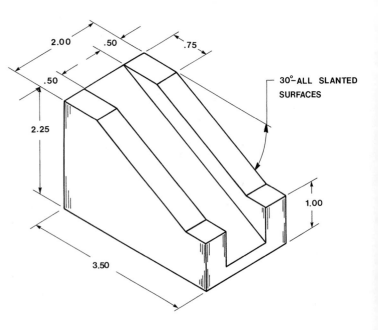

EX5-17 MILLIMETERS

EX5-19

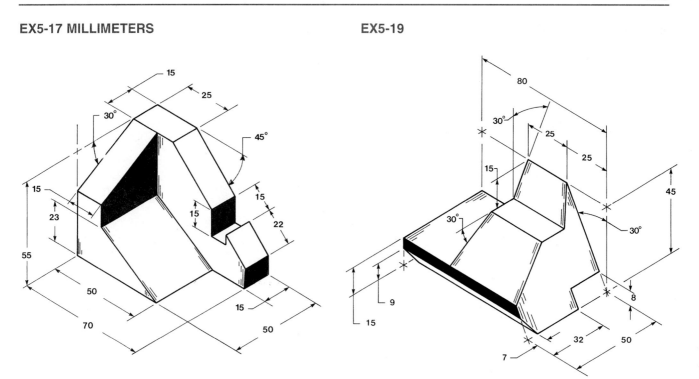

EX5-18 MILLIMETERS

EX5-20 INCHES

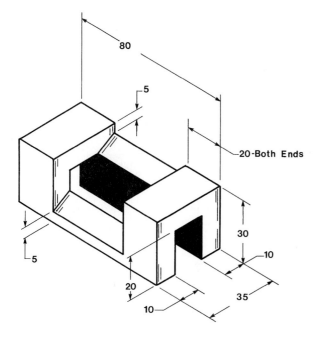

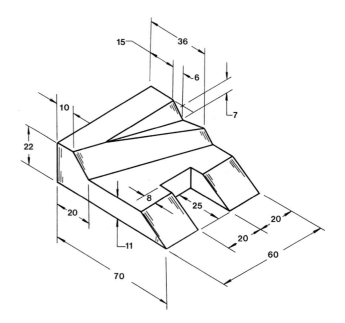

EX5-21 MILLIMETERS

EX5-23

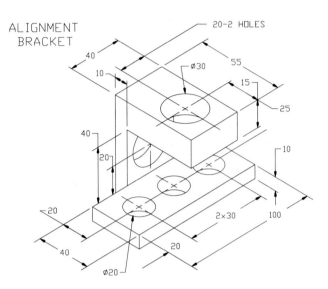

ALIGNMENT
BRACKET

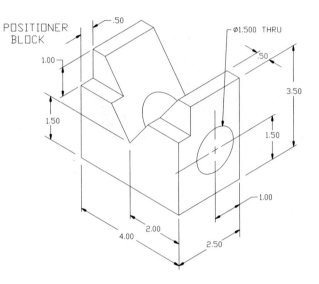

POSITIONER
BLOCK

EX5-22

EX5-24

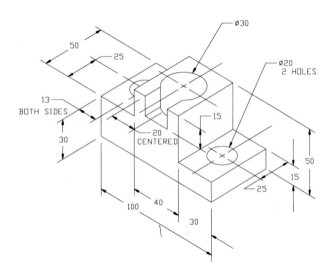

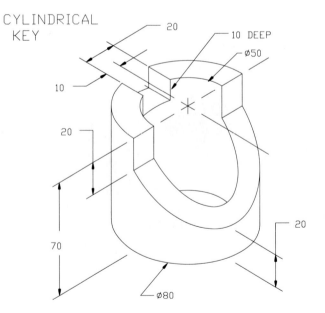

CYLINDRICAL
KEY

EX5-25 MILLIMETERS

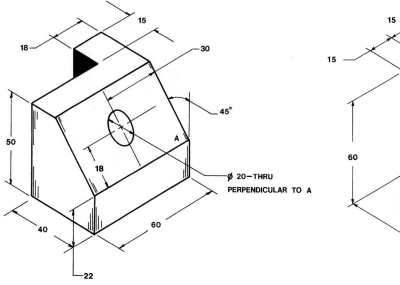

EX5-27 MILLIMETERS

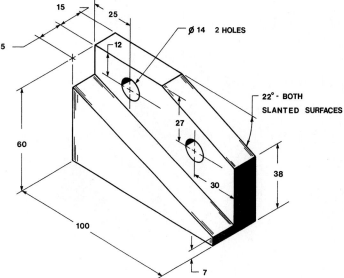

EX5-26 MILLIMETERS

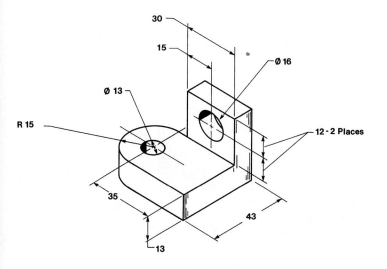

EX5-28 MILLIMETERS

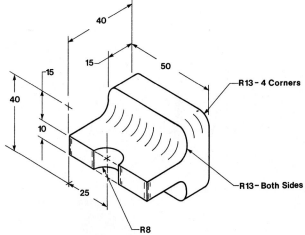

EX5-29 MILLIMETERS

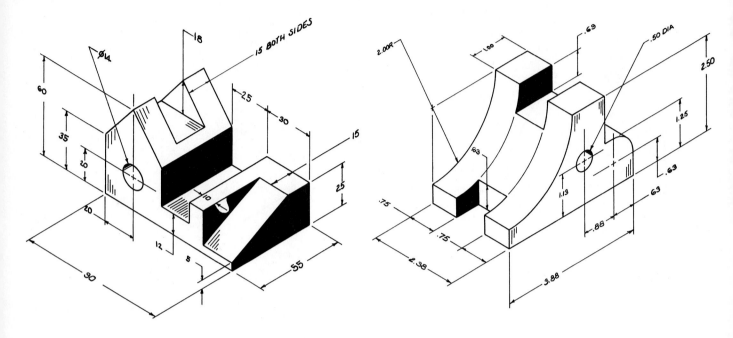

EX5-31 INCHES

EX5-30 MILLIMETERS

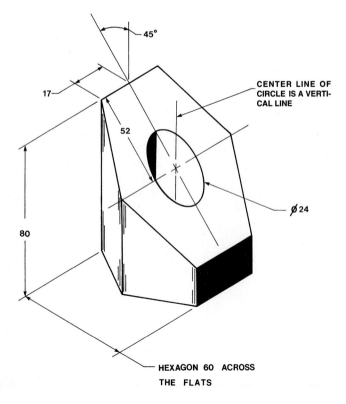

CENTER LINE OF CIRCLE IS A VERTICAL LINE

Ø 24

HEXAGON 60 ACROSS THE FLATS

EX5-32 MILLIMETERS

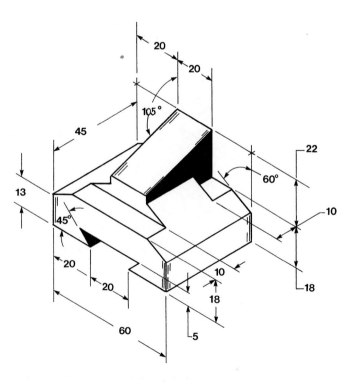

EX5-33 INCHES

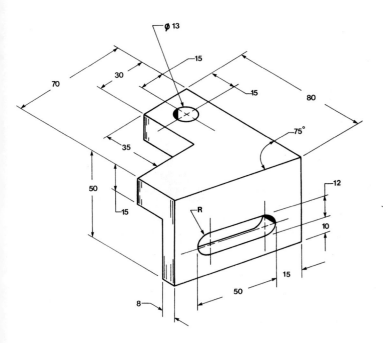

EX5-35

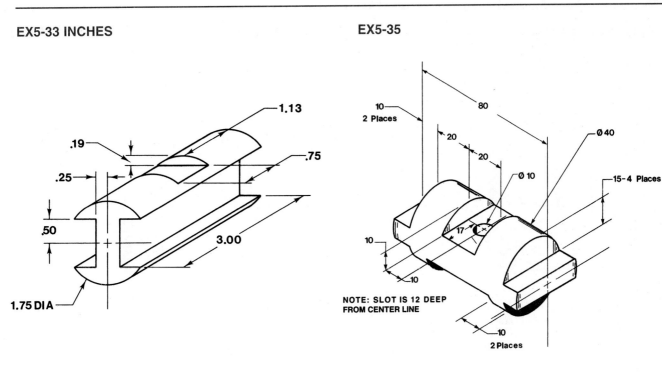

EX5-34 MILLIMETERS

EX5-36 INCHES

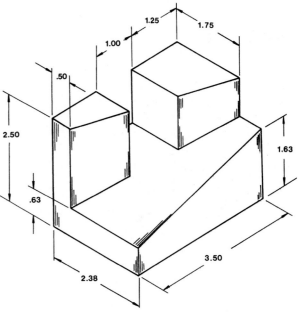

EX5-37 MILLIMETERS

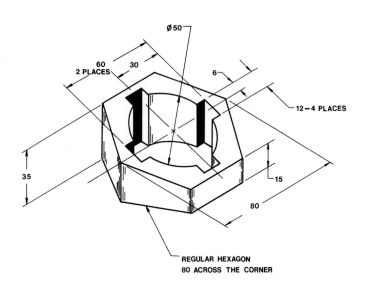

Ø50

60
2 PLACES

30

6

12 — 4 PLACES

35

15

80

REGULAR HEXAGON
80 ACROSS THE CORNER

EX5-39 MILLIMETERS

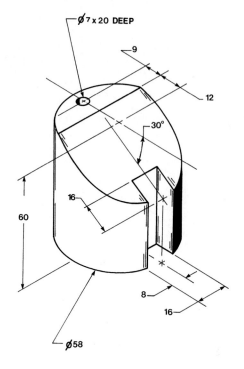

Ø 7 x 20 DEEP

9

12

30°

16

60

8

16

Ø58

EX5-38 INCHES

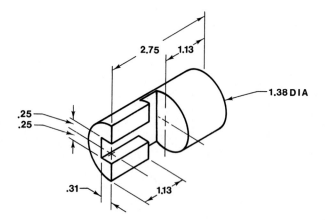

2.75   1.13

1.38 DIA

.25
.25

.31   1.13

EX5-40 INCHES

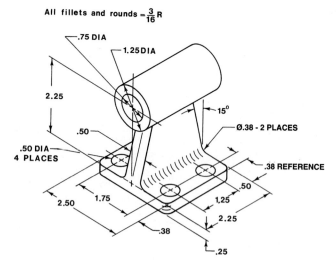

All fillets and rounds $= \frac{3}{16}$ R

.75 DIA

1.25 DIA

2.25

15°

Ø.38 - 2 PLACES

.50

.50 DIA
4 PLACES

.38 REFERENCE

.50

2.50   1.75   1.25

2.25

.38

.25

EX5-41 MILLIMETERS

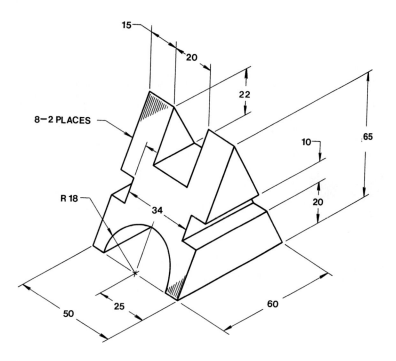

EX5-42 MILLIMETERS

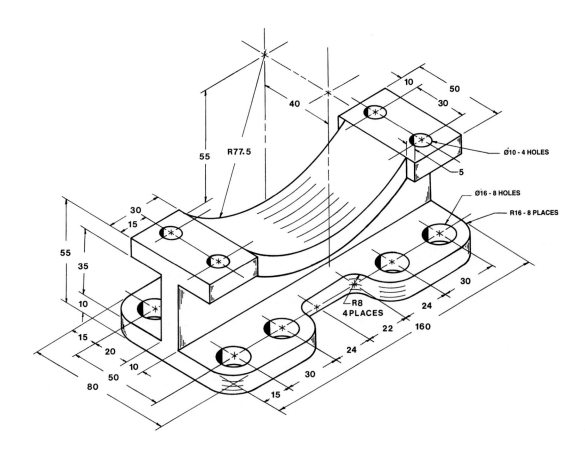

EX5-43 INCHES

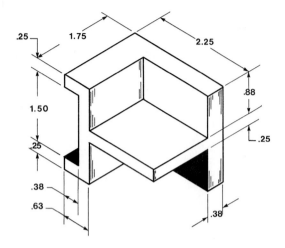

EX5-44 INCHES

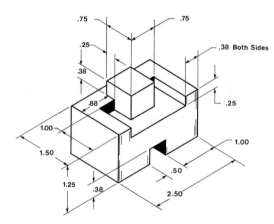

EX5-45 MILLIMETERS

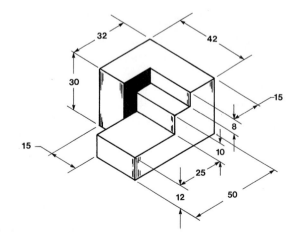

EX5-46 MILLIMETERS

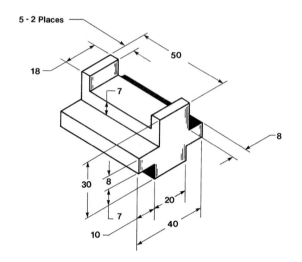

EX5-47 MILLIMETERS

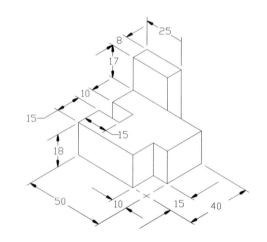

EX5-48 MILLIMETERS

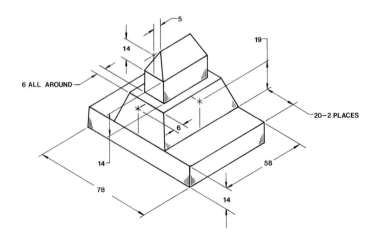

EX5-49 INCHES

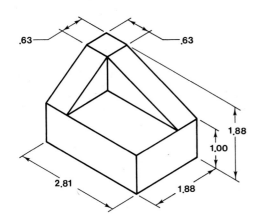

EX5-50 INCHES

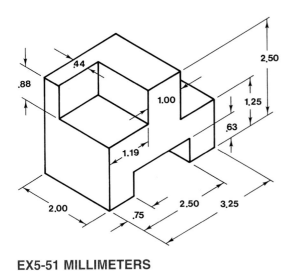

EX5-51 MILLIMETERS

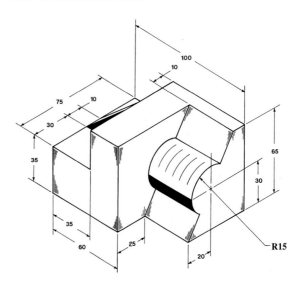

EX5-52 INCHES

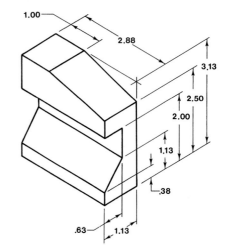

EX5-53 INCHES

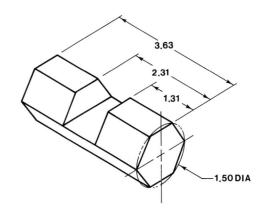

EX5-54 MILLIMETERS

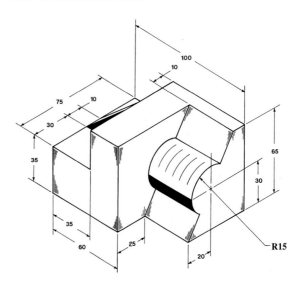

EX5-55 INCHES

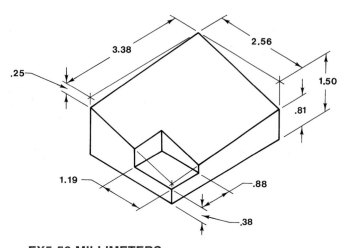

EX5-58 MILLIMETERS

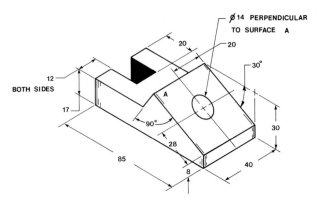

EX5-56 MILLIMETERS

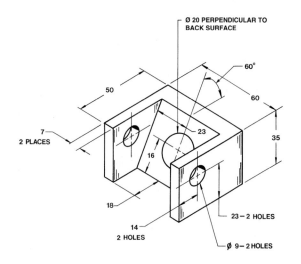

EX5-59 MILLIMETERS

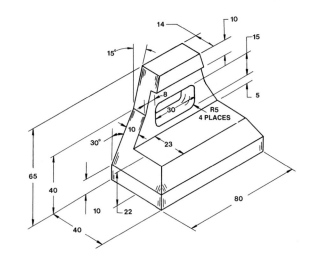

EX5-57 MILLIMETERS

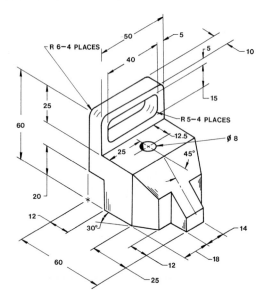

EX5-60 MILLIMETERS

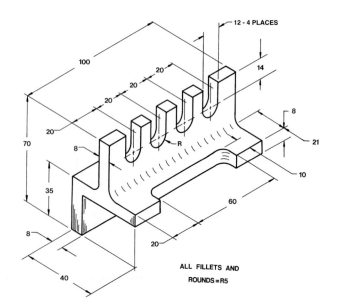

EX5-61 MILLIMETERS

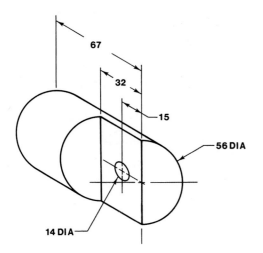

67
32
15
56 DIA
14 DIA

EX5-64 MILLIMETERS

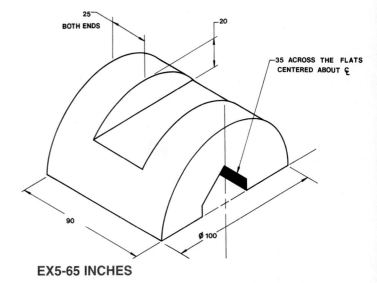

25
BOTH ENDS
20
35 ACROSS THE FLATS
CENTERED ABOUT ℄
90
Ø 100

EX5-62 MILLIMETERS

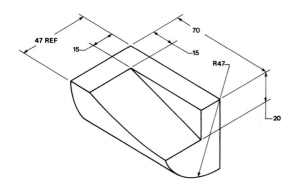

47 REF
15
70
15
R47
20

EX5-65 INCHES

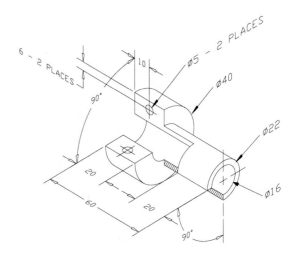

30°
2.81
Ø .50
Ø 1.56

EX5-63 MILLIMETERS

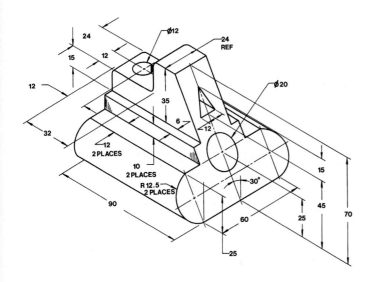

24
15
12
Ø12
24
REF
12
35
Ø20
6
12
32
12
2 PLACES
10
2 PLACES
R 12.5
2 PLACES
30°
15
90
60
45
25
70
25

EX5-66 MILLIMETERS

6 - 2 PLACES
10
Ø5 - 2 PLACES
90°
Ø40
20
20
Ø22
60
20
Ø16
90°

EX5-67 MILLIMETERS

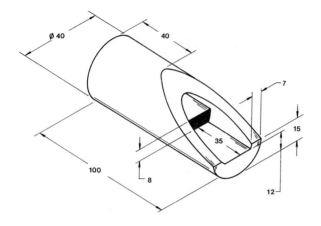

EX5-68 MILLIMETERS

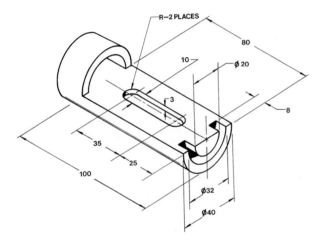

EX5-69 MILLIMETERS

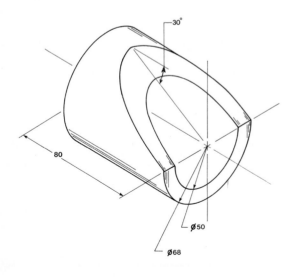

EX5-70 MILLIMETERS

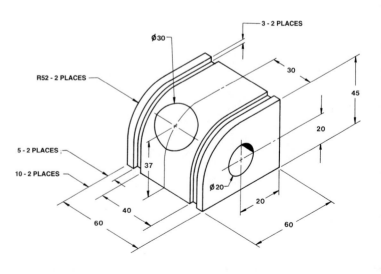

EX5-71 MILLIMETERS

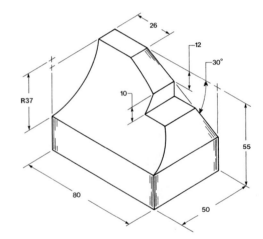

EX5-72 MILLIMETERS

EX5-73 MILLIMETERS

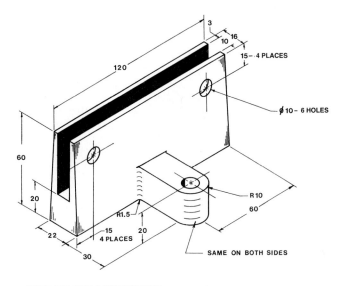

EX5-74 MILLIMETERS

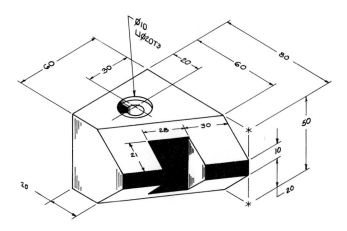

EX5-75 MILLIMETERS

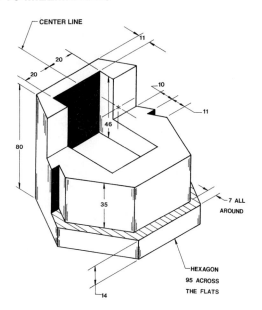

EX5-76 MILLIMETERS

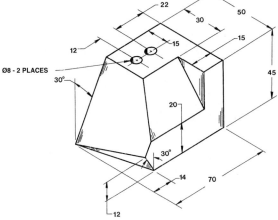

EX5-77 MILLIMETERS

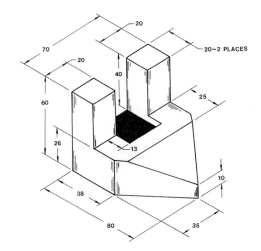

EX5-78 MILLIMETERS

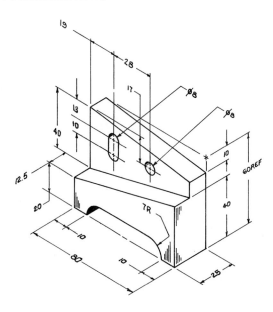

EX5-79 MILLIMETERS

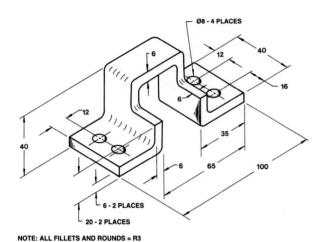

NOTE: ALL FILLETS AND ROUNDS = R3

EX5-80 MILLIMETERS

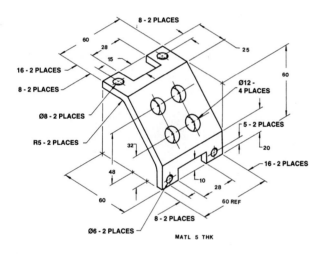

MATL 5 THK

EX5-81 MILLIMETERS

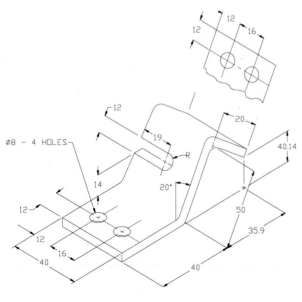

EX5-82 MILLIMETERS

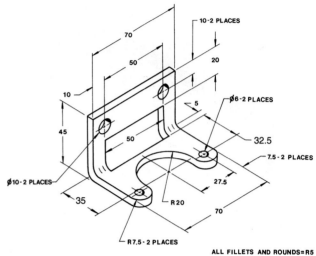

ALL FILLETS AND ROUNDS=R5
MATL 5 THK

EX5-83 MILLIMETERS

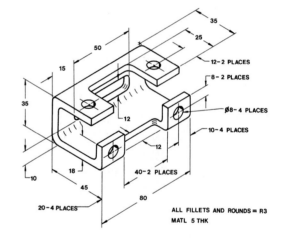

ALL FILLETS AND ROUNDS = R3
MATL 5 THK

EX5-84 MILLIMETERS

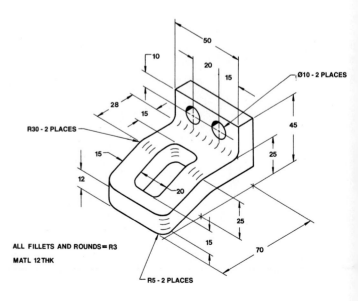

ALL FILLETS AND ROUNDS= R3
MATL 12 THK

EX5-85 MILLIMETERS

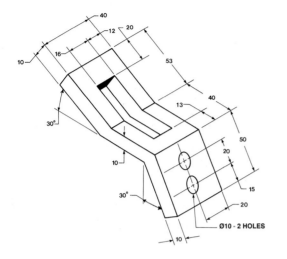

EX5-88 MILLIMETERS

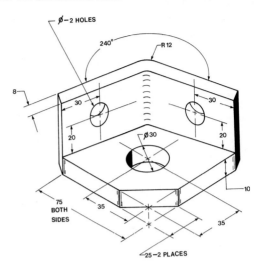

EX5-86 INCHES

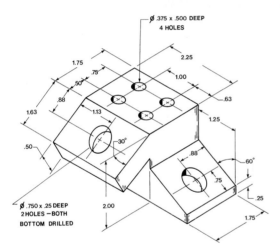

EX5-89 INCHES

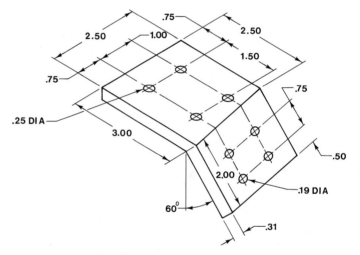

EX5-87 MILLIMETERS

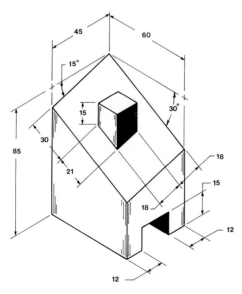

EX5-90 INCHES

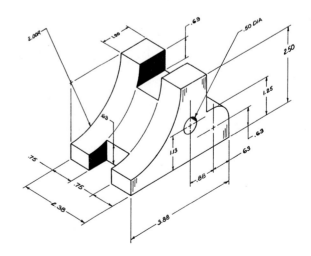

EX5-91 MILLIMETERS

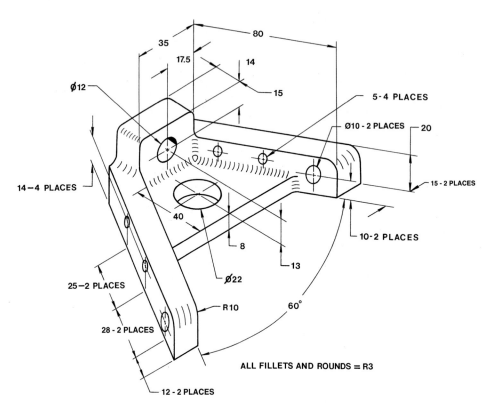

ALL FILLETS AND ROUNDS = R3

EX5-92 MILLIMETERS

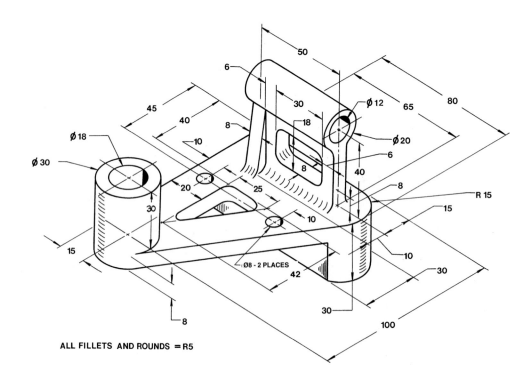

ALL FILLETS AND ROUNDS = R5

EX5-93 MILLIMETERS

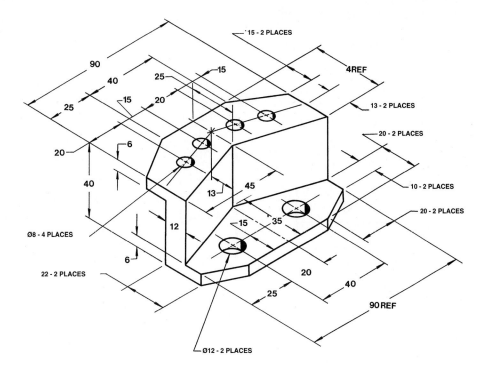

EX5-94 MILLIMETERS

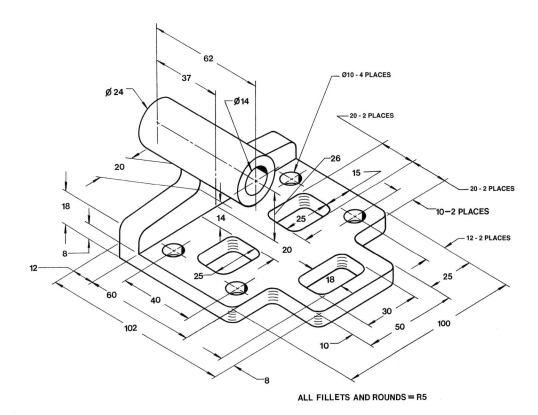

ALL FILLETS AND ROUNDS = R5

For exercise problems EX5-95 to EX5-100:

A. Sketch the given front and right-side views and add the top view.

B. Prepare a three-dimensional sketch of the object.

EX5-95

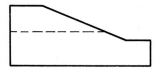
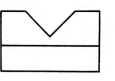

EX5-98

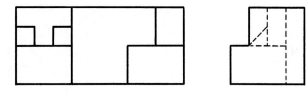

EX5-96

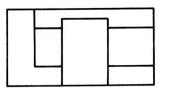
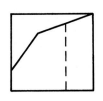

EX5-99

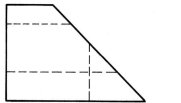
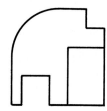

EX5-97

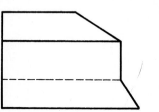
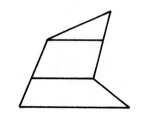

EX5-100

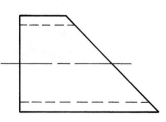
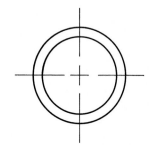

For exercise problems EX5-101 to EX5-120:
A. Redraw the given views and draw the third view.
B. Prepare a three-dimensional sketch of the object.

EX5-101 INCHES

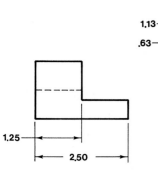
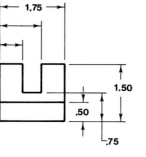

EX5-104 INCHES

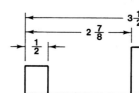
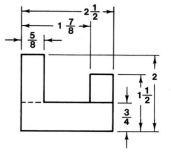

EX5-102 INCHES

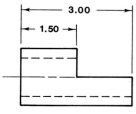
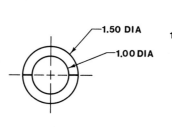

EX5-105 INCHES

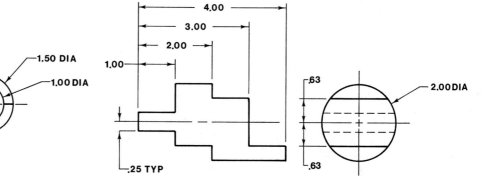

EX5-103 INCHES

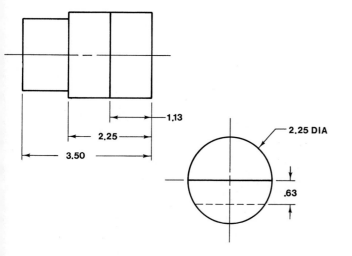

EX5-106 INCHES

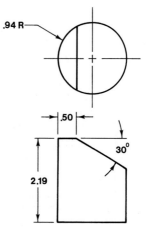

EX5-107 INCHES

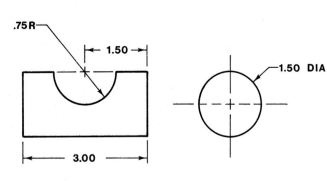

EX5-108 INCHES

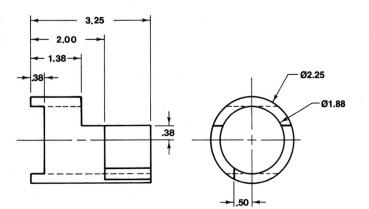

EX5-109 INCHES

All fillets and rounds $=\frac{1}{8}$ R

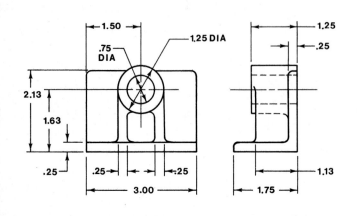

EX5-110 INCHES

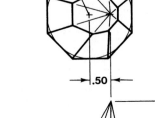

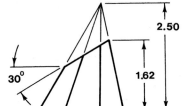

EX5-111 INCHES

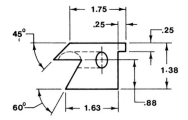

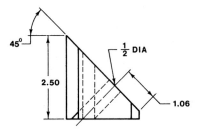

EX5-112 INCHES

All fillets and rounds $=\frac{1}{8}$ R

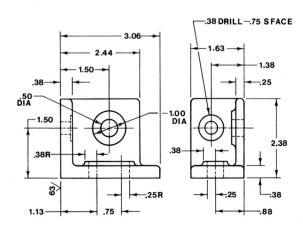

Each exercise on this page is presented on a 10mm ×10mm grid.

EX5-113

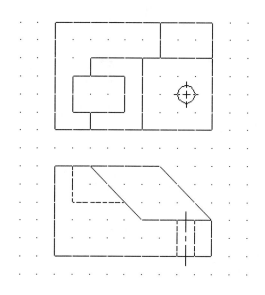

EX5-115

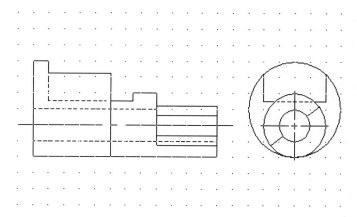

EX5-114

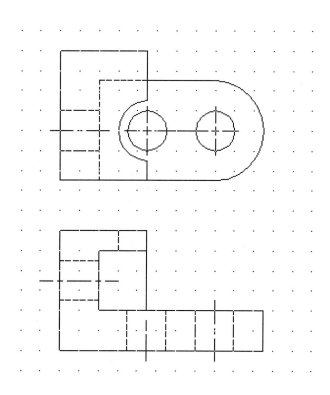

EX5-116

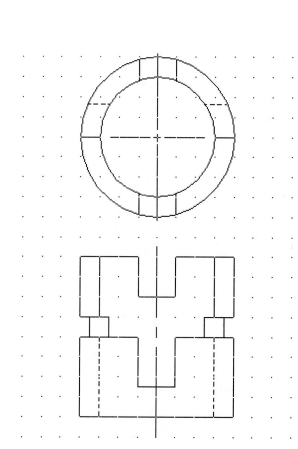

Each exercise on this page is presented on a 0.50″ × 0.50″ grid.

EX5-117

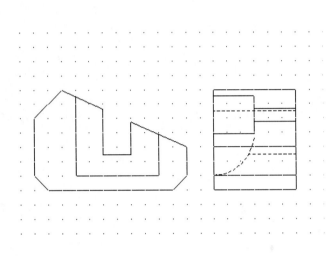

EX5-119

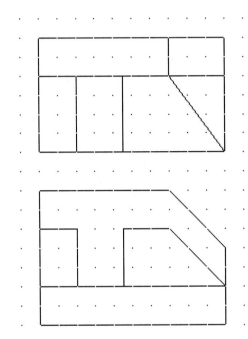

EX5-118

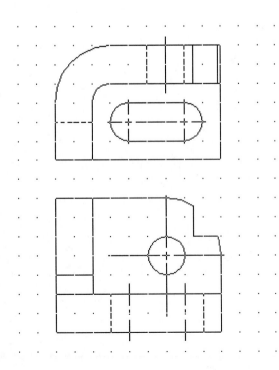

EX5-120

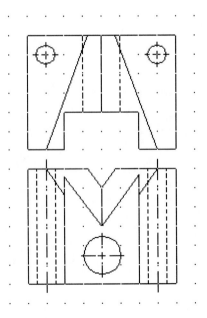

Draw the complete front, top, and side views of the two intersecting objects shown in exercise problems EX5-121 to EX5-125 based on the given complete and partially complete orthographic views.

EX5-121

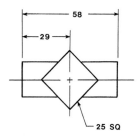

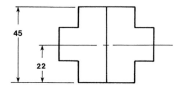 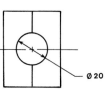

EX5-122 MILLIMETERS

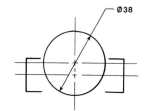

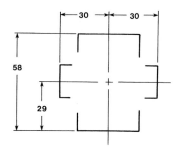 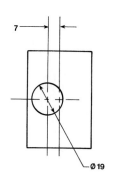

EX5-123

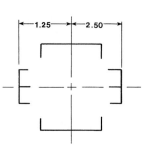

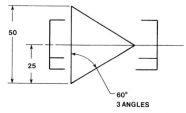 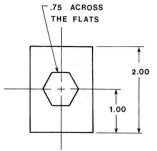

EX5-124 MILLIMETERS

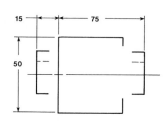 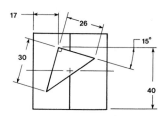

EX5-125 MILLIMETERS

EX5-127 MILLIMETERS

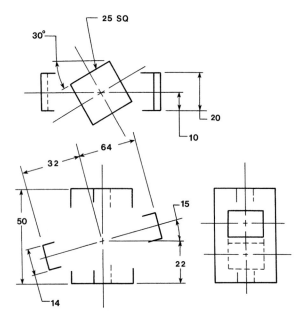

Draw the front, top, and side orthographic views of the objects given in exercise problems EX5-126 to EX5-132 based on the partially complete isometric drawings.

EX5-126 MILLIMETERS

EX5-128 MILLIMETERS

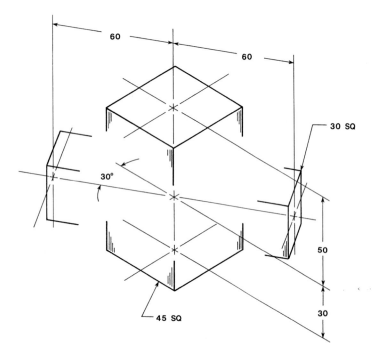

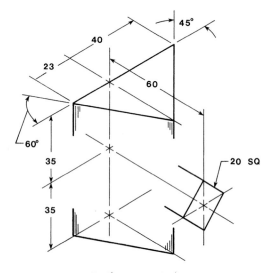

EX5-129 MILLIMETERS

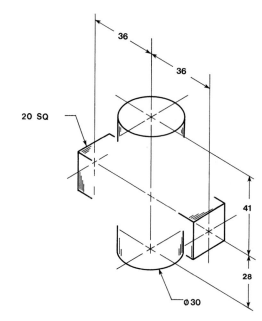

EX5-131 INCHES

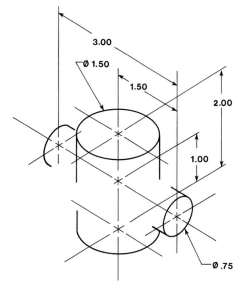

EX5-130 MILLIMETERS

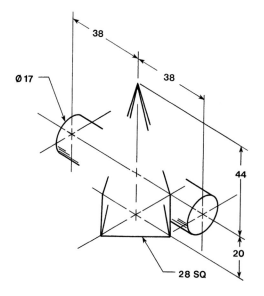

EX5-132 INCHES

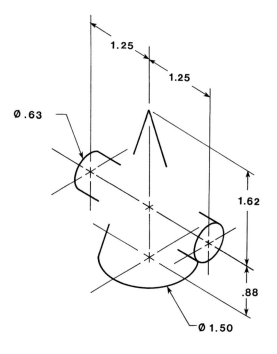

Redesign the existing objects as indicated in exercise problems EX5-133 to EX5-137, then prepare a front, top, and right-side view of the object.

EX5-133 MILLIMETERS

1. Replace the 4 existing 12 wide slots with 7 slots 16 wide.
2. Increase the distance between the slots from 20 to 24.
3. Modify the over length as needed.
4. Increase the size of the 60 slot so that it is 20 from both ends.

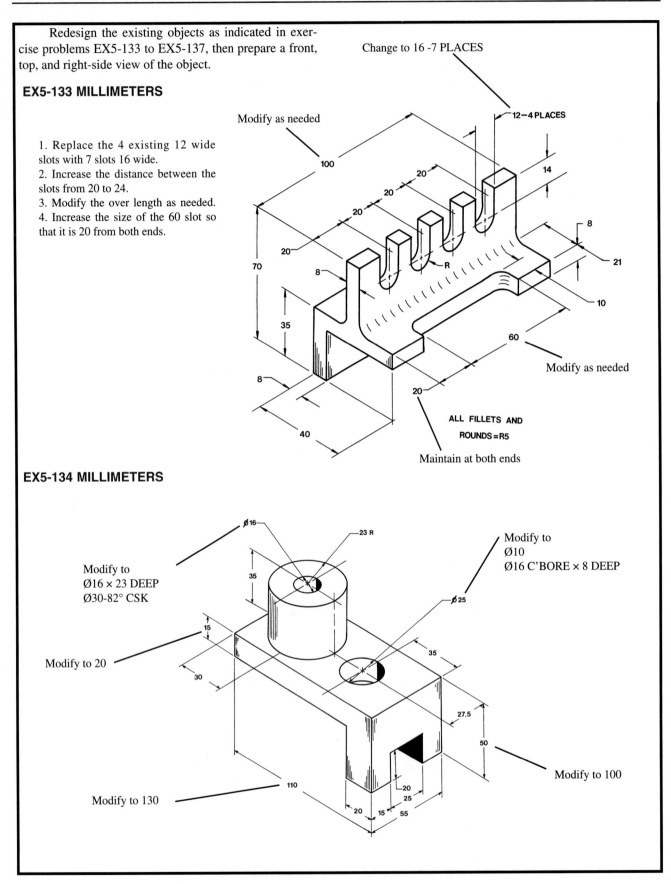

Change to 16 -7 PLACES

Modify as needed

12—4 PLACES

Modify as needed

Maintain at both ends

ALL FILLETS AND
ROUNDS = R5

EX5-134 MILLIMETERS

Modify to
Ø16 × 23 DEEP
Ø30-82° CSK

Modify to 20

Modify to 130

Modify to
Ø10
Ø16 C'BORE × 8 DEEP

Modify to 100

EX5-135 MILLIMETERS

EX5-136 MILLIMETERS

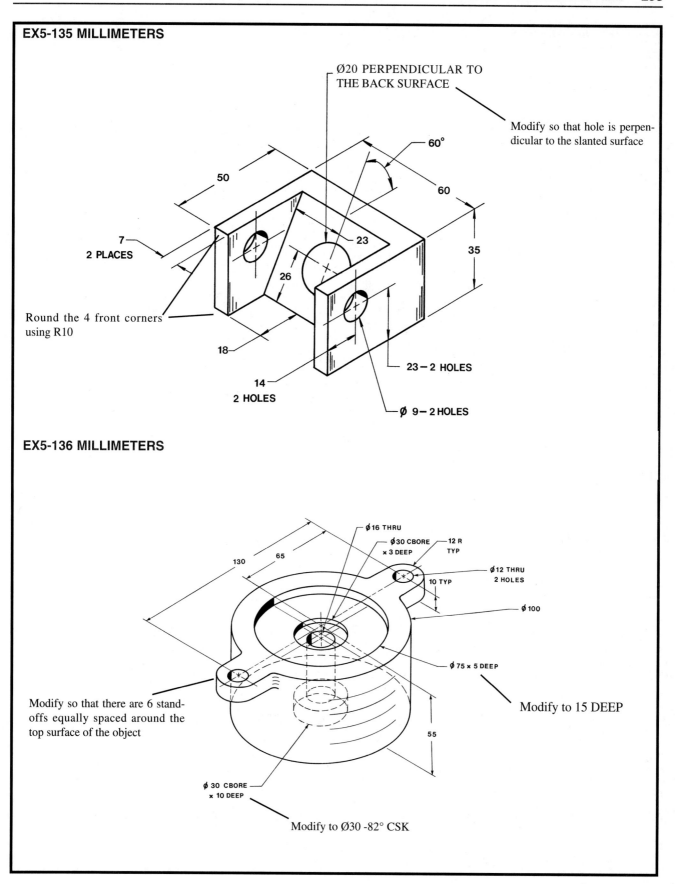

Ø20 PERPENDICULAR TO
THE BACK SURFACE

Modify so that hole is perpendicular to the slanted surface

60°

50

60

7
2 PLACES

23

35

26

Round the 4 front corners
using R10

18

14
2 HOLES

23 – 2 HOLES

Ø 9 – 2 HOLES

Ø 16 THRU

Ø 30 CBORE
x 3 DEEP

12 R
TYP

130

65

Ø 12 THRU
2 HOLES

10 TYP

Ø 100

Modify so that there are 6 stand-
offs equally spaced around the
top surface of the object

Ø 75 x 5 DEEP

Modify to 15 DEEP

55

Ø 30 CBORE
x 10 DEEP

Modify to Ø30 -82° CSK

EX5-137 MILLIMETERS

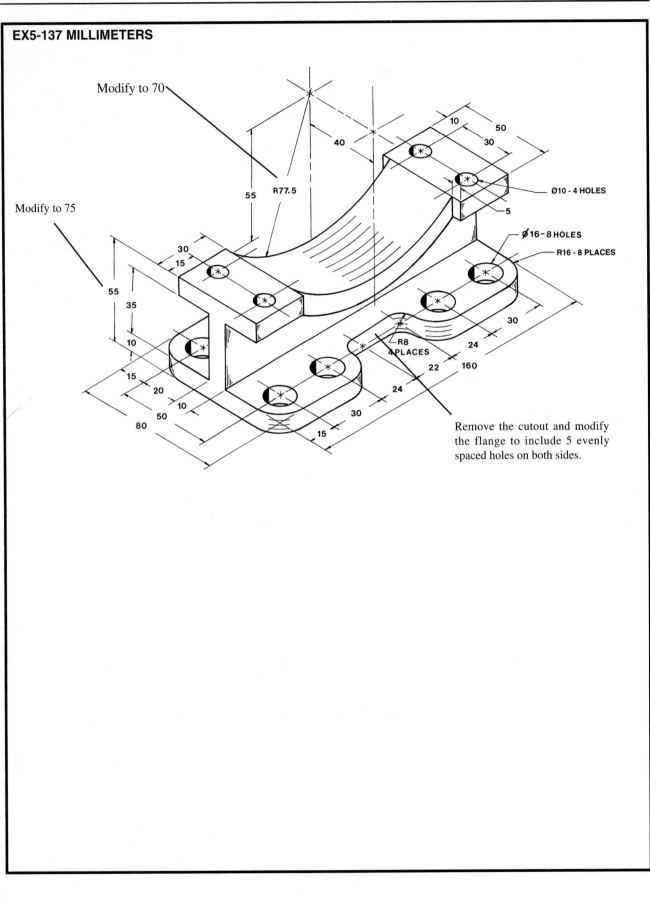

Modify to 70

Modify to 75

55

R77.5

40

10

50

30

Ø10 - 4 HOLES

5

Ø16 – 8 HOLES

R16 - 8 PLACES

30

15

55

35

10

R8
4 PLACES

30

24

22

160

15

20

10

24

50

80

30

15

Remove the cutout and modify
the flange to include 5 evenly
spaced holes on both sides.

Sectional Views

6-1 INTRODUCTION

Sectional views are used in technical drawings to expose internal surfaces. They serve to present additional orthographic views of surfaces that appear as hidden lines in the standard front, top, and side orthographic views.

Figure 6-1a shows an object intersected by a cutting plane. Figure 6-1b shows the same object with its right side and the cutting plane removed. Hatch lines were drawn on the surfaces that represent where the cutting plane passed through solid material. Also shown are the front and top orthographic views and a sectional view.

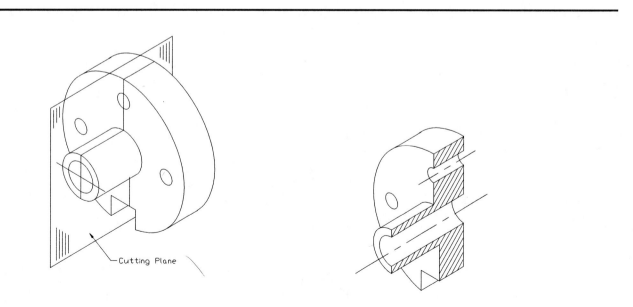

Cutting Plane

Figure 6-1a

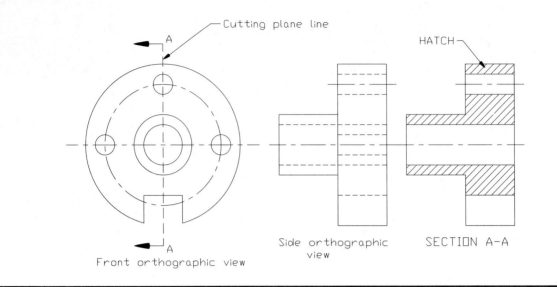

Figure 6-1b

Note the similarity between the sectional view and the cut pictorial view.

Sectional views do not contain hidden lines. The intent of using a sectional view is to clarify orthographic views that are difficult to understand because of excessive hidden lines. Figure 6-2 shows an object with a complex internal shape. The standard right view contains many hidden lines and is difficult to follow. Note how much easier it is to understand the object's internal shape when it is presented as a sectional view.

Sectional views DO include all lines that are directly visible. Figure 6-3 shows an object, a cutting plane line, and a sectional view taken along the cutting plane line. Surfaces that are directly visible are shown in the sectional view. For example, part of the large hole in the back left surface is, from the given sectional view's orientation, blocked by the shorter rectangular surface. The part of the hole that appears above the blocking surface is shown; the part behind the surface is not.

Sectional views are always viewed in the direction defined by the cutting plane arrows. Any surface that is behind the cutting plane is not included in the sectional

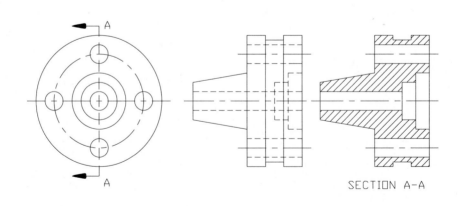

Figure 6-2

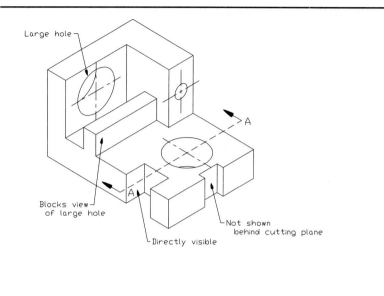

Large hole

Blocks view
of large hole

Directly visible

Not shown
behind cutting plane

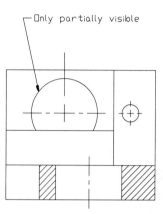

Only partially visible

Figure 6-3

view. Sectional views are aligned and oriented relative to the cutting plane lines as a side orthographic view is to the front view. The orientation of a sectional view may be better understood by placing your right hand on the cutting plane line so that your thumb is pointing up. Move your hand to the right and place it palm down. Your thumb should now be pointing to the left. Your thumb indicates the top of the view.

Drafters and designers often refer to sectional views as "sectional cuts" or simply "cuts." The terminology is helpful in understanding how sectional views are defined and created.

6-2 CUTTING PLANE LINES

Cutting plane lines are used to define the location for the sectional view's cutting plane. An object is "cut" along a cutting plane line.

Figure 6-4 shows two linetype patterns for cutting plane lines. Either pattern is acceptable, although some companies prefer to use only one linetype for all drawings to ensure a uniform appearance in all their drawings. The DASHED line pattern will be used throughout this book.

The two patterns shown in Figure 6-4 are included in AutoCAD's linetype library as DASHED and PHAN-

TOM styles. The arrow portion of the cutting plane line is created using the LEADER command listed with the DIMENSION commands or by creating a WBLOCK that includes an arrowhead and extension line.

To draw a cutting plane line -- Method I

Change a given continuous line A-A to a cutting plane line. See Figure 6-5.

1. Select the MODIFY (DOS) or EDIT (WINDOWS) pulldown menu, then PROPERTIES or use the PROPERTIES icon on the STANDARD toolbar

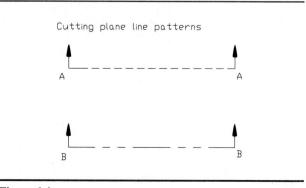

Cutting plane line patterns

A   A

B   B

Figure 6-4

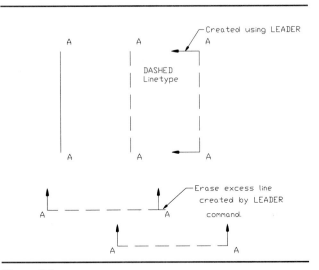

Figure 6-5

Select object(s)

2. Select line A-A, then press ENTER

The Change Properties dialog box will appear. See Figure 6-6.

3. Select LINETYPE

The Select LINETYPE dialog box will appear. See Figure 6-7. If DASHED or PHANTOM line patterns are not listed, use the LINETYPE, LOAD commands to load the linetype file.

4. Select DASHED
5. Select OK

The Change Properties dialog box will appear again with DASHED listed next to LINETYPE.

6. Select OK

To add arrows to the cutting plane line

Arrows for cutting plane lines are created using the LEADER command. The LEADER command is accessed in the DOS version via the DRAW pulldown menu, then DIMENSIONS, then LEADER. The LEADER command icon for the WINDOWS version is found on the DIMENSIONS toolbar. The Leader command is discussed in detail in Chapter 8. For cutting plane applications, typed access commands will be presented.

Arrows used in association with cutting plane lines are usually drawn slightly larger than arrows used for dimensioning.

To change the size of an arrowhead

The size of arrowheads is controlled by the DIMASZ command. The default value is 0.1800. Sizes of at least 0.25 for inch drawings and 4 for millimeter drawings are recommended.

1. Type DIMASZ in response to a Command: prompt.

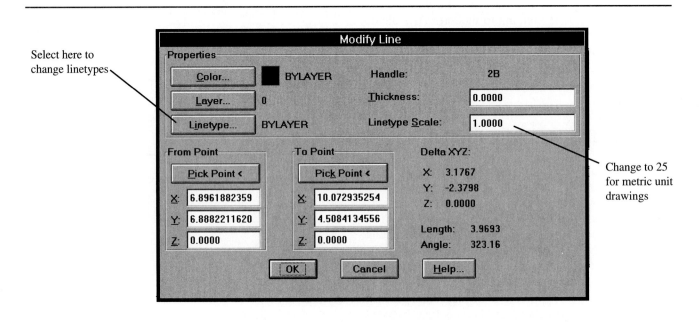

Figure 6-6

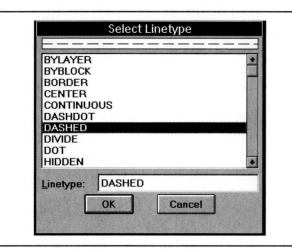

Figure 6-7

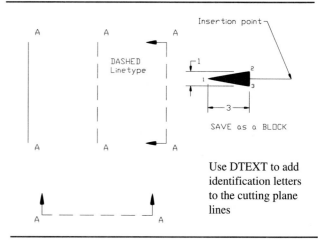

Use DTEXT to add identification letters to the cutting plane lines

Figure 6-8

New value for DIMASZ <0.1800>:

2. Type in the new value

To use a leader line to create a cutting plane line

1. Type LEADER in response to a Command: prompt.

From point:

2. Select a point on the screen

To point:

3. Select a second point

Make the length of the leader line about .50 inches or 12 millimeters.

To point(Format/Annotation/Undo)<Annotation>:

4. Type ENTER

Annotation (or RETURN for OPTIONS):

5. Type ENTER

Tolerance/Copy/Block/None/<Mtext>:

6. Type N ENTER

Use the COPY, MOVE, or ROTATE commands as needed to position the arrows on the cutting plane line.

To draw a cutting plane line -- Method II

See Figure 6-8.

1. Create a LAYER called CUTTING and set the linetype to DASHED and choose a color. Move the cutting plane line to the CUTTING LAYER. See Sections 3-27 and 5-7.
2. Create a WBLOCK called ARROW and draw an arrow as defined in Figure 6-8.
3. INSERT two ARROW BLOCKS into the CUTTING LAYER and align the arrows' base points with the ends of the line. Use OSNAP, ENDpoint to ensure accurate alignment.

The proportions of an arrowhead are 3 units to 1 unit, as shown. The scale factor and angle commands of the INSERT BLOCK sequence can be used to make the arrow of a size and angle appropriate to the drawing.

The SOLID command was used to color in the arrow. The command sequence is as follows.

To use the SOLID command

1. Select DRAW (menu), SOLID

Command: _SOLID First point:
Second point:

2. Select point 2

Third point:

3. Select point 3

Fourth point

4. Type ENTER
5. Select AutoCAD to return the Command: prompt

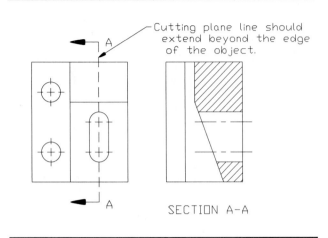

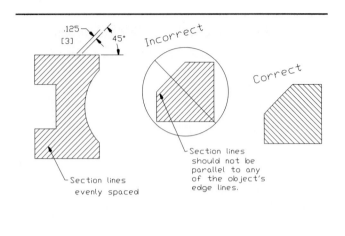

Figure 6-9

Figure 6-10

Cutting planes should extend beyond the edges of the object. See Figure 6-9. A cutting plane line should extend far enough beyond the edges of an object so that there is a clear gap between the arrowhead and the edge of the object.

If an object is symmetrical about a center line and only one sectional view is to be taken exactly aligned with the center line, the cutting plane line may be omitted.

6-3 SECTION LINES

Section lines are used to define areas that represent where solid material has been cut in a sectional view. Section lines are evenly spaced at any inclined angle that is not parallel to any existing edge line. Section lines should be visually distinct from the continuous lines that define

the boundary of the sectional view.

Figure 6-10 shows an area that includes uniform section lines evenly spaced at 45 degrees. The other area shown in Figure 6-10 includes a 45-degree edge line; therefore the section lines cannot be drawn at 45 degrees. Lines at 135 degrees (0 degrees is horizontal to the right) were drawn instead.

Figure 6-11 shows an object that contains edge lines at both 45 and 135 degrees. The section lines within this area were drawn at 60 degrees.

If two or more parts are included within the same sectional view, each part must have visually different section lines. Figure 6-12 shows a sectional view that contains two parts. Part one's section lines were spaced 3 apart at 45 degrees, and part two's were spaced 5 apart at 135 degrees (-45).

The recommended spacing for sectional lines is .125

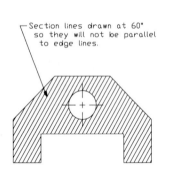

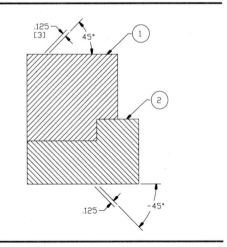

Figure 6-11

Figure 6-12

inches or 3 mm, but smaller areas may use section lines spaced closer together than larger areas. See Figure 6-13. Section lines should never be spaced so close together to look blurry or be so far apart that they are not clearly recognizable as section lines.

Evenly spaced sectional line patterns drawn at 45 degrees are called general or uniform patterns. Other patterns are available. The different section line patterns are used to help distinguish different materials. The different patterns allow the drawing reader to see what materials are used in a design without having to refer to the drawing's part list. It should be noted that not all companies use different patterns to define material differences. When in doubt, the general pattern is usually acceptable.

How to draw different section line patterns is explained in Section 6-4.

6-4 HATCH

Section lines are drawn in AutoCAD using the HATCH command. The HATCH command may be accessed for the DOS version via the DRAW pulldown menu, then HATCH, HATCH. There is a HATCH icon on the DRAW toolbar for the WINDOWS version. See Figure 6-13.

To HATCH a given area

Given an area, use the HATCH command to draw section lines. See Figure 6-14.

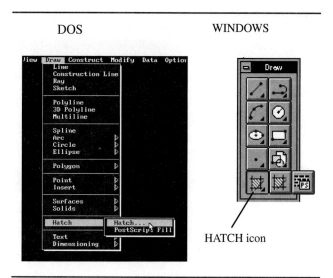

DOS   WINDOWS

HATCH icon

Figure 6-13

1. Select the HATCH command

The Boundary Hatch dialog box will appear. See Figure 6-15. The Boundary Hatch dialog box is used to select the hatch pattern and to adjust the pattern's size and angle if necessary.

The default pattern is ANSI31, which is a series of uniformly spaced 45° lines. This is a general pattern that can be used to represent any material. The ANSI31 pattern was used in the first example shown in Figure 6-14.

2. Select the Pick Points< box

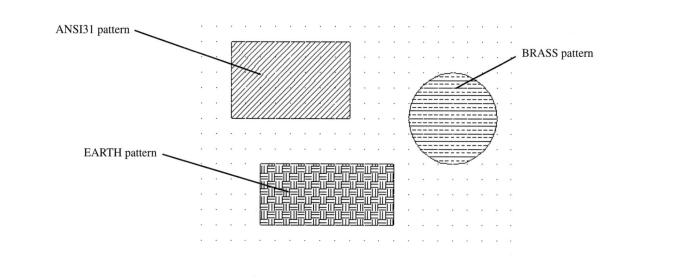

ANSI31 pattern

BRASS pattern

EARTH pattern

Figure 6-14

Preview of selected pattern

Select here to define an area to be hatched

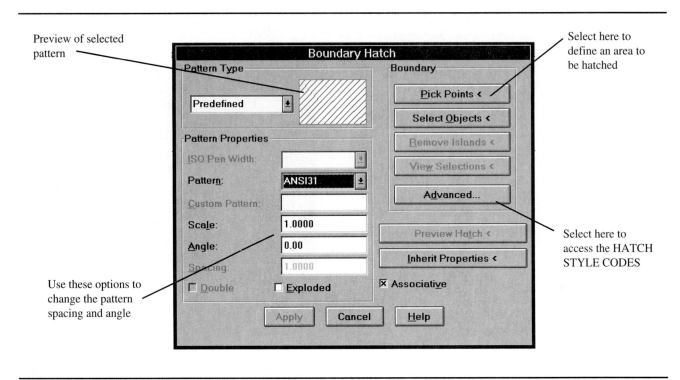

Use these options to change the pattern spacing and angle

Select here to access the HATCH STYLE CODES

Figure 6-15

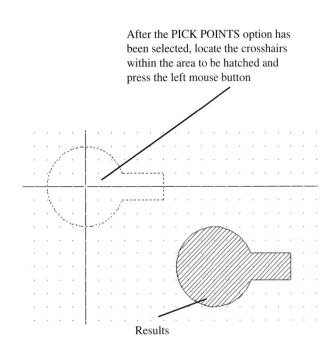

After the PICK POINTS option has been selected, locate the crosshairs within the area to be hatched and press the left mouse button

Results

Figure 6-16

The drawing will reappear.

3. Locate the crosshairs within the area to be hatched and press the left mouse button

The lines surrounding the area to be hatched will become gray. See Figure 6-16.

4. Press ENTER to signify that you are done selecting areas

The Boundary Hatch dialog box will appear again.

5. Select the Apply box.

The area will be hatched.

To change the HATCH STYLE Codes

See Figure 6-17.

1. Select the HATCH command

The Boundary Hatch dialog box will appear.

2. Select the Advanced... box

The Advanced Options dialog box will appear. See Figure 6-17.

3. Select the Style: box

There are three options: normal, outer, and ignore. The box just to the right of the Style box will preview the selected option.

4. Select the arrow button to the right of the Style box

A listing of the three options will cascade down.

5. Select the option you want
6. Select the OK box

The Boundary Hatch dialog box will reappear. Apply the hatching as described before.

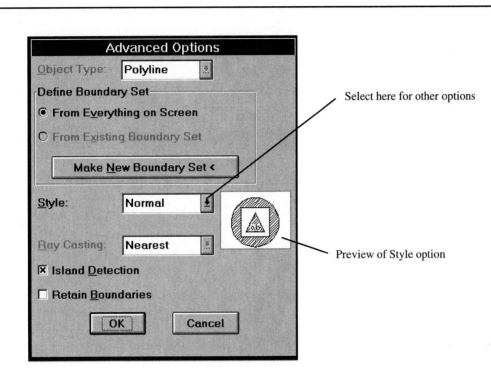

Select here for other options

Preview of Style option

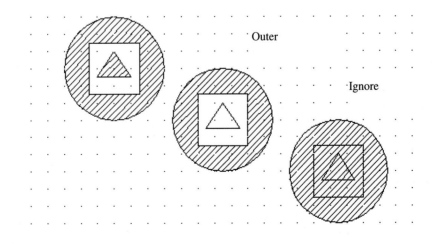

Normal

Outer

Ignore

Figure 6-17

6-5 SAMPLE PROBLEM SP6-1

Figure 6-18 shows an object with a cutting plane line. Figure 6-19 shows how a front view and a sectional view of the object were created.

1. DRAW the front orthographic view of the object and lay out the height and width of the object based on the given dimensions. Sectional views must be directly aligned with the angle of the cutting plane line. Sectional views are in fact orthographic views that are based on the angle of the cutting plane line. Information is projected to sectional views as it was projected to top and side views. In this example the cutting plane line is a vertical line, so horizontal projection lines are used to draw the sectional view.
2. DRAW the object features. No hidden lines are drawn.
3. Use HATCH to draw sectional lines within the appropriate areas.
4. ERASE or TRIM any excess lines.
5. CHANGE the color of the sectional lines as desired.
6. SAVE the drawing if desired.

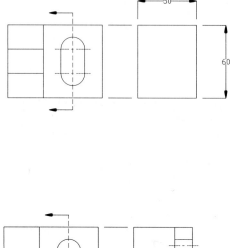

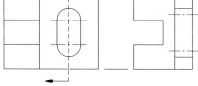

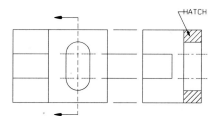

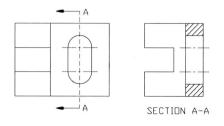

SECTION A-A

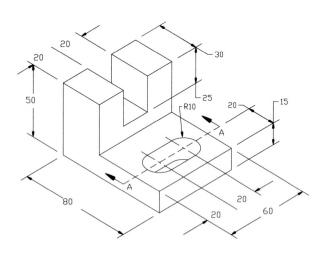

Figure 6-18

Figure 6-19

6-6 STYLES OF SECTION LINES

AutoCAD has over 50 different HATCH patterns. The different patterns can be previewed using the Choose Hatch Options dialog box explained in Section 6-4.

Most of the available options are for architectural use. The patterns can be used to create elevation drawings and add texture patterns to drawings of houses, buildings, and other structures. Technical drawings usually refer to objects made from steel, aluminum, or a composite material. There are hundreds of variations of each of these materials.

In general if you decide to assign a particular pattern to a material, clearly state which pattern has been assigned to which material on the drawing. This is best done by inserting a note on the drawing that includes a picture of the pattern and the material that it is to represent. Figure 6-20 shows a drawing note for a hatch pattern used to represent SAE 1040 steel. The representation is unique for the drawing shown.

6-7 SECTIONAL VIEW LOCATION

Sectional views should be located on a drawing behind the arrows. The arrows represent the viewing direction for the sectional view. See Figure 6-21. If it is impossible to locate sectional views behind the arrows, they may be located above or below, but still behind the arrowed portion of the cutting plane line. Sectional views should never be located in front of the arrows.

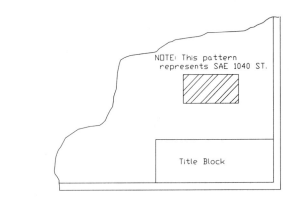

Figure 6-20

Sectional views located on a different drawing sheet than the cutting plane line must be cross-referenced back to the appropriate cutting plane line. See Figure 6-22. The boxed notation C/3 SHT 2 next to the A on the cutting plane line means that the sectional view may be found in zone C/3 on sheet 2 of the drawing.

The sectional view must be referenced back to the cutting plane line. Section G-G is referenced with the notation C/4 SHT 1, indicating the location of its cutting plane line.

The reference numbers and letters are based on a drawing area charting system similar to that used for locating features on maps. Figure EX1-14 shows a detailed picture of the referencing system. A sectional view located at

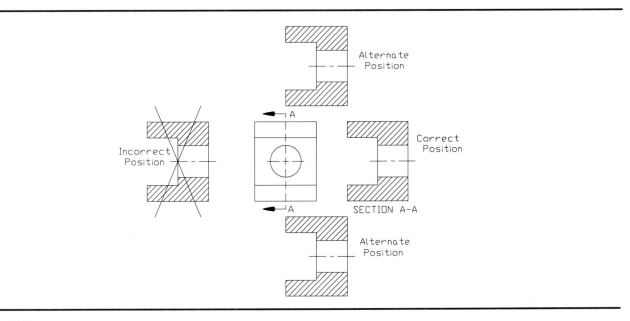

Figure 6-21

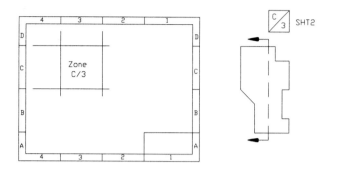

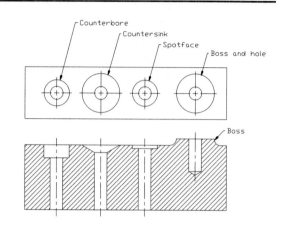

Figure 6-22

Figure 6-24

C/3 SHT 2 can be found by going to sheet 2 of the drawing, then drawing a vertical line from the box marked 3 at the top or bottom of the drawing and a horizontal line from the box marked D on the left or right edge of the drawing. The sectional view should be located somewhere near the intersection of the two lines.

point must be included on holes that do not completely penetrate the object.

A common mistake is to omit the back edge of a hole when drawing a sectional view. Figure 6-23 shows a hole drilled through an object. Note that the sectional view includes a straight line across the top and bottom edges of the view that represent the back edges of the hole.

6-8 HOLES IN SECTIONS

Figure 6-24 shows a countersunk hole, a spotface, and a hole through a boss. Again, any hole that does not completely penetrate the object must include a conical point.

Figure 6-23 shows a sectional view of an object that contains three holes. As with orthographic views, a conical

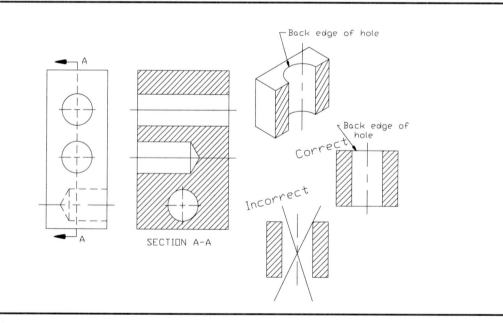

Figure 6-23

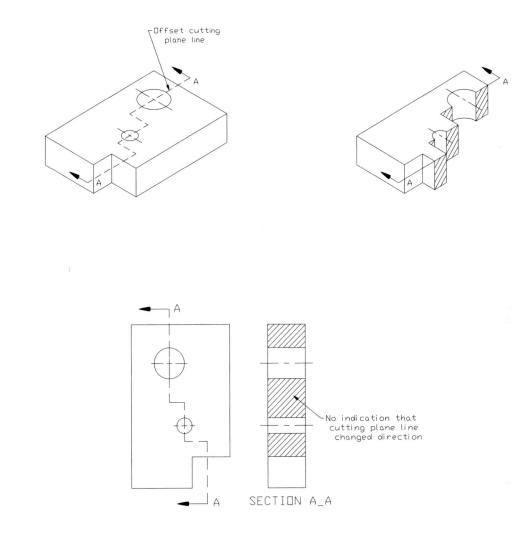

Figure 6-25

6-9 OFFSET SECTIONS

Cutting plane lines need not be drawn as straight lines across the surface of an object. They may be stepped so more features can be included in the sectional view. See Figure 6-25. In the object shown in Figure 6-25, the cutting plane line crosses two holes and an open surface directly visible that contains a hole. There is no indication in the sectional view that the cutting plane line has been offset.

Cutting plane lines should be placed to include as many features as possible without causing confusion. The intent of using sectional views is to simplify views and to clarify the drawing. Several features can be included on the same cutting plane line so that fewer views are used, giving the drawing a less cluttered look and making it easier for the reader to understand the shape of the object's features.

Figure 6-26 shows another example of an offset cutting plane line.

6-10 MULTIPLE SECTIONS

More than one sectional view may be taken off the same orthographic view. Figure 6-27 shows a drawing that includes three sectional views, all taken off a front view. Each cutting plane line is lettered. The letters are in turn used to identify the appropriate sectional view. Identifying letters are placed at the ends of the cutting plane lines,

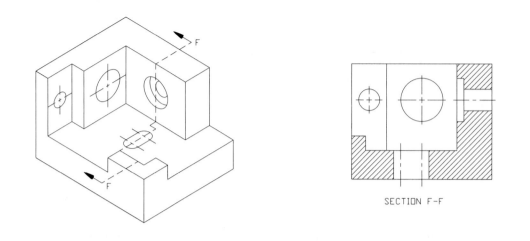

SECTION F-F

Figure 6-26

behind the arrowheads. Identifying letters are placed below the sectional view and written using the format SECTION A-A, SECTION B-B, etc. The abbreviation SECT may also be used: SECT A-A, SECT B-B.

The letters I, O, and X are generally not used to identify sectional views because they can be easily misread. If more than 23 sectional views are used, the lettering starts again with double letters: AA-AA, BB-BB, etc.

6-11 ALIGNED SECTIONS

Cutting plane lines taken at angles on circular shapes may be aligned as shown in Figure 6-28. Aligning the sectional views prevents the foreshortening that would result if the view were projected from the original cutting plane line location. A foreshortened view would not present an accurate picture of the object's surfaces.

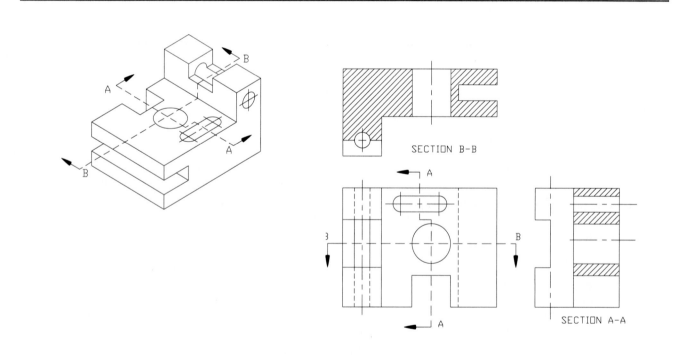

SECTION B-B

SECTION A-A

Figure 6-27

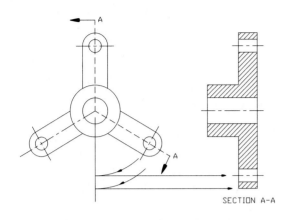

SECTION A-A

Figure 6-28

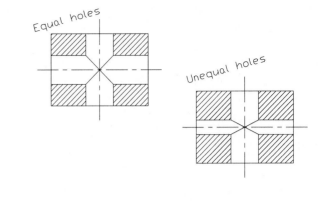

Equal holes

Unequal holes

Figure 6-30

6-12 DRAWING CONVENTIONS IN SECTIONS

The drawing conventions as explained in Chapter 5 also apply when drawing sectional views. Slots and small holes that penetrate cylindrical surfaces may be drawn as straight lines, as shown in Figure 6-29. Larger holes, that is, holes whose diameter is greater than the radius of the cylinder, should be drawn showing an elliptical curvature.

Intersecting holes are represented by crossed lines, as shown in Figure 6-30. The crossed lines are drawn from the intersecting corners of the holes.

6-13 HALF, PARTIAL, AND BROKEN-OUT SECTIONAL VIEWS

Half and partial sectional views allow a designer to show an object using an orthographic view and a sectional view within one view. A half sectional view is shown in Figure 6-31. Half the view is a sectional view, the other half a normal orthographic view including hidden lines. The cutting plane line is drawn as shown and includes an arrowhead at only one end of the line.

Figure 6-32 shows a partial sectional view. It is similar to a half sectional view, but the sectional view is taken

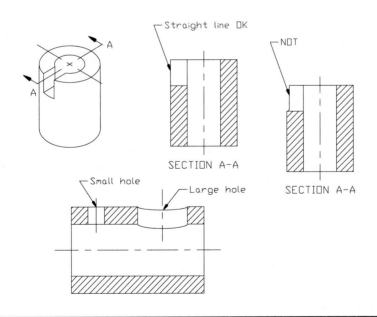

Straight line OK

NOT

SECTION A-A

SECTION A-A

Small hole

Large hole

Figure 6-29

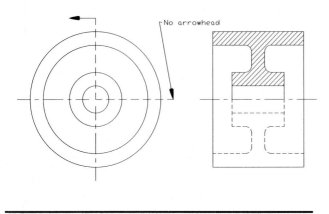

Figure 6-31

at a location other than directly on a center line or one defined by a cutting plane line. A broken line is used to separate the sectional view from the orthographic view. A broken line is a freehand line drawn using the SKETCH command.

Broken-out sectional views are like small partial views. They are used to show only small internal portions of an object. Figure 6-33 shows a broken-out sectional view. Broken lines are used to separate the broken-out section from the rest of the orthographic views.

To draw a broken line

1. Type SKETCH in response to a Command: prompt

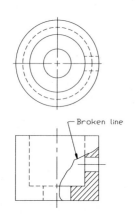

Figure 6-33

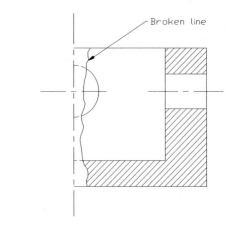

Figure 6-32

Command:_sketch
Record Increment <0.1000>:

2. ENTER

Sketch. Pen eXit Quit Record Erase Connect.

3. Press the left mouse button

<Pen down>

4. Move the crosshairs across the screen. A green freehand line will emerge from the crosshairs as they are moved
5. Press the left mouse button again

<Pen up>

The crosshairs can now be moved without producing a sketched line. If the sketched line is not acceptable, press ENTER and redraw the line.

6. Type R to record the line

23 lines recorded

The number of lines generated and recorded will depend on the length of the line and the size of the line increment.

7. Select eXit from the menu.

Command:

Do not use the right mouse button to exit the SKETCH command. If the right mouse button is pressed, a line will be drawn from the end of the sketched line to the present location of the crosshairs. Use eXit to end the SKETCH command.

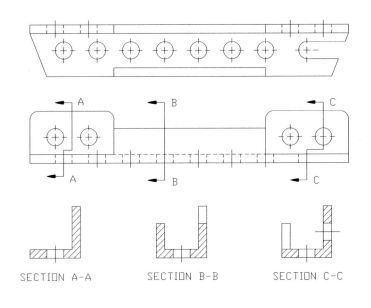

SECTION A-A   SECTION B-B   SECTION C-C

Figure 6-34

6-14 REMOVED SECTIONAL VIEWS

Removed sectional views are used to show how an object's shape changes over its length. Removed sectional views are most often used with long objects whose shape changes continuously over its length. See Figure 6-34. The sectional views are not positioned behind the arrowheads but are positioned across the drawing as shown. However, the view orientation is the same as it would be if the view were projected from the arrowheads; it is simply located in a different position in the drawing.

It is good practice to identify the cutting plane lines and the sectional views in alphabetical order. This will make it easer for the drawing's readers to find the sectional views.

6-15 BREAKS

It is often convenient to break long continuous shapes so that they take up less drawing space. There are two drawing conventions used to show breaks: freehand lines used for rectangular shapes, and S-breaks used for cylindrical shapes. See Figure 6-35. Freehand break lines are drawn using the SKETCH command as explained in Section 6-14. How to draw S-breaks is shown below.

To draw an S-break

See Figure 6-36.

1. DRAW a rectangular view of the cylindrical object and DRAW a construction line where the break is to be located. The rectangular view should include a center line.
2. DRAW two 30-degree LINES: one from the intersection of the construction line and the outside edge line of the view, and the other from the intersection of the construction line and the center line as shown.
3. DRAW an ARC using the intersection created in step 2 as the center point. MIRROR the ARC about the center line and then about the construction line.

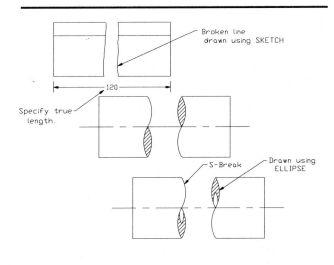

Figure 6-35

4. Use FILLET set to a small radius to smooth the corners between the ARC and the edge lines. Any small radius may be used for the FILLET, provided it produces a smooth visual transition between the ARC and the edge lines.
5. ERASE and TRIM any excess lines.
6. HATCH the area created by the two ARCS and FILLET as shown.

The COPY, MIRROR, and MOVE commands may be used to create the opposing S-break as shown in Figure 6-35. The internal shape of the tubular S-breaks are created using ELLIPSE. Position the end of the ellipse according to the thickness specifications and determine the elliptical shape by eye. TRIM the sectional lines from the inside of the inside ellipse.

6-16 SECTIONAL VIEWS OF CASTINGS

Cast objects are usually designed to include a featured called a rib. See Figure 6-37. Ribs add strength and rigidity to an object. Sectional views of ribs do not include complete section lines because this is considered misleading to the reader. Ribs are usually narrow, and a large sectioned area gives the impression of a more dense and stronger area than is actually on the casting.

There are two conventions used to present sectional views of cast ribs: one that does not draw any section lines on the ribs, and one that puts every other section line on the rib. Sectional views of castings that do not include section lines on ribs are created using HATCH for those areas that are to be hatched.

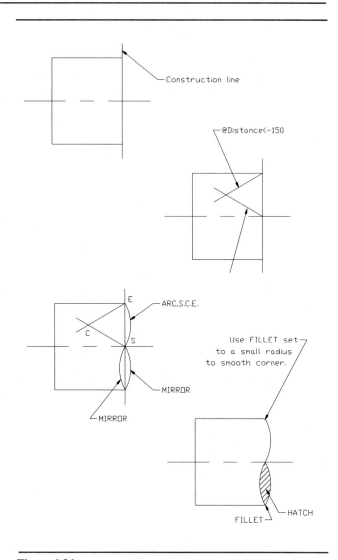

Figure 6-36

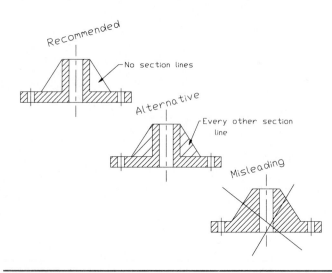

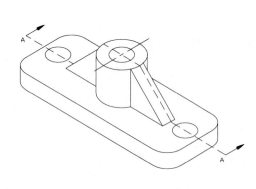

Figure 6-37

6-17 EXERCISE PROBLEMS

Draw a complete front view and a sectional view of the objects in exercise problems EX6-1 to EX6-4. The cutting plane line is located on the vertical center line of the object.

EX6-1 MILLIMETERS

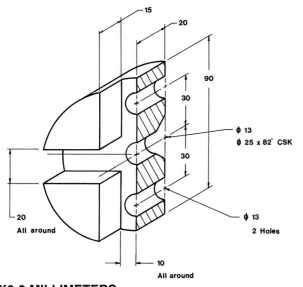

EX6-3 INCHES

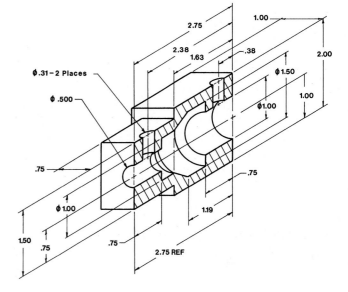

EX6-2 MILLIMETERS

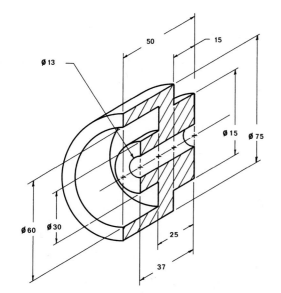

EX6-4 MILLIMETERS

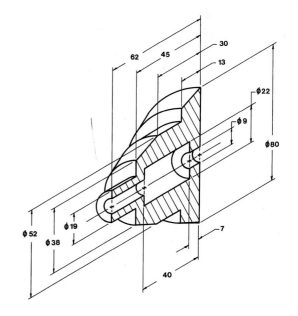

EX6-5

Draw the following sectional view using the given dimensions.

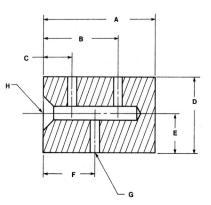

DIMENSIONS	INCHES	mm
A	3.00	72
B	2.00	48
C	.75	18
D	2.00	48
E	1.00	24
F	1.38	33
G	Ø.25	6
H	Ø.375 X 2.50 DEEP Ø.875 X 82° CSINK	Ø10 X 60 DEEP Ø24 X 82° CSINK

EX6-6

Resketch the given top view and Section A-A, then sketch Sections B-B, C-C, and D-D.

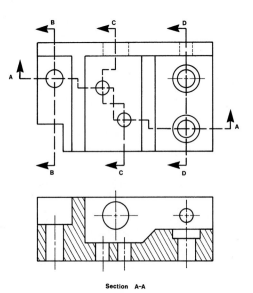

Section A-A

Resketch the front views in exercise problems EX6-7 to EX6-10 and replace the side orthographic view with the appropriate sectional view.

EX6-7

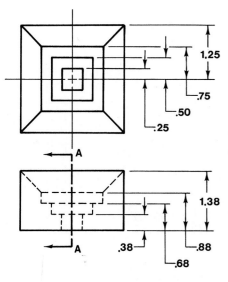

EX6-9 INCHES

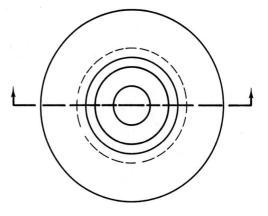
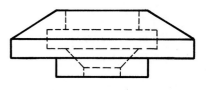

EX6-8

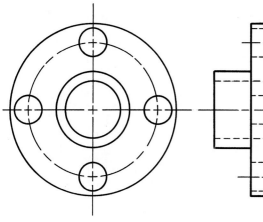
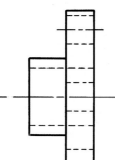

Object is symmetrical about both center lines.

EX6-10

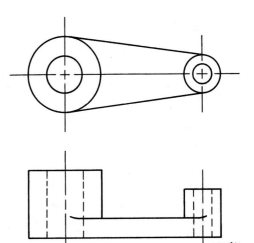

Redraw the front views in exercise problems EX6-11 to EX6-14 and replace the side orthographic view with the appropriate sectional view. The cutting plane is located on the vertical center lines of the objects.

EX6-11 INCHES

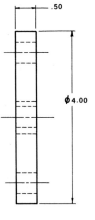
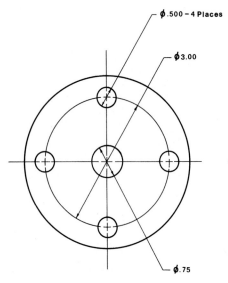

EX6-13 INCHES

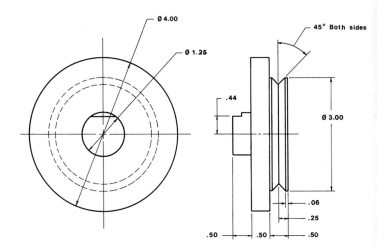

EX6-12 MILLIMETERS

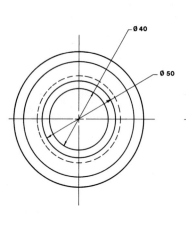
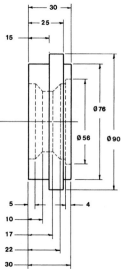

EX6-14 INCHES

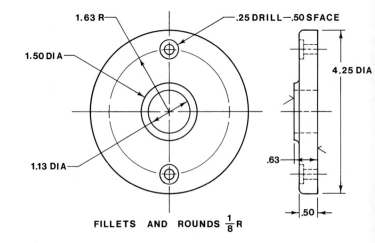

Draw the top orthographic view and the indicated sectional view in exercise problems EX6-15 to EX6-18.

EX6-15 MILLIMETERS

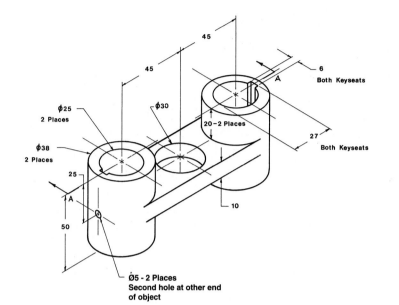

EX6-17 INCHES

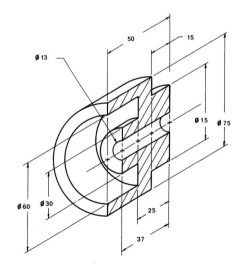

EX6-16 MILLIMETERS

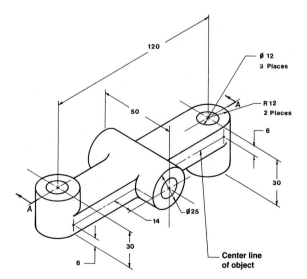

EX6-18 INCHES

Redraw the given views and add the specified sectional views in exercise problems EX6-19 to EX6-31.

EX6-19 INCHES

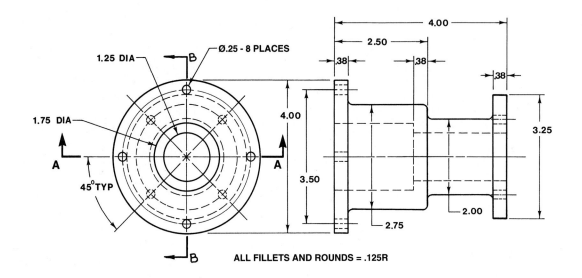

ALL FILLETS AND ROUNDS = .125R

EX6-20 MILLIMETERS

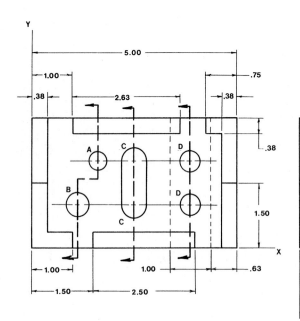

HOLE	X	Y	DIA
A	1.63	2.00	.44
B	1.13	1.00	.56
C	2.50	2.00 1.00	.63
D	3.88	2.00 1.00	.50

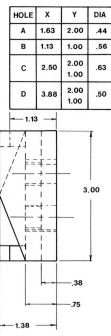

EX6-21 INCHES

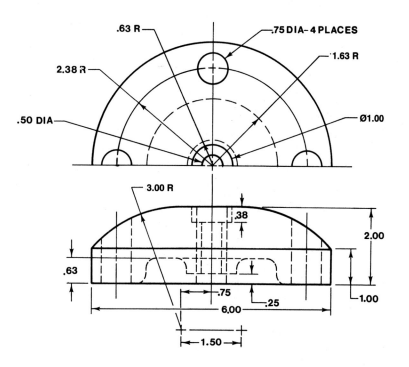

EX6-22 INCHES

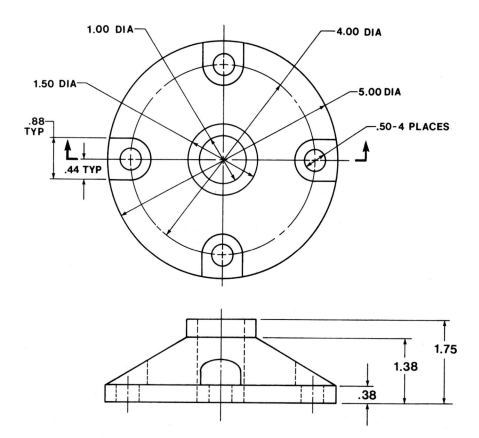

EX6-23 MILLIMETERS

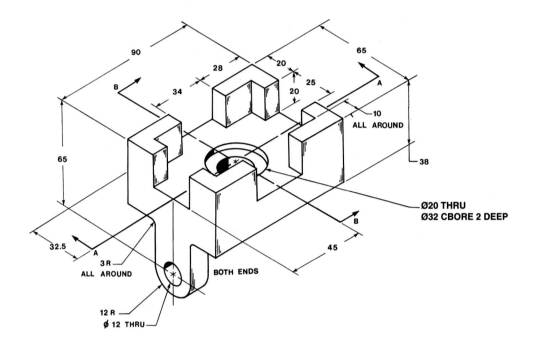

EX6-24 INCHES

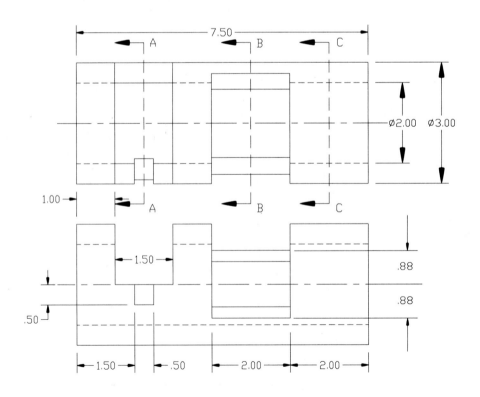

EX6-25 MILLIMETERS

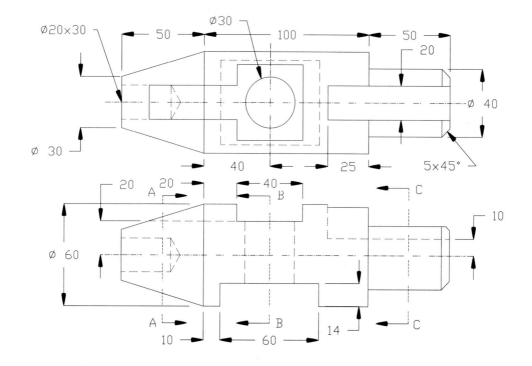

EX6-26 INCHES

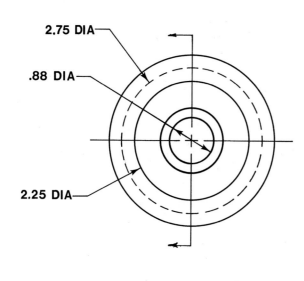

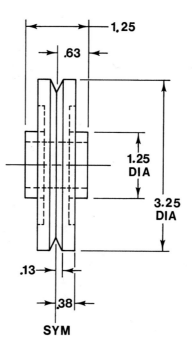

EX6-27 INCHES

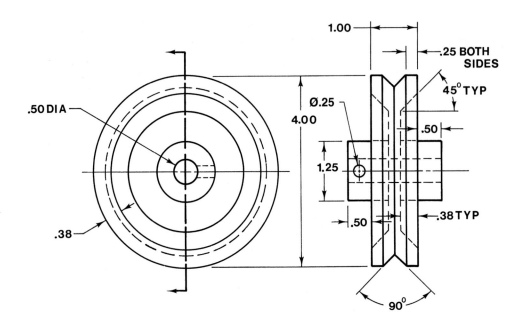

EX6-28 INCHES

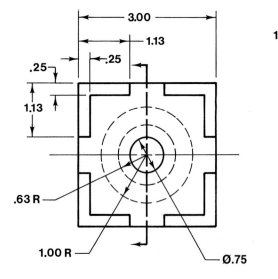

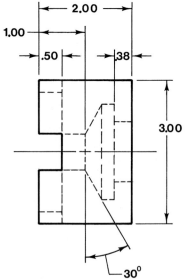

EX6-29 MILLIMETERS

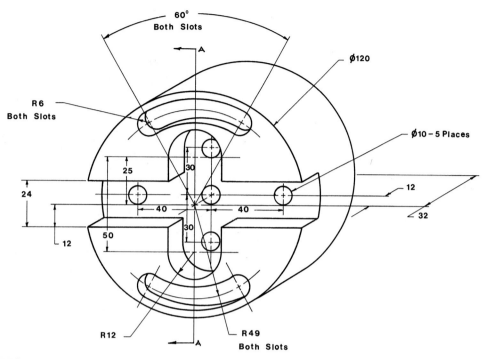

EX6-30 MILLIMETERS

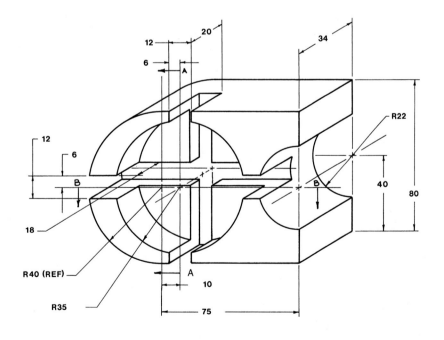

EX6-31 INCHES

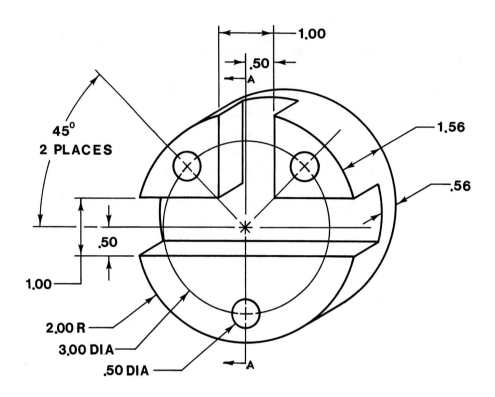

EX6-32

New customer requirements require that the part shown below be redesigned as follows. Draw a front and sectional view of the redesigned object.

1. The diameters of the Ø9 internal access holes are to be increased to Ø12.
2. The diameter of the internal cavity is to be increased to Ø30.
3. The length of the internal cavity is to be increased from 33 to 50.
4. All other sizes and distances are to be increased to maintain the same wall thickness.

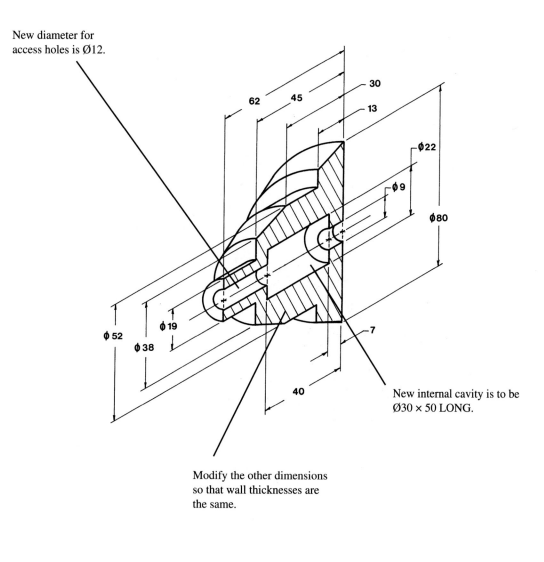

New diameter for access holes is Ø12.

New internal cavity is to be Ø30 × 50 LONG.

Modify the other dimensions so that wall thicknesses are the same.

EX6-33

The following object is to be redesigned to a new set of design requirements. Draw a top view and Section A-A of the new object.

1. Change the overall shape of the object from rectangular to square with an overall length and width of 90.
2. Add two additional extension tabs to make a total of four tabs, each centered along an edge.
3. Increase the size of the extension tabs so that they have Ø15 holes surrounded by a R15 rounded surface.
4. Change the overall height from 65 to 85 while maintaining the 20 height on the corner walls.
5. Change the center hole to Ø16,Ø24 - 82°CSK.

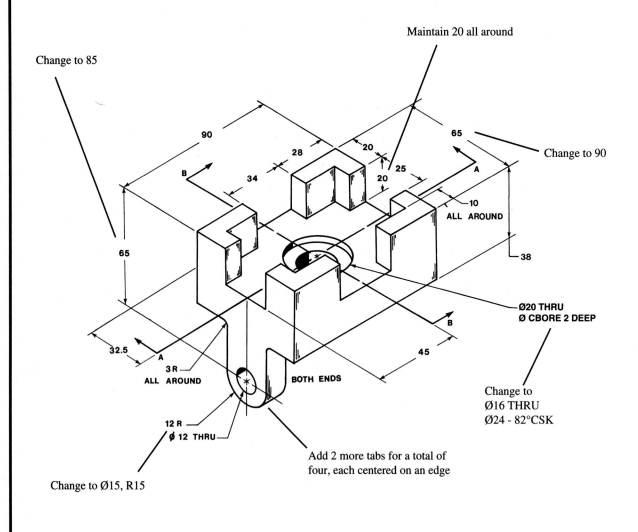

Maintain 20 all around

Change to 85

90

28

20

65

34

20

25

20

B

A

Change to 90

10
ALL AROUND

65

38

Ø20 THRU
Ø CBORE 2 DEEP

B

32.5

45

A

3 R
ALL AROUND

BOTH ENDS

Change to
Ø16 THRU
Ø24 - 82°CSK

12 R

ø 12 THRU

Add 2 more tabs for a total of
four, each centered on an edge

Change to Ø15, R15

Auxiliary Views

7-1 INTRODUCTION

Auxiliary views are orthographic views used to present true-shaped views of slanted and oblique surfaces. Slanted and oblique surfaces appear foreshortened or as edge views in normal orthographic views. Holes in the sur-

faces are elliptical, and other features are also distorted.

Figure 7-1 shows an object with a slanted surface that includes a hole drilled perpendicular to that surface. Note how the slanted surface is foreshortened in both the normal top and side views and that the hole appears as an ellipse in both of these views. The hole appears as an edge

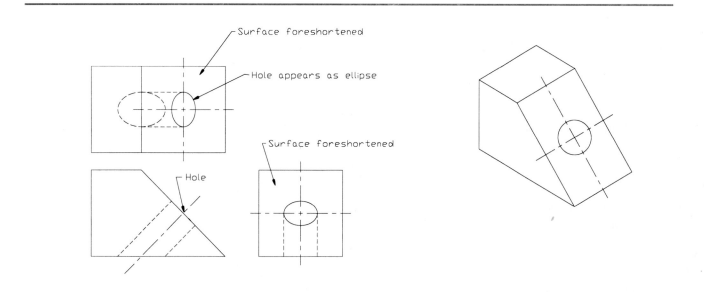

Figure 7-1

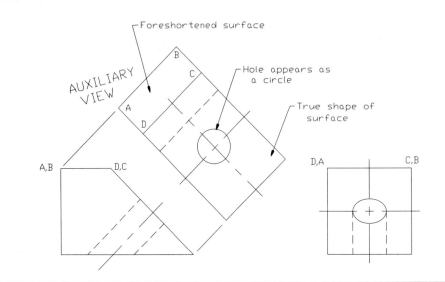

Figure 7-2

view with hidden lines in the front view, so none of the normal views show the hole as a circle.

Figure 7-2 shows the same object shown in Figure 7-1. The top and side views are the same, but the top view is replaced with an auxiliary view. The auxiliary view shows the true shape of the slanted surface, and the hole appears as a circle.

The auxiliary view in Figure 7-2 shows the true shape of the slanted surface but a foreshortened view of surface A-B-C-D. In positioning the auxiliary view so that it generated the true shape of the slanted surface, the other surfaces were foreshortened.

The book's drawing disk includes a three-dimensional drawing of the object shown in both Figure 7-1 and 7-2. The drawing's file name is F7-1. Call up the drawing and rotate it to a position that looks straight down the hole. This is the orientation for the auxiliary view.

To verify the auxiliary view shown in Figure 7-2

1. Select FILE, OPEN, A:drive,F7-1

This step assumes that the drawing disk is in the A: drive. If it is not, be sure to specify the correct drive.

2. Select the VIEW pulldown menu, then 3D DYNAMIC VIEW

Select objects:

3. Window the entire object

CAmera/TArget/Distance/POints/PAn/Zoom/ TWist/CLip/Hide/Off/Undo/<eXit>:

4. Type CA ENTER

Toggle angle in/Enter angle from XY plane<xx.xx>:

5. Rotate the object so that you are looking directly down the center line of the hole. Note how the object looks in various orientations. When you are done rotating the object, press ENTER.

Toggle angle from/Enter angle in XY from X axis<xx.xx>:

6. Rotate the object again and study how it looks at various orientations.
7. ENTER

7-2 PROJECTION BETWEEN NORMAL AND AUXILIARY VIEWS

Information about an object's features can be projected between the normal views and any additional auxiliary views by establishing reference planes. A reference plane RPT is located between the top and front views of Figure 7-3. The plane appears as a horizontal line and its location is arbitrary. In the example shown, the plane was located 10mm from the top view.

A second reference plane RPA was established parallel to the slanted surface at a location that prevents the aux-

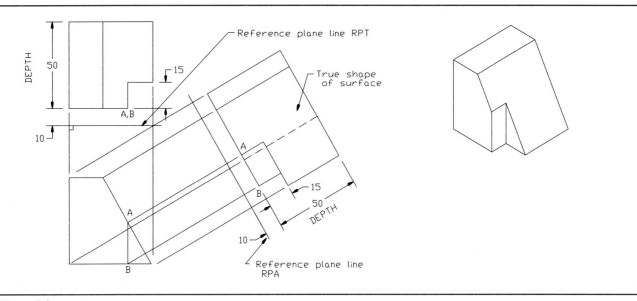

Figure 7-3

iliary view from interfering with the top view. The MOVE command can be used to move the top view further away from the front view if necessary.

Information is projected from the front view into the auxiliary view by using projection lines perpendicular to reference plane RPA.

The depth of the object is transferred from the top view to the auxiliary view. Figure 7-3 shows the 50mm depth and 15mm slot depth dimensioned in both the top and auxiliary view.

Figure 7-4 shows information projected from given front and side views into an auxiliary view. Reference planes RPS and RPA were located 10mm from and paral-

lel to the side and auxiliary views, and information is projected from the front view into the auxiliary view using lines perpendicular to plane RPA. The depth information was transferred from the side view to the auxiliary view.

Figure 7-5 shows an object that has a slanted surface in the top view. The reference plane line RPA for the auxiliary view is located parallel to the slanted surface, and another reference plane RPF (horizontal line) is established between the front and top views. Information is projected from the top view into the auxiliary view using lines perpendicular to RPA. The 30mm height measurement is transferred from the front view into the auxiliary view.

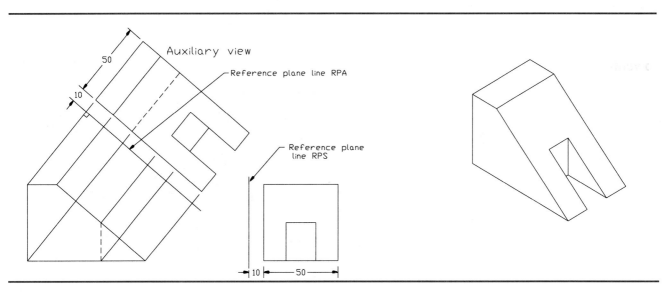

Figure 7-4

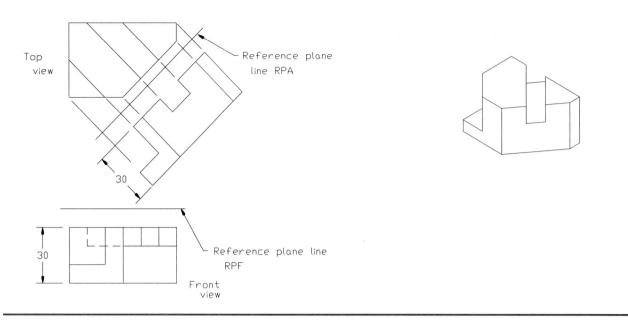

Figure 7-5

Reference plane lines and projection lines drawn perpendicular to them are best drawn by rotating the drawing's axis system, indicated by the crosshairs, so that it is parallel to the slanted surface. A separate LAYER may be created for projection lines.

To rotate the drawing's axis system

See Figure 7-6.

1. Type SNAP in response to a Command: prompt

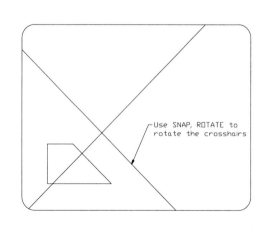

Figure 7-6

The command prompts are as follows.

Command: snap
Snap spacing or ON/OFF/Aspect/Rotate/Style <0>:

2. Select Rotate ENTER

Base point <0.0000,0.0000>:

3. Accept the default value by pressing ENTER

Rotation angle <0>:

4. Type 45 ENTER

The crosshairs will rotate 45 degrees counterclockwise. Any angle value, including negative values, may be used.

The GRID will also be rotated and the SNAP command will limit the crosshairs to spacing aligned with the rotated axis. ORTHO will limit lines to horizontal and vertical relative to the rotated axis.

The angle value entered for SNAP, ROTATE is always interpreted as an absolute value. For example, if the above procedure is repeated and a value of 60 entered, the crosshairs would advance only 15 degrees from their present location, or 60 degrees from the system's absolute 0 degree axis system.

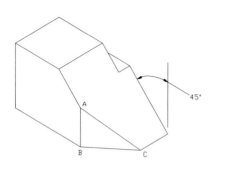

Figure 7-7

7-3 SAMPLE PROBLEM SP7-1

Figure 7-7 shows an object that includes a slanted surface. The front, top, and auxiliary views projected from the slanted surface were developed as follows. See Figure 7-8.

1. DRAW the front and top orthographic views as explained in Chapter 5.

Use the MOVE command to position the top view so that it will not interfere with the auxiliary view.

2. Establish two reference plane lines: RPT parallel to the top view (horizontal line) and RPA parallel to the slanted surface (45-degree line).

In this example the reference plane line for the top view is located along the lower edge of the view.
Use SNAP, ROTATE to establish an axis system parallel to the slanted surface. The slanted surface is 45 degrees to the horizontal. Turn ORTHO on and draw a line parallel to the slanted surface.
Option: Create a LAYER for projection lines.

3. Project lines perpendicular to RPA from the drawing's feature presented in the front view into the area of the auxiliary view. Use OSNAP, INT to ensure accuracy.
4. Use INQUIRY, DIST to determine the distance from the reference plane line RPT to the object's features.
5. Use OFFSET to draw a LINE parallel to the RPA at a distance equal to the distances of the object's features.
6. ERASE and TRIM any excess lines and SAVE the drawing if desired.

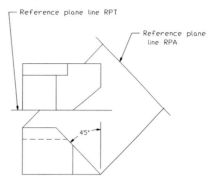

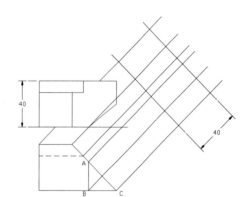

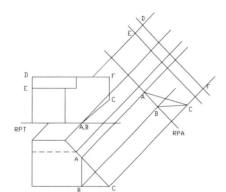

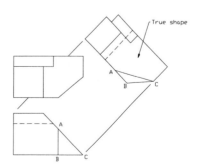

Figure 7-8

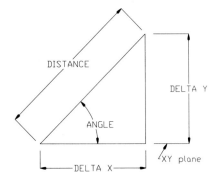

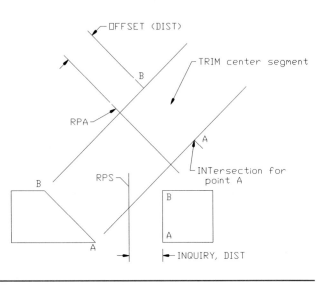

Figure 7-9

7-4 TRANSFERRING LINES BETWEEN VIEWS

Objects are often dimensioned so that only some of their edge lines are dimensioned. This means that OFFSET may not be used to transfer distances to auxiliary views until the line length is known. There are three possible methods that can be used to transfer an edge line of unknown length: measure the line length using INQUIRY, DIST and then use the determined distance with the OFFSET command, use GRIPS and ROTATE and MOVE the line, or use COPY, MODIFY, ROTATE and relocate the line. The procedures are as follows.

To measure the length of a line

1. Type DIST in response to a command prompt

Command: Dist
First point:

2. Select one end of the line. Use OSNAP, END or INT if necessary to ensure accuracy. The intersection of one of the projection lines with a reference plane is usually used.

Second point:

3. Select the other end of the line. Use OSNAP, END or INT if necessary to ensure accuracy.

The following style display will appear in the screen's prompt area.

Distance=40, Angle in X-Y Plane=45, Angle from the X-Y Plane=0
Delta X=28.2885, Delta Y=28.2885, Delta Z=0.0000

Figure 7-9 shows the meaning of the displayed distance information.

Record the distance and use it with the OFFSET command to locate the line's endpoints relative to a reference plane. See Figure 7-9.

To GRIP and MOVE a line

See Figure 7-10.

1. COPY the line and move the copy to an open area of the drawing.
2. Select the line and highlight its GRIP points by clicking the line while a Command prompt is displayed.
3. Select the line's lower endpoint.
4. For the DOS version select ROTATE from the menu; for the WINDOWS version press the ENTER key until the ROTATE commands appear on the command line

ROTATE
<Rotate angle>/ Base point/ Copy/ Undo/ Reference/ eXit:

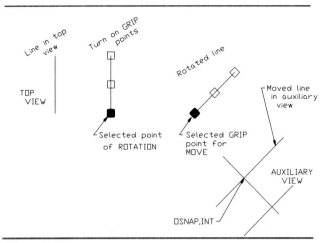

Figure 7-10

5. Type 45 ENTER

The DISTANCE (DIST) command explained above can also be used to determine the angle of a slanted surface if it is not known.

6. Select the line's lower endpoint again.
7. Select the MOVE command.
8. MOVE the line to the auxiliary view. Use OSNAP if necessary to ensure accuracy.

To ROTATE and MOVE a line

1. COPY the line and move the line to an open area of the drawing.
2. Select the GRIPS ROTATE command and rotate the line 45 degrees. See Section 3-19.
3. Select the MOVE command and relocate the line to the auxiliary view. Use OSNAP if necessary to ensure accuracy.

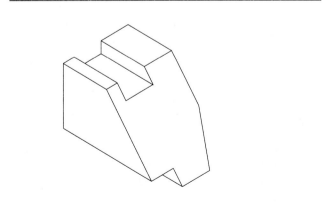

Figure 7-11

7-5 SAMPLE PROBLEM SP7-2

Figure 7-11 shows an object that contains two slanted surfaces and two cutouts. Draw a front and right-side orthographic view, and an auxiliary view. See Figure 7-12.

1. DRAW the front and side orthographic views as described in Chapter 5.
2. Define a reference plane RPS between the front and side views.
3. Use SNAP, ROTATE (37.5) to align the crosshairs with the slanted surface. The 37.5-degree value was determined using INQUIRY, DIST.
4. Draw a reference plane line RPA parallel to the slanted surface and project the features of the object into the auxiliary view area.
5. Transfer the distance measurements from RPS and the side view into the auxiliary view.

Label the various points as needed.

6. ERASE and TRIM any excess lines and SAVE the drawing if desired.

7-6 PROJECTING ROUNDED SURFACES

Rounded surfaces are projected into auxiliary views as they were projected into the normal orthographic views as described in Section 5-26. Additional lines are added to one of the normal orthographic views and then projected into the other normal view. The additional lines define a series of points that define the outside shape of the surface. The two views with the added lines are used to project and transfer the points into the auxiliary view.

7-7 SAMPLE PROBLEM SP7-3

Figure 7-13 shows a cylindrical object that includes a slanted surface. Draw the front, side, and auxiliary views.
The procedure is as follows. See Figure 7-14.

1. DRAW the front and side orthographic views.
2. DRAW a reference plane line RPS.

In this example the reference plane line was located on the side view's vertical center line.

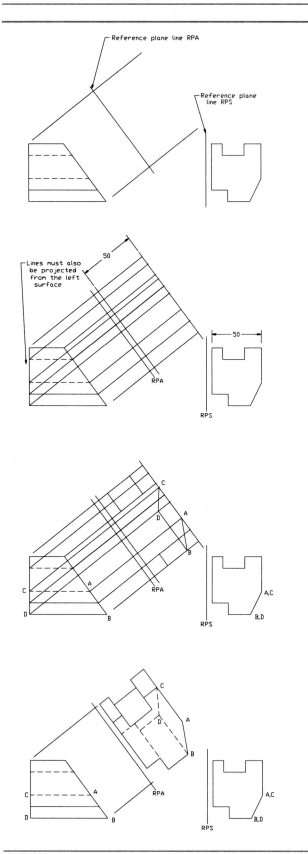

Figure 7-12

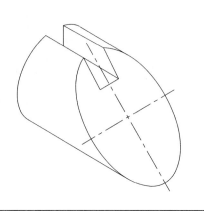

Figure 7-13

3. DRAW a reference plane line RPA parallel to the slanted surface. The reference plane line will also be used as the center line for the auxiliary view.

In this example the endpoints of both the major and minor axes of the projected elliptical auxiliary view are known as well as the angle of the auxiliary view. It is therefore not necessary to define points in the circular side view, as was done in Section 5-27. Enough information is present to draw directly the elliptical shape in the auxiliary view.

4. Draw the elliptical-shaped surfaces in the auxiliary view as shown.
5. Transfer the width and location of the slot from the side view to the auxiliary view.
6. ERASE and TRIM any excess lines and SAVE the drawing if desired.

7-8 PROJECTING IRREGULAR SURFACES

Auxiliary views of irregular surfaces are created by projecting information from given normal orthographic views into the auxiliary views in a manner similar to the way information was projected between orthographic views. See Chapter 5. The irregular surface is defined by a series of points along its edge line. The location of the points is random, although more points should be used when the curve's shape is changing sharply than where the curve tends to be smoother.

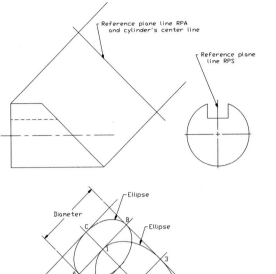

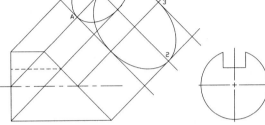

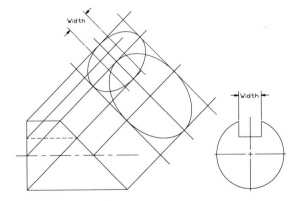

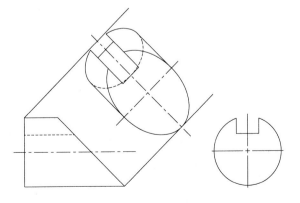

7-9 SAMPLE PROBLEM SP7-4

Figure 7-15 shows an object that includes an irregular surface. Draw a front, side orthographic view and auxiliary view of the object. The procedure is described below. See Figure 7-16.

1. DRAW the front and side views as defined in Chapter 5.
2. DRAW two reference LINES: RPF between the front and side views, and RPA parallel to the slanted surface in the side view.

Use SNAP, ROTATE to align the crosshairs with the slanted surface.

3. Define points along the irregular surface edge line in the front view and project the points into the side view using horizontal lines.
4. Project the points into the auxiliary view using lines perpendicular to line RPA. Label the points and their projection lines.
5. Transfer the depth measurements from RPS and the object's features and the points defining the irregular curve to the auxiliary view.

Use the DISTANCE (DIST) command to determine the distance from RPF to the points. Record the distances.

A = 3.00
B = 2.91
C = 2.62
D = 1.50
E = 0.30
F = 0.09
G = 0

Use OFFSET to draws lines parallel to RPA.

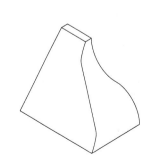

Figure 7-15

Figure 7-14

6. Use PLINE, PEDIT, FIT CURV as explained in Chapter 2 to draw the irregular curve required in the auxiliary view. Use ED VERTX to smooth the curve if necessary.

7. Project the points defined in the front view to the back surface (far right vertical line) in the side

view and project the points into the auxiliary view.

8. Use PLINE, PEDIT, FIT CURVE to draw the required irregular curve.

9. ERASE and TRIM any excess lines and SAVE the drawing if desired.

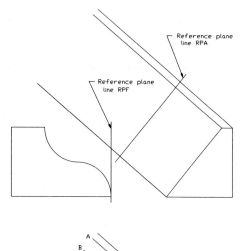

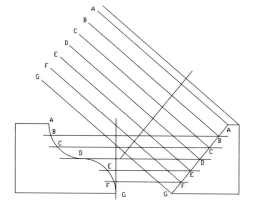

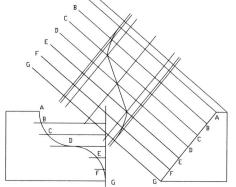

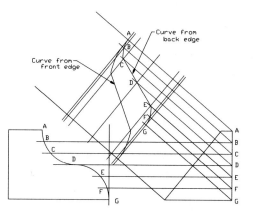

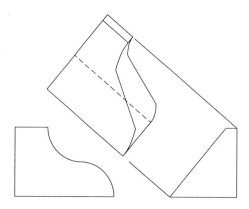

Figure 7-16

7-10 SAMPLE PROBLEM SP7-5

Figure 7-17 shows a top view and an auxiliary view of an object. Redraw the given views and add the front and right-side views. The procedure is described below.

1. DRAW a reference plane line RPA parallel to the auxiliary view and a reference plane line RPT, a horizontal line.

The object contains a dihedral angle, and the auxil-iary view is positioned to align with the vertex line of the angle. Reference plane RPA is perpendicular to the vertex of the dihedral angle's vertex.

2. Project information from the top view and transfer information from the auxiliary view into the front view.
3. Project information from the front view and transfer information from the top view to the side view.
4. ERASE and TRIM any excess lines and SAVE the drawing if desired.

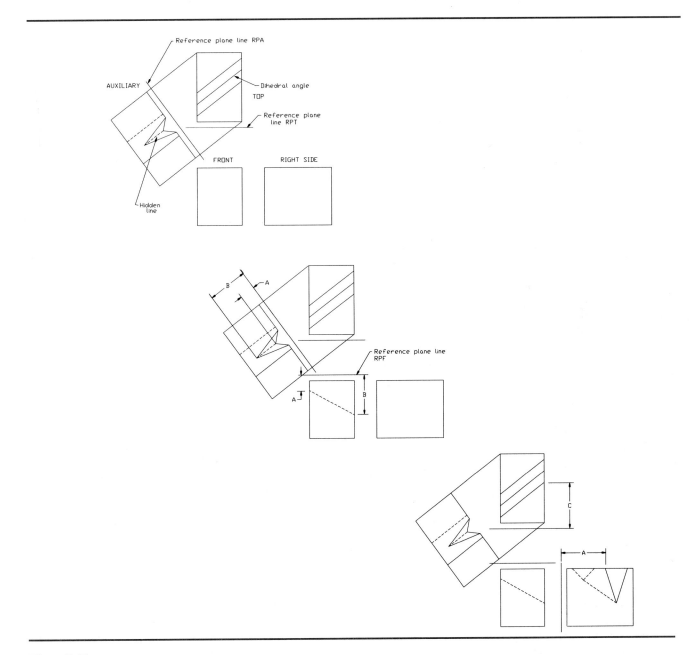

Figure 7-17

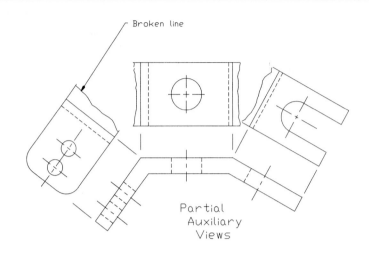

Figure 7-18

7-11 PARTIAL AUXILIARY VIEWS

Auxiliary views help present true-shaped views of slanted and oblique surfaces, but in doing so generate foreshortened views of other surfaces. It is often clearer to create an auxiliary view of just the slanted surface and omit the surfaces that would be foreshortened. Auxiliary views that show only one surface of an object are called partial auxiliary views.

Figure 7-18 shows a front view and three partial views of the object: a partial top view, and two partial auxiliary views. A broken line (see Section 6-14) may be used to show that the partial auxiliary view is part of a larger view that has been omitted. Likewise, hidden lines may or may not be included. Figure 7-19 shows front, side, and two partial auxiliary views of an object. Both the hidden lines and broken lines were omitted. If you are unsure about the interpretation of a view with hidden lines omitted, add a note to the drawing next to the partial views: ALL HIDDEN LINES OMITTED FOR CLARITY.

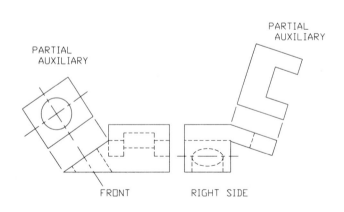

Figure 7-19

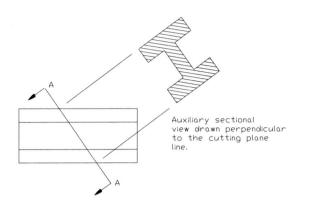

Figure 7-20

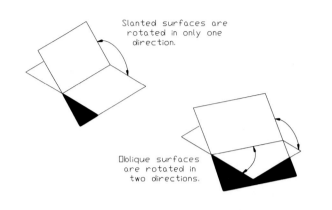

Figure 7-22

7-12 SECTIONAL AUXILIARY VIEWS

Sectional views may also be drawn as auxiliary views. Figure 7-20 shows an auxiliary sectional view. The cutting plane line is positioned across the object. A reference plane line is drawn parallel to the cutting plane line, and information is projected into the auxiliary sectional view using lines perpendicular to the cutting plane line.

Figure 7-21 shows a front, partial auxiliary, and auxiliary sectional view of an object. In this example the partial sectional view was used to help clarify the shape of the object's feature that would appear vague in the normal top or side views.

7-13 AUXILIARY VIEWS OF OBLIQUE SURFACES

The true shape of an oblique surface cannot be determined by a single auxiliary view taken directly from the oblique surface. An auxiliary view shows the true shape of a surface only when it is taken at exactly 90 degrees to the surface. The auxiliary views taken for Sample Problems 1 through 5 were taken from slanted surfaces.

Slanted surfaces are surfaces that are rotated about only one axis. See Figure 7-22. One of the orthographic views must be an edge view of the surface (the surface appears as a line) for an auxiliary view created by projecting lines perpendicular to that view to show the true shape of the surface.

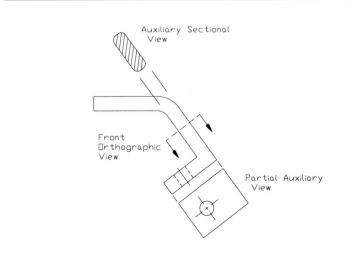

Figure 7-21

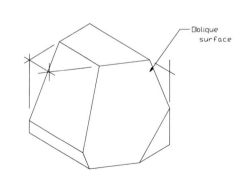

Figure 7-23

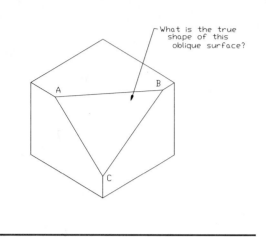

Figure 7-24

Oblique surfaces are surfaces rotated about two axes. See Figure 7-22 and Figure 7-23. This means that none of the normal orthographic views will show the oblique surface as an edge view; there is no given end view of the surface. This in turn means that an auxiliary view taken directly from one of the given views will not be perpendicular to the surface and therefore will not show the true shape of the surface. An auxiliary view that shows an edge view of the surface must first be created, then a second auxiliary taken perpendicular to one of the other normal orthographic views is needed to show the true shape of the surface.

7-14 SECONDARY AUXILIARY VIEWS

Consider the object shown in Figure 7-24. What is the true shape of surface A-B-C? An auxiliary view taken perpendicular to the surface will show its true shape, but what is the angle for a plane perpendicular to the surface?

Figure 7-25 shows the normal orthographic views of the object.

Start by choosing an edge line in the plane that is perpendicular to either the X or Y axis. Edge line A-B in the front view is a horizontal line, so it is parallel to the X axis. Take an auxiliary view aligned with the top view of the edge line (you're looking straight down the line). This auxiliary view will be perpendicular to the edge line and will generate an end view of the plane. A second auxiliary view can then be taken perpendicular to the end view that will show the true shape of the surface.

Figures 7-26a and 7-26b show how a secondary auxiliary view is created for the object shown in Figures 7-24 and 7-25. The specific procedure is as follows.

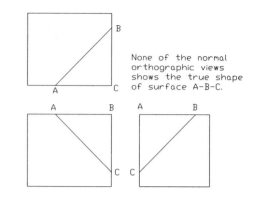

None of the normal orthographic views shows the true shape of surface A-B-C.

Figure 7-25

To draw a secondary auxiliary view

1. DRAW the normal orthographic views of the object.
2. DRAW a reference plane RPT between the front and top views.
3. EXTEND a line from the top view of line A-B in the area for the first auxiliary view.

The EXTEND command can be used by drawing a construction line slightly beyond the expected area of the first auxiliary view, then using the construction line as an EXTEND boundary line (see Chapter 2), and extending line A-B to the boundary. The construction line can then be erased.

4. DRAW a reference plane line RPA1 perpendicular to the line A-B extension.

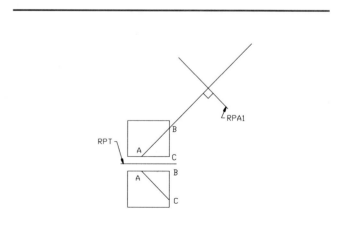

Figure 7-26a

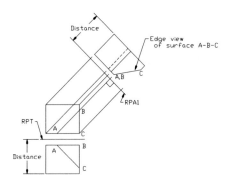

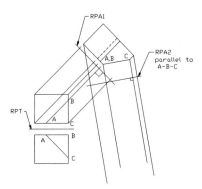

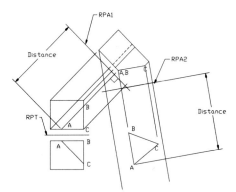

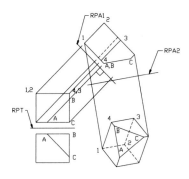

Use SNAP, ROTATE to align the crosshairs with the extension line. DISTANCE can be used to determine the line's angle if it is not known.

5. Project the feature of the object into the auxiliary view using lines perpendicular to RPA1.
6. Transfer the distance measurements from RPT and the front view as shown.
7. ERASE and TRIM any excess lines and create the first auxiliary view.

The surface A-B-C should appear as a straight line. This is an edge view of surface A-B-C.

8. Use SNAP, ROTATE and align the crosshairs with the end view of surface A-B-C. DISTANCE can be used to determine the angle of the edge view line.
9. Draw a reference plane line RPA2 parallel to the edge view of the surface.
10. Project the features of the object into the second auxiliary view using lines perpendicular to RPA2.
11. Transfer the distance measurements from RPA1 and the top view as shown.
12. ERASE and TRIM any excess lines and save the drawing if desired.

The secondary auxiliary view shows the true shape of surface A-B-C.

Figure 7-27 shows another example of a secondary auxiliary view used to show the true shape of an oblique surface. In this example the first auxiliary view was taken from line F-A in the front view because it is a vertical line

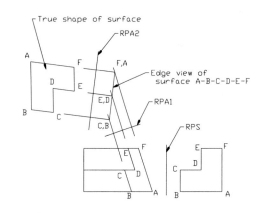

Figure 7-26b

Figure 7-27

in the side view. The distance measurements came from the top view. The procedure used is the same as described above.

The auxiliary view shown in Figure 7-27 includes only the oblique surface. This is a partial auxiliary view. The purpose of the auxiliary view is to determine the true shape of the oblique surface. All the other surfaces would be foreshortened, not their true shape, if included in the auxiliary views.

7-15 SAMPLE PROBLEM SP7-6

What is the true shape of the plane shown in Figure 7-28?

None of the edge lines are horizontal or vertical lines, so a line must be defined within the plane that is either horizontal or vertical. The added line can then be used to generate the two auxiliary views needed to define the true shape of the plane.

The procedure is as follows. See Figure 7-29.

1. DRAW a horizontal LINE from point A in the front view.

Use OSNAP, INT with ORTHO on and draw the line across the view. Use TRIM to remove the excess portion of the line.

2. Define the intersection of the new line with one of the plane's edge lines (D-C) as x.
3. Project line A-x into the top view.

Option: Create a LAYER for projection lines.

The location of point A is already known in the top view. The location of point x in the top view can be found by drawing a vertical line from point x in the front view so

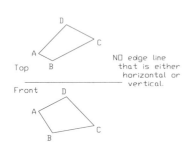

Figure 7-28

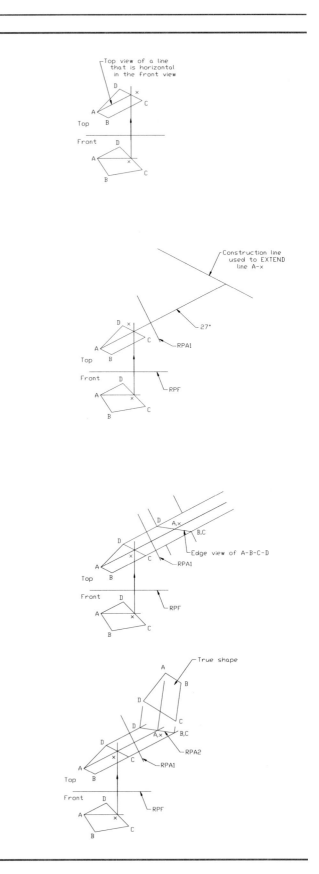

Figure 7-29

that the line intersects line D-C in the top view. Use OSNAP, INT, ORTHO to ensure accuracy.

4. EXTEND line A-x into the area for the first auxiliary view.

Draw a construction line to use as a boundary line for the EXTEND command.

5. DRAW two reference plane lines: RPT between the front and top views, and RPA1 perpendicular to the extension of line A-x.

Use SNAP, ROTATE to align the crosshairs with the extension of line A-x.

6. Project the plane's corner points into the area of the first auxiliary view from the top view. Transfer the distance measurements from RPT and the front view.

Use the DISTANCE command to determine the distance from RPF and the corner points of the surface. Use OFFSET to transfer the point distance from RPF to RPA1. Use TRIM to remove the internal portion of the offset lines. This will help clarify the drawing by removing excess lines from the auxiliary view, but will retain intersection points needed to draw lines using OSNAP, INT.

The plane should appear as a straight line, the end view of the plane.

7. DRAW a third reference plane line RPA2 parallel to the end view of the plane and project the plane's corner points into the secondary auxiliary view area.

8. Transfer the depth distances from RPA1 and the top view to RPA2 and secondary auxiliary view.

9. ERASE and TRIM any excess lines and SAVE the drawing if desired.

The secondary auxiliary view shows the true shape of surface A-B-C-D.

7-16 SECONDARY AUXILIARY VIEW OF AN ELLIPSE

Figure 7-30 shows the front and side views of an oblique surface that includes a foreshortened view of a hole, i.e., an ellipse. Also included are two auxiliary views, the second of which shows the hole as a circle.

The ellipse is projected by first determining the correct projection angle that will produce an edge view of surface A-B-C-D. In this example line B-C appears as a vertical line in the side view, so its front view can be used to project the required edge view.

It is known that the secondary view of the surface will show the hole as a circle, so only a radius value need be carried between the views. In this example point 1 in the front view was projected into the first auxiliary view and then into the second auxiliary view, thereby defining the radius of the circle.

The hole is located at the center of the surface, meaning its center lines are located on the midpoints of the edge lines in the secondary auxiliary views. If the hole's center point was not in the center of the surface, the intersections of the hole's center lines with the surface's edge lines would also have to be projected into the secondary auxiliary view to accurately locate the hole.

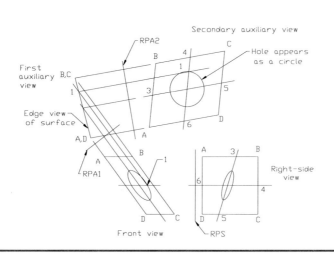

Figure 7-30

7-17 EXERCISE PROBLEMS

Given the outlines for front, side, and auxiliary views as shown, substitute one of the side views shown in exercise problems EX7-1A to EX7-1D and complete the front and auxiliary views. All dimensions are in millimeters.

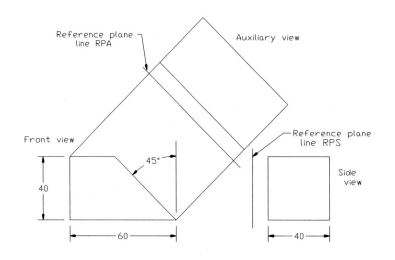

EX7-1A

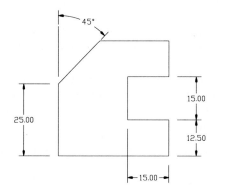

EX7-1C

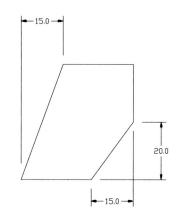

EX7-1B

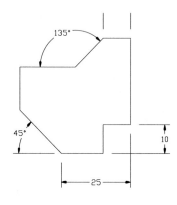

EX7-1D

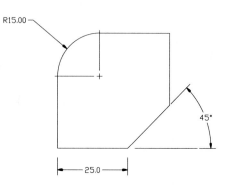

EX7-2

Given the outlines for a front, side, and auxiliary view as shown, substitute one of the side views shown in exercise problems EX7-2A to EX7-2D and complete the front and auxiliary views. All dimensions are in millimeters.

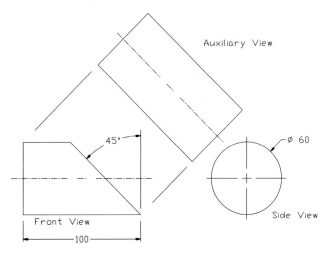

EX7-2A

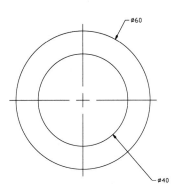

EX7-2B

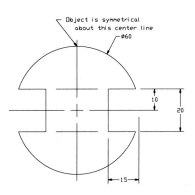

EX7-2C

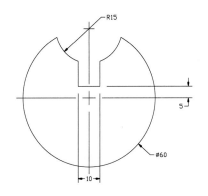

EX7-2D

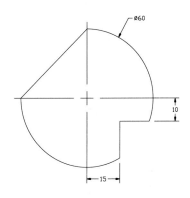

Draw two orthographic views and an auxiliary view for each of the objects in exercise problems EX7-3 to EX7-6.

EX7-3 MILLIMETERS

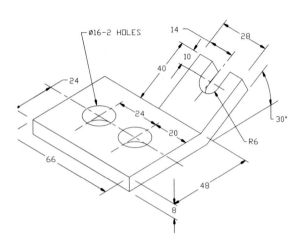

EX7-5 INCHES

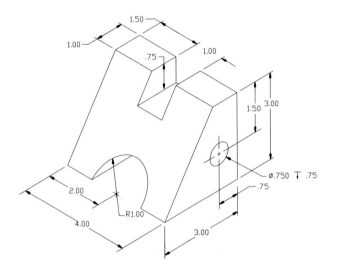

EX7-4 MILLIMETERS

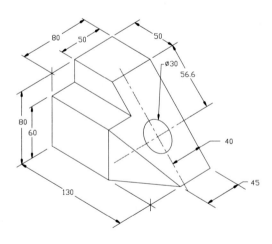

EX7-6 MILLIMETERS

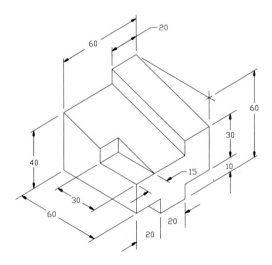

Redraw the given orthographic views in exercise problems EX7-7 to EX7-41 and add the appropriate auxiliary view.

EX7-7 MILLIMETERS

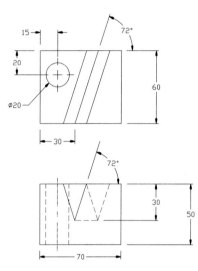

EX7-9 INCHES

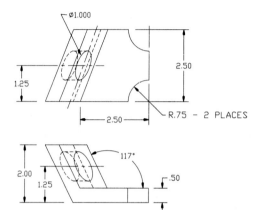

EX7-10 MILLIMETERS

EX7-8 MILLIMETERS

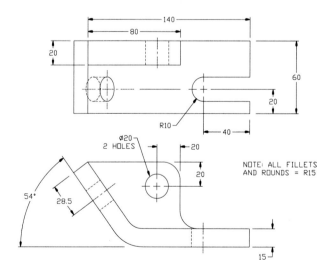

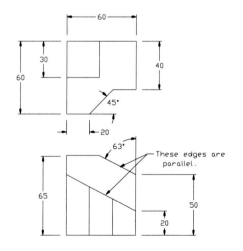

EX7-11 MILLIMETERS

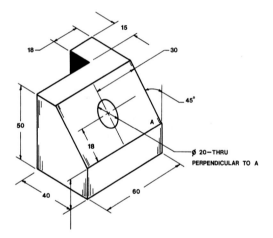

EX7-12 MILLIMETERS

EX7-13 MILLIMETERS

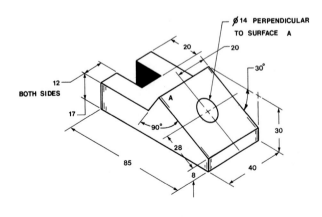

EX7-14 MILLIMETERS

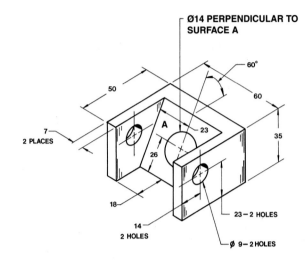

EX7-15 INCHES

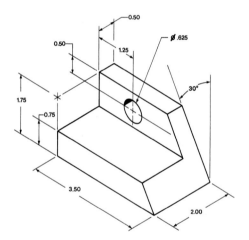

EX7-16 MILLIMETERS

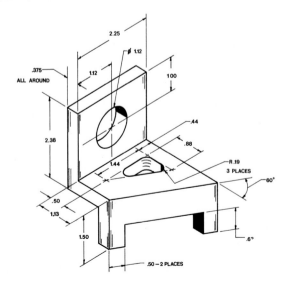

EX7-17 MILLIMETERS

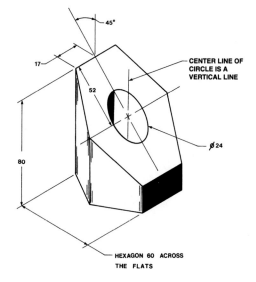

45°

17

52

CENTER LINE OF
CIRCLE IS A
VERTICAL LINE

Ø 24

80

HEXAGON 60 ACROSS
THE FLATS

EX7-20 INCHES

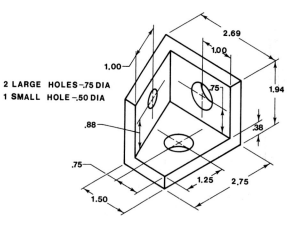

2.69

1.00

1.00

1.94

2 LARGE HOLES -.75 DIA
1 SMALL HOLE -.50 DIA

.75

.88

.38

.75

1.25

2.75

1.50

EX7-18 MILLIMETERS

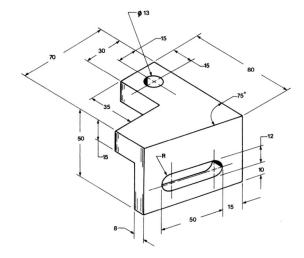

Ø 13

15

70

30

15

80

35

75°

50

15

12

R

10

8

50

15

EX7-21 MILLIMETERS

Ø 50

60
2 PLACES

30

6

12 — 4 PLACES

35

15

80

REGULAR HEXAGON
80 ACROSS THE CORNER

EX7-19 MILLIMETERS

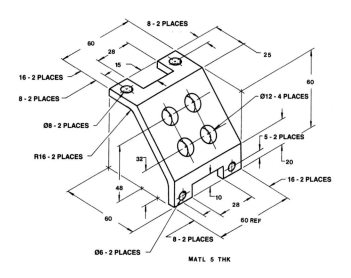

8 - 2 PLACES

60

28

25

15

16 - 2 PLACES

60

8 - 2 PLACES

Ø12 - 4 PLACES

Ø8 - 2 PLACES

5 - 2 PLACES

R16 - 2 PLACES

20

32

16 - 2 PLACES

48

10

28

60

60 REF

8 - 2 PLACES

Ø6 - 2 PLACES

MATL 5 THK

EX7-22 MILLIMETERS

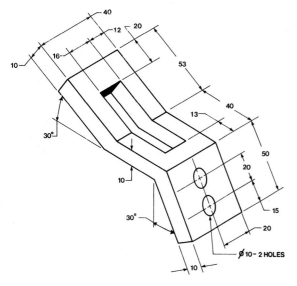

EX7-25 INCHES

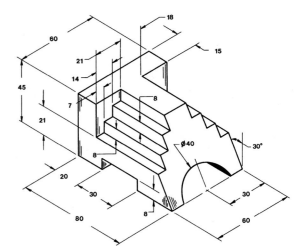

EX7-23 INCHES

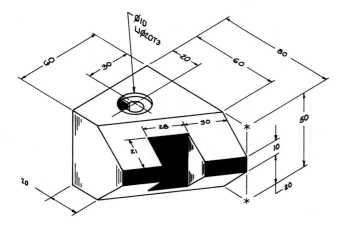

EX7-26 MILLIMETERS

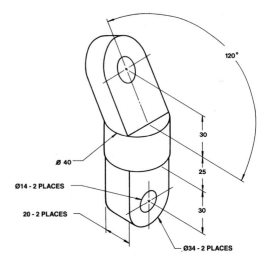

EX7-24 MILLIMETERS

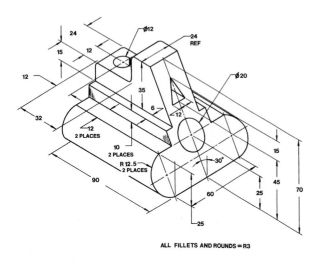

ALL FILLETS AND ROUNDS = R3

EX7-27 MILLIMETERS

EX7-28 MILLIMETERS

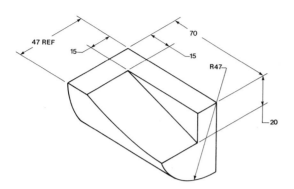

EX7-29 MILLIMETERS

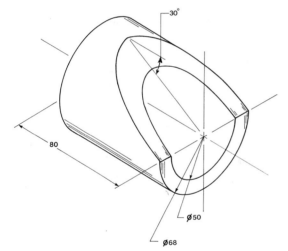

EX7-30 MILLIMETERS

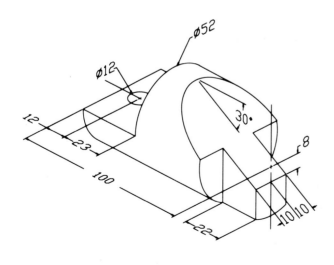

EX7-31 MILLIMETERS

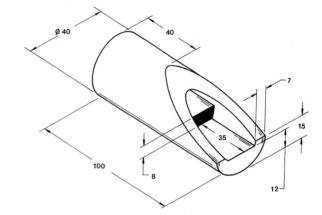

EX7-32 INCHES

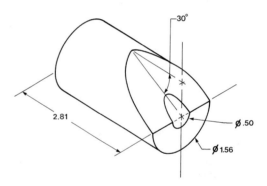

EX7-33 MILLIMETERS

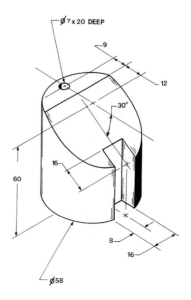

EX7-34 MILLIMETERS

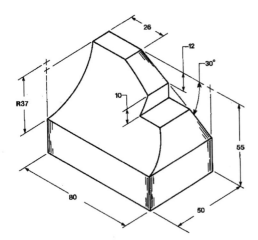

EX7-37 INCHES

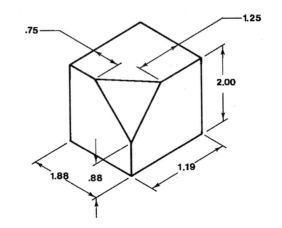

EX7-35 MILLIMETERS

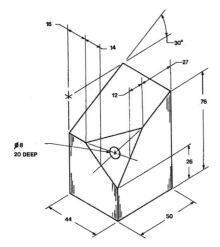

EX7-38 INCHES

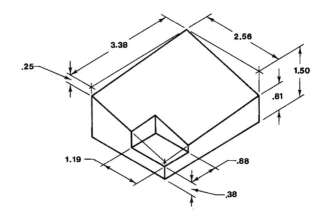

EX7-36 MILLIMETERS

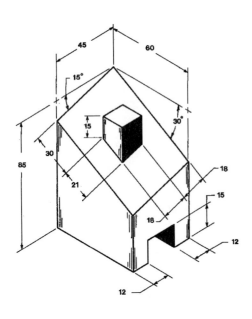

EX7-39 INCHES

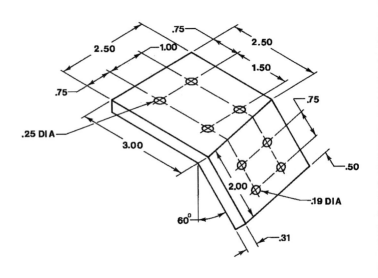

EX7-40 MILLIMETERS

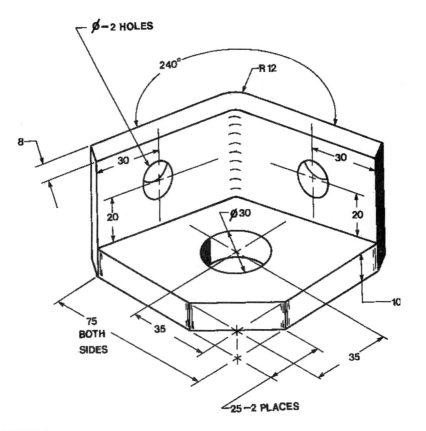

EX7-41 MILLIMETERS

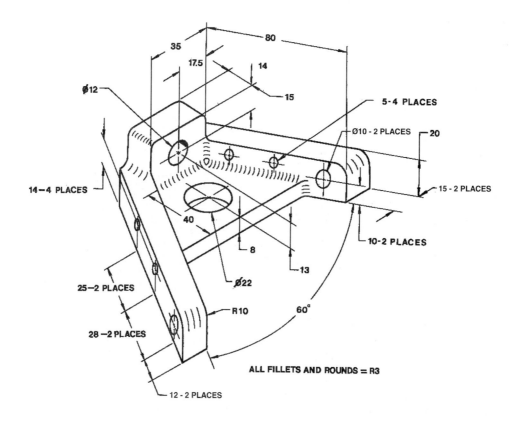

Draw at least two orthographic views and one auxiliary view for the objects in exercise problems EX7-42 to EX7-45.

EX7-42 INCHES

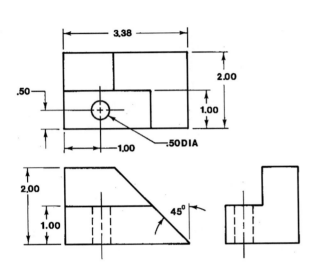

EX7-43 INCHES

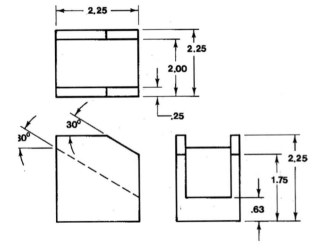

EX7-44 INCHES

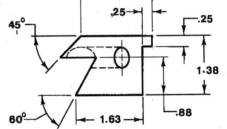

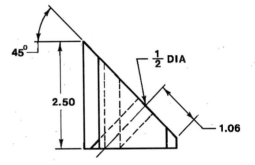

EX7-45 INCHES

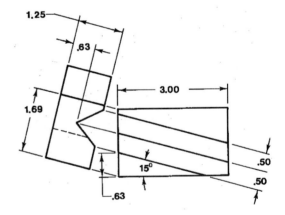

Use a secondary auxiliary view to find the true shape of the planes in exercise problems EX7-46 to EX7-51.

EX7-46 MILLIMETERS

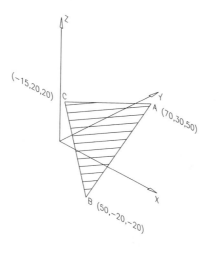

EX7-47 MILLIMETERS

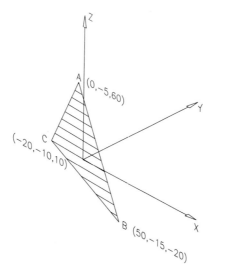

EX7-48 MILLIMETERS

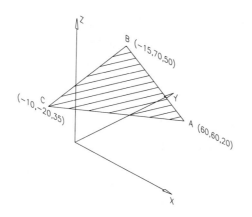

EX7-49 INCHES

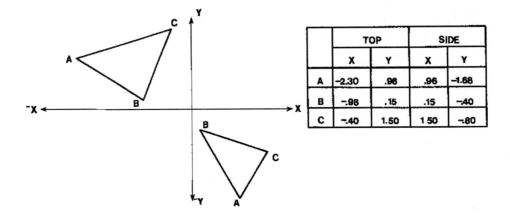

	TOP		SIDE	
	X	Y	X	Y
A	-2.30	.96	.96	-1.68
B	-.98	.15	.15	-.40
C	-.40	1.50	1.50	-.80

EX7-50 MILLIMETERS

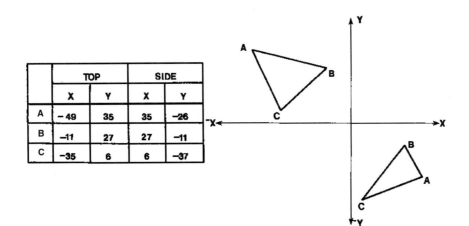

	TOP		SIDE	
	X	Y	X	Y
A	-49	35	35	-26
B	-11	27	27	-11
C	-35	6	6	-37

EX7-51 INCHES

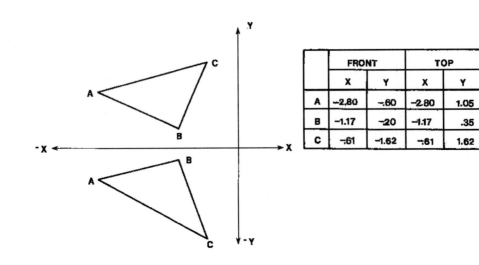

	FRONT		TOP	
	X	Y	X	Y
A	-2.80	-.60	-2.80	1.05
B	-1.17	-.20	-1.17	.35
C	-.61	-1.62	-.61	1.62

EX7-52

Redesign the following object to include 2 Ø10 holes in the slanted surface. The holes should be centered along the longitudinal axis, and spaced so that the distance between the hole's centers equals the distance from the hole's centers to the upper and lower edges of the slanted surface. The holes should be perpendicular to the slanted surface.

Draw front, top, and side views of the object plus an auxiliary view of the slanted surface.

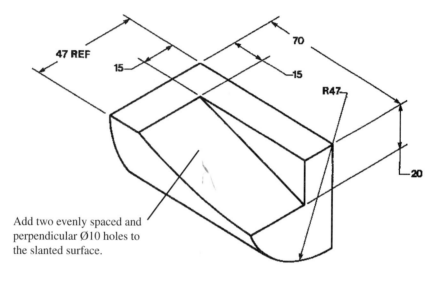

Add two evenly spaced and perpendicular Ø10 holes to the slanted surface.

EX7-53

Add a Ø.750 hole perpendicular to the oblique surface so that the hole's center point is located on the surface's center point.

Draw front, top, and auxiliary views of the object.

Add a Ø .750 hole, perpendicular to the oblique surface, and centered on the surface.

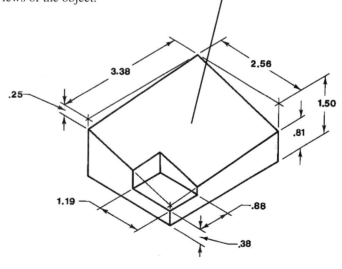

EX7-54

Redesign the following object so that the outside shape is a regular heptagon (seven-sided polygon) 80 across the flats, and the inside Ø50 hole is intersected by 6 evenly spaced slots each 12 wide.

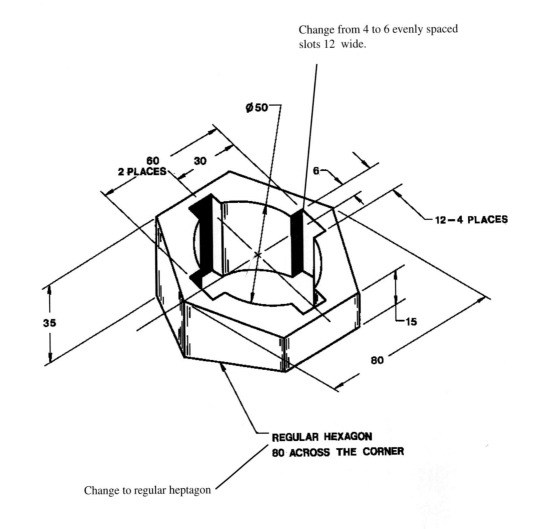

Change from 4 to 6 evenly spaced slots 12 wide.

Ø50

60
2 PLACES

30

6

12 – 4 PLACES

35

15

80

REGULAR HEXAGON
80 ACROSS THE CORNER

Change to regular heptagon

C H A P T E R 8

Dimensioning

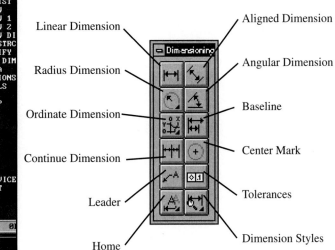

To access the DIMENSION STYLES command in the DOS version, type DDIM in
response to a Command: prompt

Figure 8-1

8-1 INTRODUCTION

This chapter explains the Dimensioning commands. See Figure 8-1. The chapter first explains dimensioning terminology and conventions, then presents an explanation of each command within the Dimensioning heading. The chapter also demonstrates how dimensions are applied to drawings and gives examples of standard drawing conventions and practices.

8-2 TERMINOLOGY AND CONVENTIONS

Some common terms

See Figure 8-2.

Dimension lines: Mechanical drawings; lines between extension lines that end with arrowheads and include a numerical dimensional value located within the line.

Architectural drawings: Lines between extension lines that end with tick marks and include a numerical dimensional value above the line.

Extension lines: Lines that extend away from an object and allow dimensions to be located off the surface of an object.

Leader lines: Lines drawn at an angle, not horizontal or vertical, that are used to dimension specific shapes such as holes. The start point of the leader line includes an arrowhead. Numerical values are drawn at the end opposite the arrowhead.

Linear dimensions: Dimensions that define the straight line distance between two points.

Angular dimensions: Dimensions that define the angular value, measured in degrees, between two straight lines.

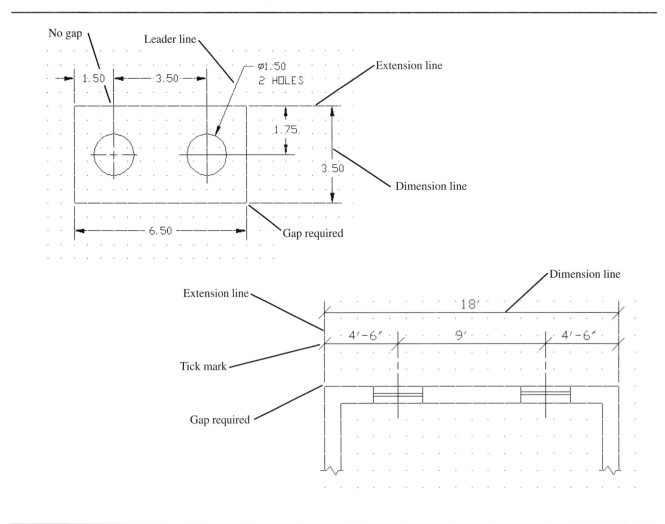

Figure 8-2

Some dimensioning conventions.

See Figure 8-3.

1. Dimension lines should be drawn evenly spaced; that is, the distance between dimension lines is uniform. A general rule of thumb is to locate dimension lines about 1/2 inch or 15 millimeters apart.
2. There should a noticeable gap between the edge of a part and the beginning of an extension line. This serves as a visual break between the object and the extension line. The visual difference between the line types can be furthered by using different colors for the two types of lines.
3. Leader lines are used to define the size of holes and should be positioned so that the arrowhead points at the center point of the hole.
4. Center lines may be used as extension lines. No gap is used when a center line is extended beyond the edge lines of an object.

5. Align dimension lines whenever possible to give the drawing a neat, organized appearance.

Some common errors

See Figure 8-4.

1. Avoid crossing extension lines. Place longer dimensions further away from the object than shorter dimensions.
2. Do not locate dimensions within cutouts; always use extension lines.
3. Do not locate any dimension close to the object. Dimension lines should be at least 1/2 inch or 15 millimeters from the edge of the object.
4. Avoid long extension lines. Locate dimensions in the same general area as the feature being defined.

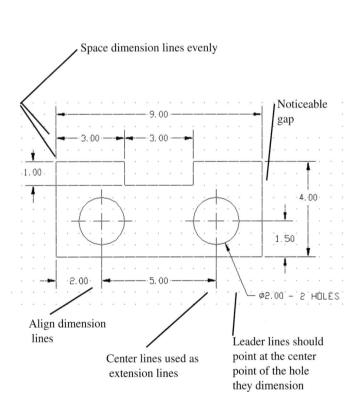

Figure 8-3

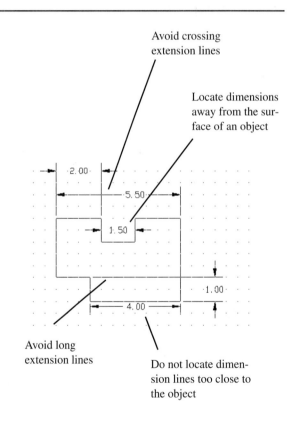

Figure 8-4

8-3 LINEAR DIMENSION

The LINEAR DIMENSION command is used to create either horizontal or vertical dimensions.

To create a horizontal dimension by selecting extension lines

See Figure 8-5.

1. Select the LINEAR DIMENSION command

   Command: _dimlinear
   First extension line origin or RETURN to select:

2. Select the starting point for the first extension line

   Second extension line origin:

3. Select the starting point for the second extension line

   Dimension line location (Text/ Angle /Horizontal/ Vertical/ Rotated):

4. Locate the dimension line location by moving the crosshairs

5. Press the left mouse button after the desired dimension line location has been selected.

The dimensional value locations shown in Figure 8-5 are the default setting locations. The location and style may be changed using the DIMENSION STYLES command discussed in Section 8-4.

To create vertical dimensions

The vertical dimension shown in Figure 8-5 was created using the same procedure demonstrated for the horizontal dimension, except that different extension line origin points were selected. AutoCAD will automatically switch from horizontal to vertical dimension lines as you move the cursor around the object.

If there is confusion between horizontal and vertical lines when adding dimensions, that is, you don't seem to be able to generate a vertical line, type v in response to the following prompt.

Dimension line location (Text/ Angle /Horizontal/ Vertical/ Rotated):

Respond by typing v ENTER. The system will now draw vertical dimension lines.

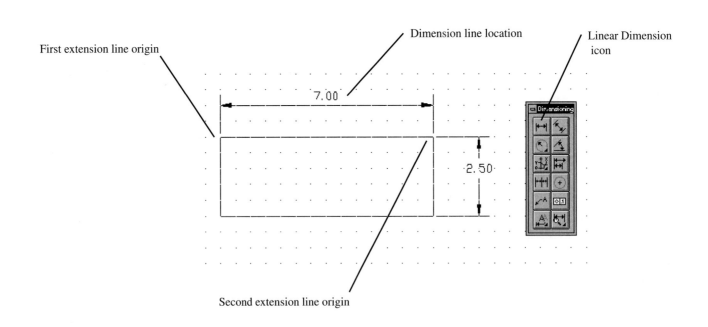

Figure 8-5

To create a horizontal dimension by selecting the distance to be dimensioned

See Figure 8-6.

1. Select the LINEAR DIMENSION command

   Command: _dimlinear
   First extension line origin or RETURN to select:

2. Press the right mouse button

   Select object to Dimension:

This option allows you to select the distance to be dimensioned directly. The option applies only to horizontal and vertical lengths. Aligned dimensions, although linear, are created using the ALIGNED DIMENSION icon.

To change the default dimension text

AutoCAD will automatically create a text value for a given linear distance. A different value or additional information may be added as follows. See Figure 8-7.

1. Select the LINEAR DIMENSION command

   Command: _dimlinear
   First extension line origin or RETURN to select:

2. Select the starting point for the first extension line

   Second extension line origin:

3. Select the starting point for the second extension line

   Dimension line location (Text/ Angle/ Horizontal/ Vertical/ Rotated):

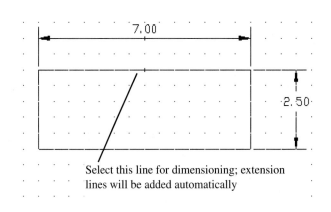

Select this line for dimensioning; extension lines will be added automatically

Figure 8-6

4. Type T ENTER

For WINDOWS the Edit MText dialog box will appear. See Figure 8-8. The "greater than, less than" symbol (<>) that appears in the open area at the top of the dialog box represents the default text. To remove the text, locate the cursor to the right of the symbols and backspace out the symbols, then type in the new text. In the example shown, the default value of 7.00 was replaced with a value of 7.000.

Information can be added before or after the default text by locating the cursor in the appropriate place and typing in the additional information. For example, locating the cursor to the right of the <> symbol and typing -2 PLACES would yield a final value of 7.00-2 PLACES on the drawing.

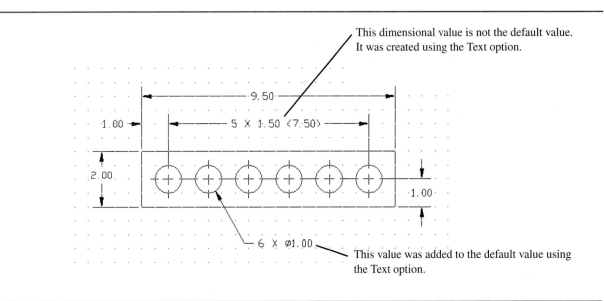

This dimensional value is not the default value. It was created using the Text option.

This value was added to the default value using the Text option.

Figure 8-7

The Edit MText dialog box can also be used to change the height of existing text using the Browse option or the color of text using the Color option. See Figures 8-9 and 8-10. Existing text files may be imported using the Import option.

Figure 8-11 shows the Import Text File dialog box. The various options within the Import Text File dialog box operate as did the options within the Save and Save As dialog boxes. See Section 2-7. The Browse option is the same as described in Section 2-8.

Figure 8-12 shows the MText Properties option. The Properties... option can be used to change the current text style, or to change the size and position of the text.

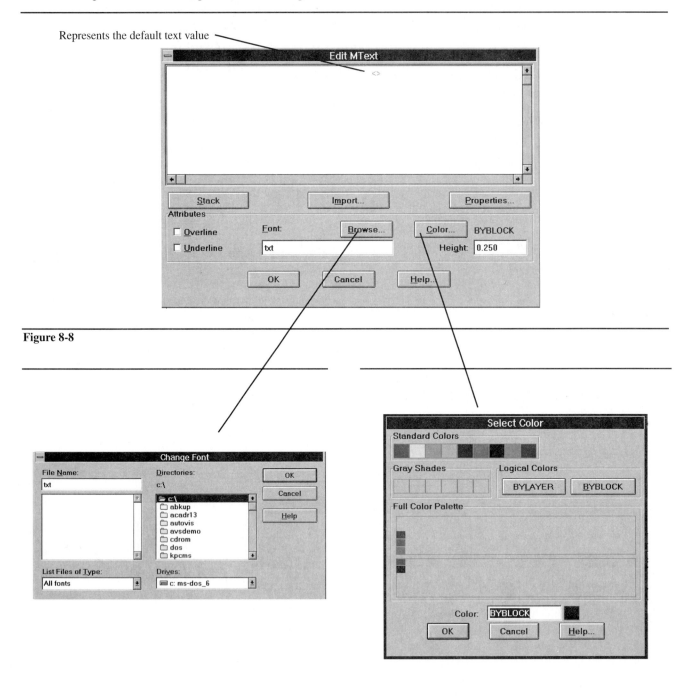

Represents the default text value

Figure 8-8

Figure 8-9

Figure 8-10

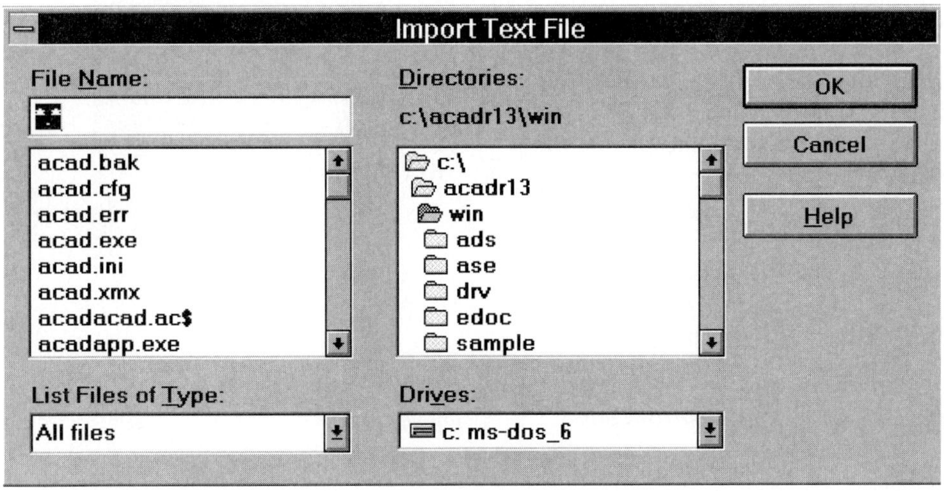

Figure 8-11

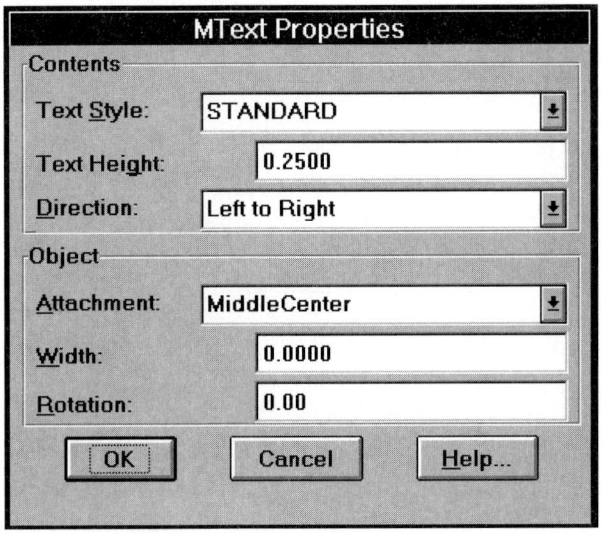

Figure 8-12

For DOS the following prompts will appear.

Dimension line location (Text/ Angle/ Horizontal/ Vertical/ Rotated):

1. Type T ENTER

Dimension text <7.000>:

This value is the value that will be added to the drawing unless a new value is entered.

2. Type 7.00 - 2 PLACES

Dimension line location (Text/ Angle/ Horizontal/ Vertical/ Rotated):

3. Locate the linear dimension by moving the crosshairs

8-4 DIMENSION STYLES

The DIMENSION STYLES command opens a group of dialog boxes that are used to control the appearance of dimensions. Figure 8-13 shows the Dimensioning toolbar with the DIMENSIONING STYLES icon from the WINDOWS version. The DIMENSION STYLES command is accessed in the DOS version by typing DDIM in response to a Command: prompt.

There is a great variety of styles used to create technical drawings. The style difference may be the result of different drawing conventions. For example, architects locate dimensions above the dimension lines, and mechanical engineers locate the dimensions within the dimension lines. AutoCAD works in decimal units for either millimeters or inches, so parameters set for inches would not be usable for millimeter drawings. The DIMENSION STYLES command allows you to conveniently choose and set dimension parameters that suit your particular drawing requirements.

Figure 8-14 shows the Dimension Styles dialog box. The Geometry..., Format..., and Annotation... options are used to change the default style settings. The changes can be saved as a new style, then recalled for future use.

To dimension using the mechanical format and decimal inches

See Figure 8-15. The units for the object shown in Figure 8-15 are decimal inches. The GRID is set at 0.50 spacing.

1. Select the DIMENSION STYLES command

The Dimension Styles dialog box will appear.

2. Select the Geometry... option

The Geometry dialog box will appear. See Figure 8-16.

3. Change the Overall Scale from 1.0000 to 2.0000

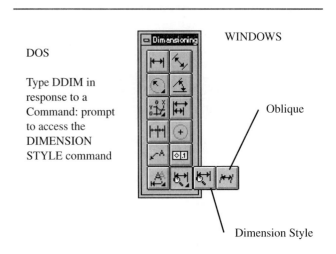

DOS

Type DDIM in response to a Command: prompt to access the DIMENSION STYLE command

WINDOWS

Oblique

Dimension Style

Figure 8-13

by locating the cursor arrow in the value box and pressing the left mouse button, then backspacing out the number 1 and typing in the number 2

All the dimensioning parameters will now be increased by a factor of two.

4. Select the OK box

The Dimension Styles dialog box will reappear.

5. Select the Format option

The Format dialog box will appear. See Figure 8-17.

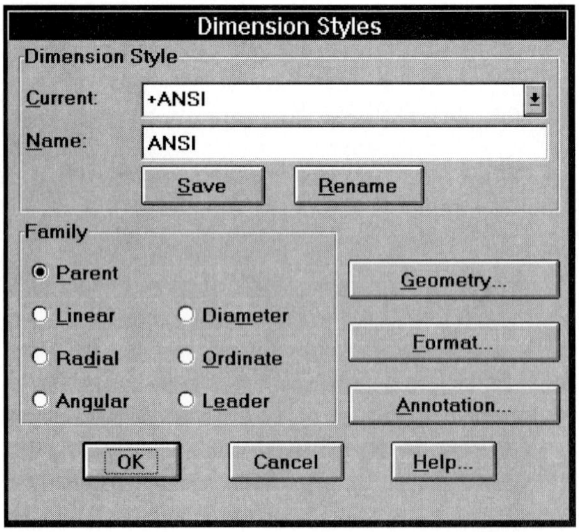

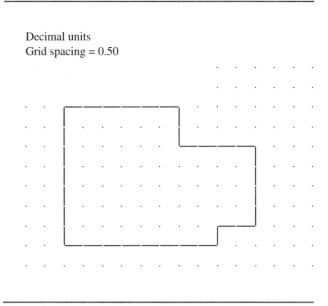

Decimal units
Grid spacing = 0.50

Figure 8-14

Figure 8-15

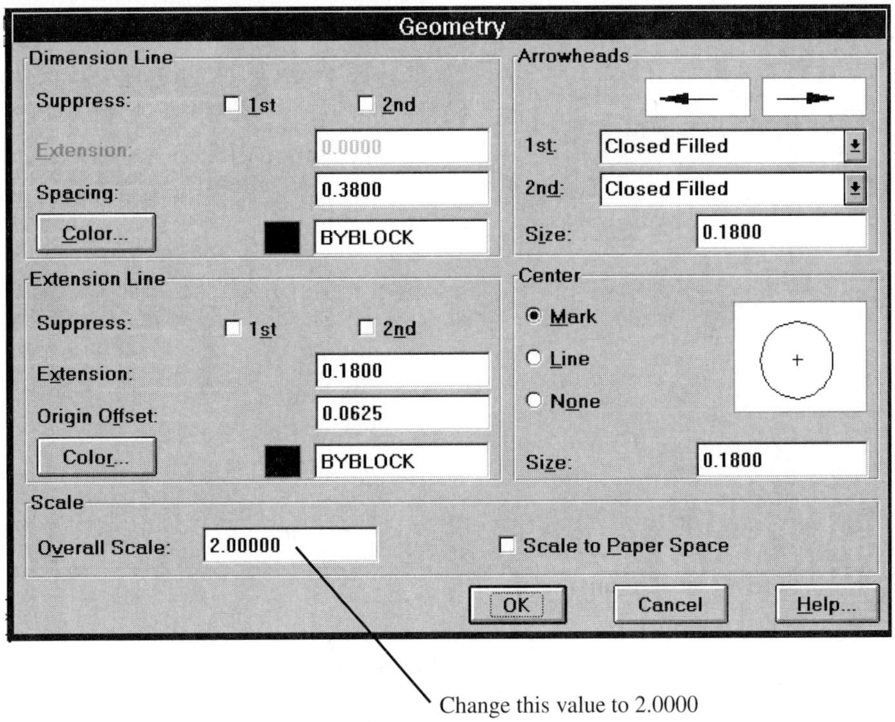

Change this value to 2.0000

Figure 8-16

6. Select the arrow box to the right of the word Above in the Vertical Justification box, and select Centered
7. Select the OK box

    The Dimension Styles options will reappear.

8. Locate the cursor arrow in the box to the right of the word ANSI in the Name: box and press the left mouse button

    A flashing cursor will appear in the box.

9. Backspace out ANSI and type in MECHINCH

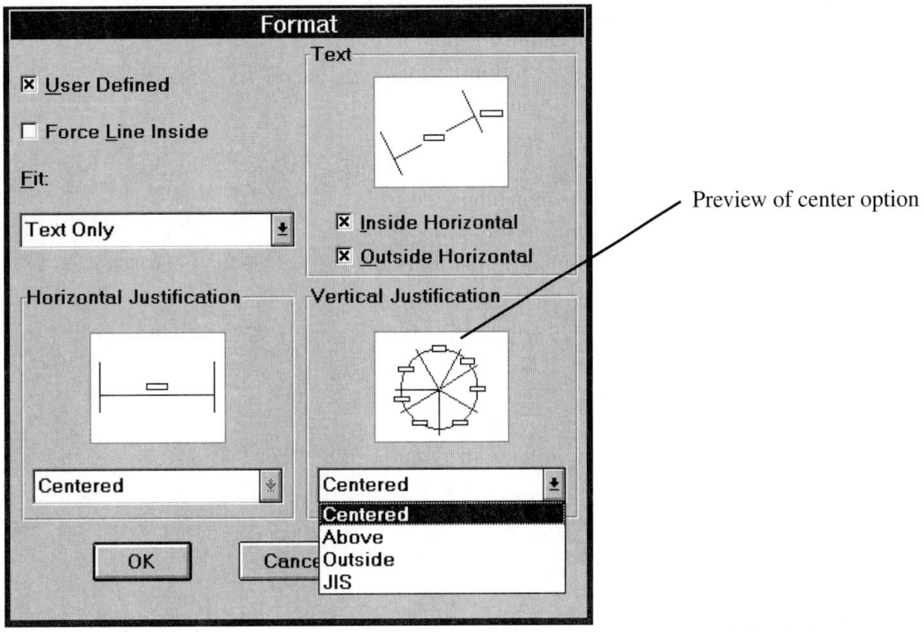

Preview of center option

Figure 8-17

Backspace out ANSI and type in MECHINCH, then Save

Dimension Styles

Dimension Style

Current: +ANSI

Name: ANSI

Save   Rename

Family

● Parent

○ Linear   ○ Diameter   Geometry...

○ Radial   ○ Ordinate   Format...

○ Angular   ○ Leader   Annotation...

OK   Cancel   Help...

Figure 8-18

See Figure 8-18. MECHINCH stands for "mechanical drawing done in decimal inches."

10. Select the Save: box.
11. Select OK

The dimensional parameters are now set. The LINEAR DIMENSION command was used to add the dimensions as shown in Figure 8-19.

To dimension using the mechanical format and millimeters

See Figure 8-20. The units for the shape are millimeters, and the GRID spacing equals 10 millimeters.

1. Select the DIMENSION STYLES command

   The Dimension Styles dialog box will appear.

2. Select the Geometry option

   The Geometry dialog box will appear.

3. Change the Overall scale factor from 1.0000 to 25.4000

   See Figure 8-21.

4. Select the OK box

   The Dimension Styles dialog box will appear

5. Change the Dimension Style Name to MECHMM

   See Figure 8-22.

6. Select the Save: box
7. Select OK

The new parameters are now set. Figure 8-23 shows a dimension created using the current MECHMM settings. Note that the dimension values includes two numerical values: 120.00 and [3048.0]. This type of dimension is called "dual dimensioning" and was originally created to allow the designer to include both inch and millimeter values for a dimension. When industry first started to shift from exclusively inch values to metric values, dual dimensions were used to convert many existing drawings to millimeters.

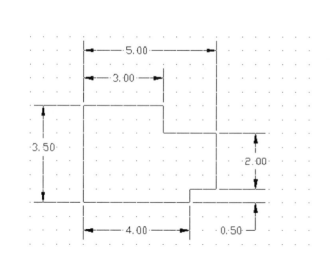

Figure 8-19

Decimal units
Grid spacing = 10
Drawing limits = 297,210

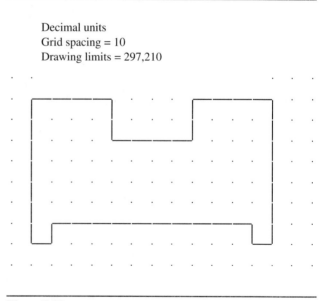

Figure 8-20

Geometry

Change the Overall Scale to 25.4 for metric unit drawings

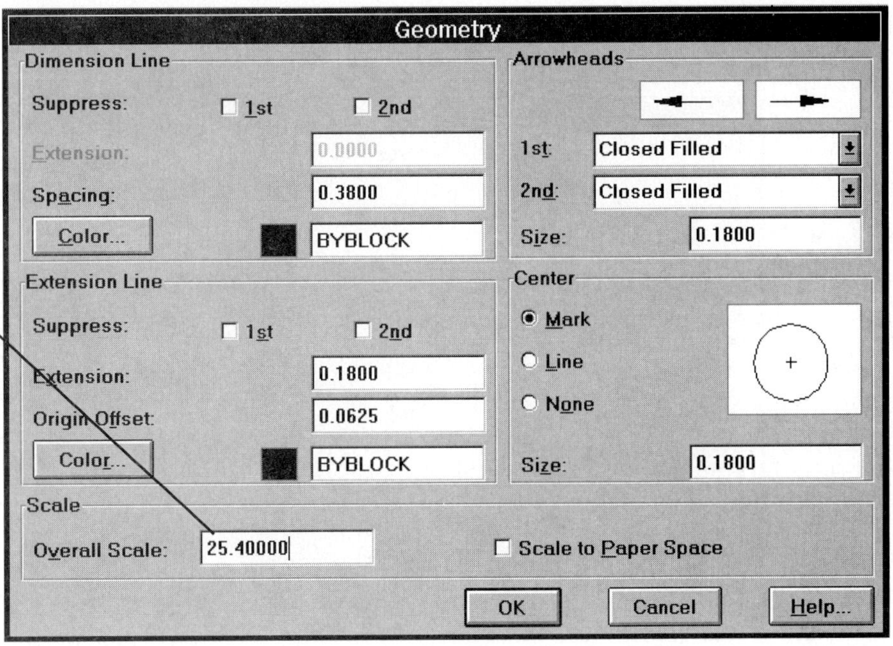

Dimension Line

Suppress: ☐ 1st   ☐ 2nd

Extension: 0.0000

Spacing: 0.3800

Color... BYBLOCK

Extension Line

Suppress: ☐ 1st   ☐ 2nd

Extension: 0.1800

Origin Offset: 0.0625

Color... BYBLOCK

Scale

Overall Scale: 25.40000

Arrowheads

1st: Closed Filled

2nd: Closed Filled

Size: 0.1800

Center

⦿ Mark
○ Line
○ None

Size: 0.1800

☐ Scale to Paper Space

OK   Cancel   Help...

Figure 8-21

It is now considered better to dimension a distance using either millimeters or inches, not both. The American National Standard publication ANSI Y14.5M-1982 includes dual dimensions in its appendix D, Former Practices, and states in section D8, "Dual dimensioning is no longer featured in this Standard."

To remove the dual dimension option

1. Select the DIMENSION STYLES command

   The Dimension Styles dialog box will appear.

2. Select the Annotation option

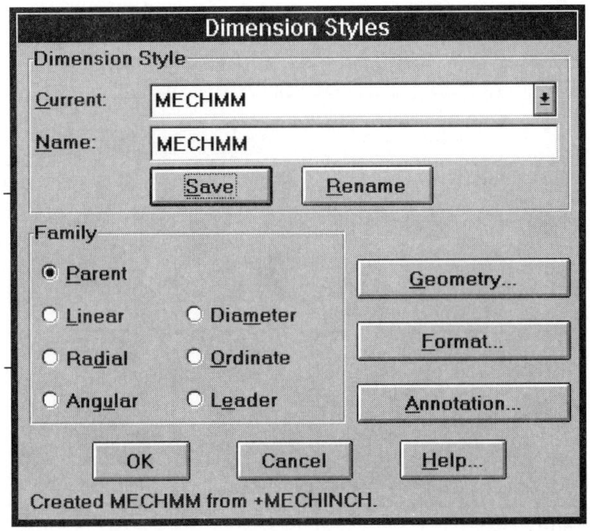

Dimension Styles

Dimension Style

Current: MECHMM

Name: MECHMM

Save   Rename

Family

⦿ Parent
○ Linear   ○ Diameter
○ Radial   ○ Ordinate
○ Angular   ○ Leader

Geometry...
Format...
Annotation...

OK   Cancel   Help...

Created MECHMM from +MECHINCH.

Figure 8-22

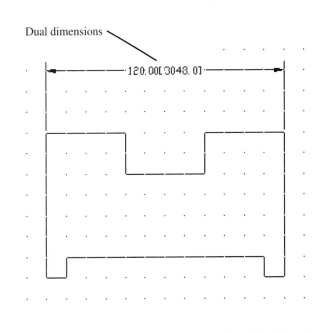

Dual dimensions

Figure 8-23

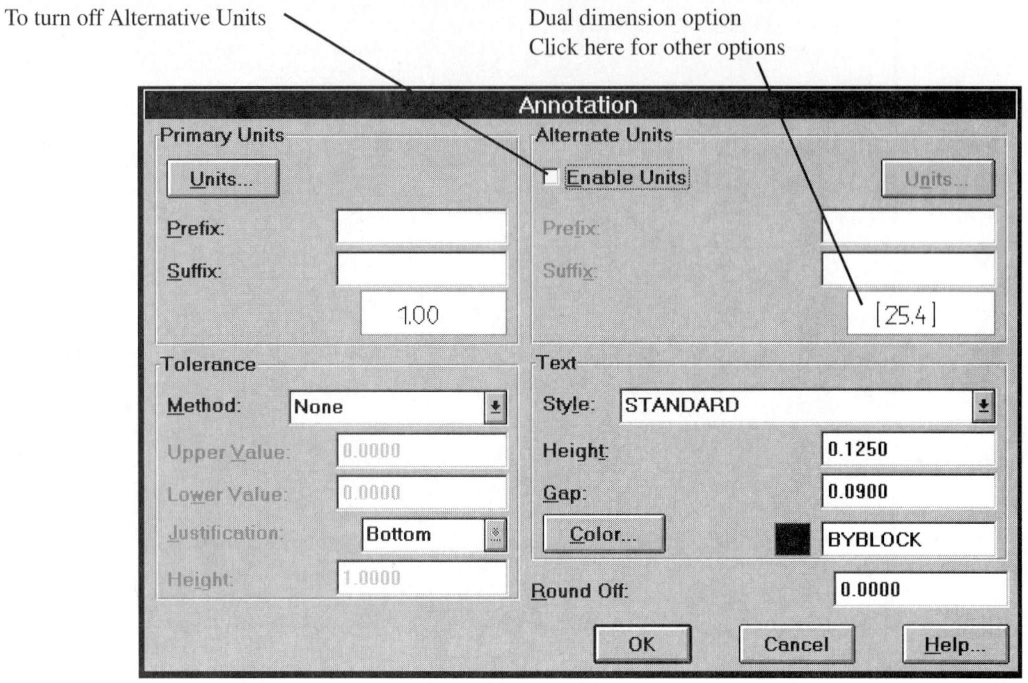

To turn off Alternative Units
Dual dimension option
Click here for other options
Annotation
Primary Units
Units...
Prefix:
Suffix:
1.00
Tolerance
Method:
None
Upper Value:
0.0000
Lower Value:
0.0000
Justification:
Bottom
Height:
1.0000
Alternate Units
Enable Units
Units...
Prefix:
Suffix:
[25.4]
Text
Style:
STANDARD
Height:
0.1250
Gap:
0.0900
Color...
BYBLOCK
Round Off:
0.0000
OK
Cancel
Help...

Figure 8-24

The Annotation dialog box will appear. See Figure 8-24.

3. Click the box to the left of the Enable Units heading within the Alternate Units box

The X should disappear, indicating that the option is now off.

4. Select OK

The Dimension Styles dialog box will appear.

5. Select Save

This will add the changes to the MECHMM dimensioning style.

6. Select OK

Dimensions may now be added using the LINEAR DIMENSIONS icon. Figure 8-25 shows the results.

7. Select OK

120.00
40.00
40.00
20.00
70.00
10.00-2 PLACES
10.00

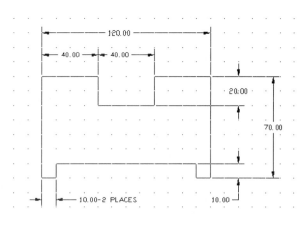

Figure 8-25

```
STANDARD TOLERANCES

        X    = ±1
      X.X    = ±0.1
     X.XX    = ±0.01
    X.XXX    = ±0.001
   X.XXXX    = ±0.0005


      X°     = ±0.1°


THESE TOLERANCES APPLY
UNLESS OTHERWISE STATED.
```

Figure 8-26

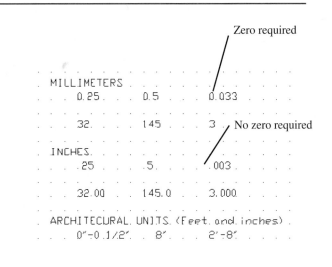

Figure 8-28

8-5 UNITS

It is important to understand that dimensional values are not the same as mathematical units. Dimensional values are manufacturing instructions and always include a tolerance, even if the tolerance value is not stated. Manufacturers use a predefined set of standard dimensions that are applied to any dimensional value without a written tolerance. Standard tolerance values differ from organization to organization. Figure 8-26 shows a chart of standard tolerances.

In Figure 8-27 a distance is dimensioned twice: once as 5.50 and a second time as 5.5000. Mathematically these two values are equal but they are not the same manufacturing instruction. The 5.50 value could, for example, have a standard tolerance of +/-.01, whereas the 5.5000 value could have a standard tolerance of +/-.0005. A tolerance of +/-.0005 is more difficult and, therefore, more expensive to manufacture than a tolerance of +/-.01.

Figure 8-28 shows examples of units expressed in millimeters, decimal inches, and architectural units. A zero is not required to the left of the decimal point for decimal inch values less than 1. Millimeter values do not require zeros to the right of the decimal point. Architectural units should always include the feet (′) and inch (″) symbols. Millimeter and decimal inch values never include symbols; the units will be defined in the title block of the drawing.

To prevent a 0 from appearing to the left of the decimal point

1. Select the DIMENSION STYLES command

   The Dimensions Styles dialog box will appear.

2. Select Annotation...

   The Annotation dialog box will appear.

3. Select Units...

   The Primary Units dialog box will appear. See Figure 8-29.

4. Click the box to the left of the word Leading within the Zero Suppression box

   An X will appear in the box, indicating that the function is on.

5. Select the OK boxes to return to the drawing

   Save the change if desired. You can now dimension using any of the dimension commands and no zeros will appear to the left of the decimal point. See Figure 8-29.

```
|——— 5.5000 ———▶|

|——— 5.50 ———▶|
```

Figure 8-27

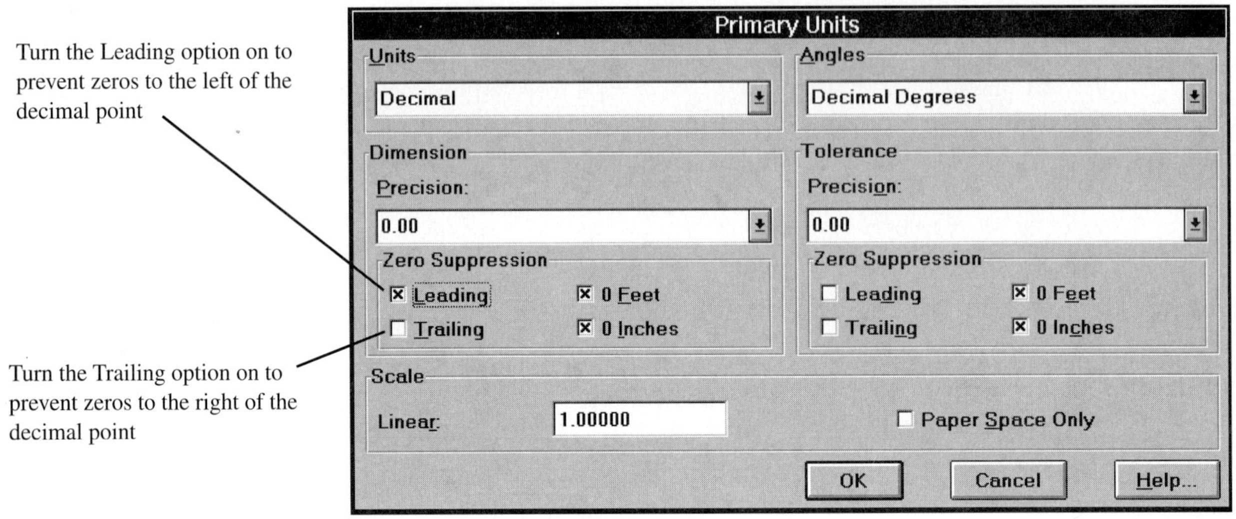

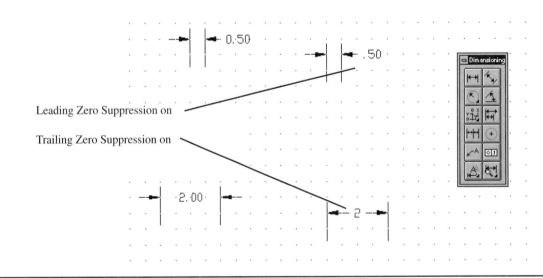

Turn the Leading option on to prevent zeros to the left of the decimal point

Turn the Trailing option on to prevent zeros to the right of the decimal point

Figure 8-29

To prevent a 0 from appearing to the right of the decimal point

1. Select the DIMENSION STYLES command

   The Dimensions Styles dialog box will appear.

2. Select Annotation...

   The Annotation dialog box will appear.

3. Select Units...

The Primary Units dialog box will appear.

4. Click the box to the left of the word Trailing within the Zero Suppression box

An X will appear in the box indicating that the function is on. Select the OK boxes to return to the drawing.

Save the changes if desired. You can now dimension using any of the dimension commands and no zeros will appear to the left of the decimal point. Figure 8-30 shows the results.

Leading Zero Suppression on

Trailing Zero Suppression on

Figure 8-30

8-6 ALIGNED DIMENSIONS

See Figure 8-31.

To create an aligned dimension

1. Select the Aligned Dimension command

   Command: _dimaligned
   First extension line origin or RETURN to select:

2. Select the first extension line origin point

   Second extension line origin:

3. Select the second extension line origin point

   Dimension line location (Text/Angle):

4. Select the location for the dimension line

The RETURN option

1. Select the Aligned Dimension command

   Command: _dimaligned
   First extension line origin or RETURN to select:

2. Press the RETURN key

   Select object to dimension

3. Select the line

   Dimension line location (Text/Angle):

4. Select the dimension line location

A response of T to the last prompt line will activate the text option. The Edit MText dialog box will appear in the WINDOWS version, and a calculated default value will be displayed between the <> symbols for the DOS version. The text option can be used to replace or supplement the default text generated by AutoCAD.

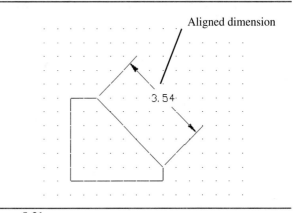

Figure 8-31

A response of A to the prompt will activate the angle option. The angle option allows you to change the angle of the text within the dimension line. See Figure 8-32. The default angle value is 0 degrees or horizontal. The example shown in Figure 8-36 used an angle of -45 degrees. The prompt responses are as follows.

Dimension line location (Text/Angle): A ENTER
Enter text angle: -45 ENTER

8-7 RADIUS AND DIAMETER DIMENSIONS

Figure 8-33 shows an object that includes both arcs and circles. The general rule is to dimension arcs using a radius dimension and circles using diameter dimensions. This convention is consistent with the tooling required to produce the feature shape. Any arc greater than 180 degrees is considered a circle and is dimensioned using a diameter.

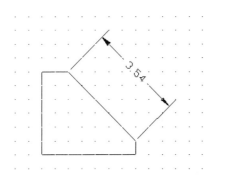

Figure 8-32

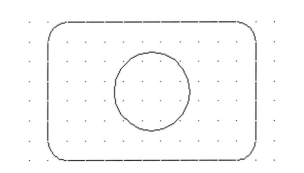

Figure 8-33

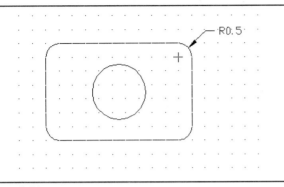

Figure 8-34

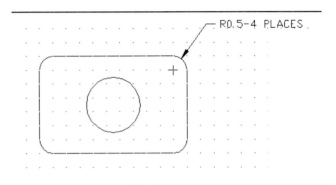

Figure 8-36

To create a radius dimension

1. Select the RADIUS DIMENSION command

   Command: _dimradius
   Select arc or circle:

2. Select the arc to be dimensioned

   Dimension line location (Text/Angle)

3. Position the radius dimension so that its leader line is not horizontal or vertical

Figure 8-34 shows the resulting dimension. The dimension text and the angle of the text can be altered using the (Text/Angle) options in the last prompt. In the example shown, it would be better to add the words 4 PLACES to the radius dimension than to include four radius dimensions.

To alter the default dimensions

1. Select the Radius dimension command

   Command: _dimradius
   Select arc or circle:

2. Select the arc to be dimensioned

   Dimension line location (Text/Angle)

3. Type T ENTER

   The Edit MText dialog box will appear in the WINDOWS version, and a calculated default value displayed between the <> symbols will appear in the DOS version.

4. Locate the flashing cursor just to the right of the <> symbol and type -4 PLACES for the WINDOWS version, or type a completely new value for the DOS version

   See Figure 8-35.

WINDOWS

DOS

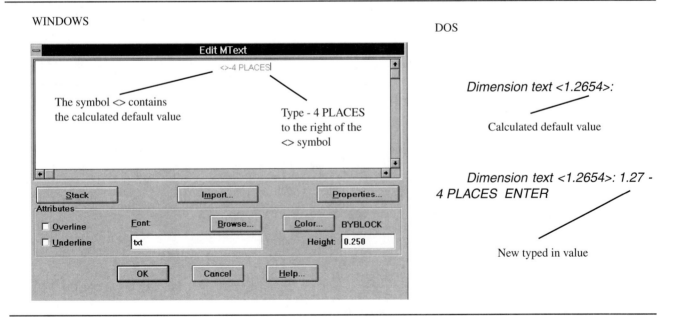

Figure 8-35

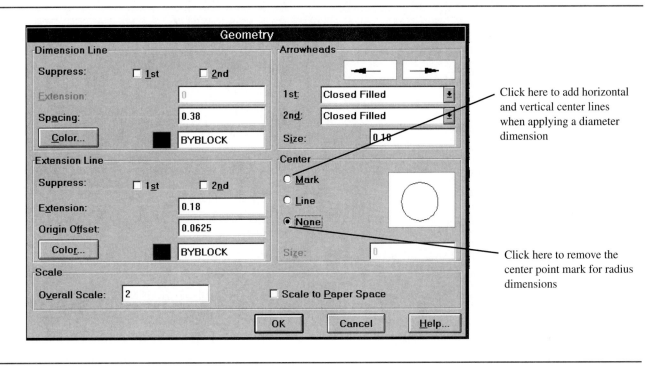

Click here to add horizontal and vertical center lines when applying a diameter dimension

Click here to remove the center point mark for radius dimensions

Figure 8-37

5. Select OK

Figure 8-36 shows the resulting dimension. The radius dimension command will automatically include a center point with the dimension. The center point can be excluded from the dimension as follows.

To remove the center mark from a radius dimension

1. Select the DIMENSION STYLES icon or type DDIM in response to a Command: prompt.

   The Dimension Styles dialog box will appear.

2. Select Geometry...

   The Geometry dialog box will appear.

3. Click the radio button to the left of the word None within the Center box

   A solid circle will appear in the button, indicating that it is on. The center mark in the circle is shown in the preview box to the right of the word None. See Figure 8-37.

4. Select the OK boxes to return to the drawing

   You will have to redimension the arc, including the text alteration. Figure 8-38 shows the results.

To create a diameter dimension

Circles require three dimensions: a diameter value plus two linear dimensions used to locate the circle's center point. AutoCAD can be configured to automatically add horizontal and vertical center lines as follows.

1. Select the DIMENSION STYLES icon or type DDIM in response to a Command: prompt

   The Dimension Styles dialog box will appear.

2. Select Geometry...

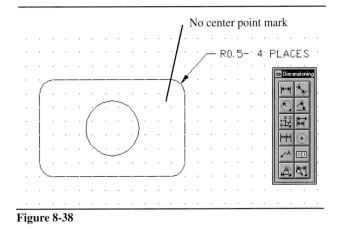

No center point mark

R0.5- 4 PLACES

Figure 8-38

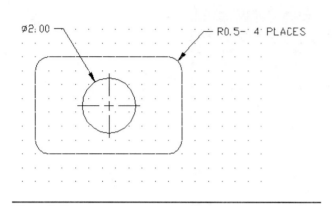

Figure 8-39

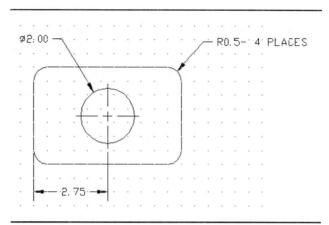

Figure 8-40

The Geometry dialog box will appear.

3. Click the radio button to the right of the word Line within the Center box

See Figure 8-37.

4. Select the OK boxes to return to the drawing
5. Select the Diameter Dimension icon

Command: _dimdiameter
Select arc or circle:

6. Select the circle

Dimension line location (Text/Angle):

7. Locate the dimension away from the object so that the leader line is neither horizontal nor vertical

Figure 8-39 shows the results.

To add linear dimensions to given center lines

1. Select the LINEAR DIMENSION icon

Command: _dimlinear
First extension line origin or RETURN to select:

2. Press the SHIFT key and the right button simultaneously, or the middle button on a three button mouse, to access the OSNAP menu
3. Select Endpoint from the OSNAP menu

First extension line origin or RETURN to select:
_endp of

4. Select the lower endpoint of the circle's vertical center line

Second extension line origin:

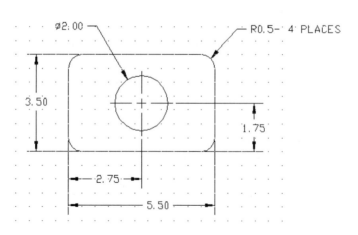

Figure 8-41

5. Use the Shift key/right button option to access the OSNAP menu and select the Endpoint option

6. Select the endpoint of the vertical edge line (the endpoint that joins with the corner arc).

Figure 8-40 shows the results.

7. Repeat the above procedure to add the vertical dimension needed to locate the circle's center point

8. Add the overall dimensions using the Linear Dimensions command

Figure 8-41 shows the results. Radius and diameter dimensions are usually added to a drawing after the linear dimensions because they are less restricted in their locations. Linear dimensions are located close to the distance they are defining, whereas radius and diameter dimensions can be located further away and use leader lines to identify the appropriate arc or circle.

Avoid crossing extension and dimension lines with leader lines. See Figure 8-42.

NOTE

The diameter symbol can be added, when using the Edit MText dialog box, by typing %%c. The characters %%c will appear on the Edit MText screen, but will be converted to the diameter symbol Ø when the text is applied to the drawing.

8-8 ANGULAR DIMENSIONS

Figure 8-43 shows four possible angular dimensions that could be created using the angular dimensions command. The extension lines and degree symbol will be added automatically.

To create an angular dimension

See Figure 8-44.

1. Select the ANGULAR DIMENSION command

Command: _dimangular
Select arc, circle, line, or RETURN:

2. Select the short vertical line on the lower right side of the object

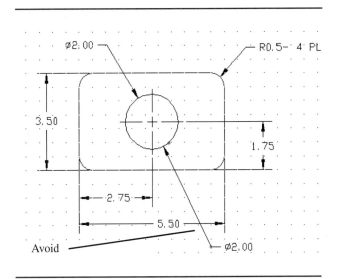

Figure 8-42

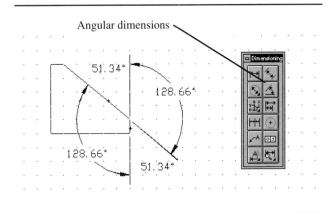

Figure 8-43

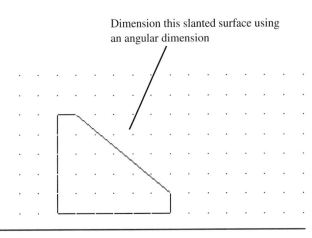

Dimension this slanted surface using an angular dimension

Figure 8-44

Second line:

3. Select the slanted line

   Dimension arc line location (Text/Angle)

4. Locate the text away from the object

Figure 8-45 shows the results. It is considered better to use two extension lines for angular dimensions and not have one of the arrowheads touch the surface of the part.

NOTE

The degree symbol can be added, when using the Edit MText dialog box, by typing %%d. The characters %%d will appear on the Edit MText screen, but will be converted to ° when the text is applied to the drawing.

Avoid overdimensioning

Figure 8-46 shows a shape dimensioned using an angular dimension. The shape is completely defined. Any additional dimension would be an error. It is tempting, in an effort to make sure a shape is completely defined, to add more dimensions, such as a horizontal dimension for the short horizontal edge at the top of the shape. This dimension is not needed and is considered double dimensioning.

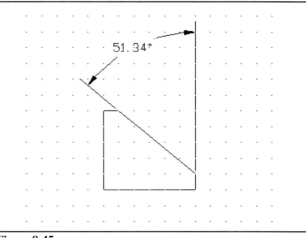

Figure 8-45

8-9 ORDINATE DIMENSIONS

Ordinate dimensions are dimensions based on an XY coordinate system. Ordinate dimensions do not include extensions, dimension lines, or arrowheads, but simply horizontal and vertical leader lines drawn directly from the features of the object. Ordinate dimensions are particularly useful when dimensioning an object that includes many small holes.

Figure 8-47 shows an object that is to be dimensioned using ordinate dimensions. Ordinate dimensions are automatically calculated from the XY origin or, in this example, the lower left corner of the screen. If the object had been drawn with its lower left corner on the origin, you could proceed directly to the ordinate dimension command, but the lower left corner of the object is currently located at X = 3, Y = 4. First move the origin to the corner of the object, then use the ordinate dimension command.

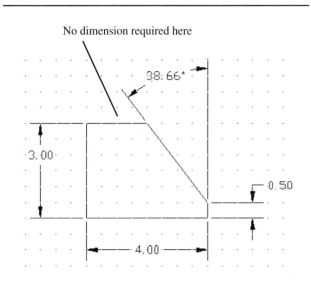

Figure 8-46

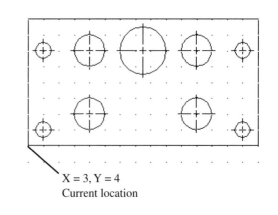

X = 3, Y = 4
Current location

Figure 8-47

The screen shown is a WINDOWS screen. The VIEW pulldown menu on the DOS screen will generate the same cascading menus.

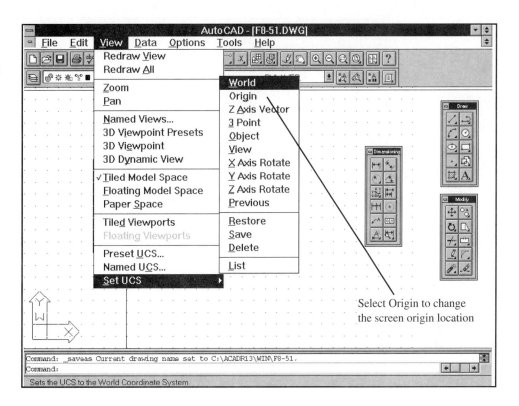

Select Origin to change the screen origin location

Figure 8-48

To move the origin

1. Select the View pulldown menu

The View pulldown menu will cascade down.

2. Select Set UCS

The Set UCS menu will appear next to the View pulldown menu. See Figure 8-48.

3. Select Origin

Origin point <0,0,0>:

4. Select the lower left corner of the object

The origin (0,0) is now located at the lower left corner of the object. This can be verified by looking at the coordinate display at the lower left corner of the screen.

The Origin icon may move to the lower left corner as shown in Figure 8-49, depending on your computer's settings. The icon can be moved back to the original screen location as follows.

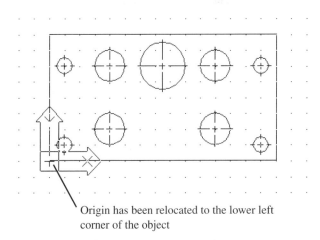

Origin has been relocated to the lower left corner of the object

Figure 8-49

The screen shown is a WINDOWS screen. The VIEW pulldown menu on the DOS screen will generate the same cascading menus.

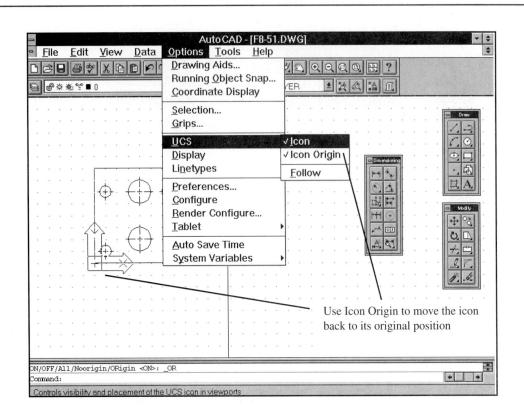

Use Icon Origin to move the icon back to its original position

Figure 8-50

To move the Origin icon

1. Select the Options pulldown menu, then UCS

The UCS menu will appear next to the Options pulldown menu. See Figure 8-50.

2. Select Icon Origin on the UCS menu

The Origin icon will relocate back to its original location.

To add ordinate dimensions to an object

The following procedure assumes that you have already used the Dimension Styles command (Section 8-4) to set the style of the dimensions to what you want.

1. Turn the ORTHO command on (press the F8 key)
2. Select the Ordinate Dimensions

Command: _dimordinate
Select feature:

3. Select the lower left corner of the object

Leader endpoint (Xdatum/Ydatum/Text):
4. Move the crosshairs to the left and select a point

The ordinate value of the point will be added to the drawing. This point should have a 0.00 value because it is the origin of the object.

5. Press the right button to restart the command and dimension the object's other features.
6. Extend the center lines across the object and add the diameter dimensions for the holes.

Figure 8-51 shows the completed drawing. The Text option of the prompt shown in step 3 can be used to modify or remove the default text value.

8-10 BASELINE DIMENSION

Baseline dimensions are a series of dimensions that all originate from a common baseline or datum line. Baseline dimensions are very useful because they help eliminate tolerance buildup associated with chain type dimensions.

Ordinate dimensions

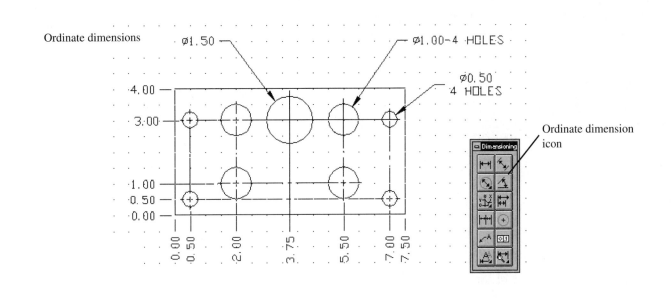

Ordinate dimension icon

Figure 8-51

Baseline dimensions

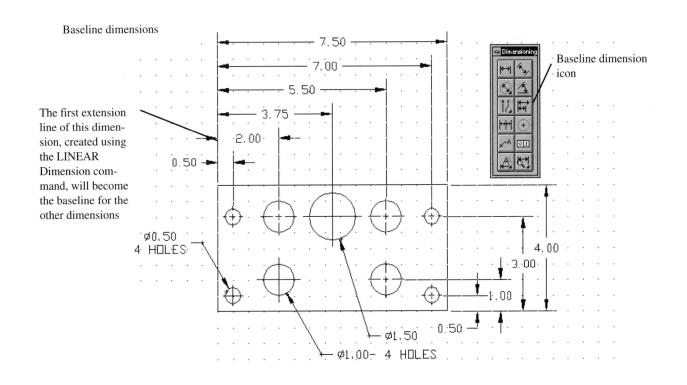

Baseline dimension icon

The first extension line of this dimension, created using the LINEAR Dimension command, will become the baseline for the other dimensions

Figure 8-52

The BASELINE command can be used only after an initial dimension has been drawn. AutoCAD will define the first extension line origin of the initial dimension selected as the baseline for all baseline dimensions.

To use the baseline dimension command

See Figure 8-52.

1. Select the LINEAR DIMENSION command

   Command: _dimlinear
   First extension line origin or RETURN to select:

2. Select the upper left corner of the object

   This selection determines the baseline.

   Second extension line origin:

3. Select the endpoint of the first circle's vertical center line; use OSNAP if needed to ensure accuracy

   Dimension line location (Text/ Angle/ Horizontal/ Vertical/ Rotated):

4. Select a location for the dimension line

   Command:

5. Select the BASELINE DIMENSION command

   Second extension line origin or RETURN to select:

6. Select the endpoint of the next circle's vertical center line

   Second extension line origin or RETURN to select:

7. Continue to select the circle center lines until all circles are located

   Second extension line origin or RETURN to select:

8. Select the upper right corner of the object
9. Type ENTER

   This will end the baseline dimension command

10. Repeat the above procedure for the vertical baseline dimensions
11. Add the circles' diameter values

The BASELINE DIMENSIONS option can also be used with the ANGULAR DIMENSION and ALIGNED DIMENSION commands.

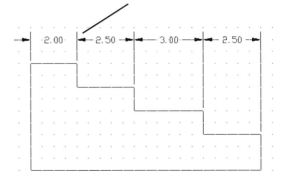

The second extension line of the previous dimension becomes the first extension line of the next dimension

Figure 8-53

8-11 CONTINUE DIMENSION

The CONTINUE DIMENSION command is used to create chain dimensions based on an initial linear, angular, or ordinate dimension. The second extension line origin becomes the first extension line origin for the CONTINUE DIMENSION.

To use the Continue Dimension command

See Figure 8-53.

1. Select the LINEAR DIMENSION command

   Command:
   First extension line origin or RETURN for select:

2. Select the upper left corner of the object

   Second extension line origin:

3. Select the right endpoint of the uppermost horizontal line

   Dimension line location (Text/ Angle/ Horizontal/ Vertical/ Rotated):

4. Select a dimension line location

   Command:

5. Select the CONTINUE DIMENSION command

   Command: _dimcontinue
   Second extension line origin or RETURN to select:

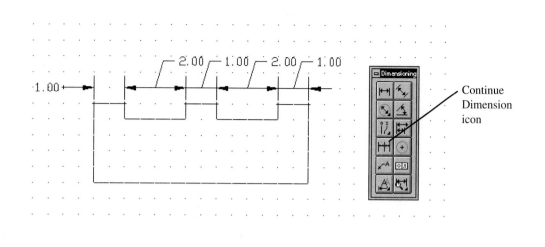

Continue
Dimension
icon

Figure 8-54

6. Select the next linear distanced to be dimensioned

Second extension line origin or RETURN to select:

7. Continue until the object's horizontal edges are completely dimensioned

AutoCAD will automatically align the dimensions. Figure 8-54 shows how the CONTINUED DIMENSION command dimension distances that are too small for both the arrowhead and dimension value are made to fit within the extension lines.

8-12 CENTER MARK

When AutoCAD first draws a circle or arc, a center mark appears on the drawing. However, these marks will disappear when the REDRAW VIEW or REDRAW ALL command is applied.

To add a permanent center mark to a given circle

See Figure 8-55.

1. Select the CENTER MARK command

Command: _dimcenter
Select arc or circle:

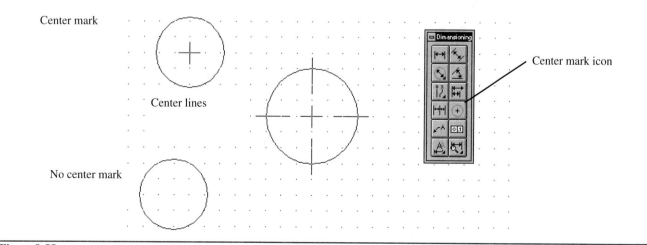

Center mark

Center lines

Center mark icon

No center mark

Figure 8-55

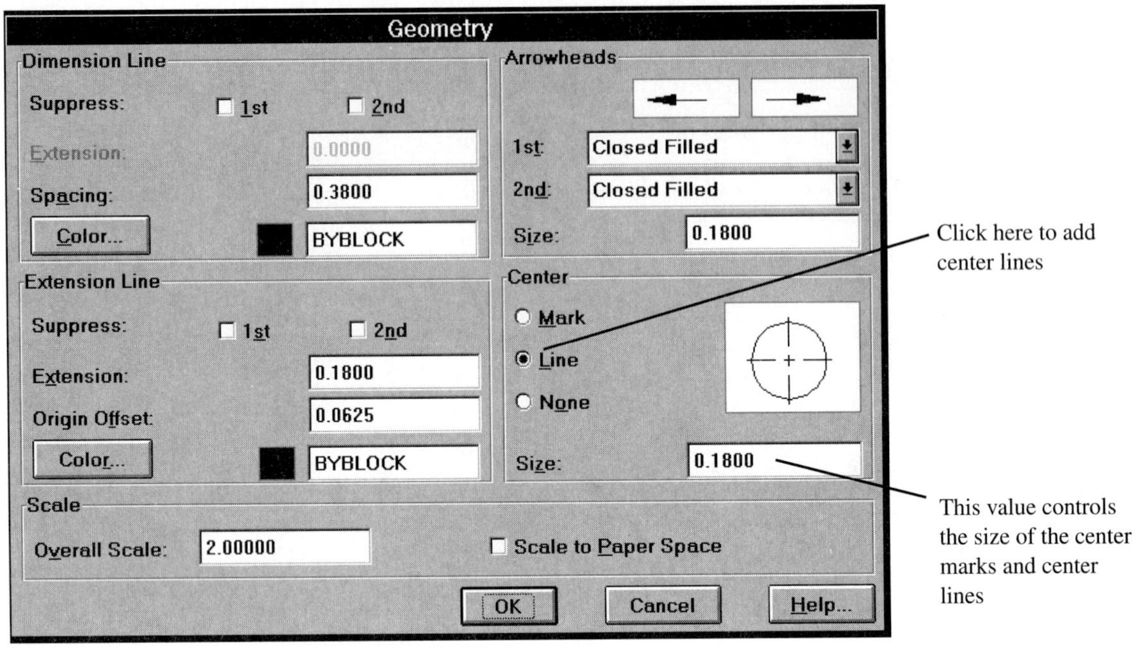

Figure 8-56

2. Select the circle

   Command:

   The CENTER MARK command can also be used to add horizontal and vertical center lines to a circle.

To add center lines to a given circle

1. Select the DIMENSION STYLES icon or type DDIM in response to a Command: prompt

   The Dimension Styles dialog box will appear

2. Select Geometry...

   The Geometry dialog box will appear. See Figure 8-56.

3. Select the radio button to the left of the word Line in the Center box

   The preview display will show horizontal and vertical center lines.

4. Select OK, OK to return to the drawing
5. Select the CENTER MARK command

   Select arc or circle:

6. Select the circle

   Horizontal and vertical center lines will appear. The size of the center mark can be controlled using the size

option in the Geometry dialog box. If the center line's size appears unacceptable, try different sizes until an acceptable size is achieved.

8-13 LEADER

Leader lines are slanted lines that extend from notes or dimensions to a specific feature or location on the surface of a drawing. They usually end with an arrowhead or dot. The RADIUS and DIAMETER DIMENSION commands automatically create a leader line. The LEADER command can be used to add leader lines not associated with radius and diameter dimensions.

To create a leader line with text

1. Select the LEADER command

   Command:_leader
   From point:

2. Select the starting point for the leader line

   This is the point where the arrowhead will appear.

   To point:

3. Select the location of the endpoint of the slanted line segment

Edit MText

ALL CORNERS TO BE R.05 MAX

Type the desired text starting here

| Stack | Import... | Properties... |

Attributes

☐ Overline   Font: Browse...   Color...   white
☐ Underline   txt   Height: 0.250

| OK | Cancel | Help... |

The screen shown is the MText WINDOWS screen. The DOS version will generate a Text screen that functions in a similar manner.

Select OK to exit the MText screen.

Select FILE, SAVE, EXIT to exit the DOS Text screen.

Figure 8-57

To point (Format/ Annotation/ Undo) <Annotation>:

4. Type ENTER

This response accepts the default Annotation response.

Annotation (or RETURN for options):

5. Type ENTER

Tolerance/Copy/Block/None/<MText>:

6. Type ENTER

The Edit MText dialog box or the DOS Text screen will appear. See Figure 8-57.

7. Type the desired text

The flashing cursor may be repositioned as needed. The initial location for the flashing cursor at the upper left corner of the text box represents the end of the leader line. Figure 8-58 shows the resulting leader line note.

8. Select the OK box for the WINDOWS version or select FILE, SAVE, EXIT for the DOS version.

The LEADER command can be used to draw curved leader lines and leader lines that end with dots. See Figure 8-59.

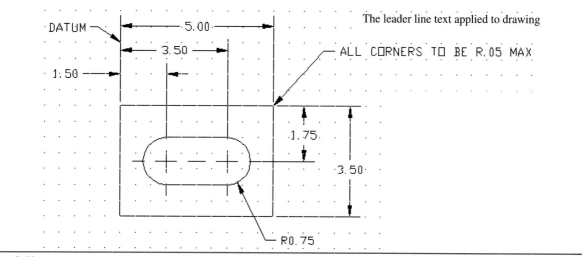

The leader line text applied to drawing

Figure 8-58

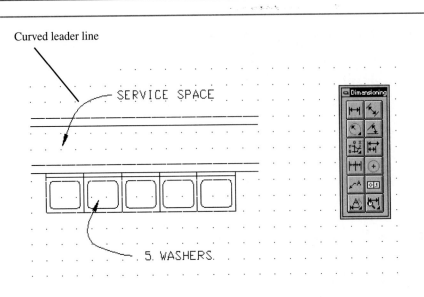

Curved leader line

Figure 8-59

To draw a curved leader line

1. Select the LEADER command

   Command: _leader
   From point:

2. Select the starting point for the leader line

   This is the point where the arrowhead will appear.

   To point:

3. Select the location of the endpoint of the slanted line segment

   Select a point just past the arrowhead.

   To point (Format/ Annotation/ Undo) <Annotation>:

4. Type F ENTER

   Spline/STraight/Arrow/None/<Exit>:

5. Type S ENTER

   To point (Format/ Annotation /Undo) <Annotation>:

   AutoCAD will shift to DRAG mode, which allows you to move the cursor around and watch the change in shape of the leader line. More than one point may be selected to define the shape.

   To point (Format/ Annotation /Undo) <Annotation>:

6. Type ENTER

   Annotation (or RETURN for options):

7. Type ENTER

   Tolerance/Copy/Block/None/<Mtext>:

8. Type ENTER

   The Edit MText dialog box or the DOS text screen will appear.

9. Type in the appropriate text
10. Select OK or select FILE, SAVE, EXIT

   The Text will appear on the drawing at the end of the LEADER line.

To draw a leader line with a dot at its end

1. Select the DIMENSION STYLES icon or type DDIM in response to a Command: prompt

   The Dimension Styles dialog box will appear.

2. Select Geometry...

   The Geometry dialog box will appear

3. Select the box with an arrow to the right of the word Closed in the Arrowheads box

   A listing of the shape options will cascade down. See Figure 8-60.

4. Select Dot

   A preview of the dot will appear in the arrowhead preview box. The size of the dot can be controlled using the Size: box.

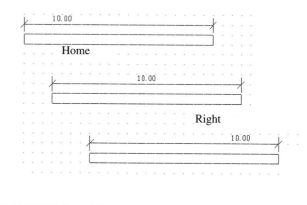

Preview will appear here

Select the Dot option

Figure 8-60

5. Select OK, OK to return to the drawing
6. Use the LEADER icon to create leader lines as described above

8-14 HOME

The HOME command is used to edit existing dimensioning text. Existing text can be moved or rotated.

For the WINDOWS version, there are five options associated with the HOME icon: HOME, ANGLE, LEFT, CENTER, and RIGHT. The same options are available in the DOS version and are accessed by selecting the MOD DIM command on the main menu, then selecting DIMT-EDIT.

To move the text of an existing dimension

1. Select the HOME or DIMTEDIT command

   Command: _dimtedit
   Select dimension:

2. Select the dimension

   Enter text location (Left/Right/Home/Angle):

Each of these options may be accessed directly by using the appropriate icon associated with the HOME icon.

3. Type h ENTER

The text will be repositioned at the center of the dimension line. The Left and Right options are used to justify text to the left or right of the dimension line. See Figure 8-61. Text can also be positioned by eye by moving the text using the cursor. When the text is located in its new position, press the left mouse button.

Figure 8-61

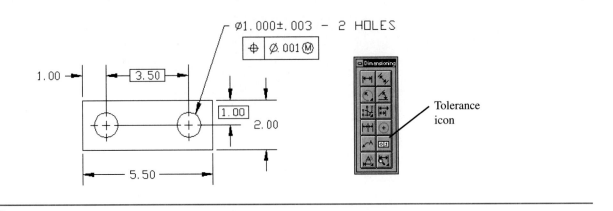

Figure 8-62

To change the angle of existing dimension text

1. Select the HOME icon

   Command: _dimtedit
   Select dimension:

2. Select the dimension

   Enter text location (Left/Right/Home/Angle):

3. Type a ENTER

   Enter text angle:

4. Type 90 ENTER

8-15 TOLERANCES

Tolerances are numerical values assigned with dimensions that define the limits of manufacturing acceptability for a distance. AutoCAD can create four types of tolerances: symmetrical, deviation, limits, and basic. The Tolerance icon located on the Dimension toolbar is used to create geometric tolerances. Geometric tolerances are discussed at length in Chapter 10. Figure 8-62 shows an example of a geometric tolerance.

8-16 DIMENSIONING HOLES

Holes are dimensioned by stating their diameters and depth, if any. The symbol Ø is used to represent diameter. It is considered good practice to dimension a hole using a diameter value because the tooling used to produce the hole is also defined in inches. A notation like 12 DRILL is considered less desirable because it specifies a machining process. Manufacturing processes should be left, whenever possible, to the discretion of the shop.

To dimension individual holes

Figure 8-63 shows three different methods that can be used to dimension a hole that does not go completely through an object. If a hole goes completely through, only the diameter need be specified. The RADIUS and DIAMETER DIMENSION commands were covered in Section 8-7. Depth values may be added using the MText dialog box or typed directly on the command line that presents a calculated default value.

Figure 8-64 shows two methods for dimensioning holes in sectional view. The single line note version is the preferred method.

Holes that go completely through an object need only their diameters defined

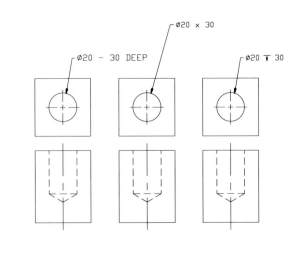

Figure 8-63

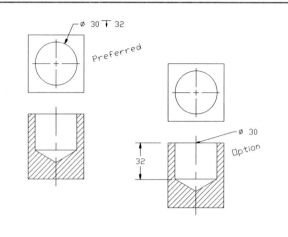

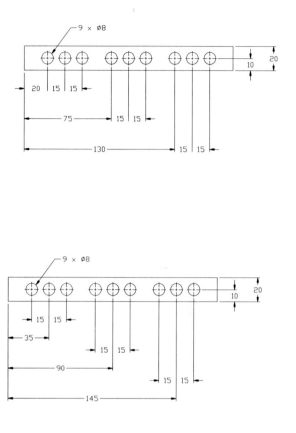

Figure 8-64

To dimension hole patterns

Figure 8-65 shows two different hole patterns dimensioned. The circular pattern includes the note Ø10-4 HOLES. This note serves to define all four holes within the object.

Figure 8-65 also shows a rectangular object that contains 5 holes of equal diameter, equally spaced from each other. The notation 5 × Ø8 specifies 5 holes of 8 diameter. The notation 4 × 20 (=80) means 4 equal spaces of 20. The (=80) notation is a reference dimension and is included for convenience. Referenced dimensions are explained in Chapter 9.

Figure 8-66 shows two additional methods for dimensioning repeating hole patterns. Figure 8-67 shows a circular hole pattern that includes two different hole diameters. The hole diameters are not noticeably different and

Figure 8-66

could be confused. One group is defined by an indicating letter (A); the other is dimensioned in a normal manner.

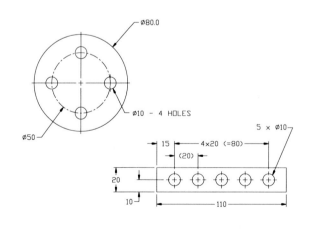

Figure 8-65

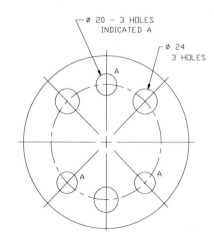

Figure 8-67

Locate shorter dimensions
closer to the object than
longer ones

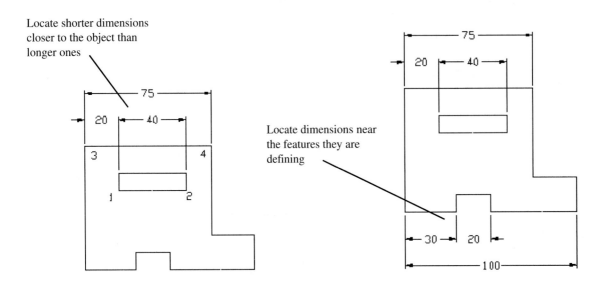

Locate dimensions near
the features they are
defining

Do not locate dimensions on the
surface of the object

Use the EXPLODE, ERASE, and
MOVE commands to reconstruct and
relocate inappropriate dimensions

Align groups of dimensions

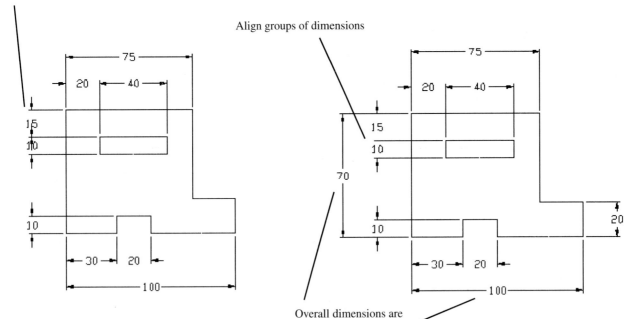

Overall dimensions are
located the furthest out

Figure 8-68

8-17 LOCATING DIMENSIONS

There are several general rules concerning the location of dimensions. See Figure 8-68.

1. Locate dimensions near the feature they are defining.
2. Do not locate dimensions on the surface of the object.
3. Align and group dimensions so they are neat and easy to follow.
4. Avoid crossing extension lines.

Sometimes it is impossible not to cross extension lines because of the complex shape of any object, but whenever possible, avoid crossing extension lines.

5. Place shorter dimensions closer to the object than longer ones.
6. Always locate overall dimensions the furthest away from the object.
7. Do not dimension the same distance twice. This is called double dimensioning and will be discussed at length in Chapter 9.

8-18 FILLETS AND ROUNDS

Fillets and rounds may be dimensioned individually or by a note. In many design situations all the fillets and rounds are the same size, so a note as shown in Figure 8-69 is used. Any fillets or rounds that have a different

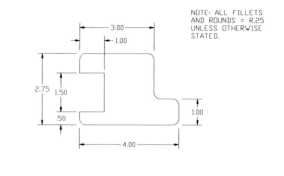

Figure 8-69

radius than that specified by the note are dimensioned individually.

See Chapter 2 for an explanation of how to draw fillets and rounds using the FILLET command.

8-19 ROUNDED SHAPES (INTERNAL)

Internal rounded shapes are called slots. Figure 8-70 shows three different methods for dimensioning slots. The end radii are indicated by the note R - 2 PLACES, but no numerical value is given. The width of the slot is dimensioned, and it is assumed that the radius of the rounded ends is exactly half of the stated width.

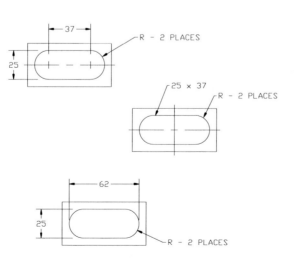

Figure 8-70

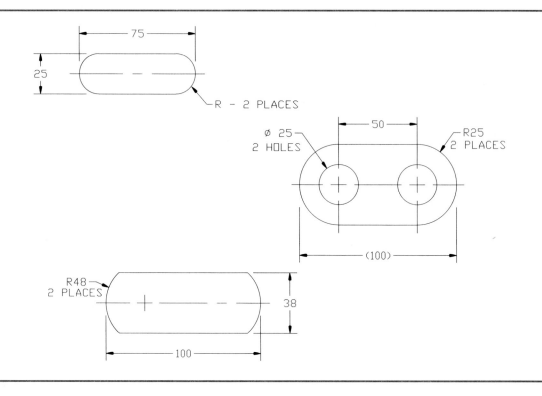

Figure 8-71

8-20 ROUNDED SHAPES (EXTERNAL)

Figure 8-71 shows two example shapes with external rounded ends. As with internal rounded shapes, the end radii are indicated but no value is given. The width of the object is given, and the radius of the rounded end is assumed to be exactly half of the stated width.

The second example in Figure 8-71 shows an object dimensioned using the object's center line. This type of dimensioning is done when the distance between the hole is more important than the overall length of the object; that is, the tolerance for the distance between the holes is more exact than the tolerance for the overall length of the object.

The overall length of the object is given as a reference dimension (100). This means that the object will be manufactured based on the other dimensions and the 100 value will be used only for reference.

Objects with partially rounded edges should be dimensioned as shown in Figure 8-71. The radii of the end features are dimensioned. The radius center point is implied to be on the object center line. The overall dimension is given; it is not referenced unless specific radii values are included.

8-21 IRREGULAR SURFACES

There are three different methods for dimensioning irregular surfaces: tabular, baseline, and baseline with oblique extension lines. Figure 8-72 shows an irregular surface dimensioned using the tabular method. An XY axis is defined using the edges of the object. Points are then defined relative to the XY axis. The points are assigned reference numbers, and the reference numbers and XY coordinate values are listed in chart form as shown.

Figure 8-73 shows an irregular curve dimensioned using baseline dimensions. The baseline method references all dimensions back to specified baselines. Usually there are two baselines, one horizontal and one vertical.

It is considered poor practice to use a center line as a baseline. Center lines are imaginary lines that do not exist on the object, and using them as baselines would make it more difficult to manufacture and inspect the finished objects.

Baseline dimensioning is very common because it helps eliminate tolerance buildup, and is easily adaptable to many manufacturing processes. AutoCAD has a special BASELINE command for use in creating baseline dimensions.

Station	1	2	3	4	5	6
X	0	20	40	55	62	70
Y	40	38	30	16	10	0

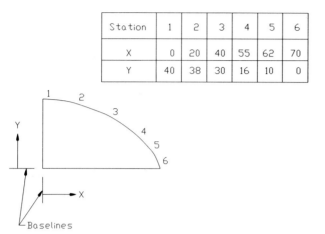

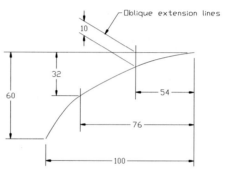

Figure 8-72

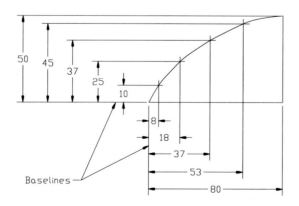

Figure 8-73

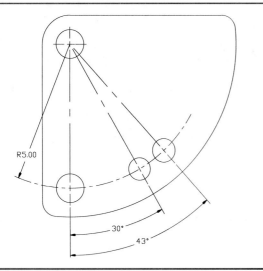

Figure 8-74

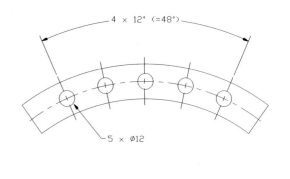

Figure 8-75

8-22 POLAR DIMENSIONS

Polar dimensions are similar to polar coordinates. A location is defined by a radius (distance) and an angle. Figure 8-74 shows an object that includes polar dimensions. The holes are located on a circular center line and their positions from the vertical center line are specified using angles.

Figure 8-75 shows an example of a hole pattern dimensioned using polar dimensions.

8-23 CHAMFERS

Chamfers are angular cuts made on the edges of objects. They are usually used to make it easier to fit two parts together. They are most often made at 45-degree angles but may be made at any angle. Figure 8-76 shows two objects with chamfers between surfaces 90 degrees apart and two examples between surfaces that are not 90 degrees apart. Either of the two types of dimensions shown for the 45-degree dimension may be used. If an angle other than 45 degrees is used, the angle and setback distance must be specified.

Figure 8-77 shows two examples of internal chamfers. Both define the knurl using an angle and diameter. Internal chamfers are very similar to countersunk holes. See Chapter 5.

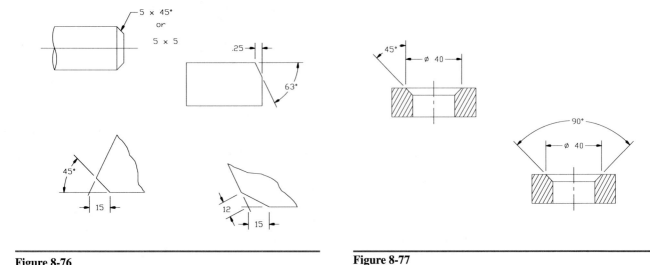

Figure 8-76

Figure 8-77

8-24 KNURLING

There are two types of knurls: diamond and straight. Knurls are used to make it easier to grip a shaft, or to rough a surface before it is used in a press fit.

Knurls are defined by their pitch and diameter. See Figure 8-78. The pitch of a knurl is the ratio of the number of grooves on the circumference to the diameter. Standard knurling tools sized to a variety of pitch sizes are used to manufacture knurls for both English and metric units.

Diamond knurls may be represented by a double hatched pattern or by an open area with notes. The HATCH command is used to draw the double hatched lines. See Chapter 6.

Straight knurls may be represented by straight lines in the pattern shown or by an open area with notes. The straight line pattern is created by projecting lines from a construction circle. The construction points are evenly spaced on the circle. Once drawn, the straight line knurl pattern can be SAVED as a WBLOCK for use on other drawings. See Chapter 3 for an explanation of WBLOCK.

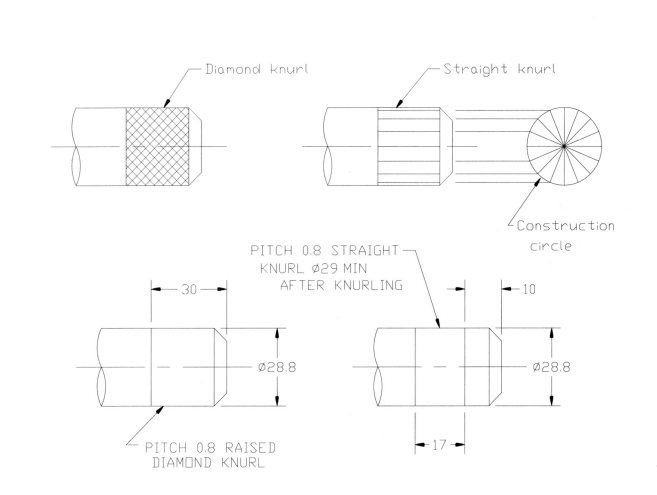

Figure 8-78

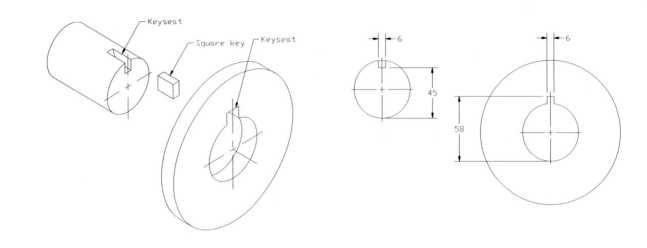

Figure 8-79

8-25 KEYS AND KEYSEATS

Keys are small pieces of material used to transmit power. For example, Figure 8-79 shows how a key can be fitted between a shaft and a gear so that the rotary motion of the shaft can be transmitted to the gear.

There are many different styles of keys. The key shown in Figure 8-79 has a rectangular cross-section and is called a SQUARE KEY. Keys fit into grooves called keyseats or keyways.

Keyways are dimensioned from the bottom of the shaft or hole as shown.

8-26 SYMBOLS AND ABBREVIATIONS

Symbols are used in dimensioning to help accurately display the meaning of the dimension. Symbols also help eliminate language barriers when reading drawings. Figure 8-80 shows dimensioning symbols and their meaning. The height of a symbol should be the same as the text height (DIMTXT or DTEXT).

Abbreviations should be used very carefully on drawings. Whenever possible, write out the full word and include correct punctuation. Figure 8-81 shows several standard abbreviations used on technical drawings.

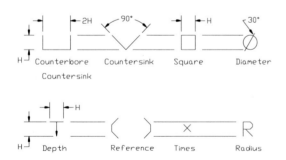

```
       AL    = Aluminum
    C'BORE   = Counterbore
       CRS   = Cold Rolled Steel
       CSK   = Countersink
       DIA   = Diameter
       EQ    = Equal
       HEX   = Hexagon
     MAT'L   = Material
       R     = Radius
       SAE   = Society of Automotive
                 Engineers
     SFACE   = Spotface
       ST    = Steel
       SQ    = Square
     REQD    = Required
```

Figure 8-80   **Figure 8-81**

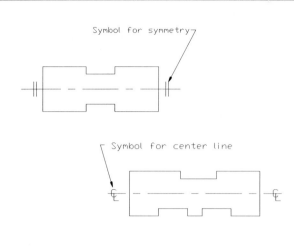

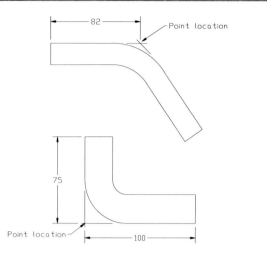

Figure 8-82

Figure 8-83

8-27 SYMMETRY AND CENTER LINE

An object is symmetrical about an axis when one side is an exact mirror image of the other. Figure 8-82 shows a symmetrical object. The two short parallel lines symbol or the note OBJECT IS SYMMETRICAL ABOUT THIS AXIS (center line) may be used to designate symmetry.

If an object is symmetrical, only half the object need be dimensioned. The other dimensions are implied by the symmetry note or symbol.

Center lines are slightly different from the axis of symmetry. An object may or may not be symmetrical about its center line. See Figure 8-82. Center lines are used to define the center of both individual features and entire objects. Use the centerline symbol when a line is a center line, but do not use it in place of the symmetry symbol.

8-28 DIMENSIONING TO POINTS

Curved surfaces can be dimensioned using theoretical points. See Figure 8-83. There should be a small gap between the surface of the object and the lines used to define the theoretical point. The point should be defined by the intersection of at least two lines.

There should also be a small gap between the extension lines and the theoretical point used to locate the point.

8-29 COORDINATE DIMENSIONS

Coordinate dimensions are used for objects that contain many holes. Baseline dimensions could also be used, but when there are many holes, baseline dimensions can create a confusing appearance and will require a large area on the drawing. Coordinate dimensions use charts that simplify the appearance, use far less space on the drawing, and are easy to understand.

Figure 8-84 shows an object that has been dimensioned using coordinate dimensions without dimension lines. Holes are identified on the drawing using letters. Holes of equal diameter use the same letter. The hole diameters are presented in chart form.

Hole locations are defined using a series of center lines referenced to baselines. The distance from the baseline to the center line is written below the center line, as shown.

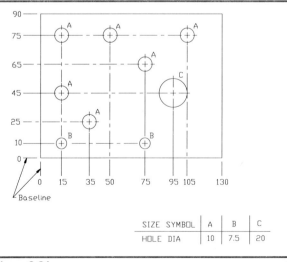

SIZE SYMBOL	A	B	C
HOLE DIA	10	7.5	20

Figure 8-84

Figure 8-85 shows an object that has been dimensioned using coordinate dimensions in tabular form. Each hole is assigned both a letter and a number. Holes of equal diameter are assigned the same letter. A chart is used to define the diameter values for each hole letter.

Hole locations are defined relative to an XY axis. A Z axis is used for depth dimensions. A chart lists each hole by its letter-number designation and specifies its distance from the X, Y, or Z axis. The overall dimensions are given using extension and dimension lines.

The side view does not show any hidden lines because if all the lines were shown, it would be too confusing to understand. A note, THIS VIEW LEFT BLANK FOR CLARITY, may be added to the drawing.

The two charts may be combined into one if desired.

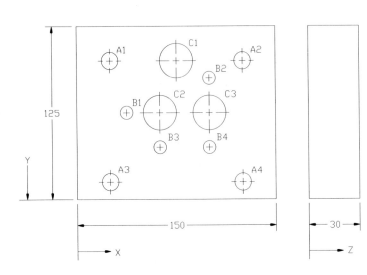

HOLE	FROM	X	Y	Z
A1	XY	15	65	THRU
A2	XY	80	65	THRU
A3	XY	15	10	THRU
A4	XY	80	10	THRU
B1	XY	25	40	12
B2	XY	65	56	12
B3	XY	40	25	12
B4	XY	65	25	12
C1	XY	48	65	THRU
C2	XY	40	40	THRU
C3	XY	65	40	THRU

HOLE	DESCRIPTION	QTY
A	Ø8	4
B	Ø5	4
C	Ø16	3

Figure 8-85

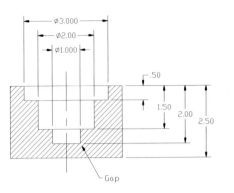

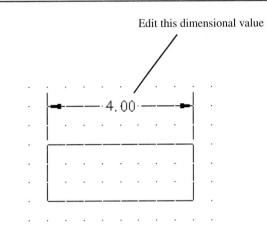

Edit this dimensional value

Figure 8-86

8-30 SECTIONAL VIEWS

Sectional views are dimensioned as are orthographic views. See Figure 8-86. The sectional lines should be drawn at an angle that allows the viewer to clearly distinguish between the sectional lines and the extension lines.

8-31 EDITING DIMENSIONS

Dimensions may be edited after they have been added to a drawing. Figure 8-87 shows a 4.00 linear dimension. You wish to change it to 4.25. The entire dimension need not be erased and redrawn, but may be edited using the EDIT TEXT command.

Figure 8-87

To change the value of an existing dimension

1. Select the EDIT TEXT icon from the MODIFY toolbar, or type DDEDIT in response to a command prompt

   Command: ddedit
   <Select an annotated object>/Undo:

2. Select the existing dimension text

The MText dialog box or the Text edit box will appear. See Figure 8-88. The <> symbol in the box represents the existing text. In this example the existing text, 4.00, is to be replaced, so backspace out the <> symbol and type in the new text.

The screen shown is for the WINDOWS version. The DOS screen functions in a similar manner.

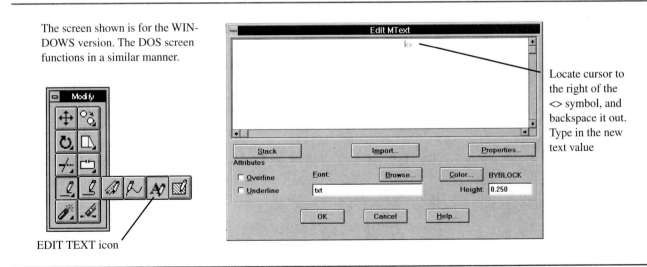

EDIT TEXT icon

Locate cursor to the right of the <> symbol, and backspace it out. Type in the new text value

Figure 8-88

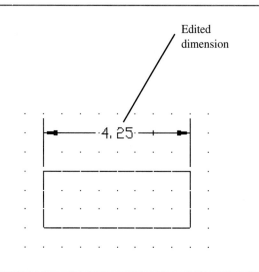

Edited dimension

Figure 8-89

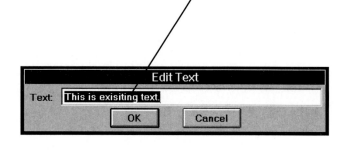

Locate the cursor anywhere in the text line and edit

Edit Text

Text: This is exisiting text.

OK   Cancel

Figure 8-90

3. Locate the cursor to the right of the <> symbol and backspace it out
4. Type 4.25
5. Select the OK box or type ENTER

Figure 8-89 shows the edited dimension.

To edit a line of text

An existing line of text can also be edited using the EDIT TEXT command. If a line of text was selected rather than an existing dimension, the EDIT TEXT dialog box will appear. See Figure 8-90. The cursor may be located anywhere in the line of text and edited as with a word processing program.

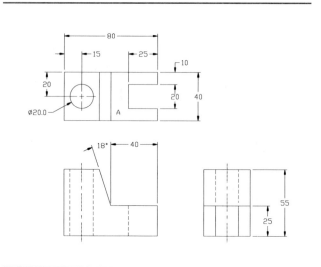

Figure 8-91

8-32 ORTHOGRAPHIC VIEWS

Dimensions should be added to orthographic views where the features appear in contour. Holes should be dimensioned in their circular views. Figure 8-91 shows three views of an object that has been dimensioned.

The hole dimensions are added to the top view, where the hole appears circular. The slot is also dimensioned in the top view because it appears in contour. The slanted surface is dimensioned in the front view.

The height of surface A is given in the side view rather than run along extension lines across the front view. The length of surface A is given in the front view. This is a contour view of the surface.

It is considered good practice to keep dimensions in groups. This makes it easier for the viewer to find dimensions.

Be careful not to double dimension a distance. A distance should be dimensioned only once per view. For example, the 30 vertical dimension located between the front and side views is an error. It creates a double dimension. The overall 65 vertical dimension to the right of the side view defines the object's height. The 35 dimension defines the distance from the bottom surface to surface A. No other dimensions are needed.

If a 30 dimension were added above the 25 dimension on the right-side view, it would be an error. The distance would be double dimensioned: once with the 25 + 30 dimension and again with the 55 overall dimension. The 25 + 30 dimensions are mathematically equal to the 55 overall dimension, but there is a distinct difference in how they affect the manufacturing tolerances. Double dimensions are explained more fully in Chapter 9.

8-33 EXERCISE PROBLEMS

Redraw the shapes in exercise problems EX8-1 to EX8-4. Locate the dimensions as shown.

EX8-1 INCHES

1. 3.00
2. 1.63
3. 45°
4. .75
5. 2.75
6. 3.63
7. 45°
8. 2.25

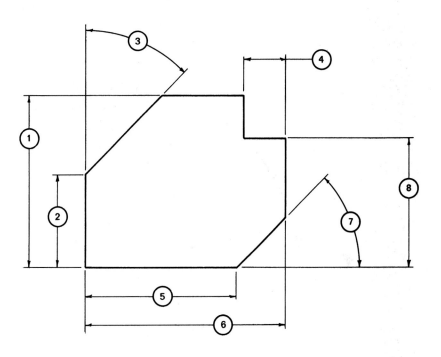

EX8-2 MILLIMETERS

1. 34
2. 17
3. 45
4. 15
5. 50
6. 80
7. R5 ALL AROUND
8. 45
9. 60
10. Ø14 - 3 PLACES
11. 15
12. 30

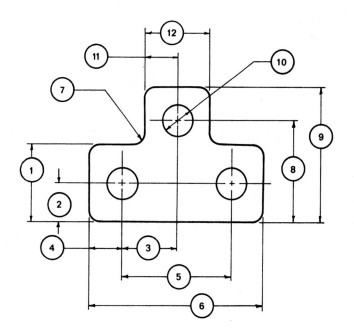

EX8-3 MILLIMETERS

1. 50
2. R44
3. 63
4. 76
5. 38
6. Ø13 - 3 PLACES
7. 39
8. 39
9. 100

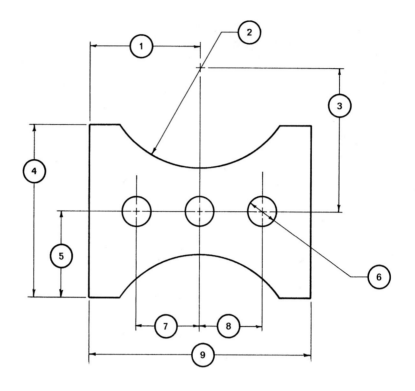

EX8-4

1. Ø30
2. Ø15
3. 10
4. 20
5. 65
6. 15
7. 35
8. 70
9. NOTE: ALL FILLETS AND ROUNDS = R5
   UNLESS OTHERWISE STATED

Note : ⑨

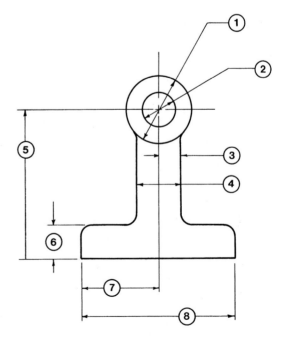

Measure and redraw the shapes in exercise problems EX8-5 to EX8-24. Add the appropriate dimensions. Specify the units and the scale of the drawing.

EX8-5

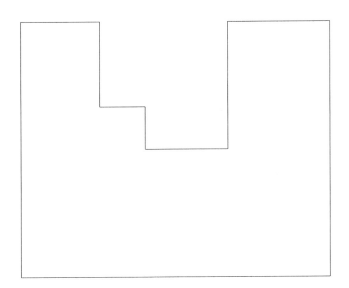

EX8-6

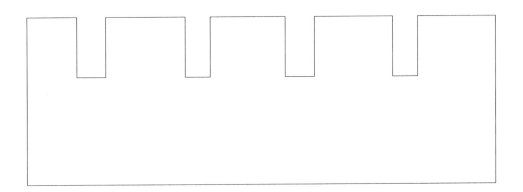

EX8-7

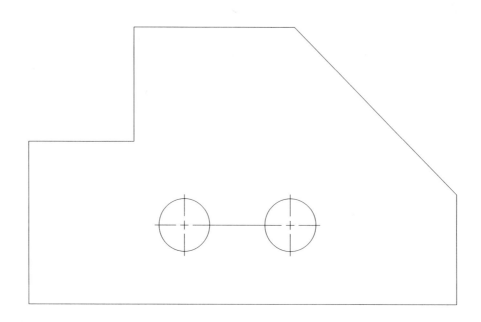

EX8-8

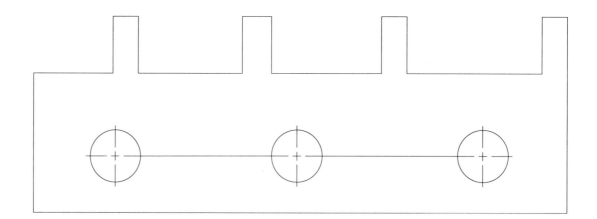

EX8-9

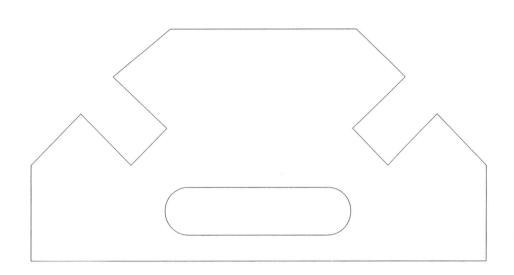

EX8-10

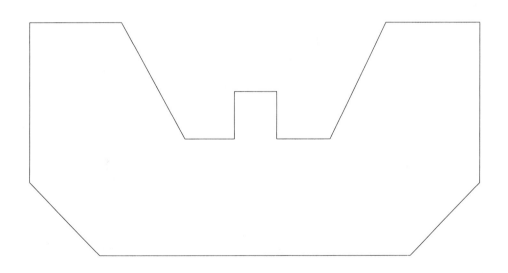

EX8-11

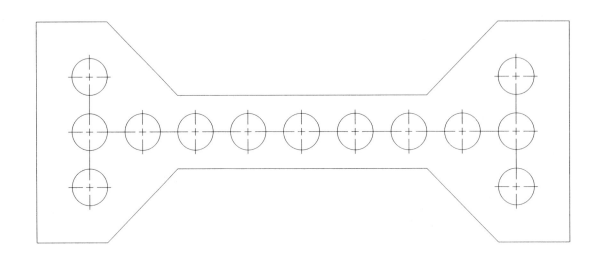

EX8-12

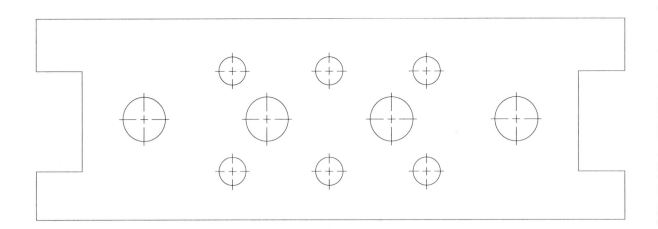

EX8-13

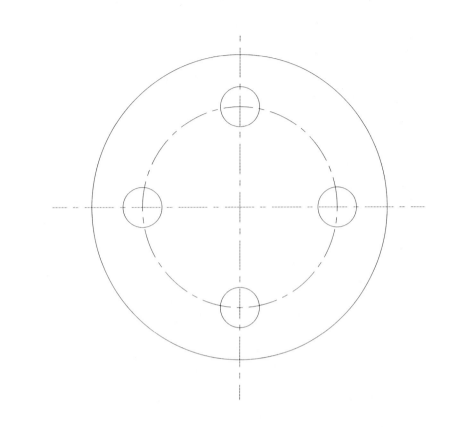

EX8-14

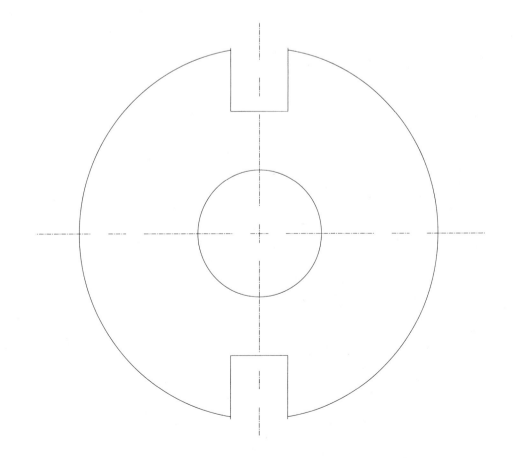

EX8-15

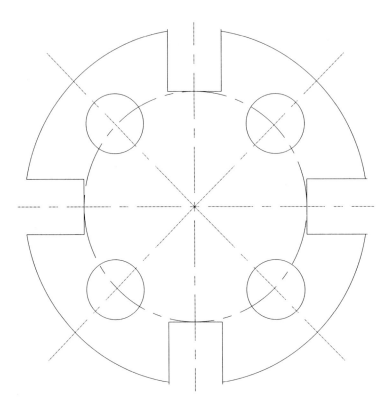

EX8-16

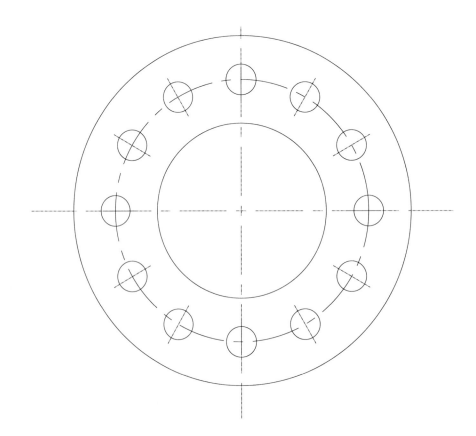

EX8-17

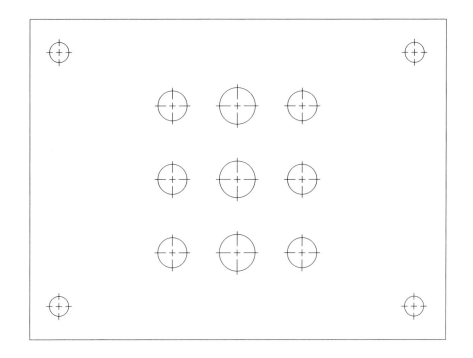

EX8-18

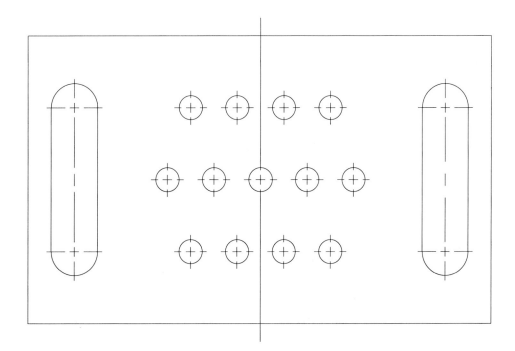

EX8-19

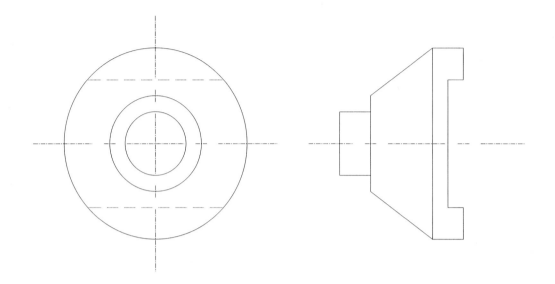

EX8-20

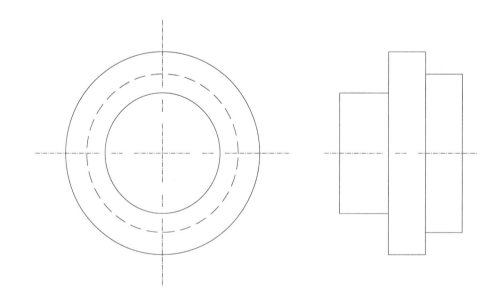

EX8-21

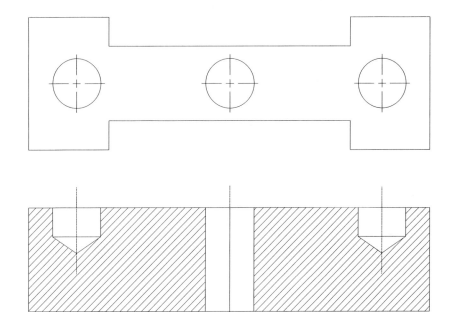

EX8-22

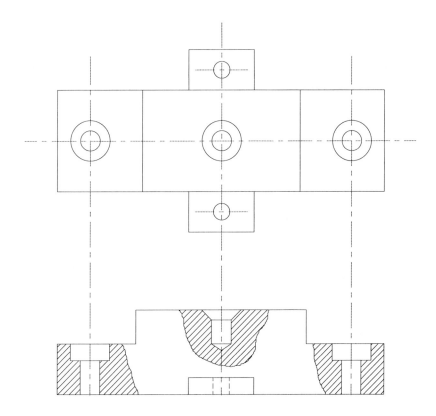

EX8-23

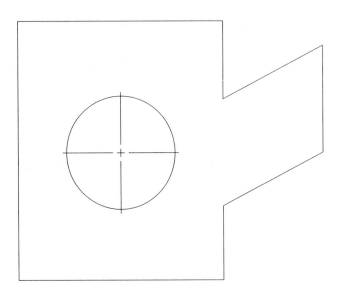

EX8-24

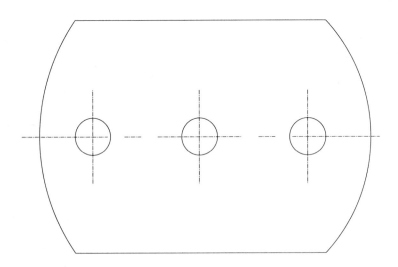

CHAPTER  9

Tolerancing

9-1 INTRODUCTION

Tolerances define the manufacturing limits for dimensions. All dimensions have tolerances either written directly on the drawing as part of the dimension or implied by a predefined set of standard tolerances that apply to any dimension without a stated tolerance.

This chapter explains general tolerance conventions and how they are applied using AutoCAD. It includes a sample tolerance study and an explanation of standard fits and surface finishes. Chapter 10 explains geometric tolerances.

9-2 DIRECT TOLERANCE METHODS

There are two methods used to include tolerances as part of a dimension: plus and minus, and limits. Plus and minus tolerances can be expressed in either bilateral or unilateral forms.

A bilateral tolerance has both a plus and minus value. A unilateral tolerance has either the plus or minus value equal to 0. Figure 9-1 shows a horizontal dimension of 60mm that includes a bilateral tolerance of plus or minus 0.1 and another dimension of 60mm that includes a bilater-

al tolerance of plus 0.2 or minus 0.1. Figure 9-1 also shows a dimension of 65mm that includes a unilateral tolerance of plus 1 minus 0.

Plus or minus tolerances define a range for manufacturing. If inspection shows that all dimensioned distances on an object fall within their specified tolerance range, the object is considered acceptable; that is, it has been manufactured correctly.

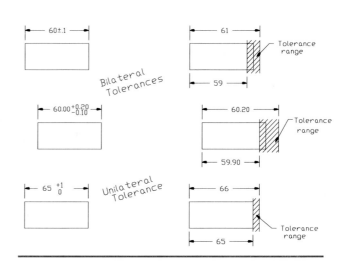

Figure 9-1

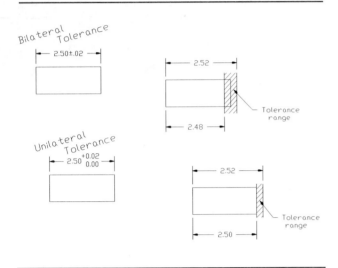

Figure 9-2

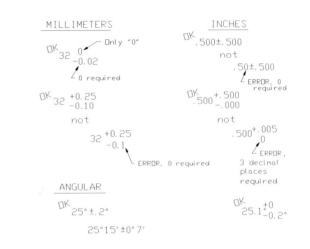

Figure 9-3

The dimension and tolerance of 60 +/–0.1 means that the distance must be manufactured within a range no greater than 60.1 or less than 59.9. The dimension and tolerance 65 +1/–0 defines the tolerance range as 65.0 to 66.0.

Figure 9-2 shows some bilateral and unilateral tolerances applied using decimal inch values. Inch dimensions and tolerances are written using a slightly different format than millimeter dimensions and tolerances, but also define manufacturing ranges for dimension values. The horizontal bilateral dimension and tolerance of 2.50 +/–.02 defines the longest acceptable distance as 2.52 inches and the shortest as 2.48. The unilateral dimension 2.50 +.02 / –.00 defines the longest acceptable distance as 2.52 and the shortest as 2.50.

9-3 TOLERANCE EXPRESSIONS

Dimension and tolerance values are written differently for inch and millimeter values. See Figure 9-3. Unilateral dimensions for millimeter values specify a zero limit by writing a single 0. A zero limit for inch values must include the same number of decimal places given for the dimension value. In the example shown in Figure 9-3, the dimension value of .500 uses a unilateral tolerance with minus zero tolerance. The zero limit is written as .000, three decimal places for both the dimension and the tolerance.

Both values in a bilateral tolerance must contain the same number of decimal places, although for millimeter values, the tolerance values need not include the same

number of decimal places as the dimension value. In Figure 9-3 the dimension value of 32 is accompanied by tolerances of +0.25 and –0.10. This form is not acceptable for inch dimensions and tolerances. An equivalent inch dimension and tolerance would be written 32.00 +.25/–.10.

Degree values must include the same number of decimal places in both the dimension value and the tolerance values for bilateral tolerances. A single 0 may be used for unilateral tolerances.

9-4 UNDERSTANDING PLUS AND MINUS TOLERANCES

A millimeter dimension and tolerance of 12 +0.2/ –0.1 means the longest acceptable distance is 12.2000...0 and the shortest 11.9000...0. The total range is .3000...0.

After an object is manufactured, it is inspected to ensure that the object has been manufactured correctly. Each dimensioned distance is measured and, if it is within the specified tolerance, is accepted. If the measured distance is not within the specified tolerance, the part is rejected. Some rejected objects may be reworked to bring them into the specified tolerance range, whereas others are simply scrapped.

Figure 9-4 shows a dimension with a tolerance. Assume five objects were manufactured using the same 12 +0.2/–0.1 dimension and tolerance. The objects were then inspected and the results were as listed. Inspected measurements are usually at least one more decimal place than that specified in the tolerance. Which objects are acceptable

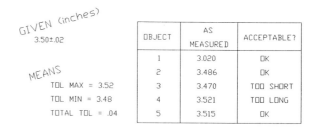

Figure 9-4

OBJECT	AS MEASURED	ACCEPTABLE?
1	12.160	OK
2	12.020	OK
3	12.203	TOO LONG
4	11.920	OK
5	11.895	TOO SHORT

GIVEN (mm)
12 +0.2 −0.1

MEANS

TOL MAX = 12.2
TOL MIN = 11.9
TOTAL TOL = 0.3

Figure 9-5

OBJECT	AS MEASURED	ACCEPTABLE?
1	3.020	OK
2	3.486	OK
3	3.470	TOO SHORT
4	3.521	TOO LONG
5	3.515	OK

GIVEN (inches)
3.50±.02

MEANS

TOL MAX = 3.52
TOL MIN = 3.48
TOTAL TOL = .04

and which are not? Object 3 is too long and object 5 is too short because their measured distances are not within the specified tolerances.

Figure 9-5 shows a dimension and tolerance of 3.50 +/–.02 inches. Object 3 is not acceptable because it is too short, and object 4 is too long.

9-5 CREATING PLUS AND MINUS TOLERANCES USING AUTOCAD

Plus and minus tolerances are added to the DIMEN-SION commands by using the DIMENSION STYLES command. The DIMENSION STYLES dialog box is accessed by typing DDIM or by selecting the DIMEN-SION STYLES icon from the DIMENSIONS toolbar. See Figure 9-6.

Tolerances may also be added to dimensions by first using the LINEAR DIMENSION command to create a dimension, then EXPLODing the dimension. The dimension can now be manipulated. The DTEXT command can be used to create the plus and minus values anywhere on the drawing screen, and the MOVE command can be used to position the plus and minus values in the appropriate locations to the right of the existing dimension. The BREAK command can be used to create a wider space in the dimension line to accept the larger dimension value. This method is acceptable for occasional use, but using the DIMENSION STYLES command to set the upper and lower values for tolerances is preferred.

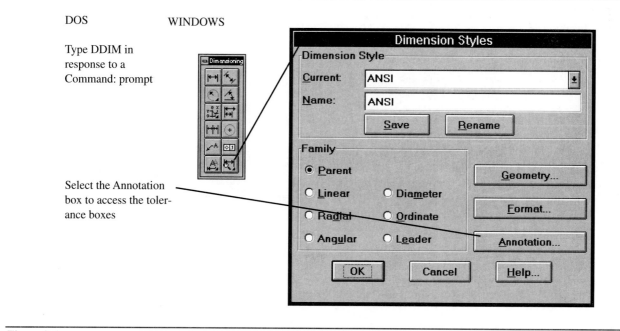

DOS

Type DDIM in response to a Command: prompt

WINDOWS

Select the Annotation box to access the tolerance boxes

Figure 9-6

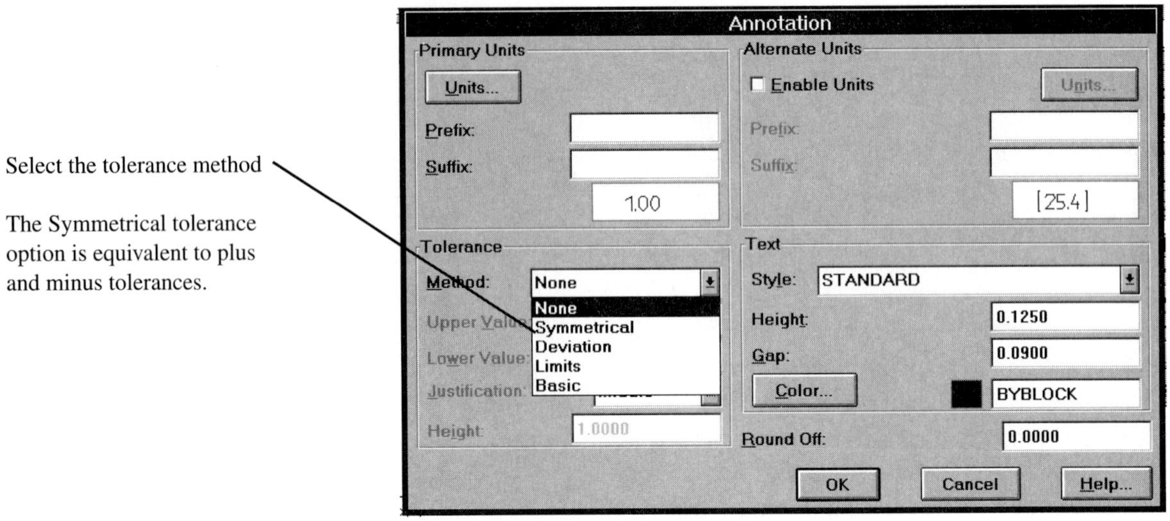

Select the tolerance method

The Symmetrical tolerance option is equivalent to plus and minus tolerances.

Figure 9-7

To create a symmetrical tolerance — inches

1. Select the DIMENSION STYLES icon or type DDIM in response to a Command: prompt

   The Dimension Styles dialog box will appear.

2. Select Annotation...

   The Annotation dialog box will appear.

3. Click the arrow box to the right of the word None in the Method: box located in the Tolerance box.

   A listing of options will cascade down. See Figure 9-7.

4. Select Symmetrical
5. Change the Upper Value to 0.0300 by locating the cursor within the Upper Value box, backspacing out the existing value, and typing in the new value.
6. Check that the Justification box reads Middle

   If it does not read Middle, use the arrow box to the right of the Justification box to change the reading. See Figure 9-8. The value displayed in the Units box will not change at this time, but the tolerance placed on the drawing will change.

7. Select OK, OK to return to the drawing

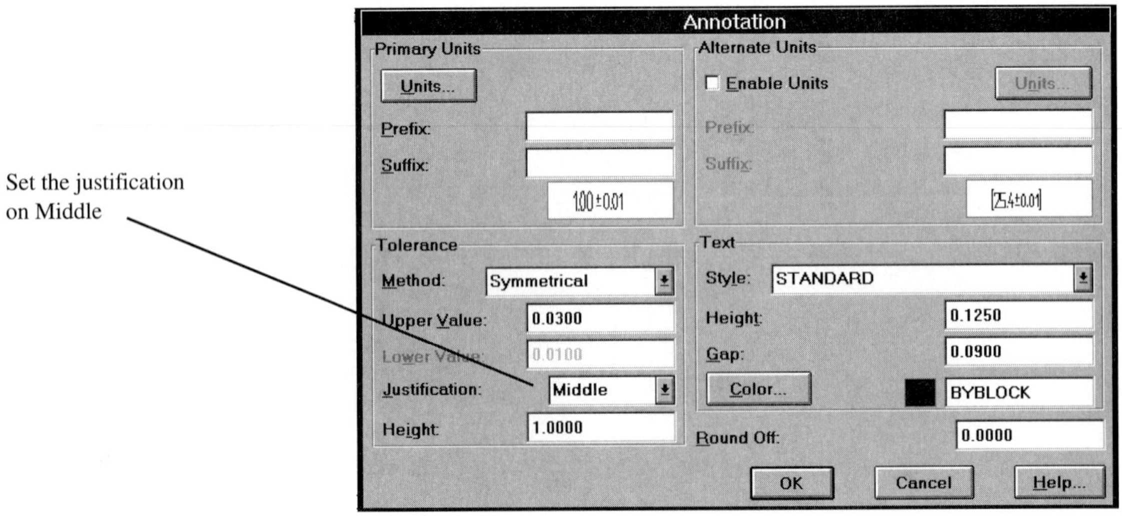

Set the justification on Middle

Figure 9-8

8. Select the LINEAR DIMENSION icon

Command:_dimlinear
First extension line or RETURN to select

9. Type ENTER

Select object to dimension:

10. Select the line

Dimension line location (Text /Angle/ Horizontal/ Vertical/ Rotated):

11. Locate the dimension line and press the left mouse button

Figure 9-9 shows the resulting dimension.

To create a symmetrical tolerance — millimeters

The object shown in Figure 9-10 is 80 millimeters long and is to have a tolerance of +/-0.02. This example assumes that the Overall Scale in the Geometry dialog box has been changed to 25.4, as explained in Section 8-4.

1. Select the DIMENSION STYLES icon or type DDIM in response to a Command: prompt

The Dimension Styles dialog box will appear.

2. Select Annotation...

The Annotation dialog box will appear.

3. Click the arrow box to the right of the word None in the Method: box located in the Tolerance box.

A listing of options will cascade down. See Figure 9-7.

4. Select Symmetrical

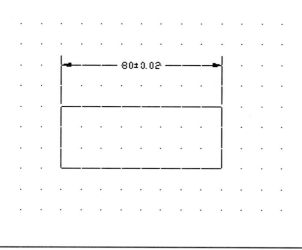

Figure 9-10

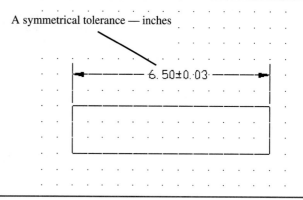

Figure 9-9

5. Change the Upper Value to 0.0200 by locating the cursor within the Upper Value box, backspacing out the existing value, and typing in the new value.

The value displayed in the Units box will not change at this time, but the tolerance placed on the drawing will change.

6. Select Units...

The primary Units dialog box will appear. See Figure 9-11.

7. Click the box to the left of the word Trailing in the Zero suppression box.

An X will appear in the box, indicating that the option is on. AutoCAD will now suppress all zeros to the right of the decimal point on the primary dimension value. It will not suppress the tolerance values.

8. Select OK, OK, OK to return to the drawing
9. Use the LINEAR DIMENSION icon to create the dimension and tolerance values.

To create a deviation tolerance

The object shown in Figure 9-12 is to have a horizontal tolerance of +.02, -.01, and a vertical tolerance of +.03, -.00.

1. Select the DIMENSION STYLES icon or type DDIM in response to a Command: prompt

The Dimension Styles dialog box will appear.

2. Select Annotation...

The Annotation dialog box will appear.

3. Click the arrow box to the right of the word None in the Method: box located in the Tolerance box.

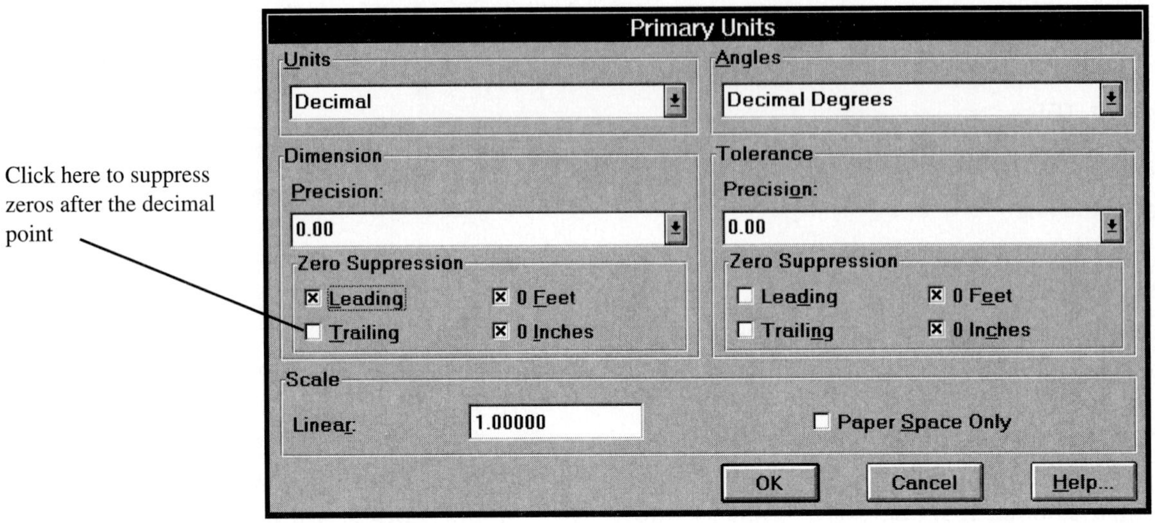

Primary Units

Units
Decimal

Angles
Decimal Degrees

Click here to suppress zeros after the decimal point

Dimension
Precision:
0.00

Zero Suppression
☒ Leading   ☒ 0 Feet
☐ Trailing   ☒ 0 Inches

Tolerance
Precision:
0.00

Zero Suppression
☐ Leading   ☒ 0 Feet
☐ Trailing   ☒ 0 Inches

Scale
Linear: 1.00000

☐ Paper Space Only

[OK]   [Cancel]   [Help...]

Figure 9-11

A listing of options will cascade down. See Figure 9-7.

4. Select Deviation
5. Change the Upper Value to 0.0200 by locating the cursor within the Upper Value box, backspacing out the existing value, and typing in the new value.

The value displayed in the Units box will not change at this time, but the tolerance placed on the drawing will change.

6. Change the Lower Value to 0.0100 by locating the cursor within the Lower Value box, backspacing out the existing value, and typing in the new value.
7. Check that the Justification box reads Middle.

If it does not read Middle, use the arrow box to the right of the Justification box to change the reading. Also use the Units option to check that the Zero Suppression for Trailing values has been turned off; that is, there is no X in the box to the left of the word Trailing.

8. Select OK, OK to return to the drawing
9. Use the LINEAR DIMENSION icon to add the appropriate dimension and tolerance.
10. Select the DIMENSION STYLES icon or type DDIM in response to a Command: prompt, then select Annotation as explained above
11. Change the Upper Value to 0.03 and the Lower Value to 0.00
12. Select OK, OK to return to the drawing

13. Use the LINEAR DIMENSIONS icon to add the vertical dimension

Figure 9-12 shows the resulting dimensions.

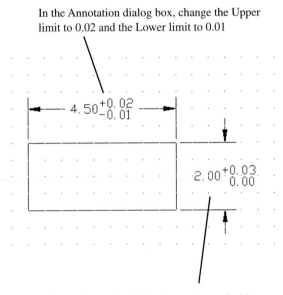

In the Annotation dialog box, change the Upper limit to 0.02 and the Lower limit to 0.01

$4.50^{+0.02}_{-0.01}$

$2.00^{+0.03}_{-0.00}$

In the Annotation dialog box, change the Upper limit to 0.03 and the Lower limit to 0.00

Figure 9-12

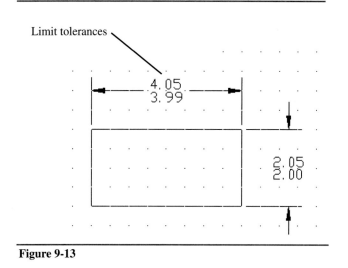

Limit tolerances

Figure 9-13

Symmetrical tolerances

50.19°±0.20°

Deviation tolerances

24.08° +0.10° −0.30°

Once defined, symmetrical and deviation tolerances will be applied to angular dimensions

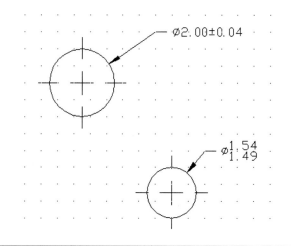

Ø2.00±0.04

Ø1.54 / 1.49

Figure 9-14

To create a limit tolerance

The object shown in Figure 9-13 is to be dimensioned using limit tolerances. The horizontal dimension limits are 4.05 to 3.99 and the vertical limits are 2.125 to 2.000.

1. Select the DIMENSION STYLES icon or type DDIM in response to a Command: prompt

The Dimension Styles dialog box will appear.

2. Select Annotation...

The Annotation dialog box will appear.

3. Click the arrow box to the right of the word None in the Method: box located in the Tolerance box.

A listing of options will cascade down. See Figure 9-7.

4. Select Limits
5. Change the Upper Value to 0.0500 by locating the cursor within the Upper Value box, backspacing out the existing value, and typing in the new value.

The value displayed in the Units box will not change, but the tolerance placed on the drawing will change.

6. Change the Lower Value to 0.0100 by locating the cursor within the Lower Value box, backspacing out the existing value, and typing in the new value.
7. Check that the Justification box reads Middle.

If it does not read Middle, use the arrow box to the right of the Justification box to change the reading. Also use the Units option to check that the Zero Suppression for Trailing values has been turned off; that is, there is no X in the box to the left of the word Trailing.

8. Select OK, OK to return to the drawing
9. Use the LINEAR DIMENSION icon to add the appropriate dimension and tolerance.
10. Select the DIMENSION STYLES icon or type DDIM in response to a Command: prompt, then select the ANNOTATION option and change the upper limit to 0.05 and the lower limit to 0.00
11. Select OK, OK to return to the drawing.
12. Use the LINEAR DIMENSION icon to add the vertical dimension to the drawing

Figure 9-14 shows examples of tolerances applied to different dimensions. Note that once defined, symmetrical and deviation tolerances will also be applied to angular dimensions.

9-6 STANDARD TOLERANCES

Most manufacturers establish a set of standard tolerances that are applied to any dimension without a specific tolerance. Figure 9-15 shows some possible standard tolerances. Standard tolerances vary from company to company. Standard tolerances are usually listed on the first page of a drawing to the left of the title block, but this location may vary.

The x value used when specifying standard tolerances means any x stated in that format. A dimension value of 52.00 would have an implied tolerance of +/−.01 because the stated standard tolerance is .xx +/−.01, so any dimension value with two decimal places has a standard implied tolerance of +/−.01. A dimension value of 52.000 would have an implied tolerance of +/−.005.

9-7 DOUBLE DIMENSIONING

It is an error to dimension the same distance twice. It is called double dimensioning. Double dimensioning is an error because it does not allow for tolerance buildup across a distance.

Figure 9-16 shows an object that has been dimensioned twice across its horizontal length: once using three 30mm dimensions and a second time using the 90mm overall dimension. The two dimensions are mathematically equal, but they are not equal when tolerances are considered. Assume that each dimension has a standard tolerance of +/−1mm. The three 30mm dimensions could create an acceptable distance of 90 +/−3 mm, or a maximum distance of 93 and a minimum distance of 87. The overall dimension of 90mm allows a maximum distance of 91 and a minimum distance of 89. The two dimensions yield different results when tolerances are considered.

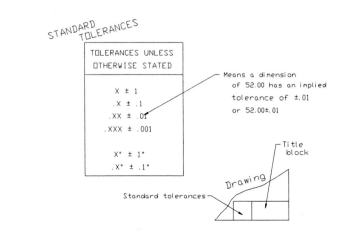

Figure 9-15

The size and location of a tolerance depends on the design objectives of the object, how it will be manufactured, and how it will be inspected. Even objects that have similar shapes may be dimensioned and toleranced very differently.

One possible solution to the double dimensioning shown in Figure 9-16 is to remove one of the 30mm dimensions and allow that distance to "float," that is, absorb the accumulated tolerances. The choice of which 30mm dimension to eliminate depends on the design objectives of the part. For this example, the far right dimension was eliminated to remove the double-dimension error.

Another possible solution to the double-dimensioning error is to retain the three 30mm dimensions and to change the 90mm overall dimension to a reference dimension. A reference dimension is used only for mathematical convenience. It is not used during the manufacturing or

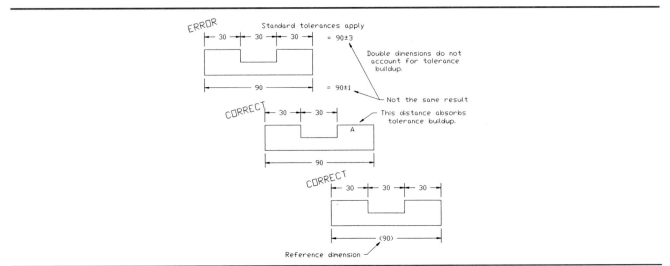

Figure 9-16

inspection process. A reference dimension is designated on a drawing using parentheses (90).

If the 90mm dimension were referenced, then only the three 30mm dimensions would be used to manufacture and inspect the object. This eliminates the double-dimension error.

9-8 CHAIN DIMENSIONS AND BASELINE DIMENSIONS

There are two systems used to apply dimensions and tolerances to a drawing: chain and baseline. Figure 9-17 shows examples of both systems. Chain dimensions dimension each feature to the feature next to it. Baseline dimensions dimension all features from a single baseline or datum.

Chain and baseline dimensions may be used together. Figure 9-17 also shows two objects that have repetitive features: one object includes two slots, and the other includes three sets of three holes. In each example, the center of the repetitive feature is dimensioned to the left side of the objects, and serves as a baseline. The sizes of the individual features are dimensioned using chain dimensions referenced to center lines.

Baseline dimensions eliminate tolerance buildup and can be related directly to the reference axis of many machines. They do tend to take up much more area on a drawing than do chain dimensions.

Chain dimensions are useful in relating one feature to another, such as the repetitive hole pattern shown in Figure 9-17. In this example the distance between the holes is more important than the individual hole's distance from the baseline.

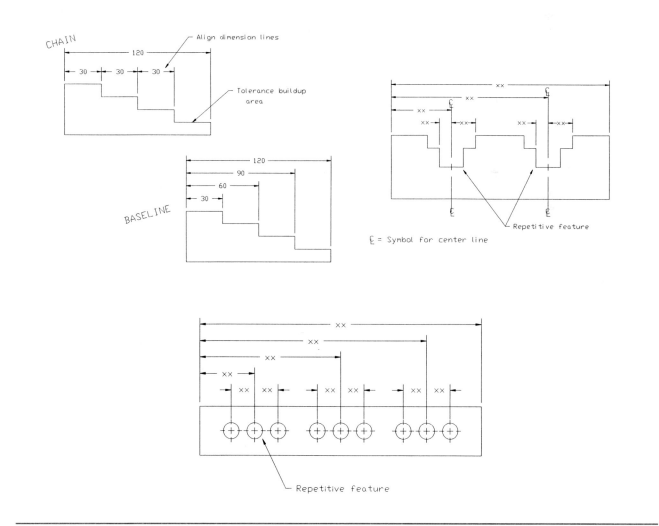

Figure 9-17

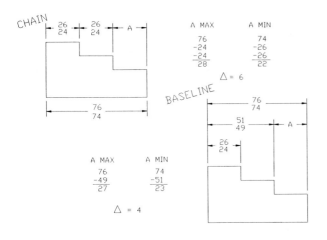

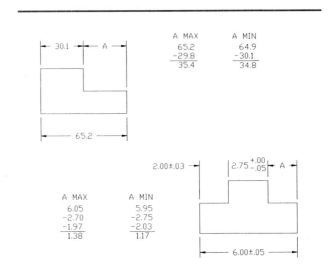

Figure 9-18

Figure 9-19

Figure 9-18 shows the same object dimensioned twice: once using chain dimensions and once using baseline dimensions. All distances are assigned a tolerance range of 2mm stated using limit tolerances. The maximum distance for surface A is 28mm using the chain system and 27mm using the baseline system. The 1mm difference comes from the elimination of the first 26-24 limit dimension found on the chain example but not on the baseline.

The total tolerance difference is 6mm for the chain and 4mm for the baseline. The baseline reduces the tolerance variations for the object simply because it applies the tolerances and dimensions differently. So why not always use baseline dimensions? For most applications, the baseline system is probably better, but if the distance between the individual features is more critical than the distance from the feature to the baseline, use the chain system.

9-9 TOLERANCE STUDIES

The term "tolerance study" is used when analyzing the effects of a group of tolerances on each other and on an object. Figure 9-19 shows an object with two horizontal dimensions. The horizontal distance A is not dimensioned. Its length depends on the tolerances of the two horizontal dimensions.

To calculate A's maximum length

Distance A will be longest when the overall distance is at its longest and the other distance is at its shortest.

$$
\begin{array}{r}
65.2 \\
-\ 29.8 \\
\hline
35.4
\end{array}
$$

To calculate A's minimum length

Distance A will be shortest when the overall length is at its shortest and the other length is at its longest.

$$
\begin{array}{r}
64.9 \\
-\ 30.1 \\
\hline
34.8
\end{array}
$$

Figure 9-19 also shows an object that includes three horizontal dimensions. Surface B is at its maximum length when the overall dimension is at its longest and the other dimensions are at their shortest. Surface B is at its minimum when the overall length is at its shortest and the other dimensions are at their longest.

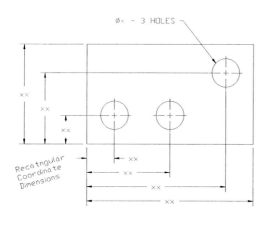

Figure 9-20

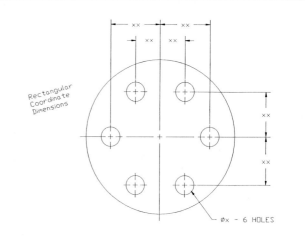

Figure 9-21

9-10 RECTANGULAR DIMENSIONS

Figure 9-20 shows an example of rectangular dimensions referenced to baselines. Figure 9-21 shows a circular object where dimensions are referenced to a circle's center lines. Dimensioning to a circle's center line is critical to accurate hole location.

9-11 HOLE LOCATIONS

When using rectangular dimensions, the location of a hole's center point is defined by two linear dimensions. The result is a rectangular tolerance zone whose size is based on the linear dimension's tolerances. The shape of the center point's tolerance zone may be changed to circular using positioning tolerancing as described in Chapter 10.

Figure 9-22a shows the location and size dimensions for a hole. Also shown is the resulting tolerance zone and the overall possible hole shape. The center point's tolerance is .2 by .3 based on the given tolerances.

The hole diameter has a tolerance of +/−.05. This must be added to the centerpoint location tolerances to define the maximum overall possible shape of the hole. The maximum possible hole shape is determined by drawing the maximum radius from the four corner points of the tolerance zone.

This means that the left edge of the hole could be as close to the vertical baseline as 12.75 or as far as 13.25.

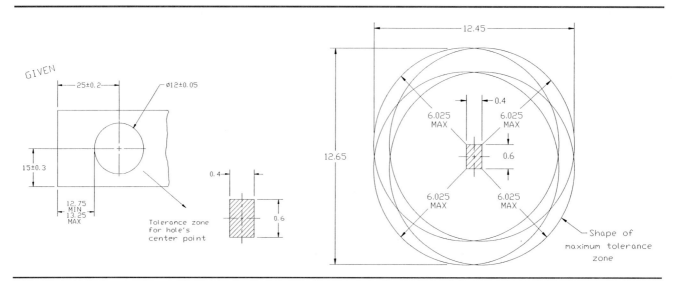

Figure 9-22a

The 12.75 value was derived by subtracting the maximum hole diameter value 12.05 from the minimum linear distance 24.80 (24.80 – 12.05 = 12.75). The 13.25 value was derived by subtracting the minimum hole diameter 11.95 from the maximum linear distance 25.20 (25.20 – 11.95 = 13.25).

Figure 9-22b shows a hole's tolerance zone based on polar dimensions. The zone has a sector shape, and the possible hole shape is determined by locating the maximum radius at the four corner points of the tolerance zone.

9-12 CHOOSING A SHAFT FOR A TOLERANCED HOLE

Given the hole location and size shown in Figure 9-22, what is the largest possible diameter shaft that will always fit into the hole?

Figure 9-23 shows the hole's centerpoint tolerance zone based on the given linear locating tolerances. Four circles have been drawn centered at the four corners on the linear tolerance zone that represent the smallest possible hole diameter. The circles define an area that represents the maximum shaft size that will always fit into the hole, regardless of how the given dimensions are applied.

The diameter size of this circular area can be calculated by subtracting the maximum diagonal distance across the linear tolerance zone (corner to corner) from the minimum hole diameter. The results can be expressed as a formula.

For linear dimensions and tolerances

Smax = Hmin – DTZ

Where:

    Smax = Maximum shaft diameter
    Hmin = Minimum hole diameter
    DTZ = Diagonal distance across the tolerance zone

In the example shown the diagonal distance is determined using the Pythagorean theorem.

$$DTZ = (.4)^2 + (.6)^2$$
$$= .16 + .36$$
$$DTZ = .72$$

The maximum shaft diameter that will always fit into the given hole is 11.23.

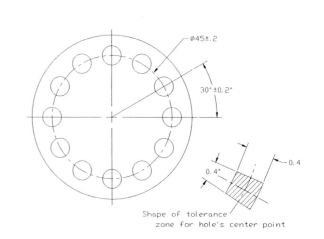

Figure 9-22b

Smax = Hmin – DTZ
    = 11.95 – .72
Smax = 11.23

This procedure represents a restricted application of the general formula presented in Chapter 10 for positioning tolerances. For a more complete discussion see Chapter 10.

Once the maximum shaft size has been established, a tolerance can be applied to the shaft. If the shaft were to have a total tolerance of .25, the minimum shaft diameter would be 11.23 – .25, or 10.98. Figure 9-23 shows a shaft dimensioned and toleranced using these values.

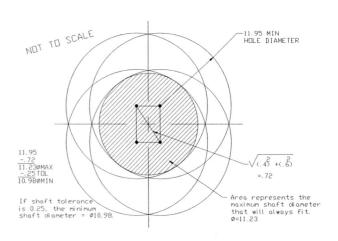

Figure 9-23

The formula presented is based on the assumption that the shaft is perfectly placed on the hole's center point. This assumption is reasonable if two objects are joined by a fastener and both objects are free to move. When both objects are free to move about a common fastener, they are called floating objects.

9-13 SAMPLE PROBLEM SP9-1

Parts A and B in Figure 9-24 are to be joined by a common shaft. The total tolerance for the shaft is to be .05. What is the maximum and minimum shaft diameter?

Both objects have the same dimensions and tolerances and are floating relative to each other.

Smax = Hmin − DTZ
= 15.93 − .85
Smax = 15.08

The shaft's minimum diameter is found by subtracting the total tolerance requirement from the calculated maximum diameter.

15.08 − .05 = 15.03

Therefore

Shaft max = 15.08
Shaft min = 15.03

9-14 SAMPLE PROBLEM SP9-2

The procedure presented in Sample Problem SP9-1 can be worked in reverse to determine the maximum and minimum hole size based on a given shaft size.

Objects AA and BB in Figure 9-25 are to be joined using a bolt whose maximum diameter is .248. What is the minimum hole size for the objects that will always accept the bolt? What is the maximum hole size if the total hole tolerance is .005?

Smax = Hmin − DTZ

In this example the Hmin is the unknown factor, so the equation is rewritten.

Hmin = Smax + DTZ
= .248 + .010
Hmin = .258

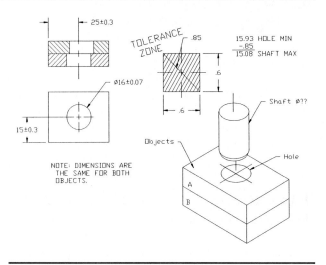

Figure 9-24

This is the minimum hole diameter, so the total tolerance requirement is added to this value.

.258 + .005 = .263

Therefore

Hole max = .263
Hole min = .258

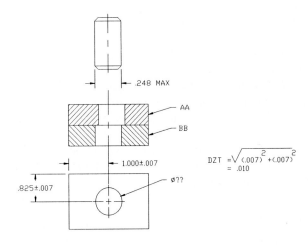

Figure 9-25

9-15 STANDARD FITS (METRIC VALUES)

Calculating tolerances between holes and shafts that fit together is so common in engineering design that a group of standard values and notations has been established. These values are listed in tables in the appendix.

There are three possible types of fits between a shaft and a hole: clearance, transitional, and interference. See Figure 9-26. There are several subclassifications within each of these categories.

A clearance fit always defines the maximum shaft diameter as smaller than the minimum hole diameter. The difference between the two diameters is the amount of clearance. It is possible for a clearance fit to be defined with zero clearance; that is, the maximum shaft diameter is equal to the minimum hole diameter.

An interference fit always defines the minimum shaft diameter as larger than the maximum hole diameter, or more simply said, the shaft is always bigger than the hole. This definition means that an interference fit is the converse of a clearance fit. The difference between the diameter of the shaft and the hole is the amount of interference.

An interference fit is primarily used to assemble objects together. Interference fits eliminate the need for threads, welds, or other joining methods. Using an interference for joining two objects is generally limited to light load applications.

It is sometimes difficult to visualize how a shaft can be assembled into a hole with a diameter smaller than the shaft's. It is sometimes done using a hydraulic press that slowly forces the two parts together. The joining process can be augmented by the use of lubricants or heat. The hole is heated, causing it to expand; the shaft is inserted; and the hole is allowed to cool and shrink around the shaft.

A transition fit may be either a clearance or interference fit. It may have a clearance between the shaft and the hole or an interference.

Figure 9-27 shows two graphic representations of twenty different standard hole/shaft tolerance ranges. The figure shows ranges for hole tolerances and shaft tolerances, and the amount of clearance or interference for each classification. The notations are based on standard international tolerance values. A specific description for each category of fit is as follows.

Clearance fits

    H11/c11 or C11/h11 = Loose running fit
    H9/d9 orD9/h9 = Free running fit
    H8/f7 or F8/h7 = Close running fit
    H7/g6 or G7/h6 = Sliding fit

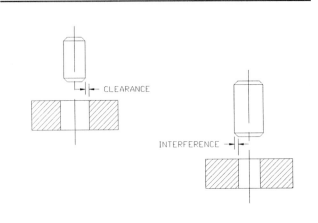

Figure 9-26

Transitional fits

    H7/h6 = Locational clearance fit
    H7/k6 or K7/h6 = Locational transition fit
    H7/n6 or N7/h6 = Locational transition fit

Interference fits

    H7/p6 or P7/h6 = Locational transition fit
    H7/s6 or S7/h6 = Medium drive fit
    H7/u6 or U7/h6 = Force fit

Not all possible sizes are listed in the tables in the appendix. Only preferred sizes are listed. Tolerances for sizes between the stated sizes are derived by going to the next nearest given size. The values are not interpolated. A basic size of 27 would use the tolerance values listed for 25. Sizes that are exactly halfway between two stated sizes may use either set of values depending upon the design requirements.

9-16 NOMINAL SIZES

The term "nominal" refers to the approximate size of an object that matches a common fraction or whole number. A shaft with a dimension of 1.500 +/−.003 is said to have a nominal size of "one and a half inches." A dimension of 1.500 +.000/−.005 is still said to have a nominal size of one and a half inches. In both examples 1.5 is the closest common fraction.

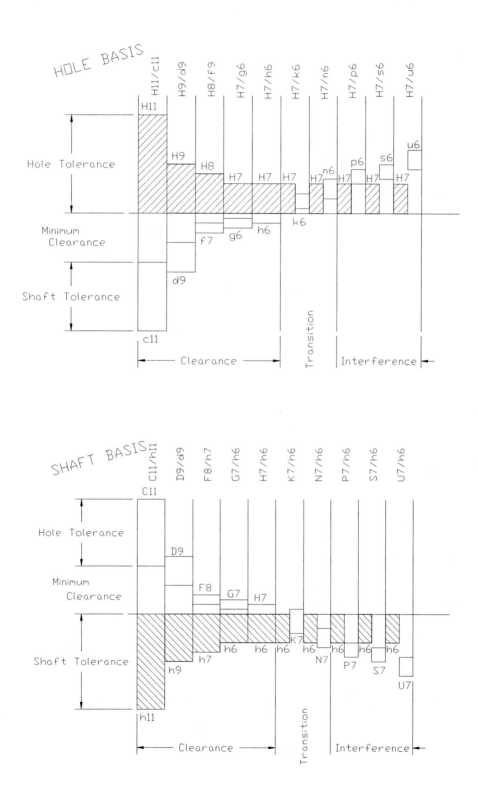

Figure 9-27

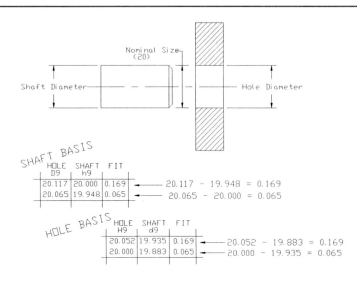

Figure 9-28

9-17 HOLE AND SHAFT BASES

One of the charts shown in Figure 9-27 applies tolerances starting with the nominal hole sizes, called hole basis; the other applies tolerances starting with the shaft nominal sizes, called shaft basis. The choice of which set of values to use depends on the design application. In general, hole basis numbers are used more often because it is more difficult to vary hole diameters manufactured using specific drill sizes than shaft sizes manufactured using a lathe. Shaft sizes may be used when a specific fastener diameter is used to assemble several objects.

Figure 9-28 shows a hole, a shaft, and a set of sample values taken from the tables found in the appendix. One of the set of values is for hole basis tolerance and the other for a shaft basis. The fit values are the same for both sets of values. The hole basis values were derived starting with a nominal hole size of 20.000, whereas the shaft basis values were derived starting with a shaft nominal size of 20.000. The letters used to identify holes are always written using capital letters and the letters for shaft values use lowercase.

9-18 SAMPLE PROBLEM SP9-3

Dimension a hole and a shaft that are to fit together using a close running fit. Use hole basis values based on a nominal size of 12mm.

Figure 9-29 shows values taken from the appropriate table in the appendix. The values may be applied directly to the shaft and hole as shown.

9-19 STANDARD FITS (INCH VALUES)

The appendix also includes tables of standard fit tolerances for inch values. The tables for inches are presented for a range of nominal values and are not for specific values, as are the metric value tables. The values may be hole or shaft basis.

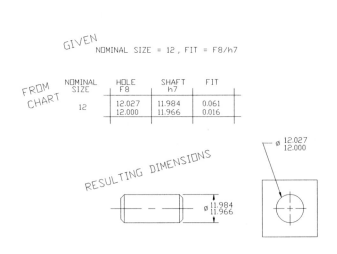

Figure 9-29

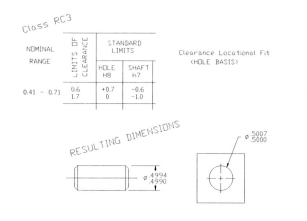

Figure 9-30

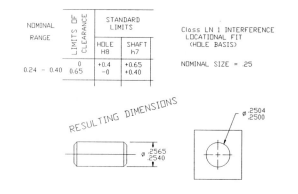

Figure 9-31

Fits defined using inch values are classified as follows

> RC = Running and sliding fits
> LC = Clearance locational fits
> LT = Transitional locational fits
> LN = Interference fits
> FN = Force fits

Each of these general categories has several subclassifications within it defined by a number. For example, Class RC1, Class RC2, through Class RC9. The letter designations are based on international tolerance standards, as are metric designations. The values are listed in thousandths of an inch. A table value of 1.1 means .0011 inches. A table value of .5 means .0005 inches.

Figure 9-30 shows a set of values for a Class RC3 fit hole basis taken from the appendix. If the values are applied to a nominal size of .5 inches, the resulting hole and shaft sizes will be as shown. Plus table values are added to the nominal value, and minus values are subtracted from the nominal value.

Nominal values that are common to two nominal ranges (0.71) may use values from either range.

9-20 SAMPLE PROBLEM SP9-4

Dimension a hole and shaft for a Class LN1 interference fit based on a nominal diameter of .25″. Use hole basis values.

Figure 9-31 shows the values for the .24 –.40 nominal range as listed in the appendix. The values are in thou-

sandths of an inch. Plus values are added to the nominal size. The resulting shaft and hole dimensions are as shown. The shaft's diameter is larger than the hole's diameter because this example calls for an interference fit.

9-21 PREFERRED AND STANDARD SIZES

It is important that designers always consider preferred and standard sizes when selecting sizes for designs. Most tooling is set up to match these sizes, so manufacturing is greatly simplified when preferred and standard sizes are specified. Figure 9-32 shows a listing of preferred sizes for metric values.

PREFERRED SIZES			
First Choice	Second Choice	First Choice	Second Choice
1		12	
1.2	1.1	16	14
1.6	1.4	20	18
2	1.8	25	22
2.5	2.2	30	28
3	2.8	40	35
4	3.5	50	45
5	4.5	60	55
6	5.5	80	70
8	7	100	90
10	9	120	110
	11		140

Figure 9-32

Consider the case of design calculations that call for a 42mm diameter hole. A 42mm diameter hole is not a preferred size. A diameter of 40mm is the closest preferred size and 45mm diameter is a second choice. A 42mm hole could be manufactured but would require an unusual drill size that may not be available. It would be wise to reconsider the design to see if a 40mm diameter hole could be used and if not, possibly a 45mm diameter hole.

A very large quantity production run could possibly justify the cost of special tooling, but for smaller runs it is probably better to use preferred sizes. Machinists will have the required drills and maintenance people will have the appropriate tools.

Figure 9-33 shows a listing of standard fractional drill sizes. Most companies now specify metric units or decimal inches. However, many standard items are still available in fractional sizes, and many older objects may still require fractional sized tools and replacement parts. A more complete listing is available in the appendix.

9-22 SURFACE FINISHES

The term "surface finish" refers to the accuracy (flatness) of a surface. Metric values are measured using micrometers (μm) and inch values are measured in microinches (μin).

The accuracy of a surface depends on the manufacturing process used to produce the surface. Figure 9-34 shows a listing of manufacturing processes and the quality of the surface finish they can be expected to produce.

Surface finishes have several design applications. Datum surfaces or surfaces used for baseline dimensioning should have fairly accurate surface finishes to help ensure accurate measurements. Bearing surfaces should have good quality surface finishes for better load distribution, and parts that operate at high speeds should have smooth finishes to help reduce friction. Figure 9-35 shows a screw head sitting on a very wavy surface. Note that the head of the screw is actually in contact with only two wave peaks, meaning all the bearing load is concentrated on the two peaks. This situation could cause stress cracks and greatly weaken the surface. A better quality surface finish would increase the bearing contact area.

Figure 9-35 also shows two very rough surfaces moving in contact with one another. The result would be excess wear to both surfaces because the surfaces touch only on the peaks, and these peaks tend to wear faster than flatter areas. Excess vibration could also result when interfacing surfaces are too rough.

Surface finishes are classified into three categories: surface texture, roughness, and lay. Surface texture is a general term that refers to the overall quality and accuracy of a surface.

Partial List of Standard Twist Drill Sizes (Fractional Sizes)					
Fraction	Decimal Equivalent	Fraction	Decimal Equivalent	Fraction	Decimal Equivalent
7/64	.1094	19/64	.2969	15/32	.4688
1/8	.1250	5/16	.3125	1/2	.5000
9/64	.1406	21/64	.3281	9/16	.5625
5/32	.1562	11/32	.3438	5/8	.6250
11/64	.1719	23/64	.3594	11/16	.6875
3/16	.1875	3/8	.3750	3/4	.7500
13/64	.2031	25/64	.3906	13/16	.8125
7/32	.2188	13/32	.4062	7/8	.8750
1/4	.2500	27/64	.4219	15/16	.9375
17/64	.2656	7/16	.4375	1	1.0000
9/32	.2812	29/64	.4531		

Figure 9-33

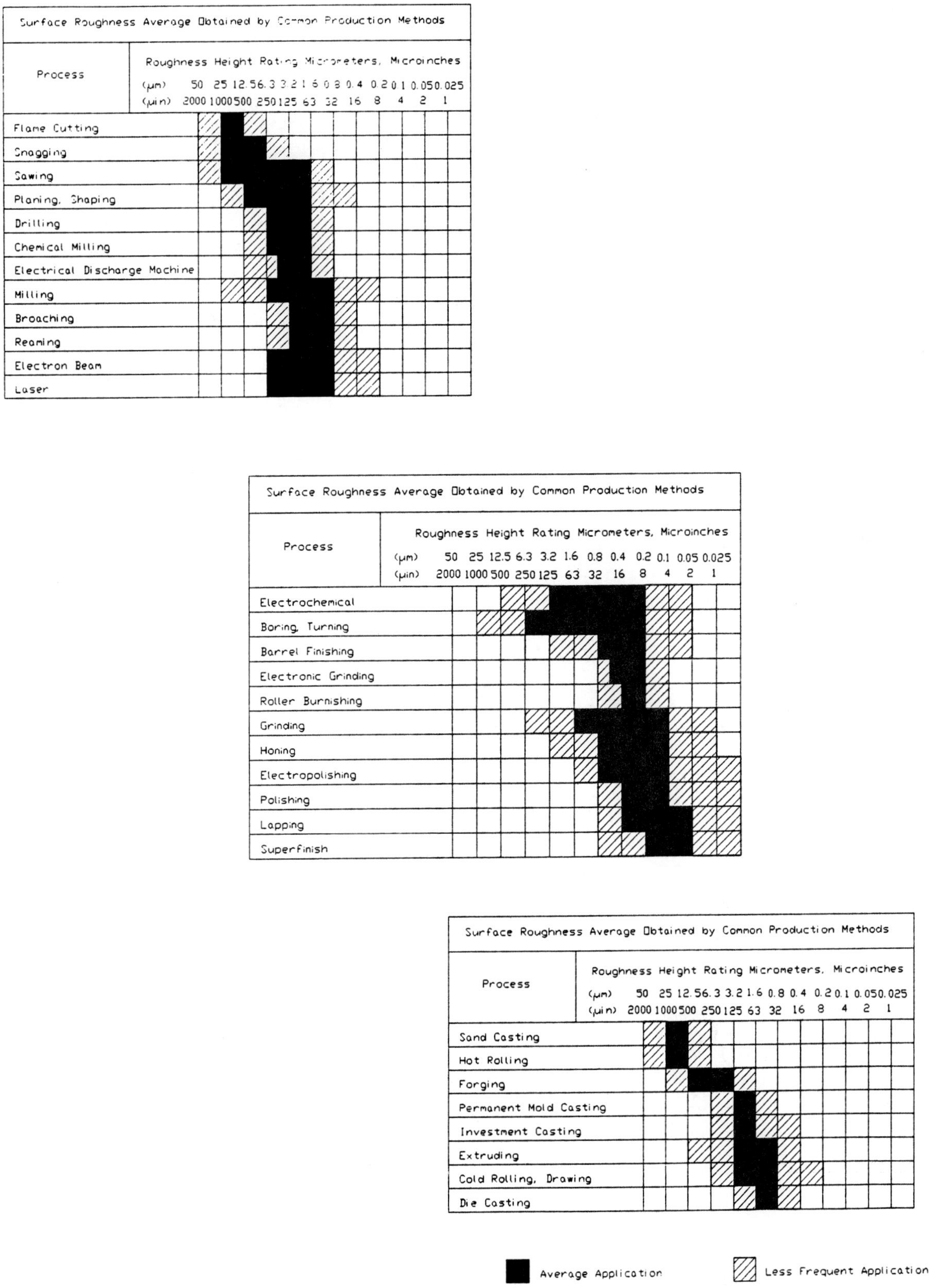

Surface Roughness Average Obtained by Common Production Methods

Process	Roughness Height Rating Micrometers, Microinches
	(μm) 50 25 12.5 6.3 3.2 1.6 0.8 0.4 0.2 0.1 0.05 0.025
	(μin) 2000 1000 500 250 125 63 32 16 8 4 2 1
Flame Cutting	
Snagging	
Sawing	
Planing, Shaping	
Drilling	
Chemical Milling	
Electrical Discharge Machine	
Milling	
Broaching	
Reaming	
Electron Beam	
Laser	

Surface Roughness Average Obtained by Common Production Methods

Process	Roughness Height Rating Micrometers, Microinches
	(μm) 50 25 12.5 6.3 3.2 1.6 0.8 0.4 0.2 0.1 0.05 0.025
	(μin) 2000 1000 500 250 125 63 32 16 8 4 2 1
Electrochemical	
Boring, Turning	
Barrel Finishing	
Electronic Grinding	
Roller Burnishing	
Grinding	
Honing	
Electropolishing	
Polishing	
Lapping	
Superfinish	

Surface Roughness Average Obtained by Common Production Methods

Process	Roughness Height Rating Micrometers, Microinches
	(μm) 50 25 12.5 6.3 3.2 1.6 0.8 0.4 0.2 0.1 0.05 0.025
	(μin) 2000 1000 500 250 125 63 32 16 8 4 2 1
Sand Casting	
Hot Rolling	
Forging	
Permanent Mold Casting	
Investment Casting	
Extruding	
Cold Rolling, Drawing	
Die Casting	

■ Average Application   ▨ Less Frequent Application

Figure 9-34

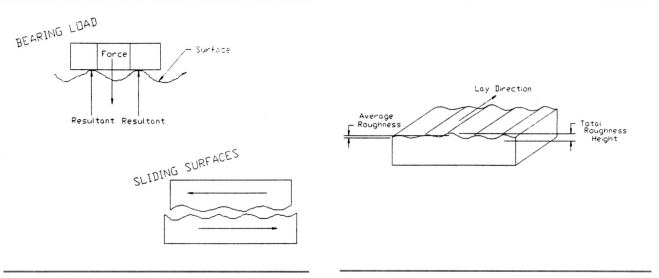

Figure 9-35

Figure 9-36

Roughness is a measure of the average deviation of a surface's peaks and valleys. See Figure 9-36.

Lay refers to the direction of machine marks on a surface. See Figure 9-37. The lay of a surface is particularly important when two moving objects are in contact with each other, especially at high speeds.

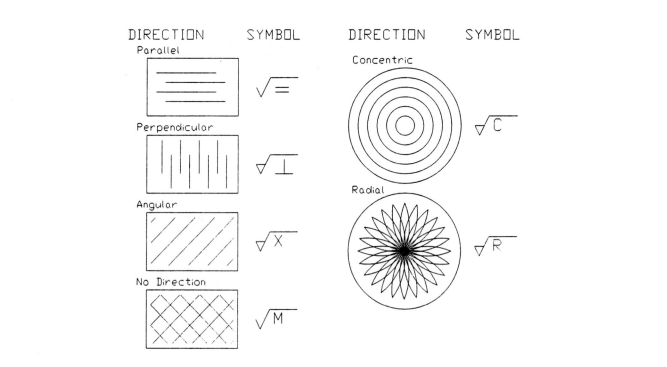

Figure 9-37

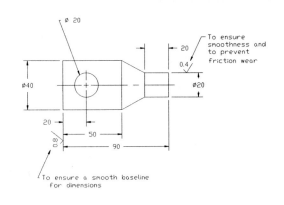

Figure 9-38

Figure 9-39

9-23 SURFACE CONTROL SYMBOLS

Surface finishes are indicated on a drawing using surface control symbols. See Figure 9-38. The general surface control symbol looks like a check mark. Roughness values may be included with the symbol to specify the required accuracy. Surface control symbols can also be used to specify the manufacturing process that can or cannot be used to produce a surface.

Figure 9-39 shows two applications of surface control symbols. In the first example a 0.8 micrometer (32 microinch) surface finish is specified on the surface that serves as a datum for several horizontal dimensions. A 0.8 μm surface finish is generally considered the minimum acceptable finish for datums.

A second finish mark with the value 0.4 micrometers is located on an extension line referring to a surface that will be in contact with a moving object. The extra flatness will help prevent wear between the two surfaces.

It is suggested that a general finish mark be drawn and saved as a WBLOCK so it can be INSERTED as needed on future drawings. Add the machine mark WBLOCK to any prototype drawings created.

FLOATING CONDITION

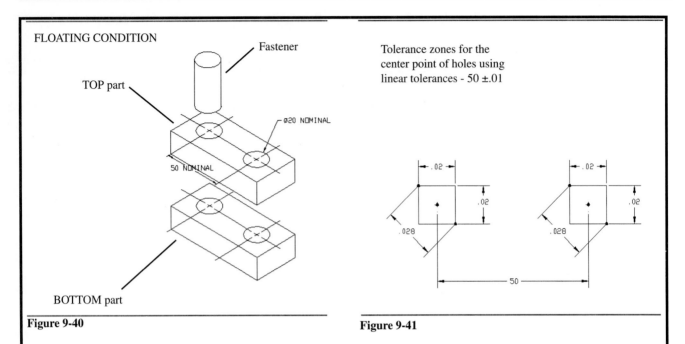

Figure 9-40

9-24 DESIGN PROBLEMS

Figure 9-40 shows two objects that are to be fitted together using a fastener such as a screw and nut combination. For this example a cylinder will be used to represent a fastener. Only two nominal dimensions are given. The dimensions and tolerances were derived as follows.

The distance between the center of the holes and the studs is given as 50 NOMINAL The term "nominal" means that the stated value is only a starting point. The final dimensions will be close to the given value, but do not have to equal it.

Assigning tolerances is an iteration process; that is, a tolerance is selected and other tolerance values are calculated from the selected initial values. If the results are not satisfactory, go back and modify the initial values and calculate again. As your experience grows, you will become better at selecting realistic initial values.

In the example shown in Figure 9-40, start by assigning a tolerance of ±.01 to both the TOP and BOTTOM parts for both the horizontal and vertical dimensions used to locate the holes. This means that there is a possible center point variation of 0.02 for both parts. The parts must always fit together, so tolerances must be assigned based on the worse case condition, or when the parts are made at the extreme ends of the assigned tolerances.

Figure 9-41 shows a greatly enlarged picture of the worst case condition created by a tolerance of ±0.1. The center point of the hole could be as much as 0.028 apart if the two center points were located at opposite corners of the tolerance zone. This means that the minimum hole

Tolerance zones for the center point of holes using linear tolerances - 50 ±.01

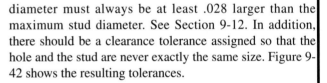

Figure 9-41

diameter must always be at least .028 larger than the maximum stud diameter. See Section 9-12. In addition, there should be a clearance tolerance assigned so that the hole and the stud are never exactly the same size. Figure 9-42 shows the resulting tolerances.

Floating condition

The TOP and BOTTOM parts shown in Figure 9-40 are to be joined by two independent fasteners; that is, the location of one fastener does not depend on the location of

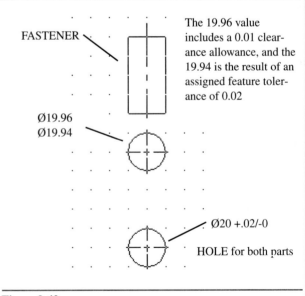

FASTENER

Ø19.96
Ø19.94

The 19.96 value includes a 0.01 clearance allowance, and the 19.94 is the result of an assigned feature tolerance of 0.02

Ø20 +.02/-0

HOLE for both parts

Figure 9-42

the other. This is call a "floating condition." This means that the tolerance zones of both the TOP and BOTTOM parts can be assigned the same values and that a fastener diameter selected to fit one part will also fit the other part.

The final tolerances were developed by first defining a minimum hole size of 20.00. An arbitrary tolerance of 0.02 was assigned to the hole and was expressed as 20.00 +0/-.02 so that the hole can never be any smaller than 20.00.

The 20.00 minimum hole diameter dictates that the maximum stud diameter can be no greater than 19.97, or .03 (the rounded off diagonal distance across the tolerance zone) less than the minimum hole diameter. A 0.01 clearance was then assigned. The clearance ensures that the hole and the stud are never exactly the same diameter. The resulting maximum allowable diameter for the stud is 19.96. Again an arbitrary tolerance of 0.02 was assigned to the stud. The final stud dimensions are 19.96 to 19.94.

The assigned tolerances ensure that there will always be at least 0.01 clearance between the stud and the hole. The other extreme condition occurs when the hole is at its largest possible size (10.02) and the stud is at its smallest (19.94). This means that there could be as much as 0.08 clearance between the parts. If this much clearance is not acceptable, then the assigned tolerances would have to be re-evaluated.

Figure 9-43 shows the TOP and BOTTOM parts dimensioned and toleranced. Any dimensions that do not include tolerances are assumed to have standard tolerances. See Figure 9-15.

Note that the top edge of each part has been assigned a surface finish. This was done to help ensure the accuracy of the 20 ±.01 dimension. If this edge surface were rough, it could affect the tolerance measurements.

This example will be done again in Chapter 10 using geometric tolerances. Geometric tolerance zones are round rather than rectangular.

Fixed condition

Figure 9-44 shows the same nominal conditions presented in Figure 9-40 but the fasteners are fixed to the TOP part. This is called the "fixed condition." In analyzing the tolerance zones for the fixed condition, two position tolerances must be considered: the positional tolerances for the holes in the BOTTOM part, and the positional tolerances for the fixed fasteners in the TOP part. This may be expressed as an equation as follows.

$$S_{max} + DTSZ = H_{min} - DTHZ$$

Where:

S_{max} = Maximum shaft (fastener) diameter
H_{min} = Minimum hole diameter
DTSZ = Diagonal distance across the shaft's center point tolerance zone
DTHZ = Diagonal distance across the hole's center point tolerance zone

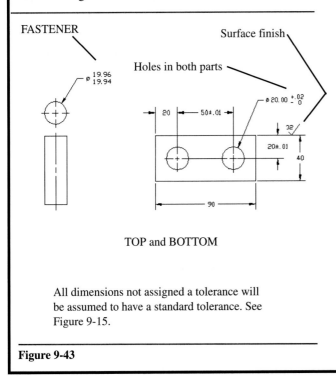

TOP and BOTTOM

All dimensions not assigned a tolerance will be assumed to have a standard tolerance. See Figure 9-15.

Figure 9-43

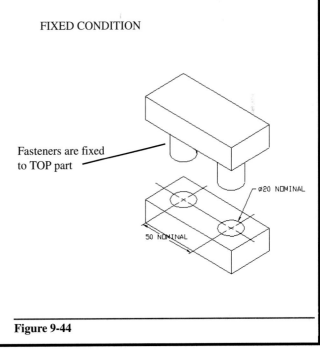

FIXED CONDITION

Fasteners are fixed to TOP part

Figure 9-44

If a dimension and tolerance of 50 ±.01 and 20±.01 are assigned to both the center distance between the holes and the center distance between the fixed fasteners, the values for DTSZ and DTHZ will be equal. The formulas can then be simplified as follows.

Smax = Hmin - 2(DTZ)

Where DTZ equals the diagonal distance across the tolerance zone. If a hole tolerance of 20.00 +0/-.02 is also defined, the resulting maximum shaft size can be determined, assuming the calculated diagonal distance of .028 is rounded off to .03. See Figure 9-45.

Smax = 20.00 - 2(.03)
    = 19.94

This means that the largest possible shaft diameter that will just fit equals 19.94. If a clearance tolerance of 0.01 is assumed to ensure that the shaft and hole are never exactly the same size, the maximum shaft diameter becomes 19.93. See Figure 9-46.

A feature tolerance of 0.02 on the shaft will result in a minimum shaft diameter of 19.91. Note that the 0.01 clearance tolerance and the 0.02 feature tolerance were

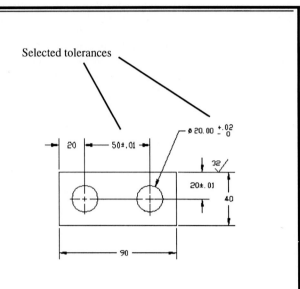

BOTTOM part

Figure 9-45

arbitrarily chosen. Other possible values could have been used.

The shaft diameter values were derived as follows.

20.00 Selected value for the minimum hole diameter
-0.03 Rounded off value for hole positional tolerance
-0.03 Rounded off value for shaft positional tolerance
-0.01 Selected clearance value

19.93 Maximum shaft diameter
-0.02 Selected tolerance value

19.91 Minimum shaft diameter

TOP part

Resulting shaft dimensions

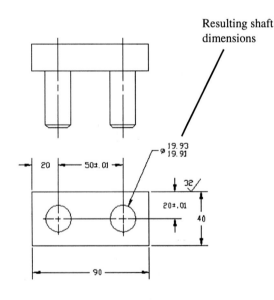

Figure 9-46

To design given a fastener size

The previous two examples started by selecting a minimum hole diameter and then calculating the resulting fastener sizes. Figure 9-47 shows a situation where the fastener size is defined, and the problem is to determine the hole sizes. Figure 9-48 shows the dimensions and tolerances for both the top and bottom parts.

Requirements:

    Clearance = .003
    Hole tolerance = .005
    Positional tolerance = .002

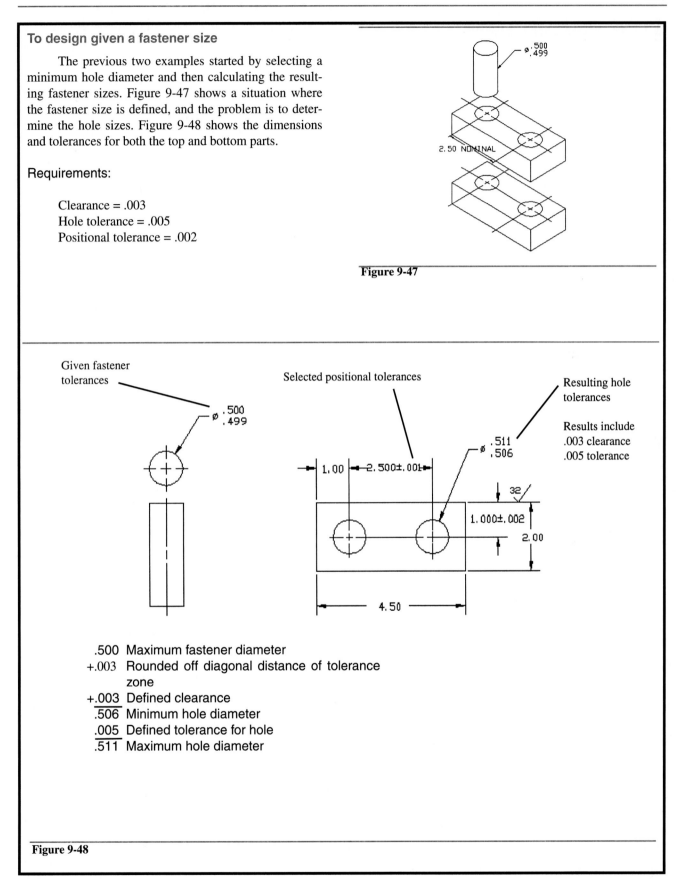

Figure 9-47

    .500 Maximum fastener diameter
+.003 Rounded off diagonal distance of tolerance zone
+.003 Defined clearance
  .506 Minimum hole diameter
  .005 Defined tolerance for hole
  .511 Maximum hole diameter

Figure 9-48

9-25 EXERCISE PROBLEMS

Redraw the figures in exercise problems EX9-1 to EX9-4 and substitute the dimensions listed in the chart in place of the appropriate circled number.

EX9-1

1. 38±0.05
2. 10±0.1
3. 5±0.05
4. $\begin{array}{l} 45.50° \\ 44.50° \end{array}$
5. 40±0.1
6. 22±0.1
7. $12 \begin{array}{l} +0 \\ -.1 \end{array}$
8. $25 \begin{array}{l} +.05 \\ -0 \end{array}$
9. $\begin{array}{l} 51.50 \\ 50.75 \end{array}$
10. 76±0.1

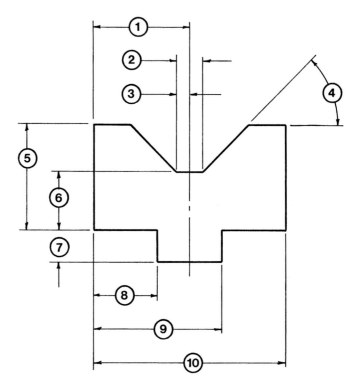

EX9-2

1. 34±0.25
2. 17±0.25
3. 25±0.05
4. $\begin{array}{l} 15.00 \\ 14.80 \end{array}$
5. 50±0.05
6. 80±0.1
7. R5±0.1 – 8 PLACES
8. 45±0.25
9. 60±0.1
10. Ø14 – 3 HOLES
11. $\begin{array}{l} 15.00 \\ 14.80 \end{array}$
12. $\begin{array}{l} 30.00 \\ 29.80 \end{array}$

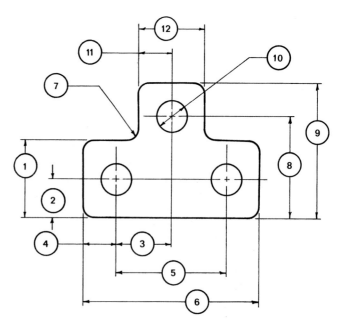

EX9-3

1. 3.00±.01

2. 1.56±.01

3. 46.50°
    45.50°

4. .750±.005

5. 2.75
    2.70

6. 3.625±.010

7. 45°±.5°

8. 2.250±.005

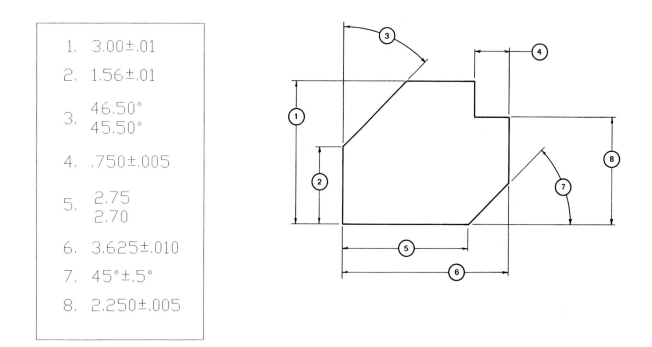

EX9-4

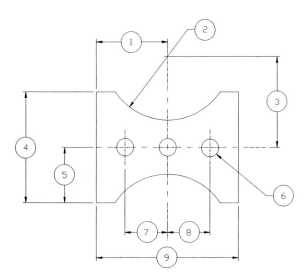

1. 50 $^{+.2}_{0}$

2. R45±.1 – 2 PLACES

3. 63.5 $^{0}_{-.2}$

4. 76±.1

5. 38±.1

6. ⌀12.00 $^{+.05}_{0}$ – 3 HOLES

7. 30±.03

8. 30±.03

9. 100 $^{+.4}_{0}$

EX9-5

Redraw the following object, including the given dimensions and tolerances. Calculate and list the maximum and minimum distances for surface A.

EX9-7

Redraw the following object, including the dimensions and tolerances. Calculate and list the maximum and minimum distances for surfaces D and E.

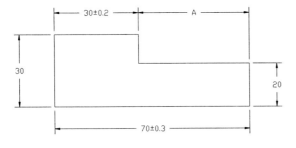

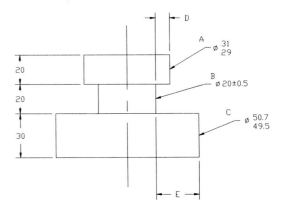

EX9-6

a. Redraw the following object, including the dimensions and tolerances. Calculate and list the maximum and minimum distances for surface A.

b. Redraw the given object and dimension it using baseline dimensions. Calculate and list the maximum and minimum distances for surface A.

EX9-8

Dimension the following object twice: once using chain dimensions and once using baseline dimensions. Calculate and list the maximum and minimum distances for surface D for both chain and baseline dimensions. Compare the results.

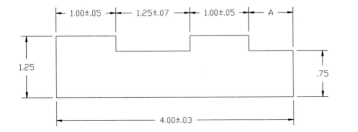

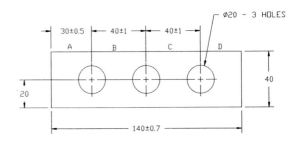

EX9-9

Redraw the following object, including the dimensions and tolerances.

1. 1.50±.02

2. 1.50±.03

3. .625±.001

4. .754
   .749

5. .625±.001

6. 2.253
   2.249

7. ⌀ .502
     .500

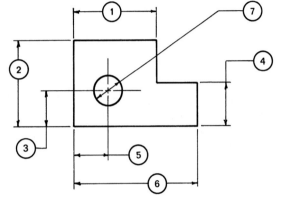

EX9-10

Redraw the following object, including the dimensions and tolerances.

Note: ⑨

1. ⌀30±0.5

2. ⌀ 15.04
     15.00

3. 10±1

4. 20±1

5. 66.50
   65.03

6. 15±0.3

7. 35±.02

8. 70±0.2

9. NOTE: ALL FILLETS AND ROUNDS = R5 UNLESS OTHERWISE STATED

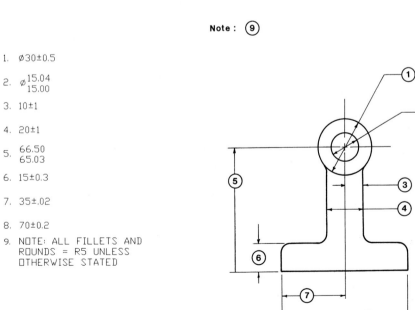

EX9-11

Redraw the following object, including the dimensions and tolerances.

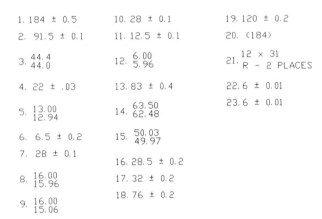

1. 184 ± 0.5

2. 91.5 ± 0.1

3. 44.4 / 44.0

4. 22 ± .03

5. 13.00 / 12.94

6. 6.5 ± 0.2

7. 28 ± 0.1

8. 16.00 / 15.96

9. 16.00 / 15.06

10. 28 ± 0.1

11. 12.5 ± 0.1

12. 6.00 / 5.96

13. 83 ± 0.4

14. 63.50 / 62.48

15. 50.03 / 49.97

16. 28.5 ± 0.2

17. 32 ± 0.2

18. 76 ± 0.2

19. 120 ± 0.2

20. (184)

21. 12 × 31 / R – 2 PLACES

22. 6 ± 0.01

23. 6 ± 0.01

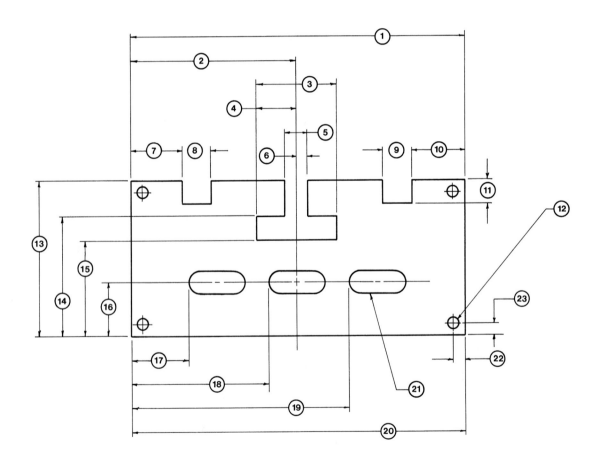

EX9-12

Redraw the following shapes, including the dimensions and tolerances. Also list the required minimum and maximum values for the specified distances.

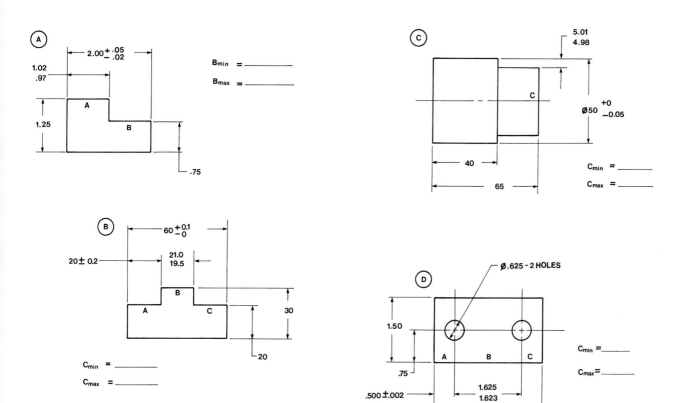

EX9-13

Redraw and complete the following inspection report. Under the Results column, classify each "AS MEASURED" value as OK if the value is within the stated tolerances, REWORK if the value indicates that the measured value is beyond the stated tolerance but can be reworked to bring it into the acceptable range, or SCRAP if the value is not within the tolerance range and cannot be reworked to make it acceptable.

INSPECTION REPORT

PART NAME AND NO: *10755002*

INSPECTOR:

DATE:

1.00 3 PLACES

BASE DIMENSION	TOLERANCES MAX	MIN	AS MEASURED	RESULTS
(1) 100 ± 0.5			99.8	
(2) ϕ^{57}_{56}			57.01	
(3) 22 ± 0.3			21.72	
(4) $^{40.05}_{39.95}$			39.98	
(5) 22 ± 0.3			21.68	
(6) $R52^{+0}_{-0.2}$			51.99	
(7) $35^{+0.2}_{-0.3}$			35.20	
(8) $30^{+0.4}_{0}$			30.27	
(9) $6.0^{+.1}_{-.2}$			5.85	
(10) 12.0 ± 0.2			11.90	

.50 —10 PLACES

EX9-14

Redraw the chart shown below and complete it based on the following information. All values are in millimeters.

A. Nominal = 16, Fit = H9/d9
B. Nominal = 30, Fit = H11/c11
C. Nominal = 22, Fit = H7/g6
D. Nominal = 10, Fit = C11/h11

E. Nominal = 25, Fit = F8/h7
F. Nominal = 12, Fit = H7/k6
G. Nominal = 3, Fit = H7/p6
H. Nominal = 19, Fit = H7/s6
I. Nominal = 27, Fit = H7/u6
J. Nominal = 30, Fit = N7/h6

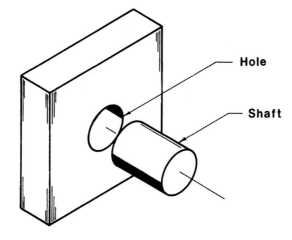

Half space

NOMINAL	HOLE		SHAFT		CLEARANCE	
	MAX	MIN	MAX	MIN	MAX	MIN
Ⓐ						
Ⓑ						
Ⓒ						
Ⓓ						
Ⓔ						

3.75
6 equal
spaces

◄— 1.5 —►◄——————— 6.0 – 6 equal spaces ———————►

EX9-15

Redraw the chart shown below and complete it based on the following information. All values are in millimeters.

A. Nominal = 0.25, Fit = Class LC5
B. Nominal = 1.00, Fit = Class LC7
C. Nominal = 1.50, Fit = Class LC10
D. Nominal = 0.75, Fit = Class RC3

E. Nominal = 1.50, Fit = Class RC6
F. Nominal = .500, Fit = Class LT2
G. Nominal = 1.25, Fit = Class LT5
H. Nominal = 0.75, Fit = Class LN3
I. Nominal = 1.63, Fit = Class FN1
J. Nominal = 2.00, Fit = Class FN4

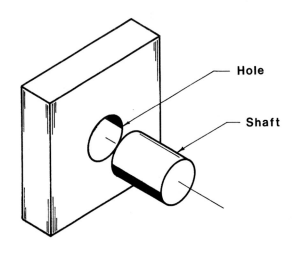

Hole

Shaft

Half space

NOMINAL	HOLE		SHAFT		CLEARANCE	
	MAX	MIN	MAX	MIN	MAX	MIN
A						
B						
C						
D						
E						

3.75
6 equal
spaces

1.5

6.0 - 6 equal spaces

Redraw the object shown in Figure EX9-16 using the given dimensions. Include the given dimensions and tolerances. Draw the chart shown and add the appropriate selected values based on the dimensions and tolerances given in exercise problems EX9-16 to EX9-19.

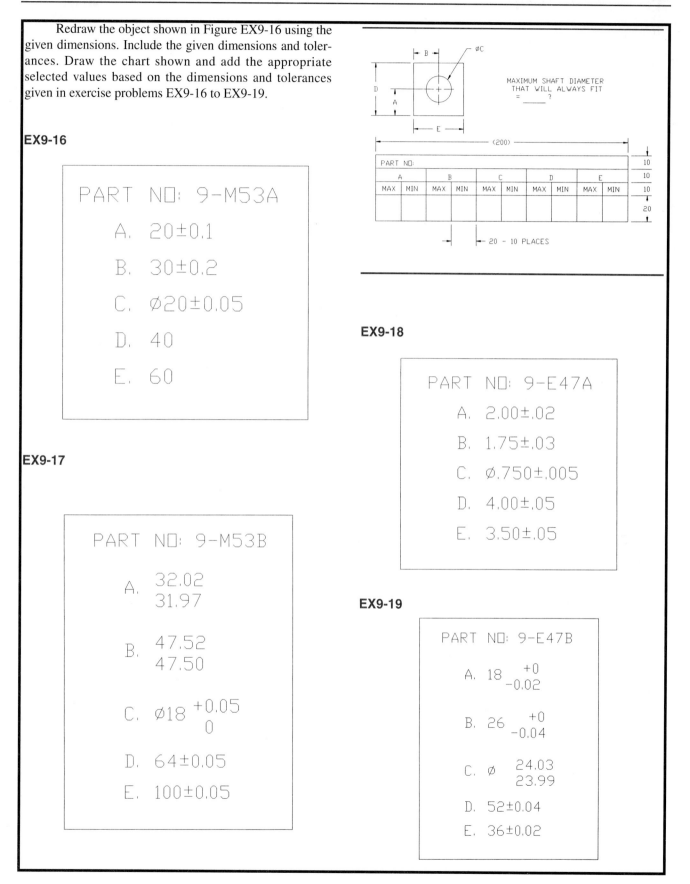

MAXIMUM SHAFT DIAMETER
THAT WILL ALWAYS FIT
= _____ ?

EX9-16

PART NO: 9-M53A

A. 20±0.1

B. 30±0.2

C. ∅20±0.05

D. 40

E. 60

EX9-17

PART NO: 9-M53B

A. 32.02
    31.97

B. 47.52
    47.50

C. ∅18 $^{+0.05}_{0}$

D. 64±0.05

E. 100±0.05

EX9-18

PART NO: 9-E47A

A. 2.00±.02

B. 1.75±.03

C. ∅.750±.005

D. 4.00±.05

E. 3.50±.05

EX9-19

PART NO: 9-E47B

A. 18 $^{+0}_{-0.02}$

B. 26 $^{+0}_{-0.04}$

C. ∅ 24.03
       23.99

D. 52±0.04

E. 36±0.02

EX9-20

Prepare front and top views of Parts 4A and 4B based on the given dimensions. Add tolerances to produce the stated maximum clearance and mismatch.

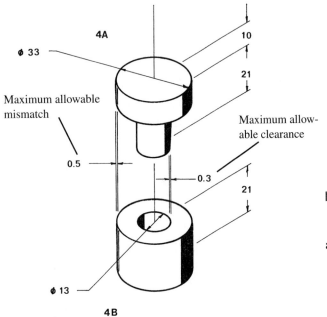

EX9-21

Redraw parts A and B and add dimensions and tolerances to meet the "UPON ASSEMBLY" requirements.

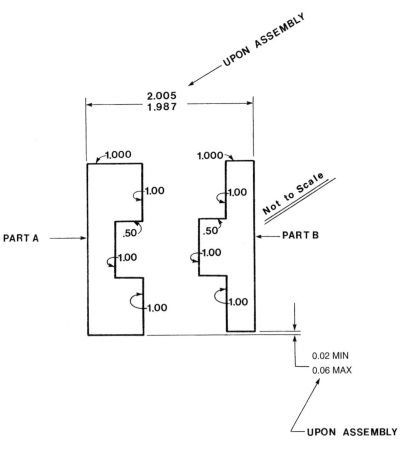

EX9-22

Draw front and top views of both given objects. Add dimensions and tolerances to meet the "FINAL CONDITION" requirements.

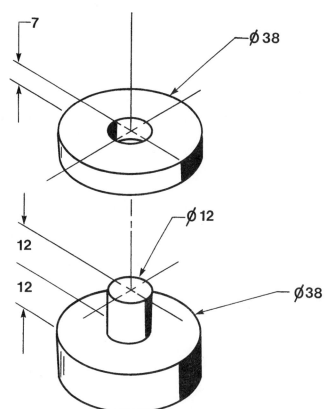

7

Ø 38

Ø 12

12

12

Ø38

FINAL CONDITION

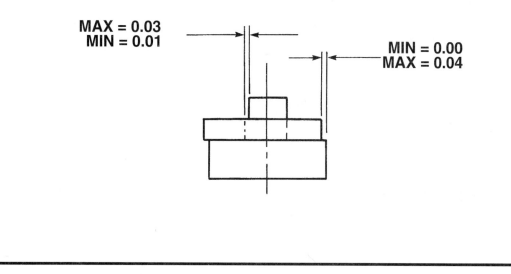

MAX = 0.03
MIN = 0.01

MIN = 0.00
MAX = 0.04

Given a TOP and BOTTOM part as shown in Figure EX9-23, satisfy the requirements given in exercise problems EX9-23 to EX9-25 so that the parts always fit regardless of orientation. All dimensions not toleranced are assumed to have standard tolerances as stated in Figure 9-15.

EX9-23 INCHES

    A. Dimension 1 is 2.00 nominal
    B. Dimension 2 is Ø.375 nominal
    C. The fasteners are to have a tolerance of .001
    D. The holes are to have a tolerance of .002
    E. The minumum allowable clearance is .003

EX9-24 MILLIMETERS

    A. Dimension 1 is 80 nominal
    B. Dimension 2 is Ø12 nominal
    C. The fasteners are to have a tolerance of 0.05
    D. The holes are to have a tolerance of 0.03
    E. The minumum allowable clearance is 0.02

EX9-25 INCHES

    A. Dimension 1 is 3.50 nominal
    B. Dimension 3 is Ø.750 nominal
    C. The studs are to have a tolerance of 0.005
    D. The holes are to have a tolerance of 0.003
    E. The minimum allowable clearance is 0.002

Given a TOP and BOTTOM part as shown in Figure EX9-26, satisfy the requirements given in exercise problems EX9-26 to EX9-28 so that the parts always fit regardless of orientation. All dimensions not toleranced are assumed to have standard tolerances as stated in Figure 9-15.

EX9-26

    A. Dimension 1 is 60 nominal
    B. Dimension 2 is Ø10 nominal
    C. The fasteners are to have a tolerance of 0.04
    D. The holes are to have a tolerance of 0.02
    E. The minumum allowable clearance is 0.02

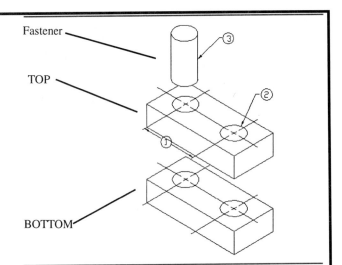

Figure EX9-23

EX9-27

    A. Dimension 1 is 3.50 nominal
    B. Dimension 3 is Ø.750 nominal
    C. The studs are to have a tolerance of 0.005
    D. The holes are to have a tolerance of 0.003
    E. The minimum allowable clearance is 0.002

EX9-28

    A. Dimension 1 is 100 nominal
    B. Dimension 2 is Ø18 nominal
    C. The fasteners are to have a tolerance of 0.02
    D. The holes are to have a tolerance of 0.01
    E. The minumum allowable clearance is 0.02

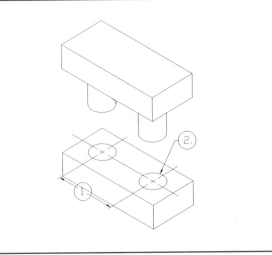

Figure EX9-26

C H A P T E R 10

Geometric Tolerances

10-1 INTRODUCTION

Geometric tolerancing is a dimensioning and tolerancing system based on the geometric shape of an object. Surfaces may be defined in terms of their flatness or roundness, or in terms of how perpendicular or parallel they are to other surfaces.

Geometric tolerancing allows a more exact definition of the shape of an object than does conventional coordinate type tolerances. Objects can be toleranced in a manner more closely related to their design function or so that their features and surfaces are more directly related to each other.

Figure 10-1 shows a square shape dimensioned and toleranced using plus and minus tolerances. The resulting tolerance zone has an outside length of 51 and an inside length of 49 square. The defined tolerance zone allows any shape that falls within in it to be deemed acceptable, or correctly manufactured. Figure 10-1 shows an exaggerated shape that fits within the defined tolerance zone and is not square, yet would be acceptable under the specified dimensions and tolerances. Geometric tolerancing could be used to more precisely define the tolerance zone so that a more nearly square shape is required.

It should be pointed out that geometric tolerancing is not a panacea for all dimensioning and tolerancing problems. In many cases coordinate tolerancing, as presented in

Chapter 9, is sufficient to accurately define an object. Unnecessary or excessive use of geometric tolerances can increase production costs. Most objects are toleranced using a combination of coordinate and geometric tolerances, depending on the design function of the object.

The key to using tolerances and types of tolerances may be simply stated as "decimal points cost money." Every tolerance should be made as loose as possible while still maintaining the design integrity of the object. If a sur-

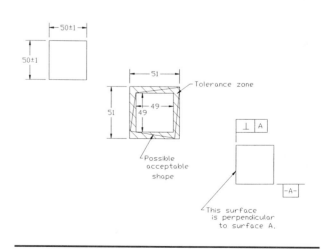

Figure 10-1

411

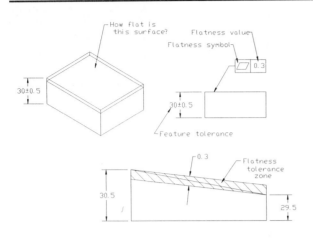

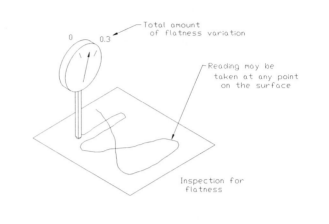

Figure 10-2

Figure 10-3

face flatness is critical to the correct functioning of the object, then of course it would require a very close tolerance. But every tolerance should be considered individually, and wherever possible loosened to make the object's manufacture easier and therefore less expensive.

10-2 TOLERANCES OF FORM

Tolerances of form are used to define the shape of a surface relative to itself. There are four classifications: flatness, straightness, roundness, and cylindricity. Tolerances of form are not related to other surfaces but apply only to an individual surface.

10-3 FLATNESS

Flatness tolerances are used to define the amount of variation permitted in an individual surface. The surface is thought of as a plane not related to the rest of the object.

Figure 10-2 shows a rectangular object. How flat is the top surface? The given plus or minus tolerances allow a variation of (+/–0.5) across the surface. Without additional tolerances the surface could look like a series of waves that vary between 30.5 and 29.5.

If the example in Figure 10-2 is assigned a flatness tolerance of 0.3, the height of the object, the feature tolerance, could continue to vary based on the 30 +/–0.5 tolerance, but the surface itself could not vary by more than 0.3. In the most extreme condition, one end of the surface could be 30.5 above the bottom surface and the other end 29.5, but the surface would still be limited to within two parallel planes 0.3 apart as shown.

To better understand the meaning of flatness, consider how the surface would be inspected. The surface would be acceptable if a gage could be moved all around the surface and never vary by more than 0.3. See Figure 10-3. Every point in the plane must be within the specified tolerance.

10-4 STRAIGHTNESS

Straightness tolerances are used to measure the variation of an individual feature along a straight line in a specified direction. Figure 10-4 shows an object with a straightness tolerance applied to its top surface. Straightness differs from flatness because straightness measurements are checked by moving a gage directly across the surface in a single direction. The gage is not moved randomly about the surface, as is required by flatness.

Straightness tolerances are most often applied to cir-

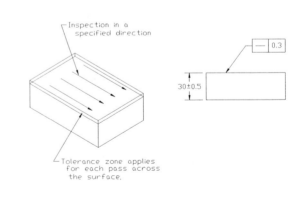

Figure 10-4

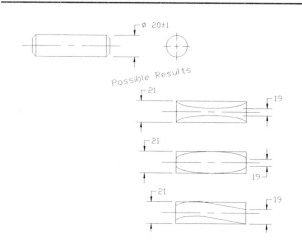

Figure 10-5

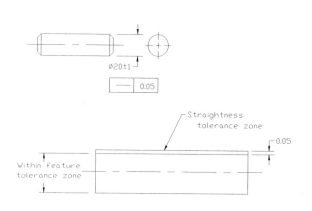

Figure 10-6

cular or matching objects to help ensure that the parts are not barreled or warped within the given feature tolerance range and would therefore not fit together well. Figure 10-5 shows a cylindrical object dimensioned and toleranced using a standard feature tolerance. The surface of the cylinder may vary within the specified tolerance range as shown.

Figure 10-6 shows the same object shown in Figure 10-5 dimensioned and toleranced using the same feature tolerance but also including a 0.05 straightness tolerance. The straightness tolerance limits the surface variation to 0.05 as shown.

10-5 STRAIGHTNESS (RFS AND MMC)

Figure 10-7 again shows the same cylinder shown in Figures 10-5 and 10-6. This time the straightness tolerance is applied about the cylinder's center line. This type of tolerance permits the feature tolerance and geometric tolerance to be used together to define a virtual condition. Virtual condition is used to determine the maximum possible size variation of the cylinder or the smallest diameter hole that would always accept the cylinder. See Section 10-19.

The geometric tolerance specified in Figure 10-7 is applied to any circular segment along the cylinder, regardless of the cylinder's diameter. This means that the 0.05 tolerance is applied equally when the cylinder's diameter measures 19 or when it measures 21. This application is called RFS, regardless of feature size. RFS conditions are specified in a tolerance either by an S with a circle around

it or implied tacitly when no other symbol is used. In Figure 10-7 no symbol is listed after the 0.05 value, so it is assumed to be applied RFS.

Figure 10-8 shows the cylinder dimensioned with an MMC condition applied to the straightness tolerance. MMC stands for "maximum material condition" and means the specified straightness tolerance (0.05) is applied only at the MMC condition or when the cylinder is at its maximum diameter size (31).

A shaft is an external feature, so its largest possible size or MMC occurs when it is at its maximum diameter. A hole is an internal feature. A hole's MMC condition occurs when it is at its smallest diameter. The MMC condition for holes will be discussed later in the chapter along with positioning tolerances.

Applying a straightness tolerance at MMC allows for

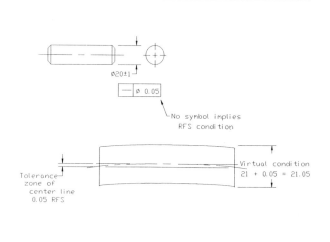

Figure 10-7

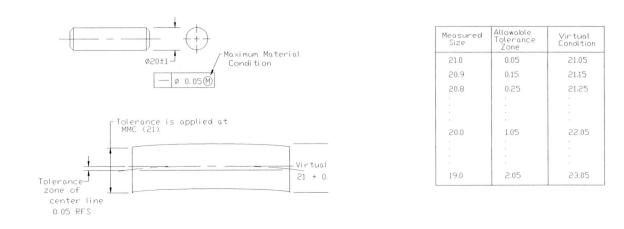

Measured Size	Allowable Tolerance Zone	Virtual Condition
21.0	0.05	21.05
20.9	0.15	21.15
20.8	0.25	21.25
.	.	.
.	.	.
.	.	.
20.0	1.05	22.05
.	.	.
.	.	.
19.0	2.05	23.05

Figure 10-8

a variation in the resulting tolerance zone. Because the 0.05 flatness tolerance is applied at MMC, the virtual condition is still 21.05, the same as with the RFS condition. However, the tolerance is applied only at MMC. As the cylinder's diameter varies within the specified feature tolerance range, the acceptable tolerance zone may vary to maintain the same virtual condition.

Figure 10-8 shows a listing of how the tolerance zone varies as the cylinder's diameter varies. When the cylinder is at its largest size or MMC, the tolerance zone equals 0.05 or the specified flatness variation. When the cylinder is at its smallest diameter, the tolerance zone

equals 2.05 or the total feature size plus the total flatness size. In all variations the virtual size remains the same, so at any given cylinder diameter value, the size of the tolerance zone can be determined by subtracting the cylinder's diameter value from the virtual condition.

Figure 10-9 shows a comparison between different methods used to dimension and tolerance a .750 shaft. The first example uses only a feature tolerance. This tolerance sets an upper limit of .755 and a lower limit of .745. Any variations within that range are acceptable.

The second example in Figure 10-9 sets a straightness tolerance of .003 about the cylinder's center line. No

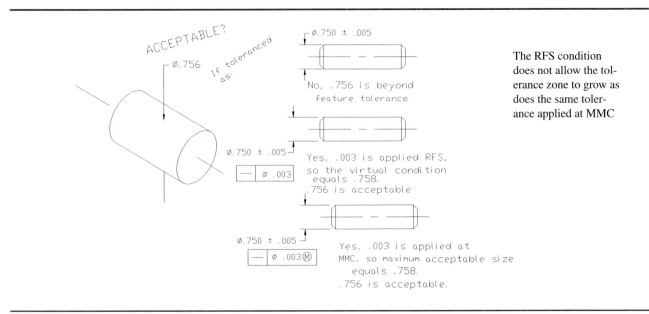

The RFS condition does not allow the tolerance zone to grow as does the same tolerance applied at MMC

Figure 10-9

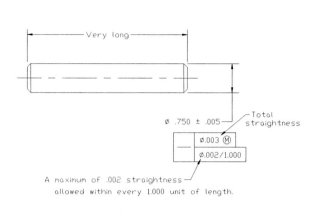

A maximum of .002 straightness
allowed within every 1.000 unit of length.

Figure 10-10

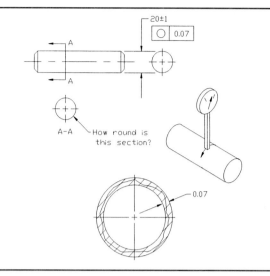

Figure 10-11

conditions are defined, so the tolerance is applied RFS. This limits the variations in straightness to .003 at all feature sizes. For example, when the shaft is at its smallest possible feature size of .745, the .003 still applies. This means that a shaft measuring .745 that had a straightness variation greater than .003 would be rejected. If the tolerance had been applied at MMC, the part would be accepted. This does not mean that straightness tolerances should always be applied at MMC. If straightness is critical to the design integrity or function of the part, then straightness should be applied in the RFS condition.

The third example in Figure 10-9 applies the straightness tolerance about the center line at MMC. This tolerance creates a virtual condition of .758. The MMC condition allows the tolerance to vary as the feature tolerance varies, so when the shaft is at its smallest feature size, .745, a straightness tolerance of .013 is acceptable (.010 feature tolerance + .003 straightness tolerance).

The fourth example in Figure 10-9 applies a 0.000 tolerance at MMC. This means that the shaft must be perfectly straight at MMC or when the shaft is at its maximum value (.755), but the tolerance can vary as the feature size varies. A 0.000 tolerance means that the MMC and the virtual conditions are equal.

Figure 10-10 shows a very long .750 diameter shaft. Its straightness tolerance includes a length qualifier that serves to limit the straightness variations over each inch of the shaft length and prevent excess waviness over the full length. The tolerance Ø.002/1.000 means that the total straightness may vary over the entire length of the shaft by .003 but that the variation is limited to .002 per 1.000 of shaft length.

10-6 CIRCULARITY

Circularity tolerances are used to limit the amount of variation in the roundness of a surface of revolution. It is measured at individual cross-sections along the length of the object. The measurements are limited to the individual cross-sections and are not related to other cross-sections. This means that in extreme conditions the shaft shown in Figure 10-11 could actually taper from a diameter of 21 to a diameter of 19 and never violate the circularity requirement. It also means that qualifications such as MMC cannot be applied.

Figure 10-11 shows a shaft that includes a feature tolerance and a circularity tolerance of 0.07. To understand circularity tolerances, consider an individual cross-section or slice of the cylinder. The actual shape of the outside

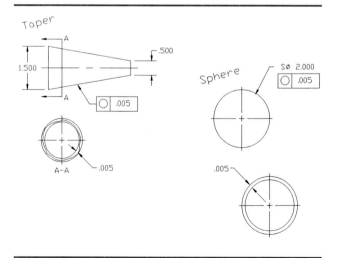

Figure 10-12

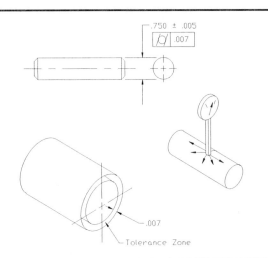

Figure 10-13

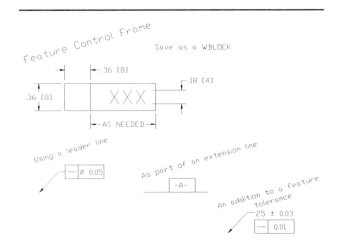

Figure 10-14

edge of the slice varies around the slice. The difference between the maximum diameter and the minimum diameter of the slice can never exceed the stated circularity tolerance.

Circularity tolerances can be applied to tapered sections and spheres, as shown in Figure 10-12. In both applications, circularity is measured around individual cross-sections, as it was for the shaft shown in Figure 10-11.

10-7 CYLINDRICITY

Cylindricity tolerances are used to define a tolerance zone both around individual circular cross-sections of an object and also along its length. The resulting tolerance zone looks like two concentric cylinders.

Figure 10-13 shows a shaft that includes a cylindricity tolerance that establishes a tolerance zone of .007. This means that if the maximum measured diameter was determined to be .755, the minimum diameter cannot be less than .748 anywhere on the cylindrical surface. Figure 10-14 shows how to draw the feature control frames that surround the tolerance symbol and size specifications.

Cylindricity and circularity are somewhat analogous to flatness and straightness. Flatness and cylindricity are concerned with variations across an entire surface or plane. In the case of cylindricity, the plane is shaped like a cylinder. Straightness and circularity are concerned with variations of a single element of a surface: a straight line across the plane in a specified direction for straightness and a path around a single cross-section for circularity.

	TYPE OF TOLERANCE	CHARACTERISTIC	SYMBOL
FOR INDIVIDUAL FEATURES	FORM	STRAIGHTNESS	—
		FLATNESS	▱
		CIRCULARITY	○
		CYLINDRICITY	⌭
INDIVIDUAL OR RELATED FEATURES	PROFILE	PROFILE OF A LINE	⌒
		PROFILE OF A SURFACE	⌓
RELATED FEATURES	ORIENTATION	ANGULARITY	∠
		PERPENDICULARITY	⊥
		PARALLELISM	//
	LOCATION	POSITION	⊕
		CONCENTRICITY	◎
	RUNOUT	CIRCULAR RUNOUT	↗
		TOTAL RUNOUT	⫽

TERM	SYMBOL
AT MAXIMUM MATERIAL CONDITION	Ⓜ
REGARDLESS OF FEATURE SIZE	Ⓢ
AT LEAST MATERIAL CONDITION	Ⓛ
PROJECTED TOLERANCE ZONE	Ⓟ
DIAMETER	⌀
SPHERICAL DIAMETER	S⌀
RADIUS	R
SPHERICAL RADIUS	SR
REFERENCE	( )
ARC LENGTH	⌒

Figure 10-15

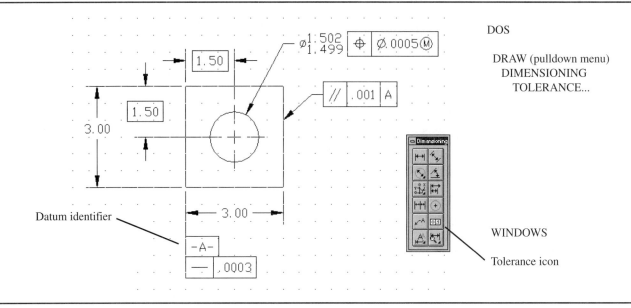

DOS

DRAW (pulldown menu)
   DIMENSIONING
      TOLERANCE...

WINDOWS

Tolerance icon

Datum identifier

Figure 10-16

10-8 GEOMETRIC TOLERANCES USING AUTOCAD

Geometric tolerances are tolerances that limit dimensional variations based on the geometric properties of an object. Figure 10-15 shows a listing of geometric tolerance symbols. Figure 10-16 shows an object dimensioned using geometric tolerances. The geometric tolerances were created as follows.

To define a datum

1. Select the TOLERANCE command

The Symbol dialog box will appear. See Figure 10-17.

Figure 10-17

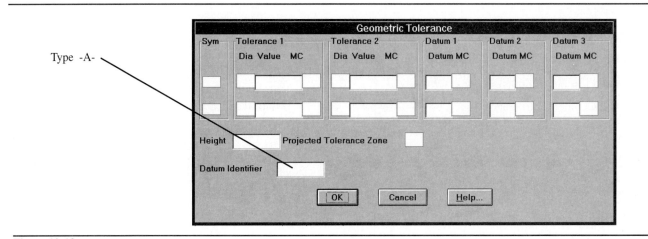

Type -A-

Figure 10-18

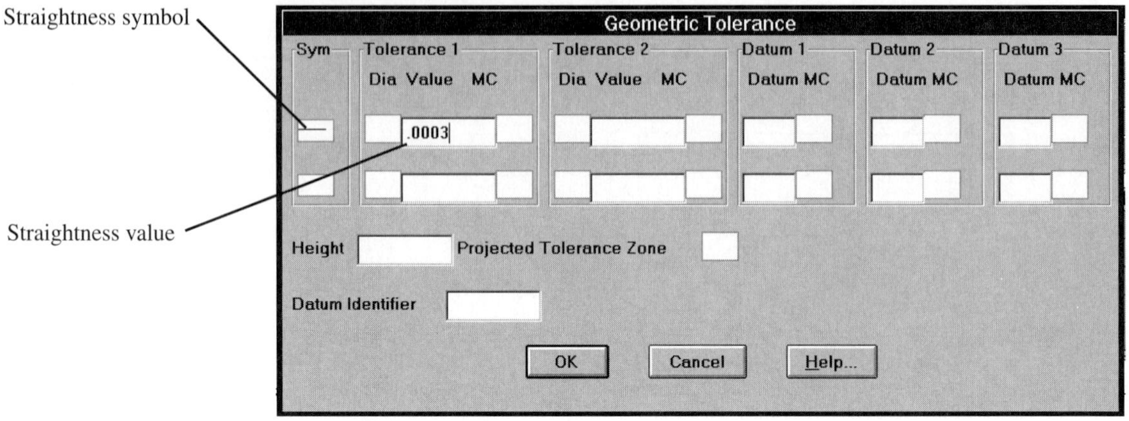

Straightness symbol

Straightness value

Geometric Tolerance

Sym	Tolerance 1	Tolerance 2	Datum 1	Datum 2	Datum 3
	Dia Value MC	Dia Value MC	Datum MC	Datum MC	Datum MC
	.0003				

Height ____   Projected Tolerance Zone ☐

Datum Identifier ____

[OK]   [Cancel]   [Help...]

Figure 10-19

2. Select OK

The Geometric Tolerance dialog box will appear. See Figure 10-18.

3. Click the Datum Identifier box and type -A-, OK

Command: _tolerance
Enter tolerance location:

4. Position the datum identifier and press the left mouse button

See Figure 10-16.

To define a straightness value

1. Select the TOLERANCE command

The Symbol dialog box will appear. See Figure 10-17.

2. Select OK

The Geometric Tolerance dialog box will appear. See Figure 10-18.

3. Select the top open box under the heading Sym

The Symbol dialog box will reappear.

4. Select the straightness symbol, then OK

The Geometric Tolerance dialog box will reappear with the straightness symbol in the first box under the heading Sym.

5. Click the open box under the word Value in the Tolerance 1 box, then type .0003, OK

See Figure 10-19.

Command: _tolerance
Enter tolerance location:

6. Position the straightness tolerance and press the left mouse button

Use the MOVE and OSNAP commands if necessary to reposition the tolerance box. See Figure 10-16.

To create a positional tolerance

A positional tolerance is used to locate and tolerance a hole in an object. Positional tolerances require base locating dimensions for the hole's center point. Positional tolerances also require a feature tolerance to define the diameter tolerances of the hole, and a geometric tolerance to define the position tolerance for the hole's center point.

To create a base dimension

See the two 1.50 dimensions in Figure 10-18 used to locate the center position of the hole.

1. Select the DIMENSION STYLES icon or type DDIM in response to a Command: prompt

The Dimension Styles dialog box will appear.

2. Select Annotation...

The Annotation dialog box will appear.

3. Select the Basic option next to the heading Method in the Tolerance box

See Figure 9-7.

4. Select OK,OK to return to the drawing
5. Use the LINEAR DIMENSION command to add the appropriate dimensions

See Figure 10-16.

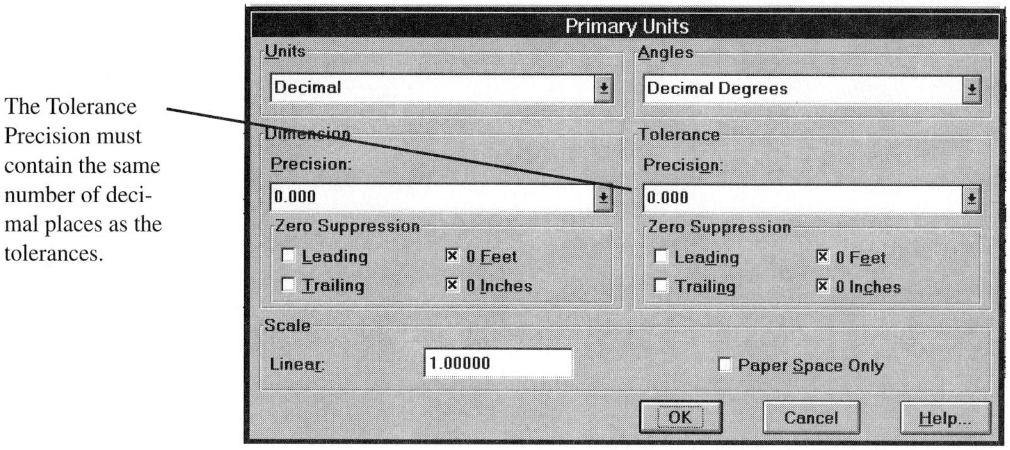

The Tolerance Precision must contain the same number of decimal places as the tolerances.

Figure 10-20

To add a feature tolerance to a hole

1. Select the DIMENSION STYLES icon or type DDIM in response to a Command: prompt

   The Dimension Styles dialog box will appear.

2. Select Annotation...

   The Annotation dialog box will appear.

3. Select the Limits option in the Method: box located in the Tolerance box.

   See Figure 9-7.

4. Change the Upper Value to 0.0020 by locating the cursor within the Upper Value box, backspacing out the existing value, and typing in the new value.

   The value displayed in the Units box will not change, but the tolerance placed on the drawing will change.

5. Change the Lower Value to 0.0010 by locating the cursor within the Lower Value box, backspacing out the existing value, and typing in the new value.

6. Check that the Justification box reads Middle.

7. Select the Units box

   The Primary units dialog box will appear.

8. Change the precision for both Dimension and Tolerance boxes to three decimal places (0.000).

   See Figure 10-20. AutoCAD will truncate any input according to the number of decimal places allowed by the precision settings. If the precision settings had been two decimal places (0.00), the resulting limit dimensions would have both been 1.50. The values defined in the third decimal place would have been ignored.

9. Select OK, OK, OK to return to the drawing

10. Select the DIAMETER DIMENSION icon

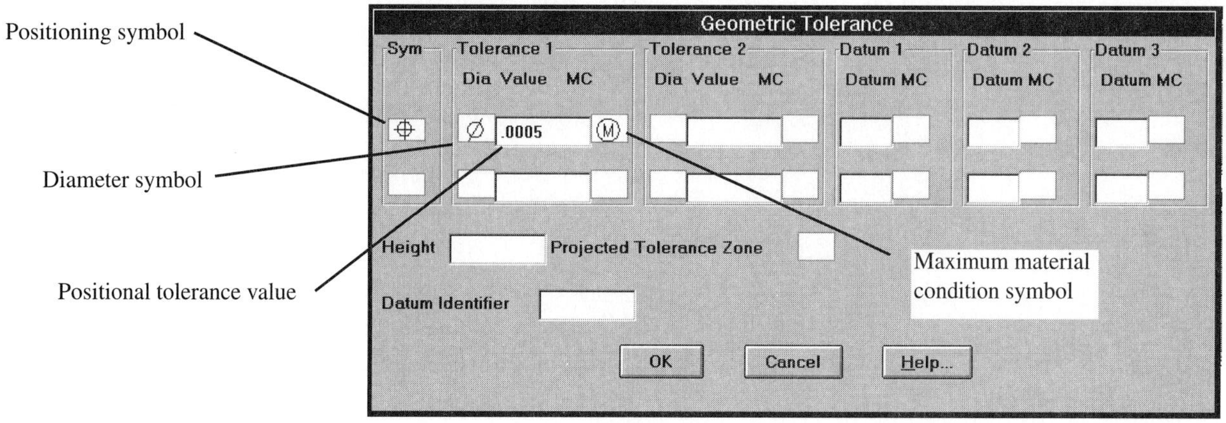

Positioning symbol

Diameter symbol

Positional tolerance value

Maximum material condition symbol

Figure 10-21

Select arc or circle:

11. Select the hole

    Dimension line location (Text/Angle):

12. Locate the diameter dimension

To add a positional tolerance to the hole's feature tolerance

1. Select the TOLERANCE command

    The Symbol dialog box will appear

2. Select the positioning tolerance symbol, then OK

    The Geometric Tolerance dialog box will appear with the positioning symbol in the first box under the Sym heading. See Figure 10-21.

3. Select the top left open box under the Dia heading in the Tolerance 1 box

    A diameter symbol will appear.

4. Select the Value box and type 0.0005

    The numbers will appear in the box.

5. Select the open box under the MC heading

    The Material Condition dialog box will appear. See Figure 10-22.

6. Select the maximum material condition symbol (the circle with an M in it)
7. Select OK

    The MMC symbol will appear in the MC box in the Geometric Tolerance dialog box.

8. Select OK

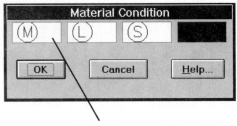

Maximum material condition symbol

Figure 10-22

Enter tolerance location:

9. Locate the tolerance box

    Use the MOVE and OSNAP commands to position the box if necessary.

To add a geometric tolerance with a leader line

1. Select the LEADER command

    Command:_leader
    From point:

2. Select the start point for the leader line (the arrowhead end)

    To point:

3. Select the other end of the leader line

    To point: (Format/ Annotation/ Undo) <Annotation>:

Parallelism symbol

Parallel tolerance value

Sym	Tolerance 1			Tolerance 2			Datum 1	Datum 2	Datum 3
	Dia	Value	MC	Dia	Value	MC	Datum MC	Datum MC	Datum MC
//		.0010					A		

Height _____ Projected Tolerance Zone

Datum Identifier _____

OK   Cancel   Help...

Figure 10-23

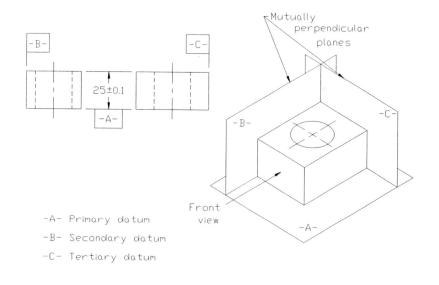

Figure 10-24

4. Type ENTER

   Annotation (or RETURN for options):

5. Type ENTER

   Tolerance/Copy/Block/None/<MText>:

6. Type T ENTER

   The Symbol dialog box will appear

7. Select the parallel symbol, then OK

   The Geometric Tolerance dialog box will appear. See Figure 10-23.

8. Select the open box under the heading Value in the Tolerance 1 box and type 0.0010
9. Select the open box under the heading Datum in the Datum 1 box, then OK

10-9 TOLERANCES OF ORIENTATION

Tolerances of orientation are used to relate a feature or surface to another feature or surface. Tolerances of orientation include perpendicularity, parallelism, and angularity. They may be applied using RFS or MMC conditions, but they cannot be applied to individual features by themselves. To define a surface as parallel to another surface is very much like assigning a flatness value to the surface. The difference is that flatness applies only within the surface; every point on the surface is related to a defined set of limiting parallel planes. Parallelism defines every point in the surface relative to another surface. The two surfaces are therefore directly related to each other, and the condition of one affects the other.

Orientation tolerances are used with locational tolerances. A feature is first located, then it is oriented within the locational tolerances. This means that the orientation tolerance must always be less than the locational tolerances. The next four sections will further explain this requirement.

10-10 DATUMS

A datum is a point, axis, or surface used as a starting reference point for dimensions and tolerances. Figure 10-24 shows a rectangular object with three datum planes labeled A, B, and C. The three datum planes are called the primary, secondary, and tertiary datums, respectively. The three datum planes are, by definition, exactly 90 degrees from each other.

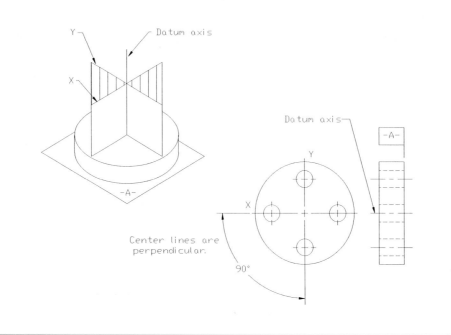

Figure 10-25

Figure 10-25 shows a cylindrical datum frame that includes three datum planes. The X and Y planes are perpendicular to each other and the base A plane is perpendicular to the datum axis between the X and Y planes.

Datums are defined on a drawing by using letters enclosed in rectangular boxes, as shown. The defining letters are written between dash lines, –A– , –B– , and –C– .

Datum planes are assumed to be perfectly flat. When assigning a datum status to a surface, be sure that the surface is reasonably flat. This means that datum surfaces should be toleranced using surface finishes, or created using machine techniques that produce flat surfaces.

10-11 PERPENDICULARITY

Perpendicularity tolerances are used to limit the amount of variation for a surface or feature within two planes perpendicular to a specified datum. Figure 10-26 shows a rectangular object. The bottom surface is assigned as datum –A– and the right vertical edge is toleranced so that it must be perpendicular within a limit of 0.05 to datum –A–. The perpendicularity tolerance defines a tolerance zone 0.05 wide between two parallel planes that are perpendicular to datum –A–.

The object also includes a horizontal dimension and tolerance of 40 +/–1. This tolerance is called a locational tolerance because it serves to locate the right edge of the

object. As with rectangular coordinate tolerances discussed in Chapter 9, the 40 +/–1 controls the location of the edge, how far away or how close it can be to the left edge, but does not directly control the shape of the edge. Any shape that falls within the specified tolerance range is acceptable. This may in fact be sufficient for a given design, but if a more controlled shape is required, a perpendicularity tolerance must be added. The perpendicularity tolerance works within the locational tolerance to ensure that the edge is not

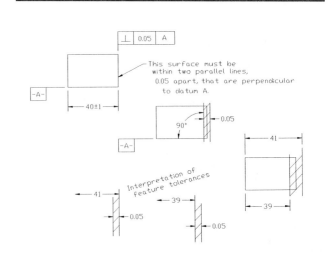

Figure 10-26

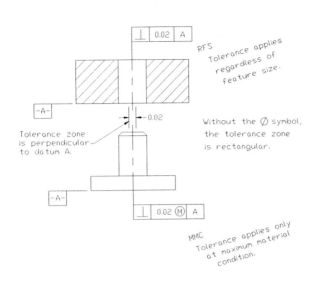

Figure 10-27

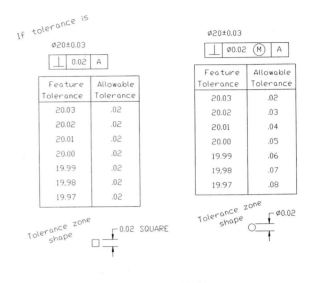

Figure 10-28

only within the locational tolerance but is also perpendicular to datum –A–.

Figure 10-26 shows the two extreme conditions for the 40 +/–1 locational tolerance. The perpendicularity tolerance is applied by first measuring the surface and determining its maximum and minimum lengths. The difference between these two measurements must be less than 0.05.

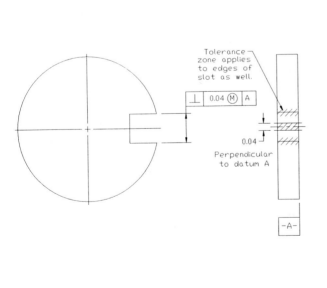

Figure 10-29

So if the measured maximum distance is 41, then no other part of the surface may be less then 41 – 0.05 = 40.05.

Tolerances of perpendicularity serve to complement locational tolerances, to make the shape more exact, so tolerances of perpendicularity must always be smaller than tolerances of location. It would be of little use, for example, to assign a perpendicularity tolerance of 1.5 for the object shown in Figure 10-26. The locational tolerance would prevent the variation from ever reaching the limits specified by such a large perpendicularity tolerance.

Figure 10-27 shows a perpendicularity tolerance applied to cylindrical features: a shaft and a hole. The figure includes examples of both RFS and MMC applications. As with straightness tolerances applied at MMC, perpendicularity tolerances applied about a hole or shaft's center line allows the tolerance zone to vary as the feature size varies.

The inclusion of the Ø symbol in a geometric tolerance is critical to its interpretation. See Figure 10-28. If the Ø symbol is not included, the tolerance applies only to the view in which it is written. This means the tolerance zone is shaped like a rectangular slice, not a cylinder, as would be the case if the Ø symbol were included. In general it is better to always include the Ø symbol for cylindrical features because it generates a tolerance zone more like that used in positional tolerancing.

Figure 10-29 shows a perpendicularity tolerance applied to a slot, a noncylindrical feature. Again the MMC specification is always for variations in the tolerance zone.

10-12 PARALLELISM

Parallelism is used to ensure that all points within a plane are within two parallel planes that are parallel to a referenced datum plane. Figure 10-30 shows a rectangular object that is toleranced so that its top surface is parallel to the bottom surface within .02. This means that every point on the top surface must be within a set of parallel planes 0.02 apart. These parallel tolerancing planes are located by determining the maximum and minimum distances from the datum surface. The difference between the maximum and minimum values may not exceed the stated 0.02 tolerance.

In the extreme condition of maximum feature size, the top surface is located 40.5 above the datum plane. The parallelism tolerance is then applied, meaning that no point on the surface may be closer than 40.3 to the datum. This is an RFS condition. The MMC condition may also be applied, thereby allowing the tolerance zone to vary as the feature size varies.

10-13 ANGULARISM

Angularism tolerances are used to limit the variance of surfaces and axes that are at an angle relative to a datum. Angularism tolerances are applied like perpendicularity and parallelism tolerances as a way to better control the shape of locational tolerances.

Figure 10-31 shows an angularism tolerance and several ways it is interpreted at extreme conditions.

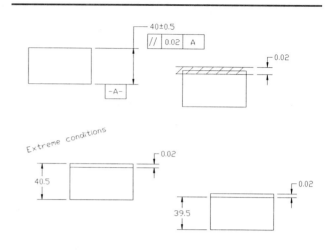

Figure 10-30

10-14 PROFILES

Profile tolerances are used to limit the variations of irregular surfaces. They may be assigned as either bilateral or unilateral tolerances. There are two types of profile tolerances: surface and line. Surface profile tolerances limit the variation of an entire surface, whereas a line profile tolerance limits the variations along a single line across a surface.

Figure 10-32 shows an object that includes a surface profile tolerance referenced to an irregular surface. The tolerance is considered a bilateral tolerance because no other specification is given. This means that all points on the surface must be located between two parallel planes 0.08 apart that are centered about the irregular surface. The measurements are taken perpendicular to the surface.

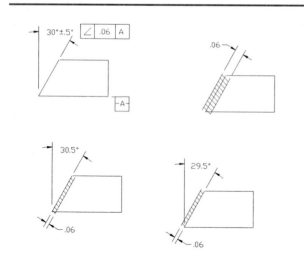

Figure 10-31

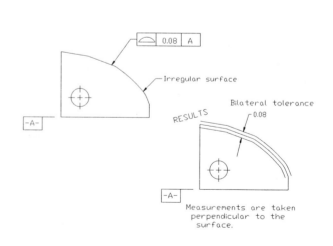

Figure 10-32

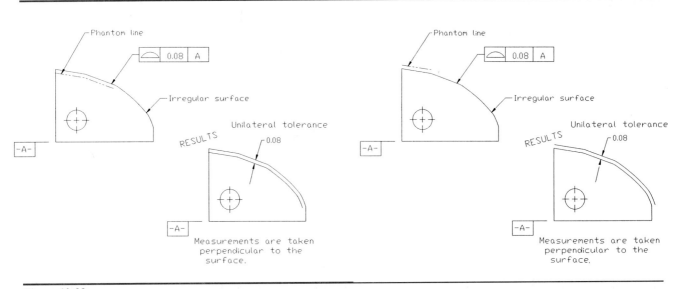

Figure 10-33

Unilateral applications of surface profile tolerances must be indicated on the drawing using phantom lines. The phantom line indicates on which side of the true profile line of the irregular surface the tolerance is to be applied. A phantom line above the irregular surface indicates that the tolerance is to be applied using the true profile line as 0 and then adding the specified tolerance range above that line. See Figures 10-33 and 10-34.

Profiles of line tolerances are applied to irregular sur-

faces, as shown in Figure 10-33. Profiles of line tolerances are particularly helpful when tolerancing an irregular surface that is constantly changing, such as the surface of an airplane wing.

Surface and line profile tolerances are somewhat analogous to flatness and straightness tolerances. A flatness and surface profile tolerance is applied across an entire surface, whereas straightness and line profile tolerances are applied only along a single line across the surface.

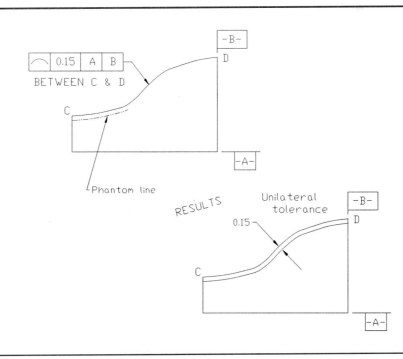

Figure 10-34

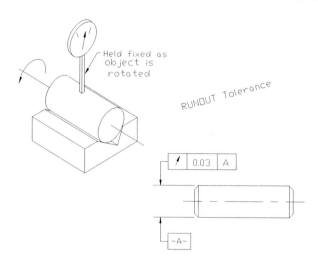

Figure 10-35

10-15 RUNOUTS

A runout tolerance is used to limit the variations between features of an object and a datum. More specifically they are applied to surfaces around a datum axis such as a cylinder or to a surface constructed perpendicular to a datum axis. There are two types of runout tolerances: circular and total.

Figure 10-35 shows a cylinder that includes a circular runout tolerance. The runout requirements are checked by rotating the object about its longitudinal axis or datum axis while holding an indicator gage in a fixed position on the object's surface.

Runout tolerances may be either bilateral or unilateral. A runout tolerance is assumed to be bilateral unless otherwise indicated. If a runout tolerance is to be unilateral, a phantom line is used to indicate to which side of the object's true surface the tolerance is to be applied. See Figure 10-36.

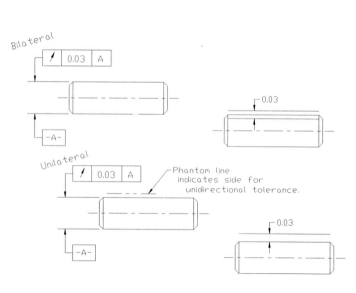

Figure 10-36

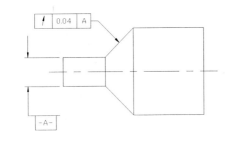

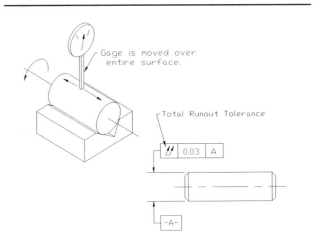

Figure 10-37

Figure 10-38

Runout tolerances may be applied to tapered areas of cylindrical objects, as shown in Figure 10-37. The tolerance is checked by rotating the object about a datum axis while holding an indicator gage in place.

A total runout tolerance limits the variation across an entire surface. See Figure 10-38. An indicator gage is not held in place while the object is rotated, as it is for circular runout tolerances, but is moved about the rotating surface.

Figure 10-39 shows a circular runout tolerance that references two datums. The two datums serve as one datum. The object can then be rotated about both datums simultaneously as the runout tolerances are checked.

10-16 POSITIONAL TOLERANCES

Positional tolerances are used to locate and tolerance holes. Positional tolerances create a circular tolerance zone for hole centerpoint locations. This differs from a rectangular shape tolerance zone created by linear coordinate dimensions. See Figure 10-40. The circular tolerance zone allows for an increase in acceptable tolerance variation without compromising the design integrity of the object. Note how some of the possible hole center points fall in an area outside the rectangular tolerance zone but are still within the circular tolerance zone. If the hole had been located using linear coordinate dimensions, center points

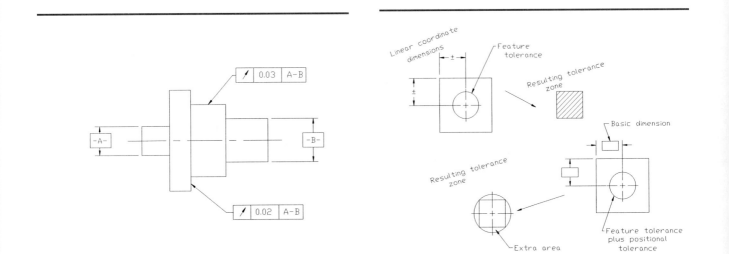

Figure 10-39

Figure 10-40

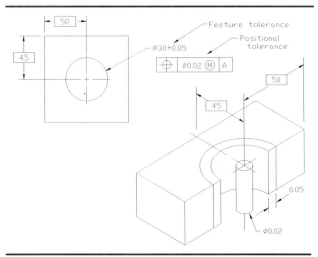

Figure 10-41

located beyond the rectangular tolerance zone would have been rejected as beyond tolerance, and yet holes produced using these locations would function correctly from a design standpoint. The centerpoint locations would be acceptable if positional tolerances had been specified. The finished hole is round, so a round tolerance zone is appropriate. The rectangular tolerance zone rejects some holes unnecessarily.

Holes are dimensioned and toleranced using geometric tolerances by a combination of locating dimensions, feature dimensions and tolerances, and positional tolerances. See Figure 10-41. The locating dimensions are enclosed in rectangular boxes and are called basic dimen-

sions. Basic dimensions are assumed to be exact.

The feature tolerances for the hole are as presented in Chapter 9. They can be presented using plus or minus or limit type tolerances. In the example shown in Figure 10-41 the diameter of the hole is toleranced using a plus and minus 0.05 tolerance.

The basic locating dimensions of 45 and 50 are assumed to be exact. The tolerances that would normally accompany linear locational dimensions are replaced by the positional tolerance. The positional tolerance also specifies that the tolerance be applied at the center line at maximum material condition. The resulting tolerance zones are as shown in Figure 10-41.

Figure 10-42 shows an object containing two holes that are dimensioned and toleranced using positional tolerances. There are two consecutive horizontal basic dimensions. Because basic dimensions are exact, they do not have tolerances that accumulate; that is, there is no tolerance buildup.

10-17 VIRTUAL CONDITION

Virtual condition is a combination of a feature's MMC and its geometric tolerance. For external features (shafts) it is the MMC plus the geometric tolerance; for internal features (holes) it is the MMC minus the geometric tolerance.

The following calculations are based on the dimensions shown in Figure 10-43.

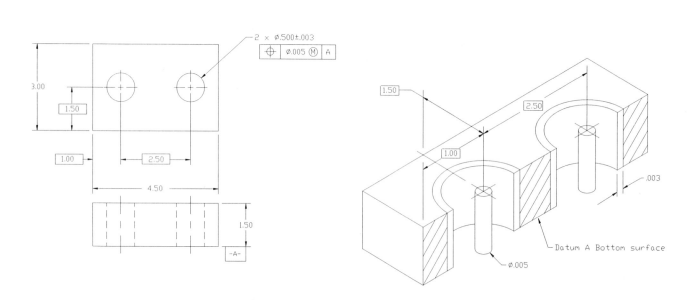

Figure 10-42

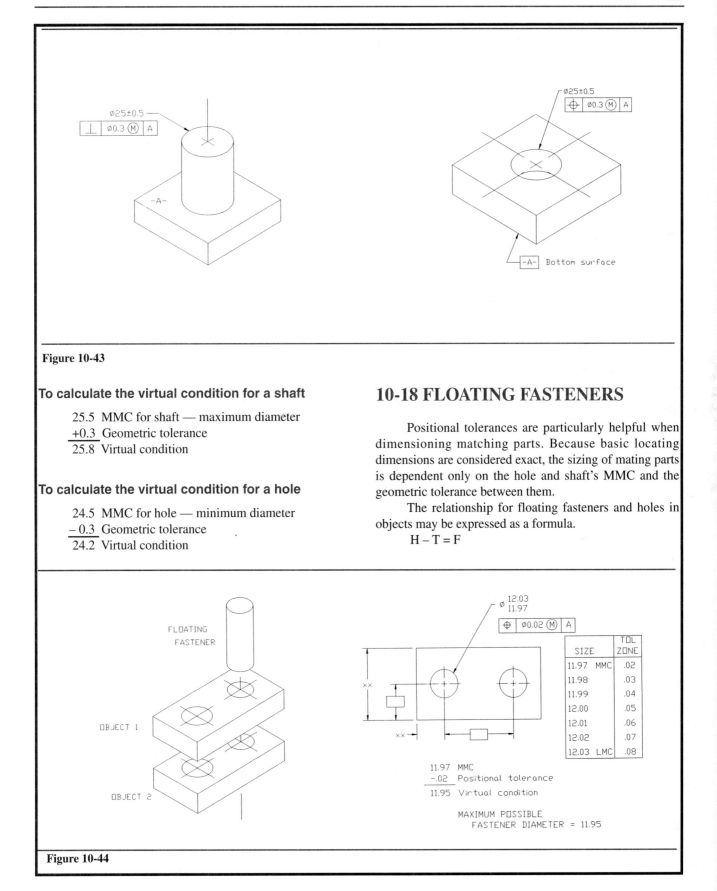

Figure 10-43

To calculate the virtual condition for a shaft

25.5	MMC for shaft — maximum diameter
+0.3	Geometric tolerance
25.8	Virtual condition

To calculate the virtual condition for a hole

24.5	MMC for hole — minimum diameter
− 0.3	Geometric tolerance
24.2	Virtual condition

10-18 FLOATING FASTENERS

Positional tolerances are particularly helpful when dimensioning matching parts. Because basic locating dimensions are considered exact, the sizing of mating parts is dependent only on the hole and shaft's MMC and the geometric tolerance between them.

The relationship for floating fasteners and holes in objects may be expressed as a formula.

$$H - T = F$$

Figure 10-44

where

H = Hole at MMC
T = Geometric tolerance
F = Shaft at MMC

A floating fastener is one that is free to move in either object. It is not attached to either object and it does not screw into either object. Figure 10-44 shows two objects that are to be joined by a common floating shaft, such as a bolt or screw. The feature size and tolerance and the positional geometric tolerance are both given. The minimum size hole that will always just fit is determined using the formula given above.

$$H - T = F$$
$$11.97 - 0.02 = 11.95$$

Therefore the shaft's diameter at MMC, the shaft's maximum diameter, equals 11.95. Any required tolerance would have to be subtracted from this shaft size.

The 0.02 geometric tolerance is applied at the hole's MMC. So as the hole's size expands within its feature tolerance, the tolerance zone for the acceptable matching parts also expands. See the table in Figure 10-44.

10-19 SAMPLE PROBLEM SP10-1

The situation presented in Figure 10-44 can be worked in reverse; that is, hole sizes can be derived from given shaft sizes.

The two objects shown in Figure 10-45 are to be joined by a .250-inch bolt. The parts are floating; that is,

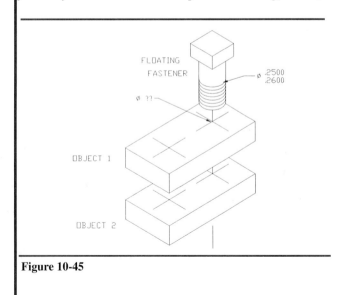

Figure 10-45

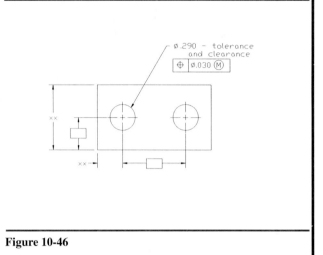

Figure 10-46

they are both free to move, and the fastener is not joined to either object. What is the MMC of the holes if the positional tolerance is to be .030?

A manufacturer's catalog specifies that the tolerance for .250 bolts is .2500 to .2600.

Rewriting the formula

$$H - T = F$$

to isolate the H yields

$$H = F + T$$
$$= .260 + .030$$
$$= .290$$

The .290 value represents the minimum hole diameter, MMC, for all four holes that would always accept the .250 bolt. Figure 10-46 shows the resulting drawing callout.

Any clearance requirements or tolerances for the hole would have to be added to the .290 value.

10-20 SAMPLE PROBLEM SP10-2

Repeat the problem presented in SP10-1 but be sure that there is always a minimum clearance of .002 between the hole and the shaft and assign a hole tolerance of .0010.

Sample problem SP10-1 determined that the maximum hole diameter that would always accept the .250 bolt was .290 based on the .030 positioning tolerance. If the minimum clearance is to be .002, the maximum hole diameter is found as follows.

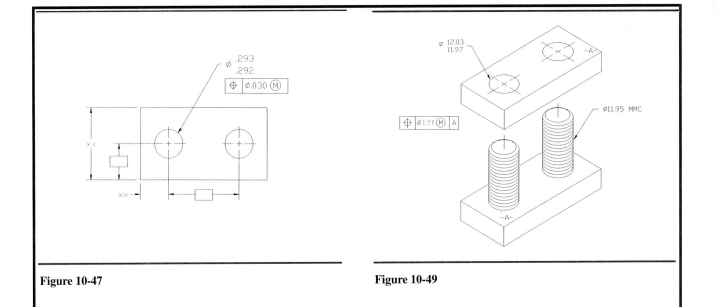

Figure 10-47

Figure 10-49

.290 Minimum hole diameter that will always
   accept the bolt (0 clearance at MMC)
+.002 Minimum clearance
.292 Minimum hole diameter including clearance

Now assign the tolerance to the hole.

.292 Minimum hole diameter
.001 Tolerance
.293 Maximum hole diameter

See Figure 10-47 for the appropriate drawing callout. The choice of clearance size and hole tolerance varies
with the design requirements for the objects.

10-21 FIXED FASTENERS

A fixed fastener is one that is attached to one of the
mating objects. See Figure 10-48. Because the fastener is
fixed to one of the objects, the geometric tolerance zone
must be smaller than that used for floating fasteners. The
fixed fastener cannot move without moving the object it is
attached to. The relationship between fixed fasteners and
holes in mating objects is defined by the formula

$$H - 2T = F$$

The tolerance zone is cut in half. This can be demonstrated by the objects shown in Figure 10-49. The same
feature sizes that were used in Figure 10-44 are assigned,
but in this example the fasteners are fixed. Solving for the
geometric tolerance yields a value as follows.

$$H - F = 2T$$

$$11.97 - 11.95 = 2T$$

$$.02 = 2T$$

$$.01 = T$$

The resulting positional tolerance is half of that
obtained for floating fasteners.

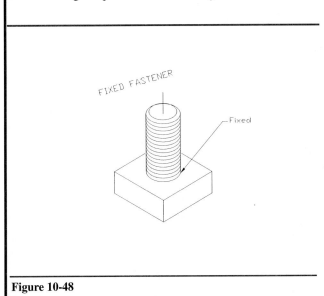

Figure 10-48

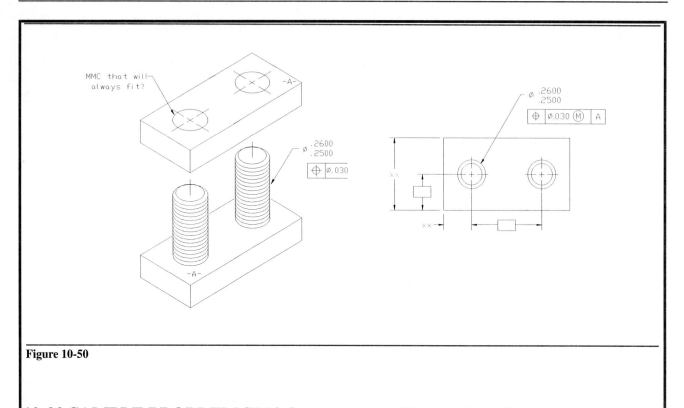

Figure 10-50

10-22 SAMPLE PROBLEM SP10-3

This problem is similar to sample problem SP10-1, but the given conditions are applied to fixed fasteners rather than floating fasteners. Compare the resulting shaft diameters for the two problems. See Figure 10-50.

A. What is the minimum diameter hole that will always accept the fixed fasteners?

B. If the minimum clearance is .005 and the hole is to have a tolerance of .002, what are the maximum and minimum diameters of the hole?

$$H - 2T = F$$

$$
\begin{aligned}
H &= F + 2T \\
&= .260 + 2(.030) \\
&= .260 + .060 \\
&= .320 \quad \text{Minimum diameter that will always accept the fixed fastener.}
\end{aligned}
$$

If the minimum clearance = .005 and the hole tolerance is .002,

.320	Virtual condition
.005	Clearance
.325	Minimum hole diameter

.325	Minimum hole diameter
.002	Tolerance
.327	Maximum hole diameter

The maximum and minimum values for the hole's diameter can then be added to the drawing of the object that fits over the fixed fasteners. See Figure 10-51.

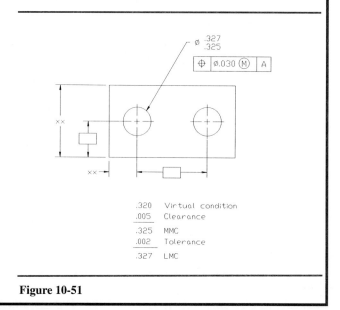

Figure 10-51

10-23 DESIGN PROBLEMS

This problem was originally done in Section 9-24 using rectangular tolerances. It is done in this section using positional geometric tolerances so that the two systems can be compared. It is suggested that Section 9-24 be reviewed before reading this section.

Figure 10-52 shows top and bottom parts that are to be joined in the floating condition. A nominal distance of 50 between hole centers and 20 for the holes has been assigned. In Section 9-24 a rectangular tolerance of ±.01 was selected and there was a minimum hole diameter of 20.00. Figure 10-53 shows the resulting tolerance zones.

The diagonal distance across the rectangular tolerance zone is .028 and was rounded off to .03 to yield a maximum possible fastener diameter of 19.97. If the same .03 value is used to calculate the fastener diameter using positional tolerance, the results will be as follows.

$$H - T = F$$

$$20.00 - .03 = 19.97$$

The results seem to be the same, but because of the circular shape of the positional tolerance zone, the manufactured results are not the same. The minimum distance between the inside edges of the rectangular zones is 49.98, or .01 from the center point of each hole. The minimum distance from the innermost points of the cir-

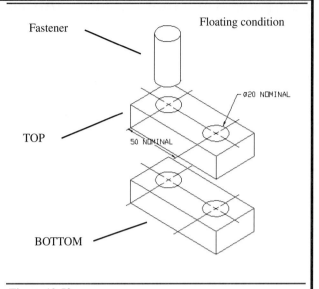

Figure 10-52

cular tolerance zones is 49.97, or .015 (half of the rounded off .03 value) from the center point of each hole. The same value difference also occurs for the maximum distance between center points, where 50.02 is the maximum distance for the rectangular tolerances and 50.03 is the maximum distance for the circular tolerances. The size of the circular tolerance zone increased further because the hole tolerances are assigned at MMC. Figure

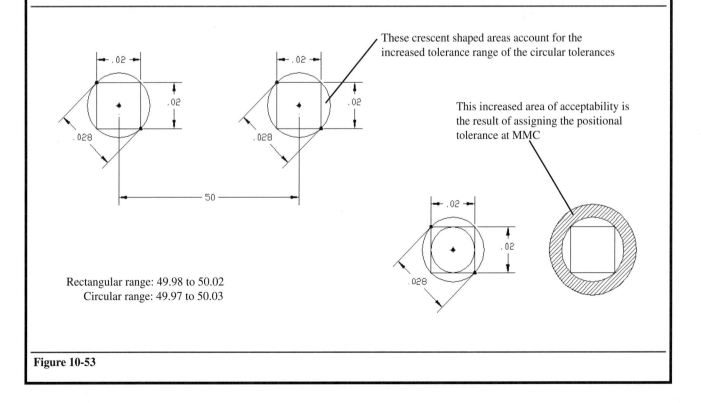

These crescent shaped areas account for the increased tolerance range of the circular tolerances

This increased area of acceptability is the result of assigning the positional tolerance at MMC

Rectangular range: 49.98 to 50.02
Circular range: 49.97 to 50.03

Figure 10-53

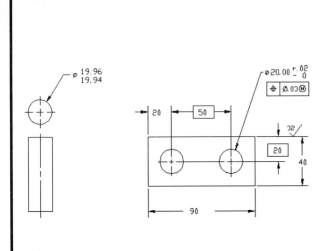

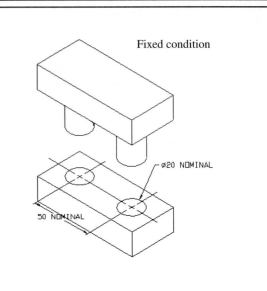

Fixed condition

Figure 10-54

Figure 10-55

10-53 shows a comparison between the tolerance zones, and Figure 10-54 shows how the positional tolerances would be presented on a drawing of either the top or bottom parts.

Figure 10-55 shows the same top and bottom parts joined together in the fixed condition. The initial nominal values are the same. If the same .03 diagonal value is assigned as a positional tolerance, the results are as follows.

$$H - 2T = F$$

$$20.00 - .06 = 19.94$$

These results appear to be the same as those generated by the rectangular tolerance zone, but the circular tolerance zone allows a greater variance in acceptable manufactured parts. Figure 10-56 shows how the positional tolerance would be presented on a drawing.

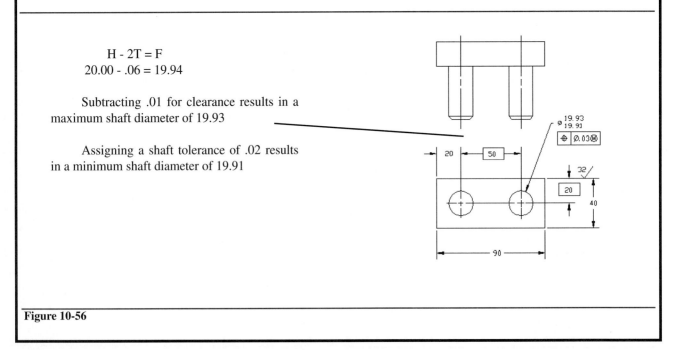

$$H - 2T = F$$
$$20.00 - .06 = 19.94$$

Subtracting .01 for clearance results in a maximum shaft diameter of 19.93

Assigning a shaft tolerance of .02 results in a minimum shaft diameter of 19.91

Figure 10-56

10-24 EXERCISE PROBLEMS

EX10-1

Redraw the object shown. Include all dimensions and tolerances.

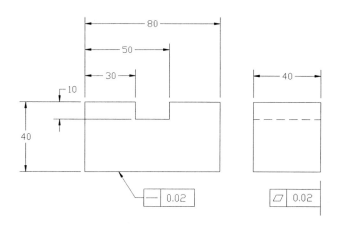

EX10-2

Redraw the following shaft and add a feature dimension and tolerance of 36±0.1 and a straightness tolerance of 0.07 about the center line at MMC.

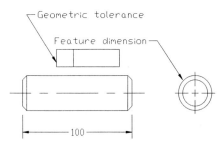

EX10-3

A. Given the shaft shown, what is the minimum hole diameter that will always accept the shaft?

B. If the minimum clearance between the shaft and a hole is equal to 0.02 and the tolerance on the hole is to be 0.6, what are the maximum and minimum diameters for the hole?

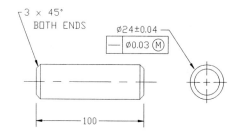

EX10-4

A. Given the shaft shown, what is the minimum hole diameter that will always accept the shaft?

B. If the minimum clearance between the shaft and a hole is equal to 0.005 and the tolerance on the hole is to be 0.007, what are the maximum and minimum diameters for the hole?

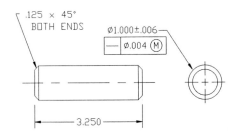

EX10-5

Draw a front and right-side view of the object shown in Figure EX10-5 and add the appropriate dimensions and tolerances based on the following information. Numbers located next to an edge line indicate the edge's length.

A. Define surfaces A, B, and C as primary, secondary, and tertiary datums, respectively.

B. Assign a tolerance of +/− 0.5 to all linear dimensions.

C. Assign a feature tolerance of 12.07 − 12.00 to the protruding shaft.

D. Assign a flatness tolerance of 0.01 to surface -A-.

E. Assign a straightness tolerance of 0.03 to the protruding shaft.

F. Assign a perpendicularity tolerance to the center line of the protruding shaft of 0.02 at MMC relative to datum -A-.

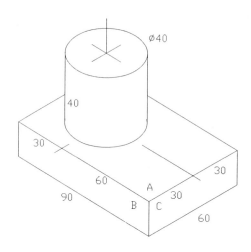

Figure EX10-5

EX10-6

Draw a front and right-side view of the object shown in Figure EX10-6 and add the following dimensions and tolerances.

A. Define the bottom surface as datum -A-.

B. Assign a perpendicularity tolerance of 0.4 to both sides of the slot relative to datum -A-.

C. Assign a perpendicularity tolerance of 0.2 to the center line of the 30 diameter hole center line at MMC relative to datum -A-.

D. Assign a feature tolerance of +/−0.8 to all three holes.

E. Assign a parallelism tolerance of 0.2 to the common center line between the two 20 diameter holes relative to datum -A-.

F. Assign a tolerance of +/−0.5 to all linear dimensions.

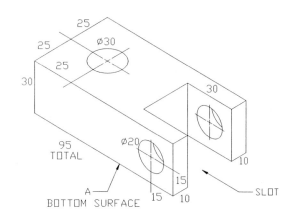

Figure EX10-6

EX10-7

Draw a circular front and the appropriate right-side view of the object shown in Figure EX10-7 and add the following dimensions and tolerances.

A. Assign datum -A- as indicated.

B. Assign the object's longitudinal axis as datum -B-.

C. Assign the object's center line through the slot as datum -C-.

D. Assign a tolerance of +/–0.5 to all linear tolerances.

E. Assign a tolerance of +/–.05 to all circular shaped features.

F. Assign a parallelism tolerance of 0.01 to both edges of the slot.

G. Assign a perpendicularity tolerance of 0.01 to the outside edge of the protruding shaft.

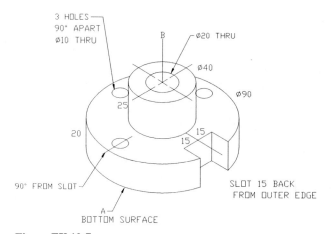

Figure EX 10-7

EX10-8

Given the two objects shown in Figure EX10-8, draw a front and side view of each. Assign a tolerance of ±0.5 to all linear dimensions. Assign a feature tolerance of ±0.4 to the shaft, and also assign a straightness tolerance of 0.2 to the shaft's center line at MMC.

Tolerance the hole so that it will always accept the shaft with a minimum clearance of 0.1 and a feature tolerance of 0.2. Assign a perpendicularity tolerance of 0.05 to the center line of the hole at MMC.

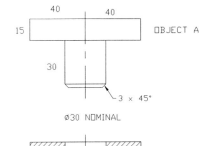

EX10-9

Given the two objects shown in Figure EX10-9, draw a front and side view of each. Assign a tolerance of +/–0.005 to all linear dimensions. Assign a feature tolerance of +/–0.004 to the shaft and also assign a straightness tolerance of 0.002 to the shaft's center line at MMC.

Tolerance the hole so that it will always accept the shaft with a minimum clearance of 0.001 and a feature tolerance of 0.002.

Figure EX10-8

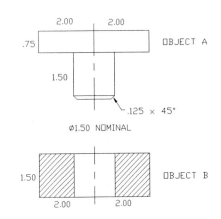

Figure EX10-9

EX10-10

Refer to parts A through G for this exercise problems. Use the format shown in Figure EX10-10 and redraw the given geometric tolerance symbols and frame as shown in the sample. Express in words (DTEXT) the meaning of each tolerance callout.

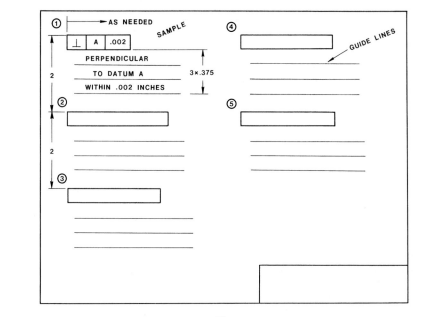

Figure EX10-10

A.

B.

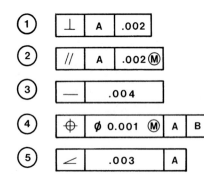

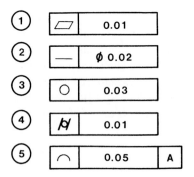

EX10-10, Continued

C.

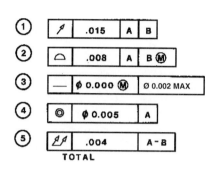

(1) | ⚡ | .015 | A | B

(2) | ⌒ | .008 | A | B Ⓜ

(3) | — | ⌀ 0.000 Ⓜ | ⌀ 0.002 MAX

(4) | ◎ | ⌀ 0.005 | A

(5) | ⚡⚡ | .004 | A - B

TOTAL

F.

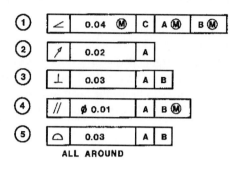

(1) | ∠ | 0.04 Ⓜ | C | A Ⓜ | B Ⓜ

(2) | ⚡ | 0.02 | A

(3) | ⊥ | 0.03 | A | B

(4) | // | ⌀ 0.01 | A | B Ⓜ

(5) | ⌒ | 0.03 | A | B

ALL AROUND

D.

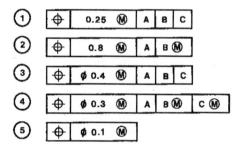

(1) | ⟐ | 0.25 Ⓜ | A | B | C

(2) | ⟐ | 0.8 Ⓜ | A | B Ⓜ

(3) | ⟐ | ⌀ 0.4 Ⓜ | A | B | C

(4) | ⟐ | ⌀ 0.3 Ⓜ | A | B Ⓜ | C Ⓜ

(5) | ⟐ | ⌀ 0.1 Ⓜ

G.

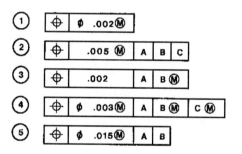

(1) | ⟐ | ⌀ .002 Ⓜ

(2) | ⟐ | .005 Ⓜ | A | B | C

(3) | ⟐ | .002 | A | B Ⓜ

(4) | ⟐ | ⌀ .003 Ⓜ | A | B Ⓜ | C Ⓜ

(5) | ⟐ | ⌀ .015 Ⓜ | A | B

E.

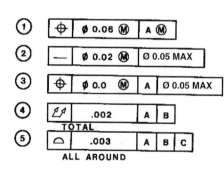

(1) | ⊕ | ⌀ 0.06 Ⓜ | A Ⓜ

(2) | — | ⌀ 0.02 Ⓜ | ⌀ 0.05 MAX

(3) | ⊕ | ⌀ 0.0 Ⓜ | A | ⌀ 0.05 MAX

(4) | ⚡⚡ | .002 | A | B

TOTAL

(5) | ⌒ | .003 | A | B | C

ALL AROUND

EX10-11

Draw front, top, and right-side views of the object in Figure EX10-11, including dimensions. Add the following tolerances and specifications to the drawing.

A. Surface 1 is datum A.

B. Surface 2 is datum B and is perpendicular to datum A within 0.1mm.

C. Surface 3 is datum C and is parallel to datum A within 0.3mm.

D. Locate a 16mm diameter hole in the center of the front surface that goes completely through the object. Use positional tolerances to locate the hole. Assign a positional tolerance of 0.02 at MMC perpendicular to datum A.

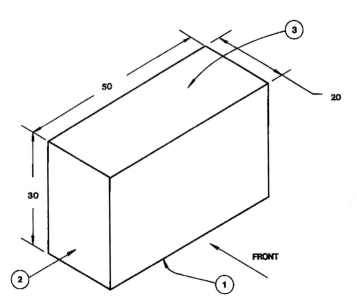

Figure EX10-11

EX10-12

Draw front, top, and right-side views of the object in Figure EX10-12, including dimensions. Add the following tolerances and specifications to the drawing.

A. Surface 1 is datum A.

B. Surface 2 is datum B and is perpendicular to datum A within .003".

C. Surface 3 is parallel to datum A within .005".

D. The cylinder's longitudinal center line is to be straight within .001" at MMC.

E. Surface 2 is to have circular accuracy within .002".

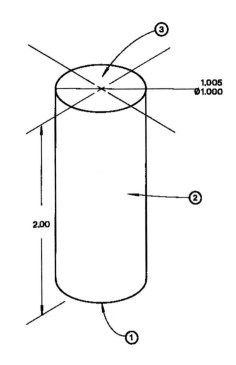

Figure EX10-12

EX10-13

Draw front, top, and right-side views of the object in Figure EX10-13, including dimensions. Add the following tolerances and specifications to the drawing.

A. Surface 1 is datum A.

B. Surface 4 is datum B and is perpendicular to datum A within 0.08mm.

C. Surface 3 is flat within 0.03mm.

D. Surface 5 is parallel to datum A within 0.01mm.

E. Surface 2 has a runout tolerance of 0.2mm relative to surface 4.

F. Surface 1 is flat within 0.02mm.

G. The longitudinal center line is to be straight within 0.02 at MMC and perpendicular to datum A.

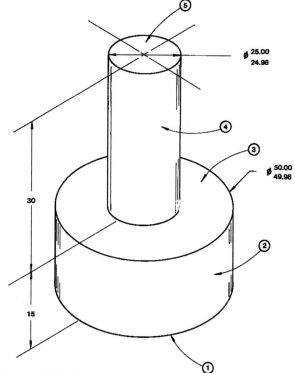

Figure EX10-13

EX10-14

Draw front, top, and right-side views of the object in Figure EX10-14, including dimensions. Add the following tolerances and specifications to the drawing.

A. Surface 2 is datum A.

B. Surface 6 is perpendicular to datum A with 0.000 allowable variance at MMC but with a 0.002" MAX variance limit beyond MMC.

C. Surface 1 is parallel to datum A within .005".

D. Surface 4 is perpendicular to datum A within .004".

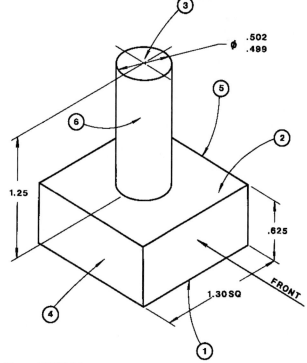

Figure EX10-14

EX10-15

Draw front, top, and right-side views of the object in Figure EX10-15, including dimensions. Add the following tolerances and specifications to the drawing.

A. Surface 1 is datum A.

B. Surface 2 is datum B.

C. The hole is located using a true position tolerance value of 0.13mm at MMC. The true position tolerance is referenced to datums A and B.

D. Surface 1 is to be straight within 0.02mm.

E. The bottom surface is to be parallel to datum A within 0.03mm.

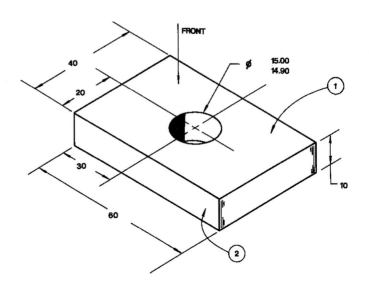

Figure EX10-15

EX10-16

Draw front, top, and right-side views of the object in Figure EX10-16, including dimensions. Add the following tolerances and specifications to the drawing.

A. Surface 1 is datum A.

B. Surface 2 is datum B.

C. Surface 3 is perpendicular to surface 2 within 0.02mm.

D. The four holes are to be located using a positional tolerance of 0.07mm at MMC referenced to datums A and B.

E. The center lines of the holes are to be straight within .01mm at MMC.

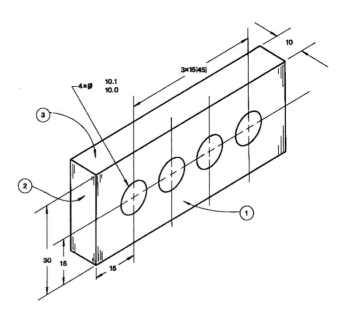

Figure EX10-16

EX10-17

Draw front, top, and right-side views of the object in Figure EX10-17, including dimensions. Add the following tolerances and specifications to the drawing.

A. Surface 1 has a dimension of 0.378-.375" and is datum A. The surface has a dual primary runout with datum B to within .005". The runout is total.

B. Surface 2 has a dimension of 1.505-1.495". Its runout relative to the dual primary datums A and B is .008". The runout is total.

C. Surface 3 has a dimension of 1.000 +/-.005 and has no geometric tolerance.

D. Surface 4 has no circular dimension but has a total runout tolerance of .006" relative to the dual datums A and B.

E. Surface 5 has a dimension of .500-.495" and is datum B. It has a dual primary runout with datum A within .005". The runout is total.

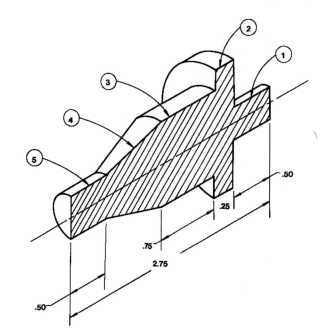

Figure EX10-17

EX10-18

Draw front, top, and right-side views of the object in Figure EX10-18, including dimensions. Add the following tolerances and specifications to the drawing.

A. Hole 1 is datum A.

B. Hole 2 is to have its circular center line parallel to datum A within 0.2mm at MMC when datum A is at MMC.

C. Assign a positional tolerance of 0.01 to each hole's center line at MMC.

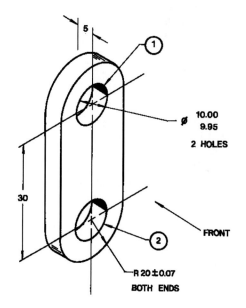

Figure EX10-18

EX10-19

Draw front, top, and right-side views of the object in Figure EX10-19, including dimensions. Add the following tolerances and specifications to the drawing.

A. Surface 1 is datum A.

B. Surface 2 is datum B.

C. The six holes have a diameter range of .502-.499" and are to be located using positional tolerances so that their center lines are within .005" at MMC relative to datums A and B.

D. The back surface is to be parallel to datum A within .002".

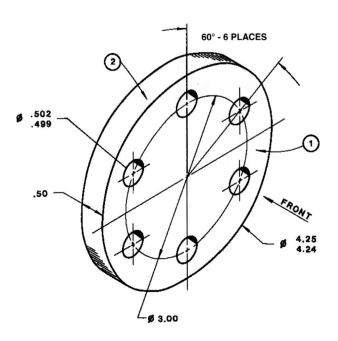

Figure EX10-19

EX10-20

Draw front, top, and right-side views of the object in Figure EX10-20, including dimensions. Add the following tolerances and specifications to the drawing.

A. Surface 1 is datum A.

B. Hole 2 is datum B.

C. The 8 holes labeled 3 have diameters of 8.4-8.3mm with a positional tolerance of 0.15mm at MMC relative to datums A and B. Also, the 8 holes are to be counterbored to a diameter of 14.6-14.4mm and to a depth of 5.0mm.

D. The large center hole is to have a straightness tolerance of 0.2 at MMC about its center line.

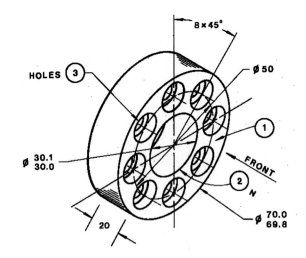

Figure EX10-20

EX10-21

Draw front, top, and right-side views of the object in Figure EX10-21, including dimensions. Add the following tolerances and specifications to the drawing.

    A. Surface 1 is datum A.

    B. Surface 2 is datum B.

    C. Surface 3 is datum C.

    D. The 4 holes labeled 4 have a dimension and tolerance of 8 +0.3,–0mm. The holes are to be located using a positional tolerance of 0.05mm at MMC relative to datums A, B, and C.

    E. The 6 holes labeled 5 have a dimension and tolerance of 6 +0.2,–0mm. The holes are to be located using a positional tolerance of 0.01mm at MMC relative to datums A, B, and C.

EX10-22

The objects on page 446 are to be toleranced using four different tolerances as shown. Redraw the charts shown in Figure EX10-22 and list the appropriate allowable tolerance for "as measured" increments of .1mm or .001". Also include the appropriate geometric tolerance drawing called out above each chart.

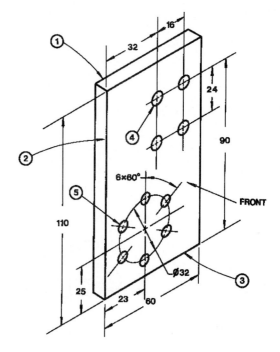

Figure EX10-21

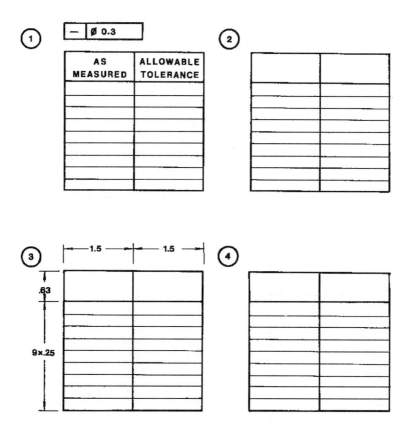

Figure EX10-22

EX10-22, Continued

A.

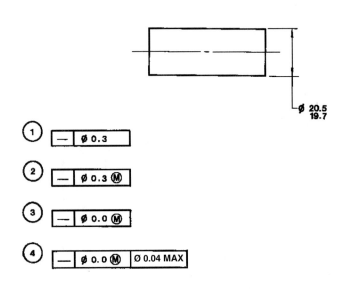

B.

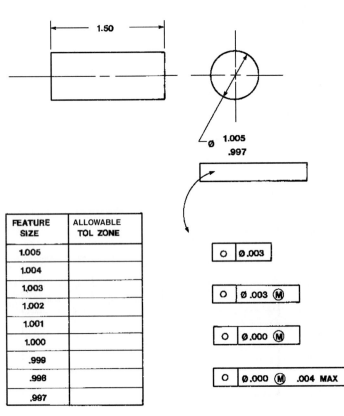

EX10-23

Dimension and tolerance Parts 1 and 2 of Figure EX10-23 so that Part 1 always fits into Part 2 with a minimum clearance of .005". The tolerance for Part 1's outer matching surface is .006".

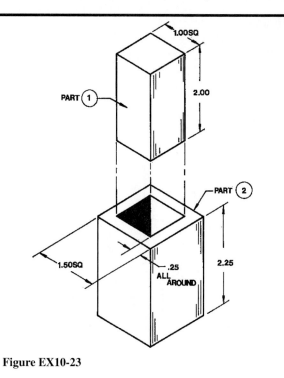

Figure EX10-23

EX10-24

Dimension and tolerance Parts 1 and 2 of Figure EX10-24 so that Part 1 always fits into Part 2 with a minimum clearance of 0.03mm. The tolerance for Part 1's diameter is 0.05mm. Take into account the fact that the interface is long relative to the diameters.

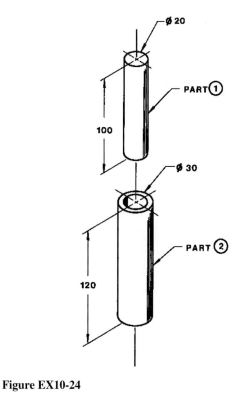

Figure EX10-24

EX10-25

Prepare front and top views of Parts 4A and 4B of Figure EX10-25 based on the given dimensions. Add geometric tolerances to produce the stated maximum clearance and mismatch.

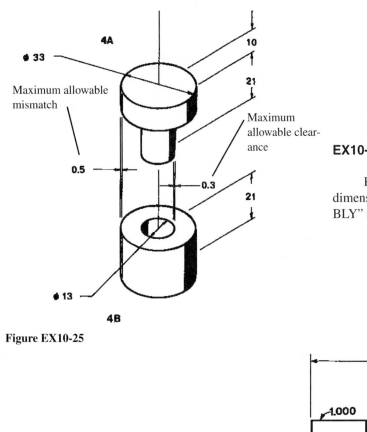

Figure EX10-25

EX10-26

Redraw parts A and B of Figure EX10-26 and add dimensions and tolerances to meet the "UPON ASSEMBLY" requirements.

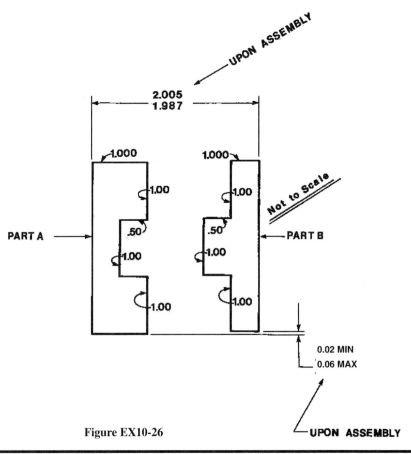

Figure EX10-26

EX10-27

Draw front and top views of both objects in Figure EX10-27. Add dimensions and geometric tolerances to meet the "FINAL CONDITION" requirements.

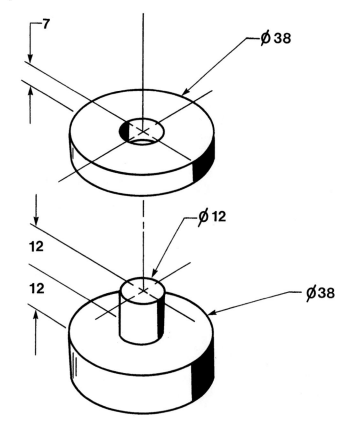

FINAL CONDITION

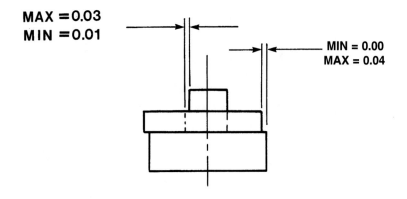

Figure EX10-27

Given top and bottom parts as shown in Figure EX10-28, satisfy the following requirements so that the parts always fit regardless of orientation. All dimensions not toleranced will be assumed to have standard tolerances as stated in Figure 9-15.

EX10-28 INCHES

A. Dimension 1. is 2.00 nominal
B. Dimension 2. is Ø.375 nominal
C. The fasteners are to have a tolerance of .001
D. The holes are to have a tolerance of .002
E. The minimum allowable clearance is .003

EX10-29 MILLIMETERS

A. Dimension 1. is 80 nominal
B. Dimension 2. is Ø12 nominal
C. The fasteners are to have a tolerance of 0.05
D. The holes are to have a tolerance of 0.03
E. The minimum allowable clearance is 0.02

EX10-30 INCHES

A. Dimension 1. is 3.50 nominal
B. Dimension 3. is Ø.750 nominal
C. The studs are to have a tolerance of 0.005
D. The holes are to have a tolerance of 0.003
E. The minimum allowable clearance is 0.002

Given top and bottom parts as shown in Figure EX10-31, satisfy the following requirements so that the parts always fit regardless of orientation. All dimensions not toleranced will be assumed to have standard tolerances as stated in Figure 9-15.

EX10-31

A. Dimension 1. is 60 nominal
B. Dimension 2. is Ø10 nominal
C. The fasteners are to have a tolerance of 0.04
D. The holes are to have a tolerance of 0.02
E. The minumum allowable clearance is 0.02

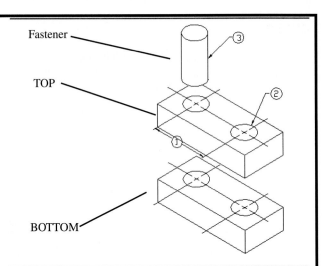

Figure EX10-28

EX10-32

A. Dimension 1. is 3.50 nominal
B. Dimension 3. is Ø.750 nominal
C. The studs are to have a tolerance of 0.005
D. The holes are to have a tolerance of 0.003
E. The minimum allowable clearance is 0.002

EX10-33

A. Dimension 1. is 100 nominal
B. Dimension 2. is Ø18 nominal
C. The fasteners are to have a tolerance of 0.02
D. The holes are to have a tolerance of 0.01
E. The minumum allowable clearance is 0.02

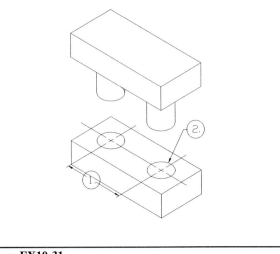

Figure EX10-31

EX10-34

Assume that there are two copies of the part in Figure EX10-34 and that these parts are to be joined together using 4 fasteners in the floating condition. Draw front and top views of the object, including dimensions and tolerances. Add the following tolerances and specifications to the drawing, then draw front and top views of a shaft that can be used to join the two objects. The shaft should be able to fit into any of the four holes.

A. Surface 1 is datum A.

B. Surface 2 is datum B.

C. Surface 3 is perpendicular to surface 2 within 0.02mm.

D. Specify the positional tolerance for the four holes applied at MMC.

E. The center lines of the holes are to be straight within .01mm at MMC.

F. The clearance between the shafts and the holes is to be .05 minimum and .10 maximum.

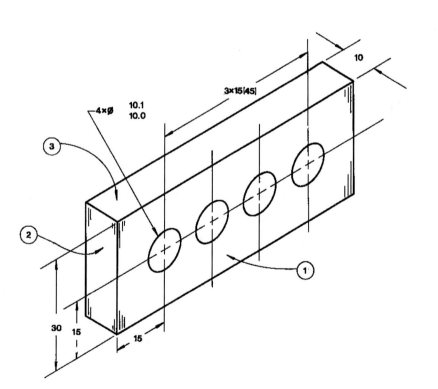

Figure EX10-34

EX10-35

Assume that there are two copies of the part in Figure EX10-35 and that these parts are to be joined together using 6 fasteners in the floating condition. Draw front and top views of the object, including dimensions and tolerances. Add the following tolerances and specifications to the drawing, then draw front and top views of a shaft that can be used to join the two objects. The shaft should be able to fit into any of the six holes.

A. Surface 1 is datum A.

B. Surface 2 is round within .003

C. Specify the positional tolerance for the six holes applied at MMC.

D. The clearance between the shafts and the holes is to be .001 minimum and .003 maximum.

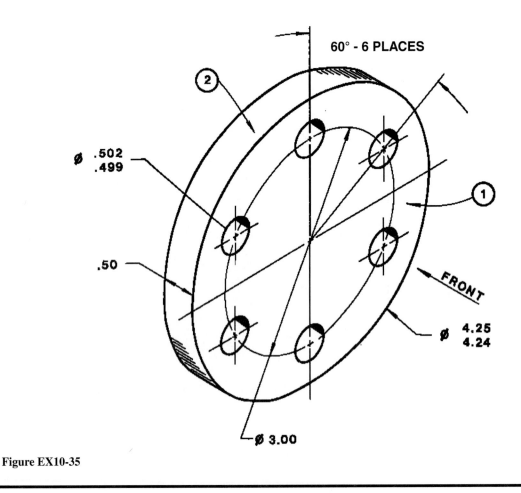

Figure EX10-35

Threads and Fasteners

11-1 INTRODUCTION

This chapter explains how to draw threads, washers, keys, and springs. It explains how to use fasteners to join parts together and explains design uses for washers, keys, and springs.

Throughout the chapter it will be suggested that BLOCKS and WBLOCKS be created of the various thread and fastener shapes. Thread representations, fastener head shapes, set screws, and both internal and external thread representations for orthographic views and sectional views are so common in technical drawings that it is good practice to create a set of WBLOCKS that can be used on future drawings to prevent having to redraw a thread shape every time it is needed.

See Chapter 3 for an explanation of the BLOCK command.

11-2 THREAD TERMINOLOGY

Figure 11-1 shows a thread. The peak of a thread is called the crest and the valley portion is called the root. The major diameter of a thread is the distance across the thread from crest to crest. The minor diameter is the distance across the thread from root to root.

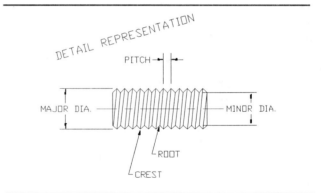

Figure 11-1

The pitch of a thread is the linear distance along the thread from crest to crest. Thread pitch is usually referred to in terms of a unit of length such as 20 threads per inch or 1.5 threads per millimeter.

11-3 THREAD CALLOUTS (METRIC UNITS)

Threads are specified on a drawing using drawing callouts. See Figure 11-2. The M at the front of a drawing

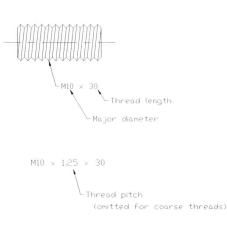

Figure 11-2

Major Dia.	Coarse		Fine	
	Pitch	Tap Drill Dia.	Pitch	Tap Drill Dia.
1.6	0.35	1.25		
2	0.4	1.6		
2.5	0.45	2.05		
3	0.5	2.5		
4	.7	3.3		
5	0.8	4.2		
6	1	5.0		
8	1.25	6.7	1	7.0
10	1.5	8.5	1.25	8.7
12	1.75	10.2	1.25	10.8
16	2	14	1.5	14.5
20	2.5	17.5	1.5	18.5
24	3	21	2	22
30	3.5	26.5	2	28
36	4	32	3	33
42	4.5	37.5	3	39
48	5	43	3	45

Figure 11-3

callout specifies that the callout is for a metric thread. Holes that are not threaded use the 0 symbol.

The number adjacent to the M is the major diameter of the thread. An M10 thread has a major diameter of 10 millimeters. The pitch of a metric thread is assumed to be a coarse thread unless otherwise stated. The callout M10 × 30 assumes a coarse thread, or 1.5 threads per millimeter. The number 30 is the thread length in millimeters. The "×" is read as "by," so the thread is called a "ten by thirty."

The callout M10 × 1.25 × 30 specifies a pitch of 1.25 threads per millimeter. This is not a standard coarse thread size, so the pitch must be specified.

Figure 11-3 shows a listing of preferred thread sizes. These sizes are similar to the standard sizes shown in Figure 9-28. A list of other metric thread sizes is included in the appendix.

Whenever possible use preferred thread sizes for designing. Preferred thread sizes are readily available and are usually cheaper than nonstandard sizes. In addition, tooling such as wrenches is also readily available for preferred sizes.

11-4 THREAD CALLOUTS (ENGLISH UNITS)

English unit threads always include a thread form specification. Thread form specifications are designated by capital letters, as shown in Figure 11-4, and are defined as follows.

UNC — Unified National Coarse

UNF — Unified National Fine

UNEF — Unified National Extra Fine

UN — Unified National, or constant pitch threads

An English unit thread callout starts by defining the major diameter of the thread followed by the pitch specification. The callout .500 – 13 UNC means a thread whose major diameter is .500 inches with 13 threads per inch. The thread is manufactured to the Unified National Coarse (UNC) standards.

There are three possible classes of fit for a thread: 1, 2, and 3. The different class specifications specify a set of manufacturing tolerances. A class 1 thread is the loosest and a class 3 the most exact. A class 2 fit is the most common.

The letter A designates an external thread, B an internal thread. The symbol × means "by" as in 2 × 4, "two by four." The thread length (3.00) may be followed by the word LONG to prevent confusion about which value represents the length.

Drawing callouts for English unit threads are sometimes shortened, such as in Figure 11-4. The callout .500 – 13UNC – 2A × 3.00 LONG is shortened to .500 – 13 × 3.00. Only a coarse thread has 13 threads per inch, and it should be obvious whether a thread is internal or external, so these specifications may be dropped. Most threads are class 2, so it is tacitly accepted that all threads are class 2

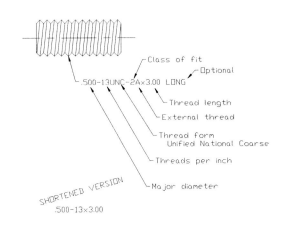

Figure 11-4

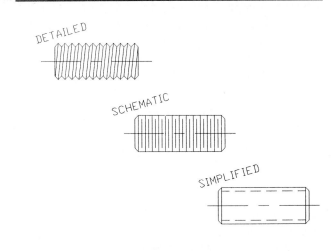

Figure 11-6

unless otherwise specified. The shortened callout form is not universally accepted. When in doubt, use a complete thread callout.

A partial listing of standard English unit threads is shown in Figure 11-5. A more complete list is included in the appendix. Some of the drill sizes listed use numbers and letters. The decimal eqivalents to the numbers and letters are listed in the appendix.

11-5 THREAD REPRESENTATIONS

There are three ways to graphically represent threads on a drawing: detailed, schematic, and simplified. Figure 11-6 shows the three representations.

Detailed representations look the most like actual threads, but are time-consuming to draw. Creating a WBLOCK of a detailed shape will help eliminate this time constraint.

Schematic and simplified thread representations are created using a series of straight lines. The simplified representation uses only two hidden lines and can be mistaken for an internal hole if it is not accompanied by a thread specification callout. The choice of which representation to use depends on individual preferences. The resulting drawing should be clear and easy to understand. All three representations may be used on the same drawing, but in general, only very large threads (those over 1.00″ or 25mm) are drawn using the detailed representation.

Ideally thread representations should be drawn with

Major Dia	Decimal	UNC		UNF		UNEF	
		Thread/in	Tap drill Dia.	Thread/in	Tap drill Dia.	Thread/in	Tap drill Dia.
#6	.138	40	#38	44	#37		
#8	.164	32	#29	36	#29		
#10	.190	24	#25	32	#21		
1/4	.250	20	7	28	3	32	.219
5/16	.312	18	F	24	1	32	.281
3/8	.375	16	.312	24	Q	32	.344
7/16	.438	14	U	20	.391	28	Y
1/2	.500	13	.422	20	.453	28	.469
9/16	.562	12	.484	18	.516	24	.516
5/8	.625	11	.531	18	.578	24	.578
3/4	.750	10	.656	16	.688	20	.703
7/8	.875	9	.766	14	.812	20	.828
1	1.000	8	.875	12	.922	20	.953
1 1/4	1.250	7	1.109	12	1.172	18	1.188
1 1/2	1.500	6	1.344	12	1.422	18	1.438

UNC = Unified National Coarse

UNF = Unified National Fine

UNEF = Unified National Extra Fine

Figure 11-5

each thread equal to the actual pitch size. This is not practical for smaller threads and not necessary for larger ones. Thread representations are not meant to be exact duplications of the threads but representations, so convenient drawing distances are acceptable.

To draw a detailed thread representation

Draw a detailed thread representation for a 1.00″ thread that is 3.00″ long. See Figure 11-7.

1. Set GRID = .5 and SNAP = .125
2. DRAW a 4.00″ center line near the center of the screen.
3. ZOOM the area around the center line.
4. DRAW a zigzag pattern .375 above the center line using the .125 snap points. Start the zigzag line .50 from the left end of the center line.
5. Use the ARRAY command to generate a total of 12 zigzags. Respond to the prompts as follows.

Command: ARRAY
Select object(s):

6. Select the zigzag line

Rectangular or polar array (R/P)<R>:

7. Type ENTER

Number of rows(- - -)<1>:

8. Type ENTER

Number of columns(III):

9. Type 12   ENTER

Distance between columns(III):

10. Type .25   ENTER
11. MIRROR the arrayed zigzag line about the center line.
12. DRAW vertical lines at both ends of the thread and two slanted lines between the thread's roots and crests as shown.
13. ARRAY both slanted lines using the same array parameters used for the zigzag line: 12 columns .25 apart.
14. Save the thread representation as a BLOCK and WBLOCK named DETLIN. Define the insertion point as shown.

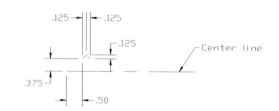

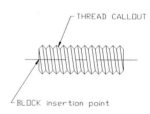

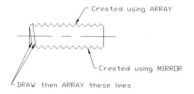

Figure 11-7

Creating BLOCKS is explained in Chapter 3.

Another technique for drawing a detailed thread representation is to draw a single thread completely and then use the COPY or ARRAY command to generate as many additional threads as is necessary.

It is recommended that you SAVE all thread WBLOCKS on a separate disk. This disk will become a

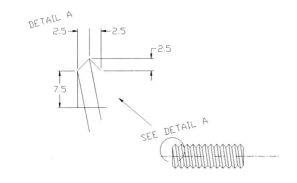

Figure 11-8

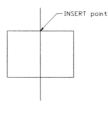

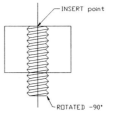

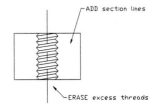

reference disk that you can use when creating other drawings that require threads.

Figure 11-8 shows a metric unit detailed thread representation. It was created using the procedure outlined above. GRID was set at 10, SNAP was set at 2.5, and the distance from the center line to the zigzag pattern is 10. DRAW and SAVE the metric detailed thread representation shown in Figure 11-8 as a WBLOCK named DETLMM.

To create an internal detailed thread representation in a sectional view

Figure 11-9 shows how to create a 1.00″ internal detailed thread representation from the WBLOCK DETLIN of the external detailed thread created above.

1. Use BLOCK, INSERT and locate the detailed WBLOCK on the drawing screen at the indicated insert point. In this example the thread is to be drawn in a vertical orientation so the block is rotated 90 degrees when it is inserted. The same scale size is used for the WBLOCK as was drawn for a 1.00″ diameter thread.
2. The thread created from WBLOCK DETLIN is longer than needed, so EXPLODE the block and then ERASE the excess lines.
3. Define the HATCH pattern as ANSI31 and apply hatching to the areas outside the thread as shown.

Figure 11-9

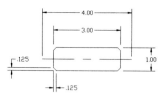

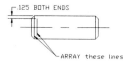

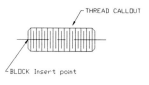

Figure 11-10

To create a schematic thread representation

Draw a schematic representation of a 1.00″ diameter thread. See Figure 11-10.

1. Set GRID to .5 and SNAP to .125
2. DRAW a 4.00 center line near the middle of the drawing screen.
3. DRAW the outline of the thread, including a chamfer, using the dimensions shown.

The chamfer was drawn in this example using the .125 snap points, but the CHAMFER command could also have been used.

The 1.00 diameter was chosen because it will make it easier to determine scale factors for the WBLOCK when inserting the representation into other drawings.

4. DRAW three vertical lines as shown.
5. Use the RECTANGULAR ARRAY command to draw 11 vertical lines across the thread. The distance between the 11 lines (COLUMNS) is .25.

A distance of –.25 would create lines to the left of the original line.

6. Save the representation as a WBLOCK named SCHMINCH. Define the insertion point as shown.

Figure 11-11 shows a metric unit version of a schematic thread representation in a sectional view. The procedure used to create the representation is the same as explained above but with different drawing limits and different values. The major diameter is 20 and the spacing between lines is 2.5 and 5 as shown. DRAW and SAVE the representation as a WBLOCK named SCHMMM.

To create an internal schematic thread representation

Figure 11-12 shows a 36mm diameter internal schematic thread representation. It was developed from the WBLOCK SCHMMM created above.

1. Set GRID = 10
   SNAP = 5
   LIMITS = 297,210
   ZOOM = ALL
2. INSERT WBLOCK SCHMMM at the indicated insert point.

The required thread diameter is 36mm. The

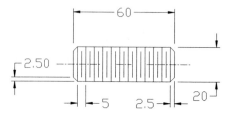

Figure 11-11

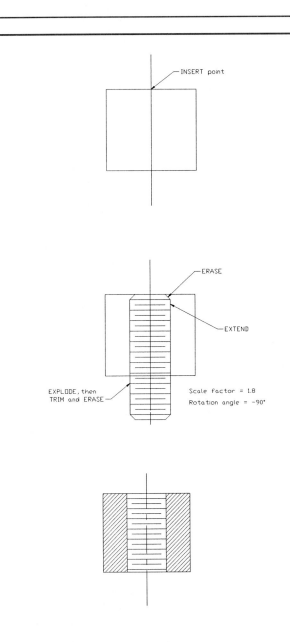

Figure 11-12

WBLOCK SCHMMM was drawn using a diameter of 20mm. This means that the block must be enlarged by using a scale factor. The scale factor is determined by dividing the desired diameter by the WBLOCK's diameter.

$$36/20 = 1.8$$

The WBLOCK must also be rotated 90 degrees to give it the correct orientation.

3. The inserted thread shape is longer than desired,

so first EXPLODE the WBLOCK and then use the ERASE, TRIM, and EXTEND commands as needed.
4. DRAW the sectional lines using HATCH ANSI31.
5. SAVE the drawing as a WBLOCK if desired.

To create a simplified thread representation

See Figure 11-13. The simplified representation looks very similar to the orthographic view of an internal hole, so it is important to always include a thread callout with the representation. In the example shown, a leader line was included with the representation. The leader serves as a reminder to add the appropriate drawing callout. If the leader line is in an inconvenient location when the WBLOCK is inserted into a drawing, the leader line can be MOVED or simply erased.

1. Set GRID = .5
     SNAP = .125
2. DRAW a 4.00 center line near the center of the screen.
3. DRAW the thread outline using the given dimensions.
4. DRAW the hidden lines using the given dimensions.
5. SAVE the thread representation as a WBLOCK named SIMPIN. Define the insertion point as shown.

Figure 11-14 shows an internal simplified thread representation in a sectional view. Note how hidden lines that cross over the sectional lines are used. The hatch must be drawn first and the hidden lines added over the pattern. If

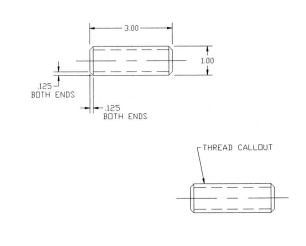

Figure 11-13

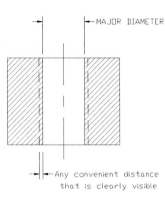

Figure 11-14

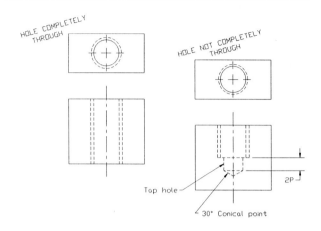

Figure 11-15

the hidden lines are drawn first, the HATCH command may not add section lines to the portion between the hidden line and the solid line that represents the edge of the threaded hole.

11-6 ORTHOGRAPHIC VIEWS OF INTERNAL THREADS

Figure 11-15 shows top and front orthographic views of internal threads. One thread goes completely through the object, the other only part way.

Internal threads are represented in orthographic views using parallel hidden lines. The distance between the lines should be large enough so that there is a clear distinction between the lines; that is, the lines should not appear to blend together or become a single, very thick line.

The circular orthographic views of threaded holes are represented by two circles: one drawn using a continuous line and the other drawn using a hidden line. The distance between the circles should be large enough to be visually distinctive. The two circles shown should both be clearly visible.

Threaded holes are created by first drilling a tap hole and then tapping (cutting) the threads using a tapping bit. Tapping bits have cutting surfaces on their side surfaces, not on the bottom. This means that if the tapping bit were forced all the way to the bottom of the tap hole, the bit could be damaged or broken. It is good design practice to make the tap hole deep enough so that a distance equivalent to at least two thread lengths (2P) extends beyond the tapped portion of the hole.

Threaded holes that do not go completely through an object must always show the unused portion of the tap

hole. The unused portion should also include the conical point. See Chapter 5.

If an internal .500 – 13 UNC thread does not go completely through an object, the length of the unused portion of the tap hole is determined as follows.

INCH/THREAD
= PITCH LENGTH = 1.00/13
= .077 inches

so

2P = 2(.077) = .15 inches

The distance .15 represents a minimum. It would be acceptable to specify a pilot hole depth greater than .15 depending on the specific design requirements.

If an internal M12 × 1.75 thread does not go completely through an object, the length of the unused portion of the tap hole is determined as follows.

2(PITCH LENGTH) = 2(1.75) = 3.50mm

11-7 SECTIONAL VIEWS OF INTERNAL THREAD REPRESENTATIONS

Figure 11-16 shows sectional views of internal threads that do not go completely through an object. Each example was created from WBLOCKs of the representations. The hatch pattern used was ANSI32. Each example includes both a threaded portion and an untapped pilot hole

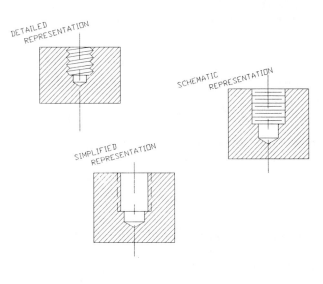

Figure 11-16

that extends approximately 2P beyond the end of the tapped portion of the hole.

When drawing a simplified representation in a sectional view, draw the hidden lines that represent the outside edges of the threads after the section lines have been added. If the lines are drawn before the section lines are added, the section lines will stop at the outside line. Section lines should be drawn up to the solid line, as shown.

11-8 TYPES OF THREADS

Figure 11-17 shows the profiles of four different types of thread: American National, square, acme, and knuckle. There are many other types of threads. In general, square and acme threads are used when heavy loading is involved. A knuckle thread can be manufactured from sheet metal and is most commonly found on a light bulb.

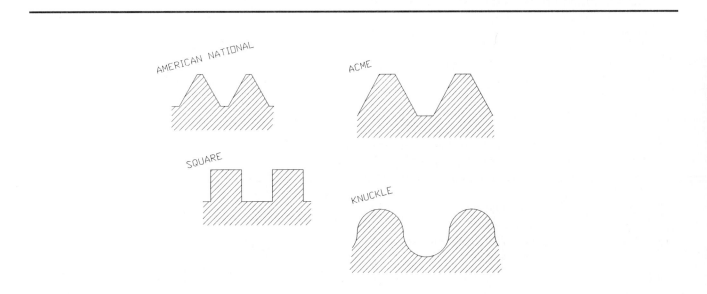

Figure 11-17

The American National thread is the thread shape most often used in mechanical design work. All threads in this chapter are assumed to be American National threads unless otherwise stated.

11-9 HOW TO DRAW AN EXTERNAL SQUARE THREAD

Figure 11-18 shows how to draw a 4.00″ long external square thread that has a major diameter of 5.25 and 2 threads per inch. The procedure is as follows.

1. Set GRID = .50
   SNAP = .125
2. DRAW two 5.00 long horizontal lines 2.00 apart and a 4.50 center line between them.
3. DRAW a rhomboid center about the center line using the given dimensions.

In this example P = .5, so .5P = .25.

4. Use the ARRAY, RECTANGULAR command to create 8 columns (2 threads per inch) .50″ apart.
5. DRAW slanted LINES 1-2 and 3-4.
6. ZOOM the upper right portion of the thread as needed.
7. DRAW a horizontal line .25 (.5P) from the outside edge of the thread as shown.
8. DRAW LINE 5-6 from the intersection of the horizontal line drawn in step 7 with line 1-2, labeled point 5, to the intersection of the tooth line 1-6 and the thread's center line.
9. TRIM the horizontal line to create line 5-7 and TRIM line 1-2 below point 5.
10. ARRAY lines 1-5, 5-6, and 5-7 using rectangular ARRAY with 8 columns −.25 apart.

The minus sign will generate a right-to-left ARRAY.

11. Repeat step 7 through step 10 for the lower portion of the thread. ARRAY 8 columns, +.25 apart. The plus sign will generate a left-to-right ARRAY.
12. ERASE any excess lines and add any necessary shaft information to the drawing.
13. SAVE the drawing as a WBLOCK named SQIN using the indicated insertion point.

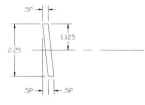

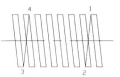

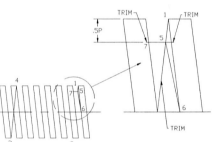

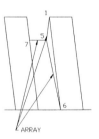

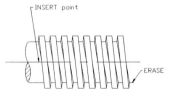

Figure 11-18

11-10 HOW TO DRAW AN INTERNAL SQUARE THREAD

Figure 11-19 shows an external 2.25 × 2 square thread. The drawing was developed from WBLOCK SQIN created in Section 11-9. The WBLOCK was rotated to the correct orientation. ERASE and TRIM were used to fit the thread within the required depth. No scale factor was needed.

11-11 HOW TO DRAW AN EXTERNAL ACME THREAD

DRAW a 2.25 × 2 × 4.00 long external ACME thread. The procedure is as follows. See Figure 11-20.

1. Set GRID = .5
     SNAP = .125
2. DRAW a 5.00 LONG horizontal center line.
3. DRAW two .5 LONG horizontal lines 1.125 above and below.

These lines establish the major diameter of the thread.

4. DRAW a single acme thread using the given dimensions. Use ZOOM to help create an enlarged working area. The first thread should start at the right end of the short horizontal line above the center line.

The width dimensions are taken along the horizontal center line of the individual thread. Each side of the thread is slanted at 14.5 degrees [.5(29)]. In this example P = .5, so .5P = .25 and .25P = .125.

5. Use the ARRAY command and draw 8 columns (2 threads per inch) .5 apart to develop the top portion of the thread.
6. COPY and MOVE the top portion of the thread to create the lower portion.

Do not use MIRROR. The lower portion of the thread is not a mirror image of the upper portion.

7. ERASE and EXTEND lines as necessary along the lower left portion of the thread to blend the thread into the shaft.

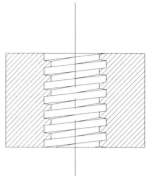

Figure 11-19

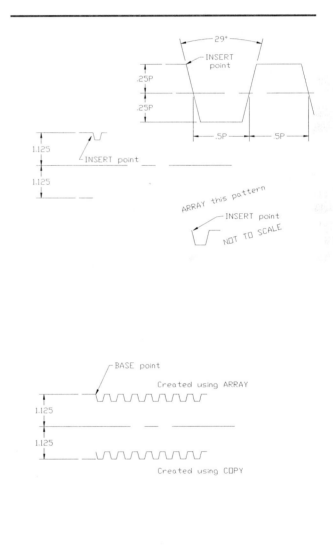

Figure 11-20, Part 1

8. DRAW two slanted lines between the thread's root lines at the left end of the thread.

9. ARRAY the lines drawn in step 8 so that there are 8 columns .5 apart.

10. DRAW two slanted lines across the thread's crest lines at the left end of the thread.

11. ARRAY the lines drawn in step 10 so that there are 8 columns .5 apart.

12. DRAW a vertical LINE at each end of the thread, establishing the thread's 4.00″ length.

13. ERASE and TRIM the excess lines from the left end of the thread.

14. COPY and TRIM a crest-to-crest line to complete the left end of the thread.

15. SAVE the drawing as a WBLOCK named ACMEIN using the indicated insert point.

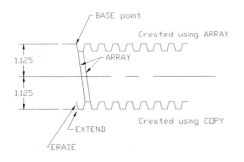

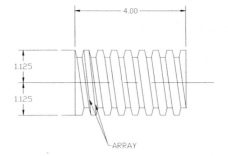

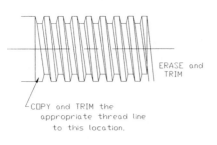

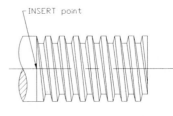

Figure 11-20, Part 2

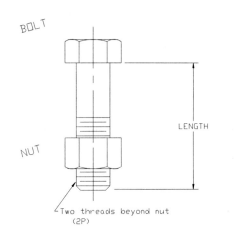

Figure 11-21

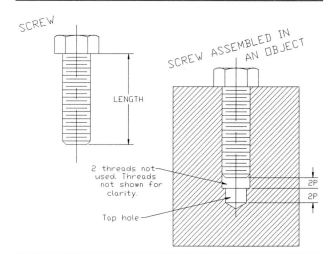

Figure 11-22

11-12 BOLTS AND NUTS

A bolt is a fastener that passes through a clearance hole in an object and is joined to a nut. There are no threads in the objects. See Figure 11-21. Note that there are no hidden lines within the nut to indicate that the bolt is passing through. Drawing convention allows for nuts to be drawn without hidden lines.

Threads on a bolt are usually made just long enough to correctly accept a nut. This is done to minimize the amount of contact between the edges of threads and the inside surfaces of the clearance holes. The sharp, knifelike thread edges could cut into the object, particularly if the application involves vibrations.

It is considered good design practice to specify a bolt length long enough to allow at least two threads to extend beyond the end of the nut. This ensures that the nut is fully attached to the bolt.

Bolt drawings can be created from WBLOCKs of threads. Remember a BLOCK must be EXPLODEd before it can be edited.

11-13 SCREWS

A screw is a fastener that assembles into an object. It does not use a nut. The joining threads are cut into the assembling object. See Figure 11-22.

Screws may or may not be threaded over their entire length. If a screw passes through a clearance hole in an object before it assembles into another object, it is good design practice to minimize the amount of threads that contact the sides of the clearance hole.

It is also considered good design practice to allow a few unused threads in the threaded hole beyond the end of an assembled screw. If a screw were forced to the bottom of a tapped hole, it might not assemble correctly or could possibly be damaged.

It is good design practice to allow at least two unused threads beyond the end of the screw. Figure 11-22 shows a schematic thread representation of a screw mounted in a threaded hole.

There is a distance of 2P (two threads) between the end of the screw and the end of the threaded portion of the hole. There should also be a 2P distance between the end of the threaded hole and the end of the pilot hole, plus the conical point of the tap hole as described in Section 11-6.

Threads are usually not drawn in a threaded hole beyond the end of an assembling screw. This makes it easier to visually distinguish the end of the screw.

Figure 11-23 shows a screw assembled into a hole drawn using the detailed, schematic, and simplified representations in a sectional view. An orthographic view of a screw in a threaded hole is also shown.

The top view shown in Figure 11-23 applies to all three representations and the orthographic view.

11-14 STUDS

A stud is a threaded fastener that both screws into an object and accepts a nut. See Figure 11-24. The thread callouts and representations for studs are the same as they are for bolts and screws.

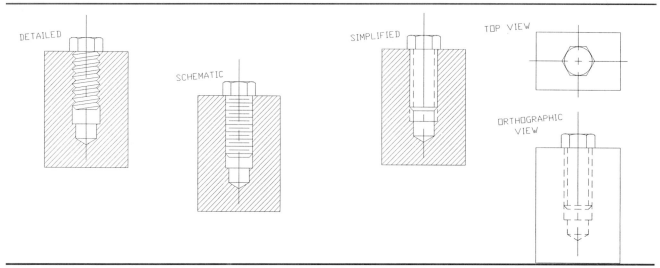

Figure 11-23

11-15 HEAD SHAPES

Bolts and screws are manufactured with a variety of different head shapes, but hexagon and square head shapes are the most common. There are many different head sizes available for different applications. Extra thick heads are used for heavy load applications and very thin heads are used for space limitation applications. The exact head size specifications are available from fastener manufacturers.

This section will show how to draw hexagon and square heads based on accepted average sizes that are functions of both the bolt and screw major diameters. It is suggested that hexagon and square head drawings be saved as WBLOCKS for both inch and millimeter values so that they can be combined with the thread WBLOCKS to form fasteners.

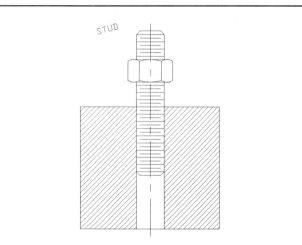

Figure 11-24

To draw a hexagon (HEX) shaped head

Draw front and top orthographic views of a hex head based on a thread with an M24 major diameter. See Figure 11-25.

1. Set LIMIT = 297,210
      GRID = 10
      SNAP = 5
2. Draw a vertical line and two horizontal lines using the given dimensions.

The two horizontal lines are used to locate the center of the head in the top view and the bottom of the head in the front view.

3. Use POLYGON and draw a hexagon distance across the flats equal to 1.5D, where D is the major diameter of the thread.

In this example a radius of 18 was used to draw the hexagon. $1.5D = 1.5(24) = 36$ is the distance across the flats of the hexagon. Use the POLYGON command to circumscribe a 6-sided polygon around a circle of radius 18.

4. OFFSET a line .67D from the lower horizontal.

This line defines the thickness of the head. The head thickness is .67D, where D is the major diameter of the thread. In this example D = 24, so .67D = .67(24) = 16.08, which can be rounded off to 16.

5. Draw projection lines from the corners of the hexagon in the top view into the front view.

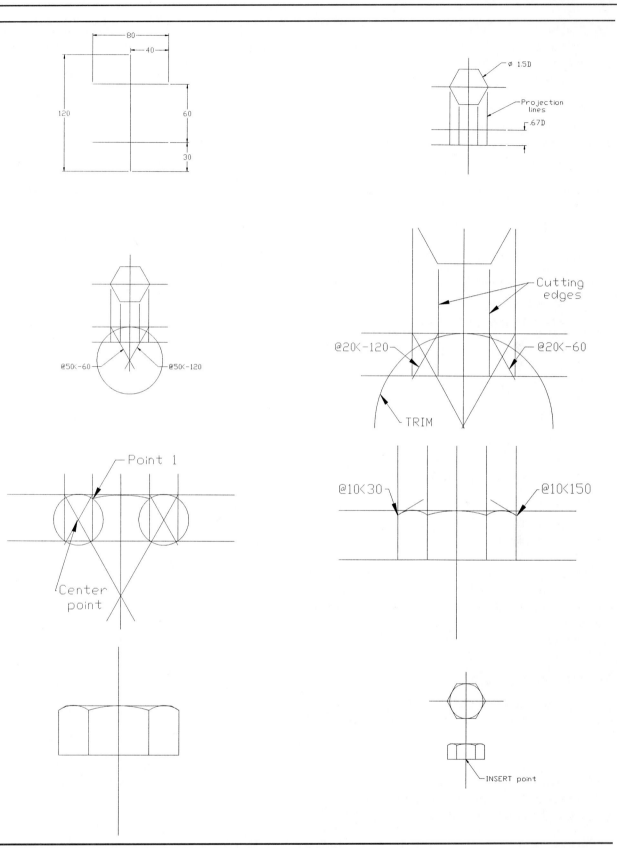

Figure 11-25

6. ZOOM the front view portion of the drawing if necessary. DRAW two 60-degree LINEs from the corners of the front view as shown so that they intersect on the vertical center line.

Use OSNAP, INTERSECTION to accurately locate the corner points. The line from the left corner uses an input of @50<–60. The line from the right corner uses the input @50<–120.

7. DRAW a CIRCLE whose center point is the intersection of the two 60-degree lines drawn in step 6 and the vertical center line, and whose radius equals the distance from the center point to the line at the top of the front view.
8. TRIM the circle so that only the arc between the inside projection lines remains.
9. DRAW two 60-degree LINES as shown using the inputs @20<–120 and @20<–60.
10. DRAW two circles centered about the intersection of the slanted lines drawn in steps 6 and 8. The radius of each circle equals the distance from the center point to the intersection of the circle drawn in step 7 and the inside projection lines labeled point 1.
11. TRIM and ERASE as needed.
12. DRAW two LINES from the intersections of the smaller arcs with the outside edge of the head. The input for the lines is @10<30 and @10<150.

These lines could have been generated using the CHAMFER command.

13. TRIM the chamfer lines to the top of the head.
14. ZOOM ALL and DRAW a CIRCLE that is circumscribed within the hexagon as shown.
15. SAVE the drawing as a WBLOCK named HEXHEAD using the indicated insert point.

To draw a square shaped head

Draw front and top orthographic views of a hex head based on a thread with a 1.00″ major diameter. See Figure 11-26.

1. Set GRID = .50
   SNAP = .25
2. DRAW two horizontal lines and a vertical line using the given dimensions.

The intersection of the top horizontal line and the vertical line will be the center point of the top view and the lower horizontal line will be the bottom edge of the head.

3. Use DRAW, POLYGON and EDIT, ROTATE (45 degrees) to create a square orientated as shown.

The distance across the square equals 1.50D or 1.50″. This means the radius for the polygon is .75.

4. OFFSET a line .67 (.67D) from the lower horizontal line.

The OFFSET distance is equal to the thickness of the head.

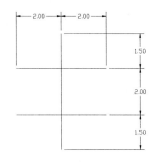

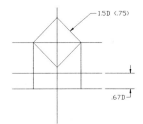

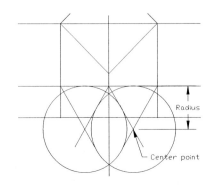

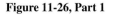

Figure 11-26, Part 1

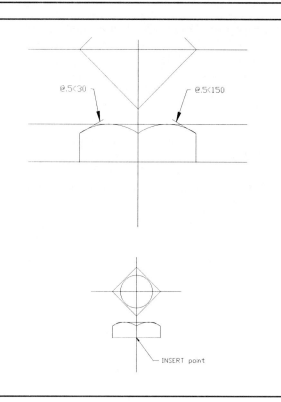

Figure 11-26, Part 2

5. Project the corners of the square in the top view into the front view.
6. ZOOM the front view and DRAW 4 60-degree LINES from the head's upper corners and intersection of the center line and the top surface of the head as shown. The inputs for the lines are @1.5<–120 and @1.5<–60. Use OSNAP, INT to ensure accuracy.
7. Use DRAW, CIRCLE, CEN, RAD and draw two circles about the center points created in step 6. TRIM the excess portions of the circle.
8. TRIM and ERASE any excess lines.
9. Add the 30-degree CHAMFER lines as shown. The LINE inputs are @.5<150 and @.5<30. Use OSNAP, INT to accurately locate the intersection between the arc and the vertical side line of the head.
10. TRIM any excess lines.
11. ZOOM the drawing back to its original size and DRAW a circle in the top view tangent to the inside edges of the square.
12. SAVE the drawing as a WBLOCK named SQHEAD using the insert point indicated.

11-16 NUTS

This section will explain how to draw hexagon and square shaped nuts. Both construction methods are based on the head shape WBLOCKS created in Section 11-15.

There are many different styles of nuts. A finished nut has a flat surface on one side that acts as a bearing surface when the nut is tightened against an object. A finished nut has a thickness equal to .88D, where D is the major diameter of the nut's thread size.

A locknut is symmetrical, with the top and bottom surface being identical. A locknut has a thickness equal to .5D, where D is the major diameter of the nut's thread size.

To draw a hexagon shaped finished nut

Draw a hexagon shaped finished nut for an M36 thread. See Figure 11-27.

1. Set LIMITS = 297,210
    GRID = 10
    SNAP = 2.5
2. Construct a vertical line that is intersected by two horizontal lines 32mm apart.

The thickness of a finished nut is .88D. In this example .88(36) = 31.68, or 32.

3. Use BLOCK, INSERT and insert the HEXHEAD WBLOCK created in Section 11-15.

The WBLOCK HEXHEAD was created for an M24 thread, so the X and Y scale factors must be increased to accommodate the large thread size. The scale factor is determined by dividing the desired size by the WBLOCK size. In this example, 36/24 = 1.5. The scale factor is 1.5. Respond to the command prompts as follows.

Command: INSERT
Block name (or ?):

4. Type HEXHEAD ENTER

Insertion point:

5. Select the indicated insertion point

X scale factor <1>/Corner/XYZ:

6. Type 1.5 ENTER

Y scale factor (default=X):

7. Type ENTER

Rotation angle <0>:

8. Type ENTER

If you have not created a WBLOCK, refer to Section 11-15 and draw a hexagon shaped head.

9. EXPLODE the WBLOCK.
10. MOVE the front view of the nut so that the top surface aligns with the top parallel horizontal line.

11. ERASE the bottom line of the front view of the nut and EXTEND the vertical line to the lower horizontal line. ERASE the top horizontal line in the front view.
12. Use OFFSET to draw a horizontal line 2mm below the bottom of the nut.

This line defines the shoulder surface of the nut. Any OFFSET distance may be used as long as the line is clearly visible. The actual shoulder surface is less than 1mm deep and would not appear clearly on the drawing.

The shoulder surface has a diameter equal to 1.5D [1.5(36) = 54] or, in this example, 54.

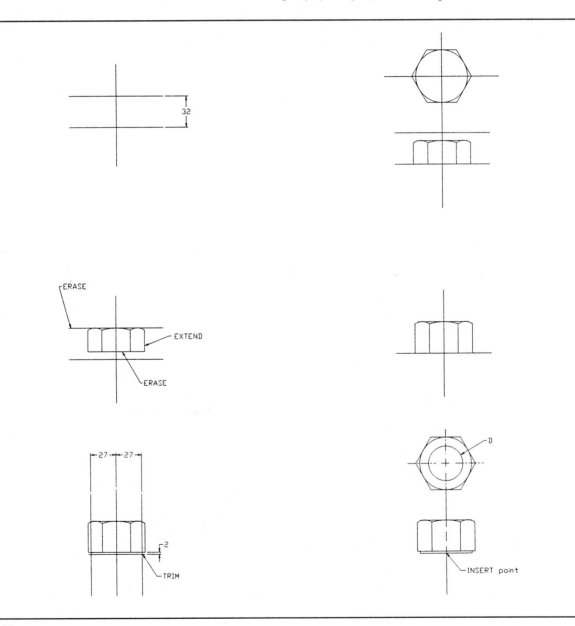

Figure 11-27

13. OFFSET the center line 27 (half of 54) to each side and TRIM the excess lines.
14. SAVE the drawing as a WBLOCK FNUTHEX. Define the insertion point as shown.

To draw a locking nut

Draw a locking nut for an M24 thread. See Figure 11-28. The HEXHEAD WBLOCK was originally drawn for an M24 thread, so no scale factor is needed.

1. Set LIMIT = 297,210
   GRID = 10
   SNAP = 5
2. Draw a vertical and two horizontal lines using the given dimensions.

The 6 distance is half the .5D [.5(24) = 12] thickness distance recommended for locknuts. Locknuts are symmetrical, so half the nut will be drawn and then MIRRORed.

3. INSERT the HEXHEAD WBLOCK at the indicated insert point.
4. EXPLODE the WBLOCK.
5. MOVE the front view of the HEXHEAD so that it aligns with the horizontal line as shown.
6. TRIM and ERASE the lines that extend beyond the lower horizontal line.
7. MIRROR the remaining portion of the front view about the lower horizontal line, then ERASE the horizontal line.
8. DRAW a CIRCLE of diameter D in the top view as shown.
9. SAVE the drawing as a WBLOCK named LNUTHEX using the indicated insert point.

The procedure explained above for hexagon shaped finish nuts and locknuts is the same for square shaped nuts. Use the WBLOCK SQHEAD in place of the HEXHEAD WBLOCK.

11-17 SAMPLE PROBLEM SP11-1

Draw and specify the mimimum threaded hole depth and pilot hole depth for an M12 × 1.75 × 50 HEX HEAD SCREW. Assemble the screw into the object shown in Figure 11-29. Use the schematic thread representation and a sectional view.

The SCHMMM WBLOCK was originally drawn for an M20 thread, so a scale factor is needed. The scale factor to reduce an M20 diameter to an M12 is 12/20 = .6.

1. INSERT the SCHMMM WBLOCK and insert it at

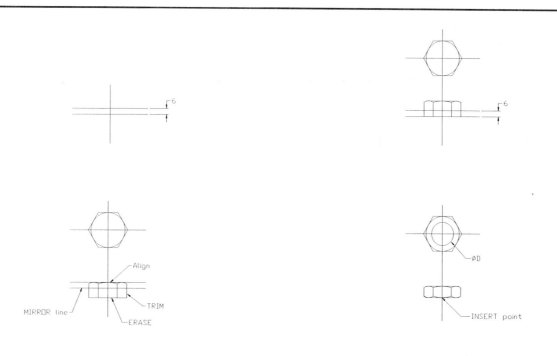

Figure 11-28

the indicated point. Use a .6 X and Y scale factor.

2. EXPLODE the BLOCK and TRIM any excess threads.
3. INSERT the HEXHEAD WBLOCK as indicated. The HEXHEAD WBLOCK was also created for an M20 thread, so the scale factor is again .6.

The thread pitch equals 1.75, so 2P = 3.5. This means that the threaded hole should be at least 50 + 3.5, or 53.5, deep to allow for two unused threads beyond the end of the screw.

The unused portion of the pilot hole should also extend 2P beyond the end of the threaded portion of the hole, so the minumum pilot hole depth equals 53.5 + 3.5 = 57.

The diameter of the tap hole for the thread is given in a table in the appendix as 10.3. For this example a diameter of 10 was used for drawing purposes. If required, the 10.3 value would be given in the hole's drawing callout.

4. DRAW the unused portion of the thread hole and pilot hole as shown. Omit the thread representation in the portion of the threaded hole beyond the end of the screw for clarity.

11-18 SAMPLE PROBLEM SP11-2

Determine the length of a .750–10UNC SQUARE HEAD bolt needed to pass through objects 1 and 2 shown in Figure 11-30. Include a hexagon shaped locknut on the end of the bolt. Allow at least two threads beyond the end of the nut. Use the closest standard bolt length and draw a schematic representation as a sectional view.

This construction is based on the WBLOCKs SCHMINCH, HEXHEAD, and LNUTHEX created in Sections 11-5 and 11-16. If no WBLOCKS are available, refer to these sections for an explanation of how to create the required shapes.

The WBLOCKs SCHMINCH, HEXHEAD, and LNUTHEX were created for a major diameter of 1.00″, so the scale factor needed to create a major diameter of .750 is .75.

1. INSERT the SCHMINCH WBLOCK at the indicated point. Use an X and Y scale factor of .75. Rotate the block –90 degrees to the correct orientation.

The WBLOCK SCHMINCH is not long enough to

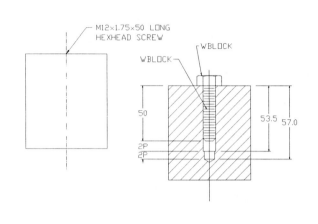

Figure 11-29

go completely through the objects, so a second WBLOCK is INSERTed below the first.

2. INSERT the SQHEAD WBLOCK at the indicated point. Use an X and Y scale factor of .75.
3. INSERT the WBLOCK LNUTHEX at the indicated point. Use an X and Y scale factor of .75.
4. EXPLODE the WBLOCKS.
5. TRIM the excess lines within the nut.
6. Calculate the minimum length for the bolt.

The total depth of objects 1 and 2 equals 1.250 + 1.625 = 2.875.

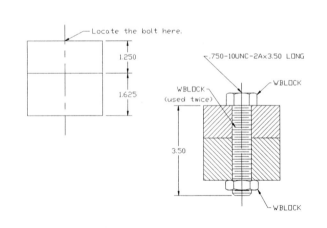

Figure 11-30

The thickness of the nut equals .88D or .88(.75) = .375.

The pitch length of the thread equals 1.00/10 = .1. So 2P = .2.

The minimum bolt length equals 2.875 + .375 + .200 = 3.450.

From the table of standard bolt lengths found in the appendix, the standard bolt length that is greater than 3.45 is 3.50, so the bolt callout can now be completed.

.750 – 10UNC – 2A × 3.50 LONG

The completed drawing with the appropriate bolt callout is shown in Figure 11-30.

11-19 STANDARD SCREWS

Figure 11-31 shows a group of standard screw shapes. The proportions given in Figure 11-30 are acceptable for general drawing purposes and represent average values. The exact dimensions for specific screws are available from manufacturers' catalogs. A partial listing of standard screw sizes is included in the appendix.

The given head shape dimensions are all in terms of D, the major diameter of the screw's thread. Information about the available standard major diameters and lengths is included in the appendix.

The choice of head shape is determined by the specific design requirements. For example, a flat head mounted flush with the top surface is a good choice when space is critical, when two parts butt against each other, or when aerodynamic considerations are involved. A round head can be assembled using a common blade screw driver, but it is more susceptible to damage than a hex head. The hex head, however, requires a specific wrench for assembly.

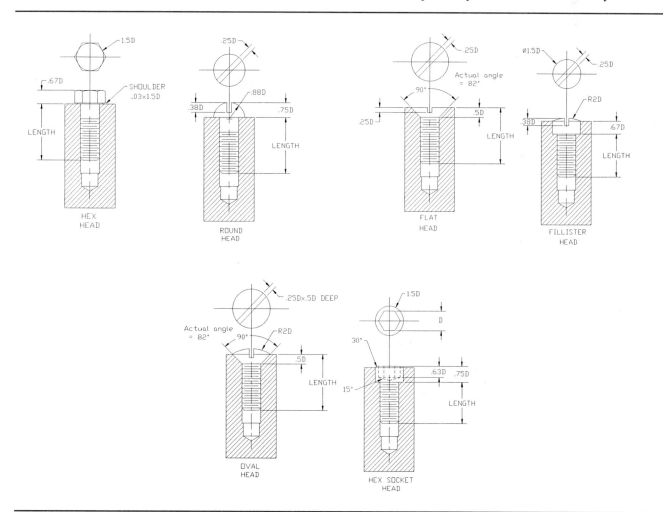

Figure 11-31

11-20 SET SCREWS

Set screws are fasteners that are used to hold parts like gears and pulleys to rotating shafts or other objects to prevent slippage between the two objects. See Figure 11-32.

Most set screws have recessed heads to help prevent interference with other parts. Many different head styles and point styles are available. See Figure 11-33.

Set screws are referenced on a drawing using the following format.

THREAD SPECIFICATION
HEAD SPECIFICATION POINT SPECIFICATION
SET SCREW

.250 - 20UNC - 2Ax1.00 LONG
SLOT HEAD FLAT POINT
SET SCREW

The words LONG, HEAD, and POINT are optional.

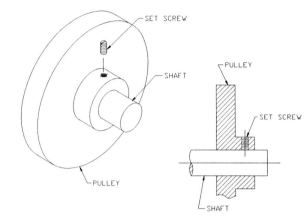

Figure 11-32

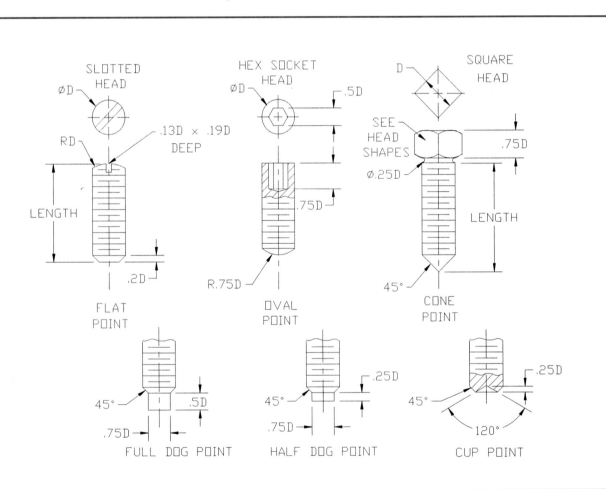

Figure 11-33

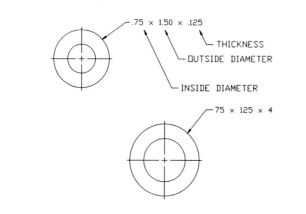

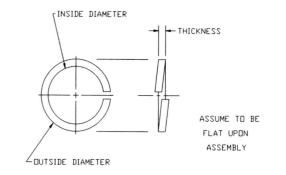

Figure 11-34

Figure 11-36

11-21 WASHERS

There are many different styles of washers available for different design applications. The three most common types of washers are plain, lock, and star. Plain washers can be used to help distribute the bearing load of a fastener or used as a spacer to help align and assemble objects. Lock and star washers help absorb vibrations and prevent fasteners from loosening prematurely. All washers are identified as follows.

Inside diameter x outside diameter x thickness

Examples of plain washers and their callouts are shown in Figure 11-34. A listing of standard washer sizes is included in the appendix.

To draw a plain washer

See Figure 11-35.

1. DRAW concentric circles for the inside and outside diameters.
2. Project lines from the circular view and draw a line that defines the width of the washer.
3. Use OFFSET to define the thickness.

Figure 11-36 shows two views of a lock washer. As the lock washer is compressed during assembly, it tends to flatten, so the slanted end portions are not usually included on the drawing. The drawing callout should include the words LOCK WASHER.

Figure 11-37 shows an internal and an external tooth lock type washer. They may also be called star washers.

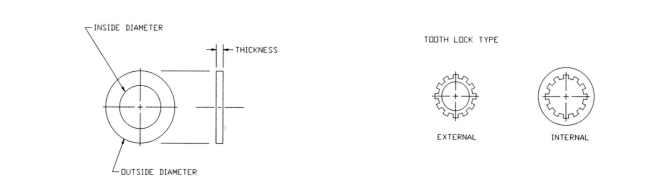

Figure 11-35

Figure 11-37

They are best drawn by first drawing an individual tooth, then using ARRAY to draw a total of 12 teeth. Because there are 12 teeth, each tooth and the space between the tooth and the next tooth require a total of 30 degrees: 15 degrees for the tooth and 15 degrees for the space between.

11-22 KEYS

Keys are used to help prevent slippage in power transmission between parts, for example, a gear and a drive shaft. Grooves called keyways are cut into both the gear and the drive shaft and a key is inserted between, as shown in Figure 11-38.

There are four common types of keys: square, Pratt & Whitney, Woodruff, and gib head. Each has design advantages and disadvantages. See Figure 11-39. A listing of standard key sizes is included in the appendix.

Square keys are called out on a drawing by specifying the width of a side SQUARE and their length. Pratt & Whitney and Woodruff keys are specified by numbers. Gib head keys are defined by a group of dimensions. See the appendix for the appropriate tables and charts of standard key sizes.

Keyways are dimensioned as shown in Figure 8-46. Note how the depth of a keyway in a shaft is dimensioned from the bottom of the shaft. Because material has been cut away, the intersection between the shaft's center line and

top outside edge does not exist. It is better to dimension from a real surface than a theoretical one. The same dimensioning technique also applies to the gear.

11-23 RIVETS

Rivets are fasteners that hold adjoining or overlapping objects together. A rivet starts with a head at one end and a straight shaft at the other. The rivet is then inserted into the object and the headless end "bucked" or otherwise forced into place. A force is applied to the headless end that changes its shape so that another head is formed holding the objects together.

There are many different shapes and styles of rivets. Figure 11-40 shows five common head shapes for rivets. Aircraft use hollow rivets because they are very lightweight. A design advantage for using rivets is that they can be drilled out and removed or replaced without damaging the objects they hold together.

Rivet types are represented on technical drawings using a coding system. See Figure 11-41. The lines used to code a rivet must be clearly visible on the drawing. Rivets are sometimes so small and the material they hold together so thin that it is difficult to clearly draw the rivets. So companies draw only the rivet's center line in the side view and identify the rivet using a drawing callout.

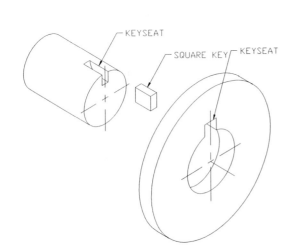

Figure 11-38

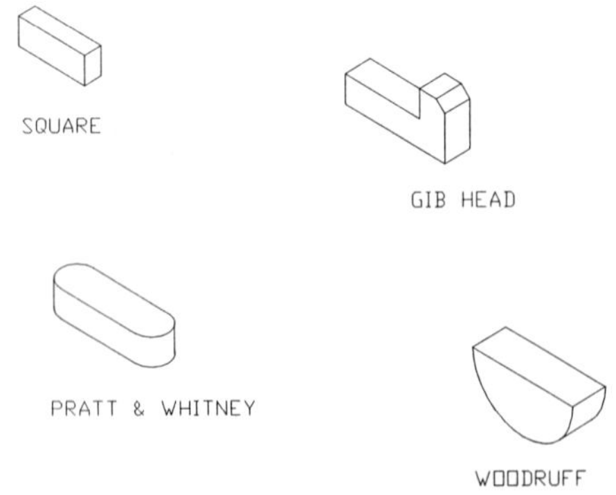

Figure 11-39

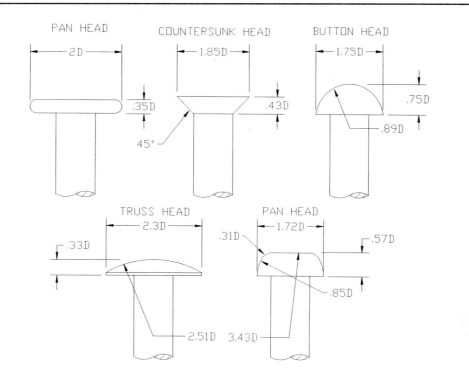

Figure 11-40

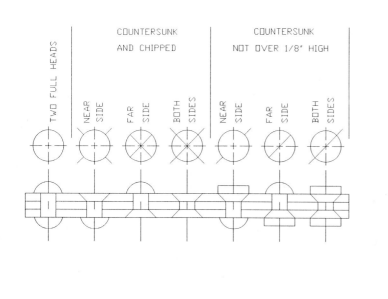

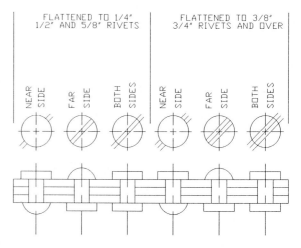

Figure 11-41

11-24 SPRINGS

The most common types of springs used on technical drawings are compression, extension, and torsional. This section explains how to draw detailed and schematic representations of springs. Springs are drawn in their relaxed position (not expanded or compressed). Phantom lines may be used to show several different positions for springs as they are expanded or compressed.

Springs are defined by the diameter of their wire, the direction of their coils, their outside diameter, the total number of coils, and their total relaxed length. Information about their loading properties may also be included. The pitch of a spring equals the distance from the center of one coil to the center of the next coil.

As with threads, the detailed representations are more difficult and time consuming to draw, but the ARRAY command shortens the drawing time considerably. Saving the representation as a WBLOCK also helps prevent having to redraw the representation for each new drawing.

Ideally the distance between coils should be exactly equal to the pitch of the spring, but this is not always practical for smaller springs. Any convenient distance between coils may be used that presents a clear, easy-to-understand representation of the spring.

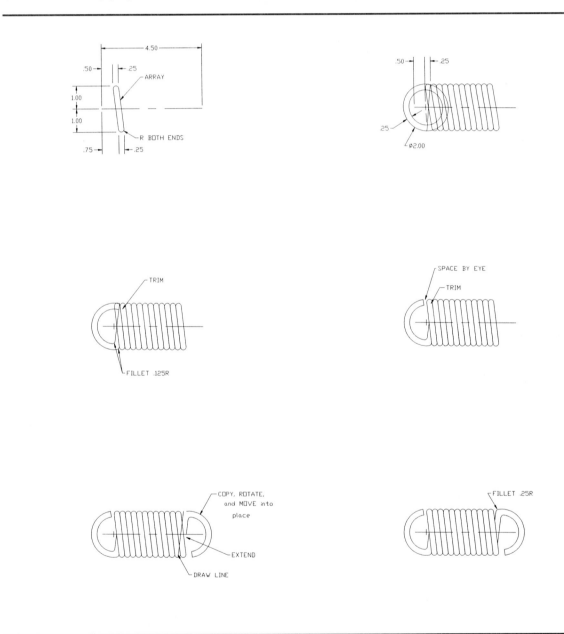

Figure 11-42

**To draw a detailed representation
of an extension spring**

Draw an extension spring 2.00″ in diameter with right-hand coils made from .250″ wire. The spring's pitch equals .25 and the total length of the coils is 3.00″. See Figure 11-42.

Because the pitch of the spring equals the wire diameter, the coils will touch each other.

1. Set GRID = .5
      SNAP = .25
2. DRAW the rounded shape of one of the coils.

The distance between the lines equals the diameter of the spring wire. The diameter of the rounded ends also equals the diameter of the wire. The coil's offset equals the spring's pitch.

3. ARRAY the coil shape.

The ARRAY used was a rectangular ARRAY with 1 row, and 12 columns .25 apart.

4. DRAW two concentric CIRCLES at the left end of the spring so that the larger circle's diameter equals the spring's diameter. The vertical center line of the circles is tangent to the left edge of the first coil.
5. DRAW a LINE across the thread offset a distance equal to one pitch. The endpoints of the line are on SNAP points.
6. TRIM the excess portion of the circles and FILLET the circles as shown.
7. TRIM the excess portion of the slanted line and cut back the end of the circles so that there is a noticeable gap between the first coil and the end of the circles. The gap distance is determined by eye.
8. COPY, ROTATE, and MOVE the circular end portion to the right end of the spring.
9. DRAW a slanted line across the furthest right coil as shown.
10. TRIM and EXTEND the LINEs as necessary and add the .25R FILLET as shown.
11. SAVE the drawing as a WBLOCK named EXTSPRNG.

**To draw a detailed representation
of a compression spring**

Draw a compression spring with 6 right-hand coils made from .25″ diameter wire. The pitch of the spring

equals .50″. The diameter of the spring is 2.00″. See Figure 11-43.

1. Set GRID = .50
      SNAP = .25
2. DRAW the rounded shape of the first left coil as shown. The diameter of the rounded ends of the coil equals the diameter of the spring's wire.
3. ARRAY the coil shape.

In this example a rectangular ARRAY was used to draw 1 row, and 6 columns .50″ apart.

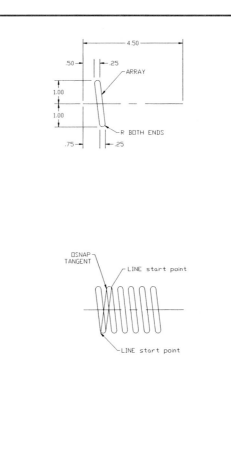

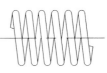

Figure 11-43

4. DRAW two slanted lines as shown.

These lines represent the back portion of the coil. They are most easily drawn from a snap point next to the rounded portion of the coil shape (this point would be the corner point of the coil if the coil were not rounded) to a point tangent to the opposite rounded end of the coil.

5. TRIM and ARRAY the slanted lines as shown.

Use rectangular ARRAY with 1 row, 6 columns .50″ apart.

6. DRAW the right end of the spring so that it appears to end just short of the spring's center line. Any convenient distance may be used.
7. DRAW the left end of the spring using COPY and copy one of the existing slanted lines. Use ZOOM if necessary to align the copied line with the coil. Draw the left end of the spring so that it appears to end just short of the center line.
8. SAVE the drawing as a WBLOCK named COMP-SPNG.

Figure 11-44 shows schematic representations of a compression and an extension spring. The distance between the peaks of the slanted lines should equal the pitch of the spring.

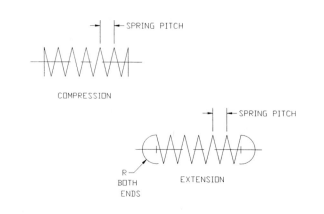

Figure 11-44

11-25 EXERCISE PROBLEMS

EX11-1

Create WBLOCKs for the following thread major diameters.
A. 1.00″ detailed representation
B. 1.00″ schematic thread representation
C. 1.00″ simplified thread representation
D. 100mm detailed representation
E. 100mm schematic thread representation
F. 100mm simplified thread representation

EX11-2

Draw a .750–10UNC – 2_ × ___ LONG thread. Include the thread callout.
A. External – 3.00 LONG
B. Internal to fit into the object shown in Figure EX11-2.
C. Use a detailed representation
D. Use a schematic representation
E. Use a simplified representation

EX11-3

Draw a .250–28UNF – 2_ × ___ LONG thread. Include the thread callout.
A. External – 1.50 LONG
B. Internal to fit into the object shown in Figure EX11-2.
C. Use a detailed representation
D. Use a schematic representation
E. Use a simplified representation

EX11-4

Draw an M36 × 4 × ___ LONG thread. Include the thread callout.
A. External – 100 LONG
B. Internal to fit into the object shown in Figure EX11-2.
C. Use a detailed representation
D. Use a schematic representation
E. Use a simplified representation

EX11-5

Draw an M12 × 1.75 × ___ LONG thread. Include the thread callout.
A. External – 40 LONG
B. Internal to fit into the object shown in Figure EX11-2.
C. Use a detailed representation
D. Use a schematic representation
E. Use a simplified representation

EX11-6

Draw a 2.75 × 2 × 5.00″ long external square thread.

EX11-7

Draw a 50 × 2 × 100mm long external square thread.

EX11-8

Draw a 3 × 1.5 × 6″ long external acme thread.

EX11-9

Draw an 80 × 1.5 × 200mm long external acme thread.

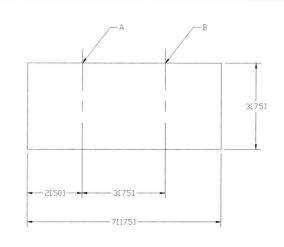

Figure EX11-2

Draw the bolts, nuts, and screws in exercise problems EX11-10 to EX11-13 assembled into the object shown in Figure EX11-2. If not given, determine the length of the fasteners using the tables given in this chapter or in the appendix. Include the appropriate drawing callout.

EX11-10

A. .500– 13UNC × ___ LONG HEX HEAD BOLT. Include a finished nut on the end of the bolt.
B. 5/8(.625)– 18UNF × 1.5 LONG HEX HEAD SCREW. Specify the diameter and length of the tap hole.
C. Draw a detailed representation.
D. Draw a schematic representation.
E. Draw a simplified representation.
F. Draw an orthographic view.
G. Draw a sectional view.

EX11-11

A. M24 – ___ LONG HEX HEAD BOLT. Include a finished nut on the end of the bolt.
B. M16 – 30 LONG HEX HEAD SCREW. Specify the diameter and length of the tap hole.
C. Draw a detailed representation.
D. Draw a schematic representation.
E. Draw a simplified representation.
F. Draw an orthographic view.
G. Draw a sectional view.

EX11-12

A. M30 × ___ LONG SQUARE HEAD BOLT. Include two locknuts on the end of the bolt.
B. M12 × 1.4 × 24 LONG SQUARE HEAD SCREW. Specify the diameter and length of the tap hole.
C. Draw a detailed representation.
D. Draw a schematic representation.
E. Draw a simplified representation.
F. Draw an orthographic view.
G. Draw a sectional view.

EX11-13

A. 1.25– 7UNC × ___ LONG SQUARE HEAD BOLT. Include two locknuts on the end of the bolt.
B. .375– 32UNEF × 1.5 LONG SQUARE HEAD SCREW. Specify the diameter and length of the tap hole.
C. Draw a detailed representation.

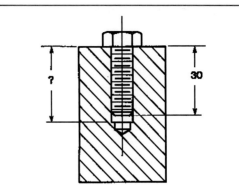

Figure EX11-14

D. Draw a schematic representation.
E. Draw a simplified representation.
F. Draw an orthographic view.
G. Draw a sectional view.

EX11-14

Redraw the sectional view shown in Figure EX11-14. Include a drawing callout that defines the threads as M12. Specify the depth of the threaded hole and the diameter and depth of the tap hole.

EX11-15

Redraw the drawing shown in Figure EX11-15. Add a drawing callout for the bolt and nut based on the following thread major diameters. Use only standard bolt lengths as defined in the appendix.
A. .375-24UNF-2A×___ LONG
B. M16 ×2×___ LONG

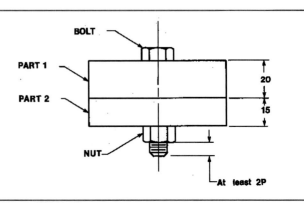

Figure EX11-15

EX11-16

Draw a front sectional view and a top orthographic view based on the drawing and table information below. Include the following set screws in the indicated holes. Include the appropriate drawing callout for each set screw.

FOR INCH VALUES:
1. .250-20UNC-2A×1.00
   SLOT HEAD, FLAT POINT
   SET SCREW
2. .375-24UNF-2A×.750
   HEX SOCKET, FULL DOG
   SET SCREW
3. #10-28UNF-2A×.625
   SQUARE, OVAL
   SET SCREW

4. #6-32UNC-2A×.50
   SLOT, CONE POINT
   SET SCREW

FOR MILLIMETER VALUES:
1. M12×20
   SLOT HEAD, FLAT POINT
   SET SCREW
2. M16×2×30
   SQUARE HEAD, HALF DOG
   SET SCREW
3. M6×20
   HEX SOCKET, CONE
   SET SCREW
4. M10×1.5×20
   CUP, SLOT
   SET SCREW

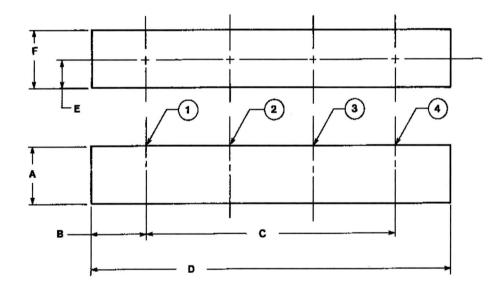

DIMENSION	INCHES	m m
A	2.00	50
B	1.00	25
C	3 X 1.00	3 X 40
D	6.5	170
E	.50	13
F	1.00	26

EX11-17

Draw a front sectional view and a top orthographic view based on the drawing and table information shown below.
  A. Use the inch values.
  B. Use the millimeter values.

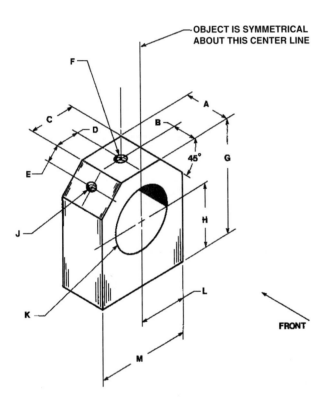

DIMENSION	INCHES	mm
A	1.00	26
B	.50	13
C	1.00	26
D	.50	13
E	.38	10
F	.190-32 UNF	M8X1
G	2.38	60
H	1.38	34
J	.164-36 UNF	M6
K	Ø1.25	Ø30
L	1.00	26
M	2.00	52

EX11-18

Redraw the drawing below as a sectional view. Select and include the drawing callouts for the nut and washer based on the following bolts. Specify the bolt lengths based on standard lengths listed in the appendix.

A. .625-11UNC-2A× ___LONG HEX HEAD BOLT
B. M16×2×____ HEX HEAD BOLT

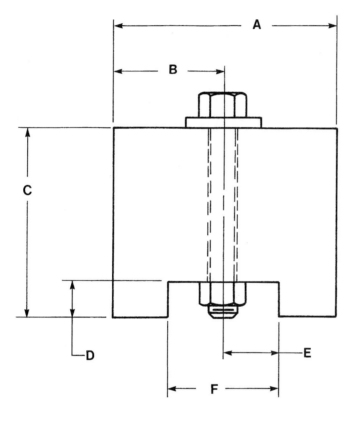

DIMENSION	INCHES	mm
A	3.00	76
B	1.50	38
C	2.50	64
D	.50	13
E	.75	19
F	1.50	38

EX11-19

Draw a front sectional view and top orthographic view based on the drawing and table information given below. Add fasteners to the labeled holes based on the following information. Include the appropriate drawing callouts. Use only standard sizes as listed in the appendix.

FOR INCHES VALUES

1. Nominal diameter = .250, UNC
   Square head bolt and nut
   A washer between the bolt head and part 23
   A washer between the nut and part 24
2. .375-24UNF-2A×1.00
   SLOT, OVAL
   SET SCREW
3. Nominal diameter = .375,UNF
   Flat head screw, 1.25 LONG

FOR MILLIMETER VALUES

1. Nominal diameter = 12, coarse
   Square head bolt and nut
   A washer between the bolt head and part 23
   A washer between the nut and part 24
2. M10×.5×20
   SQUARE HEAD, FULL DOG
   SET SCREW
3. Nominal diameter = 12, fine
   Flat head screw, 20 LONG

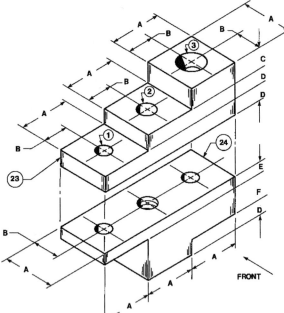

NOTE: HOLES IN PART 24 ALIGN WITH THOSE IN PART 23.

FRONT

DIMENSION	INCHES	mm
A	1.25	32
B	.63	16
C	.50	13
D	.38	10
E	.25	7
F	.63	16

EX11-20

Redraw the sectional view below and include the appropriate bolts and nuts at the locations W, X, Y, and Z. Select the bolts from the standard sizes listed in the appendix. Base the selection on the following nominal diameters.

A. .250 inches
B. 12 millimeters

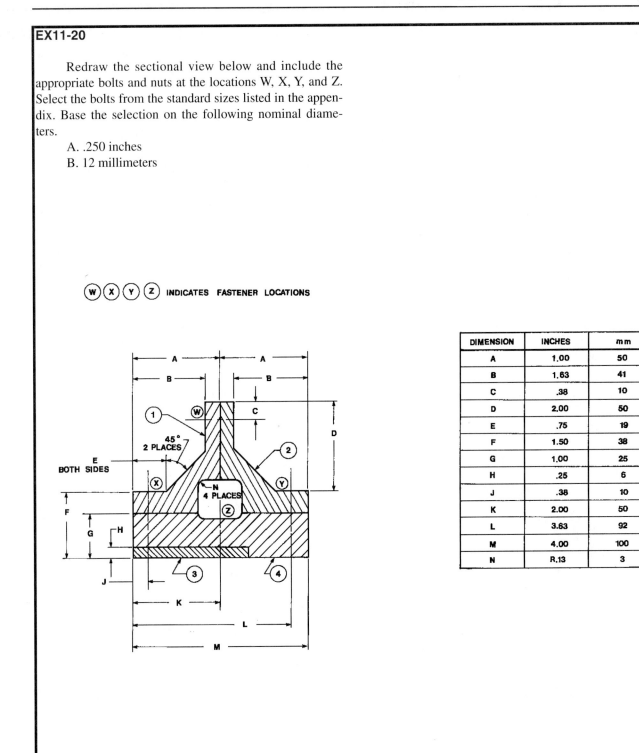

W X Y Z INDICATES FASTENER LOCATIONS

DIMENSION	INCHES	mm
A	1.00	50
B	1.63	41
C	.38	10
D	2.00	50
E	.75	19
F	1.50	38
G	1.00	25
H	.25	6
J	.38	10
K	2.00	50
L	3.63	92
M	4.00	100
N	R.13	3

EX11-21

Redraw the drawing below based on the following information. Include all bolt, nut, washer, and spring callouts. Use only standard sizes as listed in the appendix.

FOR INCH VALUES:
A. Major diameter of bolt = .375 coarse thread.
B. Add the appropriate nut.
C. Washer is .125 thick and allows a minimum clearance from the bolt of at least .125.
D. Compression springs are made from .125 diameter wire and are 1.00 long. They have an inside diameter that always clears the bolt by at least .125.
E. Parts 1 and 2 are 1.00 high and 4.00 wide.
F. Locate the bolts at least 1.00 from each end.

FOR MILLIMETER VALUES:
A. Major diameter of bolt = 12 coarse thread.
B. Add the appropriate nut.
C. Washer is 3 thick and allows a minimum clearance from the bolt of at least 2.
D. Compression springs are made from 4 diameter wire and are 24 long. They have an inside diameter that always clears the bolt by at least 3.
E. Parts 1 and 2 are 25 high and 100 wide.
F. Locate the bolts at least 25 from each end.

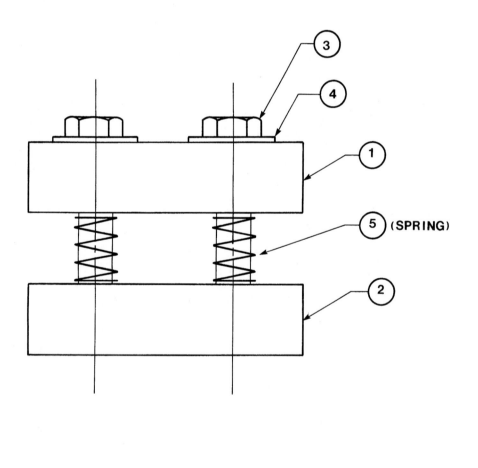

CHAPTER

Working Drawings

12-1 INTRODUCTION

This chapter explains how to create assembly drawings, parts lists, and detailed drawings. It includes guidelines for titles, revisions, tolerances, and release blocks. The chapter shows how to create a design layout, then use the layout to create assembly and detailed drawings using the LAYER command.

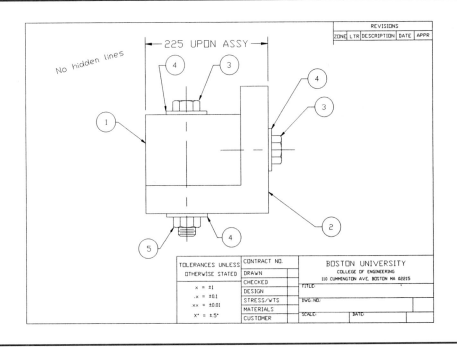

Figure 12-1

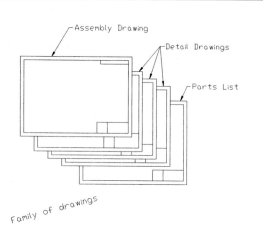

Figure 12-2

12-2 ASSEMBLY DRAWINGS

Assembly drawings show how objects fit together. See Figure 12-1. All information necessary to complete the assembly must be included on the drawing. The information may include specific assembly dimensions, torque requirements for bolts, finishing and shipping instructions, and any other appropriate company or customer specifications.

Assembly drawings are sometimes called top drawings because they are the first of a series of drawings used to define a group of parts that are to be assembled together. The group of drawings is referred to as a family of drawings. The group may include subassemblies, modification drawings, detailed drawings, and a parts list. See Figure 12-2.

Assembly drawings do not contain hidden lines. A sectional view may be used to show internal areas critical to the assembly. Specific information about the internal surfaces of objects that make up the assembly can be found on the detail drawings of the individual objects. See Figure 12-3.

Each part of an assembly is identified by an assembly or item number. Assembly numbers are enclosed in a circle or ellipse and a leader line is drawn between the assembly number and the part. Assembly numbers are unique to each assembly drawing. A part that is used in several different assemblies could have a different assembly number on each assembly drawing.

If several of the same part are used in the same assembly, each part should be assigned the same assembly number. A leader line should be used to identify each part unless the differences between the parts is obvious. In Figure 12-4 the difference between head sizes for the fasteners is obvious, so all parts need not be identified.

Assemblies should be shown in their natural or neu

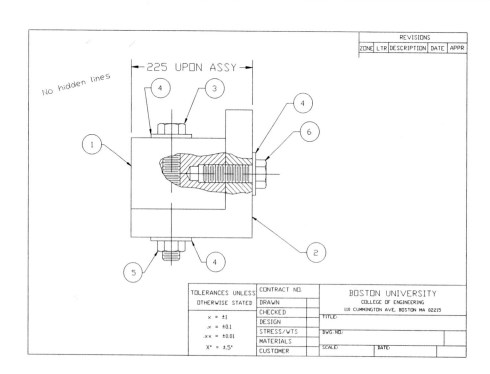

Figure 12-3

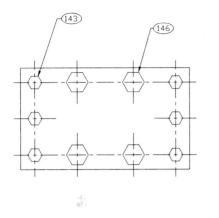

Figure 12-4

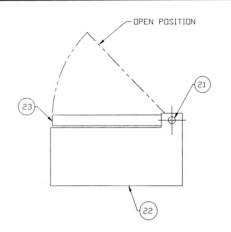

Figure 12-6

tral positions. Figure 12-5 shows a clamp in a slightly open position. It is best to show the clamp jaws partially open, not fully closed or fully open. In general, show an assembly in its most common position.

The range of motion for an assembly is shown using phantom lines. See Figure 12-6. Note how the range of motion for the hinged top piece is displayed using phantom lines.

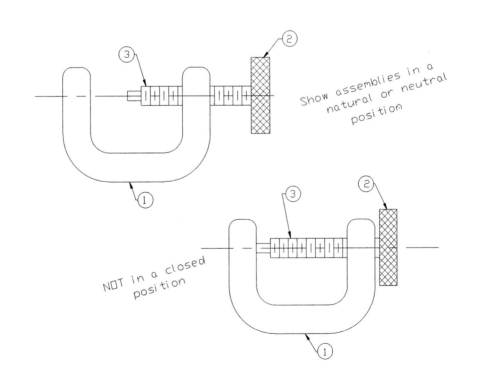

Figure 12-5

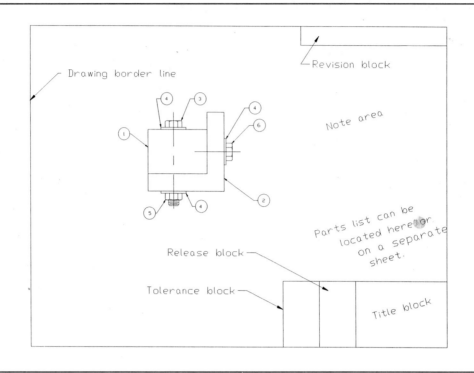

Figure 12-7

12-3 DRAWING FORMATS

Figure 12-7 shows a general format for an assembly drawing. The format varies from company to company and with the size of the drawing paper. Figure 12-8 shows two different possible formats for A sized drawings. Each of the blocks of the drawing is explained in the following sections.

It is suggested that WBLOCKS be created for all the blocks used on assembly drawings. Figures 1-42 and 1-43 show drawing formats that could be used for the exercise drawings in this book.

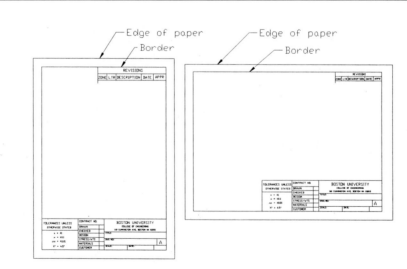

Figure 12-8

12-4 TITLE BLOCK

Title blocks are located in the lower right corner of a drawing and include, at a minimum, the drawing's name and number, the company's name, the drawing scale, the release date of the drawing, and the sheet number of the drawing. Other information may be included. Figure 12-9 shows a sample title block. Figure 12-10 shows two general formats.

Drawing titles (names)

Drawing titles should be chosen so that they clearly define the function of the part. They should be presented in the following word sequence.

Noun, modifier, modifying phrase

For example,

SHAFT, HIGH SPEED, LEFT HAND

GASKET, LOWER

Noun names may be two words if normal usage includes the two words.

GEAR BOX, COMPOSITE

SHOCK ABSORBER, LEFT

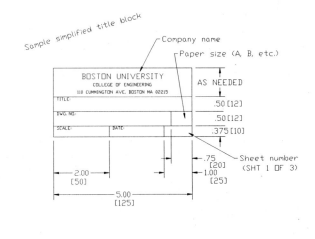

Figure 12-9

Drawing numbers

Drawing numbers are assigned by companies according to their usage requirement. The numbering system varies greatly. Usually drawing numbers are recorded in a log book to prevent duplication of numbers.

Company name

The company's name and logo are preprinted on drawing paper or are included as a WBLOCK so that they can be inserted on each drawing.

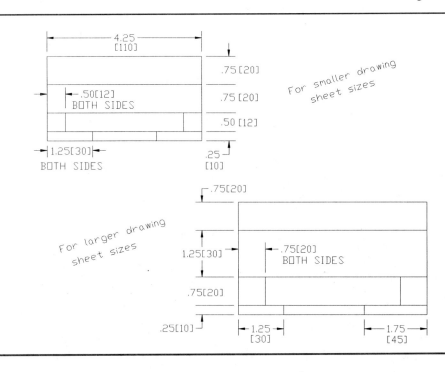

Figure 12-10

Scale

Define the scale of the drawing.

SCALE: FULL, or 1 = 1

The drawing's size is the same as the object's size.

SCALE: 2 = 1

The drawing's size is twice as large as the object's size.

SCALE: 1 = 2

The drawing's size is half as large as the object's size.

Release date

A drawing is released only after all persons required by the company's policy have reviewed and added their signature to the release block. Once released, a drawing becomes a legal document. Drawings that have not been officially released are often stamped with statements like "NOT RELEASED" or "FOR REFERENCE ONLY."

Sheet

The number of the sheet relative to the total number of sheets that make up the drawing should be stated clearly.

SHEET 2 OF 3
or
SH 2 OF 3

12-5 REVISION BLOCK

Drawings used in industry are constantly being changed. Products are improved or corrected and drawings must be changed to reflect and document these changes. Figure 12-11 shows a sample revision block.

Drawing changes are listed in the revision block by letter. Revision blocks are located in the upper right-hand corner of the drawing. See Figure 12-7. Figure 12-12 shows some possible size dimensions for revision blocks.

Each drawing revision is listed by letter in the revision block. A brief description of the change is also included. It is important that the description be as accurate and complete as possible. Revisions are often used to check drawing requirements on parts manufactured before the revisions were introduced.

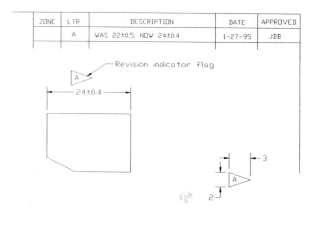

Figure 12-11

The revision letter is also added to the field of the drawing in the area where the change was made. The letter is located within a "flag" to distinguish it from dimensions and drawing notes. The flag serves to notify anyone reading the drawing that revisions have been made.

Most companies have systems in place that allow engineers and designers to make quick changes to drawings. These change orders are called engineering change orders (ECOs), change orders (COs), or engineering orders (EOs), depending on the company's preference. Change orders are documented on special drawing sheets that are usually stapled to a print of the drawing. Figure 12-13 shows a change order attached to a drawing.

After a group of change orders accumulates, they are incorporated onto the drawing. This process is called a drawing revision and is different from a revision to the drawing. Drawing revisions are usually indicated by a letter located somewhere in the title block. The revision let-

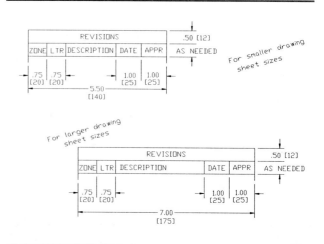

Figure 12-12

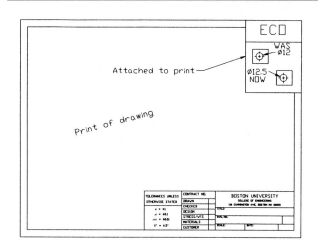

Figure 12-13

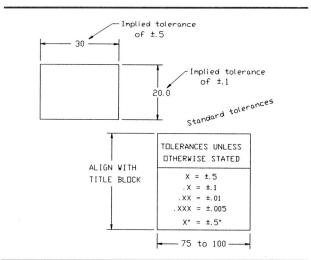

Figure 12-15

ters may be included as part of the drawing number or in a separate box in the title block. Whenever you are working on a drawing, make sure you have the latest revision and all appropriate change orders. Companies will have a recording and referencing system for listing all drawing revisions and drawing changes.

12-6 TOLERANCE BLOCKS

Most drawings include a tolerance block next to the title block that lists the standard tolerances that apply to the dimensions on the drawing. A dimension that does not include a specific tolerance is assumed to have the appropriate standard tolerance.

Figure 12-14 shows a sample tolerance block for inch

values and Figure 12-15 shows a sample tolerance block for millimeter values. In Figure 12-14 the dimension 2.00 has an implied tolerance of +/−.01. In Figure 12-15 the 30 dimension has an implied tolerance of +/−1.

12-7 RELEASE BLOCK

A release block contains a list of approval signatures or initials required before a drawing can be released for production. See Figure 12-16. The required signatures are generally as follows.

Drawn

Person that created the drawing.

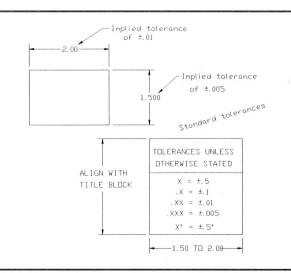

Figure 12-14

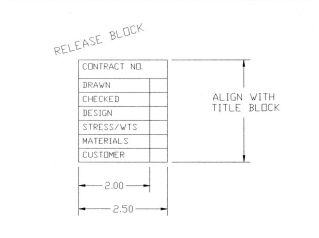

Figure 12-16

Checked

Drawings are checked for errors and compliance with company procedures and conventions. Some large companies have checking departments, whereas smaller companies have drawings checked by a senior person or the drafting supervisor.

Design

The engineer in charge of the design project. The designer and the drafter may be the same person.

Stress/Wts

The department or person responsible for the stress analysis of the design.

Materials

Usually a person in the production department checks the design and makes sure that the necessary materials and the machine times for the design are available. This person may also schedule production time.

Customer

The customer for the design may have a representative on site at the production facility to check that their design requirements are being met. For example, it is not unusual for the Air Force to assign an officer to a plant that manufactures their fighter aircraft.

12-8 PARTS LIST (BILL OF MATERIALS)

A parts list is a listing of all parts used on an assembly. See Figure 12-17. Parts lists may be located on an assembly drawing above the title block or on a separate sheet of paper. Assembly drawings done using AutoCAD often include the parts list on a separate LAYER within the drawing. Use only capital letters on a parts list.

Figure 12-18 shows two sample parts list formats, including dimensions. Parts list formats vary greatly from company to company. The dimensions are given in inches. They may be converted to millimeters using the conversion factor $1.00'' = 25.4$mm.

Parts lists serve as a way to cross-reference detail drawing numbers to assembly item numbers. They also provide a list of the materials needed for production and are very helpful for scheduling and materials purchasing.

Parts purchased from a vendor and used exactly as they are supplied, without any modification, will not have detail drawings but are included on the parts list. The washers, bolts, and screws listed on the parts list shown in Figure 12-17 would not have detail drawings. This means that the information on the parts list must be sufficient for a purchaser to know exactly what size washers, bolts, and screws to buy. The same information used to define an object on the drawing, the drawing callout, is also used on the parts list. See Chapter 11 for an explanation of drawing callouts for fasteners.

PARTS LIST

NO.	DESCRIPTION	PART NO.	MATL	NOTE	QTY
1	BLOCK, TOP	BU107S1	1020		1
2	BLOCK, BOTTOM	BU107S2	1020		1
3	M16 X 24 HEX HEAD BOLT	SPM16H	ST	▷2	1
4	20x40x3 WASHER, PLAIN	SPM-40	ST		3
5	M16 HEX NUT	2PM16N	ST		1
6	M16 X 20 HEX HEAD SCREW	SPM16HS	ST		1

Figure 12-17

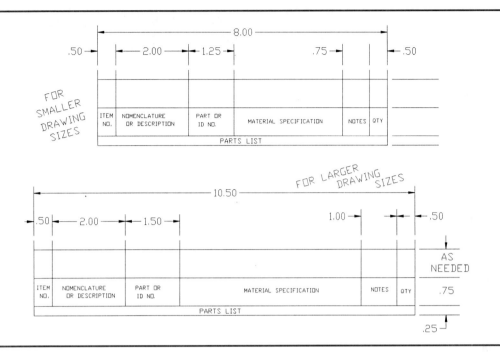

Figure 12-18

12-9 DETAIL DRAWINGS

A detail drawing is a drawing of a single part. The drawing should include all the information necessary to accurately manufacture the part, including orthographic views with all appropriate hidden lines, dimensions, toler-ances, material requirements, and any special manufacturing requirements. Figure 12-19 shows a sample detail drawing.

Detail drawings include title, release, tolerance, and revision blocks located on the drawing in the same places as they are found for assembly drawings.

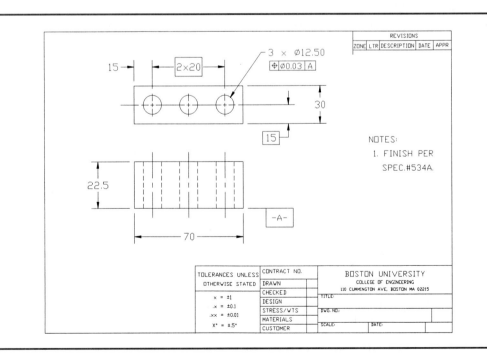

Figure 12-19

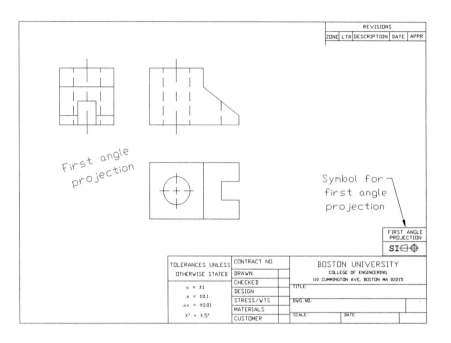

Figure 12-20

12-10 FIRST ANGLE PROJECTION

The instructions for the creation of orthographic views as presented in this book are based on third angle projection. See Chapter 5. Third angle projection is used in the United States, Canada, and Great Britain, among other countries. Many other countries such as Japan use first angle projection to create orthographic views.

Figure 12-20 shows an object and the orthographic views of the object created in first angle projection. Note that the top view in the first angle projection is the same as the top view in the third angle projection, but it is located below the front view, not above the front view as in the third angle projection. Right-side views are also the same but are located to the left of the front view in first angle projections and to the right in third angle projections.

Many companies now do business internationally. They could have manufacturing plants in one country and an assembly plant in another. Drawings can be prepared in several different countries. It is important to indicate on a drawing whether first angle or third angle projections are being used. Figure 12-21 shows the SI (International System of Units) symbols for first angle projections. The SI symbol is included on a drawing in the lower right-hand corner above the title block, as shown in Figure 12-20.

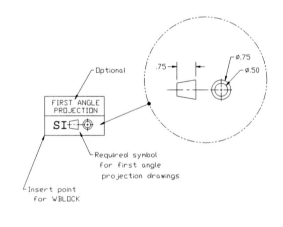

Figure 12-21

12-11 DRAWING NOTES

Drawing notes are used to provide manufacturing information that is not visual, for example, finishing instructions, torque requirements for bolts, and shipping instructions.

Drawing notes are usually located above the title block on the right side of the drawing. See Figure 12-22. Drawing notes are listed by number. If the notes apply to a specific part of the drawing, the note number is enclosed in a triangle. The note numbers enclosed in triangles are also drawn next to the appropriate area of the drawing.

12-12 DESIGN LAYOUTS

A design layout is not a drawing. It is like a visual calculation sheet used to size and locate parts as a design is developed. A design layout allows you to "build the assembly" on paper.

When drawings were created on a drawing board, an initial layout was made locating and sizing the parts. Then the individual detail drawings and the assembly drawing were traced from the layout.

The same procedure can be followed using AutoCAD. First, create a design layout on one LAYER, then either transfer the individual parts and assembly drawing to other LAYERS or create a new drawing from the layout drawing using the SAVE AS command.

The sample problem in the next section demonstrates how to first create a design layout and then use the layout to create the required detail and assembly drawings.

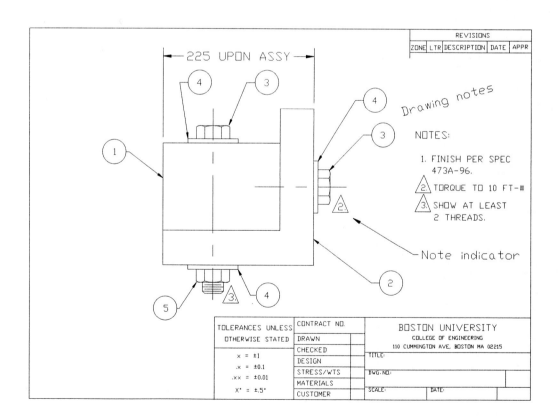

Figure 12-22

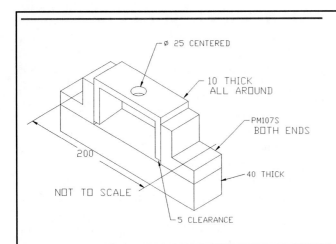

Figure 12-23

12-13 SAMPLE PROBLEM SP12-1

Figure 12-23 shows an engineer's sketch for a design problem. Prepare an assembly drawing and detail drawing of the PN123 BASE and PN124 CENTER PLATE based on the following information.

1. Parts PM107D END BRACKET are existing parts and can be used as is. Figure 12-24 shows a detail drawing of the part.
2. Locate the mounting holes for the two END BRACKETS 200mm apart, as shown in the engineer's sketch.
3. Establish the size of the BASE so that it aligns with the END BRACKETS and is 40mm thick.

4. Determine the sizes for the CENTER BRACKET so that it just fits between the end plates and has a 25mm diameter hole centered in its top surface. The CENTER BRACKET should extend 10mm above the END BRACKETS and 5mm above the BASE. The CENTER BRACKET should be 10mm thick all around.
5. Mount the END BRACKETS to the BASE using M12 FLAT HEAD screws, and attach the END BRACKETS to the CENTERED PLATE using M20 bolts with appropriate nuts.
6. Use only standard length fasteners.

To create the design layout

See Figure 12-25.

1. DRAW horizontal and vertical lines that define the top of the BASE and the distance between the mounting holes in the END BRACKETS.
2. DRAW front and top views of the END BRACKETS located using the vertical lines drawn in step 1. The vertical lines should align with the center lines of the mounting holes.
3. DRAW the BASE 40mm thick.
4. Size the CENTERED BRACKET.

Note that at this stage of the layout all lines are drawn using the same pattern. Lines can be changed to hidden lines or center lines when the detail and assembly drawings are created.

5. Add the M12 FLAT HEAD screws. A length of

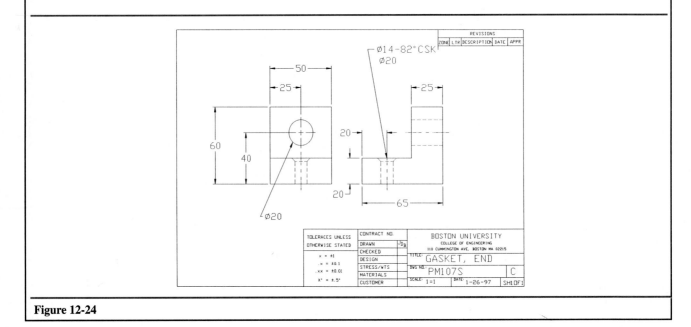

Figure 12-24

20mm was chosen from the tables in the appendix. The threaded holes in the BASE are M12 to match the screws. The tap drill size is included on the layout for reference.

6. Add the M20 × 60 bolts and nuts.

The bolt length was determined by adding 25 (END BRACKET) + 10 (CENTERED BRACKET) + 15 (nut thickness = .75D) + 2 thread pitches = 52mm. The next largest standard bolt length as listed in the appendix is 60, so an M20 × 60 bolt was specified.

7. The diameter of the clearance holes was chosen as 14 and 22 and is listed on the layout.

The design layout is complete. It may be used to create the required assembly drawing and detail drawings in either of two ways: using the LAYER command and including all the drawings under one file name, or by using the SAVE AS command to create separate drawings.

To create a drawing using LAYERS

When lines are moved from one LAYER to another,

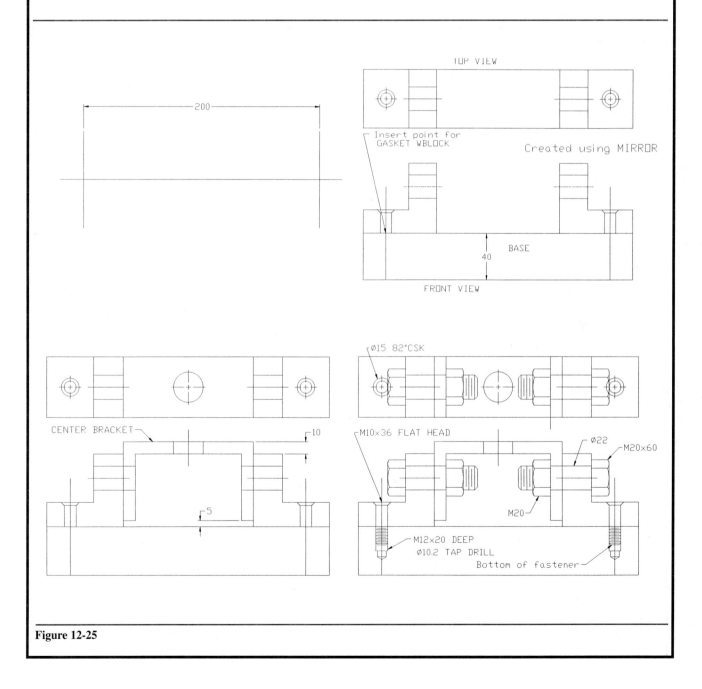

Figure 12-25

the lines will disappear from the original LAYER. This will, in essence, erase the layout drawing because all the lines will have been moved to other LAYERS. The layout may be preserved by first making a COPY of the layout, or that part of the layout you wish to transfer, then using the copy for the transfers.

To make a copy of the layout, use the COPY command. Select the entire screen and select a base point. Select the exact same point as the second point of displacement, and AutoCAD will copy the layout exactly over itself. You can then move the appropriate lines to different LAYERS.

NOTE: EXPLODE all BLOCKS before transferring them between LAYERS. A BLOCK cannot edit a BLOCK once it is moved from its original LAYER.

Create a detail drawing of the BASE by transferring the BASE from the design layout. Respond to the prompts as follows.

1. COPY the layout onto itself.

   COMMAND:_Copy
   Select objects:

2. Window the entire layout, ENTER

   <Base point or displacement>/Multiple:

3. Select a point on the screen

   Second point of displacement:

4. Select exactly the same point as used in the previous step.

5. Create the following LAYERS. See Section 3-23.

   ASSEMBLY
   END
   END-DIM
   BASE
   BASE-DIM
   CENTER
   CENTER-DIM
   PARTSLIST

   The "DIM" LAYERS will be used for the dimensions for the detail drawings. This will allow the dimensions to be shut OFF if they are not needed.

6. Transfer the BASE to a LAYER called BASE. See

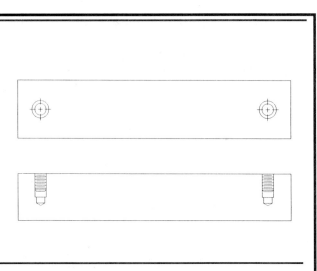

Figure 12-26

SECTION 3-23. Turn OFF all the other LAYERS. The resulting transfer should look like Figure 12-26.

It will be difficult to make a perfectly clean transfer, that is, only the lines of the BASE. If other lines appear on the transferred BASE, ERASE and TRIM them as necessary.

7. MOVE the views closer together if necessary.
8. Turn ON the BASE-DIM LAYER and make it the current LAYER. Add the appropriate dimensions, tolerances, and callouts.

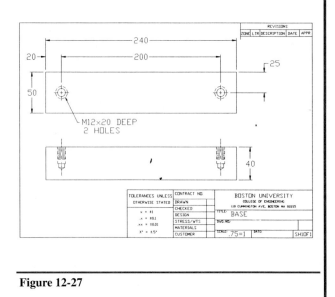

Figure 12-27

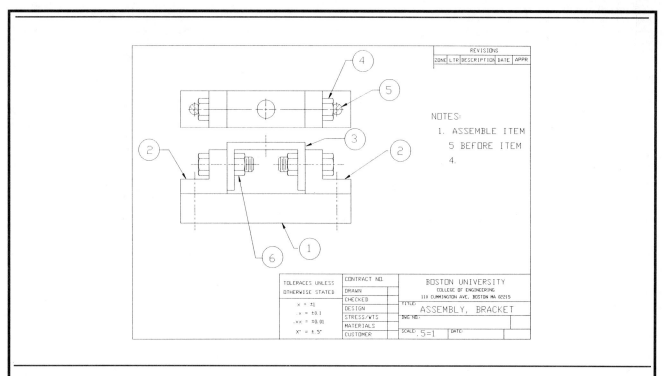

Figure 12-28

9. Create the drawing format and add the necessary information (drawing title, etc.).

The title block, etc., may be saved as a BLOCK or as part of a prototype drawing. Figure 12-27 shows the resulting drawing.

To create a drawing from a layout

Figure 12-28 shows an assembly drawing that was created from the design layout. The procedure is as follows.

1. SAVE the design layout.
2. Create the assembly drawing from the layout drawing, but use the SAVE AS command to save it under a different drawing name.
3. Add the appropriate drawing format and notes.
4. SAVE the assembly drawing using its new name.

Figure 12-29 shows a parts list for the assembly.

PARTS LIST			
ITEM NO	DESCRIPTION	MATL	QTY
1	BASE	STEEL	1
2	END BRACKET - PM107S	STEEL	2
3	CENTER PLATE	STEEL	1
4	M20×60 HEX HEAD BOLT	STEEL	2
5	M12×36 FLAT HEAD SCREW	STEEL	2
6	M20 NUT	STEEL	2

Figure 12-29

12-14 EXERCISE PROBLEMS

EX12-1

A. Draw an assembly drawing of the given objects.
B. Draw detail drawings for all nonstandard parts.

C. Prepare a parts list. Specify the length for the M10 HEX HEAD SCREW.

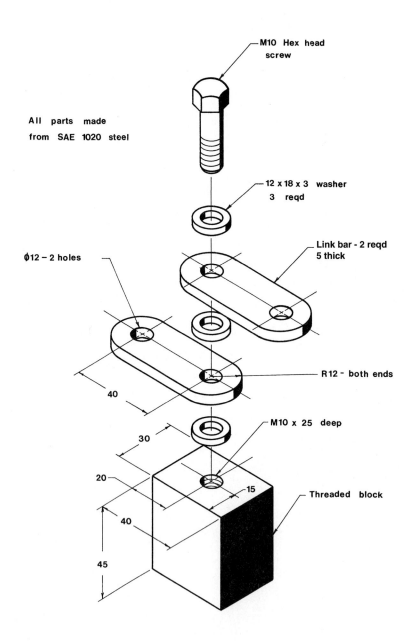

EX12-2

A. Draw an assembly drawing of the given objects.

B. Draw detail drawings for all nonstandard parts. Include positioning tolerances for all holes.

C. Prepare a parts list. Specify the diameter, thread specification, and length for the HEX HEAD SCREW.

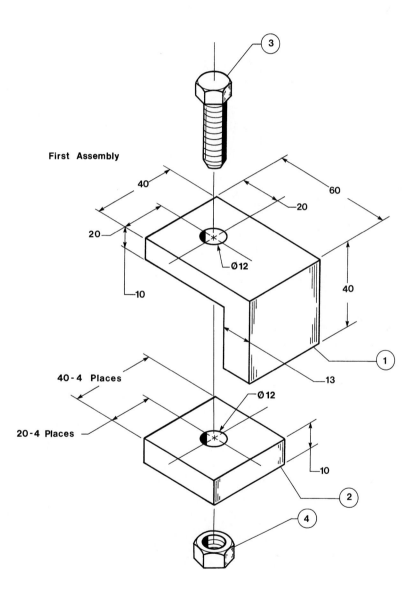

EX12-3

A. Draw an assembly drawing of the given objects.
B. Draw detail drawings for all nonstandard parts.
C. Prepare a parts list.

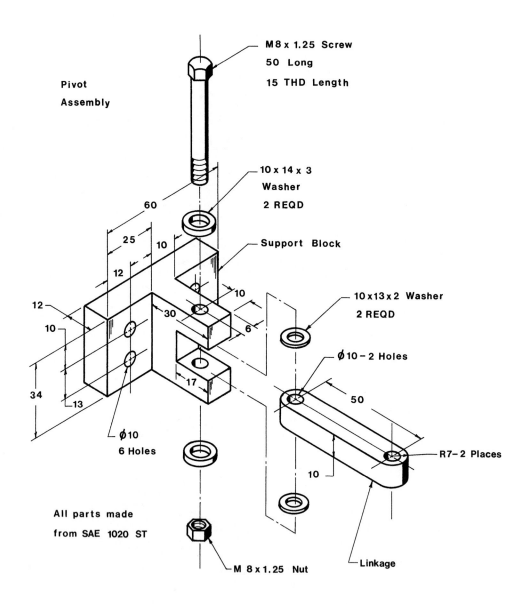

EX12-4

A. Draw an assembly drawing of the given objects.
B. Draw detail drawings for all nonstandard parts.
C. Prepare a parts list.

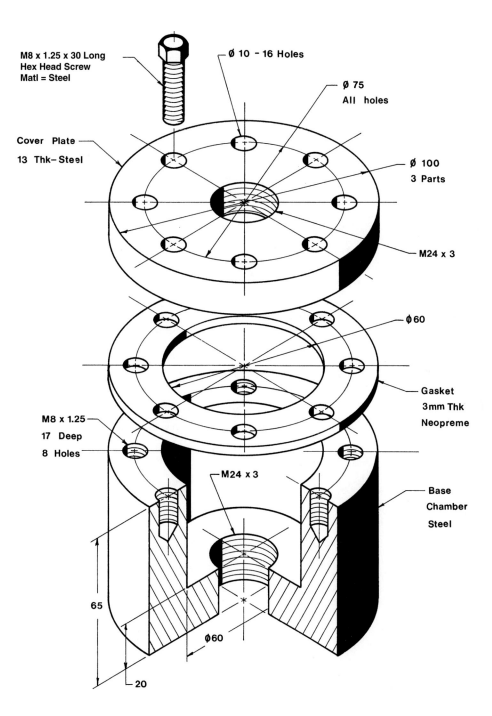

EX12-5

A. Draw an assembly drawing of the given objects.
B. Draw detail drawings for all nonstandard parts.
C. Prepare a parts list.

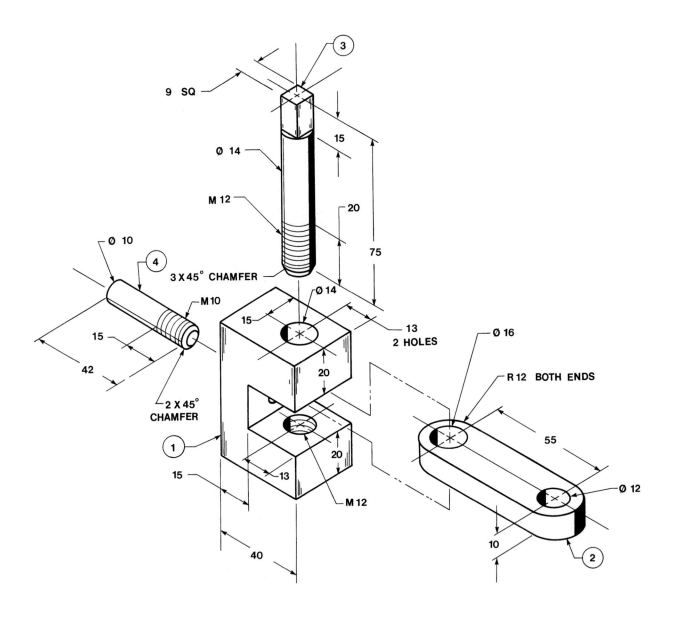

EX12-6

A. Draw an assembly drawing of the given objects.
B. Draw detail drawings for all nonstandard parts.
C. Prepare a parts list.

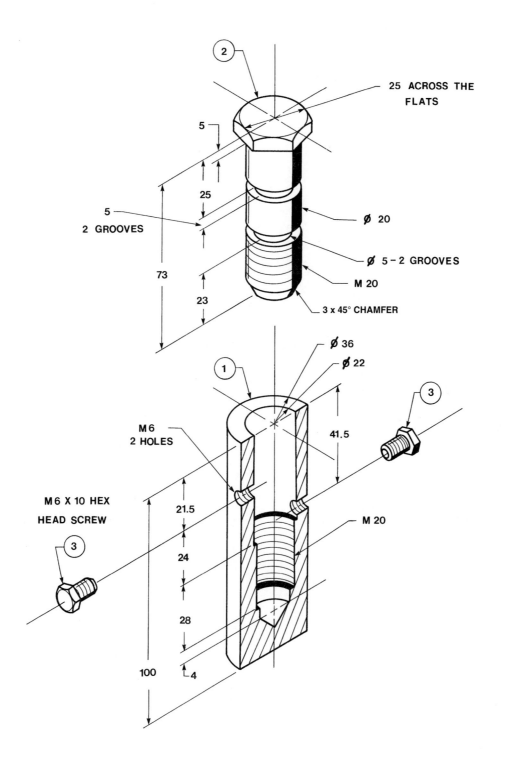

EX12-7

A. Draw an assembly drawing of the given objects.
B. Draw detail drawings for all nonstandard parts.
C. Prepare a parts list.

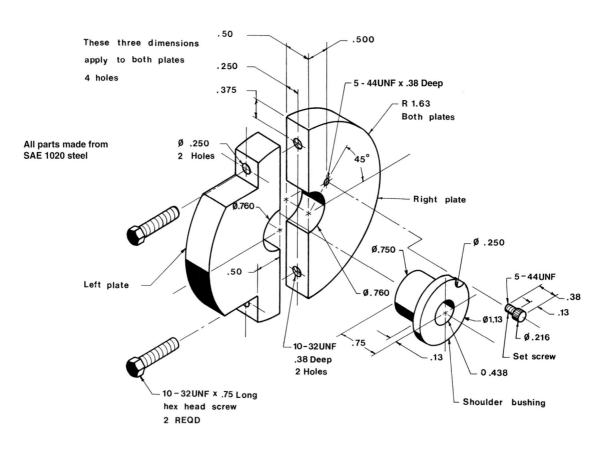

EX12-8

A. Draw an assembly drawing of the given objects.
Show the rivets in their assembled positions and shapes.
B. Draw detail drawings for all nonstandard parts.
C. Prepare a parts list.

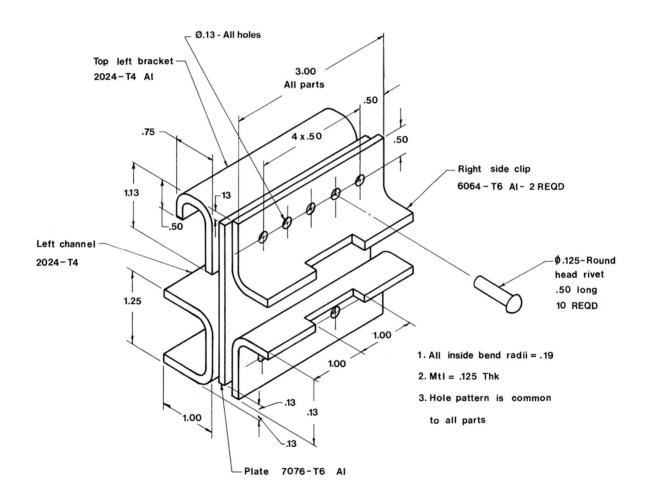

Ø.13 - All holes

Top left bracket
2024−T4 Al

3.00
All parts

.50

.75

4 x .50

.50

1.13

.13

Right side clip
6064 − T6 Al − 2 REQD

.50

Left channel
2024−T4

⌀ .125 − Round
head rivet
.50 long
10 REQD

1.25

1.00

1.00

1. All inside bend radii = .19

2. Mtl = .125 Thk

3. Hole pattern is common
   to all parts

1.00

.13

.13

.13

Plate 7076 − T6 Al

EX12-9

A. Draw an assembly drawing of the given objects.
B. Prepare a parts list.

SIMPLIFIED SURFACE GAGE

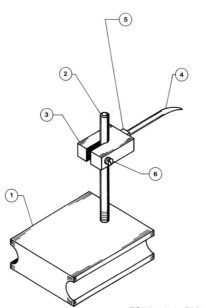

NOTE: ALL PARTS MADE
FROM SAE 1020 STEEL

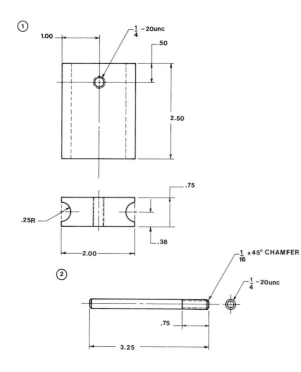

①

1.00

$\frac{1}{4}$ – 20unc

.50

2.50

.75

.25R

.38

2.00

②

$\frac{1}{16}$ × 45° CHAMFER

$\frac{1}{4}$ – 20unc

.75

3.25

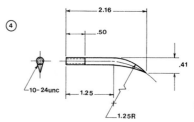

④

2.16

.50

.41

10– 24unc

1.25

1.25R

NOTE: START TAPER
.88 FROM END

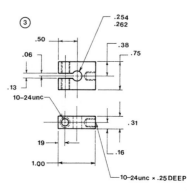

③

.254
.262

.50

.38

.06

.75

.13

10–24unc

.31

19

.16

1.00

10–24unc × .25 DEEP

EX12-10

Redraw the given objects as an assembly drawing and add two slot head, full dog set screws in the holes indicated. Add either a .625″ or 16mm bolt with the appropriate nut in the hole indicated. Add callouts for the fasteners. Specify a standard bolt length.
  A. Use the inch values.
  B. Use the millimeter values.

C. Draw the front assembly view using a sectional view.
  D. Draw the fasteners using schematic representations.
  E. Draw the fasteners using simplified representations.
  F. Prepare a parts list.
  G. Prepare detail drawings for each part.

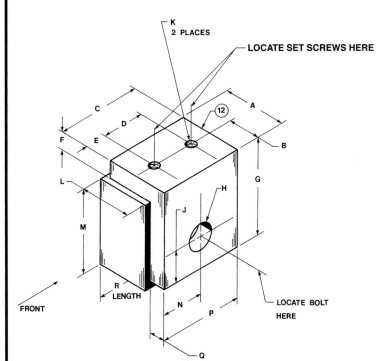

DIMENSION	INCHES	mm
A	1.50	38
B	.75	16
C	2.00	50
D	1.00	25
E	.50	12.5
F	.38	9
G	2.25	57
H	Ø.66	Ø17
J	.75	19
K	.250−20 UNC	M6
L	1.25	32
M	2.00	50
N	1.00	25
P	2.00	50
Q	.38	9
R	2.00	50

EX12-11

Redraw the given objects as an assembly drawing and add bolts with the appropriate nuts at the L and H holes. Add the appropriate drawing callouts. Specify standard bolt lengths.

A. Use the inch values.

B. Use the millimeter values.

C. Draw the front assembly view using a sectional view.

D. Draw the fasteners using schematic representations.

E. Draw the fasteners using simplified representations.

F. Prepare a parts list.

G. Prepare detail drawings for each part.

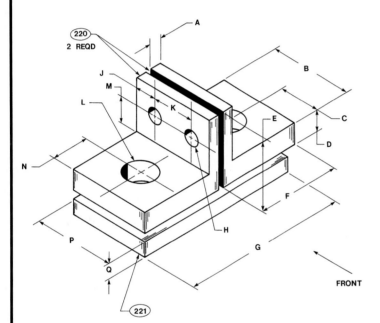

DIMENSION	INCHES	mm
A	.25	6
B	2.00	50
C	1.00	25
D	.50	13
E	1.75	45
F	2.00	50
G	4.00	100
H	Ø.438	Ø11
J	.50	12.5
K	1.00	25
L	Ø.781	Ø19
M	.63	16
N	.88	22
P	2.00	50
Q	.25	6

EX12-12

Redraw the given views and add the appropriate hex head machine screws at M and N. Use standard length screws and allow at least two unused threads at the bottom of each threaded hole. Add a bolt with the appropriate nut at hole P.

A. Use the inch values.

B. Use the millimeter values.

C. Draw the front assembly view using a sectional view.

D. Draw the fasteners using schematic representations.

E. Draw the fasteners using simplified representations.

F. Prepare a parts list.

G. Prepare detail drawings for each part.

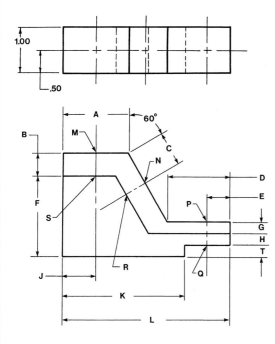

DIMENSION	INCHES	mm
A	1.50	38
B	.50	13
C	.75	19
D	1.38	35
E	.50	13
F	1.75	44
G	.25	6
H	.25	6
J	.75	19
K	2.75	70
L	3.75	96
M	Ø.31	Ø8
N	Ø.25	Ø6
P	Ø.41	Ø12
Q	Ø.41	Ø12
R	.164-32 UNF X .50 DEEP	M4 X 14 DEEP
S	.250-20 UNC X 1.63 DEEP	M6 X 14 DEEP
T	.25	6

EX12-13

Redraw the given objects as an assembly drawing and add the appropriate hex head bolts and nuts. Use only standard length bolts and include callouts for the bolts and nuts on the drawing.

A. Use the inch values.

B. Use the millimeter values.

C. Draw the front assembly view using a sectional view.

D. Draw the fasteners using schematic representations.

E. Draw the fasteners using simplified representations.

F. Prepare a parts list.

G. Prepare detail drawings for each part and include positioning tolerances for all holes.

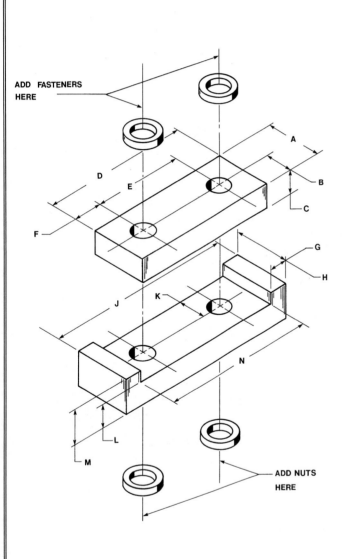

DIMENSION	INCHES	mm
A	1.25	32
B	.63	16
C	.50	13
D	3.25	82
E	2.00	50
F	.63	16
G	.38	10
H	1.25	32
J	4.13	106
K	.63	16
L	.50	13
M	.75	10
N	3.38	86

EX12-14

The objects shown below are to be assembled as shown. Select sizes for the parts that make the assembly possible. (Choose dimensions for the top and bottom blocks and then determine the screw and stud lengths.) The hex head screws (5) have a major diameter of either .375 or M10. The studs (3) are to have the same thread sizes as the screws and are to be screwed into the top part (2). The holes in the lower part (1) that accept the studs are to be clearance holes.

A. Draw an assembly drawing.

B. Draw detail drawings of each nonstandard part. Include positional tolerances for all holes.

C. Prepare a parts list.

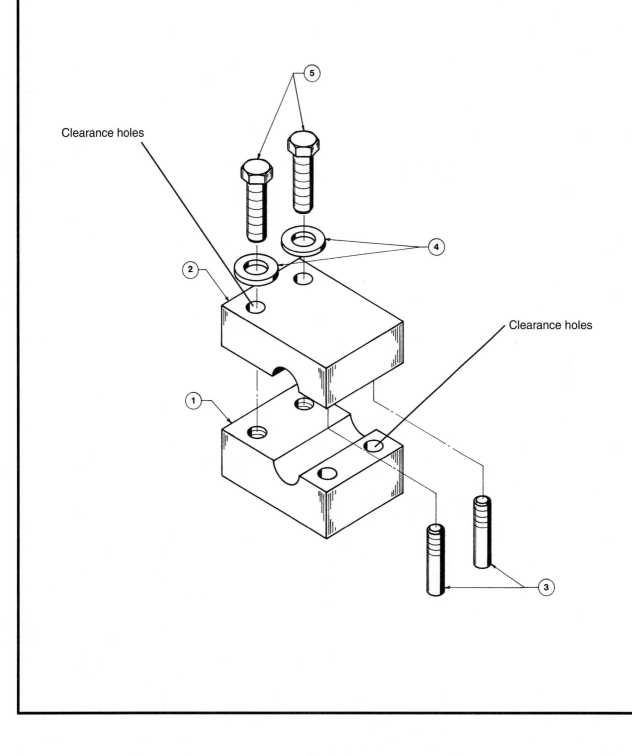

Clearance holes

Clearance holes

EX12-15

Select values for the dimensions indicated in A through J. Use either inches or millimeters. Use either .375 or M10 as the major diameter of the screws. Assemble the parts using three identical screws.

The holes in part 1 are clearance holes and the holes in part 2 are threaded.

A. Draw an assembly drawing.

B. Draw detail drawings of each nonstandard part. Include positional tolerances for all holes.

C. Prepare a parts list.

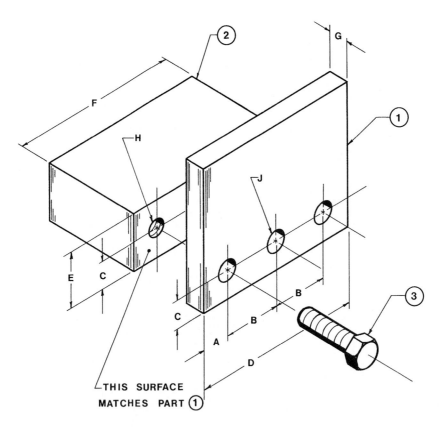

THIS SURFACE
MATCHES PART ①

EX12-16

Design an ACCESS CONTROLLER based on the information given below. The controller works by moving an internal cylinder up and down within the base so the cylinder aligns with the output holes A and B. Liquids will enter the internal cylinder from the top, then exit the base through holes A and B. Include as many holes in the internal cylinder as necessary to create the following liquid exit combinations.

1. A open, B closed
2. A open, B open
3. A closed, B open

The internal cylinder is to be held in place by an alignment key and a stop button. The stop button is to be spring loaded so that it will always be held in place. The internal cylinder will be moved by pulling out the stop button, repositioning the cylinder, then reinserting the stop button.

Prepare the following drawings.

A. Draw an assembly drawing.

B. Draw detail drawings of each nonstandard part. Include positional tolerances for all holes.

C. Prepare a parts list.

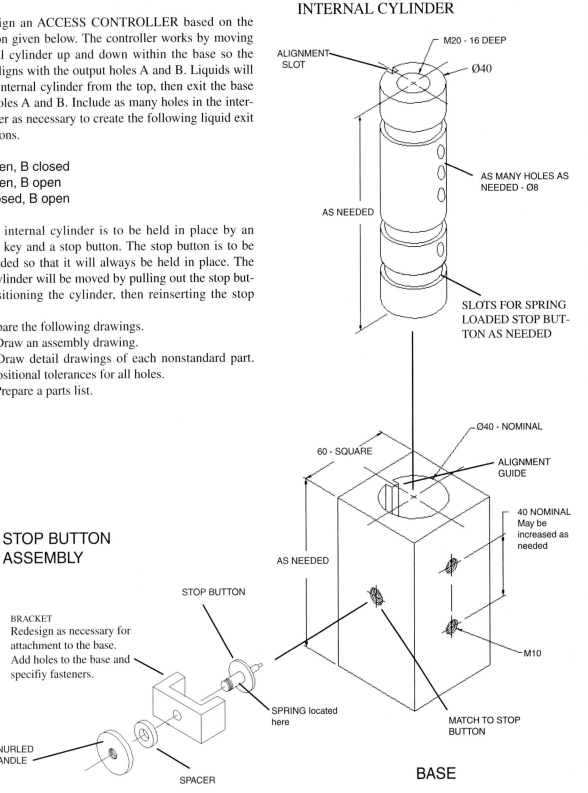

INTERNAL CYLINDER

ALIGNMENT SLOT

M20 - 16 DEEP

Ø40

AS MANY HOLES AS NEEDED - Ø8

AS NEEDED

SLOTS FOR SPRING LOADED STOP BUTTON AS NEEDED

Ø40 - NOMINAL

ALIGNMENT GUIDE

60 - SQUARE

40 NOMINAL
May be increased as needed

AS NEEDED

M10

MATCH TO STOP BUTTON

BASE

STOP BUTTON ASSEMBLY

STOP BUTTON

BRACKET
Redesign as necessary for attachment to the base. Add holes to the base and specifiy fasteners.

SPRING located here

KNURLED HANDLE

SPACER

EX12-17

Design a hand operated grinding wheel specifically for sharpening a chisel. The chisel is to be located on an adjustable rest while it is being sharpened. The mechanism should be able to be clamped to a table during operation using two thumb screws.

A standard grinding wheel is Ø6.00″ and a half inch thick, and has an internal mounting hole with a 50.00±.03 bore.

Prepare the following drawings.

A. Draw an assembly drawing.

B. Draw detail drawings of each nonstandard part. Include positional tolerances for all holes.

C. Prepare a parts list.

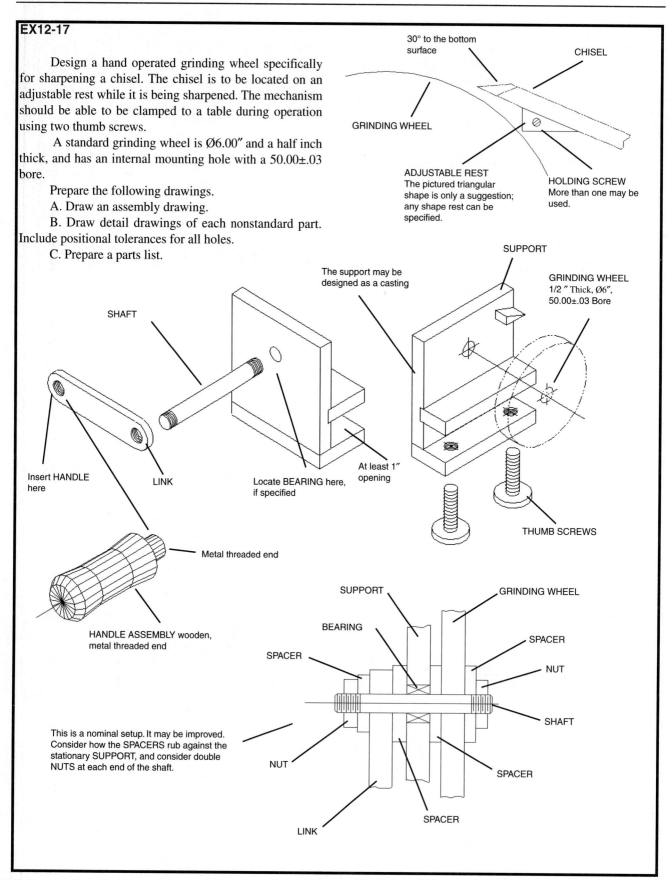

30° to the bottom surface

CHISEL

GRINDING WHEEL

ADJUSTABLE REST
The pictured triangular shape is only a suggestion; any shape rest can be specified.

HOLDING SCREW
More than one may be used.

SUPPORT

GRINDING WHEEL
1/2 ″ Thick, Ø6″,
50.00±.03 Bore

The support may be designed as a casting

SHAFT

Insert HANDLE here

LINK

Locate BEARING here, if specified

At least 1″ opening

THUMB SCREWS

Metal threaded end

HANDLE ASSEMBLY wooden, metal threaded end

This is a nominal setup. It may be improved. Consider how the SPACERS rub against the stationary SUPPORT, and consider double NUTS at each end of the shaft.

SUPPORT

BEARING

SPACER

NUT

GRINDING WHEEL

SPACER

NUT

SHAFT

SPACER

LINK

SPACER

CHAPTER 13

Gears, Bearings, and Cams

13-1 INTRODUCTION

This chapter explains how to draw and design with gears and bearings. The chapter does not discuss how to design specific gears and bearings but how to design using existing parts selected from manufacturers' catalogs. Various gear terminology is defined and design applications demonstrated.

The chapter also discusses how to design and draw a cam based on a displacement diagram. Different types of follower motion are explained as well as different types of followers.

13-2 TYPES OF GEARS

There are many types of gears, including spur, bevel, worm, helical, and rack. See Figure 13-1. Each type has its own terminology, drawing requirements, and design considerations.

13-3 GEAR TERMINOLOGY—SPUR

Below is a list of common spur gear terms and their meanings. Figure 13-2 illustrates the terms and Figure 13-3 shows a listing of relative formulas.

For spur gears using English units

Pitch Diameter (PD) – The diameter used to define the spacing of gears.

Diametral Pitch (DP) – The number of teeth per inch or millimeter.

Circular Pitch (CP) – The circular distance from a fixed point on one tooth to the same position on the next tooth as measured along the pitch circle. The circumference of the pitch circle divided by the number of teeth.

Preferred Pitches – The standard sizes available from gear manufacturers. Whenever possible, use preferred gear sizes.

Center Distance (CD) – The distance between the center points of two meshing gears.

Backlash – The difference between a tooth width and the engaging space on a meshing gear.

Addendum (a) – The height of a tooth above the pitch diameter.

Dedendum (d) – The depth of a tooth below the pitch diameter.

Whole Depth – The total depth of a tooth. The addendum plus the dedendum.

Working Depth – The depth of engagement of one gear into another. Equal to the sum of the two gear addendums.

521

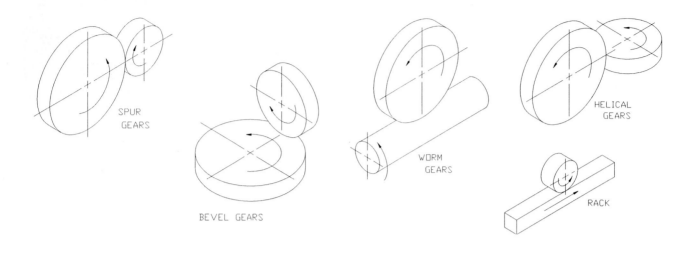

Figure 13-1

Circular Thickness – The distance across a tooth as measured along the pitch circle.

Face Width (FW) – The distance from front to back along a tooth as measured perpendicular to the pitch circle.

Outside Diameter (OD) – The largest diameter of the gear. Equals the pitch diameter plus the addendum.

Root Diameter (RD) – The diameter of the base

of the teeth. The pitch circle minus the dedendum.

Clearance – The distance between the addendum of a meshing gear and the dedendum of the mating gears.

Pressure Angle – The angle between the line of action and a line tangent to the pitch circle. Most gears have pressure angles of either 14.5 or 20 degrees.

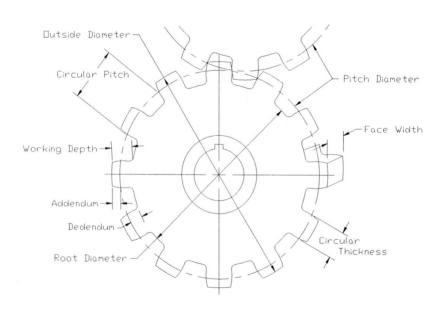

Figure 13-2

Pitch Diameter (PD)	See catalogs
Circular Pitch (CP)	$CP = \dfrac{\pi}{DP}$
Dimetral Pitch (DP)	$DP = \dfrac{\pi}{CP}$
Number of Teeth (N)	N = (PD)(DP)
Outside Diameter (OD)	See catalogs
Addendum (a)	$a = \dfrac{1}{DP}$
Dedendum (d)	d = a + .125 (for drawing purposes ONLY)
Root Diameter (RD)	RD = PD - d
Circular Thickness (CT)	$CT = \dfrac{PD}{2N}$
Face Width (F)	See catalogs

Figure 13-3

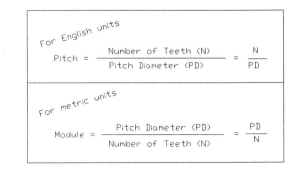

Figure 13-4

For spur gears using metric units

The terminology defined above applies to both English unit and metric unit spur gears with the exception of pitch. For English unit gears, pitch is defined as the number of teeth per inch relative to the pitch diameter. This may be expressed by the formula shown in Figure 13-4. Gears made to metric specifications are defined in terms of the amount of pitch diameter per tooth, called the gear's module. Figure 13-4 shows the formula for calculating a gear's module. Metric gears also have a slightly different tooth shape that makes them incompatible with English unit gears.

13-4 SPUR GEAR DRAWINGS

Figure 13-5 shows a drawing representation of spur gears. The individual teeth are not included in the front view but are represented by three phantom lines. The diameters of the three lines represent the outside diameter, the pitch diameter, and the root diameter.

The outside diameter and the pitch circle are usually given in manufacturers' catalogs. The root circle can be calculated from the pitch circle using the formula presented in Figure 13-3.

The side view of the gear is drawn as a sectional

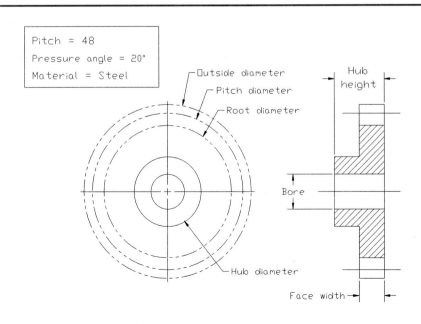

Figure 13-5

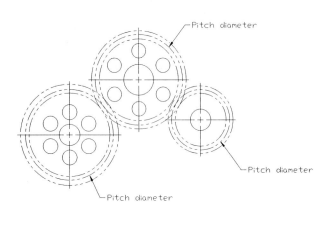

Figure 13-6

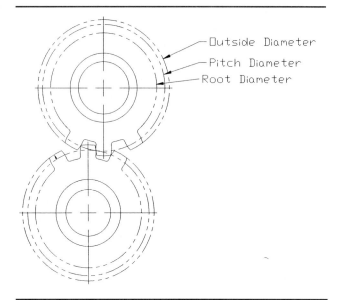

Figure 13-7

view taken along the vertical center line. The gear size is defined using the manufacturer's stock number, dimensions, and a listing of appropriate design information.

Figure 13-6 shows the front representation view of three meshing gears. The gears are positioned so that the pitch circle diameters are tangent. Ideally mating gears always mesh exactly tangent to their pitch circles.

Gear representations were developed because it was both difficult and time consuming to accurately draw individual teeth when creating drawings on a drawing board. AutoCAD can be used to create detailed gear drawings that include all teeth by using the ARRAY and BLOCK commands, among others. However, it is usually sufficient to show a few meshing teeth and use the representative center lines for the remaining portions of both gears. See Figure 13-7.

Most gear teeth shapes are based on an involute curve. Involute-based teeth fit together well, transfer forces smoothly, and can use one cutter to generate all gear tooth variations within the same pitch. Standards for tooth proportions have been established by the American National Standards Institute (ANSI) and the American Gear Manufacturer's Association (AGMA).

13-5 SAMPLE PROBLEM SP13-1

Draw a front view of a spur gear that has an outside diameter of 6.50 inches, a pitch diameter of 6.00 inches, and a root diameter of 5.25. The gear has 12 teeth.

The method presented is a simplified method and is an acceptable representation for most drawing applications. See Figure 13-8.

1. DRAW three concentric CIRCLEs of diameter 6.50, 6.00, and 5.25. Use the DIM, CENTER command to draw a center line for the circles.
2. Use the ARRAY command and create 48 ray lines as shown. Label three rays on each side of the top vertical center line as shown. Zoom the labeled area.

The number of rays should equal 4 times the number of teeth to be drawn. Two adjoining sectors are used to define the width of the tooth, and the next two adjacent sectors are used to define the space between teeth.

3. DRAW a CIRCLE whose center point is at the intersection of the pitch circle and the ray labeled 2, and whose radius is determined by the distance from the center point to the intersection of the pitch circle and the ray labeled −1.
4. Repeat step 3 using the intersection of the pitch circle and the point labeled −2 as the center point.
5. Use the FILLET command to draw a radius at the base of the tooth. Select the side of the tooth as one of the lines for the FILLET and the root circle as the other line.

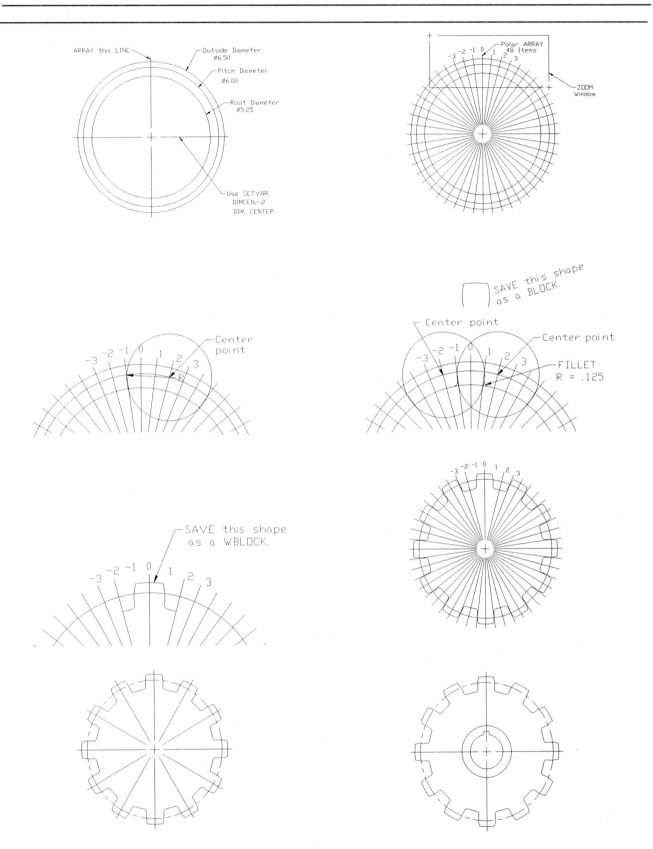

Figure 13-8

Both the circle and ray line will be within the selected cursor, but AutoCAD will select the last entity drawn so the circle will be selected.

The tooth shape can be saved as a WBLOCK named TOOTH and used when drawing other gears. Only the lines that represent the top of the gear and the two side sections need to be SAVED. A different sized gear will have a different root diameter and new FILLETS can be drawn that align with the new root circle.

6. Use the TRIM and ERASE commands to remove excess lines and create the tooth shape between rays –2 and 2 as shown.

This tooth shape may be saved as a WBLOCK and used when drawing other gears.

7. ARRAY the tooth shape about the gear's center point.
8. ERASE the excess ray lines and change the pitch circle to a center line.
9. DRAW the gear's bore hole or center hole and hub as required.

13-6 SAMPLE PROBLEM SP13-2

Figure 13-9a shows two meshing gears. In the example shown, the larger gear has a diameter of 6.00 inches with 24 teeth; the smaller gear has a diameter of 3.00 inches and 12 teeth. The drawing utilizes the WBLOCK created in Sample Problem SP13-1 as follows.

The circular thickness of the WBLOCK tooth as measured along the pitch diameter equals 1/12 the circumference of the pitch diameter.

$(1/12)(\Pi \ PD)$

where PD = 6, for the gear in SP13-1

$(1/12)(\Pi \ 6) = \Pi/2$

$= 1.57''$

The large gear requires 24 teeth on a pitch diameter of 6, or twice as many teeth as the gear used to create the WBLOCK. The teeth on the 24 tooth gear must be half the size of the tooth created in the WBLOCK. The teeth on the smaller gear must be the same size as the teeth on the larger gear.

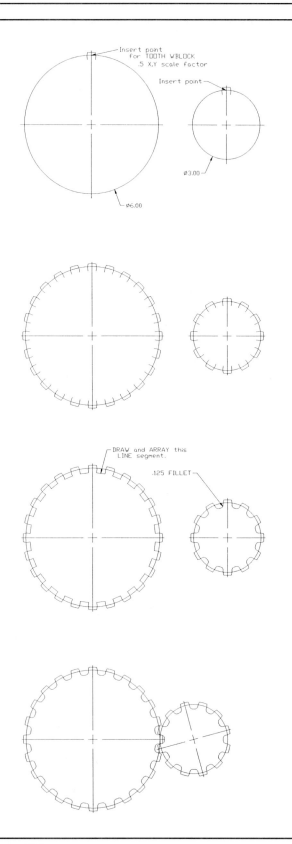

Figure 13-9a

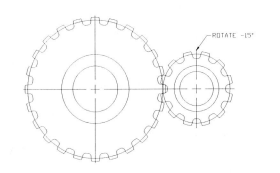

Figure 13-9b

To draw meshing spur gears

See Figure 13-9b.

1. DRAW two CIRCLEs of diameter 6.00 and 3.00 inches. Include the circles' center lines. Use SETVAR, DIMCEN, set to −.2.

The gears will be drawn separately, then meshed.

2. INSERT the TOOTH WBLOCK on both gears as shown on the pitch diameter. Use an X and Y scale factor of .5. EXPLODE the WBLOCK.

3. Use the ARRAY command to create the required 24 and 12 teeth.
4. DRAW a LINE between the roots of two of the teeth as shown. Use the ARRAY command to create the root circle. Add the FILLET to each tooth base.

The line in this example is a straight line acceptable for smaller gears. If more accuracy of shape is required, draw a complete root circle, then trim all of it away except the portion between two tooth roots. ARRAY this sector between all the other teeth.

5. Use the ROTATE command to orient the small gear with the large gear.

Each tooth on the large gear requires 360/24 = 15 degrees. Rotate the smaller gear 15 degrees.

6. Use the MOVE command to position the small gear.

The pitch circles of the two gears should be tangent.

7. ROTATE the smaller gear's center line −15 degrees.
8. Add the center hubs to both gears as shown.

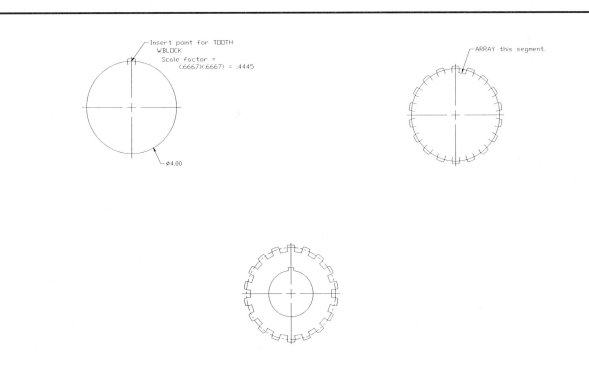

Figure 13-10

13-7 SAMPLE PROBLEM SP13-3

Figure 13-10 shows a gear that has a pitch diameter of 4.00 with 18 teeth. The TOOTH WBLOCK can be used as follows.

The WBLOCK is first reduced to accommodate the smaller diameter.

1. DRAW a CIRCLE with a 4.00-inch diameter. Include center lines.
2. INSERT the WBLOCK using an X and Y scale factor of .4445.

The scale factor was derived by first considering the ratio between the number of teeth on the gear used to create the TOOTH WBLOCK (12) and the number of teeth on the desired gear, 18, or 12/18 = .6667. The ratio between the diameters is also considered: 4.00/6.00 = .6667. The two ratios are multiplied together (.6667)(.6667) = .4445.

3. Use the ARRAY command to create the required 18 teeth.
4. DRAW a LINE between the end lines of two of the teeth, then ARRAY the line 18 times around the gear.

The LINE may be drawn as a straight LINE for small gears or as an ARC for larger gears. The ARC may be created by drawing a CIRCLE, then using the TRIM command to create the desired length.

5. Add the center hub as required.

The same WBLOCK can be used for metric gears using the conversion factor 1.00 inch = 2.54 millimeters. It is probably easier to create a separate WBLOCK for a metric tooth.

13-8 SELECTING SPUR GEARS

When two spur gears are engaged, the smaller gear is called the pinion gear and the larger gear is called simply the gear. The relationship between the relative speed of two mating gears is directly proportional to the gears' pitch diameters. Also, the number of teeth on a gear is proportional to the gear's pitch diameter. This means that the ratio of speed between two meshing gears is equal to the ratio of the number of teeth on the two gears. If one gear has 40 teeth and the other 20, the speed ratio between the two gears is 2:1.

For gears to mesh properly, they must have the same pitch and pressure angle. Gear manufacturers present their gears in charts that include a selection of gears with common pitches and pressure angles. Figure 13-11 shows a sample spur gear listing from Berg's B92 Precision Mechanical Components Catalog. The charts also include dimensional values for the outside diameter of the gear, the pitch diameter, and the face width; and information about the bore; center hub, if appropriate; and the gear's material. The listing is set up to give the designer a wide choice in selecting gears. For example, the chart shows 12 different combinations of gears that could be used to create a 2:1 ratio between gears.

13-9 CENTER DISTANCE BETWEEN GEARS

The center distance between meshing spur gears is needed to align the gears properly. Ideally, gears mesh exactly on their pitch diameters, so the ideal center distance between two meshing gears is equal to the sum of the two pitch radii, or the sum of the two diameters divided by 2.

CD = (PD1 + PD2)/2

If two gears were chosen from the chart in Figure 13-11, and one had 30 teeth and a pitch diameter of .9375, and the second had 60 teeth and a pitch diameter of 1.8750, the center distance between the gears would be

CD = (.9375 + 1.8750)/2 = 2.8125

The center distances of gears is dependent on the tolerance of the gears' bores, the tolerance of the supporting shafts, and the feature and positional tolerance of the holes in the shaft's supporting structure. The following sample problem shows how these tolerances are considered and applied when matching two spur gears.

13-10 SAMPLE PROBLEM SP13-4

An electric motor generates power at 1750 rpm. Reduce this speed by a factor of 2 using steel metric gears with a module of 1.5 and a pressure angle of 20 degrees. Figure 13-12 shows a listing of gears. Determine the center distance between the gears and specify the shaft sizes required for both gears.

Gear number A 1C22MYKW150 50A and number A 1C22MKYW150 100A were selected from the chart shown in Figure 13-12. The pinion gear has 50 teeth and

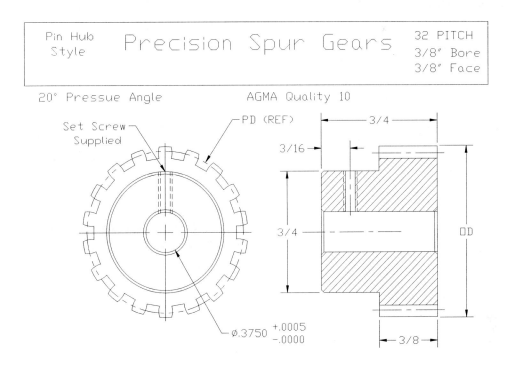

Pin Hub Style	Precision Spur Gears	32 PITCH 3/8" Bore 3/8" Face

20° Pressue Angle   AGMA Quality 10

303 STAINLESS STEEL STOCK NUMBER	BRONZE ALLOY 464 STOCK NUMBER	BERG QUALITY #10 OR BETTER PER AGMA STANDARD 2000-A88 (FORMERLY 390.03)		
		NO. OF TEETH	PITCH DIAMETER	OUTSIDE DIAMETER
P32S34-20	P32B34-20	20	.6250	.687
P32S34-24	P32B34-24	24	.7500	.812
P32S34-28	P32B34-28	28	.8750	.937
P32S34-30	P32B34-30	30	.9375	1.000
P32S34-32	P32B34-32	32	1.0000	1.062
P32S34-36	P32B34-36	36	1.1250	1.187
P32S34-40	P32B34-40	40	1.2500	1.312
P32S34-48	P32B34-48	48	1.5000	1.562
P32S34-56	P32B34-56	56	1.7500	1.812
P32S34-60	P32B34-60	60	1.8750	1.937
P32S34X-64	P32B34X-64	64	2.0000	2.062
P32S34X-72	P32B34X-72	72	2.2500	2.312
P32S34X-80	P32B34X-80	80	2.5000	2.562
P32S34X-96	P32B34X-96	96	3.0000	3.062
P32S34X-112	P32B34X-112	112	3.5000	3.562
P32S34X-128	P32B34X-128	128	4.0000	4.062
P32S34X-160	P32B34X-160	160	5.0000	5.062

An X in a number indicates two piece construction (some dimensions may vary).
W.M. Berg, Inc., 499 Ocean Avenue, East Rockaway, New York, 11518
Telephone 516-596-1700

Figure 13-11

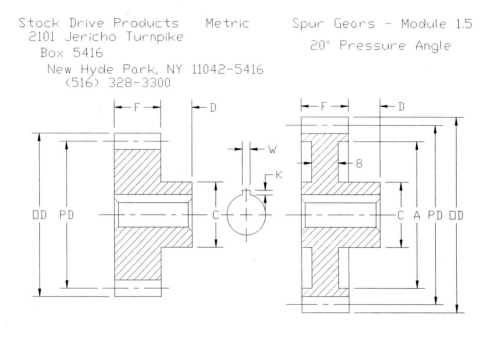

Stock Drive Products   Metric   Spur Gears — Module 1.5
2101 Jericho Turnpike   20° Pressure Angle
Box 5416
New Hyde Park, NY 11042-5416
(516) 328-3300

FIG. 1   FIG. 2

Catalog Number	Fig No.	No. of Teeth	P.D.	O.D.	B* Bore (H7)	F Face Width	C Hub Dia	D Hub Proj	A Dia	W Dim	K Dim
A 1C22MYKW150 20A		20	30	33	14		25			5	2.3
A 1C22MYKW150 24A		24	36	39	16		30				
A 1C22MYKW150 25A		25	37.5	40.5	18	18	32				
A 1C22MYKW150 28A		28	42	45			36				
A 1C22MYKW150 30A		30	45	48							
A 1C22MYKW150 32A	1	32	48	51						6	2.8
A 1C22MYKW150 36A		36	54	57							
A 1C22MYKW150 40A		40	60	63				14			
A 1C22MYKW150 48A		48	72	75			40				
A 1C22MYKW150 50A		50	75	78	20						
A 1C22MYKW150 56A		56	84	87		16					
A 1C22MYKW150 60A		60	90	93					76		
A 1C22MYKW150 64A		64	96	99					82		
A 1C22MYKW150 70A		70	105	108					91		
A 1C22MYKW150 72A	2	72	108	111					94		
A 1C22MYKW150 80A		80	120	123	25		50		106	8	3.3
A 1C22MYKW150 100A		100	150	153					136		

* Gears with 14, 16, and 18mm bores have a tolerance of +.018, +.000.
  20 and 25mm bores have a tolerance of +.021, −.000.

Figure 13-12

the large gear has 100, so if the pinion gear is mounted on the motor shaft, the larger gear will turn at 875 rpm, or half the 1750 motor speed.

1/2 = x/1750

x = 1750/2 = 875 rpm

The specific design information for the selected gears is as follows.

PINION GEAR
    PD = 75
    OD = 78
    N = 50
    Bore = 20 +.021, − .000
    Tolerance = H7

LARGE GEAR
    PD = 150
    OD = 153
    N = 100
    Bore = 25 +.021, − .000
    Tolerance = H7

The center distance between the gears is equal to the sum of the two pitch diameters divided by 2.

(PD1 + PD2)/2 =

(75 + 150)/2 = 112.5mm

The manufacturer's catalog lists the bore tolerance as an H7. One gear has a nominal bore diameter of 20 and the other 25. Standard fit tolerances for metric values are discussed in Chapter 9 and appropriate tables are included in the appendix.

Tolerance values for a sliding fit (H7/g6) hole bases were selected for this design application. This means that the shaft tolerances are 19.993 and 19.980 for the pinion gear and 24.993 and 24.980 for the large gear.

13-11 COMBINING SPUR GEARS

Gears may be mounted on the same shaft. Gears on a common shaft have the same turning speed. Combining gears on the same shaft enables the designer to develop larger gear ratios within a smaller space.

Combining gears can also be used to help reduce the size of gear ratios between individual gears and the amount of space needed to create the reductions. Figure 13-13 shows a four-gear setup and the number of teeth on each gear. Gears B and C are mounted on the same shaft. Gear A is the driver gear and is turning at a speed of 1750 rpm. The speed of gear D is determined as follows.

The ratio between gears A and B is

48/72 = .6667

The speed of gear B is therefore

1750 x .6667 = 1166.7 rpm

Gears B and C are on the same shaft, so they have the same speed. Gear C is turning at 1166.7 rpm.

The ratio between gears C and D is

24/48 = .5000

The speed of gear D is therefore

1166.7 x .5000 = 583 rpm

The ratio between gears A and D is 3:1.

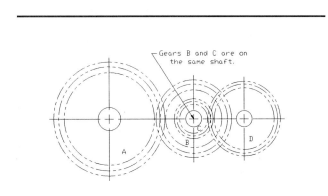

Figure 13-13

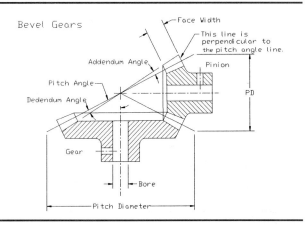

Figure 13-14

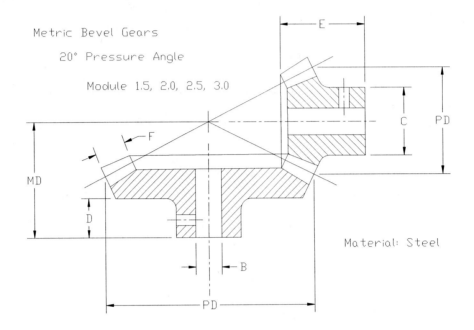

Stock Drive Products

Metric Bevel Gears

20° Pressure Angle

Module 1.5, 2.0, 2.5, 3.0

Material: Steel

Catalog Number	Module	No. of Teeth	Ratio	PD	OD	B* Bore (H8)	F Face Width	E Length	C Hub Dia	D Hub Proj	MD Dim
A 1C 3MYK 15018	1:5	18		27	29.7	8	9.8	23	22	12.5	40.74
A 1C 3MYK 15036		36		54	55.4	10		18.5	30	10	26.75
A 1C 3MYK 20018	2:0	18		36	39.6	9	12.6	29	28	15	53.12
A 1C 3MYK 20036		36	1:2	72	73.8	12		24	36	13	35.21
A 1C 3MYK 25018	2.5	18		45	49.5	12	16.7	35	36	17	64.29
A 1C 3MYK 25036H		36		90	92.2	14		29	50	15	42.55
A 1C 3MYK 30018	3.0	18		54	59.4	12	20	40	41	18	75.27
A 1C 3MYK 30036H		36		108	110.7	16		36	60	19	52.32

* Gears with: 8, 9, 10mm bores have a tolerance of +.022, −.000
　　　　　　　12, 14, 16mm bores have a tolerance of +.027, −.000.

Figure 13-15

13-12 GEAR TERMINOLOGY — BEVEL

Bevel gears align at an angle with each other. An angle of 90 degrees is most common. Bevel gears use much of the same terminology as spur gears but with the addition of several terms related to the angles between the gears and the shape and position of the teeth. Figure 13-14 defines the related terminology.

Bevel gears must have the same pitch or module value and have the same pressure angle for them to mesh properly. Manufacturers' catalogs usually list bevel gears in matched sets designated by their ratios that have been predetermined to fit together correctly. Figure 13-15 shows a sample listing of matched set bevel gears using inch values and Figure 13-16 shows a listing for millimeter values.

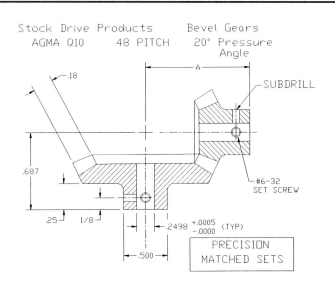

Catalog Number	Ratio	No. of Teeth	PD	A	Material
S1346Z-48S30A030	1:1	30 / 30	.625	.687	St Steel Aluminum
S1346Z-48S30S030	1:1	30 / 30	.625	.687	St Steel
S1346Z-48A30A030	1:1	30 / 30	.625	.687	Aluminum
S1346Z-48S30A045	1:1-1/2	30 / 45	.625 / .937	.812	St Steel Aluminum
S1346Z-48S30S045	1:1-1/2	30 / 45	.625 / .937	.812	St Steel
S1346Z-48A30A045	1:1-1/2	30 / 45	.625 / .937	.812	Aluminum
S1346Z-48S30A060	1:2	30 / 60	.625 / 1.250	.937	St Steel Aluminum
S1346Z-48S30S060	1:2	30 / 60	.625 / 1.250	.937	St Steel
S1346Z-48A30A060	1:2	30 / 60	.625 / 1.250	.937	Aluminum
S1346Z-48S30A090	1:3	30 / 90	.625 / 1.875	1.250	St Steel Aluminum
S1346Z-48S30S090	1:3	30 / 90	.625 / 1.875	1.250	St Steel
S1346Z-48S30A090	1:3	30 / 90	.625 / 1.875	1.250	Aluminum
S1346Z-48S30A120	1:4	30 / 120	.625 / 2.500	1.531	St Steel Aluminum
S1346Z-48S30S120	1:4	30 / 120	.625 / 2.500	1.531	St Steel
S1346Z-48A30A120	1:4	30 / 120	.625 / 2.500	1.531	Aluminum

Figure 13-16

13-13 HOW TO DRAW BEVEL GEARS

Bevel gears are usually drawn by working from dimensions listed in manufacturers' catalogs for specific matching sets. The gears are drawn using either a sectional view or a half sectional view that shows the profiles of the two gears. Figure 13-17 shows a matching set of bevel gears that were drawn from the information given in Figure 13-15.

The procedure used to draw the gears, based on information given in manufacturers' catalogs, is as follows.

To draw a matched set of beveled gears

1. DRAW a perpendicular centerline pattern and use the OFFSET command to define the pitch diameters of the pinion and gear.
2. EXTEND the pitch diameter lines and DRAW LINES from the center point to the intersections as shown.

These lines are called the face angle lines. The ends of beveled gears are drawn perpendicular to the face angle lines. Gear manufacturers do not always include the outside diameter values with matching sets of gears. The val-

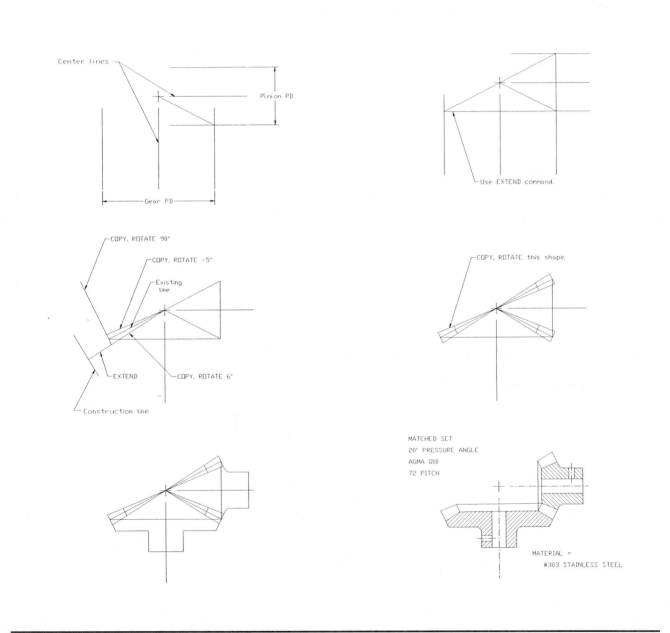

Figure 13-17

ues are sometimes listed with data for the individual gears elsewhere in the catalog. If the outside diameter values are not given, they can be conservatively estimated by drawing the addendum angle approximately –5.0 degrees from the face angle and the dedendum 6.0 degrees from the face angle.

The perpendicular end lines may be constructed using the COPY and ROTATE commands. COPY the existing face angle line directly over the existing line, then ROTATE the line 90 degrees from the face angle line.

Use the EXTEND command to extend the rotated lines as needed. Add a construction line to help define an intersection between the dedendum ray line and the face line perpendicular to the face angle line. TRIM and ERASE any excess lines.

3. Use the COPY and ROTATE commands to COPY the face shape and ROTATE it into the two other positions shown.
4. Use the given dimensions to complete the profiles. ERASE and TRIM lines as necessary.
5. DRAW the bore holes and holes for the set screws based on the manufacturer's specifications.
6. Use the HATCH command to DRAW the appropriate hatch lines.

The two gears should have HATCH patterns at different angles. In this example the HATCH pattern on the pinion is at 90 degrees to the pattern on the gear.

13-14 WORM GEARS

A worm gear setup is created using a cylindrical gear called a worm and a circular matching gear called a worm gear. See Figure 13-18. As with other types of gears, worm gears must have the same pitch and pressure angle to mesh correctly. Manufacturers list matching worms and worm gears together in their catalogs. Figure 13-19 on page 536 shows a gear manufacturer's listing for a worm gear and the appropriate worms.

Worm gears are drawn using the representation shown in Figure 13-19 or using sectional views as shown in Figure 13-20. The worm teeth shown can be drawn using the procedure explained in Chapter 11 for Acme threads.

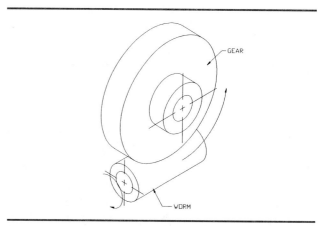

Figure 13-18

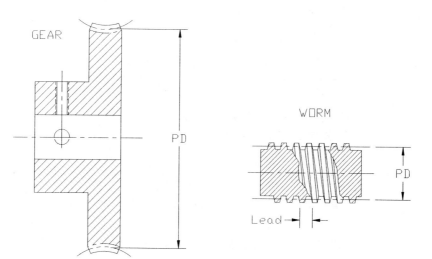

Figure 13-20

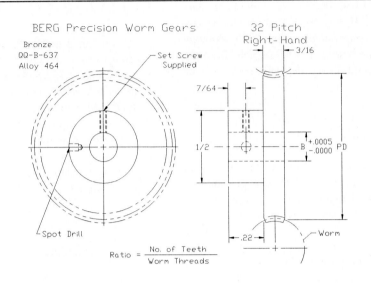

BERG Precision Worm Gears

$$\text{Ratio} = \frac{\text{No. of Teeth}}{\text{Worm Threads}}$$

FOR SINGLE THREAD WORM		FOR DOUBLE THREAD WORM			
CIRCULAR PITCH .0982		CIRCULAR PITCH .1963		NO. OF	PITCH
HELIX ANGLE 4° – 5'		HELIX ANGLE 8° – 8'		TEETH	DIA
PRESSURE ANGLE 14-1/2°		PRESSURE ANGLE 20°			
STOCK NUMBER		STOCK NUMBER			
W32B29-S20		W32B29-D20		20	.625
W32B29-S30		W32B29-D30		30	.938
W32B29-S40		W32B29-D40		40	1.250
W32B29-S50		W32B29-D50		50	1.562
W32B29-S60		W32B29-D60		60	1.875
W32B29-S80		W32B29-D80		80	2.500
W32B29-S96		W32B29-D96		96	3.000
W32B29-S100		W32B29-D100		100	3.125
W32B29-S120		W32B29-D120		120	3.750
W32B29-S180		W32B29-D180		180	5.625

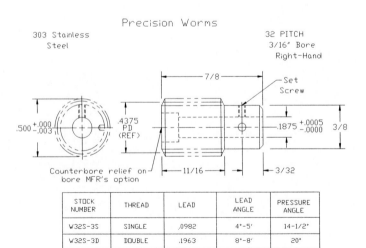

Precision Worms

STOCK NUMBER	THREAD	LEAD	LEAD ANGLE	PRESSURE ANGLE
W32S-3S	SINGLE	.0982	4°-5'	14-1/2°
W32S-3D	DOUBLE	.1963	8°-8'	20°

Figure 13-19

The relationship between worm gears is determined by the lead of the worm thread. The lead of a worm thread is similar to the pitch of a thread discussed in Chapter 11. Worm threads may be single, double, or quadruple. If a worm has a double thread, it will advance the gear twice as fast as a worm with a single thread.

13-15 HELICAL GEARS

Helical gears are drawn as shown in Figure 13-21. The two gears are called the driver and the driven, as indicated. Figure 13-22 shows a manufacturer's listing of compatible helical gears.

Helical gears may be manufactured with either left- or right-hand threads. Left- and right-hand threads are used to determine the relative rotation direction of the gears.

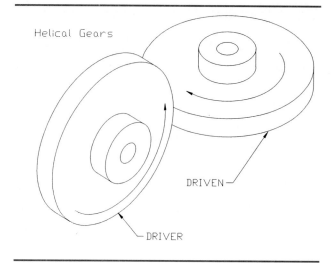

Figure 13-21

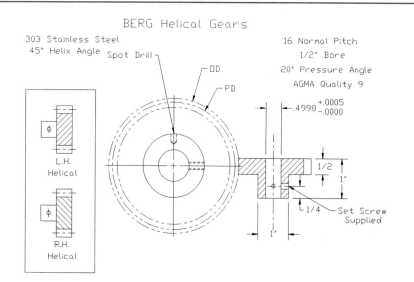

STOCK NUMBER		NO. OF TEETH	PITCH DIAMETER	OUTSIDE DIAMETER
RIGHT-HAND	LEFT-HAND			
H16S38-R12	H16S38-L12	12	1.060	1.185
H16S38-R16	H16S38-L16	16	1.4142	1.539
H16S38-R20	H16S38-L20	20	1.7677	1.892
H16S38-R24	H16S38-L24	24	2.1213	2.246
H16S38-R32	H16S38-L32	32	2.8284	2.953
H16S38-R40	H16S38-L40	40	3.5355	3.660
H16S38-R48	H16S38-L48	48	4.2426	4.367

Figure 13-22

13-16 RACKS

Racks are gears that have their teeth in a straight row. Racks are used to change rotary motion into linear motion. See Figure 13-23. Racks are usually driven by a spur gear called a pinion.

One of the most common applications of gear racks is the steering mechanism of an automobile. Rack and pinion steering helps create a more positive relationship between the rotating steering wheel and the linear input to the car's wheel than did the mechanical linkages used on older model cars.

Figure 13-24 shows a manufacturer's listing for racks and a second listing of compatible pinion gears. The rack and pinions must have the same pitch and pressure angle for them to mesh correctly.

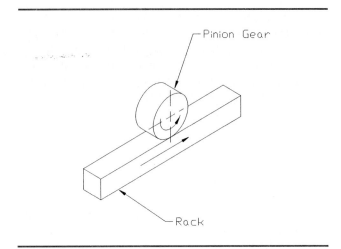

Figure 13-23

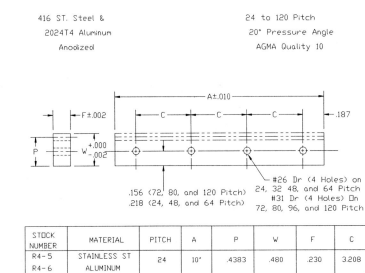

Berg Precision Racks

416 ST. Steel &
2024T4 Aluminum
Anodized

24 to 120 Pitch
20° Pressure Angle
AGMA Quality 10

STOCK NUMBER	MATERIAL	PITCH	A	P	W	F	C
R4-5	STAINLESS ST	24	10"	.4383	.480	.230	3.208
R4-6	ALUMINUM						
R4-9	STAINLESS ST	32	10"	.4487	.480	.230	3.208
R4-10	ALUMINUM						
R4-11	STAINLESS ST	48	9"	.4592	.480	.230	2.879
R4-12	ALUMINUM						
R4-15	STAINLESS ST	64	7"	.4644	.480	.230	2.208
R4-16	ALUMINUM						
R4-17	STAINLESS ST	72	5"	.3411	.355	.167	1.541
R4-18	ALUMINUM						
R4-19	STAINLESS ST	80	5"	.3425	.355	.167	1.541
R4-20	ALUMINUM						
R4-21	STAINLESS ST	96	3"	.3446	.355	.167	.875
R4-22	ALUMINUM						
R4-23	STAINLESS ST	120	3"	.3467	.355	.167	.875
R4-24	ALUMINUM						

Figure 13-24

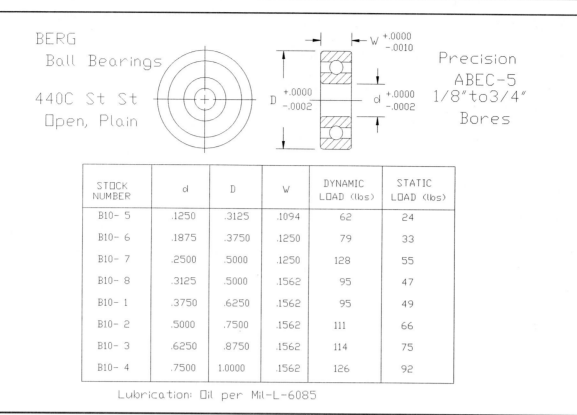

STOCK NUMBER	d	D	W	DYNAMIC LOAD (lbs)	STATIC LOAD (lbs)
B10- 5	.1250	.3125	.1094	62	24
B10- 6	.1875	.3750	.1250	79	33
B10- 7	.2500	.5000	.1250	128	55
B10- 8	.3125	.5000	.1562	95	47
B10- 1	.3750	.6250	.1562	95	49
B10- 2	.5000	.7500	.1562	111	66
B10- 3	.6250	.8750	.1562	114	75
B10- 4	.7500	1.0000	.1562	126	92

Lubrication: Oil per Mil-L-6085

Figure 13-25

13-17 BALL BEARINGS

Ball bearings are used to help eliminate friction between moving and stationary parts. The moving and stationary parts are separated by a series of balls that ride in a "race."

Figure 13-25 shows a manufacturer's listing for ball bearings that includes applicable dimensions and tolerances. There are many other types and sizes of ball bearings available.

Ball bearings may be drawn as shown in Figure 13-25 or by using one of the representations shown in Figure 13-26. It is recommended that the representations be drawn and saved as WBLOCKS for use on future drawings.

The outside diameter of the bearings listed in Figure 13-25 has a tolerance of +.0000/−.0002. The same tolerance range applies to the center hole. These tight tolerances are manufactured because this type of ball bearing is usually assembled using a force fit. See Chapter 9 for an explanation of fits. Ball bearings are available that do not assemble using force fits.

The following sample problem shows how ball bearings can be used to support the gear's shafts.

13-18 SAMPLE PROBLEM SP13-5

Figure 13-27 shows two spur gears and a dimensioned drawing of a shaft used to support both gears. Design a support plate for the shafts. Use ball bearings to support the shafts. Specify dimensions and tolerances for the support plate and assume that the bearings are to be fitted into the support plate using an LN2 medium press fit. The tolerance for the center distance between the gears is to be +.001, −.000.

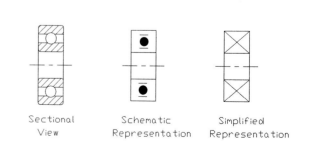

Sectional View   Schematic Representation   Simplified Representation

Figure 13-26

The maximum interference permitted for an LN2 medium press fit is .0011. See the fits tables in the appendix. For purposes of calculation, the bearing is considered the shaft and the holes in the support plate the hole.

Maximum interference occurs when the shaft (bearing) is at its maximum diameter and the hole (support plate) is at its minimum. The maximum shaft diameter, the maximum diameter of the bearing, is .5000 as defined in the manufacturer's listing. This means that the minimum hole diameter should be .5000 – .0011 = .4989. An LN2 fit has a hole tolerance of +.0007, so the maximum hole size should be .4989 + .0007 = .4996.

The minimum interference or the difference between the minimum shaft diameter and the maximum hole diameter is .4998 – .4996 = .0002. There will always be at least .0002 interference between the ball bearing and the hole.

The bore of the selected bearing, listed in Figure 13-25, has a limit tolerance of .2500 – .2498. The shafts specified in Figure 13-27 have a limit tolerance of .2497-.2495. This means that there will always be a slight clearance between the shafts and the bore hole.

The nominal center distance between the two gears is 3.000 inches. The given tolerance for the center distance is +.001, –.000. This tolerance can be ensured by assigning a positional tolerance of .0005 to each of the two holes applied at maximum material condition at the center line. The base distance between the two holes is defined as 3.0000. The maximum center distance, including the positional tolerance, is 3.0000 + .0005 = 3.0005, and the minimum is 3.0000 – .0005 = 2.9995, or a total maximum tolerance of .001.

Figure 13-28 shows a detailed drawing of the support plate.

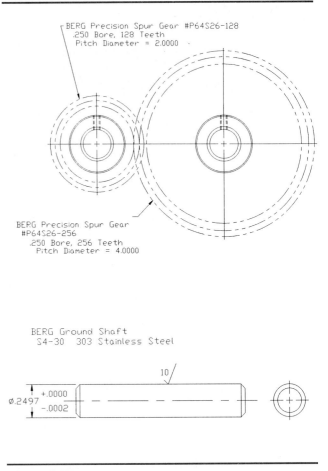

Figure 13-27

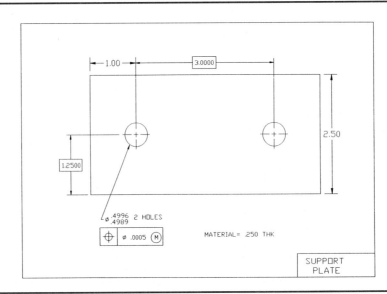

Figure 13-28

13-19 BUSHINGS

A bushing is a cylindrically shaped bearing that helps reduce friction between a moving part and a stationary part. Bushings have no moving parts like a ball bearing. Bushings are usually made from oil impregnated bronze or teflon. Figure 13-29 shows a manufacturer's listing for bronze bushings and Figure 13-30 shows a listing for teflon bushings.

Bushings are cheaper than ball bearings but they wear over time, particularly if the application is high speed or one with heavy loading. Bushings are usually pressed into a supporting plate. Gear shafts must always have clearance from the inside diameters of bushings.

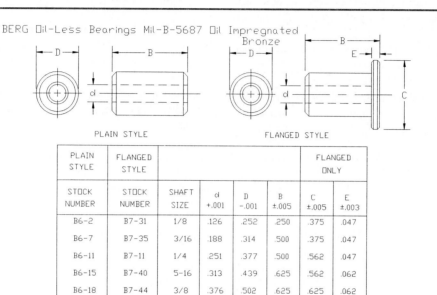

BERG Oil-Less Bearings Mil-B-5687 Oil Impregnated Bronze

PLAIN STYLE   FLANGED STYLE

PLAIN STYLE	FLANGED STYLE					FLANGED ONLY	
STOCK NUMBER	STOCK NUMBER	SHAFT SIZE	d +.001	D −.001	B ±.005	C ±.005	E ±.003
B6-2	B7-31	1/8	.126	.252	.250	.375	.047
B6-7	B7-35	3/16	.188	.314	.500	.375	.047
B6-11	B7-11	1/4	.251	.377	.500	.562	.047
B6-15	B7-40	5-16	.313	.439	.625	.562	.062
B6-18	B7-44	3/8	.376	.502	.625	.625	.062
B6-23	B7-49	1/2	.501	.627	.750	.875	.062

Figure 13-29

BERG Teflon Bearings MIL-P-9468

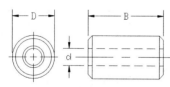

PLAIN STYLE

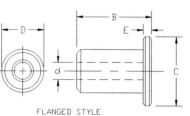

FLANGED STYLE

PLAIN STYLE	FLANGED STYLE					FLANGED ONLY	
STOCK NUMBER	STOCK NUMBER	SHAFT SIZE	d +.001	D −.001	B ±.005	C ±.005	E ±.003
	B9-3	1/8	.126	.252	.250	.312	.047
B8-5	B9-6	3/16	.188	.315	.250	.375	.047
B8-11	B9-11	1/4	.251	.377	.500	.500	.047
B8-14	B9-15	5/16	.313	.439	.500	.562	.093
B8-19	B9-19	3/8	.376	.502	.625	.687	.093
B8-23	B8-29	1/2	.501	.628	.750	.875	.125

Figure 13-30

13-20 SAMPLE PROBLEM SP13-6

Figure 13-31 shows two support plates used to support and align a matched set of bevel gears. The gears selected are numbered S1346Z–48S30S060 in the BERG listings presented in Figure 13-16. The calculations are similar to those presented above for Sample Problem SP13-5 but with the addition of tolerance for the holes and machine screws used to join the two perpendicular support plates together.

Figure 13-31 shows an assembly drawing of the two gears along with appropriate bushings, Stock Number B6-11 from Figure 13-29, and shafts and supporting Parts 1 and 2. The figure also shows detailed drawings of the two support plates with appropriate dimensions and tolerances.

The bushings are fitted into the support plates using an FN1 fit. The fit tables in the appendix define the maximum interference for an FN1 fit as .0075 and the minimum interference as .0001. The outside diameter of the bushing has a tolerance of .3770 – .3760, per Figure 13-29. The feature tolerances for the holes in the support parts are found as follows.

Shaft max – hole min = interference max

Shaft min – hole max = interference min

The feature tolerance for the hole is therefore .3750 - .3695.

The positional tolerance is determined as described in SP13-5 and is based on a tolerance of .001 between gear centers.

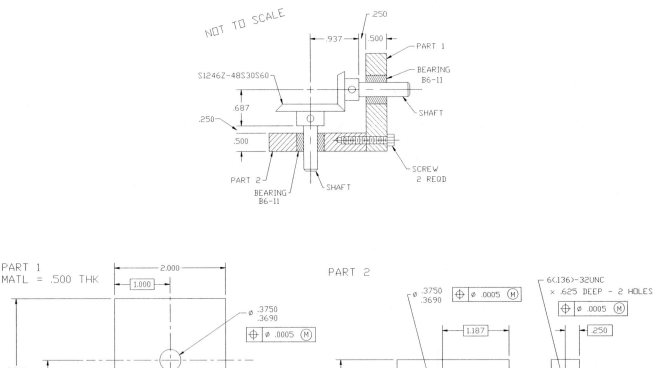

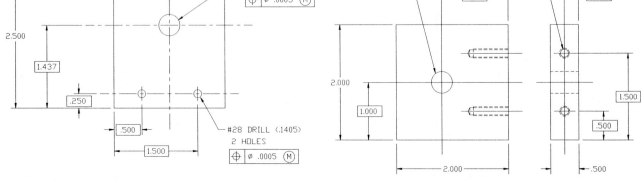

Figure 13-31

PART 1

13-21 CAM DISPLACEMENT DIAGRAMS

A displacement diagram is used to define the motion of a cam follower. Displacement diagrams are set up as shown in Figure 13-32. The horizontal axis is marked off in 12 equal spaces that represent 30 degrees on the cam. The vertical axis is used to define the linear displacement of the follower and is defined using either inches or millimeters.

The vertical axis of a displacement diagram must be drawn to scale because once defined, the vertical distances are transferred to the cam's base circle to define the cam's shape. Figure 13-32 shows distances A, B, and C on both the displacement diagram and cam. The distances define the follower displacement at the 30, 60, and 90 degree marks, respectively.

The horizontal axis may use any equal spacing to indicate the angle because the vertical distances will be transferred to the cam along ray lines. The lower horizontal line represents the circumference of the base circle.

Figure 13-33 shows a second displacement diagram. Note how the distance between the 60 and 90 degree lines has been further subdivided. The additional lines are used to more accurately define the cam's motion. Additional degree lines are often added when the follower is undergoing a rapid change of motion.

The term "dwell" means the cam follower does not move either up or down as the cam turns. Dwells are drawn as straight horizontal lines on a displacement diagram. Note the horizontal line between the 90 and 210 degree lines on the displacement diagram shown in Figure 13-33. Dwells are drawn as sectors of constant radius on the cam.

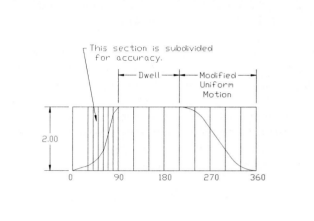

Figure 13-33

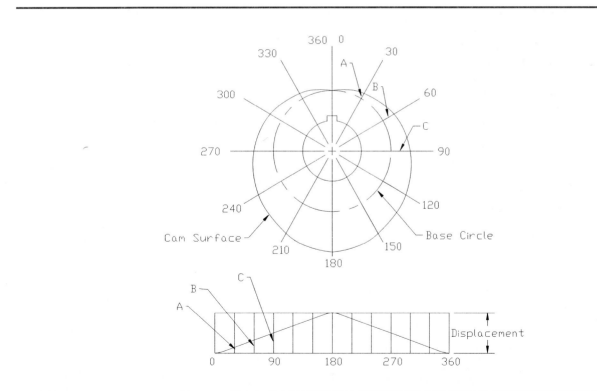

Figure 13-32

To set up a displacement diagram

See Figure 13-34. The given dimensions are in inches. The values in the brackets, [ ], are in millimeters.

1. Set GRID = .5 [10]

    SNAP = .25 [5]

2. DRAW a horizontal LINE 6 [120] long.
3. DRAW a vertical LINE 2 [40] from the left end of the horizontal line as shown.

The length 2 [40] was chosen arbitrarily for this example. The vertical distance should be equal to the total displacement of the follower.

4. Use the ARRAY command to create a rectangular array with 12 columns .5 [10] apart. DRAW a horizontal LINE across the top of the diagram.
5. Label the horizontal axis in degrees, with each vertical line representing 30 degrees, and the vertical axis in inches [millimeters] of displacement.

13-22 CAM MOTIONS

The shape of a cam surface is designed to move a follower through a specific distance. The surface also determines the acceleration, deceleration, and smoothness of motion of the follower. It is important that a cam surface be shaped to maintain continuous contact with the follower. Several standard cam motions are defined below.

Uniform motion

Uniform motion is drawn as a straight line on a displacement diagram. See Figure 13-35. The follower rises the same distance for each degree of rotation by the cam.

Modified uniform motion

Modified uniform motion is similar to uniform motion but has a curved radius shape added to each end of the line to facilitate a smooth transition from the uniform motion to another type of motion or a dwell section.

Figure 13-36 shows how to create a modified uniform motion on a displacement diagram. The procedure is as follows.

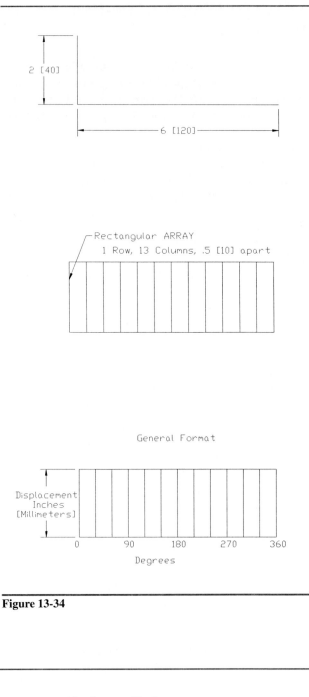

Figure 13-34

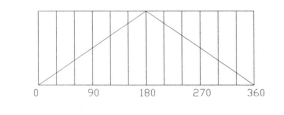

Figure 13-35

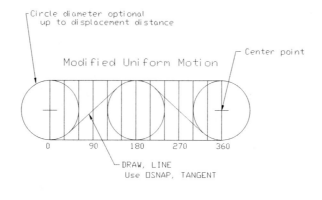

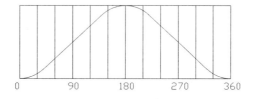

Figure 13-36

1. Set up a displacement diagram as presented in Section 13-21.
2. DRAW two ARCs or CIRCLEs of radius no greater than half the required displacement.

Any radius value can be used. In general, the larger the radius, the smoother the transition. In the example shown, a radius equal to half the total displacement was used.

3. Use OSNAP, TANGENT, and DRAW a LINE between the two ARCs.
4. ERASE and TRIM any excess lines.

Harmonic motion

Figure 13-37 shows how to create a harmonic cam motion. The procedure is as follows.

1. Set up a displacement diagram as presented in Section 13-21.
2. Draw a semicircle aligned with the left side of the displacement diagram. The diameter of the semicircle equals the total height of the dis-

placement.
3. Use the ARRAY command or the LINE command with relative coordinate inputs and DRAW rays every 30 degrees on the circle as shown. Label the rays from 0 to 180 degrees in 30-degree segments.
4. Use OSNAP, INTERSECTION with ORTHO ON (F8), and DRAW projection LINEs from the intersections of the rays with the circumference of the circle across the displacement diagram.
5. DRAW a POLYLINE starting at the lower left corner of the diagram and connecting the intersections of like angle lines.

For this example, the horizontal line from the circle's 30-degree increment intersects with the vertical line from the 30-degree mark on the displacement diagram.

6. Use POLYEDIT, FIT CURVE, to change the straight POLYLINE into a smooth curved line.
7. Project the same lines to the far side of the diagram to define the deceleration harmonic motion path.

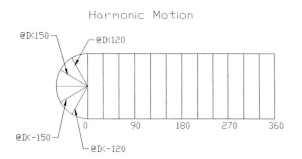

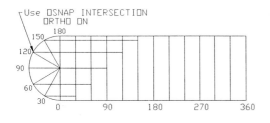

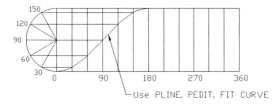

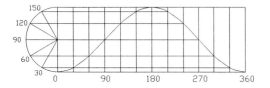

Figure 13-37

Uniform acceleration and deceleration

Uniform acceleration and deceleration is based on the knowledge that acceleration is related to distance by the square of the distance. Acceleration is measured in distance per second squared. Distances of units 1, 2, and 3 may be expressed as 1, 4, and 9, respectively.

Uniform acceleration and deceleration motions create smooth transitions between various displacement heights and are often used in high-speed applications.

Figure 13-38 shows how to create a uniform acceleration cam motion. The procedure is as follows.

1. Set up a displacement diagram as presented in Section 13-21.
2. DRAW a horizontal construction line to the left and align it with the bottom horizontal line of the displacement diagram.
3. Use the ARRAY command and create 1 column, 19 rows, .1111 apart.

The 19 rows create 18 spaces. The uniform motion shape will be created by combining 6 horizontal steps (30, 60, 90, 120, 150, 180 degrees) and the squares of six vertical steps (1, 4, 9, 4, 1, 0).

The vertical spacing is symmetrical about the center line of the displacement diagram, so the original spacing is 1, 2, 3, 2, 1. The square of these values is used to create the uniform acceleration and deceleration.

The .1111 value was derived by dividing the displacement distance by the number of spaces, 2.00/18 = .1111.

4. Label the stack of vertical construction lines as shown.
5. Use the EXTEND command to extend the horizontal construction lines so that they intersect the appropriate vertical degree line.
6. Use the PLINE, PEDIT, FIT CURVE commands to create a smooth, continuous curve between the 0 and 180 degree lines.

The same line many be used to create a deceleration curve as shown.

13-23 CAM FOLLOWERS

There are two basic types of cam followers: ones that roll as they follow the cam's surface, and others that have a fixed surface that slides in contact with the cam surface. Figure 13-39 shows an example of a roller follower and a

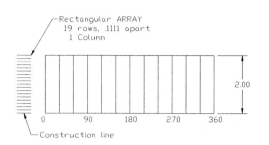

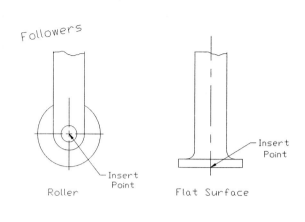

Followers

Roller — Insert Point

Flat Surface — Insert Point

Figure 13-39

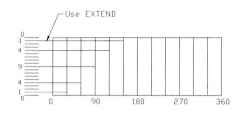

Use EXTEND

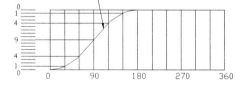

PLINE, PEDIT, FIT CURVE

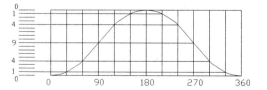

Figure 13-38

fixed or flat surface follower. The flat surface type followers are limited to slow moving cams with low force requirements.

Followers are usually spring loaded to help keep them in contact with the cam surface during operation. Springs were discussed in Section 11-26.

13-24 SAMPLE PROBLEM SP13-7

Design a cam that rises 2.00 inches over 180 degrees using harmonic motion, dwells for 60 degrees, then descends 2.00 inches in 90 degrees using modified uniform motion, and dwells the remaining 30 degrees. The base circle for the cam is 3.00 inches in diameter and the follower is a roller type with a 1.00-inch diameter. The cam will rotate in a counterclockwise direction. The center hole is .75 inches in diameter with a .125 × .875 keyway. See Figures 13-40 and 13-41.

1. Set up a displacement diagram as described in Section 13-21.
2. Define a path between the 0 and 180 degree vertical lines using the method described for harmonic motion. Draw the required circle on the left end of the diagram as shown.
3. Draw a horizontal line from the 180- to 240-degree line.

This line defines the follower's dwell.

4. DRAW two ARCS of .50 radius, one tangent to the top horizontal line of the displacement diagram and the second tangent to the bottom line.

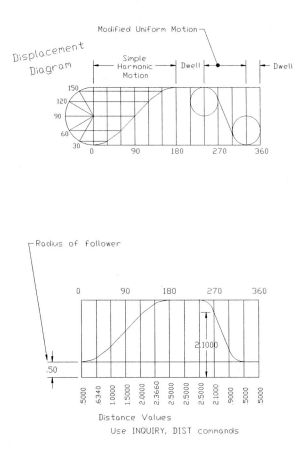

Figure 13-40

DRAW one ARC on the 240-degree line and the other on the 330-degree line as shown. In this example the arcs have a radius equal to .25 of the total displacement. Any convenient radius value could be used.

5. Use the OSNAP, TANGENT commands and DRAW a LINE tangent to the two ARCS.
6. ERASE and TRIM any excess lines and constructions.

This completes the displacement diagram. The follower distances are now transferred to the cam's base circle to define the surface shape. See Figure 13-41.

7. DRAW two concentric CIRCLES of 3.00 and 8.00 diameters.

The 3.00 diameter is the base circle. The 8.00 diame-

ter circle value is derived from the radius of the base circle plus the maximum displacement plus the radius of the follower, 1.50 + 2 + .5 = 4.00 radius or 8.00 diameter.

8. Use the SETVAR, DIMCEN, −.2, DIM, CENTER commands to draw the center lines for the 8.00 CIRCLE.
9. Use the ARRAY command and polar array the top portion of the vertical center line 12 times around the full 360 degrees.
10. Label the ray lines as shown.

Note that the top vertical ray line is labeled both as 0 and 360.

11. Transfer the follower distances from the displacement diagram to the cam drawing.

There are several different techniques that can be used to transfer the distances.

The DIM, VERTICAL or INQUIRY, DIST command could be used to determine the displacement distances. Use the OSNAP, INTERSECTION commands to ensure accuracy. In this example the measured distance values are listed below the displacement diagram in Figure 13-40. The .50 addition to the bottom of the diagram is to account for the .50 follower radius. Note how the distance of 2.1000 was measured.

The distance values can be used to draw lines from the base circle along the appropriate ray line on the cam drawing using relative coordinate values. The values for this example are as follows.

```
 .5000-(0)    @.5000<90
 .6340-(30)   @.6340<60
1.0000-(60)   @1.0000<30
1.5000-(90)   @1.5000<0
2.0000-(120)  @2.0000<–30
2.3660-(150)  @2.3660<–60
2.5000-(180)  @2.5000<–90
2.5000-(210)  @2.5000<–120
2.5000-(240)  @2.5000<–150
2.1000-(270)  @2.1000<180
 .9000-(300)  @.9000<150
 .5000-(330)  @.5000<120
```

LINES could be drawn over the existing vertical lines between the base line and the displacement path on the displacement diagram. The MOVE, ROTATE or GRIPS, ROTATE command could be used to transfer the lines to the base circle and appropriate ray line.

12. DRAW CIRCLEs of diameter .50, representing the roller follower, with their center points on the ends of the lines created in step 11.

Note that these lines and their endpoints are not visible on the screen because they are drawn directly over the existing ray lines. The OSNAP, ENDPOINT command should be used to locate the circle's center point.

13. Use the DRAW, POLYLINE command and draw a line tangent to the follower at each ray line.

The tangent point for each ray may not be exactly on the ray line.

14. Use the MODIFY, POLYEDIT, SPLINE commands to create the cam surface.
15. DRAW the center hole and keyway using the given dimensions.
16. SAVE the drawings if desired.

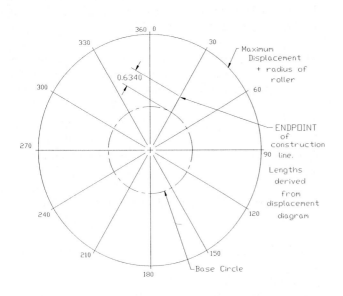

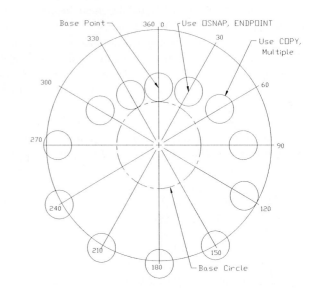

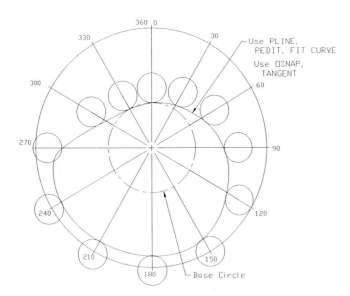

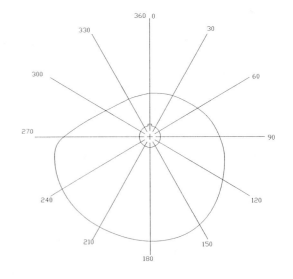

Figure 13-41

13-25 EXERCISE PROBLEMS

EX13-1 INCHES

Draw a spur gear with 24 teeth on a 4.00 pitch circle. The fillets at the base of each tooth have a radius of .0625. Locate a 1.00 diameter mounting hole in the center of the gear.

EX13-2 MILLIMETERS

Draw a spur gear with 36 teeth on a 100 pitch circle. The fillets at the base of each tooth have a radius of 3. Locate a 20 diameter mounting hole in the center of the gear.

EX13-3

Use the information presented in Figure 13-11 and draw front and side sectional views of gear number P32S34-60.

EX13-4

Use the information presented in Figure 13-12 and draw front and side sectional views of gear number A 1C22MYKW150-64A.

EX13-5

Use the information presented in Figure 13-15 and draw a sectional view of bevel gears A 1C 3 MYK 30018 and A 1C 3MYK 30036H.

EX13-6

Use the information presented in Figure 13-16 and draw a sectional view of the matched set of bevel gears S1346Z-48S30A120.

EX13-7

Use the information presented in Figure 13-19 and draw front and side views of a set of worm gears.

EX13-8

Use the information presented in Figure 13-22 and draw a front view of a matched set of helical gears.

EX13-9

Use the information presented in Figure 13-24 and draw a front view of a set of rack and pinion gears.

EX13-10

Draw a displacement diagram and appropriate cam based on the following information.

Dwell for 60 degrees, rise 1.00 inch using harmonic motion over 180 degrees, dwell for 30 degrees, then descend 1.00 using harmonic motion over 90 degrees.

The cam's base circle is 4.00 inches in diameter. Include a 1.25 inch center mounting hole.

EX13-11

Draw a displacement diagram and appropriate cam based on the following information.

Dwell for 60 degrees, rise 30 millimeters using harmonic motion over 180 degrees, dwell for 30 degrees, then descend 30 millimeters using harmonic motion over 90 degrees.

The cam's base circle is 120 millimeters in diameter. Include a 20-millimeter center mounting hole.

EX13-12

Draw a displacement diagram and appropriate cam based on the following information.

Rise 1.25 inches over 180 degrees using uniform acceleration motion, dwell for 60 degrees, descend 1.25 inches over 90 degrees using modified uniform motion, dwell for 30 degrees.

The cam's base circle is 3.25 inches in diameter. Include a .75 diameter center mounting hole.

EX13-13

Draw a displacement diagram and appropriate cam based on the following information.

Rise 20 millimeters over 180 degrees using uniform acceleration motion, dwell for 60 degrees, descend 20 millimeters over 90 degrees using modified uniform motion, dwell for 30 degrees.

The cam's base circle is 80 millimeters in diameter. Include a 16 diameter center mounting hole.

EX13-14

Draw a displacement diagram and appropriate cam based on the following information.

Rise .60 inches in 90 degrees using harmonic motion, dwell for 30 degrees, rise .60 inches in 60 degrees using modified uniform motion, dwell 60 degrees, descend 1.20 inches using uniform deceleration in 120 degrees.

The cam's base circle is 3.20 inches in diameter. Include a 1.75 diameter center mounting hole.

EX13-15

Draw a displacement diagram and appropriate cam based on the following information.

Rise 16 millimeters in 90 degrees using harmonic motion, dwell for 30 degrees, rise 16 millimeters in 60 degrees using modified uniform motion, dwell 60 degrees, descend 32 millimeters using uniform deceleration in 120 degrees.

The cam's base circle is 84 millimeters in diameter. Include a 20 diameter center mounting hole.

DESIGN EXERCISES

EX13-16

An electrical motor operates at 1750 rpm. Design a gear system that includes at least 4 spur gears and reduces the motor speed by a ratio of 4:1.

Draw the gear setups. Assume that the center distances have a tolerance of +.001,−.000 and the support shafts have tolerances of +.0000, −.0002 or their metric equivalent.

A. Draw an assembly drawing showing the gears in their assembled positions.

B. Support the gear shafts with either bushings or ball bearings press fitted into the support plate. The support plate is to be 0.50″ or 12 mm thick. The length and width dimensions are arbitrary.

C. Draw detail drawings of the required support plates. Included dimensions and tolerances. Locate all support holes using positional tolerances.

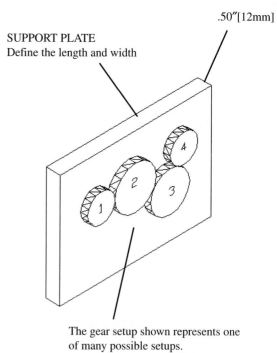

.50″[12mm]

SUPPORT PLATE
Define the length and width

The gear setup shown represents one of many possible setups.
Consider mounting two gears on the same shaft to save space.

See the tables in Chapter 13 and in the appendix for gear, shaft, and bearing selections.

EX13-17

An electric motor operates at 3600 rpm. Design a gear system that includes at least 4 spur gears (more may be used if needed) and reduces the motor speed to between 400 to 500 rpm.

Enclose the gears in a box made from .50″ [12mm] plates, assembled using flathead screws. There should be at least three screws per edge on the box.

Extend the shafts for the input and output at least .50[12] from the box. The other shafts should end at the edge of the box. Mount each shaft using two ball bearings, one mounted in each support plate.

Assume that the center distances have a tolerance of +.001,–.000 and the support shafts have tolerances of +.0000, –.0002, or their metric equivalent.

A. Draw an assembly drawing showing the gears in their assembled positions.

B. Support the gear shafts with ball bearings press fitted into the support plate. The support plate is to be 0.50″ or 12 mm thick. The length and width dimensions are arbitrary, but there should be at least .25 [6] clearance between the GEARS and the SUPPORT PLATE.

C. Draw detail drawings of the required support plates. Included dimensions and tolerances. Locate all support holes using positional tolerances.

The figure shown represents half the gear box. The other half includes another END, TOP, and SUPPORT PLATE.

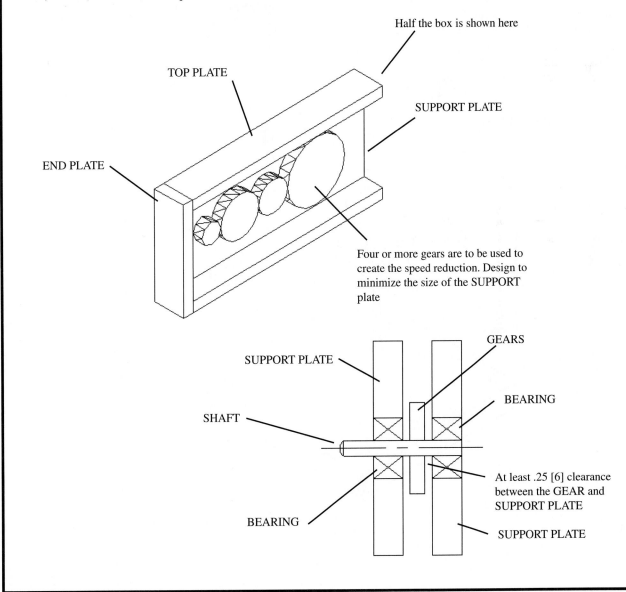

Half the box is shown here

TOP PLATE

SUPPORT PLATE

END PLATE

Four or more gears are to be used to create the speed reduction. Design to minimize the size of the SUPPORT plate

GEARS

SUPPORT PLATE

SHAFT

BEARING

BEARING

At least .25 [6] clearance between the GEAR and SUPPORT PLATE

SUPPORT PLATE

EX13-18

The figure below shows a general setup for matched bevel gears. Complete the design for a gear box with a ratio of 3:1 between the two gears. Select appropriate bearings and fasteners. Dimension and tolerance the shaft sizes and each of the six supporting plates. Extend the input and output shafts at least 1.00″ [24mm] beyond the surface of the box.

Assume that the center distances have a tolerance of +.001,−.000 and the support shafts have a tolerance of +.0000, −.0002, or their metric equivalent.

The figure shown represents half the gear box. The other half includes another three plates without the holes for the shafts. There should be at least three screws in each edge of the box.

A. Draw an assembly drawing showing the gears in their assembled positions.

B. Support the gear shafts with ball bearings press fitted into the support plate. The support plate is to be 0.50″ or 12 mm thick. The length and width dimensions are arbitrary, but there should be at least .375 [10] clearance between the gears and the support plates.

C. Draw detail drawings of the required support plates. Included dimensions and tolerances. Locate all support holes using positional tolerances.

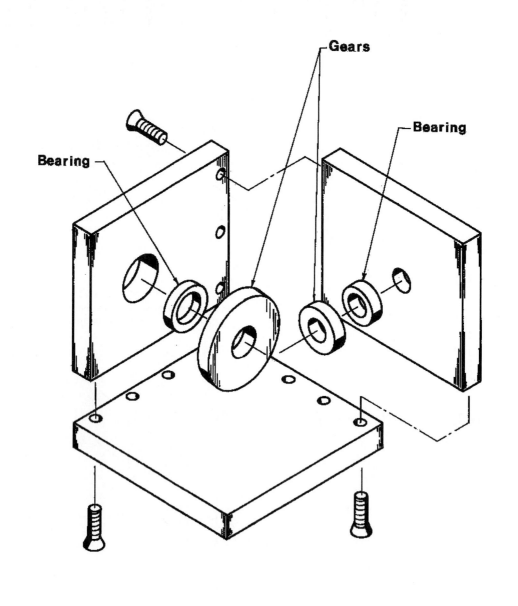

Fundamentals of 3D Drawing

14-1 INTRODUCTION

This chapter introduces the fundamental concepts needed to produce 3D drawings using AutoCAD. The chapter shows how to change viewpoints and how to create, save, and work with user defined coordinate systems called user coordinate systems, or UCSs.

The chapter will demonstrate how to use both the View and UCS toolbars. It will also show how to create orthographic views from given 3D objects using the View toolbar.

14-2 THE WORLD COORDINATE SYSTEM

AutoCAD's absolute coordinate system is called the world coordinate system (WCS). The default settings for the WCS position it so you are looking at the system 90 degrees to its XY plane. See Figure 14-1. The Z axis is also perpendicular to the XY plane, or directly aligned with your viewpoint. This setup is ideal for 2D drawings and is called a plan view. All your drawings up to now have been done in this orientation.

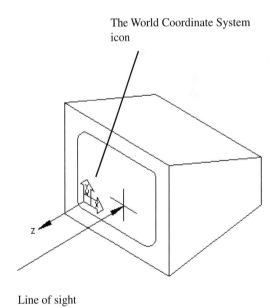

The World Coordinate System icon

Line of sight

Figure 14-1

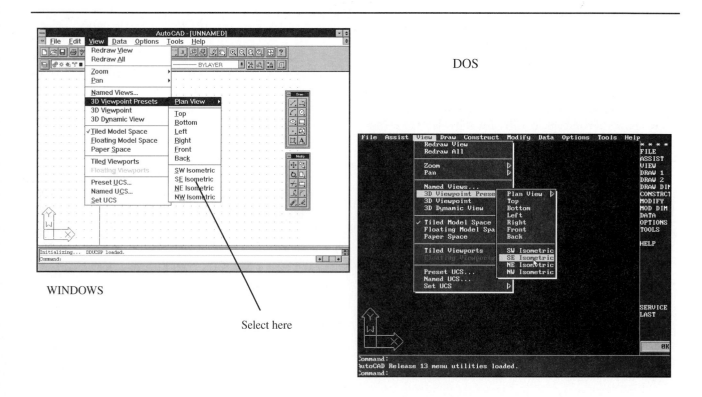

Figure 14-2

Figure 14-3

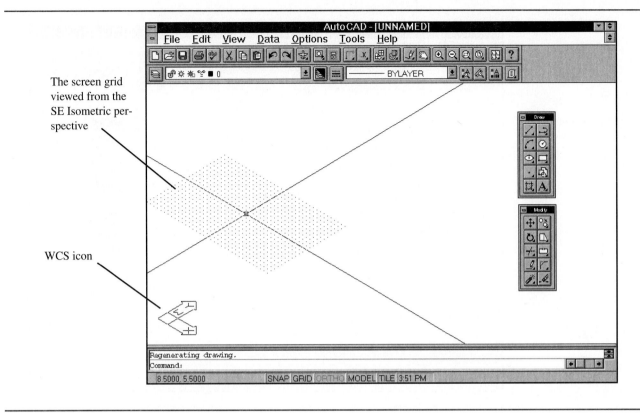

The screen grid viewed from the SE Isometric perspective

WCS icon

Figure 14-4

Figure 14-2 shows a standard drawing screen setup oriented so that you are looking directly down on the XY plane of the world coordinate system. Note the icon in the lower left corner of the screen. The W indicates that it is the WCS, and the X and Y indicate the orientation of these axes. The WCS icon will always be present when you are in the WCS.

14-3 VIEWPOINTS

The orientation of the WCS may be changed by changing the drawing's viewpoint. There are two ways to change the viewpoint: use the View pulldown menu or the View toolbar.

To change the viewpoint using the View pulldown menu

This exercise assumes that the screen includes a grid. The grid serves to help define a visual orientation.

1. Select the View pulldown menu
2. Select 3D Viewpoint Presets

See Figure 14-3. The current WCS orientation is the Plan View setting.

3. Select SE Isometric

The drawing will now be oriented as shown in Figure 14-4. Note the change in the WCS icon. It is important to remember that you are still in the WCS, but are merely looking at it from a different perspective. This concept may be verified by drawing some simple shapes. Figure 14-5 shows a rectangular shape created using the LINE command, and a circle created using the CIRCLE command. These shapes are 2D shapes drawn on the WCS.

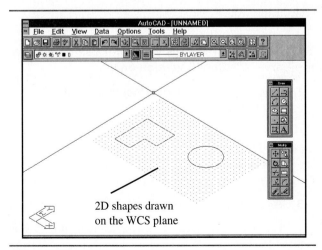

2D shapes drawn on the WCS plane

Figure 14-5

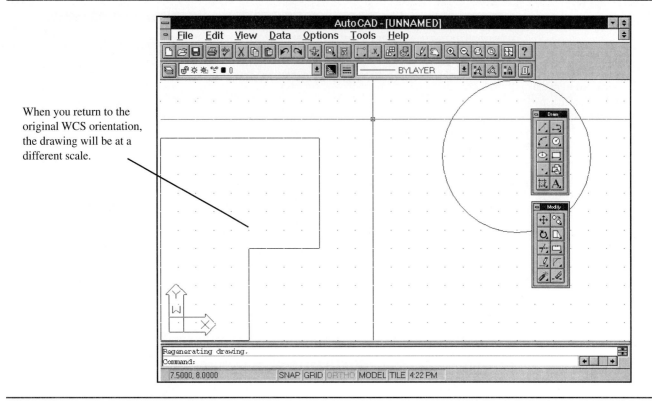

When you return to the original WCS orientation, the drawing will be at a different scale.

Figure 14-6

To return to the original WCS orientation

1. Select the View pulldown menu
2. Select 3D Viewpoint Presets, Plan View, World

See Figure 14-6. The drawing will reappear on the screen at a different scale than was originally defined.

3. Select the Zoom All command

See Figure 14-7. If the Zoom All command does not produce a satisfactory scale, type ZOOM and specify a scale factor: .75, .50, etc.

To change the drawing's viewpoint using the View toolbar — WINDOWS version only

1. Select the Tools pulldown menu
2. Select Toolbars, then View

The View toolbar will appear on the screen. It can be moved and reshaped as described in Chapter 1. Figure 14-8 shows both the View toolbar and the View, 3D Viewpoint Presets menus. The same commands are included in both.

3. Select the SE Isometric View icon

The screen will return to the same orientation as was achieved using the SE Isometric command listed on the

View pulldown menu, Figure 14-4. The scale will be larger, so use the ZOOM command to achieve a smaller scale.

4. Type ZOOM ENTER

All/Center/Dynamic/Extents/Left/Previous/Vmax/ Window/<Scale(X/XP)>:

5. Type .75 ENTER

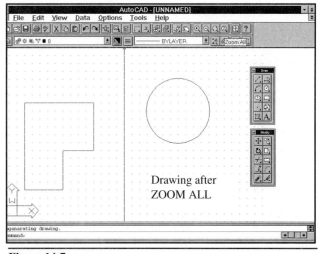

Drawing after ZOOM ALL

Figure 14-7

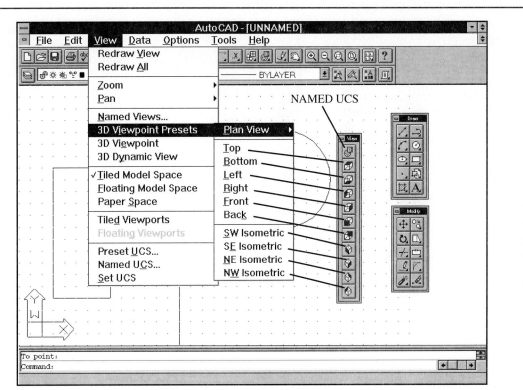

NAMED UCS

DOS
Use the View pull-down menu to access the view-point commands

WINDOWS
The viewpoint commands may be accessed using either the pulldown menus or the View toolbar.

Figure 14-8

To return to the original WCS orientation

1. Select the Top View command

The original plan view orientation will return to the screen. Use the ZOOM command to reduce the drawing's scale size if necessary. In Figure 14-9 a zoom scale factor of .5 was used.

It is suggested that you try several of the View tool-bar commands and watch how the WCS icon and grid pattern change. Remember the Top View command will return the Plan view WCS orientation.

14-4 USER COORDINATE SYSTEMS (UCSs)

User coordinate systems are coordinate systems that you define relative to the WCS. Drawings often contain several UCSs. UCSs can be saved and recalled.

Figure 14-10 shows a wedge orientated using the SE Isometric View icon. This section assumes that a wedge shape already exists on the screen and will create a UCS aligned with the slanted surface of the wedge.

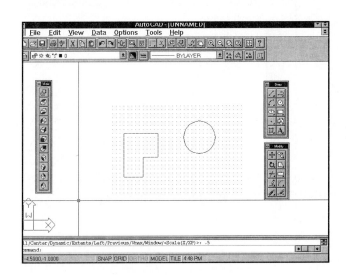

Zoom factor = .5

Figure 14-9

To create a UCS

1. Select the View pulldown menu
2. Select Set UCS

The UCS toolbar will appear on the screen. As with viewpoints, UCS related commands can be accessed in the WINDOWS version either through a toolbar or through pulldown menus. Figure 14-11 shows both the UCS toolbar and the UCS pulldown menus.

3. Select the 3 Point option

*Origin/Zaxis/3point/OBject/View/X/Y/ZPrev/
Restore/Save/Del/?/<World>:_3
Origin point <0,0,0>:*

4. Select the lower right corner of the wedge

*Point on positive portion of the X-axis
<10.0000,3.5000,0.0000>:*

The given coordinate values are the coordinate values of the new origin point relative to the WCS. See Figure 14-12.

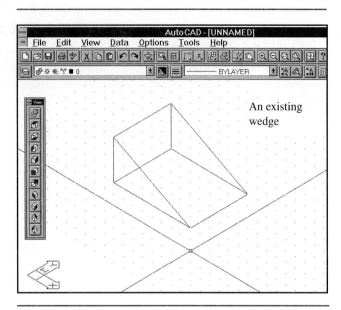

An existing wedge

Figure 14-10

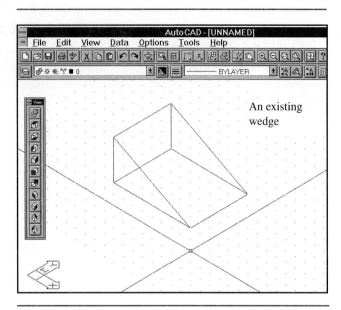

Preset UCS

Named UCS

The screen shown is for the WINDOWS version. The VIEW pulldown menu in the DOS version will yield the same menus.

The UCS commands may be accessed using either the View pull-down menu or the UCS toolbar.

Figure 14-11

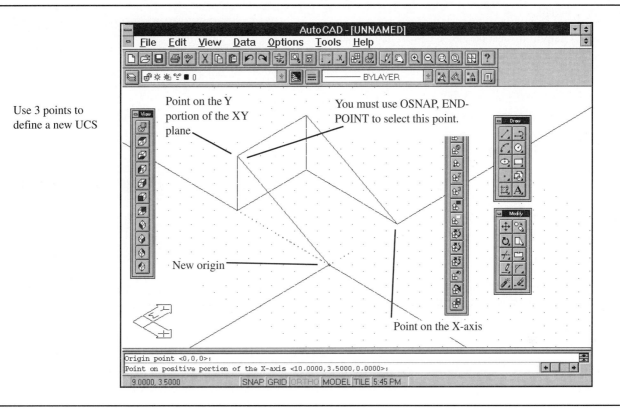

Figure 14-12

5. Select the lower right corner of the wedge

Point on the positive-Y portion of the UCS XY plane <8,3.5,0.0>:

6. Use Object Snap, Endpoint option and select the upper left corner of the wedge.

It is imperative that the Endpoint option of the OBJECT SNAP command be used to locate the point. The crosshairs will move only in the current coordinate plane. In this exercise we are still in the WCS because the new UCS has not been completely defined yet. If you were to try to select the upper corner of the wedge visually, that is, by moving the crosshairs so that they appeared to be located on the corner, you would get an incorrect result. The selected point would actually be a point on the WCS directly behind the corner point.

NOTE:
The OBJECT SNAP command must be used to select points not in the current coordinate system.

Figure 14-13 shows the reorientated coordinate system.

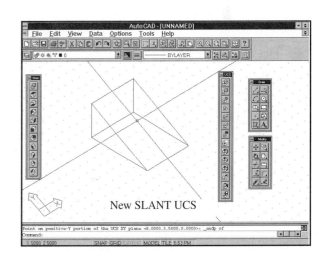

Figure 14-13

To save a UCS

It is helpful to save defined UCSs so that if they are needed again during the preparation of the drawing, they will not have to be redefined.

1. Select the Save UCS command

Origin/Zaxis/3point/OBject/View/X/Y/ZPrev/ Restore/Save/Del/?/<World>:_s
?/Desired UCS name:

2. Type Slant ENTER

Command:

To return to the WCS using named UCSs

1. Select the Named UCS command

The UCS Control dialog box will appear. See Figure 14-14. Note that the Slant UCS is the current UCS.

2. Select *WORLD* in the UCS Names box
3. Select Current

The word Current will move from the SLANT line to the *WORLD* line

4. Select OK

The original WCS will return to the screen.

To return to the WCS directly

1. Select the World UCS icon or the World command on the Set UCS menu

14-5 WORKING WITH UCSs

Drawing with AutoCAD in 3D is limited to the UCS orientation. You can draw only in the current UCS, such as the circle shown in Figure 14-15. You cannot draw a circle on the slanted surface of the wedge or on the side or back surfaces of the wedge using the current UCS orientation. You must draw on a surface orientated to the surface you wish to work on.

To draw on a slanted surface

To draw on the slanted surface shown in Figure 14-15, we must first move to a UCS orientated to the slanted surface. A UCS named SLANT was created in the previous section, so we will return to that UCS and then draw a circle. The procedure is as follows.

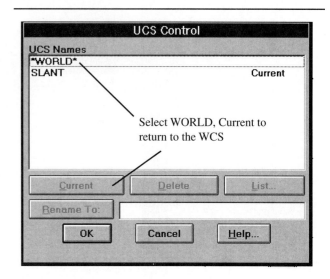

Figure 14-14

1. Select the NAMED UCS icon

The UCS Control dialog box will appear. See Figure 14-16.

2. Select the SLANT UCS and make it the Current3. Select OK

The screen will be reorientated to the SLANT UCS settings.

4. Use the CIRCLE to draw circle

See Figure 14-17.

5. Select the World UCS icon to return to the original drawing orientation.

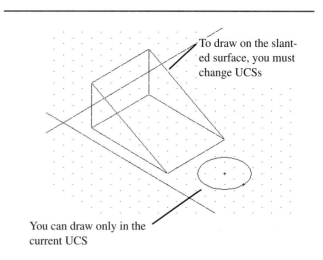

Figure 14-15

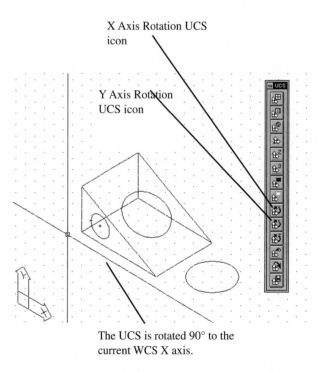

Fugure 14-16

To draw on a surface perpendicular to the X axis

The side surface of the wedge is perpendicular to the WCS. To draw on the side surface we must reorientate the current surface UCS to be aligned with the side surface. In addition, we must also align the origin of the axis with the side surface.

1. Select the X Axis Rotation UCS command

   Origin/Zaxis/3point/OBject/View/X/Y/ZPrev/ Restore/Save/Del/?/<World>:_x
   Rotation angle about X axis <0.00>:

2. Type 90 ENTER

The drawing icon in the lower left corner of the screen will shift positions, and the letter W will disappear from the icon because the drawing is no longer in the WCS.

3. Select the Origin command

   Origin/Zaxis/3point/OBject/View/X/Y/ZPrev/ Restore/Save/Del/?/<World>:_o
   Origin point<0,0,0>:

4. Use OSNAP, ENDPOINT (shift key, right mouse button), and select the lower left corner of the wedge.

The origin has now been shifted. This can be verified by locating the crosshairs on the lower left corner of the wedge and checking the coordinate display at the bottom of the screen.

5. Use the CIRCLE command to draw a circle on the side surface of the wedge

   See Figure 14-18.

6. Select the World command to return the drawing to its original WCS orientation

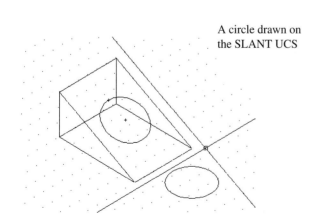

A circle drawn on the SLANT UCS

Figure 14-17

X Axis Rotation UCS icon

Y Axis Rotation UCS icon

The UCS is rotated 90° to the current WCS X axis.

Figure 14-18

To draw a circle on the back surface of the wedge

1. Select the Y Axis Rotation from the Set UCS menu

   Origin/Zaxis/3point/OBject/View/X/Y/ZPrev/
   Restore/Save/Del/?/<World>:_y
   Rotation angle about the Y axis <0.00>:

2. Type 90 ENTER

   The drawing icon in the lower left corner of the screen will shift positions, and the letter W will disappear from the icon because the drawing is no longer in the WCS.

3. Select the Origin command

   Origin/Zaxis/3point/OBject/View/X/Y/ZPrev/
   Restore/Save/Del/?/<World>:_o
   Origin point<0,0,0>:

4. Use OSNAP, ENDPOINT (shift key, right mouse button), and select the lower left corner of the wedge.
5. Use the CIRCLE command to draw a circle on the side surface of the wedge

   See Figure 14-19.

14-6 PRESET UCSs

AutoCAD includes a group of preset UCS orientations. Figure 14-20 shows the UCS Orientation dialog box. The preset orientations are set up to help generate standard orthographic views. The icons in the dialog box can also be used to return to the last previous UCS you were working on, or to return to the WCS.

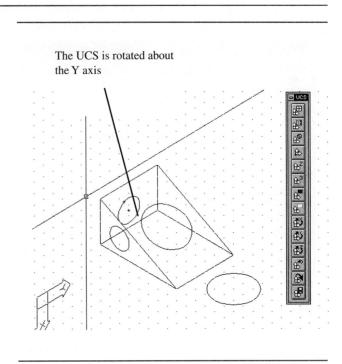

The UCS is rotated about the Y axis

Figure 14-19

Figure 14-21 shows an L-shaped object. This section assumes that a 3D L-shaped object, as shown in Figure 14-21, already exists on the screen. The WINDOWS toolbars shown in Figure 14-21 are directly equivalent to the commands listed in the View and Set UCS menus under the View pulldown menus.

To avoid visual errors

When working in 3D, it is important to remember that you cannot rely on visual inputs to locate shapes. What

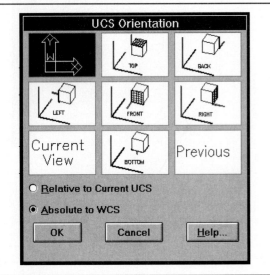

Figure 14-20

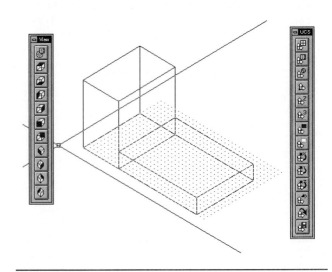

Figure 14-21

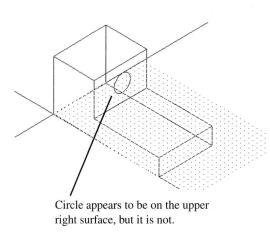

Circle appears to be on the upper
right surface, but it is not.

Figure 14-22

you see may be misleading. For example, Figure 14-22
shows a circle that appears to be drawn on the upper right
surface of an L-shaped object. In fact, the circle is not
located on the surface; it only appears to be on the surface.
Figure 14-23 shows a top view of the same drawing. The
circle is actually drawn behind the surface and off the
object. It appears to be located on the surface because of
the line of sight of the current viewpoint orientation. This
visual distortion can be avoided by ensuring that the origin
for the current UCS is located on the plane where you are
working.

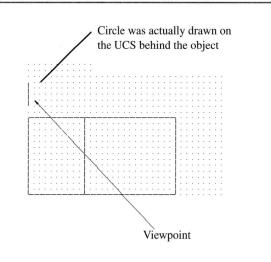

Circle was actually drawn on
the UCS behind the object

Viewpoint

Figure 14-23

To locate the screen icon on the current origin

To help avoid visual errors based on an incorrectly
located origin, it is best to set the screen icon so that it is
located directly on the current origin.

1. Select the Options pulldown menu

   See Figure 14-24.

2. Select UCS
3. Select Icon Origin

The Icon Origin option will locate the screen
icon on the current UCS origin

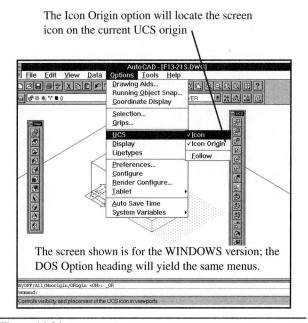

The screen shown is for the WINDOWS version; the
DOS Option heading will yield the same menus.

Figure 14-24

The screen icon has been relocated to
the current UCS origin

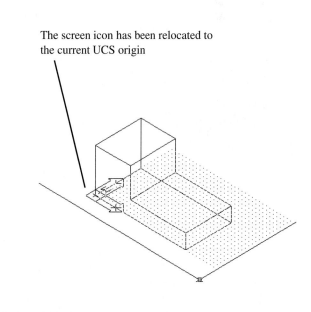

Figure 14-25

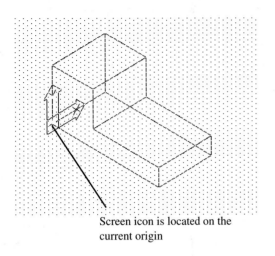

Screen icon is located on the
current origin

Figure 14-26

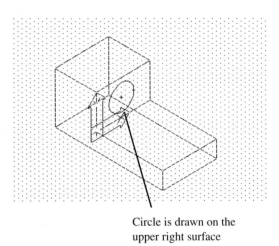

Circle is drawn on the
upper right surface

Figure 14-28

There should be a check mark to the left of the word Icon. After Icon Origin has been selected, there should be check marks next to both the words Icon and Icon Origin. The screen icon should move to the current origin: 0,0,0 on the WCS. See Figure 14-25.

To draw in the right plane of an object using preset UCSs

This section will draw a circle on the inside right plane of the object shown in Figure 14-21.

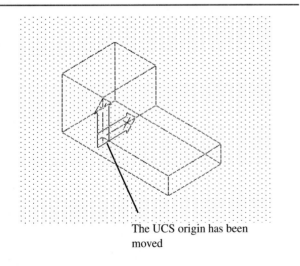

The UCS origin has been
moved

Figure 14-27

1. Select the Preset UCS command

   The UCS Orientation dialog box will appear.

2. Select the RIGHT option, then OK

   The screen icon and grid pattern will change as shown in Figure 14-26. It is important to note that the origin of current RIGHT UCS is still located at the 0,0,0 point on the WCS. If you try to draw now, the shapes will be located on a plane aligned with the 0,0,0 origin. The origin must be moved before you can draw on the inside right surface of the object.

3. Select the Origin UCS command

   Origin/Zaxis/3point/OBject/View/X/Y/ZPrev/Restore/Save/Del/?/<World>:_o
   Origin point<0,0,0>:

4. Use OSNAP, ENDPOINT (shift key, right mouse button) and select the lower left corner of the inside right surface

   The origin of the RIGHT UCS is now located at the lower left corner of the inside right surface of the object. The screen icon will move to this new origin location. See Figure 14-27.

5. Use the CIRCLE command to draw a circle as shown in Figure 14-28.

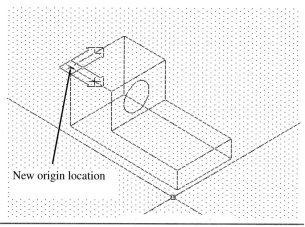

Figure 14-29

New origin location

To draw more complex shapes on UCSs

In this section, a slot shape will be drawn on the upper top surface of the object shown in Figure 14-28. The shape can be drawn directly on the surface once a UCS has been established, but in this exercise we will change the view orientation to create a 2D drawing surface.

1. Select the World command
2. Select the Origin command

Origin/Zaxis/3point/OBject/View/X/Y/ZPrev/
Restore/Save/Del/?/<World>:_o
Origin point<0,0,0>:

3. Use OSNAP, ENDPOINT (shift key, right mouse button) and select the lower left corner of the upper top surface

The screen icon will shift to the designated origin corner. See Figure 14-29.

4. Select the Top View command
5. Type Zoom ENTER

All/Center/Dynamic/Extents/Left/Previous/Vmax/
Window/<Scale(X/XP)>:

6. Type .5 ENTER

A top view of the object will appear on the screen as shown in Figure 14-30.

7. Use the LINE, CIRCLE, and TRIM commands to create the slot shape shown in Figure 14-31.
8. Select the SE Isometric View command

The object will appear oversized. Use the ZOOM command to reduce its appearance and size.

9. Type Zoom ENTER

All/Center/Dynamic/Extents/Left/Previous/Vmax/
Window/<Scale(X/XP)>:

10. Type .5 ENTER

Your screen should look like Figure 14-32. Use the VIEW, PAN commands to reposition the object if desired, or move the toolbars if necessary to give an unobstructed view of the object.

11. Select the World command to return to the original WCS orientation

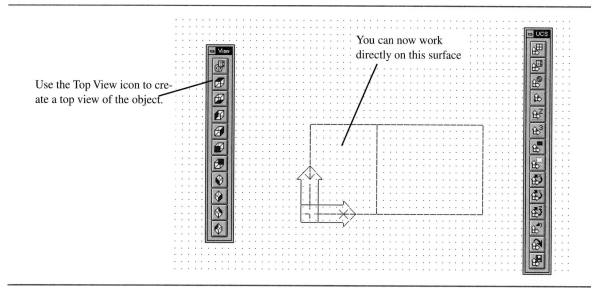

Use the Top View icon to create a top view of the object.

You can now work directly on this surface

Figure 14-30

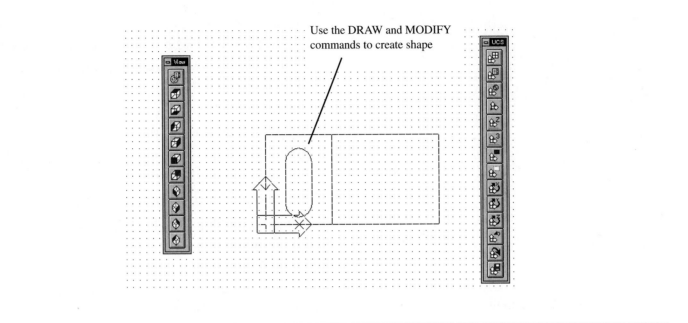

Use the DRAW and MODIFY
commands to create shape

Figure 14-31

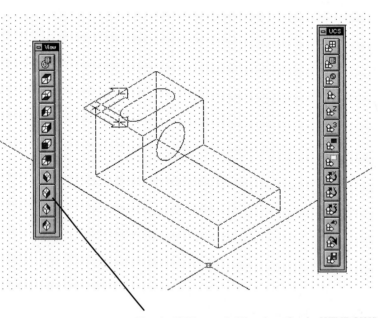

Use the SE Isometric View icon for the WINDOWS
version, or the SE Isometric command on theView,
3D Viewpoint Presets to return to the original view
orientation

Figure 14-32

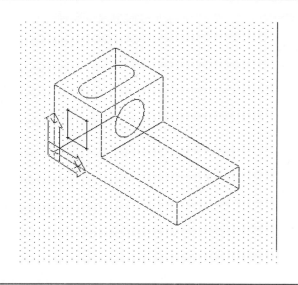

Figure 14-33

To draw on the FRONT surface

1. Select the Presets UCS command

   The UCS Orientation dialog box will appear.

2. Select the FRONT option, OK

   The screen icon will appear at the lower left corner of

the front surface because this corner of the object was originally located on the origin of the WCS. It is not necessary to relocate the origin.

3. Use the RECTANGLE or LINE command to draw a rectangular shape on the FRONT surface as shown in Figure 14-33.

   The rectangle will appear to be out of visual perspective as you draw it, but it will be drawn in the correct orientation after the corner points are defined.

4. Use the World command to return to the original WCS orientation.

14-7 ORTHOGRAPHIC VIEWS

Once a 3D object has been created, orthographic views may be taken directly from the object. The screen is first split into four ports, each showing the 3D object. The viewpoint of three of the ports will be changed to create the front, top, and right-side views of the object.

1. Select the View pulldown menu

   See Figure 14-34.

2. Select Tiled Viewports, 4 Viewports

The screen shown is for the WINDOWS version; the View heading on the DOS version will yield the same pulldown menus

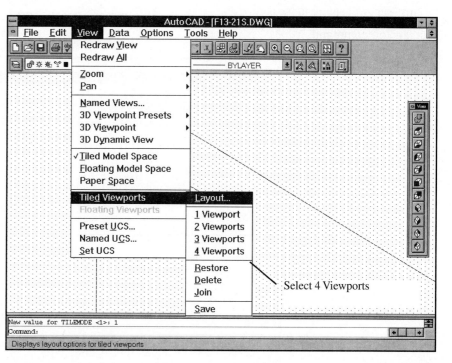

Figure 14-34

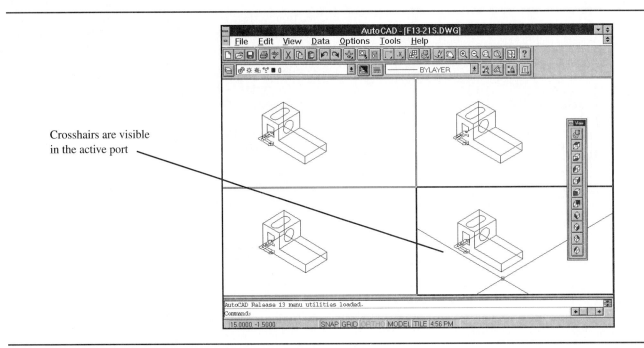

Crosshairs are visible in the active port

Figure 14-35

See Figure 14-35. Note that crosshairs are visible in only the lower left view port. An arrow will appear if the cursor is moved into any other port.

3. Move the cursor into the top left port and press the left mouse button

The crosshairs will appear in the port.

4. Select the Top command

An oversized top view of the object will appear in the port.

5. Type Zoom ENTER

All/Center/Dynamic/Extents/Left/Previous/Vmax/Window/<Scale(X/XP)>:

6. Type .75 ENTER

See Figure 14-36.

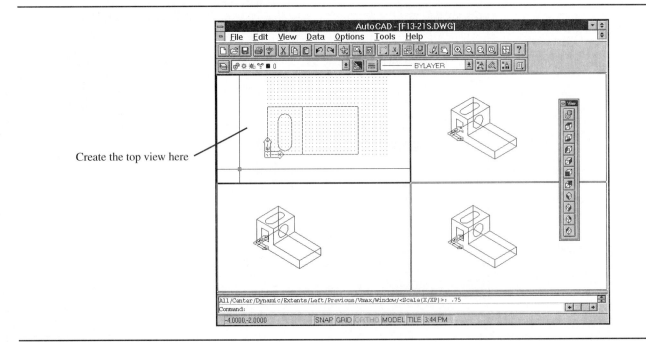

Create the top view here

Figure 14-36

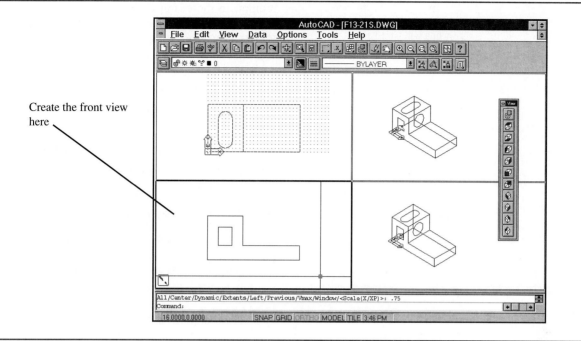

Create the front view here

Figure 14-37

7. Move the cursor into the lower left port and press the left mouse button.

The crosshairs will appear in the port.

8. Select the Front View command
9. Type Zoom, ENTER, then .75 ENTER

See Figure 14-37.

10. Move the cursor to the lower right port and press the left mouse button
11. Select the Right View command
12. Type Zoom ENTER, then .75 ENTER

See Figure 14-38.

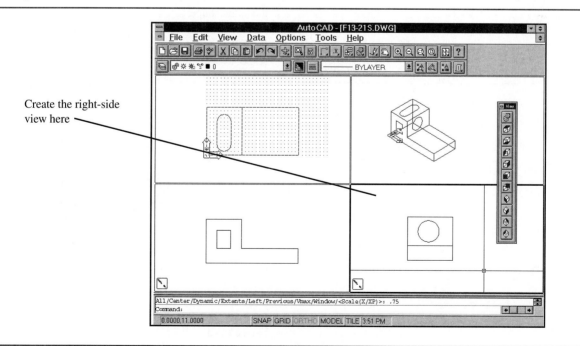

Create the right-side view here

Figure 14-38

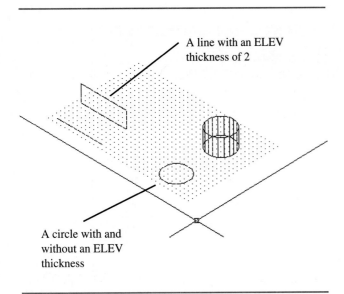

A line with an ELEV thickness of 2

A circle with and without an ELEV thickness

Figure 14-39

14-8 ELEV

The ELEV (elevation) command is used to create surfaces from 2D drawing commands. Figure 14-39 shows a line and a circle drawn as normal 2D entities and then drawn a second time with the ELEV command thickness set for 2. The LINE command generates a plane perpendicular to the plane of the original line, and the CIRCLE command generates a cylinder perpendicular to the plane of the base circle.

To use the ELEV command

There is no icon for the ELEV command. It is accessed by typing ELEV in response to a Command:

prompt. In the example shown below, GRID and SNAP have .5 spacing using decimal units, and there is an SE ISOMETRIC viewpoint.

Command:

1. Type ELEV

   New current elevation <0.0000>:

   The current elevation is the base plane for the constructions. In this example the base plane is the current XY (WCS) plane, that is, the plane with the grid.

2. Type ENTER

   New current thickness <0.0000>:

   The thickness defines the height of the generated planes. It is currently set at 0.0000, so any shapes drawn have no thickness. They are two dimensional.

3. Type 3 ENTER

   The height of the elevation is now set for 3.

4. Select the LINE command

   Command: _line From point:

5. Draw the box shape shown in Figure 14-40.

   The shape shown in the figure is not a box, but is four perpendicular planes. There is no top or bottom surface. This can be seen more clearly in Figure 14-41, which shows a rendering of the surfaces. Chapter 15 shows how to add a 3D FACE to objects, closing in the top and bottom, and Chapter 16 shows how to create a solid object of the same shape.

   Figure 14-42 shows a hexagon and an arc drawn with the ELEV command set at a thickness value of 2 and 4, respectively.

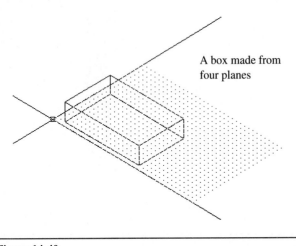

A box made from four planes

Figure 14-40

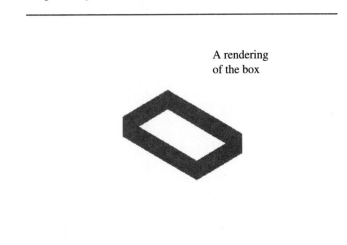

A rendering of the box

Figure 14-41

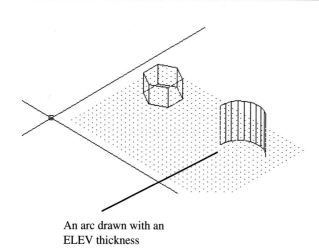

An arc drawn with an
ELEV thickness

Figure 14-42

To draw a curve using ELEV

See Figure 14-43.

1. Type ELEV

New current elevation <0.0000>:

2. Type ENTER

New current thickness <0.0000>:

3. Type 5 ENTER
4. Select the POLYLINE command

Command: _pline

From point:

5. Draw a ployline approximately like the one shown in Figure 14-43
6. Select the EDIT POLYLINE icon from the Modify toolbar

Command: _pedit Select polyline:

7. Select the Polyline

Close/ Join/ Width/ Edit vertex/ Fit/ Spline Decurve/ Ltype gen/ Undo/ eXit/ <X>:

8. Type F ENTER

See Figure 14-44.

14-9 USING THE ELEV COMMAND TO CREATE OBJECTS

The ELEV command can be used along with different UCSs to create 3D objects. The objects will actually be open ended plane structures. The following procedure shows how to create the object shown in Figure 14-45. The drawing shown was created with GRID and SNAP set to .5 using decimal units and with an SE ISOMETRIC viewpoint.

To draw the box

1. Type ELEV ENTER

New current elevation <0.0000>:

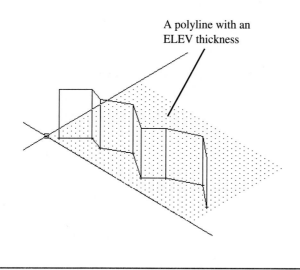

A polyline with an
ELEV thickness

Figure 14-43

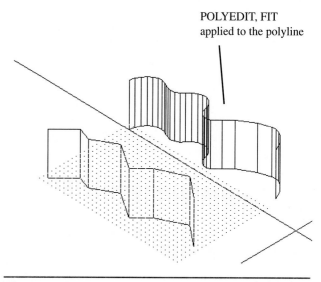

POLYEDIT, FIT
applied to the polyline

Figure 14-44

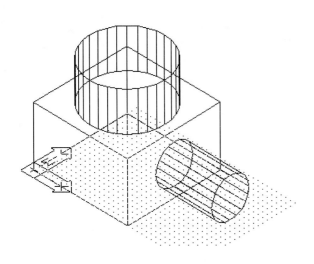

Figure 14-45

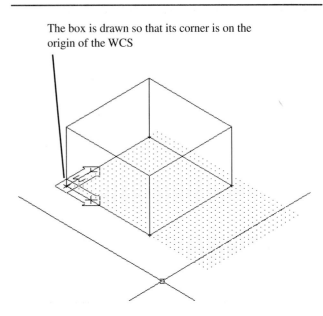

The box is drawn so that its corner is on the origin of the WCS

Figure 14-46

2. Type ENTER

   New current thickness <0.0000>:

3. Type 6 ENTER

   Command:

4. Select the LINE command and draw a 10 x 10 box as shown in Figure 14-46

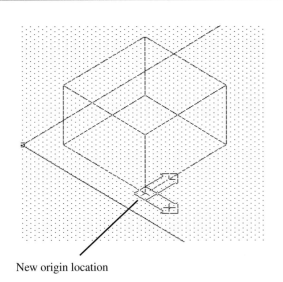

New origin location

Figure 14-47

To create a new UCS

1. Select the ORIGIN command

   Origin point <0,0,0>:

2. Select the lower right corner as shown in Figure 14-47

3. Type ENTER

   Origin/ZAxis/3point/OBject/View/X/Y/Z/Prev/Restore/Save/Del/?/<World>:

4. Type 3 ENTER

   Origin point:

5. Type ENTER

   Point on positive portion of the X-axis <1.0000,0.0000,0.0000>:

6. Use OSNAP, ENDPOINT and select the right corner of the box

   Point on positive-Y portion of the UCS XY plane <-1.0000,0.0000,0.0000>:

7. Use ONSAP, ENDPOINT and select the end of the line directly above the origin

   Your screen should look like Figure 14-48.

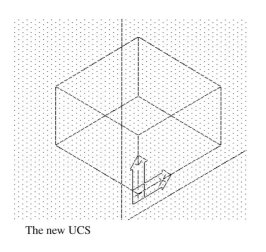

The new UCS

Figure 14-48

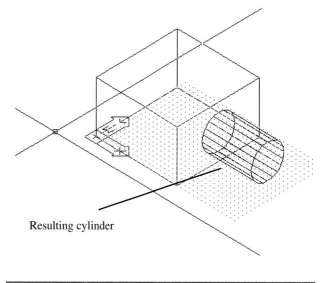

Resulting cylinder

Figure 14-49

To draw the right cylinder

This cylinder will be 6 units long, so there is no need to change the ELEV thickness setting.

1. Select the CIRCLE command and draw a cylinder centered on the right face of the box

The coordinate values for the cylinder's center point will be 5,3 and the radius value = 2.00.

To draw the top cylinder

First return the drawing to the original WCS XY axis, then change the location of the XY plane so the top cylinder can be drawn in the correct position.

1. Select the PRESET UCS command and select the WCS box, then OK

Your screen should look like Figure 14-49.

2. Type ELEV ENTER

New current elevation <0.0000>:

3. Type 6 ENTER

The value 6 was used because this is the thickness of the box.

New current thickness <0.0000:

4. Type 4 ENTER

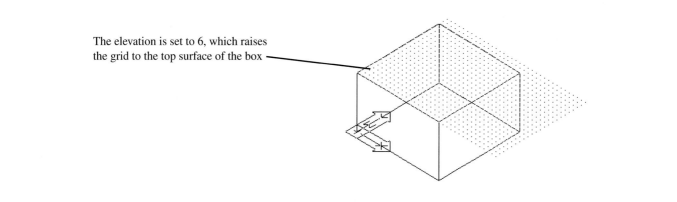

The elevation is set to 6, which raises the grid to the top surface of the box

Figure 14-50

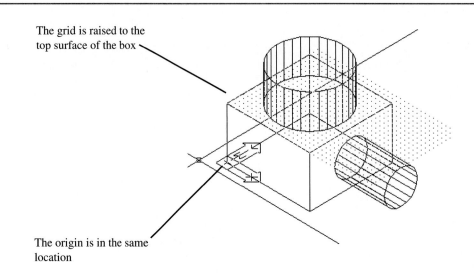

The grid is raised to the top surface of the box

The origin is in the same location

Figure 14-51

Notice the shift in the GRID pattern. The WCS origin icon is still located at the same place, but the grid origin is on the top surface. See Figure 14-50. Positions on the top surface may be located using the displayed coordinate values.

5. Select the CIRCLE command and draw the cylinder as shown in Figure 14-51

The cylinder's center point is at 5,5 and its radius = 4.

6. Type ELEV ENTER

   New current elevation <6.0000>:

7. Type 0 ENTER

   New current thickness <4.0000>:

8. Type 0 ENTER

The object should look like the one shown in Figure 14-45.

14-10 EXERCISE PROBLEMS

Exercise problems EX14-1 to EX14-3 require you to draw 2D shapes on various surfaces of 3D objects. All 2D shapes should be drawn at the center of the surfaces on which they appear.

A. Draw the 2D shapes as shown.

B. Divide the screen into 4 viewports, and create a front, top, and right-side orthographic view for each object.

EX14-1 INCHES

All circles are Ø4.00

The box is 12 × 12 × 8

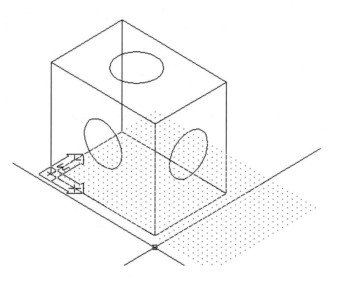

EX14-2 MILLIMETERS

The three big circles are Ø60

The small circle is Ø30

The lower box is 150 × 100 × 30

The upper box is 150 × 80 × 80

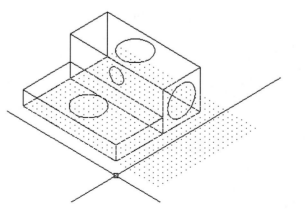

EX14-3 INCHES

The three circles are Ø5.00

The box is 8 × 8 × 4

Both wedges have 8 × 8 bases
and are 4 high

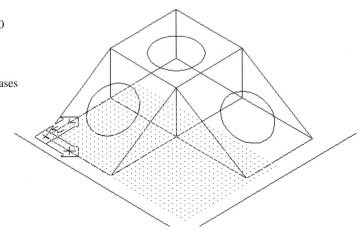

EX14-4 MILLIMETERS

Draw a wire frame model of
the following object using the
ELEV command.

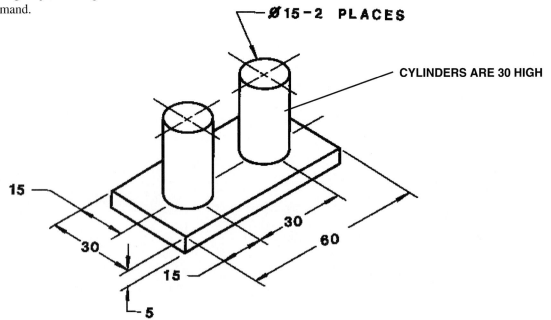

EX14-5 MILLIMETERS

Draw a wire frame model of the following object using the ELEV command.

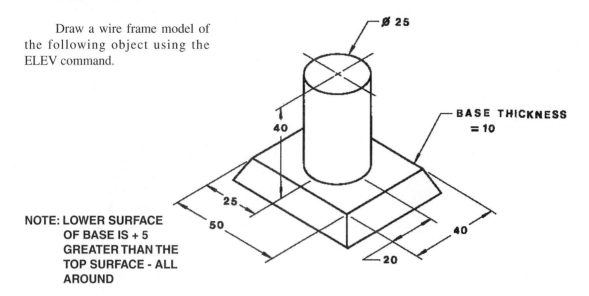

NOTE: LOWER SURFACE
OF BASE IS + 5
GREATER THAN THE
TOP SURFACE - ALL
AROUND

EX14-6 MILLIMETERS

Draw a wire frame model of the following object using the ELEV command.

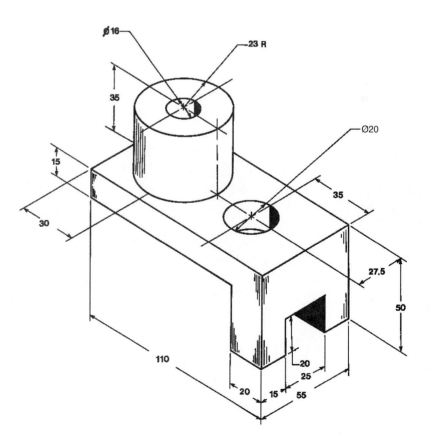

EX14-7 INCHES

Draw the three boxes positioned as shown using the ELEV command. The length, width, and height for each box is as follows.

    a. X = 6, Y = 5, Z = 2
    b. X = 4, Y = 4, Z = 4
    c. X = 5, Y = 2, Z = 1

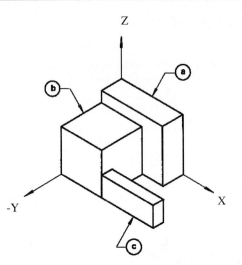

EX14-8 INCHES

Draw the three boxes shown centered about the Z axis using the ELEV command. The length, width, and height for each box is as follows.

    a. X = 8, Y = 8, Z = 1
    b. X = 6, Y = 6, Z = 2
    c. X = 2, Y = 2, Z = 6

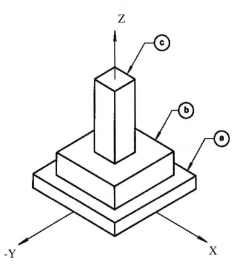

EX14-9 MILLIMETERS

Draw the three cylinders as shown using the ELEV command. Center the cylinders about the Z axis. The sizes of the cylinders are as follows.

    a. Ø = 10
    b. Ø = 20
    c. Ø = 35

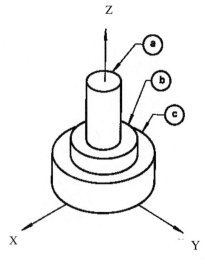

EX14-10 FEET

Draw the three boxes positioned as shown using the ELEV command. The length, width, and height for each box is 2 × 2 × 5.

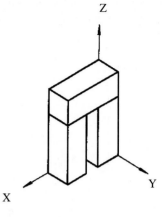

EX14-11 MILLIMETERS

Draw the boxes as shown using the ELEV command.

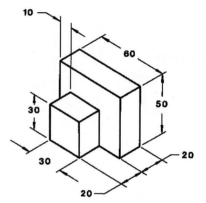

EX14-12 INCHES

Draw the following cylinders using the ELEV command and based on the given orientations.

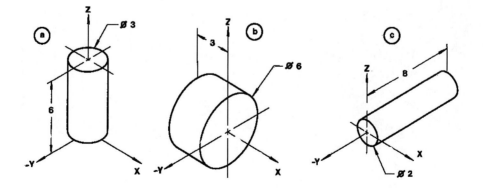

Draw the objects in exercise problems EX14-13 to EX14-16 using the ELEV command.

EX14-13 MILLIMETERS

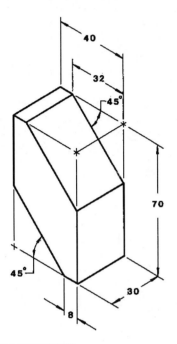

EX14-15 MILLIMETERS

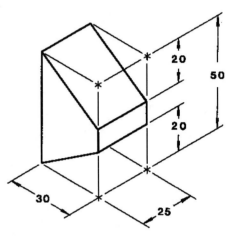

EX14-14 MILLIMETERS

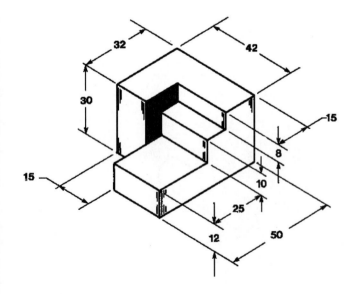

EX14-16 MILLIMETERS

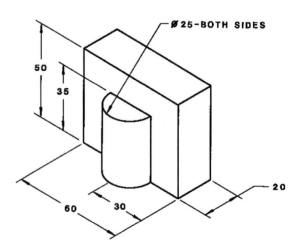

CHAPTER

Surface Modeling

15-1 INTRODUCTION

This chapter introduces surface modeling. Surface modeling creates 3D objects by joining surfaces together. The SURFACE commands are accessed in the WINDOWS version using the SURFACE toolbar (see Figure 15-1 WINDOWS) and in the DOS version via the DRAW pulldown menu, SURFACES commands (see Figure 15-1 DOS). Both versions can access the SURFACE command by using the DRAW 2, SURFACES commands on the screen menus. AutoCAD's surface commands generate what AutoCAD calls "faceted surfaces using a polygonal mesh." This means that the curved surfaces generated are only mathematical approximations and not true, smooth surfaces. The approximations are, however, very accurate and present a minimal visual distortion.

Surface modeling is different from solid modeling. Surface modeling deals only with individual surfaces, whereas solid modeling deals with entire solid shapes. A box created as a surface model is comprised of six surfaces. A box created using solid modeling is a solid object with six sides. Surface models cannot be unioned or subtracted as can solid models.

Surface modeling is particularly well suited for drawing complex 3D meshes, such as might be found on a surface profile map, or for the transition area between an airfoil and fuselage on an aircraft.

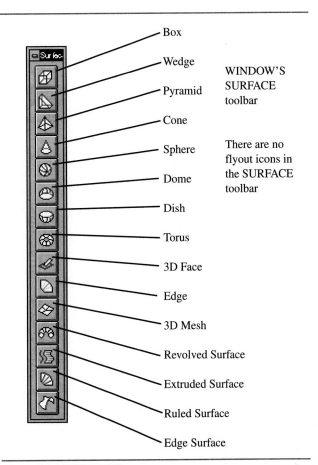

WINDOW'S SURFACE toolbar

There are no flyout icons in the SURFACE toolbar

Figure 15-1 WINDOWS

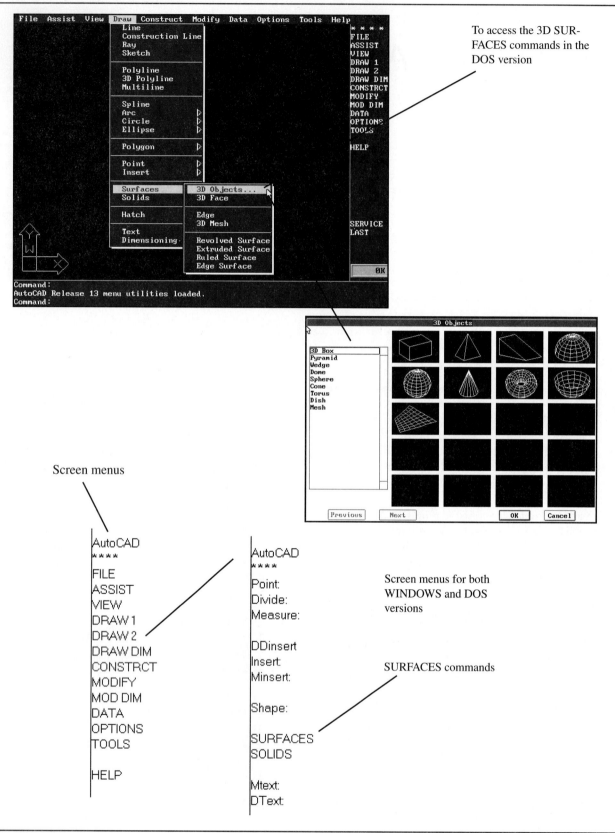

To access the 3D SUR-
FACES commands in the
DOS version

Screen menus

AutoCAD
****

FILE
ASSIST
VIEW
DRAW 1
DRAW 2
DRAW DIM
CONSTRCT
MODIFY
MOD DIM
DATA
OPTIONS
TOOLS

HELP

AutoCAD
****

Point:
Divide:
Measure:

DDinsert
Insert:
Minsert:

Shape:

SURFACES
SOLIDS

Mtext:
DText:

Screen menus for both
WINDOWS and DOS
versions

SURFACES commands

Figure 15-1 DOS

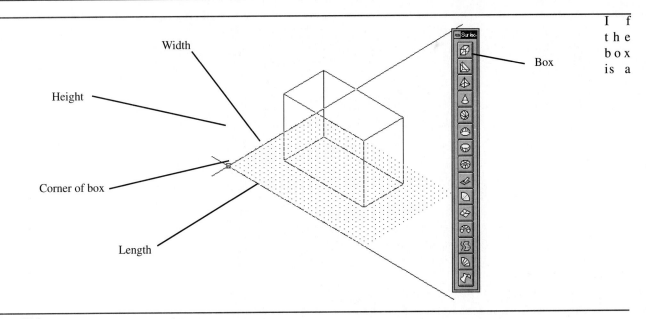

Figure 15-2

15-2 BOX

The BOX command is used to draw a box comprised of six surfaces. See Figure 15-2. The command sequence is as follows.

To draw a box

1. Select the BOX command

   Command: ai_box
   Corner of box:

2. Select a corner location for the box

   In the example shown, the coordinate display was used to locate the corner point on 3,4. The corner could have been defined using a 3D coordinate value (X,Y,Z).

3. Move the cursor until the cursor display reads 3,4, then press the left mouse button

   Length:

4. Type 10 ENTER

   The length could also be determined by moving the crosshairs and either picking a random point, using OSNAP to align with an existing entity, or using the values displayed in the coordinate display box.

   Cube/<Width>:

5. Type 5 ENTER

cube, enter a C response instead of a width value. AutoCAD will automatically take the length value and apply it to the width and height, skipping the width and height prompts in the sequence.

   Height:

6. Type 7 ENTER
7. Rotation angle about the Z axis:

   AutoCAD is now in a dynamic mode, meaning that as you move the crosshairs, the box will rotate about a Z axis projected out of the original corner point.

8. Type 0 ENTER

15-3 WEDGE

The wedge in this example will be drawn aligned with the box drawn in Section 15-2. See Figure 15-3.

To draw a wedge

1. Select the WEDGE command

   Command: ai_wedge
   Corner of wedge:

2. Use OSNAP, ENDPOINT (press the shift key and right mouse button simultaneously) and select the lower right corner of the box

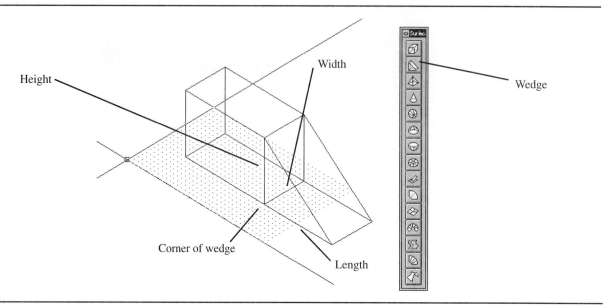

Figure 15-3

Length:

3. Move the crosshairs away from the corner until the coordinate display reads 21.5,4, then press the left mouse button

Width:

4. Use OSNAP, ENDPOINT and select the upper right corner of the box

Height:

5. Use OSNAP, ENDPOINT and select the upper right corner of the box.

Rotation angle about the Z axis:

6. Type 0 ENTER

The box and the wedge are not joined objects. They each have a surface that occupies the same space, but they are still two individual entities.

7. Clear the screen using the ERASE command, then use VIEW, REDRAW to refresh the screen.

15-4 PYRAMID

There are several different types of pyramids. Pyramids may have triangular, rectangular, or square bases. Any polygon can be used as the base of a pyramid, but the Surfaces toolbar commands are limited to rectangular bases. Polygons with more points can be used with the solid modeling options.

A tetrahedron is a pyramid made from three triangles. Pyramids that have their apexes located directly over the center point of their base polygons are called right pyramids. Pyramids whose apexes are not located directly over the center point of their base polygons are called oblique pyramids. Pyramids with their top sections removed are called truncated pyramids, and pyramids whose tops are line and not point apexes are called ridged pyramids.

To draw a rectangular pyramid

See Figure 15-4.

1. Select the PYRAMID command

   Command: ai_pyramid
   First base point:

2. Type 0,0 ENTER

   Second base point

3. Press F8 to turn the ORTHO command on
4. Move the crosshairs to the 8,0 point, and press the left mouse button

   Third base point:

5. Move the crosshairs to the 8,10 point and press the left mouse button

   Tetrahedron/<Fourth base point>:

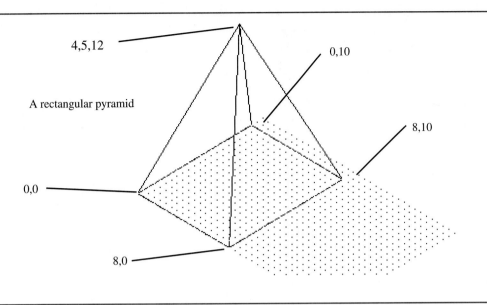

4,5,12

0,10

A rectangular pyramid

8,10

0,0

8,0

Figure 15-4

6. Move the crosshairs to the 0,10 point and press the left mouse button

Ridge/Top/<Apex point>:

The apex point location requires a Z component. All of the previous points have been in the same XY plane, so only an X and Y coordinate point was necessary. The apex point can be located randomly; that is, you can simply move the crosshairs and select a point, but this procedure can be visually misleading. It is better to use either coordinate values or the OSNAP command to locate a pyramid's apex.

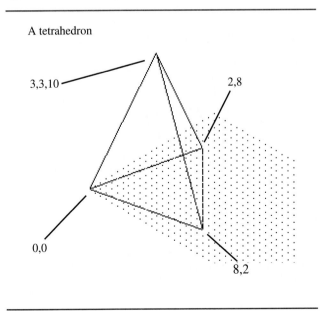

A tetrahedron

3,3,10

2,8

0,0

8,2

Figure 15-5

7. Type 4,5,12 ENTER

A negative Z value could have been entered.

To draw a tetrahedron

See Figure 15-5.

1. Select the PYRAMID command

Command: ai_pyramid
First base point:

2. Type 0,0 ENTER

Second base point

3. Type 8,2

Third base point:

4. Type 2,8

Tetrahedron/<Fourth base point>:

5. Type T ENTER

Top/<Apex point>:

6. Type 3,3,10 ENTER

To draw a truncated pyramid

See Figure 15-6.

1. Select the PYRAMID command

Pyramid

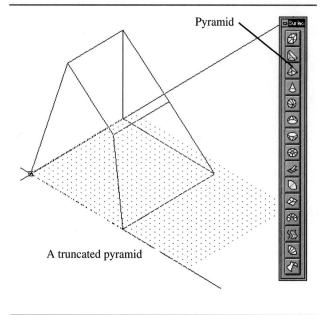

A truncated pyramid

Figure 15-6

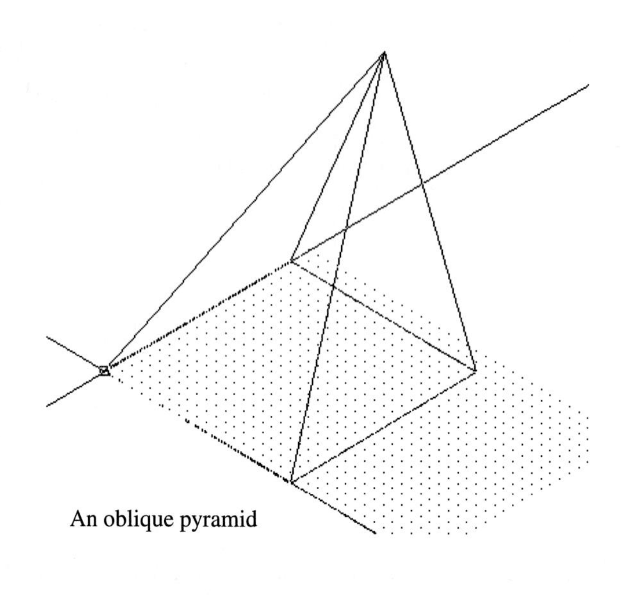

An oblique pyramid

Figure 15-7

Command: ai_pyramid
First base point:

2. Type 0,0 ENTER

   Second base point:

3. Type 10,0 ENTER

   Third base point:

4. Type 10,10 ENTER

   Tetrahedron/<Fourth base point>:

5. Type 0,10 ENTER

   Ridge/Top/<Apex point>:

6. Type T ENTER

   First top point:

7. Type 2,2,10 ENTER

   Remember top points are not in the base plane and therefore require a Z component to their coordinate values. Also note that a line will appear from the crosshairs to the corner point whose top point is being defined.

   Second top point:

8. Type 7,2,6 ENTER

   Third top point:

9. Type 7,8,6 ENTER

   Fourth top point:

10. Type 2,8,10 ENTER

To draw an oblique pyramid

   See Figure 15-7.

1. Select the PYRAMID command

   Command: ai_pyramid
   First base point:

2. Type 0,0 ENTER

   Second base point:

3. Type 10,0 ENTER

   Third base point:

4. Type 10,10 ENTER

   Tetrahedron/<Fourth base point>:

5. Type 0,10 ENTER

   Ridge/Top/<Apex point>:

6. Type 5,10,12 ENTER

   This apex point is located over the center point of the rear line in the base polygon. Any apex not located over the base polygon's center point is classified as an oblique pyramid.

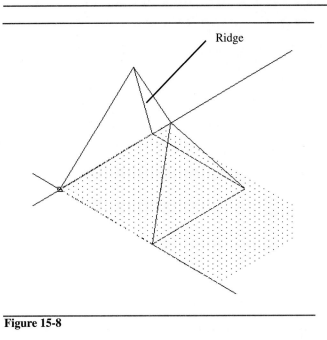

Figure 15-8

3. Type 10,0 ENTER

   Third base point:

4. Type 10,10 ENTER

   Tetrahedron/<Fourth base point>:

5. Type 0,10 ENTER

   Ridge/Top/<Apex point>:

6. Type R ENTER

   First ridge point:

7. Type 3,5,10 ENTER

   Second ridge point:

8. Type 7,5,7 ENTER

15-5 CONES

See Figure 15-9.

To draw a cone

1. Select the CONE command

   Command: ai_cone
   Base center point:

2. Type 5,5 ENTER

The cone's center point could also have been selected by locating a point using the crosshairs, then pressing the left mouse button.

To draw a ridged pyramid

See Figure 15-8.

1. Select the PYRAMID command

   Command: ai_pyramid
   First base point:

2. Type 0,0 ENTER

   Second base point:

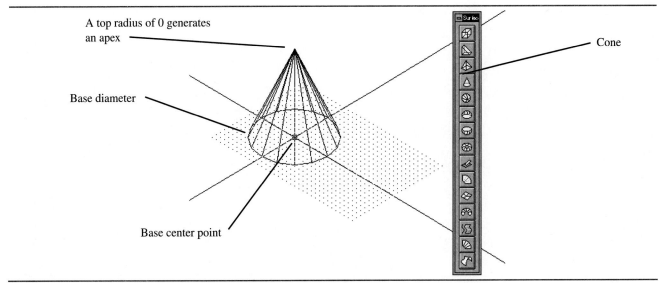

Figure 15-9

Diameter/<radius> of base:

3. Type 4 ENTER

Diameter/<radius> of top <0>:

A top radius of 0 will create a cone with an apex. A radius value other than 0 will create a truncated cone.

4. Type ENTER

Height:

5. Type 9 ENTER

Number of segments <16>:

The number of segments defines the number of facets used to show the cone. The more segments, the smaller each segment will be, and the resulting cone will appear smoother. However, a large number of segments will use more memory and will require more time to process. The default value of 16 is a good compromise between visual accuracy and drawing speed.

6. Type ENTER

To draw a truncated cone

See Figure 15-10.

1. Select the CONE command

Command: ai_cone
Base center point:

2. Type 5,5 ENTER

Diameter/<radius> of base:

3. Type 6 ENTER

Diameter/<radius> of top <0>:

4. Type 3 ENTER

Height:

5. Type 8 ENTER

Number of segments:

6. Type ENTER

15-6 SPHERE

See Figure 15-11.

To draw a sphere

In this example, the sphere will be drawn above the XY plane.

1. Select the SPHERE command

Command: ai_sphere
Center of sphere:

2. Type 5,5,5

Diameter/<radius>:

3. Type 5 ENTER

Number of longitudinal segments <16>:

4. Type ENTER

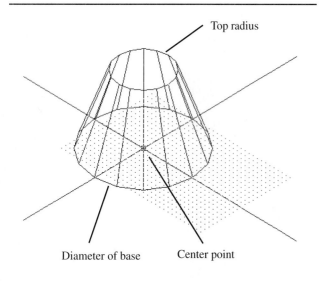

Top radius

Diameter of base   Center point

Figure 15-10

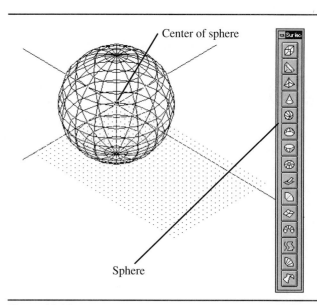

Center of sphere

Sphere

Figure 15-11

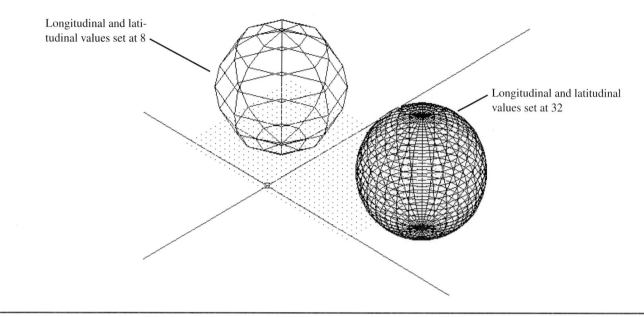

Figure 15-12

Number of latitudinal segments <16>:

The number of longitudinal and latitudinal segments controls the number of facets that will show on the sphere. Longitudinal lines are equivalent to vertical lines. Latitudinal lines are equivalent to horizontal lines. The more segments defined, the smoother the resulting sphere, but more line segments will increase the drawing time needed to generate the sphere.

Figure 15-12 shows two spheres; one drawn with 8 longitudinal and latitudinal segments, and one drawn with 32 longitudinal and latitudinal segments. Note the differences in the overall smoothness of the visual presentation.

15-7 DOME

A dome is a semisphere, or the top half of a sphere. See Figure 15-13.

To draw a dome

1. Select the DOME command

   Command: ai_dome
   Center of dome:

2. Type 5,5 ENTER

   Diameter/<radius>:

3. Type 8 ENTER

   Number of longitudinal segments <16>:

4. Type ENTER

   Number of latitudinal segments <8>:

5. Type ENTER

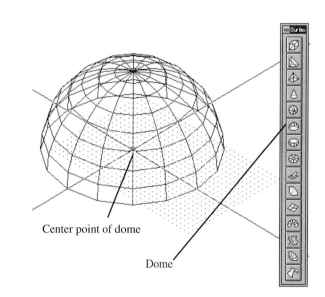

Center point of dome

Dome

Figure 15-13

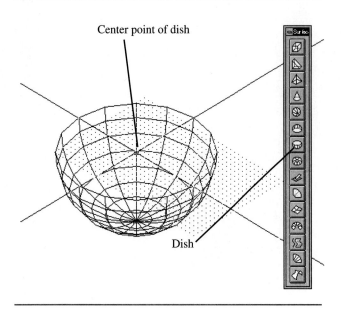

Center point of dish

Dish

Figure 15-14

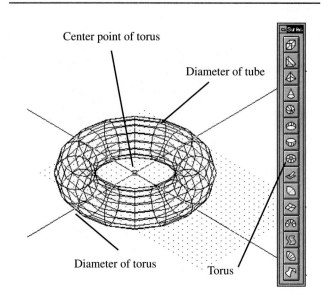

Center point of torus

Diameter of tube

Diameter of torus

Torus

Figure 15-15

15-8 DISH

A dish is a semisphere, or the bottom half of a sphere. See Figure 15-14.

To draw a dish

1. Select the DISH command

   Command: ai_dome
   Center of dome:

2. Type 5,5 ENTER

   Diameter/<radius>:

3. Type 7 ENTER

   Number of longitudinal segments <16>:

4. Type ENTER

   Number of latitudinal segments <8>:

5. Type ENTER

15-9 TORUS

A torus is a donutlike shape. See Figure 15-15.

To draw a torus

1. Select the TORUS command

   Command: ai_torus
   Center of torus:

2. Type 5,5 ENTER

   Diameter/<radius> of torus:

3. Type 6 ENTER

   Diameter/<radius> of tube:

4. Type 1.5 ENTER

   The radius of a torus is the distance from the center point to the outside edge of the torus, as measured along the center plane.

   Segments around the tube circumference <16>:

5. Type ENTER

   Segments around the torus circumference <16>:

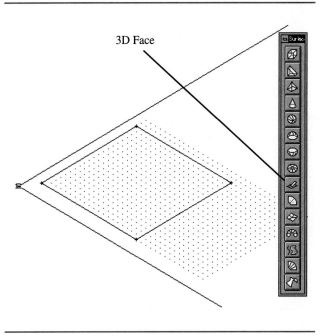

3D Face

Figure 15-16

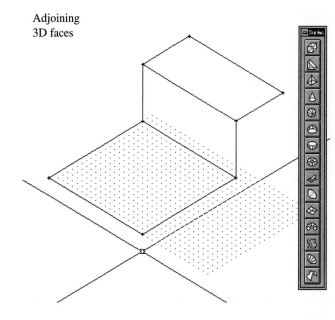

Adjoining
3D faces

Figure 15-17

15-10 3D FACE

A 3D face is a plane. 3D faces may be created as individual planes or as adjoining groups of planes. A 3D face can be added to an existing 3D object to close in an open area, or to create a transition between existing objects.

To draw a single 3D face

In this example we will select points on a grid. Coordinate values can also be used to define the 3D face's corner points. See Figure 15-16.

1. Select the 3D FACE command

   Command: _3dface First point:

2. Select the 0,0 point on the grid

   Use the coordinate display at the lower left of the screen to verify the point location.

   Second point:

3. Select 10,0

   Third point:

4. Select 10,10

   Fourth point:

5. Select 0,10

   Third point:

   This point assumes that you will also be creating an adjacent plane, but because you are not, enter a null value.

6. Type ENTER

To draw adjoining 3D faces

In this example we will draw three adjoining planes, each 90 degrees to the other. See Figure 15-17.

1. Select the 3D FACE command

   Command: _3dface First point:

2. Type 0,0 ENTER

   Second point:

3. Type 10,0 ENTER

   Third point:

4. Type 10,10 ENTER

   Fourth point:

5. Type 0,10 ENTER

   Third point:

6. Type 0,10,5 ENTER

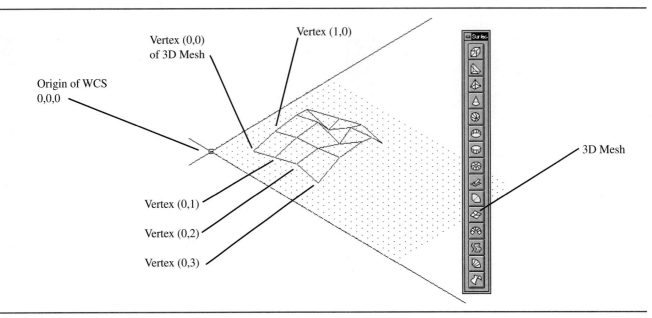

Figure 15-18

The adjoining plane will be perpendicular to the line on the Y axis.

Fourth point:

7. Type 10,10,5 ENTER

Third point:

8. Type 10,15,5 ENTER

Fourth point:

9. Type 0,15,5 ENTER
10. Type ENTER

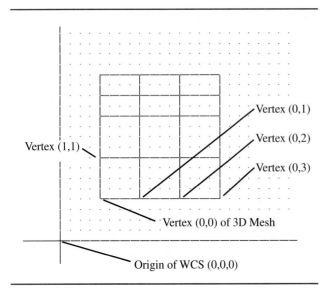

Figure 15-19

15-11 3D MESH

The 3D MESH command defines a surface by defining a series of points on the surface. Mesh surfaces are usually irregular surfaces, that is, not flat. See Figure 15-18.

The points used to define a mesh surface are located in terms of an M,N axis. First the number of points in both the M and N directions is defined, then each point is automatically assigned a vertex notation. The vertex notation 0,2 means first row, that is, the first line in the M direction, and the third column, third line in the N direction. The first line in both the M and N directions is labeled 0. Figure 15-19 is a top view of the finished 3D mesh.

Coordinate values for each mesh point are expressed in terms of their X,Y,Z values relative to the existing XY plane.

To draw a 3D mesh

1. Select the 3D MESH command

   Command: _3dmesh
   Mesh M size:

2. Type 5 ENTER

   Mesh N size:

3. Type 4 ENTER

   Vertex (0,0):

This prompt is asking for the first point value on the MN axis. It is not a numerical input, but rather a point location definition relative to the MN axis. Note that the numbers are enclosed by (), meaning they are not default values.

4. Type 2,2,0 ENTER

This input establishes the corner of the mesh surface at the 2,2,0 point on the current XYZ axis.

Vertex (0,1):

5. Type 4,2,.5 ENTER

Vertex (0,2):

6. Type 6,2,1 ENTER

Vertex (0,3):

7. Type 8,2,.5 ENTER

Vertex (1,0):

8. Type 2,4,.5 ENTER

Vertex (1,1):

9. Type 4,4,1 ENTER

Vertex (1,2):

10. Type 6,4,1.2 ENTER

Vertex (1,3):

11. Type 8,4,1.5 ENTER

Vertex (2,0):

12. Type 2,6,.75

Vertex (2,1):

13. Type 4,6,1.2 ENTER

Vertex (2,2):

14. Type 6,6,.5

Vertex (2,3):

15. 8,6,1.7 ENTER

Vertex (3,0):

16. Type 2,7,.7 ENTER

Vertex (3,1):

17. Type 4,7,.1 ENTER

Vertex (3,2):

18. Type 6,7,1.3 ENTER

Vertex (3,3):

19. Type 8,7,1.5 ENTER

Vertex (4,0):

20. Type 2,8,0 ENTER

Vertex (4,1):

21. Type 4,8,.5 ENTER

Vertex (4,2):

22. Type 6,8,1 ENTER

Vertex (4,3):

23. Type 8,8,.5 ENTER

15-12 REVOLVED SURFACE

A revolved surface is created by revolving a given shape about an axis of revolution. Cones, cylinders, spheres, toruses, and ellipsoids are all shapes that can be created as revolved surfaces. AutoCAD can also create unusual shapes by revolving polylines.

To create a cylinder

A cylinder can be created by revolving a line around another line. The resulting cylinder is not a solid cylinder, but a cylindrical shape with open ends. It is analogous to a rolled sheet of paper. Figure 15-20 shows two lines that will be used to construct a cylinder.

1. Select the REVOLVED SURFACE command

Command:_revsurf
Select curve path:

The curve path is the line that will be revolved. In this example it is the shorter of the two lines.

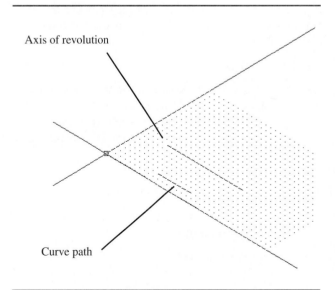

Axis of revolution

Curve path

Figure 15-20

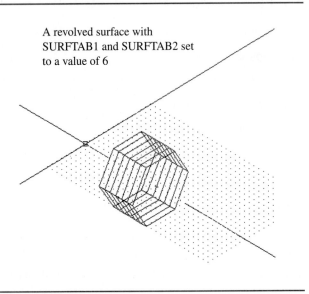

A revolved surface with SURFTAB1 and SURFTAB2 set to a value of 6

Figure 15-21

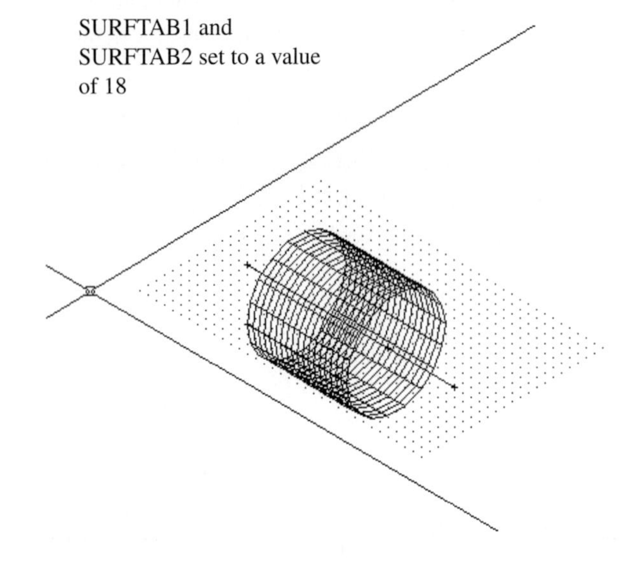

SURFTAB1 and SURFTAB2 set to a value of 18

Figure 15-22

2. Select the shorter line

Select the axis of revolution:

3. Select the longer line

Start angle <0>:

Revolved shapes need not be 360 degrees. They can be started at and ended at any angle.

4. Type ENTER

Included angle (+=ccw, −=cw) <Full circle>:

This prompt reminds you that the counterclockwise direction is the positive direction. Either positive or negative values may be entered. The default value is a full circle, or 360 degrees.

5. Type ENTER

See Figure 15-21. Note that the resulting cylinder doesn't look like a cylinder. This is because the default system variables SURFTAB1 and SURFTAB2 are set too small for this example. Their values must be increased to produce a smooth looking cylinder.

To change SURFTAB1 and SURFTAB2

1. Type SURFTAB1 ENTER in response to a Command: prompt

Command: Surftab1

New value for SURFTAB1 <6>:

2. Type 18 ENTER

Command:

3. Type SURFTAB2 ENTER

Command: surftab2

New value for SURFTAB2 <6>:

4. Type 18 ENTER

The values may also be changed by using the System Variables option in the Options pulldown menu.

The surftab variables are now reset from a value of 6 to a value of 18. Figure 15-22 shows the resulting cylinder created using the Revolved Surface command.

Figure 15-23 shows a cylinder drawn perpendicular to the XY plane. The lines used to define the surface of revolution were defined using the XYZ values of the line's end points. For example, the shorter vertical line was drawn between points 0,0,0 and 0,0,5.

Figure 15-23 also shows a partial cylinder that was created by not revolving the line a full 360 degrees. The cylinder shown was created by revolving a line 120 degrees.

Figure 15-24 shows an object that was created by first drawing a polyline, then revolving the polyline around an axis of revolution. Any curved shape can be used to create a surface of revolution. A torus, for example, can be created by revolving a circle around an axis of revolution.

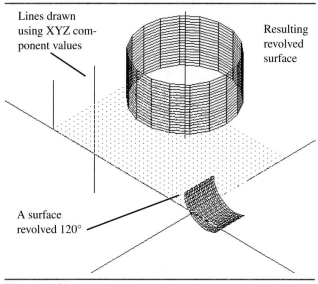

Lines drawn using XYZ component values

Resulting revolved surface

A surface revolved 120°

Figure 15-23

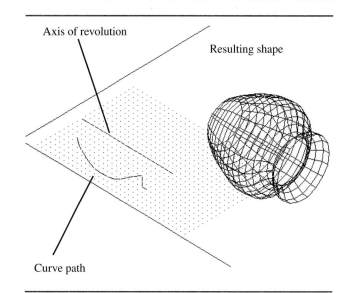

Axis of revolution

Resulting shape

Curve path

Figure 15-24

15-13 EXTRUDED SURFACE

An extruded surface creates an object by tracking a given shape along a direction vector. Only straight lines can be used as direction vectors. A curved line may be specified as a direction vector, but AutoCAD will draw a straight line from the first point to the last point on the curve and use that straight line as the direction vector.

Extruded surfaces often involve objects drawn in two different planes. The following example will create a cylinder by extruding a circle along a straight line. The circle will be drawn in a plane perpendicular to the plane of the line.

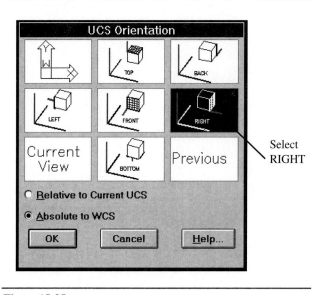

Select RIGHT

Figure 15-25

To draw an extruded surface

1. Use the LINE command in the Draw toolbar to draw a line in the current XY plane (WCS)
2. Select the View pulldown menu, then Preset UCS...

The UCS orientation dialog box will appear. See Figure 15-25.

3. Select the RIGHT UCS

The screen grid pattern will shift to the new UCS orientation.

4. Select the ORIGIN UCS icon from the UCS toolbar
5. Use the OSNAP, ENDPOINT commands to define the start point of the line as the new origin for the RIGHT UCS.

See Figure 15-26.

6. Use the CIRCLE command on the Draw toolbar to draw a circle about the start point of the line

See Figure 15-27.

7. Return to the WCS by selecting the View pulldown menu, then PRESET UCS..., WORLD, OK
8. Select the EXTRUDED SURFACE icon on the Surface toolbar

Command: _tabsurf
Select curve path:

9. Select the circle

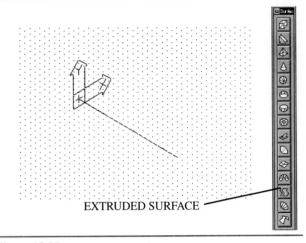

EXTRUDED SURFACE

Figure 15-26

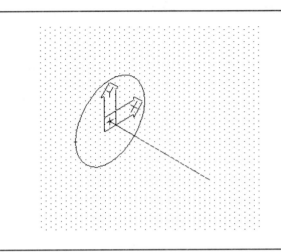

Figure 15-27

Select direction vector:

10. Select the line

Figure 15-28 shows the resulting extruded surface. The circle has been extended in the direction and length of the line. The cylinder is drawn perpendicular to the base plane, which was established as the RIGHT UCS with its origin at the start point of the line. Had the same procedure been followed, but the other end of the line selected as the origin, the cylinder would have covered the line.

Figure 15-29 shows a polyline that has been edited to form a curve. The EXTRUDED SURFACE command was then applied using a line perpendicular to the plane of the polyline as a direction vector.

15-14 RULED SURFACE

A ruled surface is created between two existing curves or between a point and a curve.

To draw a ruled surface between two curves

See Figure 15-30.

1. Select the RULED SURFACE command

Command:_rulesurf
Select the defining curve:

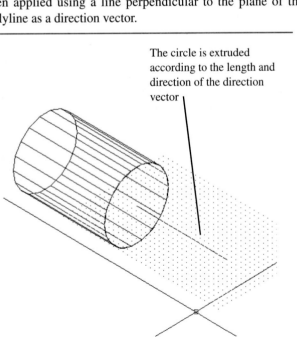

The circle is extruded according to the length and direction of the direction vector

Figure 15-28

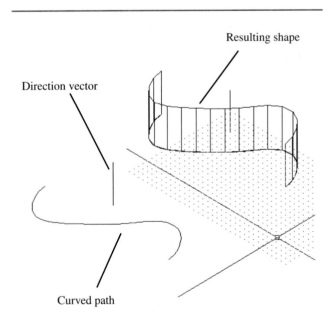

Resulting shape

Direction vector

Curved path

Figure 15-29

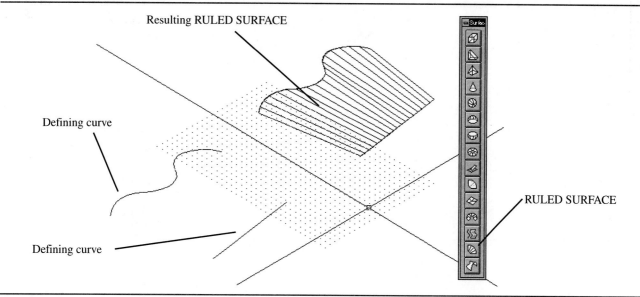

Resulting RULED SURFACE

Defining curve

Defining curve

RULED SURFACE

Figure 15-30

2. Select the straight line

Select second defining line:

Ruled surfaces are selection sequence dependent. Figure 15-31 shows two ruled surfaces created from the same defining curves. The differences between the resulting surfaces is the result of different selection point locations. The selection points for the defining curves for the lower left surface were the left end of each line. The selection points for the upper surface were the left end of the curved line and the right end of the straight line.

Figure 15-32 shows a ruled surface drawn between curves drawn in different planes. The left curve was drawn in the RIGHT preset UCS and the right curve was drawn in the WCS.

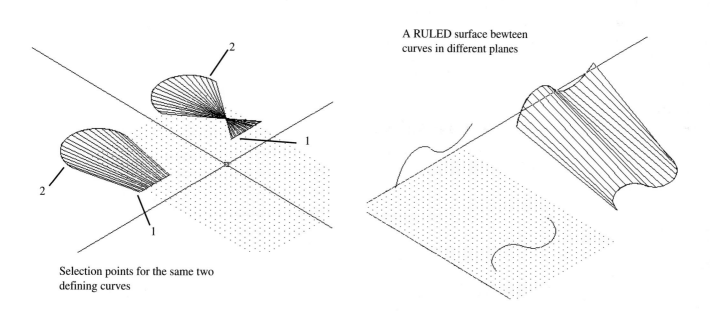

Selection points for the same two defining curves

A RULED surface bewteen curves in different planes

Figure 15-31

Figure 15-32

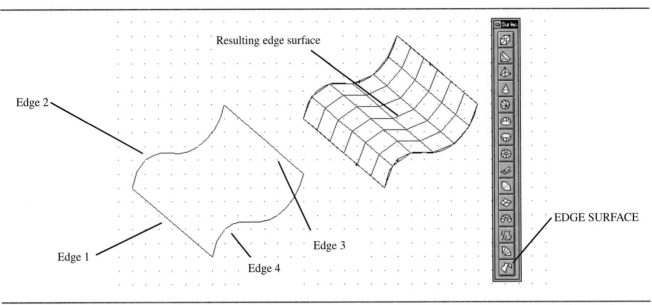

Resulting edge surface

Edge 2

Edge 1

Edge 3

Edge 4

EDGE SURFACE

Figure 15-33

15-15 EDGE SURFACE

The EDGE SURFACE command is used to create a surface among four existing adjoining lines. See Figure 15-33.

1. Select the EDGE SURFACE command

   Command: _edgesurf
   Select edge 1:

2. Select one of the lines

   Select edge 2:

3. Select a second line

Select edge 3:

4. Select a third line

Select edge 4:

5. Select a fourth line

The edge surface shown in Figure 15-33 was created with a SURFTAB setting of 6. Note how the surface contains a 6 by 6 pattern of rectangles. Figure 15-34 shows an edge surface created on the same four lines, but with SURFTAB1 and SURFTAB2 set to 18. Note the difference in visual appearance.

Figure 15-35 shows an edge surface created between three 3D polylines edited to form splines and a single straight line. Both SURFTABS were set at 18.

SURFTAB1 = 18
SURFTAB2 = 18

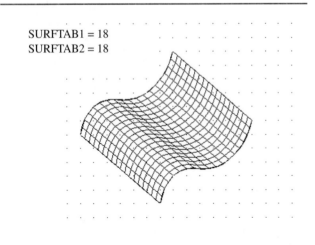

Figure 15-34

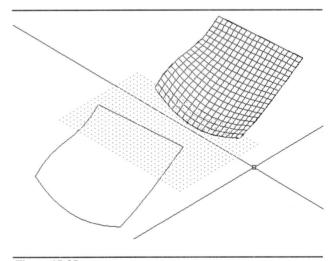

Figure 15-35

15-16 COMBINING SURFACES

Figure 15-36 shows an object created by combining two surfaces: a cylinder and a truncated cone. The procedure is as follows. The object will be centered around the 0,0 point on the XY axis.

To draw the truncated cone

1. Set the GRID and SNAP spacing for .5, and select DECIMAL UNITS
2. Select the SE ISOMETRIC icon from the Views toolbar or the VIEWPOINT PRESETS dialog box and set the values for 315° and 30°.
3. Select the VIEW pulldown menu, then PAN, POINT, and move the grid pattern to the center of the screen. (The icon that looks like a hand on the STANDARD toolbar accesses the PAN command)
4. Select the ZOOM command and create a zoom window around the 0,0,0 point
5. Select the CONE command

   Base center point:

6. Type 0,0,0 ENTER

   Diameter/<radius> of base:

7. Type D ENTER

   Diameter of base:

8. Type 1.38 ENTER

   Diameter/<radius> of top <0>:

9. Type D ENTER

   Diameter of top <0>:

10. Type .62 ENTER

    Height:

11. Type .75 ENTER

    Number of segments <16>:

12. Type ENTER

See Figure 15-37. Use the ZOOM WINDOW command again, if necessary, to approximate the screen size shown.

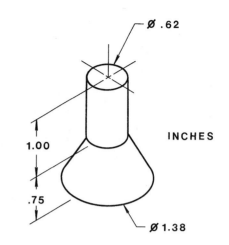

Ø .62

INCHES

1.00

.75

Ø 1.38

Figure 15-36

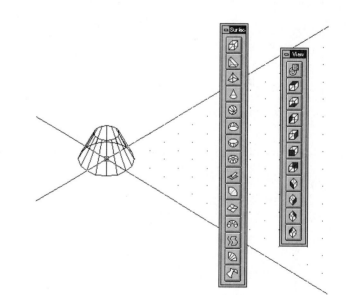

Figure 15-37

Draw two circles

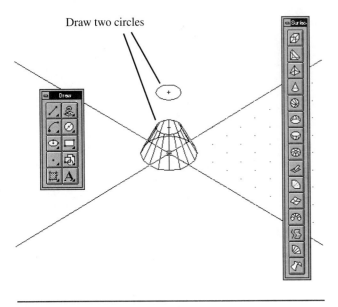

Figure 15-38

Resulting shape

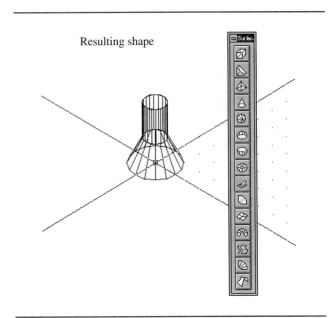

Figure 15-39

The problem now requires that a cylinder be joined to the top of the truncated cone. The ELEV command can be used to create a cylinder located on top of the cone, but in this example, two circles will be drawn, then joined, using the RULED SURFACE command. The cone was created using a Surface command and has no top surface. The RULED SURFACE command requires an edge, and the top of the cone does not constitute an edge, so a circle must be added at the top of the cone.

To add the cylinder to the top of the cone

1. Select the CIRCLE CENTER DIAMETER command

   Command: _circle 3P/2P/TTR/<Center point>:

2. Type 0,0,.75 ENTER

   Diameter/Radius <0.3100>: _d diameter <0.6200>:

3. Type ENTER

   There is no visual change in the object, although a tick mark should appear at the center point of the circle. The circle and the top of the cone occupy the same space.

4. Type ENTER again to restart the CIRCLE command sequence

   CIRCLE 3P/2P/TTR/<Center point>:

5. Type 0,0,1.75 ENTER

Diameter/<Radius>: <0.3100>:

See Figure 15-38.

To create the cylinder

1. Select the RULED SURFACE command

   Select the first defining curve:

2. Select the top circle

   Select the second defining curve:

3. Select the circle drawn on the top surface of the cone.

   See Figure 15-39. The density of line segments in the cylinder occurs because the SURFTAB settings are at 18.

15-17 USING SURFACES WITH A UCS

Figure 15-40 shows a dimensioned object. The following section shows how the object was created as a surface model.

To draw the box portion

1. Set the GRID and SNAP spacing for .5, and select DECIMAL UNITS

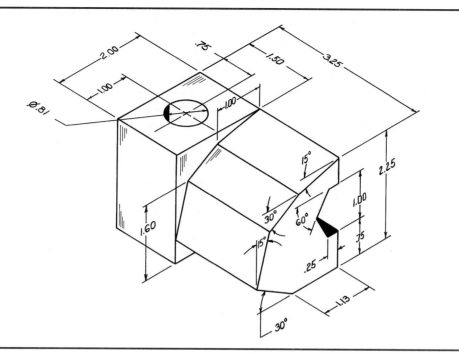

Figure 15-40

2. Select the SE ISOMETRIC icon from the Views toolbar or use the VIEWPOINT PRESETS dialog box and set the view to 315° and 30°.
3. Select the VIEW pulldown menu, then PAN, POINT, and move the grid pattern to the center of the screen
4. Select the ZOOM command and create a zoom window around the 0,0,0 point
5. Select the BOX command

   Corner of box:

6. Type 0,0,0

   Length:

7. Type 1.50 ENTER

   Cube/<Width>:

8. Type 2.00 ENTER

   Height:

9. Type 2.25

   Rotation angle about Z axis:

10. Type 0 ENTER

    See Figure 15-41. The size values for the box were taken from the given dimensions in Figure 15-40. Use the ZOOM command again, if necessary, to approximate the size shown in Figure 15-40.

To add the hole to the object

The hole could be created using the ELEV command, but in this example, the RULED SURFACE command will be used.

1. Select the CIRCLE CENTER DIAMETER command

   Command: _circle 3P/2P/TTR/<Center point>:

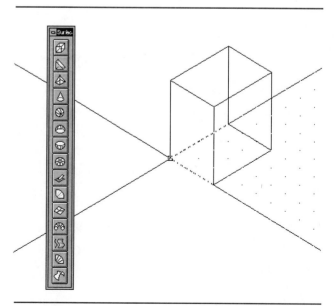

Figure 15-41

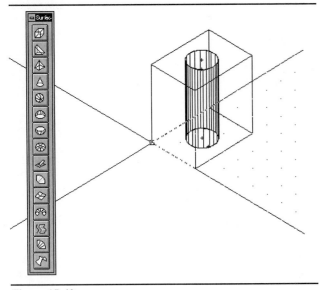

Figure 15-42

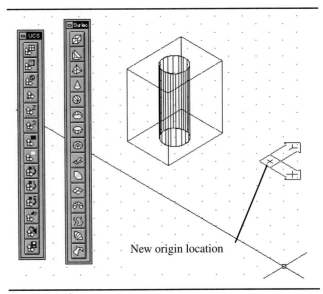

New origin location

Figure 15-43

2. Type .75,1.00,0 ENTER

The hole location came from the given dimensions.

Diameter/Radius <0.3100>: _d Diameter <.6200>:

3. Type .81 ENTER
4. Type ENTER again to restart the CIRCLE command sequence

CIRCLE 3P/2P/TTR/<Center point>:

5. Type .75,1.00, 2.25 ENTER

This will locate the second circle on the top surface of the box.

Diameter/<Radius> <0.4050>:

6. Type ENTER
7. Select the RULED SURFACE command

Select first defining curve:

8. Select the lower circle

Select the second defining curve:

9. Select the upper circle

See Figure 15-42.

To create the extended portion of the object

This construction requires that a new UCS be established with its origin at the 3.25,2.00,0 point on the WCS (current UCS).

1. Select the ORIGIN command

Origin point:

2. Type 3.25,2,0 ENTER

Command:

See Figure 15-43. The screen icon is on the new origin.

3. Type ENTER again

Origin/ZAxis/3point/OBject/View/Z/Y/Z/Prev/ Restore/Save/Del/?/<World>:

4. Type 3 ENTER

Origin point <0.0.0>:

5. Type ENTER

Point on the positive portion of the x-axis <1.0000,0.0000,0.0000>:

6. Type 0,-2,0 ENTER

A Y value is entered because of the new origin location. This value will position the new UCS so that the construction of the object's extended portion will be in the positive quadrant of the UCS.

Point on the positive-Y portion of the UCS XY plane <1.0000,0.0000,0.0000>:

7. Type 0,0,2.25

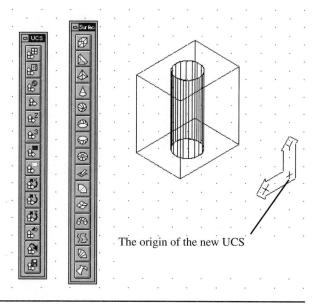

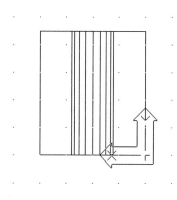

The origin of the new UCS

The RIGHT view of the new UCS

Figure 15-44

Figure 15-45

The new UCS is now defined as indicated by the screen icon shift. See Figure 15-44. A value of 1 could have been used rather than 2.25. Any value in the positive Y direction is acceptable.

To draw the end shape of the object

1. Select the RIGHT VIEW icon from the View toolbar or from the UCS orientation dialog box (see Figure 15-25)

    Grid too dense to display
    Command:

2. Type ZOOM ENTER

    All/Center/Dynamic/Extents/Left/Previous/Vmax/Window/<Scale(X/XP)>:

3. Type 2 ENTER

    See Figure 15-45.

4. Use the Draw and Modify commands to create the needed shape

    Figure 15-46 shows the untrimmed construction of the extension shape. Remember, you are working in the new UCS, and even though the box lines appear to be in

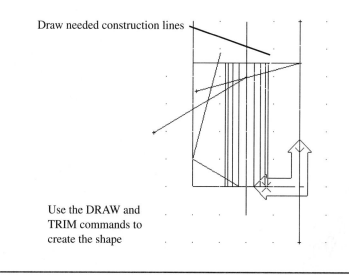

Draw needed construction lines

Use the DRAW and
TRIM commands to
create the shape

Figure 15-46

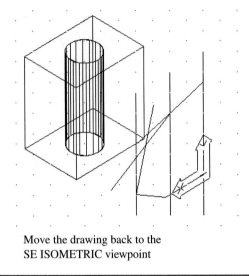

Move the drawing back to the
SE ISOMETRIC viewpoint

Figure 15-47

the same plane, they are not. You cannot use them as part of the construction process. They are visible, but not usable in this plane. Figure 15-47 shows the same construction viewpoint. Horizontal and vertical construction lines were added to the UCS plane so that the OSNAP and LINE commands could be used. Lines were also drawn using relative coordinate values. Figure 15-48 shows the final trimmed shape with the construction lines erased. Figure 15-49 shows the completed shape with the internal cutout added.

15-19 EXERCISE PROBLEMS

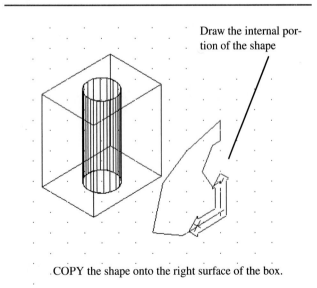

COPY the shape onto the right surface of the box.

Figure 15-49

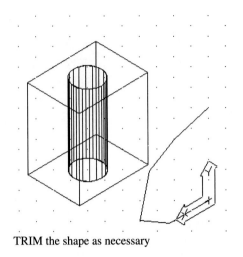

TRIM the shape as necessary

Figure 15-48

5. Use the COPY command to create an identical shape located on the right surface of the box.

Use OSNAP, ENDPOINT to ensure accuracy.

6. Use the RULED SURFACE command to generate surfaces between the two shapes

If necessary, set the SURFTABS to a value of 6. Also use the zoom command to help select the correct lines. Figure 15-50 shows the finished drawing of the object orientated to the WCS.

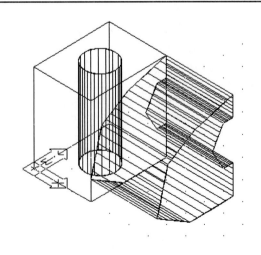

The final object located on the WCS

Figure 15-50

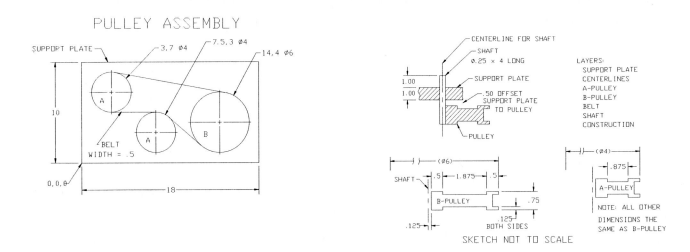

Figure 15-51

15-18 A SAMPLE PROBLEM

The following section explains in detail how to draw the pulley assembly shown in Figure 15-65 on page 613. When creating a complex design or drawing of an object, it is best to start with a freehand sketch and locate all the important assembly and insertion points. A freehand sketch is not required, but it provides a quick and easy way to become familiar with the drawing requirements, resulting in a more efficient drawing approach. Figure 15-51 shows a design sketch for the pulley assembly. Note how the sizes and shapes are defined, center point locations for the pulleys are given in terms of coordinate values, shaft sizes and locations are defined, and assembly points are also defined using coordinate values.

It is also good practice to draw each part on its own LAYER. This allows individual parts to be shown or not shown as needed during the construction. The following LAYERS are recommended. See Section 3-27 for an explanation of the LAYER command.

Select the LAYER icon to access the Layer Control dialog box, or use the DATA pulldown menu to access the LAYER command, then the LAYER CONTROL dialog box, and create the following LAYERS. See Figure 15-52 and Section 3-27.

LAYER - COLOR - LINETYPE

CONSTRUCTION - white - continuous
CENTERLINES - white - center lines
PLATE - white - continuous
A-PULLEY - blue - continuous
B-PULLEY - cyan - continuous
SHAFT - red - continuous
BELT - yellow - continuous

To draw the SUPPORT PLATE

See Figure 15-53. The drawing uses decimal units.

1. Set GRID and SNAP = 1 and the viewpoint for SE ISOMETRIC
2. Access the LAYER CONTROL dialog box using the LAYER icon (WINDOWS) or the LAYER command under the DATA pulldown menu (DOS)
3. Select the PLATE LAYER
4. Select the BOX command, then draw a 1 x 18 x 10 box with its lower front corner on the 0,0,0 origin of the WCS

WINDOWS	DOS
LAYER CONTROL icon	Use DATA pulldown menu, then LAYERS

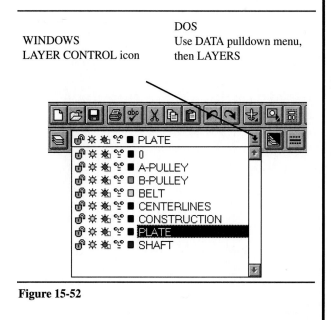

Figure 15-52

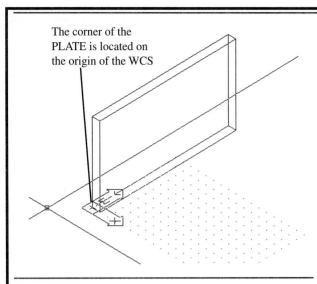

The corner of the PLATE is located on the origin of the WCS

Figure 15-53

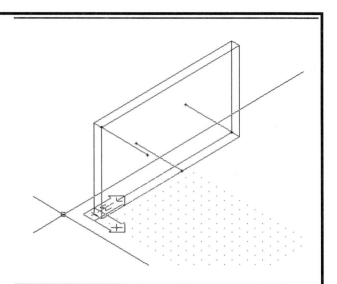

Figure 15-54

To draw the pulley center lines

See Figure 15-54.

1. Access the LAYER CONTROLS dialog box
2. Select the CENTERLINES LAYER
3. Select the LINE command

Draw the three pulley center lines, using coordinate values based on the dimensions given in Figure 15-51. Each shaft is to be 4″ long, so the center lines should be greater than 4″ long. A length of 6″ was chosen. The center lines should start at a point 1″ beyond one end of the shaft and end 1″ beyond the other end.

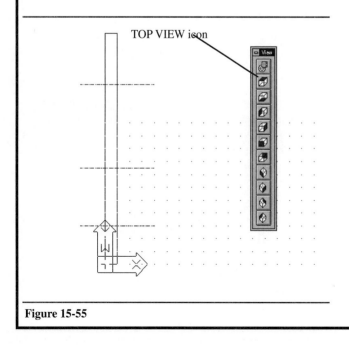

TOP VIEW icon

Figure 15-55

The centerline coordinate points are as follows.

1. From point: -2,3,7 to point: 4,3,7
2. From point: -2,7.5,3 to point: 4,7.5,3
3. From point: -2,14,4 to point: 4,14,4

To draw the A and B pulley profiles

The profiles of the pulleys will be draw on the CONSTRUCTION LAYER and from a TOP viewpoint. The top view will give the drawing a 2D appearance and make it visually easier to draw the profiles. The ELEV command will be used to position the working planes for the profiles at the correct height above the WCS XY plane.

1. Select the TOP view command

The view will change to a top view of the plate. See Figure 15-55.

2. Select the OPTIONS pulldown menu (WINDOWS) or the DATA pulldown menu (DOS), then DRAWING AIDS...

The Drawing Aids dialog box will appear.

3. Change the SNAP setting to .125

The .125 value was chosen because it is the length of the smallest distance on the pulley's profile.

4. Select the ZOOM WINDOW command and zoom the plate and pulley center lines
5. Select the LAYER command, then select the CONSTRUCTION LAYER

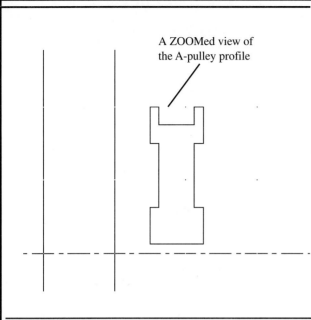

A ZOOMed view of the A-pulley profile

Figure 15-56

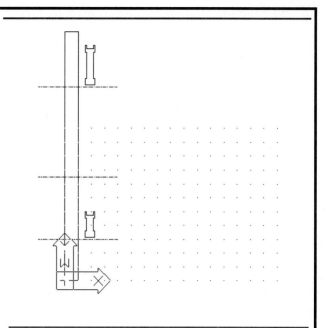

Figure 15-57

At this time you can also turn off any LAYERS that you find visually confusing.

The profiles of the pulleys will be drawn using POLYLINE, then the REVOLVED SURFACE command will be used to generate the final pulley shapes. The POLYLINE construction will be done on the CONSTRUCTION LAYER, and the REVOLVED SURFACE command will be applied to the profiles on the A-PULLEY and B-PULLEY LAYERS.

6. Type ELEV and set the new current elevation to 7 and the new current thickness to 0.0000.

The value of 7 was derived from the centerline location of the first A-pulley, which according to the sketch in Figure 15-51 has a Y component of 7. The chosen orientation on the WCS changes the component value to the Z axis.

7. Select the POLYLINE command and draw the A-pulley profile.

The new current elevation of 7 has raised the working plane of the drawing so that it is aligned with the pulley's center line. This means you can draw the pulley directly. Turn the ORTHO command (F8) on if desired to help produce the required horizontal and vertical lines of the profile. See Figure 15-56.

8. Type ELEV and change the new current elevation to 4
9. Use the ZOOM ALL command to return the drawing to its original size, then use the ZOOM

WINDOW command to enlarge the area for the B-pulley
10. Access the LAYER CONTROL dialog box and select the B-PULLEY LAYER
11. Use POLYLINE to draw the B-pulley's profile
12. Type ELEV and change the new current elevation to 0.

Turn the ORTHO command off, if it was turn on. See Figure 15-57.

To COPY the A-pulley's profile

The assembly requires two A-pulleys, and it is easier to COPY the existing profile than to redraw it. The pulleys are located at two different Z planes so you cannot make the copy directly. The displacement points must be defined in terms of their XYZ component values relative to the WCS.

1. Select the COPY command.

   Select objects:

2. Select the A-pulley profile

   <Base point or displacement>/Multiple:

3. Type 1.5,3,7 ENTER

   Second point of displacement:

4. Type 1.5,7.5,3 ENTER

   See Figure 15-58.

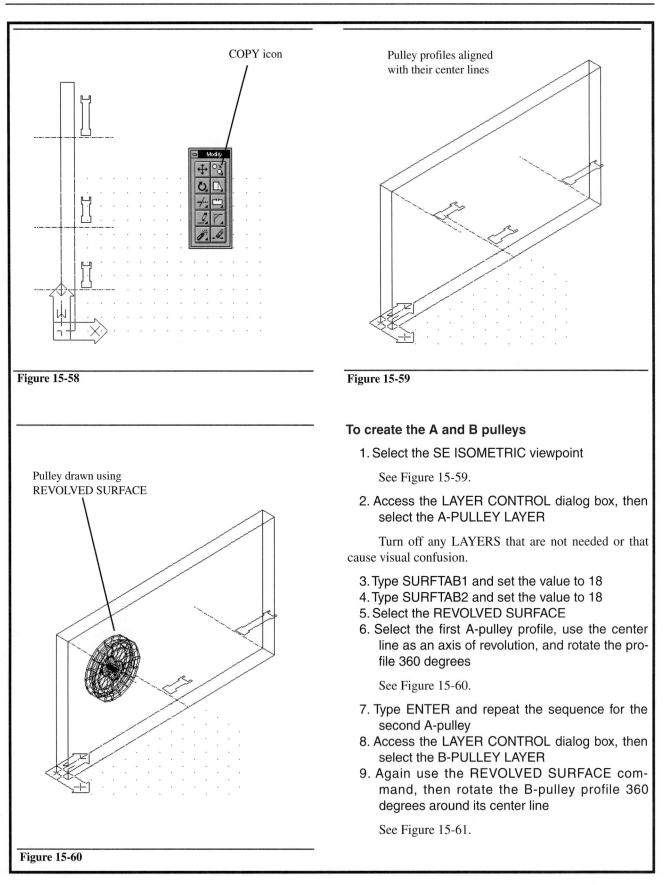

COPY icon

Figure 15-58

Pulley profiles aligned
with their center lines

Figure 15-59

Pulley drawn using
REVOLVED SURFACE

Figure 15-60

To create the A and B pulleys

1. Select the SE ISOMETRIC viewpoint

   See Figure 15-59.

2. Access the LAYER CONTROL dialog box, then select the A-PULLEY LAYER

   Turn off any LAYERS that are not needed or that cause visual confusion.

3. Type SURFTAB1 and set the value to 18
4. Type SURFTAB2 and set the value to 18
5. Select the REVOLVED SURFACE
6. Select the first A-pulley profile, use the center line as an axis of revolution, and rotate the profile 360 degrees

   See Figure 15-60.

7. Type ENTER and repeat the sequence for the second A-pulley
8. Access the LAYER CONTROL dialog box, then select the B-PULLEY LAYER
9. Again use the REVOLVED SURFACE command, then rotate the B-pulley profile 360 degrees around its center line

   See Figure 15-61.

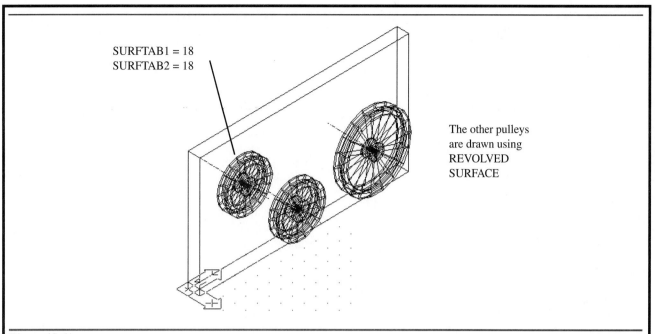

SURFTAB1 = 18
SURFTAB2 = 18

The other pulleys
are drawn using
REVOLVED
SURFACE

Figure 15-61

To draw the shafts

The three shafts are each 4″ long and are perpendicular to the face of the support plate. The PRESET RIGHT view will be used to create a viewpoint perpendicular to the face of the support plate, then the ELEV command can be used to draw the shafts.

1. Select the PRESET UCS command, then select the RIGHT UCS
2. Select the RIGHT view command

See Figure 15-62. The origin will not move and is located at the lower left corner of the support plate. Remember that the working plane of this view is the back face of the support plate, even though you are looking at the front face.

3. Type ELEV ENTER

   New current elevation <0.0000>:

4. Type -1 ENTER

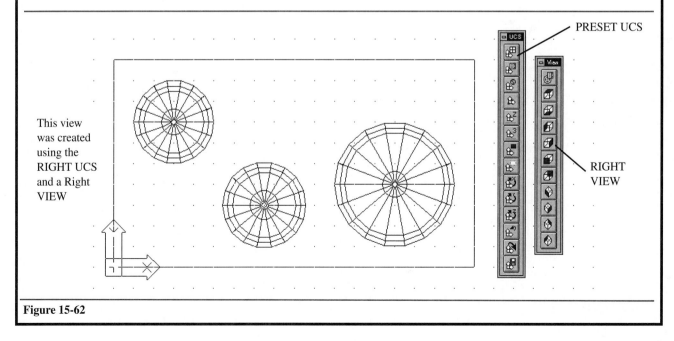

PRESET UCS

This view
was created
using the
RIGHT UCS
and a Right
VIEW

RIGHT
VIEW

Figure 15-62

This value moves the working plane 1″ back from the back face of the support plate.

New current thickness <0.0000>:

5. Type 4 ENTER

The value 4 is the length of the shafts.

6. Select the DIAMETER CIRCLE command

Command:_Circle 3P/2P/TTR/<Center point>:

7. Type 3,7,0 ENTER

The 3,7 XY component values were obtained from the design sketch, Figure 15-51. The Z component is 0 because the working plane has been set to align with the end of the shaft.

Radius/<Diameter>:

8. Type .25 ENTER
9. Type ENTER

Command:_Circle 3P/2P/TTR/<Center point>:

10. Type 7.5,3,0 ENTER

Radius/<Diameter>:

11. Type .25 ENTER
12. Type ENTER

Command:_Circle 3P/2P/TTR/<Center point>:

13. Type 14,4,0 ENTER

Radius/<Diameter>:

14. Type .25 ENTER

To draw the belt

The belt is .50 wide and can be created by constructing the required shape using the CIRCLE, OSNAP TANGENT, LINE, and TRIM commands. The working plane will be moved to a plane .625 from the face of the support plate, and the current elevation thickness set to .50. The .625 value was derived by adding the distance from the front face of the support plate to the edge of the pulleys (.50), and the .125 distance from the edge of the pulleys to the edge of the belt.

The drawing should still be in the RIGHT view orientation. See Figure 15-62.

1. Type ELEV

New current elevation <-1.0000>:

2. Type 1.625 ENTER

The additional 1″ is the thickness of the plate (1.000 + 0.625). The origin that you are working from is still located at the original 0,0,0 point of the WCS.

New current thickness <4.0000>:

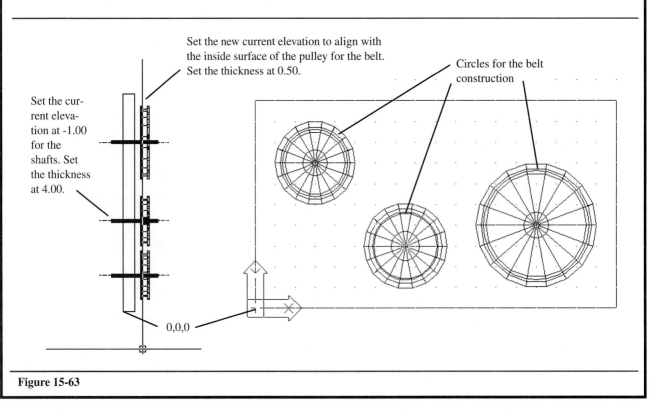

Set the new current elevation to align with the inside surface of the pulley for the belt. Set the thickness at 0.50.

Circles for the belt construction

Set the current elevation at -1.00 for the shafts. Set the thickness at 4.00.

0,0,0

Figure 15-63

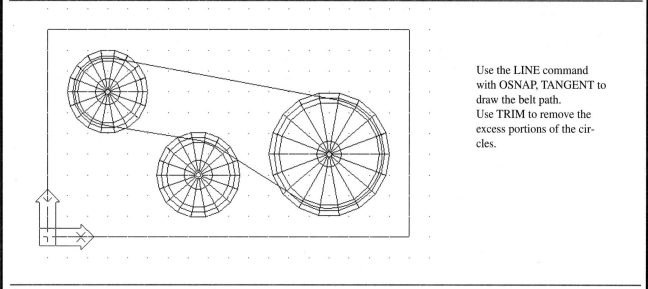

Figure 15-64

Use the LINE command with OSNAP, TANGENT to draw the belt path.
Use TRIM to remove the excess portions of the circles.

3. Type .5 ENTER
4. Access the LAYER CONTROL dialog box, then the BELT LAYER

Turn off any LAYERS that you find visually confusing.

5. Select the OPTIONS pulldown menu, then DRAWING AIDS...
6. Set the GRID value for 1.00 and the SNAP value for .50
7. Select the CIRCLE RADIUS command, and draw three circles as shown in Figure 15-63.

The center point coordinate values are 3,7,0; 7.5,3,0; and 14,4,0: the same points used as the center points for the shafts. Again the Z component is 0 because the working plane has been moved using the ELEV command.

The radius values of 1.625 and 2.625 were derived from the design sketch, Figure 15-51, and define the location on the pulley surfaces where the belt interfaces.

8. Draw the belt path by drawing lines between the circles using the OSNAP, TANGENT command
9. Use the TRIM command to remove the excess portions of the circles

See Figure 15-64.

To create the final assembly drawing

1. Select the LAYER command and turn on all LAYERS except the CONSTRUCTION LAYER
2. Select the PRESET UCS command, then select the WCS box, OK
3. Select the SE ISOMETRIC command

The final drawing appears in Figure 15-65.

4. Select the FILE pulldown menu, then SAVE AS
5. Save the drawing as PULLEYS

The drawing will be used again in Chapter 16 when rendering is discussed.

Finished drawing

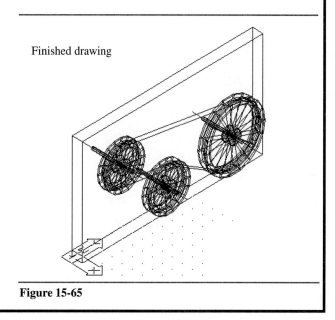

Figure 15-65

Draw surface models of the objects in exercise problems
EX15-1 to EX15-3.

EX15-1 INCHES

EX15-2 INCHES

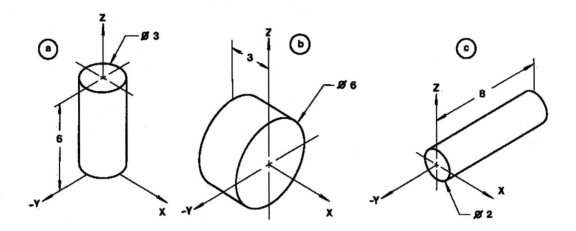

EX15-3 INCHES

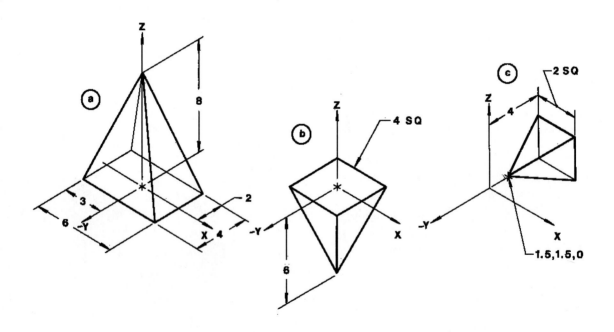

EX15-4 INCHES

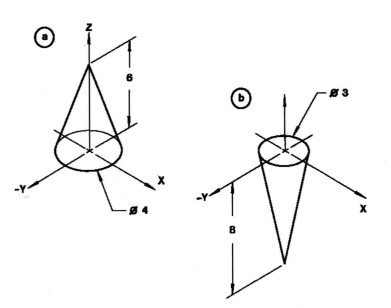

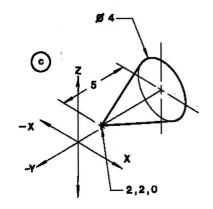

Draw the three boxes positioned as shown. The length, width, and height for each box is as follows.
- a. X = 6, Y = 5, Z = 2
- b. X = 4, Y = 4, Z = 4
- c. X = 5, Y = 2, Z = 1

EX15-5 INCHES

Draw the three boxes as shown centered about the Z axis. The length, width, and height for each box is as follows.
- a. X = 8, Y = 8, Z = 1
- b. X = 6, Y = 6, Z = 2
- c. X = 2, Y = 2, Z = 6

EX15-6 INCHES

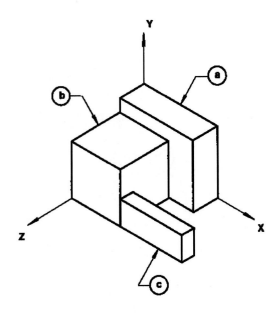

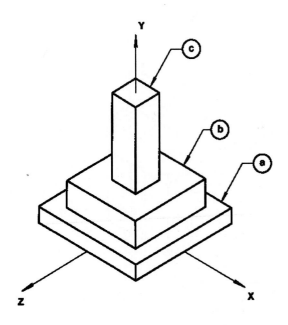

Draw the three cylinders shown below centered about the Y axis positioned as shown. The sizes of the cylinders are as follows. Use either the REVOLVED SURFACE or RULED SURFACE commands.

    a. Diameter = 2, height = 4
    b. Diameter = 4, height = 1
    c. Diameter = 6, height = 2

EX15-7 INCHES

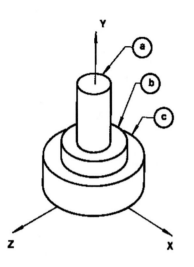

Draw the three boxes positioned as shown. The length, width, and height for each box is 2 × 2 × 5.

Draw surface models of the objects shown in exercise problems EX15-8 to EX15-27.

EX15-8 FEET

EX15-9 MILLIMETERS

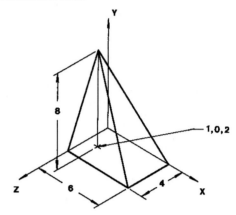

EX15-10 MILLIMETERS

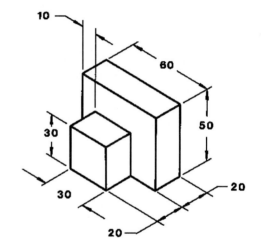

EX15-11 MILLIMETERS

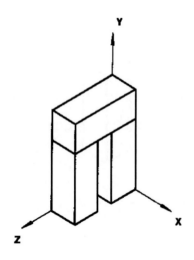

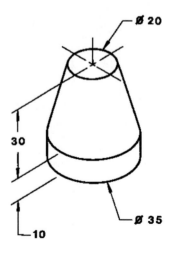

EX15-12 MILLIMETERS

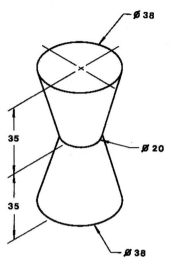

EX15-15 MILLIMETERS

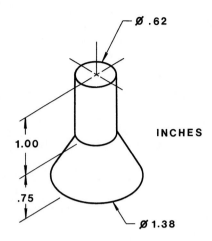

EX15-13 MILLIMETERS

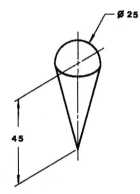

EX15-16 MILLIMETERS

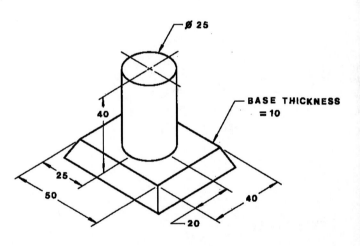

NOTE: LOWER SURFACE OF BASE
IS +5 GREATER THAN TOP
SURFACE - ALL AROUND

EX15-14 MILLIMETERS

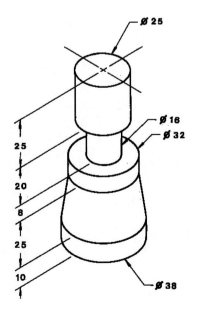

EX15-17 MILLIMETERS

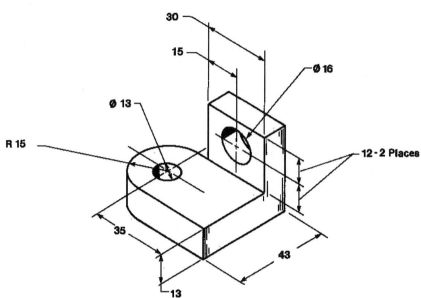

EX15-18 MILLIMETERS

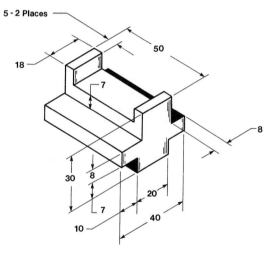

EX15-20 INCHES

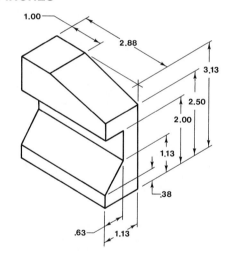

EX15-19 FEET

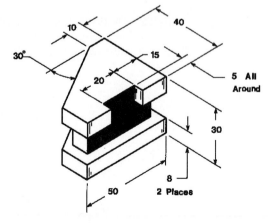

EX15-21 MILLIMETERS

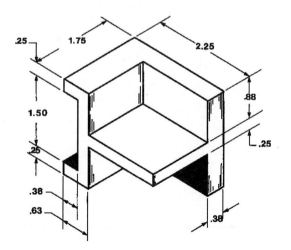

EX15-22 MILLIMETERS

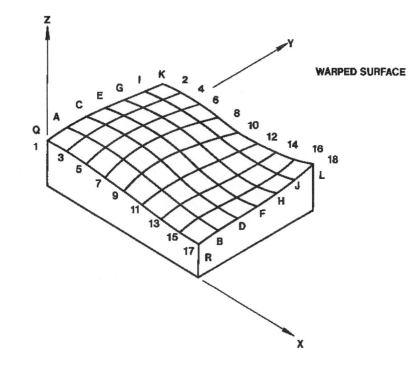

WARPED SURFACE

LINE Q R			
N	X	Z	Y
1	0	20.0	0
3	10	20.4	0
5	20	20.0	0
7	30	19.6	0
9	40	17.8	0
11	50	16.8	0
13	60	16.0	0
15	70	15.0	0
17	80	14.8	0

LINE A B			
N	X	Z	Y
1	0	20.5	10
3	10	21.5	10
5	20	22.0	10
7	30	21.5	10
9	40	20.5	10
11	50	18.0	10
13	60	16.5	10
15	70	15.8	10
17	80	15.2	10

LINE C D			
N	X	Z	Y
1	0	20.0	20
3	10	21.2	20
5	20	22.2	20
7	30	22.7	20
9	40	21.3	20
11	50	17.8	20
13	60	16.0	20
15	70	15.5	20
17	80	15.8	20

LINE E F			
N	X	Z	Y
1	0	19.3	30
3	10	20.8	30
5	20	22.0	30
7	30	22.5	30
9	40	20.5	30
11	50	17.5	30
13	60	15.8	30
15	70	15.0	30
17	80	16.0	30

LINE G H			
N	X	Z	Y
1	0	17.5	40
3	10	19.0	40
5	20	20.3	40
7	30	20.0	40
9	40	18.8	40
11	50	16.3	40
13	60	15.2	40
15	70	15.4	40
17	80	16.8	40

LINE I J			
N	X	Z	Y
1	0	16.5	50
3	10	18.0	50
5	20	18.8	50
7	30	17.8	50
9	40	16.6	50
11	50	15.5	50
13	60	15.3	50
15	70	16.0	50
17	80	18.0	50

LINE K L			
N	X	Z	Y
1	0	15.0	60
3	10	16.5	60
5	20	17.0	60
7	30	14.5	60
9	40	13.8	60
11	50	14.3	60
13	60	15.6	60
15	70	17.5	60
17	80	20.0	60

EX15-23 MILLIMETERS

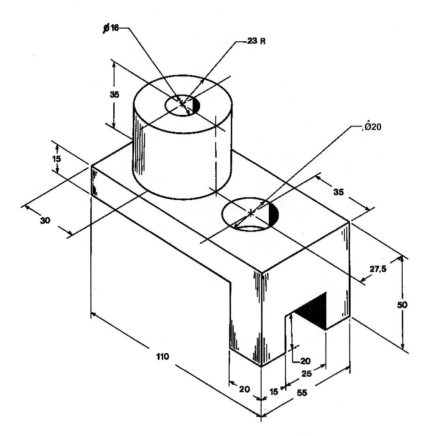

EX15-24 INCHES

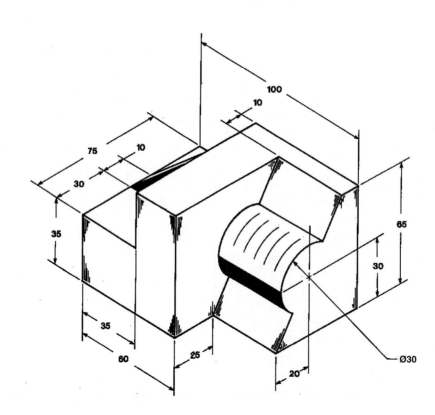

EX15-25 INCHES

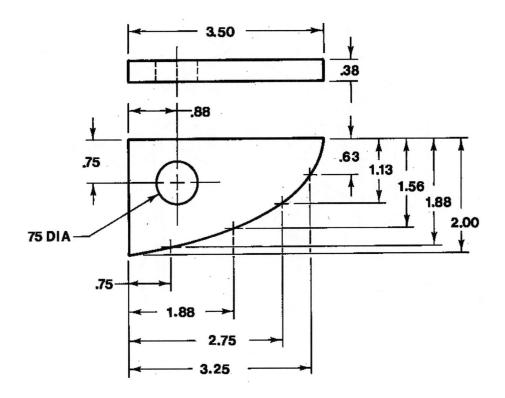

EX15-26 MILLIMETERS

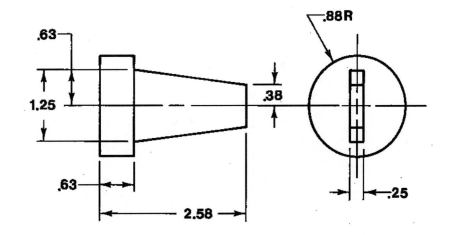

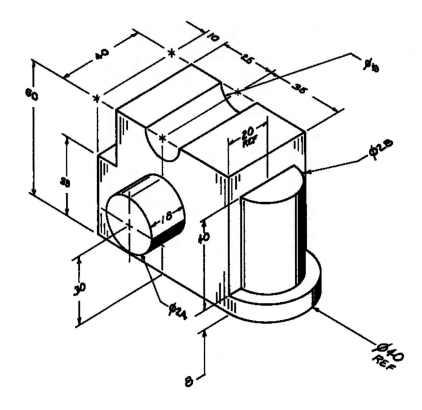

EX15-27 MILLIMETERS

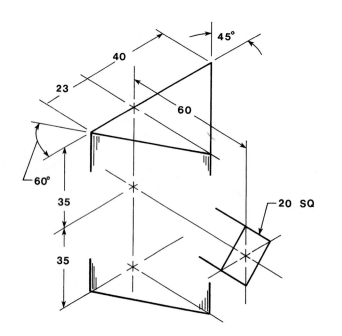

EX15-28 MILLIMETERS

Draw the pulley assembly defined by the following design sketch.

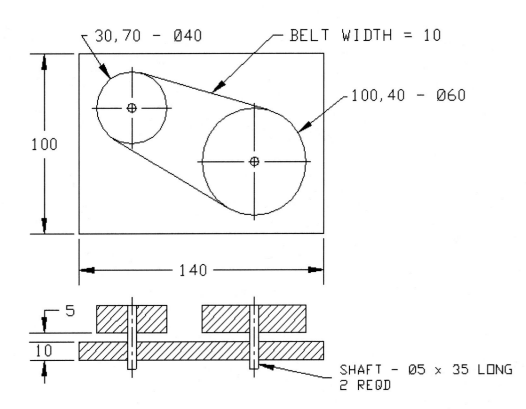

30,70 – Ø40

BELT WIDTH = 10

100,40 – Ø60

100

140

5

10

SHAFT – Ø5 × 35 LONG
2 REQD

PULLEY PROFILES

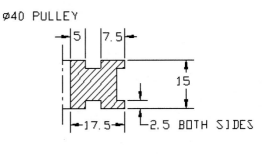

Ø40 PULLEY

5   7.5

15

17.5   2.5 BOTH SIDES

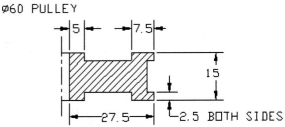

Ø60 PULLEY

5   7.5

15

27.5   2.5 BOTH SIDES

EX15-29 MILLIMETERS

Draw the following pulley assembly as defined in the following design sketch. The pulley profile sizes are as defined in exercise problem EX15-28.

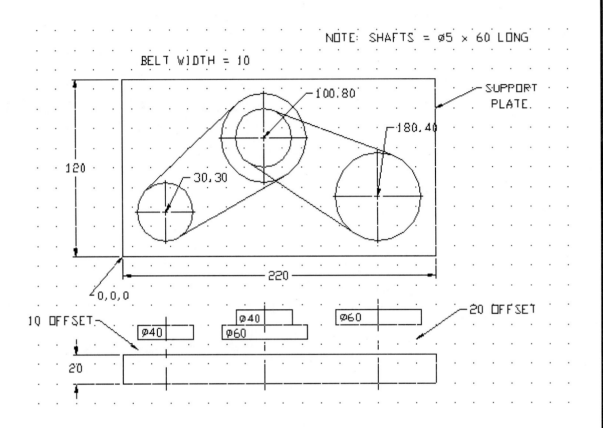

EX15-30

Build a scale model of an airplane or car, measure the model relative to a defined 0,0,0 reference point, and create a surface model of the object's outside surfaces.

CHAPTER 16

Solid Modeling

16-1 INTRODUCTION

This chapter introduces solid modeling. The solid modeling commands can be accessed in the WINDOWS version using the SOLIDS toolbar and in the DOS version using the DRAW pulldown, then the SOLIDS command. See Figure 16-1 DOS and Figure 16-1 WINDOWS.

Figure 16-1 DOS

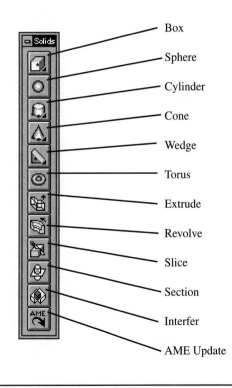

Figure 16-1 WINDOWS

625

Solid modeling allows you to create objects as solid entities. Solid models differ from the surface models created in the last chapter because solid models have density and are not merely joined surfaces.

Solid models are created by joining together, unioning, basic primitive shapes: boxes, cylinders, wedges, etc., or by defining a shape as a polyline line and extruding it into a solid shape. Solid primitives may also be subtracted from one another. For example, to create a hole in a solid box, draw a solid cylinder, then subtract the cylinder from the box. The result will be an open volume in the shape of a hole.

The first part of the chapter deals with the SOLIDS individual commands. The second part gives examples of how to create solid objects by joining primitive shapes and changing UCSs.

16-2 BOX

Figure 16-2 shows the two BOX options: CENTER and CORNER. The CENTER command is used to draw a box by first locating its center point. The CORNER command is used to draw a box by first locating one of its corner points.

To draw a BOX using the CENTER command

See Figure 16-3.

1. Select the CENTER BOX command

Command:_box
Center/<Corner of box> <0,0,0>:_ce
Center of box <0,0,0>:

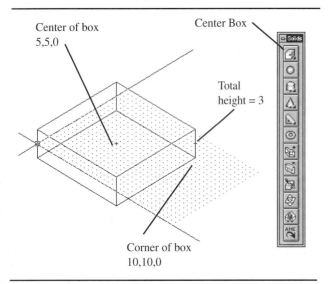

Center of box
5,5,0

Center Box

Total
height = 3

Corner of box
10,10,0

Figure 16-3

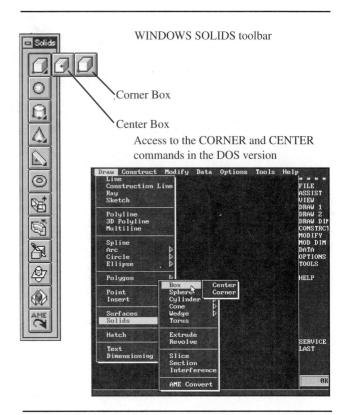

WINDOWS SOLIDS toolbar

Corner Box

Center Box

Access to the CORNER and CENTER
commands in the DOS version

Figure 16-2

2. Type 5,5,0 ENTER or locate the center point using the coordinate display at the lower left of the screen

Cube/Length/<corner of box>:

3. Type 10,10,0 ENTER

Height:

4. Type 3 ENTER

The box is centered about the 5,5,0 point. The size of the box along the XY plane is defined by the distance from the center point (5,5,0) to the right corner of the box (10,10,0). The height input of 3 represents half the total height of 6 centered about the XY plane.

To draw a BOX using the CORNER command

See Figure 16-4.

1. Select the CORNER BOX command

Command:_box
Center/<Corner of the box> <0,0,0>:

2. Type ENTER

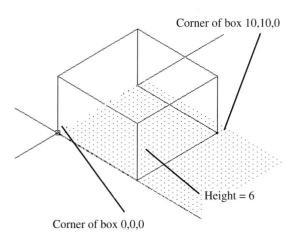

Figure 16-4

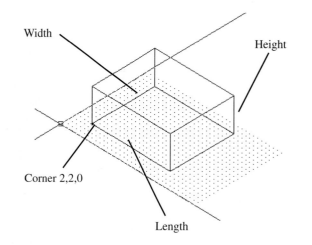

Figure 16-5

This means that the corner of the box will be located on the 0,0,0 point of the XY plane.

Cube/Length/<corner of box>:

3. Type 10,10,0 ENTER

Height:

4. Type 6 ENTER

The box shown in Figure 16-4 has its bottom surface aligned with the XY plane, whereas the XY plane passes through the middle of the box shown in Figure 16-3.

To draw a BOX from given dimensions

See Figure 16-5. Draw a box with a length of 10, a width of 8, and a height of 4, with its corner at the 2,2,0 point.

1. Select the CORNER BOX command

Command: _box
Center/<Corner of the box> <0,0,0>:

2. Type 2,2,0 ENTER

Cube/Length/<corner of box>:

3. Type L ENTER

Length:

4. Type 10 ENTER

Width:

5. Type 8 ENTER

Height:

6. Type 4 ENTER

To draw a cube

See Figure 16-6.

1. Select the CORNER BOX command

Command: _box
Center/<Corner of the box> <0,0,0>:

2. Type ENTER

Cube/Length/<corner of box>:

3. Type C ENTER

Length:

4. Type 7.5 ENTER

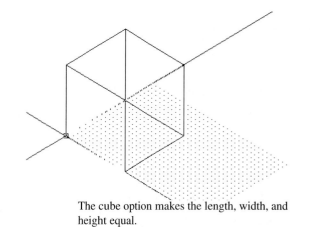

The cube option makes the length, width, and height equal.

Figure 16-6

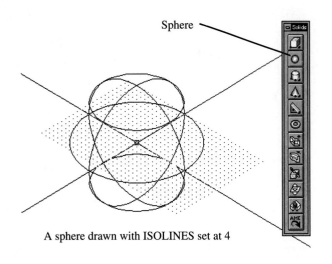

A sphere drawn with ISOLINES set at 4

Figure 16-7

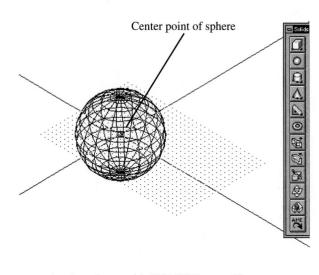

A sphere drawn with ISOLINES set at 18

Figure 16-8

16-3 SPHERE

The visual accuracy of solids depends on the settings of the ISOLINES command. The sphere shown in Figure 16-7 was drawn with an ISOLINES setting of 4. For this section the ISOLINES setting will be changed to 18.

To change the ISOLINES settings

1. Type ISOLINES ENTER

   There is no icon for the ISOLINES command.

   New value for isolines <4>;

2. Type 18 ENTER

   Command:

   The new value is now in place and will be used for all solids drawn until it is changed or a new drawing is started.

To draw a sphere

See Figure 16-8.

1. Select the SPHERE command

   Center of sphere <0,0,0>:

2. Type 5,5,0 ENTER

   Diameter/<Radius> of sphere:

3. Type 4 ENTER

16-4 CYLINDER

There are two options associated with the CYLINDER command: ELLIPTICAL and CENTER. See Figure 16-9. This means cylinders may be drawn with either elliptical or circular base planes. The base elliptical shape is drawn using the same procedure as was outlined for the ELLIPSE command in Chapter 3.

To draw a cylinder with an elliptical base

See Figure 16-10. The sequence described below uses coordinate value input. The same points could have been selected by moving the crosshairs and pressing the left mouse button.

1. Select the ELLIPTICAL CYLINDER command

   Command:_cylinder
   Elliptical/<center point> <0,0,0>:_e
   Center/<Axis endpoint>:

2. Type 0,0,0 ENTER

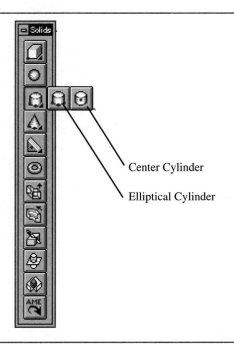

Figure 16-9

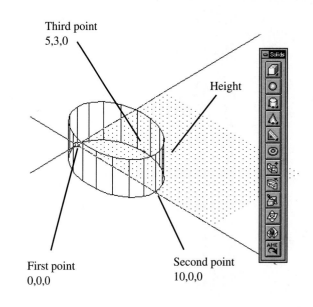

Figure 16-10

This input will locate one end of the base axis on the 0,0,0 point of the XY plane.

Axis endpoint 2:

3. Type 10,0,0

This input will locate the axis line along the X axis.

Other axis distance:

Note that the line dragging from the crosshairs has one end centered on the axis just defined.

4. Type 5,3.5,0 ENTER

Center of other end/<Height>:

5. Type 4 ENTER

An elliptical base can also be defined by first defining a center point for the ellipse, then defining the length of the radii of the major and minor axes.

To draw a cylinder with a circular base

See Figure 16-11.

1. Select the CENTER CYLINDER command

Command: _cylinder
Elliptical/<center point> <0,0,0>:

2. Type 5,5,0 ENTER

Diameter/<Radius>:

3. Type 4 ENTER

Center of other end/<Height>:

4. Type 6 ENTER

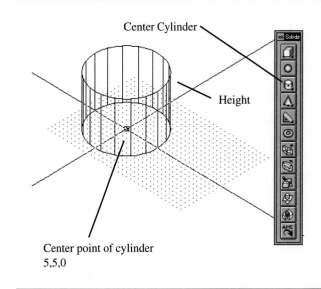

Figure 16-11

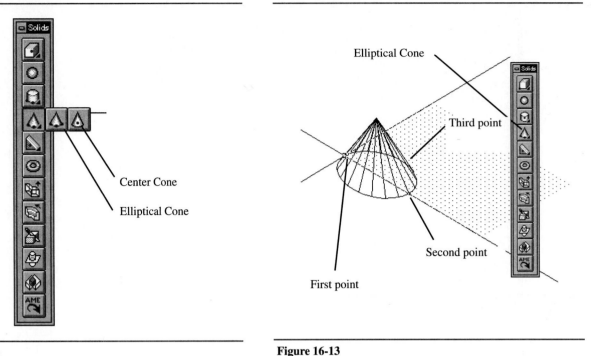

Figure 16-12

Figure 16-13

16-5 CONES

There are two options associated with the CONE command: ELLIPTICAL and CENTER. See Figure 16-12. This means that cones can be drawn with either an elliptical or circular base plane. The base elliptical shape is drawn using the same procedure as was outlined for the ELLIPSE command in Chapter 3. The CONE command cannot be used to draw truncated cones. Truncated cones are created by subtracting the top portion of the cone.

To draw a CONE with an elliptical base

See Figure 16-13.

1. Select the ELLIPTICAL CONE command

   Command:_cone
   Elliptical/<center point> <0,0,0>:_e
   Center/<Axis endpoint>:

2. Type 0,0,0 ENTER

   This input will locate one end of the ellipse axis at the 0,0,0 point of the XY plane.

   Axis point 2:

3. Type 8,0,0

Other axis distance:

Note that the line dragging from the crosshairs has one end centered on the axis just defined.

4. Type 3 ENTER

   Apex/<Height>:

5. Type 6 ENTER

A response of A to the Apex/<Height>: prompt allows you to select the height of the cone using the crosshairs.

To draw a cone with a circular base

See Figure 16-14.

1. Select the CENTER CONE command

   Command:_cone
   Elliptical <center point> <0,0,0>:

2. Type 5,5,0 ENTER

   Diameter/<Radius>:

3. Type 3 ENTER

   Apex/<Height>:

4. Type 7 ENTER

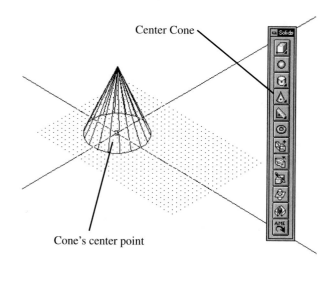

Center Cone

Cone's center point

Figure 16-14

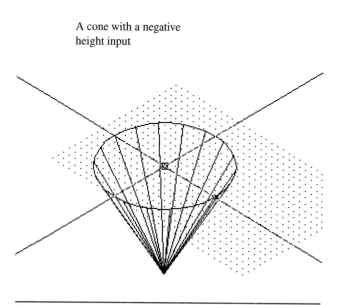

A cone with a negative
height input

Figure 16-15

A response of A to the Apex/<Height>: prompt allows you to select the height of the cone using the crosshairs. Figure 16-15 shows a cone drawn using a negative height input.

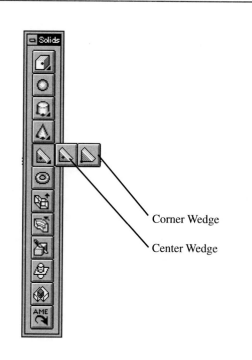

Corner Wedge

Center Wedge

Figure 16-16

16-6 WEDGE

There are two options associated with the WEDGE command: CENTER and CORNER. See Figure 16-16.

To draw a wedge by defining its center point

See Figure 16-17.

1. Select the CENTER WEDGE command

   Command:_Wedge
   Center/<Center of wedge> <0,0,0>:_ce
   Center of wedge <0,0,0>:

2. Type 5,5,0 ENTER

   Cube/Length/<Corner of wedge>:

3. Type 10,10,0 ENTER

   Height:

4. Type 4 ENTER

The wedge shown in Figure 16-17 is centered about the XY plane; that is, part of the wedge is above the plane, and part is below. This is not easy to see even with the grid shown. The far right corner of the wedge is actually located below the grid at the 10,10 point. Figure 16-17 also shows a side view of the same wedge with a line drawn on the XY plane added. Note how the line bisects the height line of the wedge.

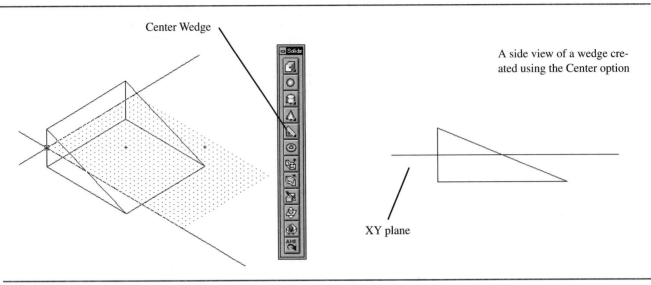

Center Wedge

A side view of a wedge created using the Center option

XY plane

Figure 16-17

To draw a wedge by defining its corner point

See Figure 16-18.

1. Select the CORNER WEDGE command

Command:_wedge
Center/<Corner> <0,0,0>:

2. Type ENTER

This input will locate the corner of the wedge on the 0,0,0 point of the XY plane.

Cube/Length/<other corner>:

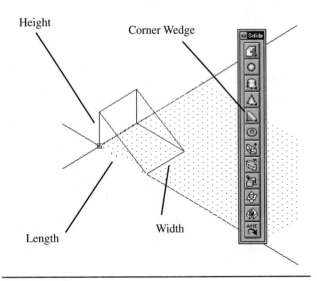

Height

Corner Wedge

Length

Width

Figure 16-18

The default response to this command defines the diagonal corner of the wedge's base. In this example, the wedge's base will be defined using length and width inputs.

3. Type L ENTER

Length:

4. Type 5 ENTER

Width:

5. Type 4 ENTER

Height:

6. Type 3 ENTER

To draw a wedge using selected points

See Figure 16-19.

1. Select the CORNER WEDGE command

Command:_wedge
Center/<Corner> <0,0,0>:

2. Type ENTER

This input will locate the corner of the wedge on the 0,0,0 point of the XY plane.

Cube/Length/<other corner>:

3. Type L ENTER

Length:

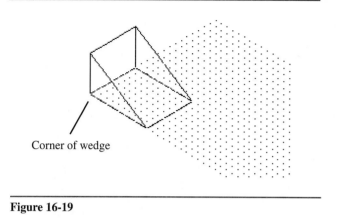

Corner of wedge

Figure 16-19

4. Select the 0,0 point on the XY plane by moving the crosshairs to that point and pressing the left mouse button

   Length: Second point:

5. Select a point on the X axis

The length input values are measured only along the X axis. If you had selected a point within the XY plane, the resulting length distance would have been the X component of the selected point relative to the first point selected. The width distances are measured only in the Y direction, and the height distances in the Z direction.

   Width:

6. Select the 0,0 point

   Width: Second point:

7. Select a point on the Y axis

   Height:

8. Select the 0,0 point

   Height: Second point:

9. Select a point in the Z direction

The technique of drawing a wedge by selecting points is best used when another object already exists and the OSNAP command can be used to align the selection points with the existing object.

To align a wedge with an existing wedge

This example serves to illustrate how you can use different inputs to position a wedge. Figure 16-19 shows a wedge. The problem is to draw another wedge with its back surface aligned with the back surface of the existing wedge.

1. Select the CORNER WEDGE command

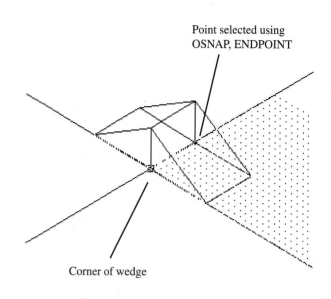

Point selected using OSNAP, ENDPOINT

Corner of wedge

Figure 16-20

   Command: _wedge
   Center/<Corner of wedge> <0,0,0>:

2. Select OSNAP, ENDPOINT and select the corner of the existing wedge

   Cube/Length/<other corner>:

3. Type L ENTER

   Length:

4. Type -5 ENTER

   Width:

5. Select OSNAP, ENDPOINT and select the corner point

   Width: _endp of Second point:

6. Select the other corner of the Y axis

   Height:

7. Type 3 ENTER

See Figure 16-20. The construction could also have been achieved by using the COPY command to create a second wedge, the ROTATE command to rotate the new wedge 180 degrees, and the MOVE command to align the wedge with the existing wedge. Use OSNAP, ENDPOINT to ensure exact alignment.

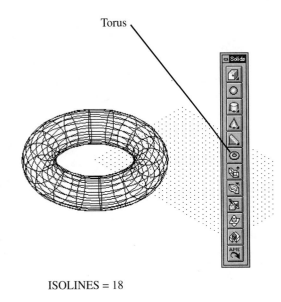

ISOLINES = 18

Figure 16-21

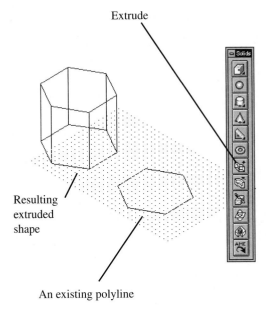

Figure 16-22

16-7 TORUS

A torus is a donutlike shape. See Figure 16-21.

To draw a torus

1. Select the TORUS command

   Command: _torus
   Center of torus <0,0,0,>:

2. Type ENTER

   This input will locate the center of the torus at the 0,0,0 point on the XY plane.

   Diameter/<Radius> of torus:

3. Type 5 ENTER

   Diameter/<Radius> of tube:

4. Type 1.5 ENTER

   The torus shown in Figure 16-21 was created with ISOLINES set at 18.

16-8 EXTRUDE

The EXTRUDE command is used to extend existing 2D shapes into 3D shapes.

NOTE

The EXTRUDE command can be applied only to a polyline.

To extrude a 2D POLYLINE

Figure 16-22 shows a hexagon drawn using the POLYGON command. All shapes drawn using the POLYGON command are automatically drawn as a polyline, so the hexagon can be extruded. How to draw a polygon is discussed in Chapter 3.

1. Select the EXTRUDE command

   Command: _extrude
   Select objects:

2. Select the hexagon

   Select objects:

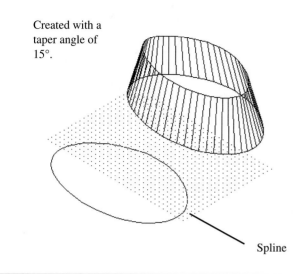

Created with a
taper angle of
15°.

Spline

Figure 16-23

This shape was creatd as
individual line segments,
then joined to form a polyline.

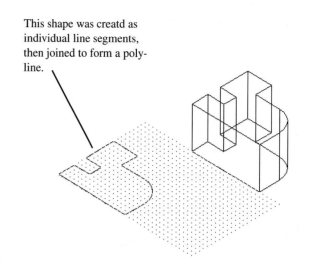

Figure 16-24

3. Type ENTER

   Path/<Height of Extrusions>:

4. Type 6 ENTER

   Extrusion taper angle <0>:

5. Type ENTER

Figure 16-23 shows an irregular spline and an extrusion created from the spline. The procedure is as outlined above with a 15 response to the Extrusion taper angle prompt.

To create a polyline from line segments

Figure 16-24 shows a 2D shape that was created using the LINE, SEGMENTS, and ARC commands. The object must be converted to a polyline before it can be extruded.

1. Select the EDIT POLYGON command from the MODIFY pulldown menu in the DOS version, or the MODIFY toolbar in the WINDOWS version

   Command: _pedit Select polyline:

2. Select any one of the lines in the 2D shape

   Object selected is not a polyline
   Do you want to turn it into one? <Y>:

3. Type ENTER

   Close/ Join/ Width/ Edit Vertex/ Fit/ Spline/ Decurve /Ltype gen/ Undo/ eXit <X>:

4. Type J ENTER

   Select objects:

5. Window the entire object

   Select objects: Other corner: 11 found
   Select objects:

6. Type ENTER

   10 Segments added to polyline
   Close/ Join/ Width /Edit Vertex/ Fit/ Spline/ Decurve/ Ltype gen/ Undo/ eXit <X>:

7. Select the EXTRUDE command and create an extrusion 5 units high with a 0 degree taper angle

16-9 REVOLVE

The REVOLVE command is used to create a solid 3D object by rotating a 2D shape around an axis of revolution. Figure 16-25 shows a torus created by rotating a circle around a straight line. The density of the resulting object is controlled by the ISOLINES command. In this example ISOLINES is set at 18.

To create a REVOLVE object

This procedure assumes that the curve path (2D shape) and the line that will be used as the axis of revolution already exist on the drawing.

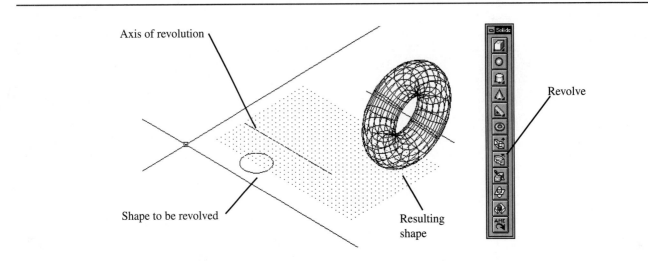

Figure 16-25

1. Select the REVOLVE command

   Command: _revolve
   Select objects:

2. Select the circle

   Select objects;

3. Press the right mouse button

   Axis of revolution — Object/X/Y/<Start point axis>:

4. Select one end of the line used as the axis of revolution

   Use OSNAP, ENDPOINT to ensure accuracy.

   <End point of Axis>:

5. Select the other end of the axis line

   Angle of revolution <full circle>:

6. Type ENTER

16-10 SLICE

The SLICE command is used to remove part of an existing solid object. The plane of the slice can be defined using several different methods.

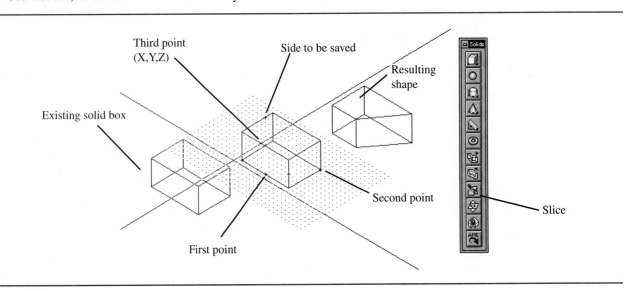

Figure 16-26

To SLICE an object — 3 points

See Figure 16-26.

1. Select the SLICE command

   Command: _slice
   Select objects:

2. Select the box

   Select objects:

3. Type ENTER

   Slicing plane by object/Zaxis/View/XY/YZ/ZX/ <3 points>:

4. Type ENTER

This input means that the cutting plane for the slice will be defined using three points. This is a similar process to that used to define a UCS in Chapter 13.

   1st point on plane:

5. Select a point

In this example a first point was selected along the X axis of the box.

   2nd point on plane:

6. Select the far right corner of the box

The OSNAP, ENDPOINT command can be used to ensure accuracy.

   3rd point on plane:

7. Select the third point on the plane

In this example a coordinate value (X,Y,Z) was used to define the third point. Remember, the crosshairs move only on the XY plane, so either OSNAP commands or an X,Y,Z coordinate value must be used to define the point. It cannot be defined by moving the crosshairs and selecting a point.

   Both sides/<Point on desired side of the plane>:

8. Select a point on the part of the object you want to remain

In this example the far left corner was selected. Figure 16-26 shows the resulting 3D shape.

To SLICE an object — Z axis

The Z axis option allows you to specify a slicing plane by defining a line with its origin on the Z axis and its other end in an XY plane. The resulting slice will be generated normal to the defining line. See Figure 16-27.

1. Select the SLICE command

   Command: _slice
   Select objects:

2. Select the box

   Select objects:

3. Type ENTER

   Slicing plane by object/Zaxis/View/XY/YZ/ZX/ <3 points>:

4. Type Z ENTER

   Point on plane:

5. Type 5,0,4 ENTER

This point could also have been selected using the crosshairs.

   Point on Z-axis (normal) of the plane:

6. Select a point on the Z axis

In this example the point 0,0,2 was selected. Again the point could have been selected using the crosshairs.

   Both sides/<Point on desired side of the plane>:

7. Select a point on the object on the side of the plane you want to keep

In this example, a point on the Y axis was selected. Figure 16-27 shows the resulting sliced object.

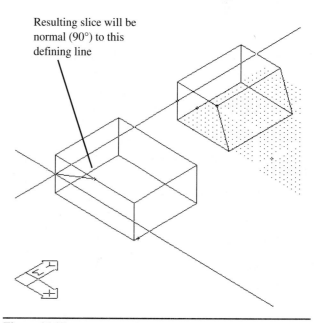

Resulting slice will be normal (90°) to this defining line

Figure 16-27

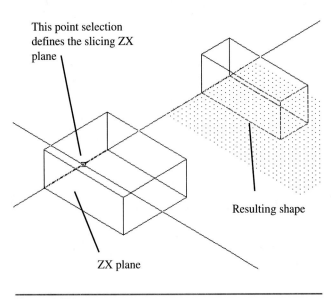

This point selection defines the slicing ZX plane

ZX plane

Resulting shape

Figure 16-28

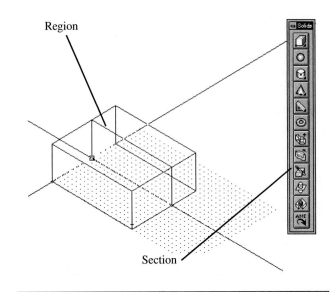

Region

Section

Figure 16-29

To SLICE an object — ZX

The SLICE command lists three plane options: XY, YZ, and ZX. Each of these options allows you to take slices parallel to these principal planes. See Figure 16-28.

1. Select the SLICE command

   Command: _slice
   Select objects:

2. Select the box

   Select objects:

3. Type ENTER

   Slicing plane by object/Zaxis/View/XY/YZ/ZX/<3 points>:

4. Type ZX ENTER

   Point on the zx plane <0,0,0>:

   This prompt is asking for the location of the ZX slicing plane. The plane will be drawn parallel to the ZX plane based at the 0,0,0 origin, so select a point along the Y axis.

5. Select a point on the Y axis

   Both sides/<Point on desired side of the plane>:

6. Select a point on the object on the side of the plane you want to keep

16-11 SECTION

The SECTION command is used to define a region within an existing solid. The regions are defined in the same manner as are slicing planes discussed in the previous section. See Figure 16-29.

1. Select the SECTION command

   Command: _section
   Select objects:

2. Select the box

   Select objects:

3. Type ENTER

   Slicing plane by object/Zaxis/View/XY/YZ/ZX/<3 points>:

4. Type ZX ENTER

   Point on the zx plane <0,0,0>:

   This prompt is asking for a location parallel to the ZX plane based at the 0,0,0 origin. The defining point for the region will be a point along the Y axis.

5. Select a point on the Y axis

   Figure 16-29 shows the resulting region. The region is an independent object or plane. This can be verified by erasing the box. After the box is erased, the region will remain.

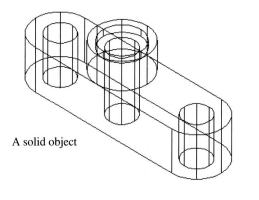

A solid object

Figure 16-30

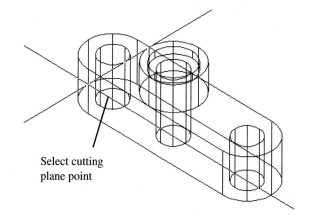

Select cutting plane point

Figure 16-31

To create a sectional view from a solid object

Figure 16-30 shows a solid object. Use the SECTION command to create a sectional view along the longitudinal center line of the object.

1. Select the SECTION command

   Command:_section
   Select objects

2. Select the object

   Select objects:

3. Type ENTER

Slicing plane by object/Zaxis/View/XY/YZ/ZX/<3 points>:

4. Type ZX ENTER

   Point on the zx plane <0.00>:

5. Locate a point on the object for the sectional cutting plane

See Figure 16-31. See Chapter 6 for section view terminology. The section cutting plane will appear on the object. See Figure 16-32.

6. Select the MOVE command and move the cutting plane away from the solid object.

See Figure 16-33. In order to apply HATCH lines to the just created sectional view, a UCS aligned to the sectional view must be created.

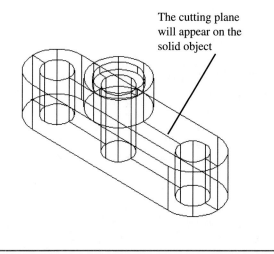

The cutting plane will appear on the solid object

Figure 16-32

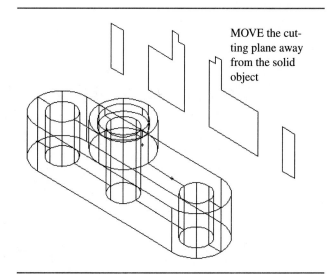

MOVE the cutting plane away from the solid object

Figure 16-33

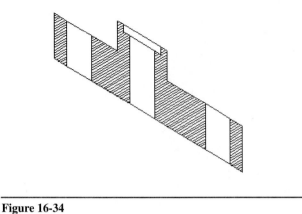

Figure 16-34

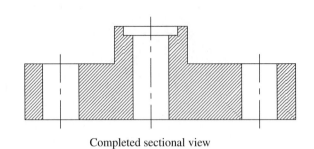

Completed sectional view

Figure 16-36

7. Select the SET UCS command, then 3 points
8. Select the lower left corner of the sectional view as the origin, the lower right corner as the second point, and the upper left corner as the third point.

Use OSNAP ENPOINT to ensure accuracy of the point selections.

9. Select the HATCH command, then SELECT OBJECTS and select the appropriate areas on the sectional view
10. Add the appropriate missing lines

See Figure 16-34. See Chapter 6 for instructions on the HATCH command.

11. Create a LAYER called SECTION and use the

CHANGE PROPERTIES command to move the sectional view to the SECTION LAYER

See Figure 16-35.

12. Turn off the 0 LAYER, and turn on the SECTION LAYER and make it the current LAYER

Only the sectional view should be seen on the screen.

13. Select the 3D VIEWPOINT PRESET command, then the FRONT command

If the sectional view appears too large for the screen, use the ZOOM command to reduce the view's size.

14. Add the appropriate center lines

Figure 16-36 shows the resulting sectional view.

Locate the sectional view on its own LAYER

Modify Region		
Properties		
Color... ■ BYLAYER	Handle:	37
Layer... SECTION	Thickness:	0.0000
Linetype... BYLAYER	Linetype Scale:	1.0000

| OK | Cancel | Help... |

Figure 16-35

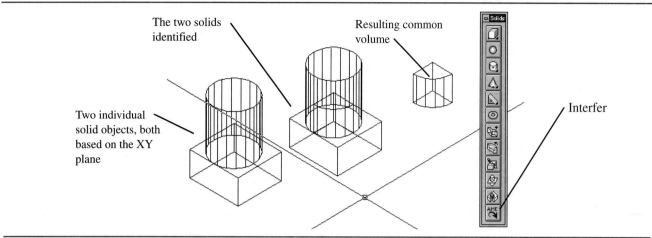

Figure 16-37

16-12 INTERFER

The INTERFER command is used to define a volume common to two or more existing solid objects. Figure 16-37 shows a solid cylinder and box that intersect each other. They were both drawn on the XY plane. The following procedure will define the volume common to both of them.

1. Select the INTERFER command

   Command: -interfere Select the first set of solids:
   Select objects:

2. Select the box

   Select objects:

3. Type ENTER or press the right mouse button

   Select the second set of solids:
   Select objects:

4. Select the cylinder

   Select objects:

5. Type ENTER or press the right mouse button

   Create interference solids ? <N>:

6. Type Y ENTER

   The common volume is now defined but difficult to see.

7. Select the ERASE icon from the Modify toolbar and erase the box and cylinder.

   Figure 16-37 shows the resulting common volume.

16-13 UNION AND SUBTRACTION

Solid objects may be combined to form more complex objects. Objects can be added together using the UNION command and subtracted from each other using the SUBTRACT command. A volume common to two or more objects may be defined using the INTERSECTION command. For the WINDOWS version, the icons for these three commands are located on the Modify toolbar. For the DOS version, the commands are under the CONSTRUCTION pulldown menu. See Figure 16-38.

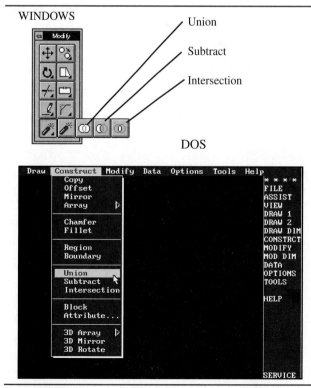

Figure 16-38

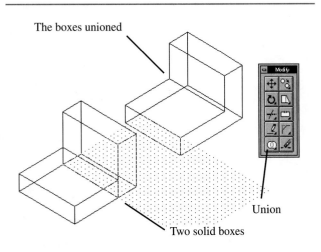

The boxes unioned

Union

Two solid boxes

Figure 16-39

To UNION two objects

Figure 16-39 shows two solid boxes.

1. Select the UNION command

    Command: -union
    Select objects:

2. Select the two boxes

Note the changes in the boxes after they have been unioned. The solid object is no longer two boxes but an L-shaped object.

To SUBTRACT an object

Figure 16-40 shows the L-shaped bracket formed above. This exercise will add a hole to the front surface. Holes are created in solid objects by subtracting solid cylinders from the existing objects.

1. Select the CENTER CYLINDER command

    Command: _cylinder
    Elliptical/<center point> <0,0,0>:

2. Select a point approximately in the middle of the front surface

Remember, the crosshairs move only in the XY plane, so you can select a point only on the bottom surface of the box.

    Diameter/<Radius>:

3. Select a radius for the cylinder

    Center of other end/<Height>:

4. Type 5 ENTER

The height of the cylinder was deliberately drawn higher than the top surface of the bracket to illustrate the fact that the two heights need not be equal for the SUBTRACTION command. The only requirement is that the cylinder be equal to or greater than the height of the box surface.

5. Select the SUBTRACT command

    Command: _subtract Select solids and regions to subtract from...

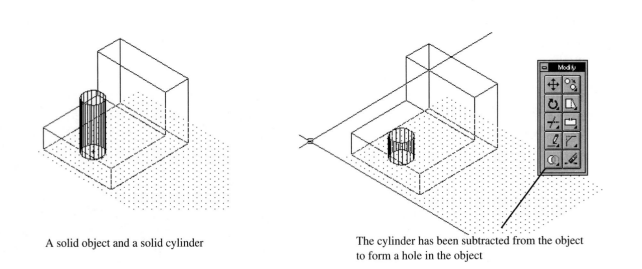

A solid object and a solid cylinder

The cylinder has been subtracted from the object to form a hole in the object

Figure 16-40

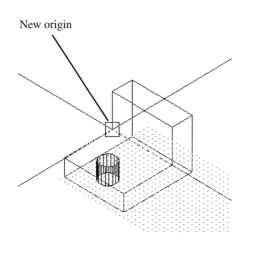

New origin

Figure 16-41

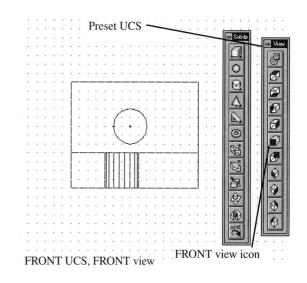

Preset UCS

FRONT UCS, FRONT view   FRONT view icon

Figure 16-42

Select objects:

This prompt is asking you to define the main object, that is, the object you want to remain after the subtraction.

6. Select the L-shaped bracket

Select objects:

7. Type ENTER

Select solids and regions to subtract...
Select objects:

This prompt is asking you to define the object you want removed by the subtraction.

8. Select the cylinder

Select objects:

9. Type ENTER

16-14 SOLID MODELING AND UCSs

In this section we will again work with the L-shaped bracket and add a hole to the upper surface. The procedure is to create a new UCS with its origin at the left intersection of the two perpendicular surfaces, then create and subtract a cylinder. See Figure 16-41.

1. Select the ORIGIN UCS command

Command: _ucs
Origin/Zaxis/3point/OBject/View/X/Y/Z/Prev/
Restore/Save/Del/?/<World>: _o
Origin point <0,0,0>:

2. Use OSNAP, ENDPOINT and select the new origin

See Figure 16-41.

3. Select the PRESET UCS command
4. Select the FRONT UCS command
5. Select the FRONT VIEW command
6. Select the CENTER CYLINDER command

Command: _cylinder
Elliptical/<center point>: <0,0,0>:

7. Select a center point in the approximate center of the surface

Diameter/<Radius>:

8. Select a radius for the cylinder

Center of other end/<Height>:

9. Type -5 ENTER

See Figure 16-42. The negative value is required to project the cylinder into the back surface. The direction on the Zaxis is determined using the right-hand rule.

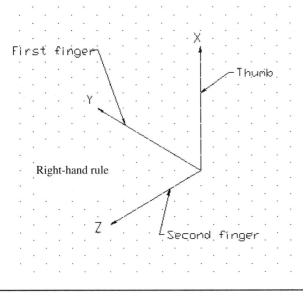

Figure 16-43

A cylinder drawn with a
height of –5 in the new UCS

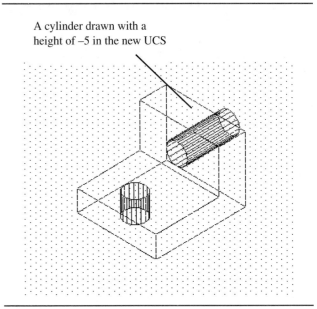

Figure 16-44

Figure 16-43 shows the right-hand rule. The positive direction of a Z axis relative to a given XY plane is determined by aligning your thumb with the X axis so that the end of your thumb is pointing in the positive X direction. Align your first finger with the Y axis so that it is pointing in the positive Y direction. Extend your second finger so

that it is perpendicular to the plane formed by your thumb and first finger. This is the positive Z direction.

10. Select the SE ISOMETRIC VIEW command
11. Type ZOOM and enter a .5 scale factor

See Figure 16-44.

12. Select the SUBTRACT command

Command: _subtract Select solids and regions to subtract from...
Select objects:

13. Select the L-shaped bracket

Select objects:

14. Type ENTER

Select solids and regions to subtract...
Select objects:

15. Select the cylinder

Select objects:

16. Type ENTER

Figure 16-45 shows the resulting solid object.

Resulting shape

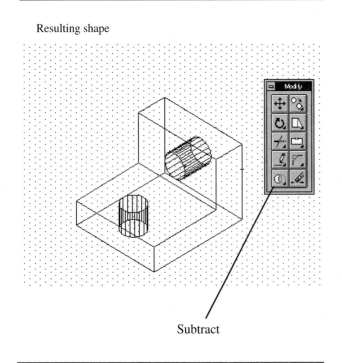

Subtract

Figure 16-45

16-15 COMBINING SOLID OBJECTS

Figure 16-46 shows a dimensioned object. The following section explains how to create the object as a solid model. There are many different ways to create a solid model. The sequence presented here was selected to demonstrate several different input options.

To set up the drawing

Set up the drawing as follows

UNITS = decimal
DRAWING LIMITS = 297,210
GRID = 10
SNAP = 10
VIEW = SE ISOMETRIC
TOOLBARS (WINDOWS) = Draw, Modify, Solids, View, and UCS

The object is relatively small so use ZOOM WINDOW to create a size that you find visually comfortable.

To draw the first box

The size specifications for this box are based on the given dimensions

1. Select the CORNER BOX command

   Command: _box
   Center/<Corner of box> <0,0,0>:

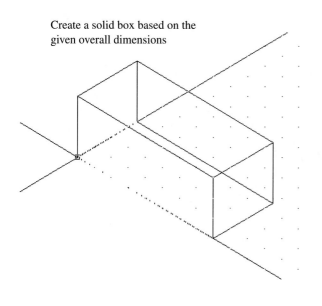

Create a solid box based on the given overall dimensions

Figure 16-47

Figure 16-46

2. Select the 0,0,0 point on the WCS

   Cube/Length/<other corner>:

3. Type L ENTER

   Length:

4. Type 80 ENTER

   Width:

5. Type 35 ENTER

   Height:

6. Type 30 ENTER

   See Figure 16-47.

To create the internal open volume

The volume will be created by subtracting a second box from the first box.

1. Select the CORNER BOX command

   Command: _box
   Center/<Corner of box> <0,0,0>:

Create the rectangular cutout by subtracting a second solid box

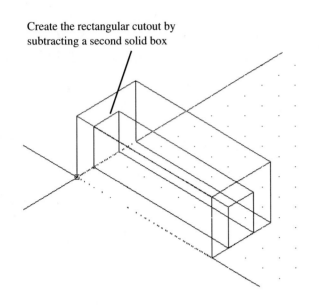

Figure 16-48

Resulting shape after the subtraction

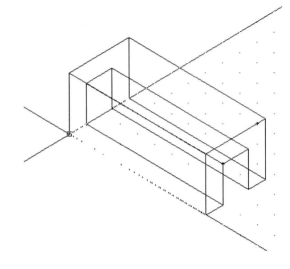

Figure 16-49

2. Select the 0,10,0 point on the WCS

The point 0,10,0 was selected based on the given 10mm dimension. The point can be selected using the crosshairs because it is on the grid located on the XY plane.

Cube/Length/<other corner>:

3. Type L ENTER

Length:

4. Type 80 ENTER

Width:

5. Type 15 ENTER

Height:

6. Type 20 ENTER

See Figure 16-48.

7. Select the SUBTRACT command

Command: _subtract Select solids and regions to subtract from...
Select objects:

8. Select the first box

Select objects:

9. Type ENTER

Select solids and regions to subtract...
Select objects:

10. Type ENTER

See Figure 16-49.

To create the wedge shaped cutout

The wedge shaped cutout will be created by first drawing a wedge based on the given dimensions, then moving the wedge into the correct location. A small box will be unioned to the wedge and both will be subtracted from the first box.

1. Select the CORNER WEDGE command

Command: _wedge
Center/<Center of wedge> <0,0,0>:

2. Type 20,35,25 ENTER

This corner point locates the corner of the wedge on the back surface of the first box, 5mm below the top surface as specified by the given dimensions.

Cube/Length/<other corner>:

3. Type L ENTER

Length:

4. Type 35 ENTER

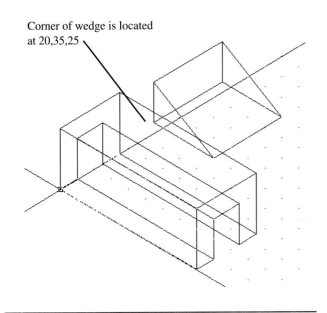

Corner of wedge is located
at 20,35,25

Figure 16-50

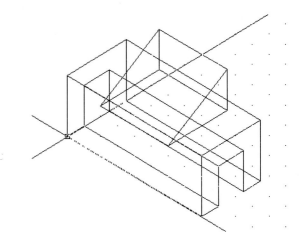

Use the ROTATE command to
reposition the wedge

Figure 16-51

The WEDGE command always interprets a length dimension as being along the current X axis. In this example, the wedge will be rotated 90 degrees into place, so the 35mm length must be equal to the width of the object.

Width:

5. Type 40 ENTER

Height:

6. Type 20 ENTER

See Figure 16-50.

To ROTATE the wedge in the XY plane

1. Select the ROTATE command

   Command:_rotate
   Select objects:

2. Select the wedge

   Select objects:

3. Type ENTER

   Base point

4. Use OSNAP, ENDPOINT and select the corner point of the wedge

   You may have to turn the SNAP command off temporarily to select the point.

<Rotation angle>/Reference:

5. Type -90 ENTER

See Figure 16-51. The counterclockwise direction is the positive direction.

To rotate the wedge along the X axis

The ROTATION command will rotate only in the current XY plane, so a new UCS is required.

1. Select the ORIGIN UCS command

   Command:_ucs
   Origin/Zaxis/3point/OBject/View/X/Y/Z/Prev/
   Restore/Save/Del/?/<World>:_o
   Origin point <0,0,0>:

2. Use OSNAP, ENDPOINT and select the new origin

   See Figure 16-52.

3. Select the PRESET UCS command
4. Select the RIGHT UCS command
5. Select the ROTATE command

   Command:_rotate
   Select objects:

6. Select the wedge

   Select objects;

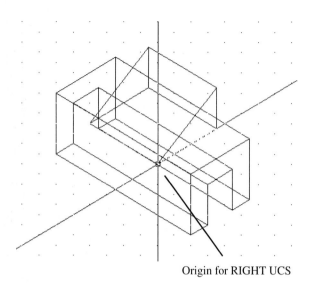

Origin for RIGHT UCS

Figure 16-52

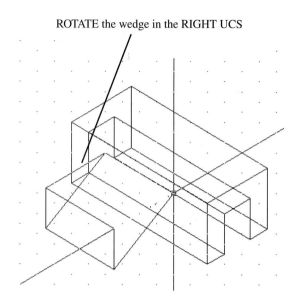

ROTATE the wedge in the RIGHT UCS

Figure 16-53

7. Type ENTER

   Base point:

8. Use OSNAP, ENDPOINT and select the new origin, or type 0,0,0 ENTER

   <Rotation angle>/Reference:

9. Type 180 ENTER

   See Figure 16-53.

To relocate the wedge

1. Select the MOVE command

   Command: _move
   Select objects:

2. Select the wedge

   Select objects:

3. Type ENTER

   Base point or displacement:

4. Type 0,0,0 ENTER

   Second point of displacement

5. Type 35,0,0 ENTER

   The displacement inputs serve to move the wedge 35mm along the current X axis. Remember, you are in the RIGHT UCS.

6. Select the WORLD command

   See Figure 16-54.

Use the MOVE command to reposition the wedge

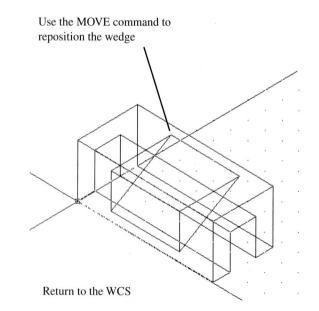

Return to the WCS

Figure 16-54

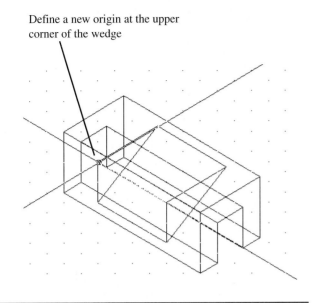

Define a new origin at the upper corner of the wedge

Figure 16-55

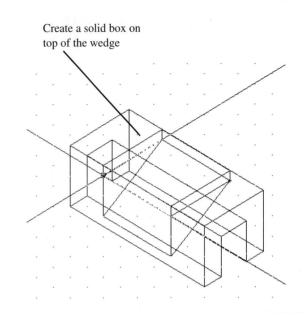

Create a solid box on top of the wedge

Figure 16-56

To add a small box to the wedge

The wedge is located 5mm from the top surface of the first box. A small box will be added to reach the top surface of the first box.

1. Select ORIGIN command

    Command: _ucs
    Origin/Zaxis/3point/OBject/View/X/Y/Z/Prev/
    Restore/Save/Del/?/<World>:_o
    Origin point <0,0,0>:

2. Use OSNAP, ENDPOINT and select the new origin

    See Figure 16-55.

3. Select the CORNER BOX command

    Command:_box
    Center/<Corner of box> <0,0,0>:

4. Type ENTER

    The corner of the box could have been defined directly relative to the WCS as point 20,0,25.

    Cube/Length/<other corner>:

5. Use OSNAP, ENDPOINT and select the diagonal corner from the origin

    Height:

6. Type 5 ENTER

    See Figure 16-56.

7. Select the WCS command

To SUBTRACT the wedge and small box

1. Select the SUBTRACT command

    Command: _subtract Select solids and regions to subtract from...
    Select objects:

2. Select the first box

    Select objects:

3. Type ENTER

    Select solids and regions to subtract...
    Select objects:

4. Select the small box

    Select objects:

5. Select the wedge

    Select objects:

6. Type ENTER

    See Figure 16-57.

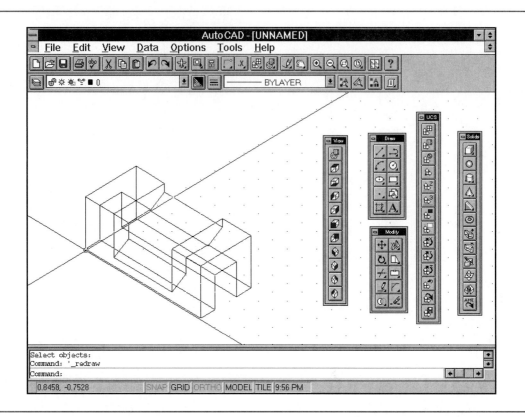

Figure 16-57

7. Type HIDE ENTER

See Figure 16-58.

8. Type REGEN ENTER

The REGEN command will return the screen to a wire frame type of object display.

9. SAVE the drawing

16-16 INTERSECTING SOLIDS

Figure 16-59 shows an incomplete 3D drawing of a cone and a cylinder. The problem is to complete the drawing in 3D and show the front, top, and right side orthographic views of the intersecting objects. If this problem were to be done by hand on a drawing board, it would require extensive projection between views, as well as a high degree of precision in the line work. Done as a solid model, the problem is much simpler and serves to show the strength of solid modeling as a design tool.

The solid model of the object with the HIDE command applied

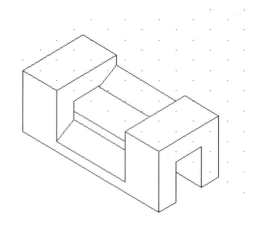

Figure 16-58

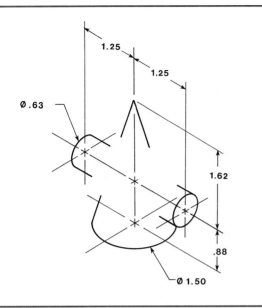

Figure 16-59

To set up the drawing

Set up the drawing screen as follows.

GRID = 0.50
SNAP = 0.50
UNITS = decimal
VIEW = SE ISOMETRIC
TOOLBARS (WINDOWS) = Solids, View, UCS,
   Modify
ISOLINES = 18

See Figure 16-60. The objects are small, so use the ZOOM WINDOW command to create a comfortable visual size.

To draw the cone

1. Select the CENTER CONE command

   Command: _cone
   Elliptical/<center point> <0,0,0>:

2. Type ENTER

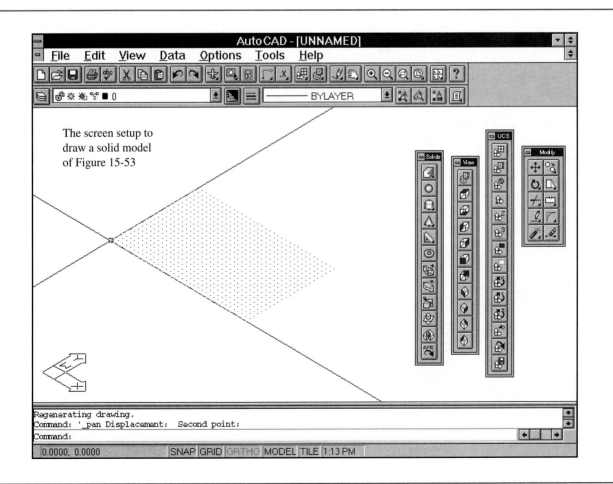

Figure 16-60

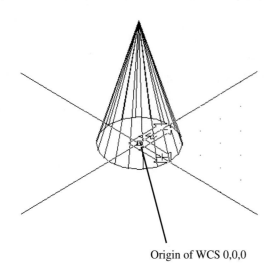

Origin of WCS 0,0,0

Figure 16-61

The center point of the cone will be located on the origin of the WCS.

Diameter/<Radius>:

3. Type D ENTER

Diameter:

A solid cylinder drawn in the RIGHT UCS

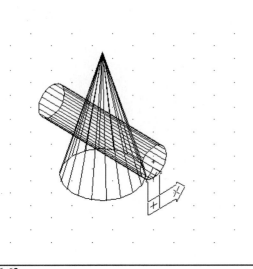

Figure 16-63

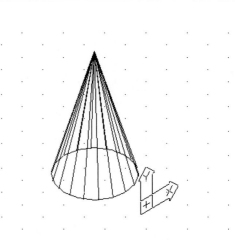

Origin for RIGHT UCS set at 1.25,0,0

Figure 16-62

4. Type 1.50

Apex/<Height>:

5. Type 2.50 ENTER

See Figure 16-61.

To draw the cylinder

1. Select ORIGIN UCS command

Command: _ucs
Origin/Zaxis/3point/OBject/View/X/Y/Z/Prev/
Restore/Save/Del/?/<World>: _o
Origin point <0,0,0>:

2. Type 1.25,0,0 ENTER

This input locates the origin in the same plane as the end of the cylinder.

3. Select the PRESET UCS command, then the RIGHT UCS, OK

See Figure 16-62.

4. Select the CENTER CYLINDER command

Command: _cylinder
Elliptical/<center point> <0,0,0>:

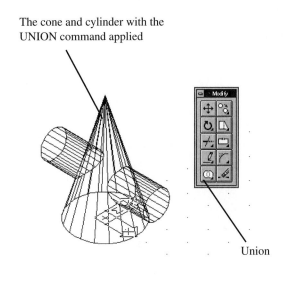

The cone and cylinder with the UNION command applied

Union

Figure 16-64

5. Type 0,.88,0

Diameter/<Radius>:

6. Type D ENTER

Diameter:

7. Type .63 ENTER

Center of other end/<Height>:

8. Type -2.50 ENTER

The negative value is used based on the right-hand rule applied to the RIGHT UCS. See Figure 16-63.

To complete the 3D drawing

1. Select the UNION command

Command:_union
Select objects:

2. Select the cone

Select objects:

3. Select the cylinder

Select objects:

4. Type ENTER

Command:

5. Select the WCS command

See Figure 16-64.

To create the viewports for the orthographic views

1. Select the VIEW pulldown menu
2. Select Tiled Viewports, then 4 Viewports

See Figure 16-65 and Figure 16-66.

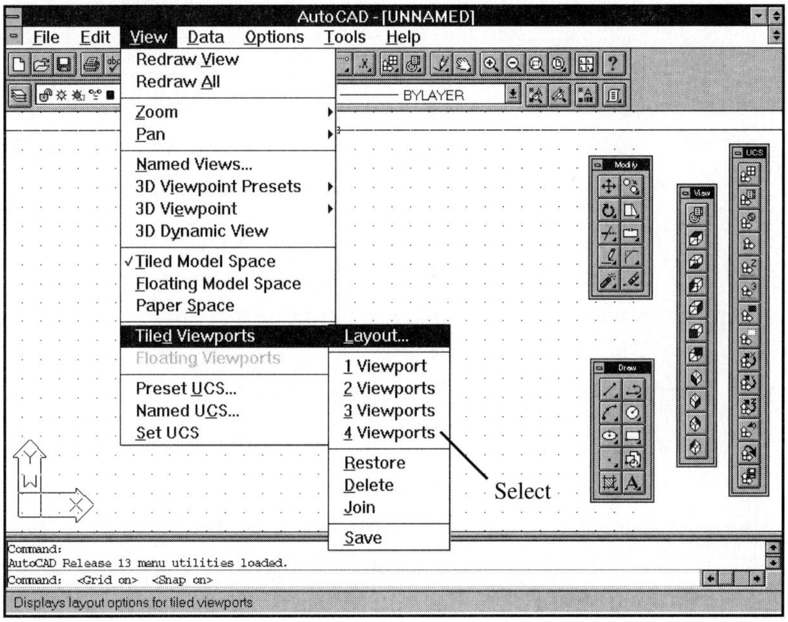

The screen shown is for the WINDOWS version. The DOS version's VIEW pull-down menu will yield the same submenus.

Figure 16-65

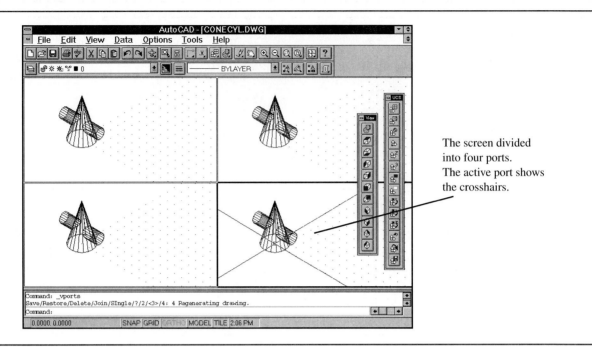

The screen divided into four ports. The active port shows the crosshairs.

Figure 16-66

To create a top orthographic view

1. Move the cursor into the top left port and press the left mouse button.

   The crosshairs will appear in the port.

2. Select the TOP VIEW command

   An oversized top view of the objects will appear.

3. Type ZOOM ENTER

   All/Center/Dynamic/Extents/Left/Previous/Vmax/ Window/<Scale(X/XP)>:

4. Type 4 ENTER

   See Figure 16-67.

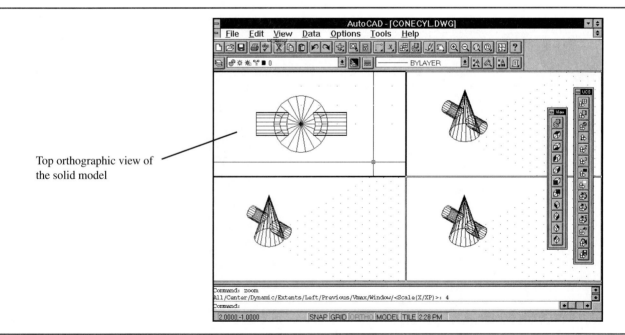

Top orthographic view of the solid model

Figure 16-67

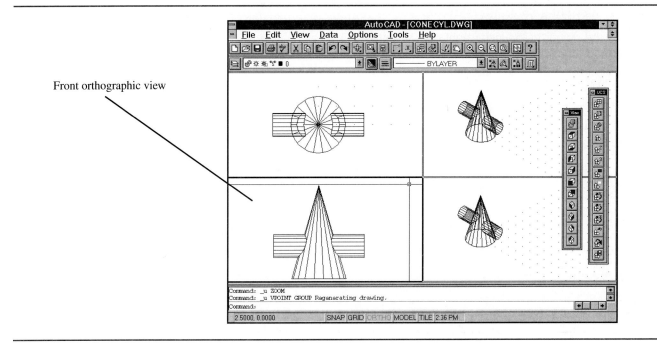

Front orthographic view

Figure 16-68

To create the front orthographic view

1. Move the cursor into the lower left port and press the left mouse button

   The crosshairs will appear in the port.

2. Select the FRONT VIEW command
3. Type ZOOM ENTER

All/Center/Dynamic/Extents/Left/Previous/Vmax/ Window/<Scale(X/XP)>:

4. Type 4 ENTER

   See Figure 16-68. Use VIEW (pulldown), PAN, POINT to align the views if necessary.

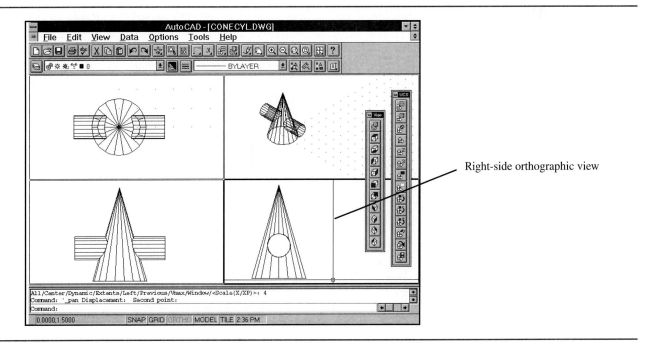

Right-side orthographic view

Figure 16-69

To create the right-side orthographic view

1. Move the cursor to the lower right port and press the left mouse button
2. Select the RIGHT VIEW command
3. Type ZOOM ENTER
4. Type 4 ENTER

See Figure 16-69. Use VIEW (pulldown), PAN, POINT to align the views if necessary.

16-17 SOLID MODELS OF CASTINGS

Figure 16-70 shows a casting. Note that the object includes rounded edges. These rounded edges can be created on a solid model using the FILLET command found on the Modify toolbar. The FILLET command was explained in Chapter 3.

This example will be presented without specific dimensions, and will use a generalized approach to creating the model.

To draw the basic shape

The basic shape will first be drawn in 2D, then extruded into the 3D solid model

1. Set up the drawing screen as needed
2. Draw the basic shape using the CIRCLE command and then the LINE command along with the OSNAP, TANGENT option.
3. Use TRIM to remove any excess lines.

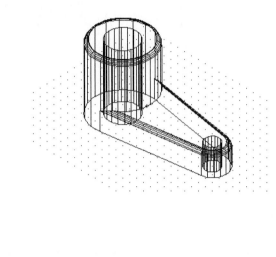

Figure 16-70

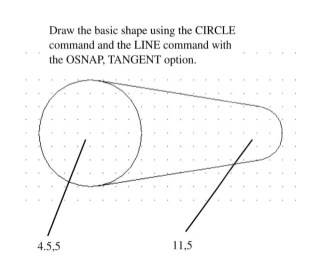

Draw the basic shape using the CIRCLE command and the LINE command with the OSNAP, TANGENT option.

4.5,5   11,5

Figure 16-71

See Figure 16-71. It is important to know the center point location for the two circles in terms of their XY components. In this example the center point location for the large circle is 4.5,5, and the location for the small circle is 11,5.

To create a polyline from the basic shape

Only polylines can be extruded; some of the lines in the basic shape must be formed into a polyline. The large circle can be extruded, so it need not be included as part of the polyline. However, the polyline must be a closed area, and so it will need part of the circle. The needed circular segment can be created by drawing a second large circle directly over the existing circle and then using the TRIM command to remove the excess portion. Remember that two lines can occupy the same space in AutoCAD drawings.

1. Use the CIRCLE command and draw a second large circle directly over the first circle
2. Use the TRIM command to remove the excess portion of the circle

Figure 16-72 shows the resulting shape that will be joined to form a polyline.

3. Select VIEW (pulldown), REDRAW VIEW to return the original large circle to the screen
4. Select the EDIT POLYLINE command

Command: _pedit Select polyline:

Join these lines together to
form a polyline

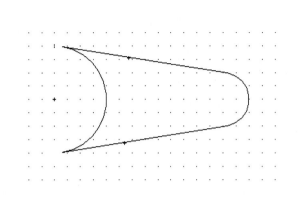

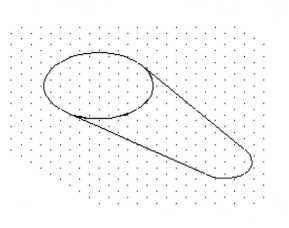

The SE ISOMETRIC viewpoint

Figure 16-72

Figure 16-73

5. Select the remaining portion of the small circle

   Object is not a polyline
   Do you want to turn it into one? <Y>

6. Type ENTER

   Close/ Join/ Width/ Edit vertex/ Fit/ Spline/
   Decurve /Ltype gen/ Undo/ eXit/ <X>:

7. Type J ENTER

   Select objects:

8. Select the line segments for the polyline

The arc portion of the large circle created in step 2 can be selected just like the other line segments. AutoCAD will select the last entity created if two or more entities occupy the same space.

Close/ Join/ Width/ Edit vertex/ Fit/ Spline/
Decurve/ Ltype gen/ Undo/ eXit/ <X>:

9. Type ENTER

To extrude the shape

1. Select the SE ISOMETRIC command
2. Type ZOOM ENTER
3. Type .75 ENTER

   See Figure 16-73.

4. Select the EXTRUDE command

   Command:_extrude
   Select objects:

5. Select the polyline, and assign a height and 0 degree taper

   See Figure 16-74.

   Command:

6. Type ENTER

   Select objects:

7. Select the large circle

   Select the circle a point away from the polyline arc. See Figure 16-75.

The polyline with the EXTRUDE
command applied

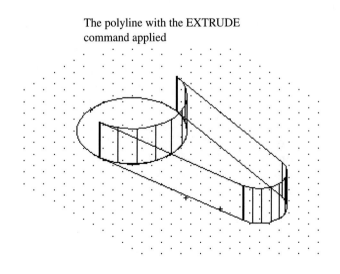

Figure 16-74

The circle is
extruded to form a
cylinder

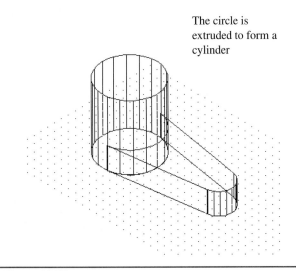

Figure 16-75

Solid cylinders are created then
subtracted to form holes

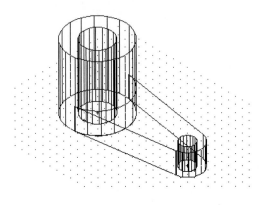

Figure 16-76

To add the holes

Create the holes by subtracting cylinders from the
object.

1. Select the CENTER CYLINDER command

Command: _cylinder
Elliptical/<center point> <0,0,0>:

2. Type 4.5,5,0

This value came from step 3 in the "To draw the
basic shape" section.

3. Enter the appropriate diameter and height values

Command:

4. Type ENTER

Elliptical/<center point> <0,0,0>:

5. Type 11,5,0
6. Enter the appropriate diameter and height values

See Figure 16-76.

7. Select the UNION command and join the large
cylinder portion of the object to the polyline portion
8. Select the SUBTRACT command and subtract
the cylinder from the basic shape

See Figure 16-77.

To create the rounded edges

1. Select the FILLET command

Command: _fillet
(TRIM mode) Current fillet radius = 0.2500
Polyline/Radius/Trim/<Select first object>:

Type R and enter the appropriate radius value if
necessary.

2. Select the outside edge of the top surface of the
large back cylindrical portion of the object

ENTER radius <0.2500>:

Object with the cylinders
subtracted

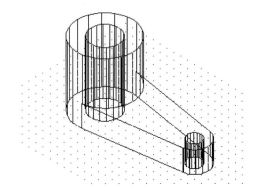

Figure 16-77

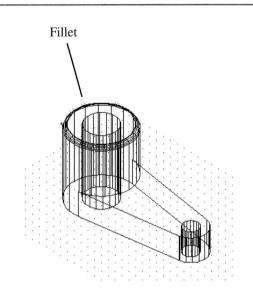

Fillet

Figure 16-78

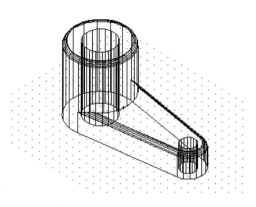

Finished object

Figure 16-79

3. Type ENTER

   Chain/Radius/<Select edge>:

4. Type ENTER

   See Figure 16-78.

5. Use the FILLET command to create a fillet along the top edges of the object as shown in Figure 16-79

Note that the arc edge line between the large cylindrical portion of the object and the extended flat area can- not be filleted.

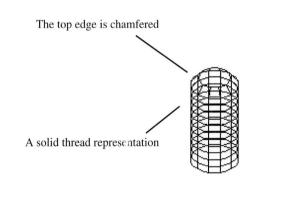

The top edge is chamfered

A solid thread representation

Figure 16-80

16-18 THREADS REPRESENTATIONS IN SOLID MODELS

This section explains how to draw thread representations for solid models. The procedure presented represents only a thread. It is not an actual detailed solid drawing of a thread. As with the thread representations presented in Chapter 11 for 2D drawings, 3D representations are acceptable for most applications.

1. Select the CENTER CYLINDER command and draw a cylinder

In the example shown, a cylinder of diameter 3 and a height of 6 was drawn centered about the 0,0,0 point of the WCS. See Figure 16-80.

2. Draw a circle with a diameter equal to the diameter of the cylinder using the same center point that was originally used to create the cylinder

3. Select the 3D ARRAY command

   Select object:

4. Select the circle

   Select object:

5. Type ENTER

   Number of rows (___)<1>:

6. Type ENTER

Number of columns: (lll)<1>:

7. Type ENTER

Number of levels:

8. Type 11 ENTER

The number 11 is used because the cylinder is 6 units high, and in this example circles representing threads will be spaced .5 apart. The top edge of the thread will be chamfered.

Distance between levels: (...):

9. Type .5 ENTER
10. Select the CHAMFER command and draw a .5x.5 chamfer around the top edge of the cylinder

16-19 LIST

The LIST command is used to display database information for a drawn solid object. Figure 16-81 shows a solid object and Figure 16-82 shows the information displayed for the object when the LIST command is used.

A solid object

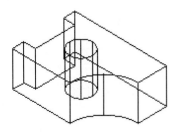

Figure 16-81

16-20 MASSPROP

The MASSPROP command is used to display information about the structural characteristics of an object. Figures 16-83 and 16-84 show the MASSPROP information for the object shown in Figure 16-81. To access the MASSPROP command, type MASSPROP in response to a Command: prompt.

The LIST icon

— BYLAYER

LIST information

```
AutoCAD Text Window
Edit

Command: '_redraw
Command: Other corner:
Command:
Command:
Command: _list
Select objects: Other corner: 1 found

Select objects:
                    3DSOLID    Layer: 0
                              Space: Model space
                     Handle = 2B
     Bounding Box: Lower Bound X = 0.0000    , Y = 0.0000    , Z = 0.0000
                   Upper Bound X = 8.0000    , Y = 5.5000    , Z = 3.0000


Command:
Command:
Command: _list
Select objects: Other corner: 1 found

Select objects:
                    3DSOLID    Layer: 0
                              Space: Model space
                     Handle = 2B
     Bounding Box: Lower Bound X = 0.0000    , Y = 0.0000    , Z = 0.0000
                   Upper Bound X = 8.0000    , Y = 5.5000    , Z = 3.0000
Command:
```

Figure 16-82

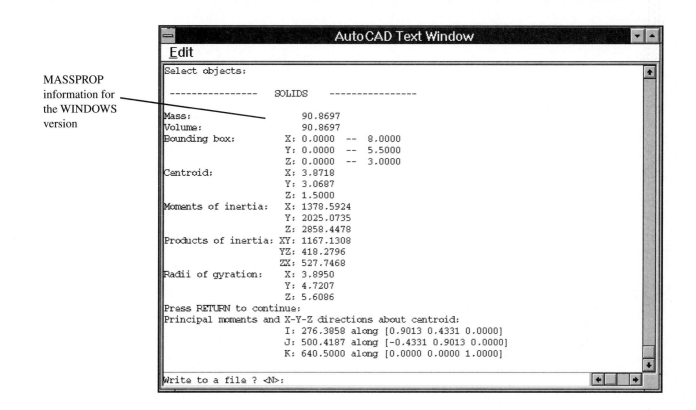

MASSPROP
information for
the WINDOWS
version

Figure 16-83

MASSPROP informa-
tion for the DOS version

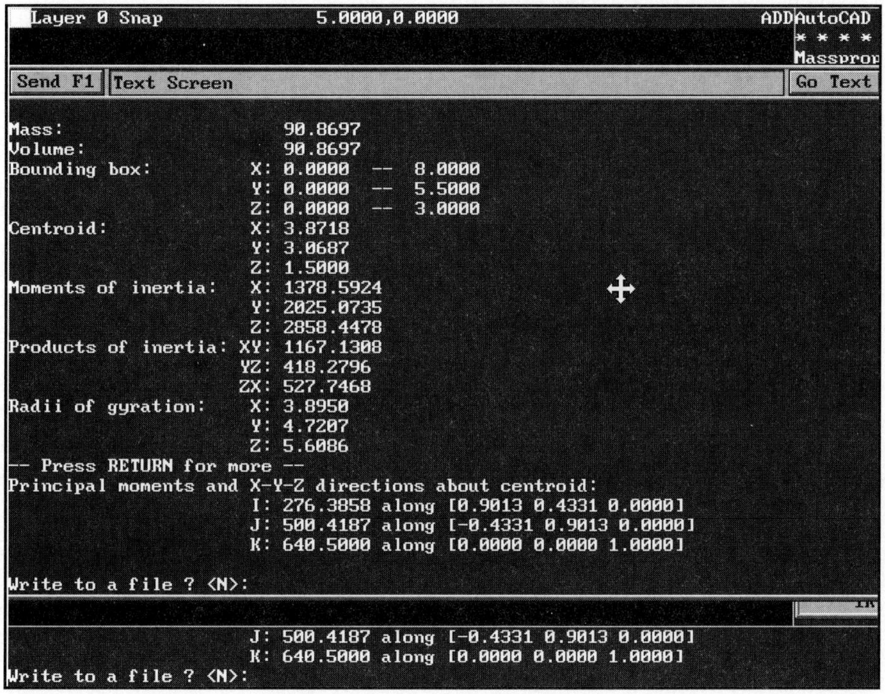

Figure 16-84

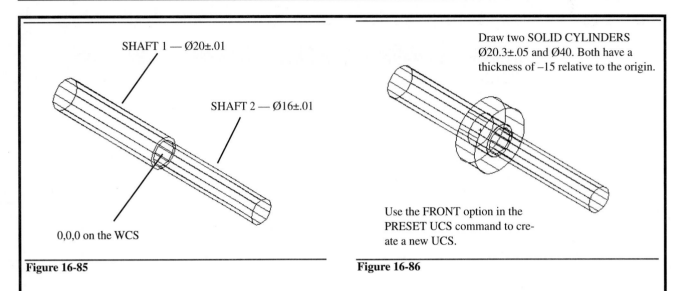

SHAFT 1 — Ø20±.01

SHAFT 2 — Ø16±.01

0,0,0 on the WCS

Figure 16-85

Draw two SOLID CYLINDERS Ø20.3±.05 and Ø40. Both have a thickness of −15 relative to the origin.

Use the FRONT option in the PRESET UCS command to create a new UCS.

Figure 16-86

16-21 DESIGN PROBLEM

Design a coupling that will hold together the two shafts shown in Figure 16-85. The coupling is to be cylindrical and have an outside diameter of 40. It should also include two threaded holes for M4 setscrews to hold the shafts in place. The final design was created as follows.

The two shafts are positioned on the screen so that the intersection of their center lines is at the 0,0,0 point on the WCS. This was done to make it easier to determine any required coordinate points.

Assume that anaylsis has determined that the inside diameters of the coupling should be Ø20.3±.05 and Ø16.3±.05.

1. Select the PRESET UCS command from the VIEW pulldown menu

2. Select the FRONT option from the UCS orientation dialog box

See Figure 14-20 in Section 14-6. This step will create a new UCS perpendicular to the longitudinal axis of the two shafts. The origin for the UCS is located on the 0,0,0 point of the WCS.

3. Select the SOLID CENTER CYLINDER command and draw two cylinders with their center points located at the 0,0,0 point

The diameter of the smaller cylinder is Ø16.3 and the diameter of the larger cylinder is Ø40, and both have a height of -15. See Figure 16-86.

4. SUBTRACT the smaller cylinder from the larger cylinder

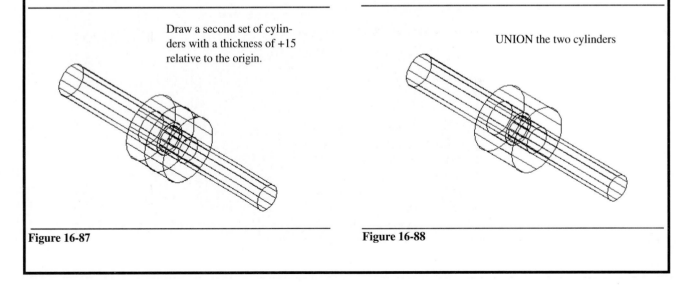

Draw a second set of cylinders with a thickness of +15 relative to the origin.

Figure 16-87

UNION the two cylinders

Figure 16-88

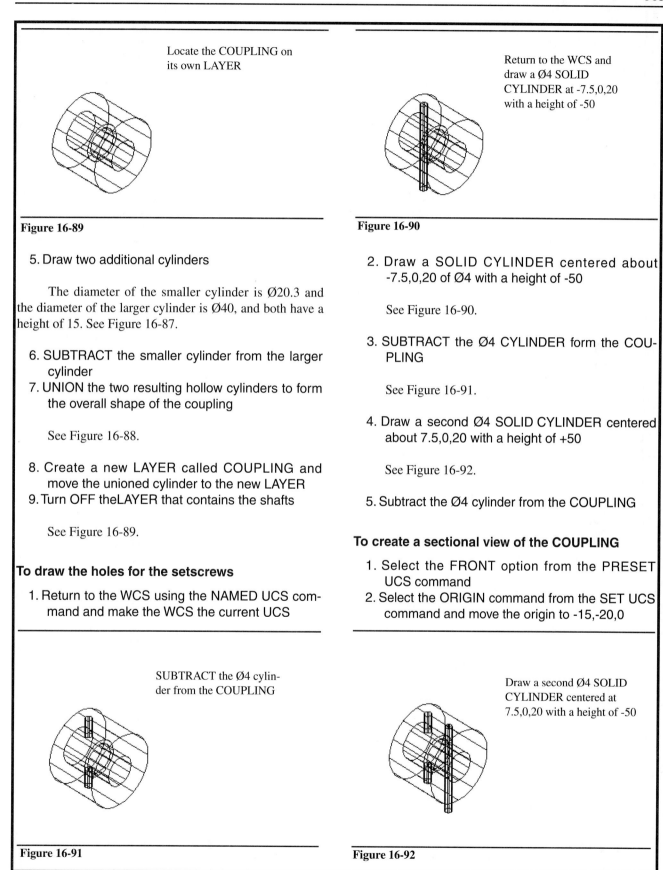

Locate the COUPLING on
its own LAYER

Figure 16-89

5. Draw two additional cylinders

The diameter of the smaller cylinder is Ø20.3 and
the diameter of the larger cylinder is Ø40, and both have a
height of 15. See Figure 16-87.

6. SUBTRACT the smaller cylinder from the larger
   cylinder
7. UNION the two resulting hollow cylinders to form
   the overall shape of the coupling

See Figure 16-88.

8. Create a new LAYER called COUPLING and
   move the unioned cylinder to the new LAYER
9. Turn OFF theLAYER that contains the shafts

See Figure 16-89.

To draw the holes for the setscrews

1. Return to the WCS using the NAMED UCS command and make the WCS the current UCS

SUBTRACT the Ø4 cylin-
der from the COUPLING

Figure 16-91

Return to the WCS and
draw a Ø4 SOLID
CYLINDER at -7.5,0,20
with a height of -50

Figure 16-90

2. Draw a SOLID CYLINDER centered about
   -7.5,0,20 of Ø4 with a height of -50

See Figure 16-90.

3. SUBTRACT the Ø4 CYLINDER form the COU-
   PLING

See Figure 16-91.

4. Draw a second Ø4 SOLID CYLINDER centered
   about 7.5,0,20 with a height of +50

See Figure 16-92.

5. Subtract the Ø4 cylinder from the COUPLING

To create a sectional view of the COUPLING

1. Select the FRONT option from the PRESET
   UCS command
2. Select the ORIGIN command from the SET UCS
   command and move the origin to -15,-20,0

Draw a second Ø4 SOLID
CYLINDER centered at
7.5,0,20 with a height of -50

Figure 16-92

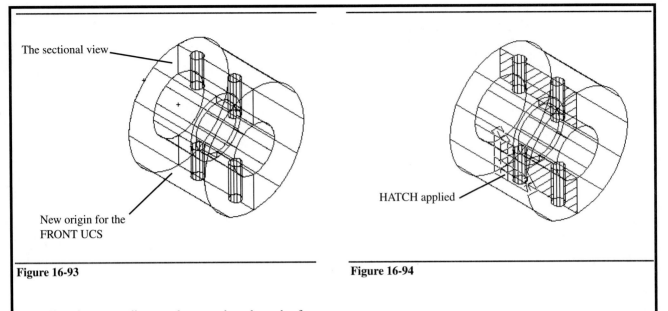

The sectional view

New origin for the
FRONT UCS

HATCH applied

Figure 16-93

Figure 16-94

The given coordinate values are based on the fact that the new FRONT UCS has its initial location at the WCS 0,0,0 point.

3. Select the SECTION command

Select object:

4. Select the coupling

Section plane by Object/ Zaxis/ View/ XY/ YZ/ ZY/ <3 points>:

5. Type XY ENTER

Point on XY plane <0,0,0>:

6. Type ENTER

See Figure 16-93. The default 0,0,0 point can be accepted because the origin for the FRONT UCS was moved from its original location.

To HATCH the sectional plane

1. Select the HATCH command

The BOUNDARY HATCH dialog box will appear. See Chapter 6 for an explanation of the HATCH command.

2. Set the Scale factor equal to 15, then select the Select objects: box

Select objects:

3. Select the sectional plane

The BOUNDARY HATCH dialog box will reappear.

4. Select the Apply box

The sectional plane will be hatched. See Figure 16-94. In Figure 16-94 the UCS icon is located on the UCS's origin in the FRONT orientation.

To dimension the COUPLING

The COUPLING will be dimensioned by using a sectional view and a 3D view. The screen must first be divided into two viewports in Paper space. Model space will then be used to manipulate the objects individually. The drawing will be returned to Paper space and the dimensions applied.

Paper space treats the screen as one sheet of paper and does not acknowledge individual screen ports. Model space treats each port as an individual drawing, allowing each port to be manipulated independently of the others.

1. For the WINDOWS version, double click the word MODEL at the bottom of the screen or select the VIEW pulldown menu, then the PAPER SPACE command for either version

See Figure 16-95. The screen will go blank, signifying a blank sheet of paper. You must now define the port sizes.

2. Select the FLOATING VIEWPORTS command from the VIEW pulldown menu

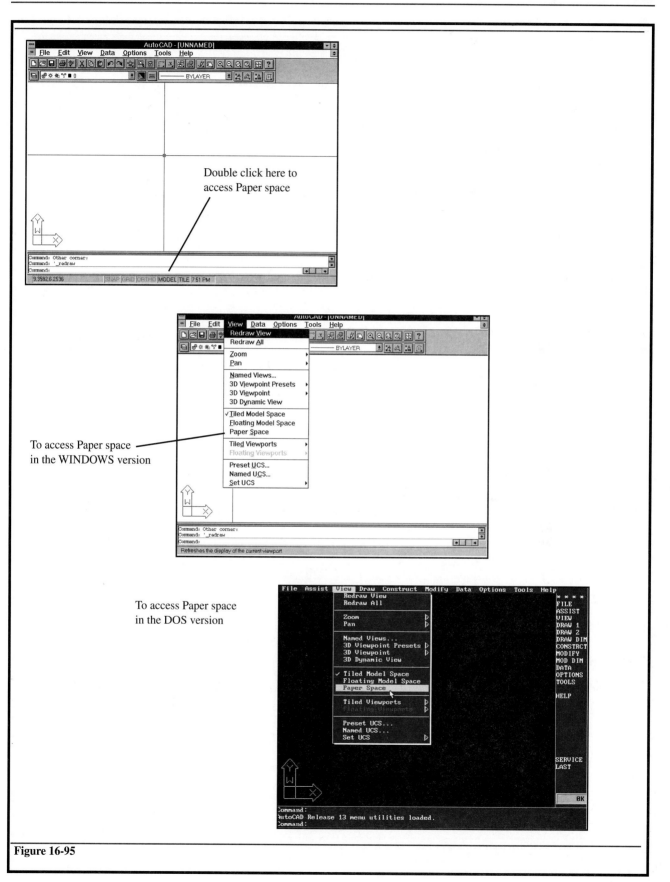

Figure 16-95

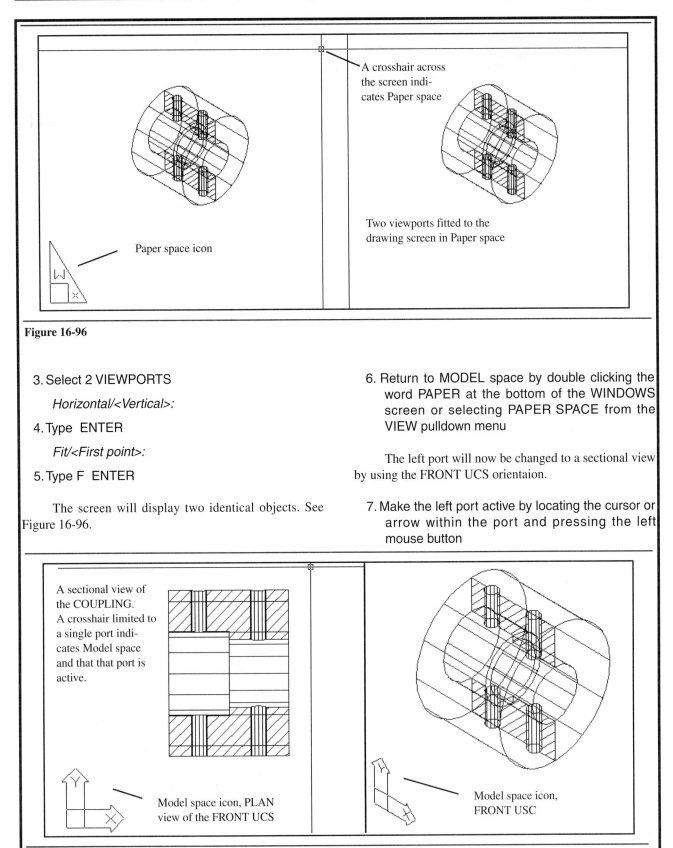

Figure 16-96

3. Select 2 VIEWPORTS

   Horizontal/<Vertical>:

4. Type ENTER

   Fit/<First point>:

5. Type F ENTER

   The screen will display two identical objects. See Figure 16-96.

6. Return to MODEL space by double clicking the word PAPER at the bottom of the WINDOWS screen or selecting PAPER SPACE from the VIEW pulldown menu

   The left port will now be changed to a sectional view by using the FRONT UCS orientaion.

7. Make the left port active by locating the cursor or arrow within the port and pressing the left mouse button

A crosshair across the screen indicates Paper space

Two viewports fitted to the drawing screen in Paper space

Paper space icon

A sectional view of the COUPLING. A crosshair limited to a single port indicates Model space and that that port is active.

Model space icon, PLAN view of the FRONT UCS

Model space icon, FRONT USC

Figure 16-97

8. Select the FRONT option from the PRESET UCS command

9. Select the PLAN view from the 3D VIEWPOINT PRESETS command from the VIEW pulldown menu

The COUPLING will appear as a sectional view in the left port. Use the ZOOM command to create a visually comfortable size. Don't forget to leave room for the dimensions. See Figure 16-97.

10. Return to Paper space
11. Select the DIMENSION STYLES command

See Chapter 8 for an explanation of the DIMENSION STYLES command. The DIMENSIONS dialog box will appear.

12. Select the GEOMETRY box

See Figure 16-98.

13. Turn on the SCALE TO PAPER SPACE option
14. Make any other changes necessary to the DIMENSION STYLES dialog box
15. Dimension the COUPLING

Turn on the SCALE TO PAPER SPACE option

Figure 16-98

Figure 16-99 shows the final dimensioned COUPLING. AutoCAD's ability to combine 3D and 2D views of any object allows both types of views to be used within the same drawing, giving a clearer understanding of both an object's size and shape.

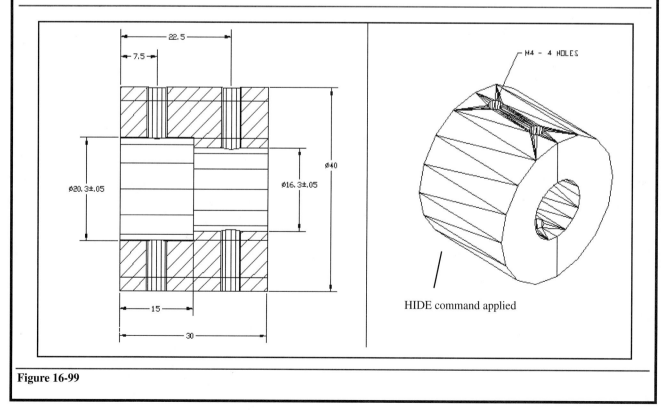

Figure 16-99

16-22 EXERCISE PROBLEMS

Draw the objects in exercise problems EX16-1 to EX16-27 as follows:

A. Draw each as a 3D solid model.

B. Create front, top, and right-side orthographic views from the solid.

C. Dimension the orthographic views.

EX16-1 INCHES

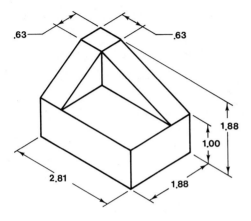

EX16-2 INCHES

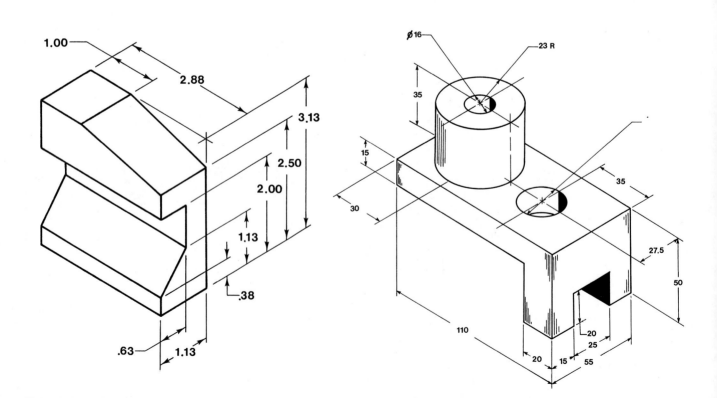

EX16-3 MILLIMETERS

EX16-4 MILLIMETERS

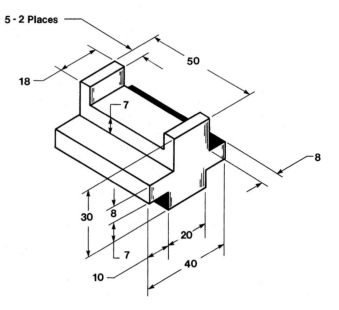

EX16-5 INCHES

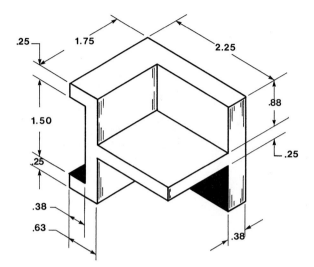

EX16-7 INCHES

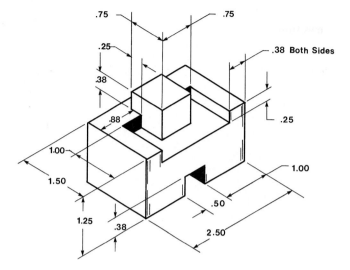

EX16-6 MILLIMETERS

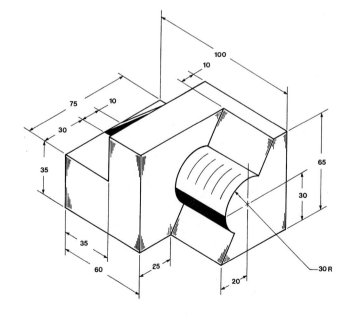

EX16-8 MILLIMETERS

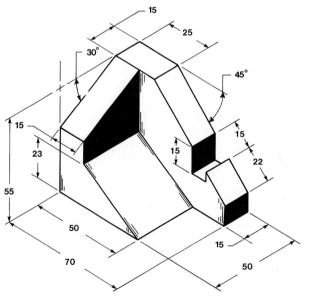

EX16-9 INCHES

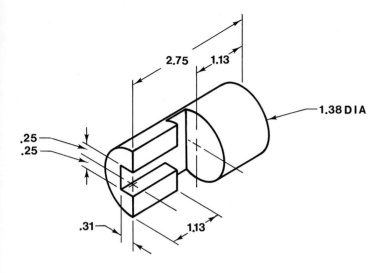

EX16-11 MILLIMETERS

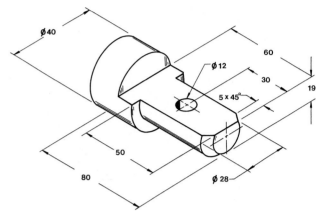

EX16-10 MILLIMETERS

EX16-12 MILLIMETERS

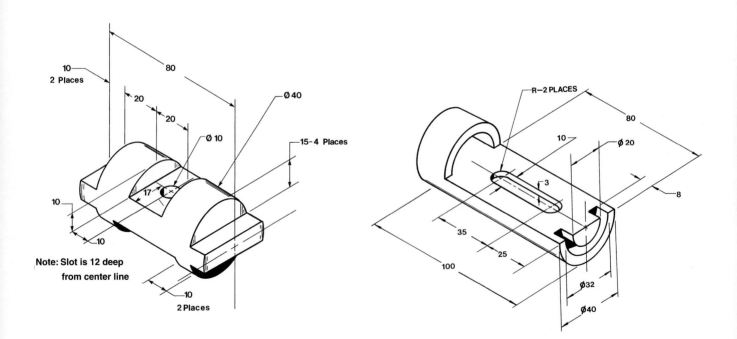

Note: Slot is 12 deep from center line

EX16-13 MILLIMETERS

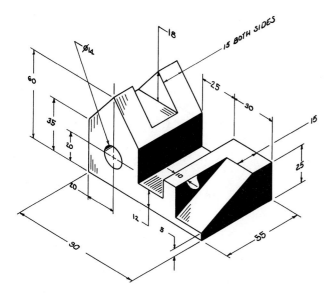

EX16-15 INCHES

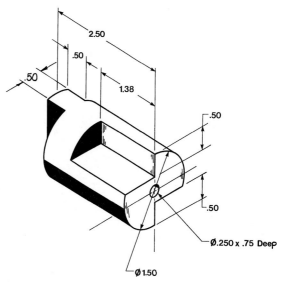

EX16-14 INCHES

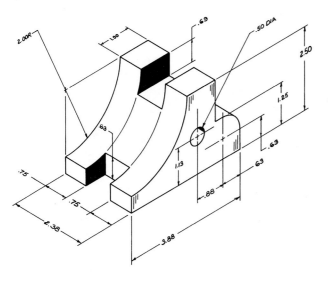

EX16-16 MILLIMETERS

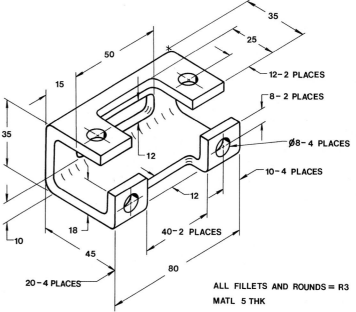

EX16-17 MILLIMETERS

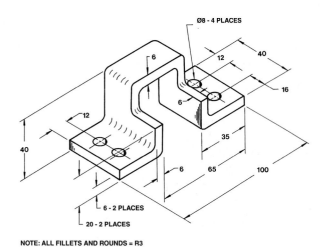

NOTE: ALL FILLETS AND ROUNDS = R3

EX16-19 MILLIMETERS

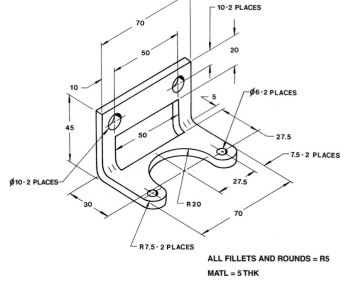

ALL FILLETS AND ROUNDS = R5
MATL = 5 THK

EX16-18 MILLIMETERS

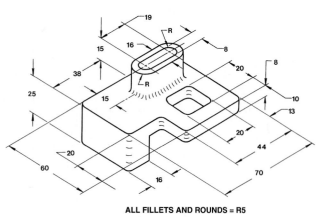

ALL FILLETS AND ROUNDS = R5
MATL = 5 THK

EX16-20 MILLIMETERS

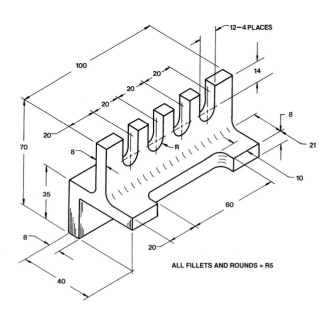

ALL FILLETS AND ROUNDS = R5

EX16-21 INCHES

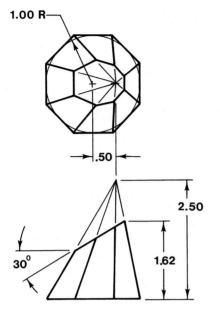

EX16-23 INCHES

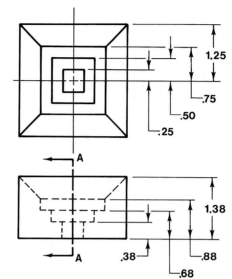

Object is sym-
metrical about
both center lines

EX16-22 INCHES

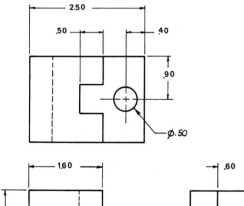

EX16-24 INCHES

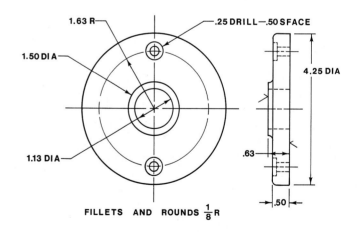

EX16-25 MILLIMETERS

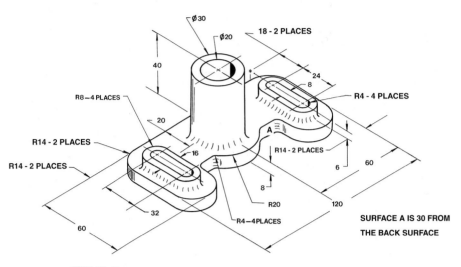

NOTE: ALL FILLETS AND ROUNDS= R3

EX16-26 MILLIMETERS

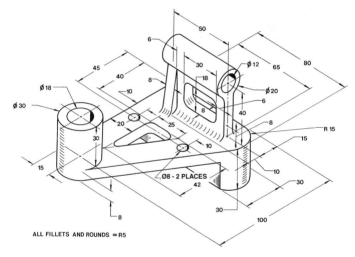

ALL FILLETS AND ROUNDS = R5

EX16-27 MILLIMETERS

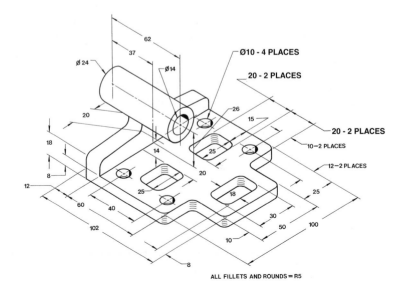

ALL FILLETS AND ROUNDS = R5

Draw the objects in exercise problems EX16-28 to EX16-31 as solid models, then use the SECTION command to create the indicated sectional views.

EX16-28 MILLIMETERS

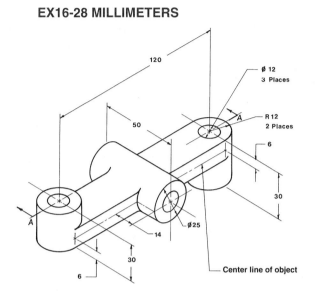

EX16-30 MILLIMETERS

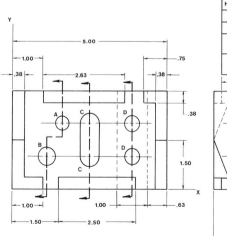

EX16-29 MILLIMETERS

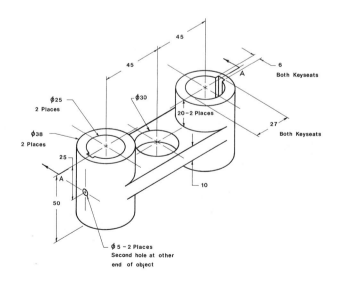

EX16-31 INCHES

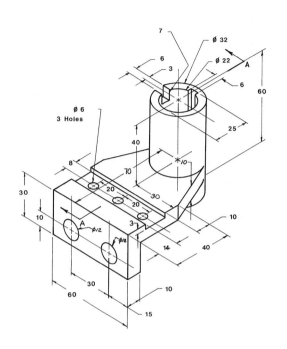

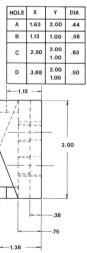

HOLE	X	Y	DIA
A	1.63	2.00	.44
B	1.13	1.00	.56
C	2.50	2.00 1.00	.63
D	3.88	2.00 1.00	.50

Redraw the assemblies in exercise problems EX16-32 to EX16-34 as solid models with the individual parts located in their assembled positions.

EX16-32 MILLIMETERS

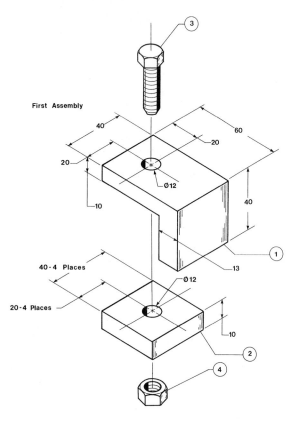

EX16-34 MILLIMETERS

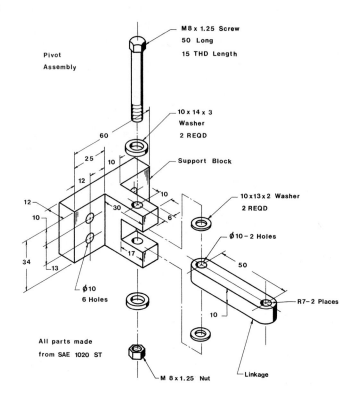

EX16-33 MILLIMETERS

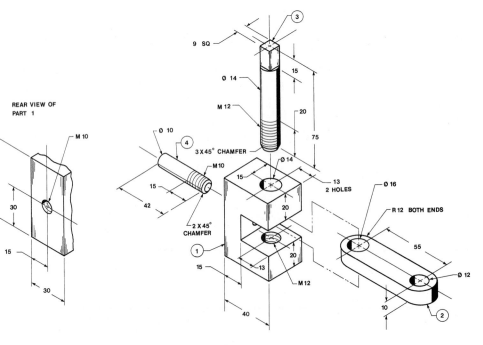

Prepare a solid model and three dimensioned orthographic views of the intersecting objects in exercise problems EX16-35 to EX16-40.

EX16-35

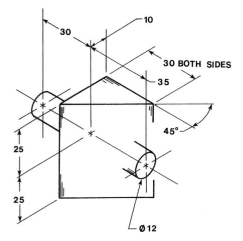

EX16-36 INCHES

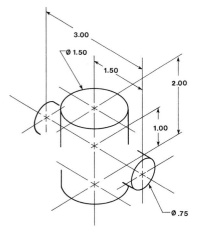

EX16-37 MILLIMETERS

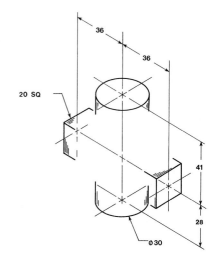

EX16-38 INCHES

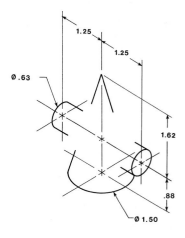

EX16-39 MILLIMETERS

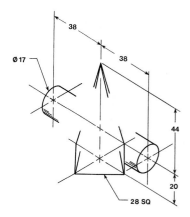

EX16-40 MILLIMETERS

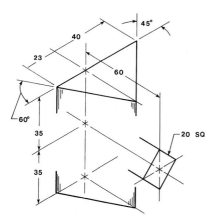

EX16-41

Redraw the given objects as solid models and add bolts with the appropriate nuts at the L and H holes. Add the appropriate drawing callouts. Specify standard bolt lengths.

A. Use the inch values.

B. Use the millimeter values.

C. Draw the front assembly view using a sectional view.

D. Prepare orthographic assembly views from the solid models.

E. Prepare a parts list.

F. Prepare detail drawings for each part.

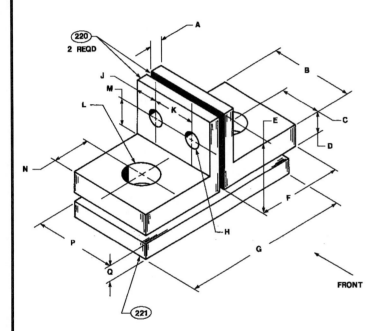

FRONT

DIMENSION	INCHES	mm
A	.25	6
B	2.00	50
C	1.00	25
D	.50	13
E	1.75	45
F	2.00	50
G	4.00	100
H	⌀.438	⌀11
J	.50	12.5
K	1.00	25
L	⌀.781	⌀19
M	.63	16
N	.88	22
P	2.00	50
Q	.25	6

EX16-42

Redraw the given objects as solid models. Add the appropriate hex head machine screws at M and N. Use standard length screws and allow at least two unused threads at the bottom of each threaded hole. Add a bolt with the appropriate nut at hole P.

A. Use the inch values.

B. Use the millimeter values.

C. Draw the front assembly view using a sectional view.

D. Prepare orthographic assembly views from the solid models.

E. Prepare a parts list.

F. Prepare detail drawings for each part.

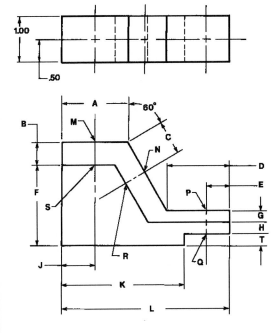

DIMENSION	INCHES	mm
A	1.50	38
B	.50	13
C	.75	19
D	1.38	35
E	.50	13
F	1.75	44
G	.25	6
H	.25	6
J	.75	19
K	2.75	70
L	3.75	96
M	⌀.31	⌀8
N	⌀.25	⌀6
P	⌀.41	⌀12
Q	⌀.41	⌀12
R	.164-32 UNF X .50 DEEP	M4 X 14 DEEP
S	.250-20 UNC X 1.63 DEEP	M6 X 14 DEEP
T	.25	6

EX16-43

Redraw the given objects as solid models and add the appropriate hex head bolts and nuts. Use only standard length bolts and include callouts for the bolts and nuts on the drawing.

A. Use the inch values.

B. Use the millimeter values.

C. Draw the front assembly   using a sectional view.

D. Prepare orthographic ass   y views from the solid models.

E. Prepare a parts list.

F. Prepare detail drawings for   h part and include positioning tolerances for all holes.

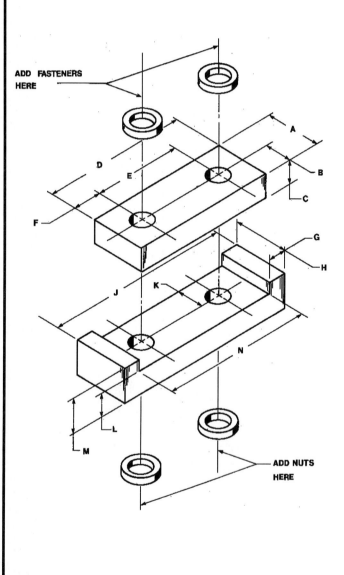

DIMENSION	INCHES	mm
A	1.25	32
B	.63	16
C	.50	13
D	3.25	82
E	2.00	50
F	.63	16
G	.38	10
H	1.25	32
J	4.13	106
K	.63	16
L	.50	13
M	.75	10
N	3.38	86

EX16-44

The objects below are to be assembled as shown. Select sizes for the parts that make the assembly possible. (Choose dimensions for the top and bottom blocks and then determine the screw and stud lengths.) The hex head screws (5) have a major diameter of either .375 or M10. The studs (3) are to have the same thread sizes as the screws and are to be screwed into the top part (2). The holes in the lower part (1) that accept the studs are to be clearance holes.

A. Draw the objects as solid models.

B. Draw an assembly drawing.

C. Draw detail drawings of each nonstandard part. Include positional tolerances for all holes.

D. Prepare a parts list.

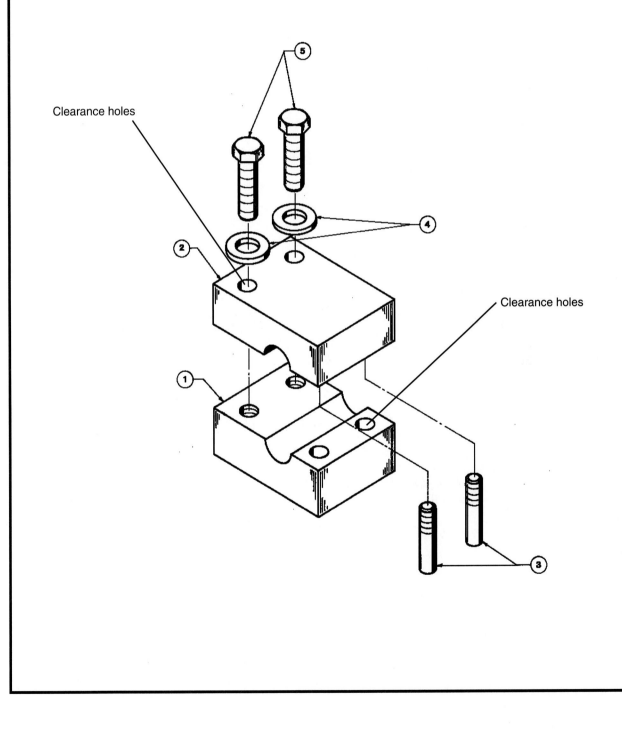

DESIGN

EX16-45

Select values for the dimensions indicated in A through J. Use either inches or millimeters. Use either .375 or M10 as the major diameter of the screws. Assemble the parts using three identical screws.

The holes in part 1 are clearance holes and the holes in part 2 are threaded.

A. Draw the objects as solid models.
B. Draw an assembly drawing.
C. Draw detail drawings of each nonstandard part. Include positional tolerances for all holes.
D. Prepare a parts list.

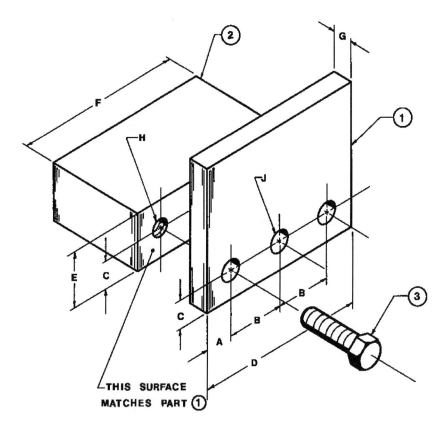

THIS SURFACE
MATCHES PART ①

EX16-46

Design an access controller based on the information given below. The controller works by moving an internal cylinder up and down within the base to align with the output holes A and B. Liquids will enter the internal cylinder from the top, then exit the base through holes A and B. Include as many holes in the internal cylinder as necessary to create the following liquid exit combinations.

1. A open, B closed
2. A open, B open
3. A closed, B open

The internal cylinder is to be held in place by an alignment key and a stop button. The stop button is to be spring loaded so that it will always be held in place. The internal cylinder will be moved by pulling out the stop button, repositioning the cylinder, then reinserting the stop button.

Prepare the following drawings.

A. Draw the objects as solid models.

B. Draw an assembly drawing.

C. Draw detail drawings of each nonstandard part. Include positional tolerances for all holes.

D. Prepare a parts list.

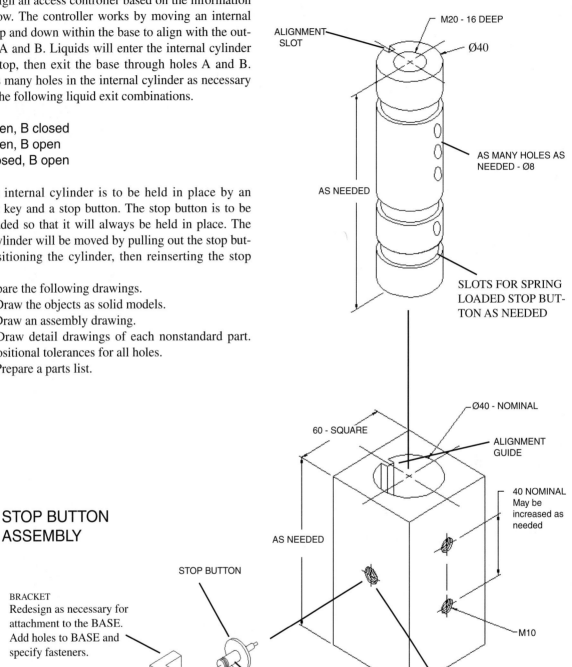

INTERNAL CYLINDER

STOP BUTTON ASSEMBLY

BASE

EX16-47

Design a hand-operated grinding wheel specifically for sharpening a chisel. The chisel is to be located on an adjustable rest while it is being sharpened. The mechanism should be able to be clamped to a table during operation using two thumb screws.

A standard grinding wheel is Ø6.00″, is a half inch thick, and has an internal mounting hole with a 50.00±.03 bore.

Prepare the following drawings.

A. Draw a solid model assembly drawing.

B. Draw detail drawings of each nonstandard part. Include positional tolerances for all holes.

C. Prepare a parts list.

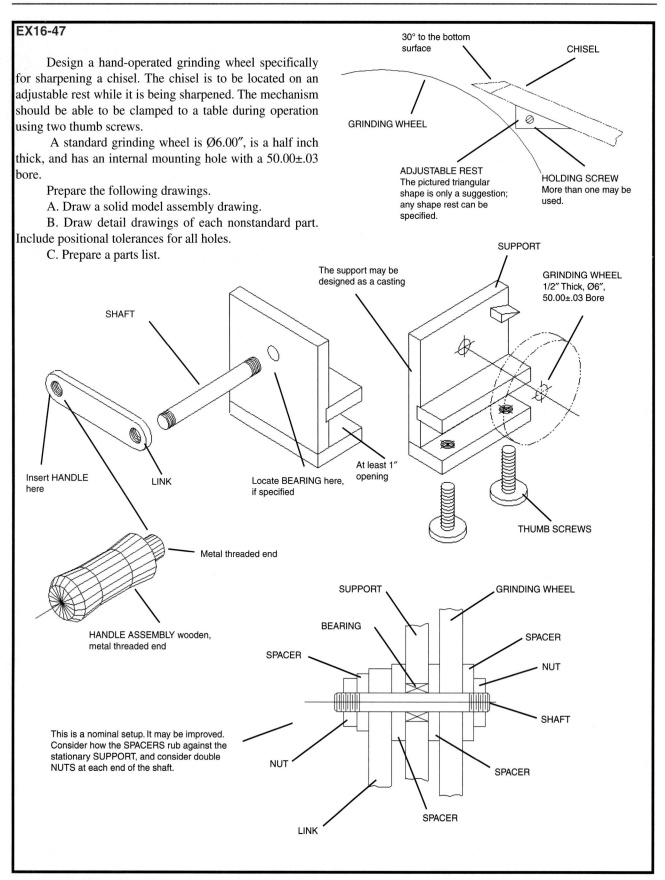

30° to the bottom surface

CHISEL

GRINDING WHEEL

ADJUSTABLE REST
The pictured triangular shape is only a suggestion; any shape rest can be specified.

HOLDING SCREW
More than one may be used.

SUPPORT

GRINDING WHEEL
1/2″ Thick, Ø6″, 50.00±.03 Bore

SHAFT

The support may be designed as a casting

Insert HANDLE here

LINK

Locate BEARING here, if specified

At least 1″ opening

THUMB SCREWS

Metal threaded end

HANDLE ASSEMBLY wooden, metal threaded end

This is a nominal setup. It may be improved. Consider how the SPACERS rub against the stationary SUPPORT, and consider double NUTS at each end of the shaft.

SUPPORT

GRINDING WHEEL

BEARING

SPACER

SPACER

NUT

SHAFT

NUT

SPACER

SPACER

LINK

Descriptive Geometry

17-1 INTRODUCTION

Descriptive geometry is the study of points, lines, and planes in space to determine their location and true shapes. Classic descriptive geometry solutions involve using projection between both standard and auxiliary orthographic views. This chapter will introduce these solutions and show how they can be done using AutoCAD. The chapter will also introduce some different approaches to the problems using AutoCAD's 3D capabilities.

17-2 ORTHOGRAPHIC PROJECTION

Figure 17-1 shows a point P located in space represented by the box. The front, top, and right-side orthographic views of the point are used to define the location of the point by relating the point's location to the sides of the box or the orthographic planes. The point's locations in the orthographic views are related to each other using a projection rectangle. The front and side views are related

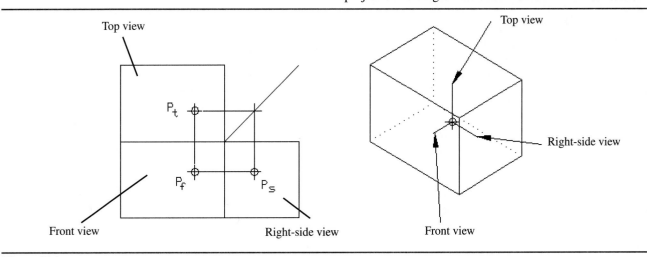

Figure 17-1

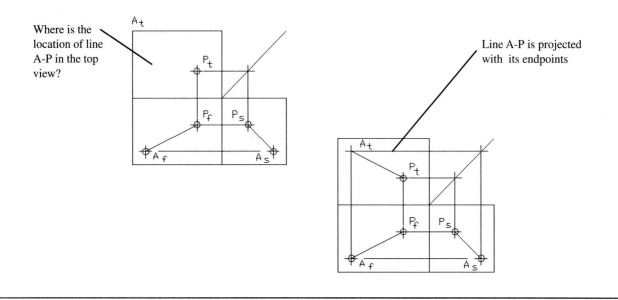

Where is the location of line A-P in the top view?

Line A-P is projected with its endpoints

Figure 17-2

by a horizontal line, the top and front views by a vertical line, and the top and side by a combination of a horizontal line and a vertical line.

Each orthographic view is two dimensional and includes two pieces of locating information. For example, if the bottom surface of the box representing space were on an XY axis, the top view would locate the point using its X,Y coordinates, the front view the X,Z coordinates, and the side the Y,Z coordinates. This means that any two views will generate the X,Y,Z coordinate values for the point. This also means that if any two orthographic views are defined, the other orthographic view, or an auxiliary view, can be derived from the defined views.

To create a third view from two existing views

Figure 17-2 shows the front and side view of a line A-P. The location of the line in the top view can be determined by projecting the endpoints of the line. If the line were curved, it could not be projected by using just its endpoints. Other points must be defined and then projected.

To project a curved line

Figure 17-3 shows the front and top views of a curved line. The side view was derived as follows.

1. Draw vertical lines between the front and top views so that they intersect both the front and top views of the curved line

In this example two vertical lines were drawn.

2. Label the intersections between the vertical lines and the front and top views of the curved line

These intersections are defined points on the curved line common to both views of the line.

3. Project the points into the side view
4. Use the POLYLINE command to join the end points and the newly defined points with a polyline
5. Use the EDIT POLYLINE command, then the FIT option to change the straight polyline into a curved line through all the defined points

The resulting elliptically shaped line is the side view of the original curved line.

To project a plane

Flat planes may be projected with their corner points. Projecting a plane's corner points projects the plane's edge lines, and in turn the entire plane. Figure 17-4 shows the projection of a plane 1-2-3-4 from given top and front views into the side view.

Only flat planes can be projected in this manner. Warped or compound surfaces must be projected by defining points on the plane's surface and then projecting the individual points, similar to the method demonstrated for curved lines.

What is the shape
of line A-B in the
side view?

Define some
additional points
in the front view
and project them
into the top view

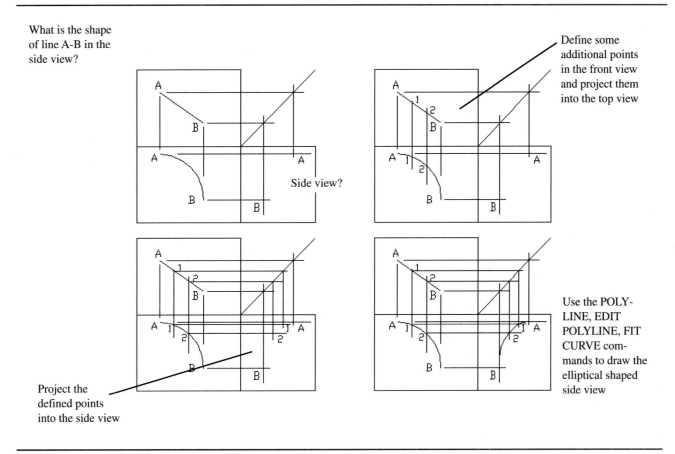

Side view?

Use the POLY-
LINE, EDIT
POLYLINE, FIT
CURVE com-
mands to draw the
elliptical shaped
side view

Project the
defined points
into the side view

Figure 17-3

Project a plane by projecting its corner points

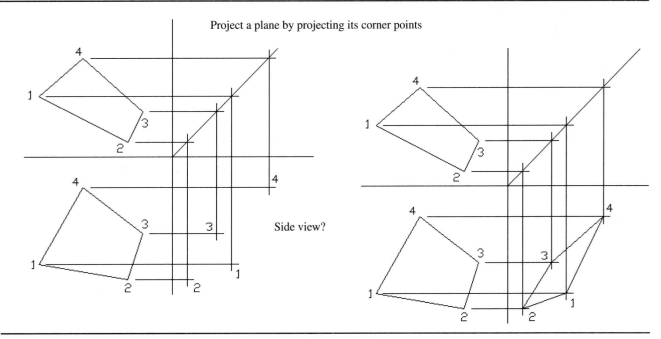

Side view?

Figure 17-4

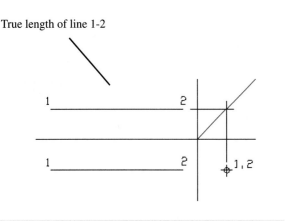

True length of line 1-2

Figure 17-5

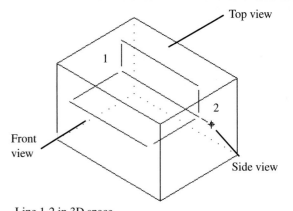

Line 1-2 in 3D space

Figure 17-6, Part 1

17-3 TRUE LENGTH OF A LINE

An orthographic view of a line shows only the true length of the line if the line is exactly parallel to the orthographic view's plane. Figure 17-5 shows three orthographic views of a line. Note that the side view is a point, or the end view of a line. If one of the views of a line is an end view, it means that a view 90° to the end view is a true length view. In the example shown, both the front and top views are true length views.

To determine the true length of a line

Figure 17-6, Parts 1 and 2, shows three views of line 1-2. None of the views is parallel to the front, top, or side orthographic plane, so none of the views is a true length view. A true length view can be created by defining an auxiliary orthographic plane parallel to one of the views of the line and then projecting the line into that view. The procedure is as follows.

1. Use the OFFSET command and create a line parallel to the side view at any distance from the side view

This line is a reference plane line for an auxiliary view parallel to the side view of line 1-2.

2. Type SNAP ENTER

Snap spacing or ON/OFF/Aspect/Rotate/Style/ <0.2500>:

3. Type R ENTER

Base point<0.0000,0.0000>:

4. Use the OSNAP, ENDPOINT option and select point 2 in the side view

Base point<0.0000,0.0000>: _endp of Rotation angle<0.00>:

5. Use the OSNAP, ENDPOINT option and select point 1 in the side view

The crosshairs will align with the side view of line 1-2.

6. Draw lines perpendicular to the two endpoints of the auxiliary plane reference line
7. Use the SNAP, ROTATION option and return the crosshairs to their normal horizontal and vertical orientation

Set the base point value to 0.0000,0.0000 and the angle of rotation to 0.

8. Use the OSNAP, ENDPOINT and PERPENDICULAR options to draw lines from the endpoints of the front view of the line perpendicular to the reference plane line between the front and side views
9. Type DIST to access the DISTANCE command
10. Use the DIST command to determine the lengths of the perpendicular lines drawn in step 8
11. Use the OFFSET command to draw lines parallel to the auxiliary reference plane line at distances equal to the distances determined in step 10

In the example shown, the distances are represented by distances A and B.

12. Draw an auxiliary view of line 1-2 between the offset line and the lines drawn perpendicular to the auxiliary plane reference line as shown
13. Erase any excess lines

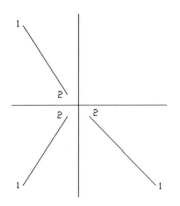

Orthographic views of line 1-2.
What is the true length of the line?

Use SNAP, ROTATE and align the cross-hairs with the side view of line 1-2.

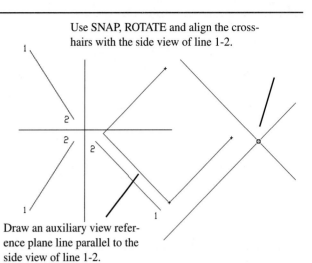

Draw an auxiliary view refer-ence plane line parallel to the side view of line 1-2.

Projection lines into the auxil-iary view perpendicular to the reference plane line

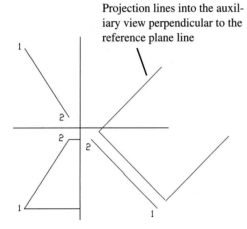

Draw lines from the line's endpoints perpendicular to the vertical axis line. Use the DIST command to determine the distances from the points to the vertical reference line.

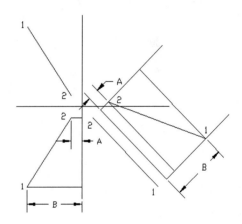

Use OFFSET to transfer the distances determined in the last step into the auxiliary view.

This is the true length of line 1-2

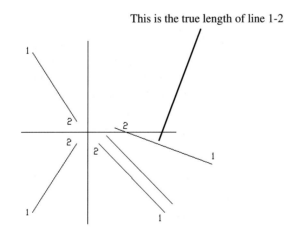

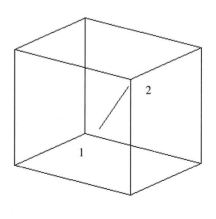

Line 1-2 in 3D space

Figure 17-6, Part 2

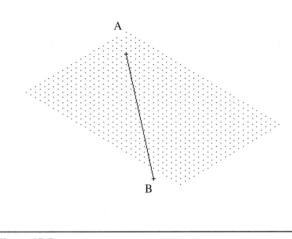

Figure 17-7

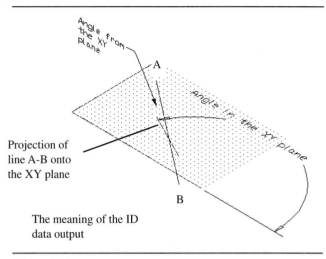

The meaning of the ID
data output

Figure 17-9

To determine the properties of a line using AutoCAD

Figure 17-7 shows a line A-B in 3D space. The location of the line's endpoints and the line's true length can be determined using the ID (identification) and DIST (distance) commands.

1. Type ID in response to a Command: prompt

    Point:

2. Use OSNAP, ENDPOINT and select endpoint A

    Point: _endp of X = 6.0000 Y = 5.0000 Z = 4.0000

These coordinate values are the location of point A relative to the WCS origin.

3. Type ENTER to restart the ID command

    Point:

4. Use OSNAP, ENDPOINT and select endpoint B

    Point: _endp of X = 12.0000 Y = 2.0000 Z = -3.0000

5. Type DIST in response to a Command: prompt

First point

6. Use OSNAP, ENDPOINT and select point A

    First point: _endp of Second point:

7. Use OSNAP, ENDPOINT and select point B

Figure 17-8 shows the resulting value readout that will appear in the command area of the screen. The distance value, 9.6954, is the true length of the line. The values listed as delta values are the changes in the individual component values. For example, the X value for point A is 6, and the B value is 12. The change in the values equals 6. Likewise, the Y value for point A is 5 and for the B value 2. The delta value is -3 measured from point A to point B. Figure 17-9 shows the meaning of the two given angle values.

To determine the true length of a line using the rotation method

Figure 17-10 shows the front and top views of a line A-B. The true length of the line can be determined by rotating the line so that one of the views of the line is parallel to one of the orthographic planes. The other view will then be a true length.

Data generated by the ID command

```
Distance = 9.6954,   Angle in XY Plane = 333.43,   Angle from XY Plane = 313.78
Delta X = 6.0000,   Delta Y = -3.0000,   Delta Z = -7.0000
Command:
```

Figure 17-8

1. Select the ROTATE command

   Select objects:

2. Select the front view of line A-B

   Select objects:

3. Type ENTER

   Base point:

4. Use OSNAP, ENDPOINT and select point A

   <Rotation angle>/Reference:

5. Rotate line A-B so that it is parallel to the reference plane line between the two views

   This rotation can be done by eye. The line will be smooth only when it is perfectly horizontal or vertical or parallel to one of the orthographic view reference plane lines. If the rotation is to be done in another type of orthographic plane, use OFFSET to create a line parallel to the required orthographic view through one of the point's endpoints, then align the rotated line to the offset line.

6. Turn ORTHO on and draw a horizontal line from point B in the top view
7. Draw a vertical line from point B in the front view as shown in Figure 17-10

   The intersection of the lines is the new location for point B.

8. Draw a line in the top view from point A to the new point B

   This line is the true length of line A-B.

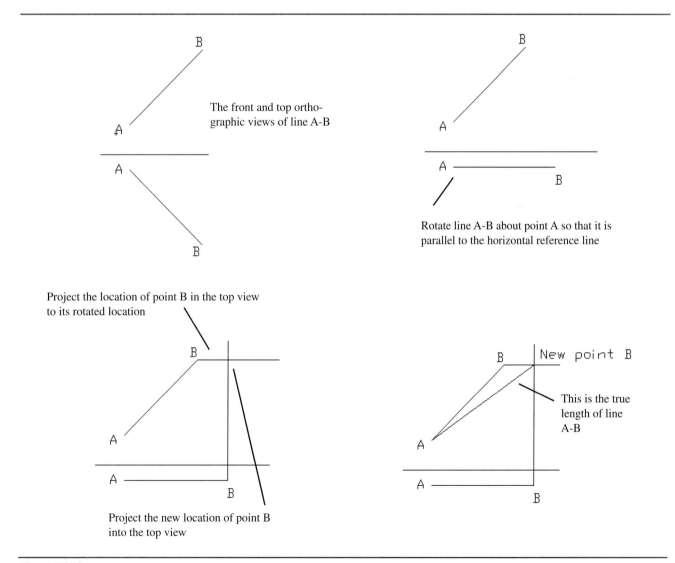

The front and top orthographic views of line A-B

Rotate line A-B about point A so that it is parallel to the horizontal reference line

Project the location of point B in the top view to its rotated location

Project the new location of point B into the top view

New point B

This is the true length of line A-B

Figure 17-10

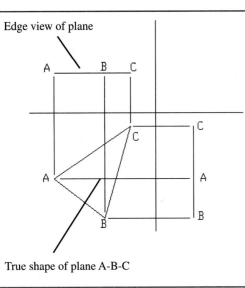

Edge view of plane

True shape of plane A-B-C

Figure 17-11

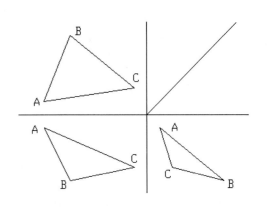

None of the given views are true shaped

Figure 17-12

17-4 THE TRUE SHAPE OF A PLANE

Figure 17-11 shows three views of a plane A-B-C. The top and side views appear as single lines, or as edge views of the plane. This means that the front view is a view perpendicular to the plane: a view of the plane's true shape.

Figure 17-12 shows three views of a plane A-B-C. None of the views appears as a straight line, so none of the views is the true shape of the plane. All the views are distorted.

The true shape of the plane can be determined by creating an auxiliary orthographic view parallel to the plane. This is done by first creating an auxiliary view that defines an edge view of the plane (a straight line), and then taking a second auxiliary view perpendicular to the first.

To create a secondary auxiliary view of a plane

In this example, only the front and top views will be used. To define an edge view of the plane, we need a reference line that defines the true angle between the plane and the orthographic reference axis. None of the edge lines is parallel to the orthographic axis; there is no appropriate reference line. A plane contains an infinite number of lines, so a line can be drawn parallel to the orthographic axis in one of the views, then projected into the other view to yield a correct reference line. See Figure 17-13, Parts 1 to 3.

To create an edge view of a plane

1. Draw a horizontal line A-x in the top view

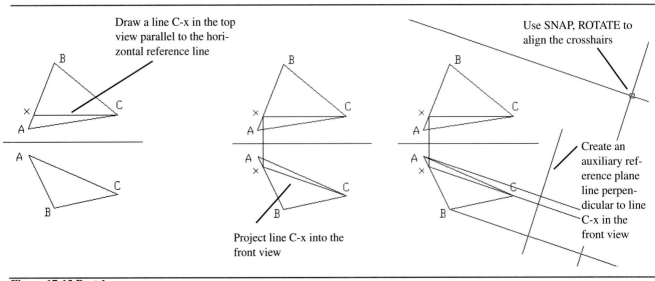

Draw a line C-x in the top view parallel to the horizontal reference line

Project line C-x into the front view

Use SNAP, ROTATE to align the crosshairs

Create an auxiliary reference plane line perpendicular to line C-x in the front view

Figure 17-13, Part 1

Any horizo   wit in the plane can be used. It is simply convenien   t o ie end of the line on a known corner point.

2. Project the   the front view
3. Type SNAP   ons e to a Command: prompt

   Snap spac   ON/OFF/Aspect/Rotate/Style <0.5000>:

4. Type R EN

   Base point   0,0 0000>:

5. Use OSNAF   POINT and select point x

   Base point   00,0.0000>: _endp of Rotation angle <0.00>:

6. Select point

   The crosshai   rotate and align with line A-x.

7. Turn ORTHC   and draw a line to the right of and perpenc   iar to line A-x

This is a reference plane line for the first auxiliary view.

8. Draw projection lines parallel to line A-x from points A and B in the front view into the auxiliary view
9. Turn ORTHO off and draw a line from the corner point in the top view to the reference line between the front and top views
10. Use the DIST command to determine the lengths of the projected lines drawn in step 9
11. Record the lengths and then use OFFSET to create lines parallel to the auxiliary view reference line in the auxiliary view plane
12. Use the appropriate intersections to draw the edge view of plane A-B-C

The distances measured in step 9 determine where along the projected lines created in step 8 the corner points are located in the auxiliary view

13. ERASE the offset lines and TRIM the projection lines using the edge view as a cutting edge line

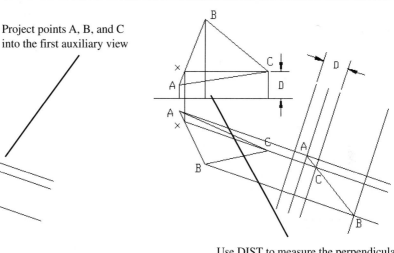

Project points A, B, and C into the first auxiliary view

Use DIST to measure the perpendicular distances from the endpoints in the top view to the horizontal reference plane line, then use OFFSET to transfer the distances to the first auxiliary view

The edge view of plane A-B-C

Figure 17-13, Pa

To create a secondary auxiliary view perpendicular to the edge view of the plane

1. Use the SNAP, ROTATE command to reposition the crosshairs so that they are aligned with the edge view line
2. Draw a line parallel to and above the edge view line

This line is the reference plane line for the secondary auxiliary view.

3. Turn ORTHO on and draw projection lines from the corner point of the plane in the first auxiliary view into the second auxiliary view

4. Use the DIST command to determine the distance from the corner point in the front view to the first auxiliary view reference line
5. Use the OFFSET command to transfer these distances to the secondary auxiliary view
6. Draw lines between the appropriate intersections to create the secondary auxiliary view of plane A-B-C
7. ERASE any excess lines

The secondary auxiliary view is the true shape of plane A-B-C.

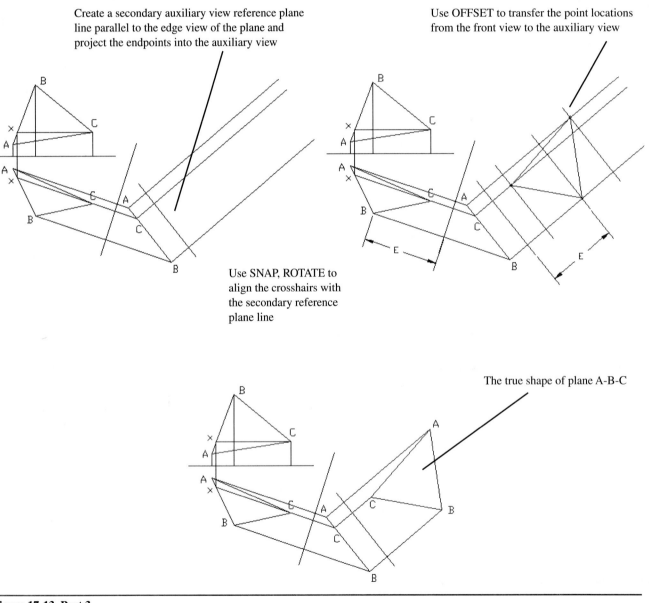

Create a secondary auxiliary view reference plane line parallel to the edge view of the plane and project the endpoints into the auxiliary view

Use OFFSET to transfer the point locations from the front view to the auxiliary view

Use SNAP, ROTATE to align the crosshairs with the secondary reference plane line

The true shape of plane A-B-C

Figure 17-13, Part 3

To determine the true shape of a plane using AutoCAD

Figure 17-14 shows a plane A-B-C in 3D space. The true shape of the plane can be determined by creating a UCS aligned with the plane and then taking a plane view of the UCS.

1. Select the SET UCS command, then the 3 POINT option

Origin point <0,0,0>:

2. Use OSNAP, ENDPOINT and select point A

Point on the positive portion of the X-axis <>:

3. Use OSNAP, ENDPOINT and select point B

Point on the positive portion of the UCS XY plane <>:

4. Use OSNAP, ENDPOINT and select point C

The coordinate system will change, creating a UCS aligned with the plane. In the example shown, the UCS icon was located on the UCS's origin.

5. Select the 3D VIEWPOINT PRESETS command, then PLAN VIEW, then CURRENT

The view shown is the true shape of plane A-B-C.

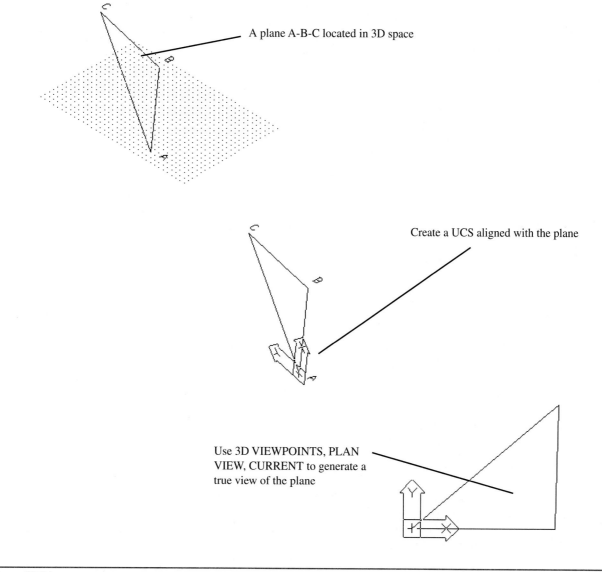

A plane A-B-C located in 3D space

Create a UCS aligned with the plane

Use 3D VIEWPOINTS, PLAN VIEW, CURRENT to generate a true view of the plane

Figure 17-14

17-5 LOCATING A LINE IN A PLANE

Figure 17-15 shows the front and top views of plane A-B-C and a line 1-2 in the top view. Line 1-2 may be located in the front view as follows.

1. Define the intersection points of the line with the edge lines of the plane as x and y
2. Project points x and y into the front view

This is done by drawing vertical lines from the inter-section points in the top view into the front view through the appropriate edge lines. In this example point x is on edge line A-C and point y is on A-B.

3. Draw a line between points x and y in the front view
4. Draw vertical lines (ORTHO) from the endpoints of the line into the front view
5. Use the EXTEND command to extend line x-y to the projection lines from the endpoints 1 and 2

Line 1-2 is now defined in the front view.

The given views
of plane A-B-C
and line 1-2

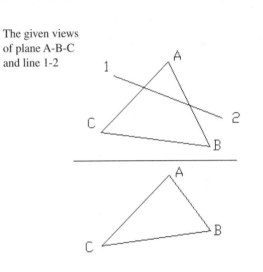

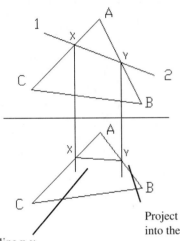

Draw line x-y

Project points x and y
into the front view

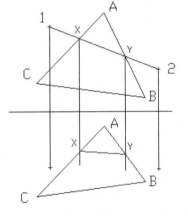

Use OSNAP, ENDPOINT and ORTHO to
project line 1-2's endpoint into the front
view

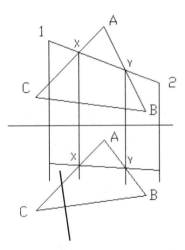

Use EXTEND to extend line x-y to the projection
lines for points 1 and 2
This the front view of line 1-2

Figure 17-15

To locate a line not in a plane

The line need not actually intersect the plane. Figure 17-16 shows a line 1-2 in the top view that does not intersect plane A-B-C. The line can be located in the front view as follows.

1. Project the endpoints into the front view

At this point the exact location of the endpoints is unknown, so draw the line into the front view, past the front view of the plane.

2. Use the EXTEND command and extend line 1-2 into the plane so that it crosses at least two edge lines

3. Label the intersection points x and y, and project them into the front view
4. Draw a line between points x and y in the front view
5. Use the EXTEND command and extend line x-y in the front view to the projection line for endpoint 2
6. Use the endpoint projection lines to TRIM line 1-2 to its correct length in both the front and top views
7. ERASE any excess lines

The given views of plane
A-B-C and line 1-2

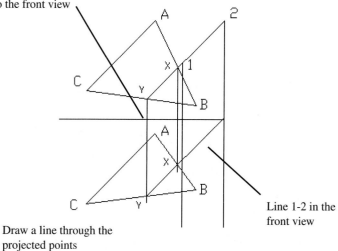

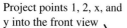

Use EXTEND to extend
line 1-2 into the plane,
crossing at least two edge
lines

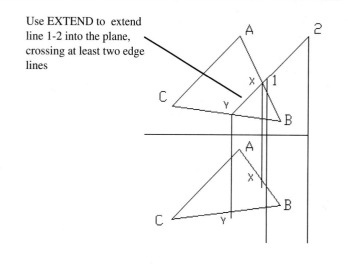

Project points 1, 2, x, and
y into the front view

Draw a line through the
projected points

Line 1-2 in the
front view

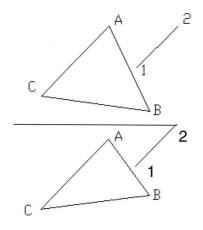

Figure 17-16

17-6 LOCATING A POINT IN A PLANE

Figure 17-17 shows front and top views of a plane A-B-C. A point P is shown in the top view. The location of the point can be determined by drawing a line from one of the plane's corner points through point P, and intersecting one of the plane's edge lines. This line can then be projected into the front view. It is known that the point's location in the front view is directly below the top view location, so the intersection of a vertical line from the point location in the top view with the projected line in the front view defines the point's location in the front view.

1. Draw a line from corner point A to point P
2. Use the EXTEND command and extend line A-P to the edge of the plane

3. Label the intersection point with the edge line x
4. Project line A-x into the front view

   Use OSNAP to ensure accuracy.

5. Project point P into the front view by drawing a vertical line from point P in the top view so that it intersects line A-x in the front view.

The intersection point is the location of point P in the front view.

The above method can also be used to determine the location of a point relative to a known plane. In Figure 17-18, a point is located to the right of plane A-B-C. The point can be located relative to the plane by drawing a line from the point to a corner point of the plane that intersects an edge line. The line can then be projected into the other views, and the point can be projected using the line. See Figure 17-18.

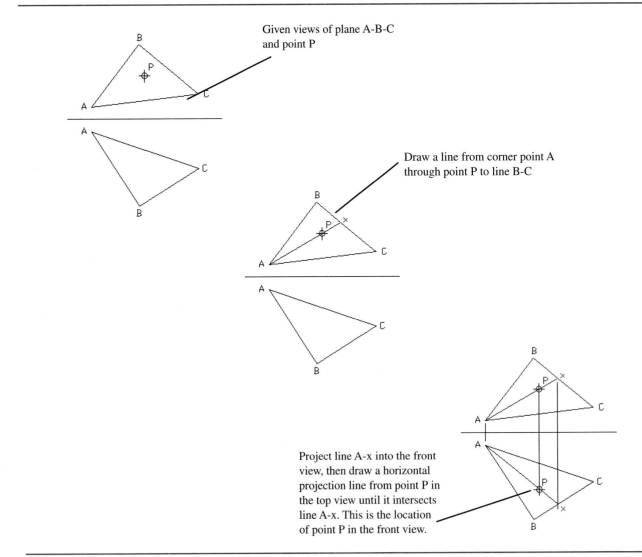

Given views of plane A-B-C and point P

Draw a line from corner point A through point P to line B-C

Project line A-x into the front view, then draw a horizontal projection line from point P in the top view until it intersects line A-x. This is the location of point P in the front view.

Figure 17-17

Given views of plane A-B-C and a point

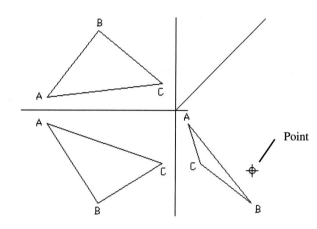

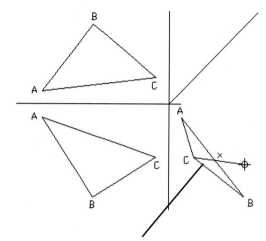

Point

Draw a line from the point to the plane so that the line crosses one edge line and intersects one of the plane's corner points

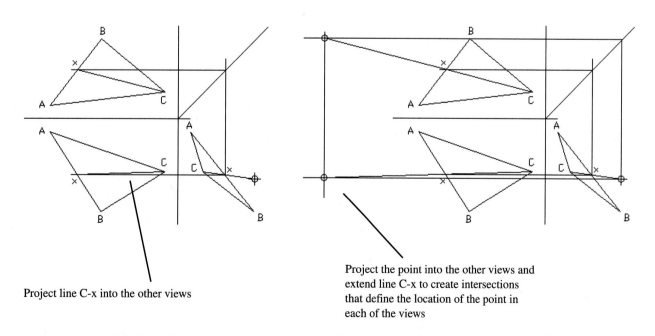

Project line C-x into the other views

Project the point into the other views and extend line C-x to create intersections that define the location of the point in each of the views

Figure 17-18

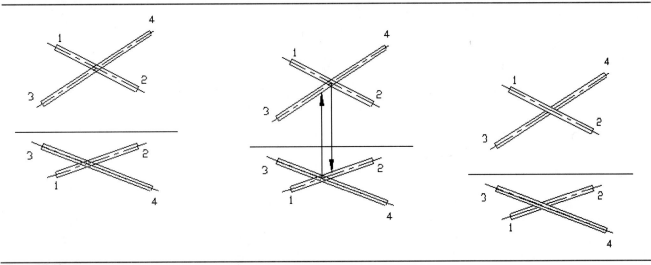

Figure 17-19

17-7 VISIBILITY OF A LINE

When working in two-dimensional orthographic views, it is sometimes difficult to determine the relative position of two lines with respect to each other. In the example presented here, solid bars were used rather than lines so it would be easier to see the visual distinction between the lines' relative locations.

Figure 17-19 shows two intersecting bars. Which bar is closer in the top view and which is closer in the front view?

For the top view

If the intersection point of lines 1-2 and 3-4 in the top view is projected into the front view by drawing a vertical line downward, the projection line intersects line 1-2 before it intersects line 3-4. Remember that objects near

the top of the front view are higher than those near the bottom of the view. If line 1-2 is intersected first, it must be higher than line 3-4 at the intersection point in the top view.

For the front view

If the intersection of lines 1-2 and 3-4 in the front view is projected into the top view by drawing a vertical line upward, the projection line intersects line 3-4 first, indicating that line 3-4 is in front of line 1-2. Points near the bottom of the top view are closer than those located in the top portion of the view.

Figure 17-19 shows the resulting intersections with their visibility displayed.

Figure 17-20 shows two lines in 3D space. They were both drawn as solid cylinders so that their relative positions can be more easily seen.

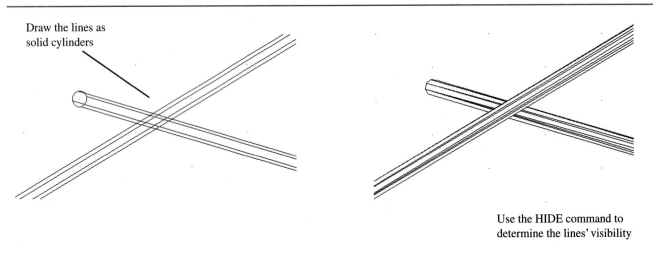

Draw the lines as solid cylinders

Use the HIDE command to determine the lines' visibility

Figure 17-20

To determine the lines' visibility using AutoCAD

1. ZOOM the intersecting area
2. Type HIDE ENTER

It can be clearly seen that line 1-2 is above line 3-4 from this viewpoint. Different viewpoints would yield different results. This may be verified by returning to the original ZOOM scale, then using the ZOOM command again and creating a window that includes both lines in their entirety. Use the 3D DYNAMIC VIEW command to rotate the lines about the screen, so you can see their relative positions and different viewpoints. If you are unsure about the lines' visibility at any orientation, use the HIDE command to see the current visibility. See Figure 17-20. The REGEN command will always return the lines to their original wire frame visibility.

17-8 PIERCING POINTS

Figure 17-21, Parts 1 and 2, shows front and top views of a plane A-B-C and line 1-2. What is the position of the line relative to the plane? There are three possible results. The line pierces the plane, the line is parallel to the

plane, or the line is within the same plane as the designated plane. There are two methods that can be used to determine whether the line does or does not pierce the plane: cutting plane method, or auxiliary view method.

Cutting plane method

1. Complete line 1-2 across the top view
2. Label the intersection points with the plane's edge lines as x and y

Think of this line as representing the top edge of a plane that includes the line 1-2.

3. Project points x and y into the front view and draw line x-y
4. Complete line 1-2 in the front view

The intersection of lines 1-2 and x-y in the front view define the piercing point between the line and the plane.

5. Project the piercing point into the top view

The visibility of the line relative to the plane can be determined by using the method explained in Section 17-9 for the visibility of lines. Note the intersection of lines A-C

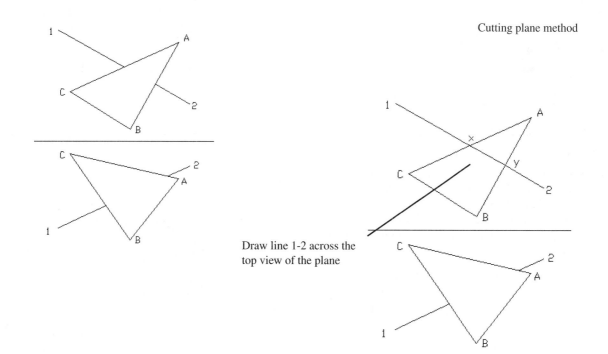

Given front and top views of plane A-B-C and line 1-2

Cutting plane method

Draw line 1-2 across the top view of the plane

Figure 17-21, Part 1

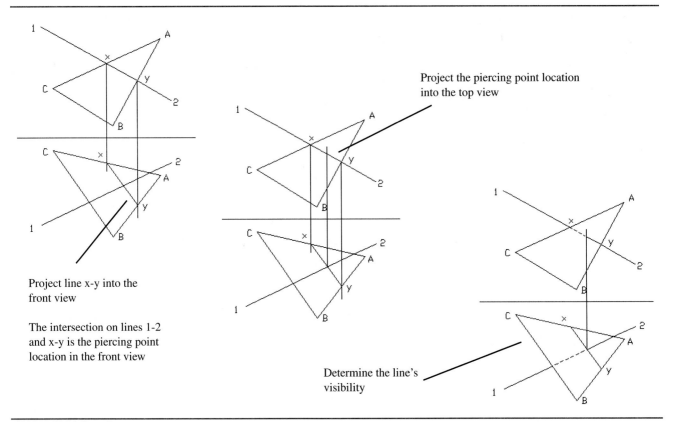

Project line x-y into the front view

The intersection on lines 1-2 and x-y is the piercing point location in the front view

Project the piercing point location into the top view

Determine the line's visibility

Figure 17-21, Part 2

and 1-2 in the top view, intersection x. Follow the projection line from the intersection down to the front view. Line A-C is intersected before line 1-2, indicating that line A-C is higher than line 1-2. Likewise, the projection of the intersection between lines C-B and 1-2 in the front view strikes line C-B first, indicating that line C-B is closer to the viewer in the front view.

Auxiliary view method

Figure 17-22 shows the same front and top views of plane A-B-C and line 1-2 that were used to explain the cutting plane method in Figure 17-21. In this example, the piercing point location will be determined using an auxiliary view that shows the edge view of the plane. See Section 17-5 for a more detailed explanation of auxiliary views.

1. Determine the projection angle for the plane's edge view by drawing a horizontal line in one of the views and then projecting it into the other view

In this example, horizontal line C-x was drawn in the top view, then projected into the front view.

2. Use the SNAP, ROTATION axis and align the

crosshairs with the front view of line C-x
3. Extend line C-x into an area for the auxiliary view
4. Draw a line perpendicular to the extension of line C-x

The perpendicular line is the reference plane line for the auxiliary view.

5. Project the endpoints of the plane into the auxiliary plane
6. Draw a line between the projected endpoints

The result should be a straight line, or the edge view of plane A-B-C.

7. Project line 1-2 into the auxiliary view
8. Complete the views of line 1-2 in both the top and front views
9. Project the piercing point location back to the front and top views

The auxiliary view generates the piercing point location on line 1-2, and because the location of line 1-2 is known in both the front and top views, the point locations in those views can be found using projection.

The visibility of the line relative to the plane can be determined as explained for the cutting plane method.

Given views of plane A-B-C and
line 1-2

Define a line C-x parallel to
the horizontal reference line

Project line C-x into the
front view

Create an auxiliary view perpendicular to the front view of
line C-x

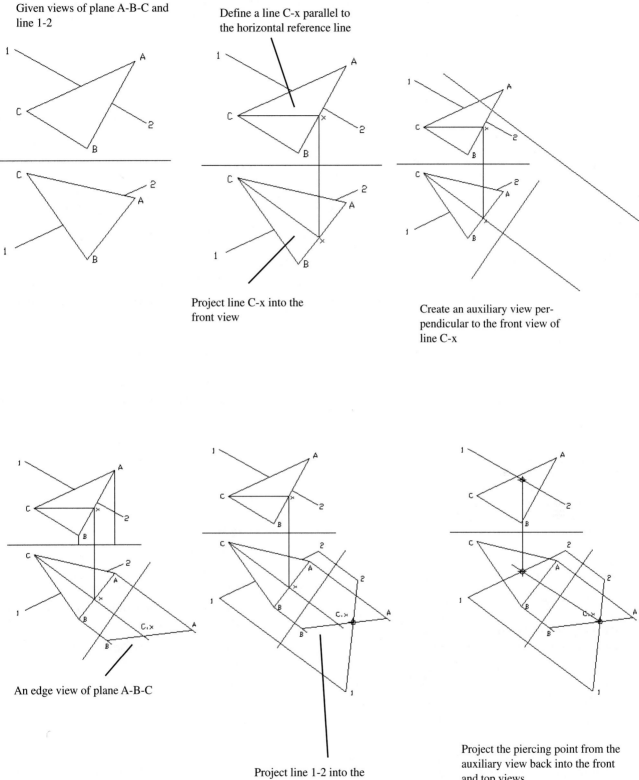

An edge view of plane A-B-C

Project line 1-2 into the
auxiliary view

Project the piercing point from the
auxiliary view back into the front
and top views

Figure 17-22

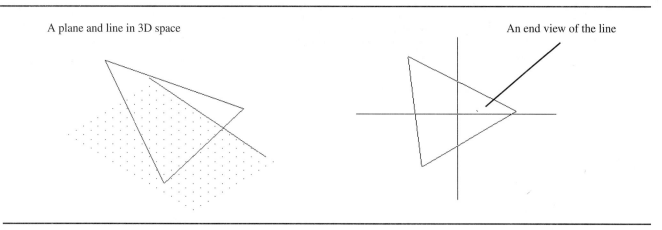

A plane and line in 3D space   An end view of the line

Figure 17-23

To determine if a plane and a line intersect using AutoCAD

Figure 17-23 shows a plane and a line in 3D. We can determine if the line pierces the plane, but not the piercing point's exact location, by using the 3D DYNAMIC VIEW command. In this example, the plane and line are not solids; they are surface models.

1. Select the 3D DYNAMIC VIEW command

Select objects:

2. Select the plane edge lines and the line

CAmera/TArget/Distance/POints/ PAn/Zoom/TWist/Clip/Hide/Off/Undo/<eXit>:

3. Type CA ENTER
4. Move the objects around until an end view of the line is found

The endpoint of line 1-2 will appear as a point. If the point appears within plane A-B-C, then the line pierces the plane.

To determine the piercing point of a line and a plane using AutoCAD's solid modeling

In this example the corner points of the plane and the endpoints of the line are used to create solid models, then the INTERSECT command is used to determine the location of the piercing point relative to the WCS. See Figure 17-24.

1. Use the DRAW command and draw the edge lines of the plane using the given coordinate values
2. Select the SET UCS command and create a UCS aligned with the plane

3. Select the POLYEDIT command and change the drawn lines into a polyline

The EDIT POLYLINE command cannot be applied to planes that are not parallel to the current UCS.

4. Select the EXTRUDE command and create a solid plane .00001 thick (height of extrusion)
5. SAVE the UCS and return to the WCS
6. Select the CYLINDER, CENTER command
7. Draw a cylinder between the two known endpoints of the line of radius .00001

Because the thickness and radius values are so small, the plane and line will appear as they did as surface models.

8. ZOOM the approximate area of the piercing point
9. Use the INTERSECTION command to determine the piercing point

The piercing point for two solid models is their common volume. It will appear as a small dot on the screen after the INTERSECTION command has been applied. Be

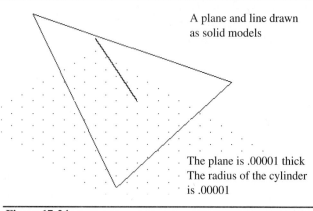

A plane and line drawn as solid models

The plane is .00001 thick
The radius of the cylinder is .00001

Figure 17-24

```
┌─────────────────────────────────────────────────────────────┐
│ ─                    AutoCAD Text Window              ▼ ▲   │
├─────────────────────────────────────────────────────────────┤
│ E̲dit                                                        │
├─────────────────────────────────────────────────────────────┤
│Command: '_zoom                                           ▲  │
│                                                             │
│All/Center/Dynamic/Extents/Left/Previous/Vmax/Window/<Scale(X/XP)>: _w│
│First corner: Other corner:                                  │
│Command:                                                     │
│Command:                                                     │
│Command: _intersect                                          │
│Select objects: 1 found                                      │
│                                                             │
│Select objects: 1 found                                      │
│                                                             │
│Select objects:                                              │
│                                                             │
│                                                             │
│Command: '_redrawall                                         │
│Command:  <Grid off> list                                    │
│                                                             │
│Select objects: 1 found                                      │
│                                                             │
│Select objects:                                              │
│               3DSOLID   Layer: 0                            │
│                         Space: Model space                  │
│                    Handle = 47                              │
│    Bounding Box: Lower Bound X = 7.5092  , Y = 5.4929  , Z = 5.0054│
│                 Upper Bound X = 7.5092  , Y = 5.4930  , Z = 5.0054│
│                                                          ▼  │
├─────────────────────────────────────────────────────────────┤
│Command:                                    ◄ █    ►        │
└─────────────────────────────────────────────────────────────┘
```

Location of the intersection between the
cylinder and the plane, the piercing point

Figure 17-25

sure to turn off GRID if it is on, so that the intersection volume can be seen.

10. Type LIST ENTER
11. Select the common volume (the dot that represents the common volume)

Figure 17-25 shows the resulting AutoCAD Text Window and the X,Y,Z coordinate values relative to the WCS. There are two values listed for the Y coordinate. Use the upper value to verify the location of the piercing point. If you were working with the plane's UCS, the resulting values would be relative to that UCS.

If you need to work with the piercing point, first use the point command to define the point as an entity. Then it can be used as a selected object.

17-9 DISTANCE BETWEEN A LINE AND A POINT

Figure 17-26, Parts 1 and 2, shows the front and top views of a line 1-2 and point P. The shortest distance between the point and line is determined by taking a secondary auxiliary view of the line, which will be a point

view of the line. The shortest possible distance can then be measured directly between the end view and the point.

1. Use the OFFSET command to create a line parallel to the top view of line 1-2

This line is the first auxiliary view reference plane line.

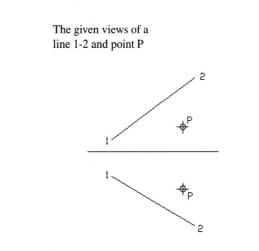

The given views of a
line 1-2 and point P

Figure 17-26, Part 1

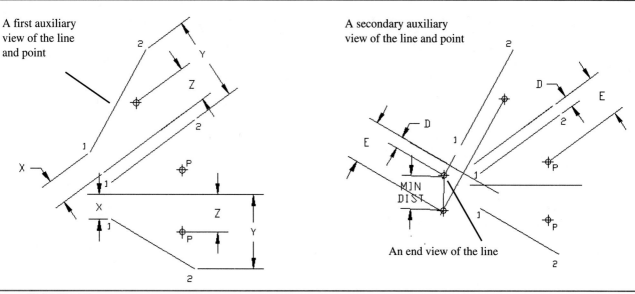

Figure 17-26, Part 2

2. Project line 1-2 and point P into the first auxiliary view
3. Use the SNAP, ROTATE option and align the crosshairs with the first auxiliary view of line 1-2
4. Create a secondary auxiliary view that shows the end view of the line

The distance between the edge view of the line and the point in the secondary auxiliary view is the minimum distance between the point and the line. See Section 17-5 for a more detailed explanation of auxiliary views.

To determine the minimum distance between a line and a point using 3D AutoCAD

Figure 17-27 shows a line 1-2 and point P. The minimum distance between the point and the line is determined as follows.

1. Select the SET UCS, 3 POINT command

   Origin point <0.0000,0.0000>:

2. Use OSNAP, ENDPOINT and select point 1

   Point on the positive portion of the X-axis:

3. Use OSNAP, ENDPOINT and select point 2

   Point on the positive-Y portion of the UCS XY plane:

4. Use OSNAP, NEAREST and select point P
5. Select the 3D VIEWPOINT PRESETS, PLAN VIEW, CURRENT command
6. Select the LINEAR DISTANCE command

   First extension line origin or RETURN to select:

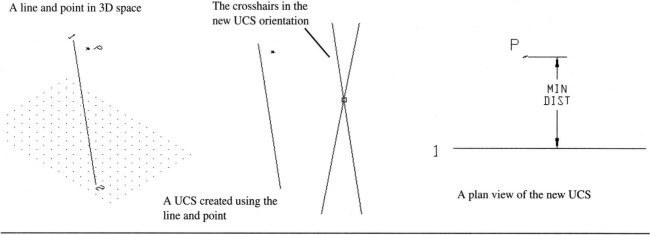

A line and point in 3D space

The crosshairs in the new UCS orientation

A UCS created using the line and point

A plan view of the new UCS

Figure 17-27

Given views of two lines

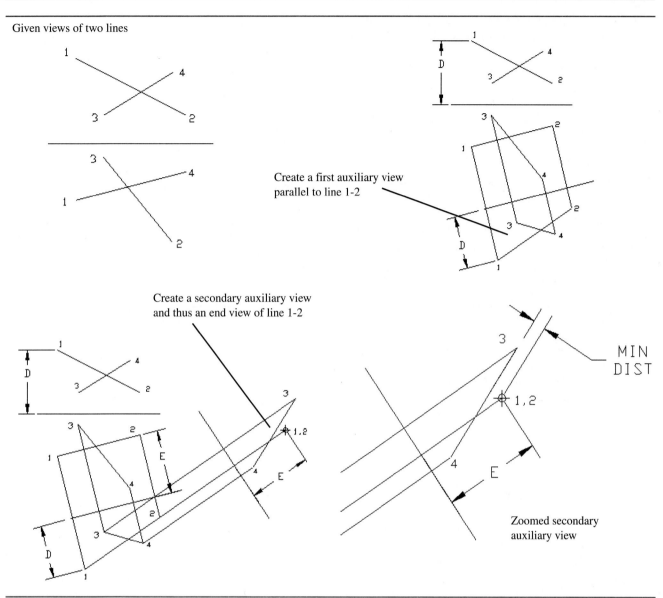

Create a first auxiliary view parallel to line 1-2

Create a secondary auxiliary view and thus an end view of line 1-2

Zoomed secondary auxiliary view

MIN DIST

Figure 17-28

7. Use OSNAP, NEAREST and select point P

   Second extension line origin:

8. Use OSNAP, PERPENDICULAR and select line 1-2

17-10 DISTANCE BETWEEN TWO LINES

Figure 17-28 shows the front and top views of lines 1-2 and 3-4.

The minimum distance between the lines can be determined by using a secondary auxiliary view to create an end view of one of the lines. The minimum distance can then be measured by drawing a line from the point end view of the line perpendicular to the other line.

The secondary auxiliary view method

1. Use the SNAP, ROTATE command to align the crosshairs with the front view of line 1-2

2. Draw a reference plane line for the first auxiliary view parallel to the front view of line 1-2, then project both lines' endpoints into the auxiliary view from the front view

3. Use the OSNAP, ROTATE command and align the crosshairs with the first auxiliary view of line 1-2
4. Create the edge plane line for the secondary auxiliary view by drawing a line perpendicular to the first auxiliary view of line 1-2
5. Project both lines' endpoints into the secondary auxiliary view

Line 1-2 should appear as a point or end view of the line.

6. Draw a line from the end view perpendicular to the view of line 3-4
7. Use the LINEAR, ALIGNED dimension command to measure the length of the perpendicular line

The distance found in step 7 will be the minimum distance between the two lines.

Using AutoCAD's 3D capabilities

Figure 17-29 shows two lines in 3D space. The minimum distance between them may be determined by rotating the lines until one appears as an end view, then measuring the perpendicular distance between the end view and the other line. The OSNAP commands cannot be applied in this situation. The resulting distance is an approximation. It is, however, a very close approximation.

1. Select the 3D DYNAMIC VIEW command
2. Select the two lines

   CAmera/TArget/Distance/POints/Pan/Zoom/ TWist/CLip/Hide/Off/Undo/<eXit>:

3. Type CA ENTER
4. Rotate the lines until one appears as a point
5. Type X ENTER to exit the 3D DYNAMIC VIEW command
6. Zoom the area around the end view and draw a line from the end view perpendicular to the line

Draw the line by eye; that is, select the endpoints on the screen. Do not use OSNAP.

7. Use the DIST command to determine the length of the line

This distance will be the approximate minimum distance between the two lines.

Two lines in 3D space

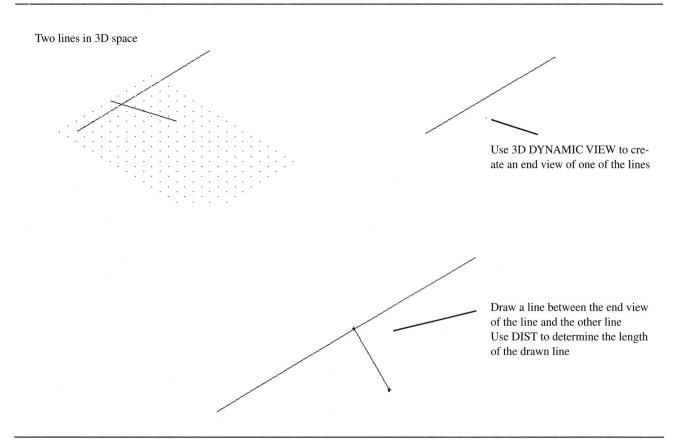

Use 3D DYNAMIC VIEW to create an end view of one of the lines

Draw a line between the end view of the line and the other line
Use DIST to determine the length of the drawn line

Figure 17-29

17-11 ANGLE BETWEEN A PLANE AND A LINE

Figure 17-30 shows front and top views of a plane A-B-C and a line 1-2. The true angle between them can be determined by taking several auxiliary views so that the plane appears as an edge view and the line appears as a true length. See Section 17-6 for additional explanation of how to create the end view of a plane.

The auxiliary view method

1. Create a first auxiliary view that shows plane A-B-C as an end view (a straight line)

This view shows the edge view of the plane but not the true length of the line, so the angle between them is not a true angle.

2. Draw a secondary auxiliary view of the line and plane that shows the true shape of the plane
3. Draw a third auxiliary view so that its edge plane line is parallel to the secondary auxiliary view of line 1-2

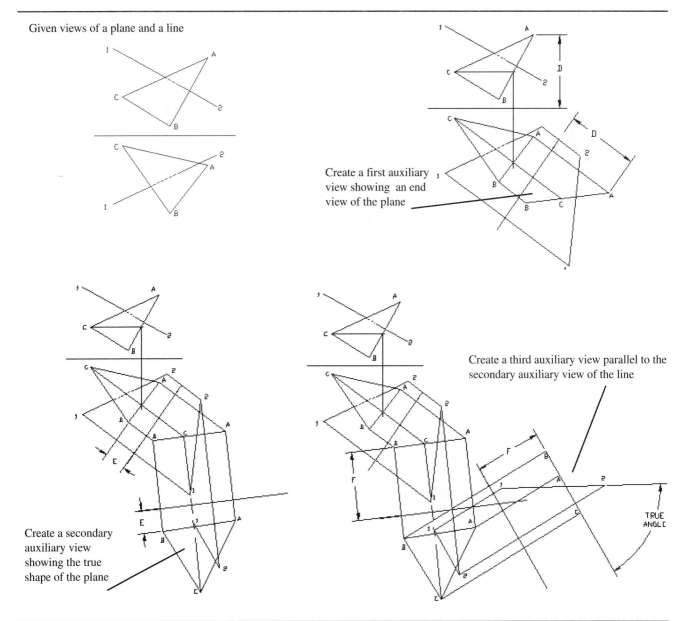

Given views of a plane and a line

Create a first auxiliary view showing an end view of the plane

Create a secondary auxiliary view showing the true shape of the plane

Create a third auxiliary view parallel to the secondary auxiliary view of the line

TRUE ANGLE

Figure 17-30

A plane and a line in 3D space

Create a UCS aligned with the plane

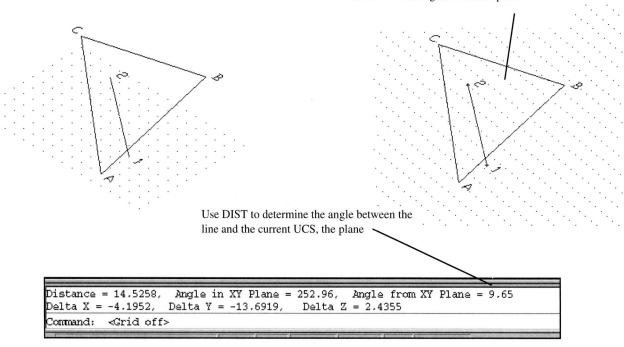

Use DIST to determine the angle between the
line and the current UCS, the plane

```
Distance = 14.5258,  Angle in XY Plane = 252.96,  Angle from XY Plane = 9.65
Delta X = -4.1952,  Delta Y = -13.6919,   Delta Z = 2.4355
Command:  <Grid off>
```

Figure 17-31

Using 3D AutoCAD

Figure 17-31 shows a plane A-B-C and a line 1-2 in 3D space. The angle between them can be determined by first defining a UCS aligned with the plane, then using the DIST command.

1. Select the SET UCS, 3 POINT command and define a UCS aligned with plane A-B-C

    Use OSNAP, ENDPOINT to ensure accuracy.

2. Type DIST in response to a Command: prompt
3. Use OSNAP, ENDPOINT and select points 1 and 2

The value listed in the command box at the bottom of the screen for "Angle from XY plane" is the angle between the line and the plane. In this example, the angle from the XY plane is defined as 9.65°. See Figure 17-31. If the endpoints had been selected in the opposite sequence, the resulting angular value would have been 350.35°, or the complementary angle of the 9.65° initially determined.

17-12 ANGLE BETWEEN TWO PLANES

Figure 17-32 shows front and top views of two intersecting planes A-B-C and B-C-D. The true angle between the planes can be determined by using a secondary auxiliary view positioned to show an edge view of each plane. This can be done only by aligning the secondary view so that it shows an end view of the line common to the two planes.

The auxiliary view method

1. Create a first auxiliary view aligned with line B-C, the line common to both planes
2. Create a secondary auxiliary view perpendicular to the projection line aligned with line B-C in the first auxiliary view

The resulting auxiliary view shows end views of both planes.

3. Use the ANGULAR dimension command to determine the angle between the two planes

Given views of two intersecting planes

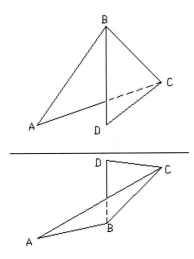

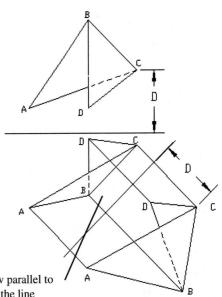

Create a first auxiliary view parallel to the front view of line B-C, the line common to both planes

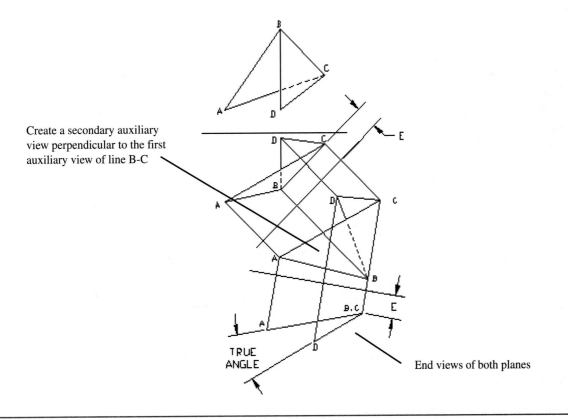

Create a secondary auxiliary view perpendicular to the first auxiliary view of line B-C

TRUE ANGLE

End views of both planes

Figure 17-32

Using AutoCAD's solid modeling

Figure 17-33 shows two planes in 3D space: A-B-C and D-E-F. The planes were drawn using the LINE command. The endpoints were defined by X,Y,Z coordinate values. This example will explain how to determine the angle between the planes using solid modeling.

The two planes will be changed to solid models 0.00001 thick, then unioned to determine their intersection line, if any. A UCS will then be created and aligned with the common intersection line. A PLAN view of this UCS's LEFT PRESET UCS view will yield an edge view of both planes, which in turn can be used to determine the angle between the planes. The origin icon will appear in most of the illustrations to help clarify the different UCSs used.

1. Use the SET UCS command and create a UCS aligned with plane A-B-C, with point A as the origin
2. Select the EDIT POLYLINE command

    Command: _pedit Select polyline:

3. Select line A-B

    Object selected is not a polyline.

    Do you want to turn it into one? <Y>

4. Type ENTER

    Close/Join/ Width/ Edit vertex/ Fit/ Spline/ Decurve/ Ltype gen/ Undo/ eXit <X>:

5. Type J ENTER

    Select objects:

6. Select the three lines in plane A-B-C

    Close/ Join/ Width/ Edit vertex/ Fit/ Spline/ Decurve/ Ltype gen/ Undo/ eXit <X>:

7. Type ENTER to return to a Command: prompt
8. Select the EXTRUDE command

    Select objects:

9. Select plane A-B-C

    Path/<Height of Extrusion>:

10. Type .00001 ENTER

    Extrusion taper angle <0>:

11. Type ENTER

There will be no visible change in the plane, but it is now a solid, very thin model.

12. Use the SET UCS command and create a UCS aligned with plane D-E-F, with point D as the origin
13. Change plane D-E-F into a solid model as explained above for plane A-B-C
14. Used the NAMED UCS command, and make the WCS the current UCS
15. Use the UNION command to join the two planes (solid models) together

A line will appear on the planes. This is their common intersection line.

16. Type HIDE to see how the two planes intersect
17. Type REGEN ENTER to return to a wire frame view of the planes

In this example, the intersection line is labeled 1-2.

18. Use the SET UCS command and create a third UCS aligned with the intersection line 1-2
19. Select point 1 as the origin, point 2 as a point on the positive portion of the Xaxis, and point D as a point on the positive portion of the Xaxis.
20. Select the PRESET UCS command, then select a LEFT UCS orientation
21. Select the 3D VIEWPOINT PRESETS, PLAN VIEW, CURRENT

The planes will appear as two intersecting lines.

22. Use the ANGULAR DIMENSION command to determine the angle between the two planes

17-13 INTERSECTION

AutoCAD's solid modeling capabilities are particularly well suited to solving intersection problems. Examples of 2D solutions to intersection problems are presented in Chapter 5, and solid model solutions are presented in Chapter 16.

17-14 FURTHER STUDY

Students interested in further study of descriptive geometry are referred to *Descriptive Geometry*, by Pare, Loving, and Hill, published by Macmillan Publishing Co., Inc., New York, New York.

Two planes in 3D space

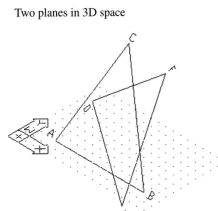

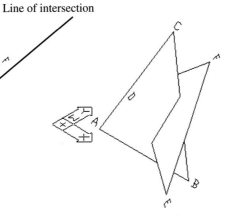

Create a UCS aligned with one of the planes
Change the plane to a solid .00001 thick

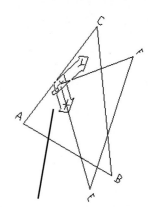

Create a second UCS aligned with the other plane
Change the plane to a solid .00001 thick

Line of intersection

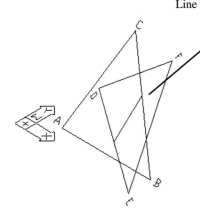

UNION the two solid planes

The HIDE command may be used to verify the intersection
Use REGEN to return to the original drawing

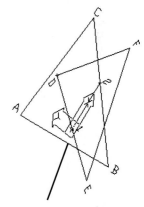

Create a third UCS aligned with the intersection line

Use PRESET UCS to create a FRONT view of the UCS aligned with the intersection line

ANGLE BETWEEN PLANES

Use ANGULAR DIMENSION to determine the angle between the planes

Figure 17-33

17-15 EXERCISE PROBLEMS

For exercise problems EX17-1 to EX17-12:

A. Locate the line or plane in the missing view.

B. Determine the true length of the line.

C. Determine the true shape of the plane.

The grid spacing for the dot background is either .5″ or 10mm.

EX17-1

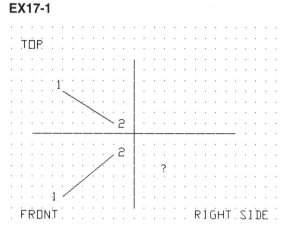

EX17-4

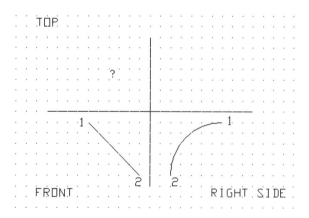

EX17-2

EX17-5

EX17-3

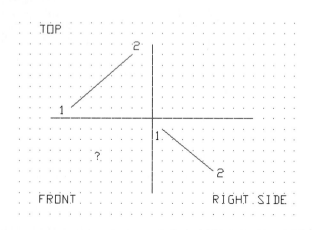

EX17-6

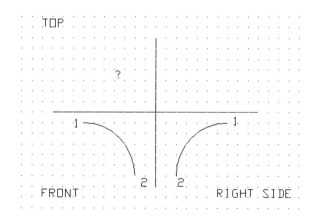

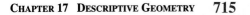

EX17-7

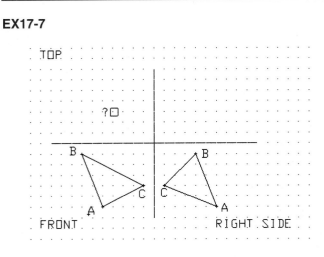

EX17-10 INCHES, SCALE 4:1

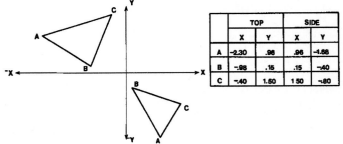

	TOP		SIDE	
	X	Y	X	Y
A	-2.30	.96	.96	-1.88
B	-.98	.15	.15	-.40
C	-.40	1.50	1.50	-.80

EX17-8

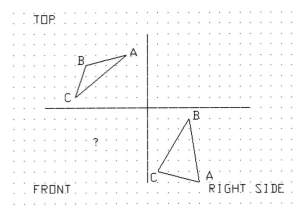

EX17-11 MILLIMETERS, SCALE 3:1

	TOP		SIDE	
	X	Y	X	Y
A	-49	35	35	-26
B	-11	27	27	-11
C	-35	6	6	-37

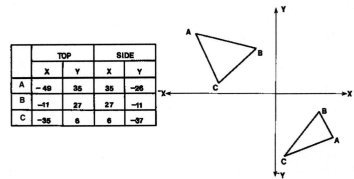

EX17-9

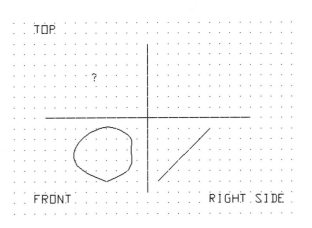

EX17-12 INCHES, SCALE 4:1

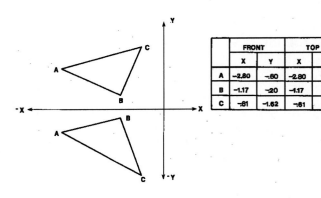

	FRONT		TOP	
	X	Y	X	Y
A	-2.80	-.60	-2.80	1.05
B	-1.17	-.20	-1.17	.35
C	-.61	-1.62	-.61	1.62

Find the true shape of the triangular planes in exercise problems EX17-13 to EX17-16. The three corner points of the planes are defined as A, B, and C with the following coordinate values.

EX17-13 INCHES

A = 2,6,5
B = 3,2,-4
C = 6,5,1

EX17-14 INCHES

A = 0,7,3
B = 8,0,-1
C = 5,5,-6

EX17-15 MILLIMETERS

A = 50, 50,125
B = 175,50,-100
C = 150,125,25

EX17-16 MILLIMETERS

A = 20,200,80
B = 200,0,-30
C = 120,120,-160

Determine the length of each of the lines in exercise problems EX17-17 to EX17-20 and the minimum distance between the two lines. The lines are defined as A-B and C-D.

EX17-17 INCHES

A = 1,1,1
B = 8,8,-3

C = 3,4,5
D = 9,6,-7

EX17-18 INCHES

A = 2,6,-4
B = 7,1,6

C = 0,1,3
D = 8,6,-2

EX17-19 MILLIMETERS

A = 30,20,20
B = 200,200,-70

C = 60,100,130
D = 200,150,-170

EX17-20 MILLIMETERS

A = 50,150,-100
B = 180,20,150

C = 0,20,70
D = 200,150,-60

Determine the minimum distance between the points and planes in exercise problems EX17-21 to EX17-24.

EX17-21 INCHES

Plane:

A = 1,6,4
B = 3,3,-4.5
C = 6,5,0

Point:

P = 4,3,6

EX17-22 INCHES

Plane:

A = 0,7,3
B = 7,1,-1
C = 5,5,-6

Point:

P = 2,3,5

EX17-23 MILLIMETERS

Plane:

A = 55,150,120
B = 75,50,-100
C = 140,130,20

Point:

P = 100,60,130

EX17-24 MILLIMETERS

Plane:

A = 20,180,85
B = 200,0,-35
C = 120, 130,-150

Point:

P = 50,75,130

Determine the true shape of each plane in exercise problems EX17-25 to EX17-30 and the perpendicular distance from the point to the plane.

EX17-25 INCHES

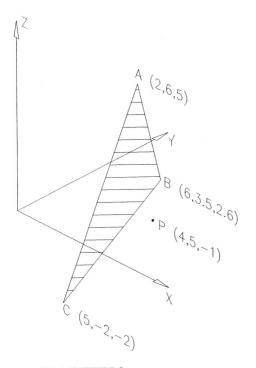

EX17-27 MILLIMETERS

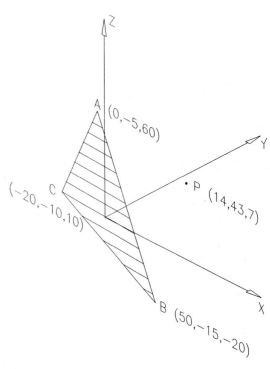

EX17-26 MILLIMETERS

EX17-28 INCHES

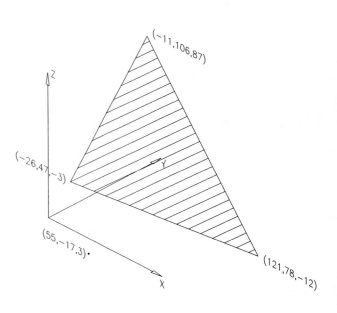

EX17-29 INCHES

Determine the intersection line and angle of intersection between the planes in exercise problems EX17-31 to EX17-34.

EX17-31 INCHES

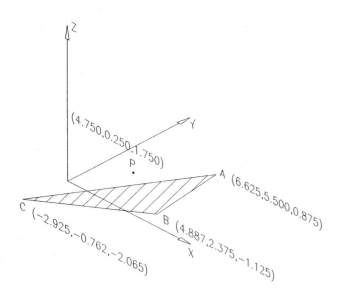

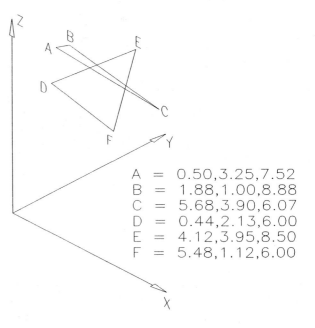

A = 0.50,3.25,7.52
B = 1.88,1.00,8.88
C = 5.68,3.90,6.07
D = 0.44,2.13,6.00
E = 4.12,3.95,8.50
F = 5.48,1.12,6.00

EX17-30 MILLIMETERS

EX17-32 MILLIMETERS

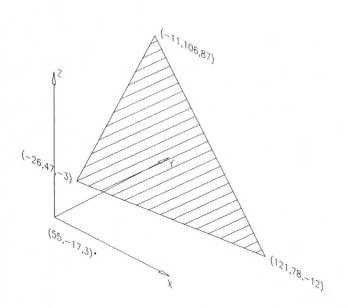

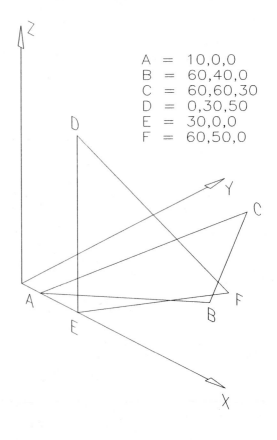

A = 10,0,0
B = 60,40,0
C = 60,60,30
D = 0,30,50
E = 30,0,0
F = 60,50,0

EX17-33 MILLIMETERS

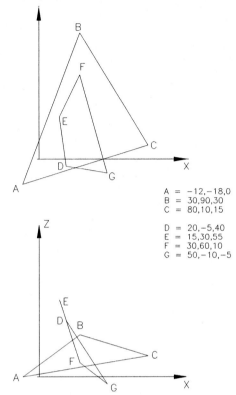

A = −12,−18,0
B = 30,90,30
C = 80,10,15

D = 20,−5,40
E = 15,30,55
F = 30,60,10
G = 50,−10,−5

EX17-34 MILLIMETERS

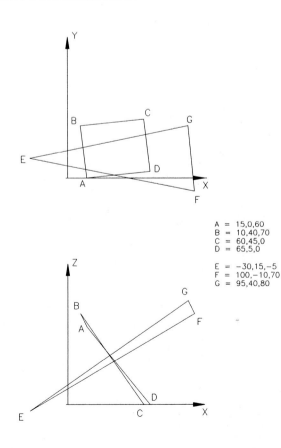

A = 15,0,60
B = 10,40,70
C = 60,45,0
D = 65,5,0

E = −30,15,−5
F = 100,−10,70
G = 95,40,80

Determine the minimum distance between the given lines in exercise problems EX17-35 to EX17-36.

EX17-35 MILLIMETERS

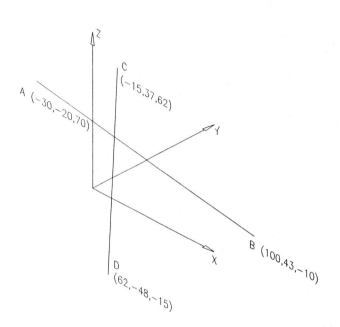

EX17-36 MILLIMETERS

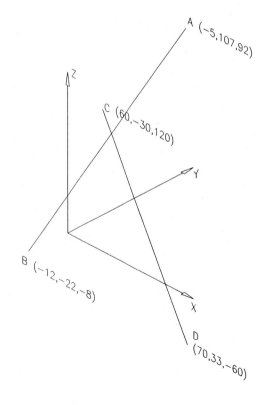

Determine the minimum distance between the given line and the point in exercise problems EX17-37 to EX17-40.

EX17-37 MILLIMETERS

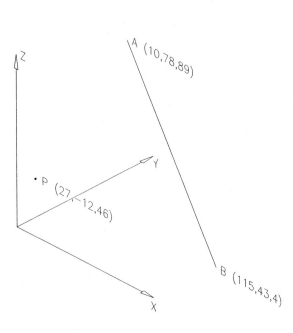

EX17-39 INCHES

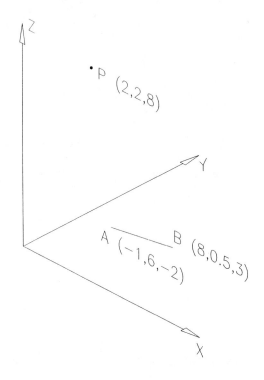

EX17-38 INCHES

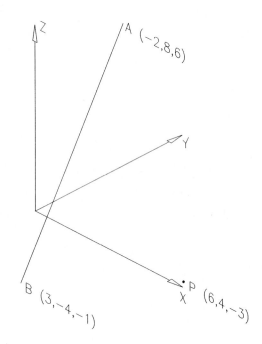

EX17-40 MILLIMETERS

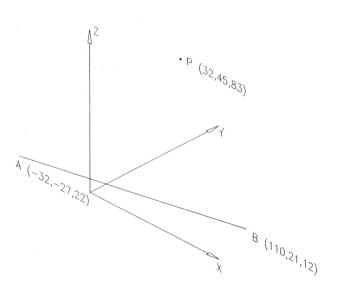

In exercise problems EX17-41 to EX17-45, determine the point on the plane where the line intersects. Label the point and specify its x,y,z coordinate relative to the WCS.

EX17-41 INCHES

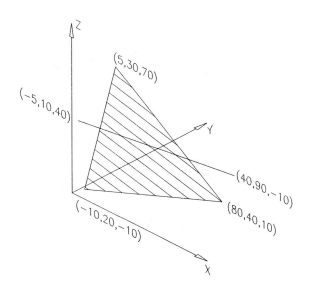

EX17-43 MILLIMETERS

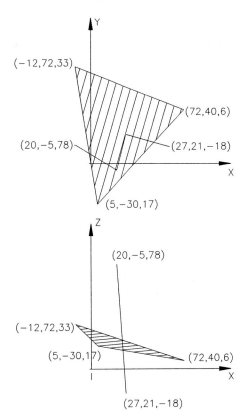

EX17-42 MILLIMETERS

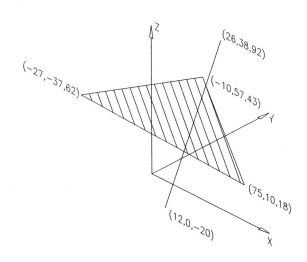

EX17-44 IINCHES

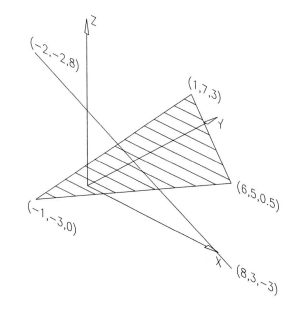

EX17-45 MILLIMETERS

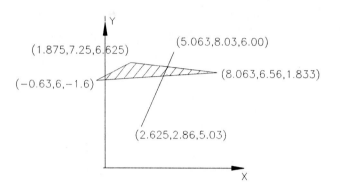

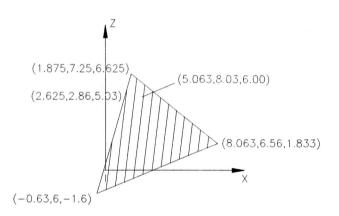

EX17-46

A pole 19.7 feet high is supported by three guy wires. Wire 1 is attached to the pole 1.00 feet from the top, wire 2 is attached 2.00 feet from the top, and wire 3 is attached 2′6″ from the top. The location of the pole and the location of the ground positions of the three guy wires are defined below. What is the true length of each of the guy wires?

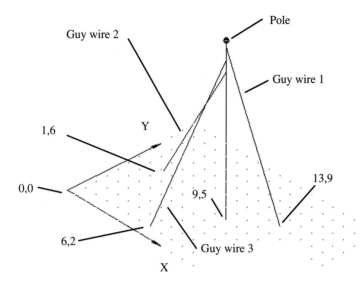

EX17-47

A work platform is to be added to the cowling of a helicopter. It is to fold down, giving access to the transmission area, and supplying a place for the mechanic to sit while working. The platform is to be 24″ by 24″.

Two support wires will be required to support the mechanic's weight and tools. The wires are to attach to the platform 1″ in from each of the outside edges and attach to the cowling 6″ to the left and right of the the top edge of the platform opening as shown.

What is the true length of the support wires?

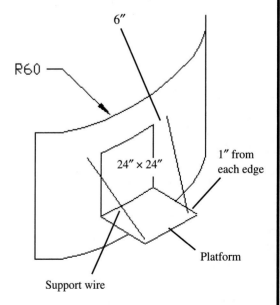

EX17-48

A satellite for scientific experiments involving the solar wind is to be made in an approximate spherical shape. The diameter of the sphere is 20cm, but the top and bottom portions have to be truncated so that they are 19cm apart. See below.

The satellite is to be made from 6 rows of 8 flat panels with straight edges The satellite is symmetrical about its central horizontal axis. The symmetry allows the satellite to be made from just three different sized panels.

What is the true shape of each of the three different panels?

Solar Wind Satellite

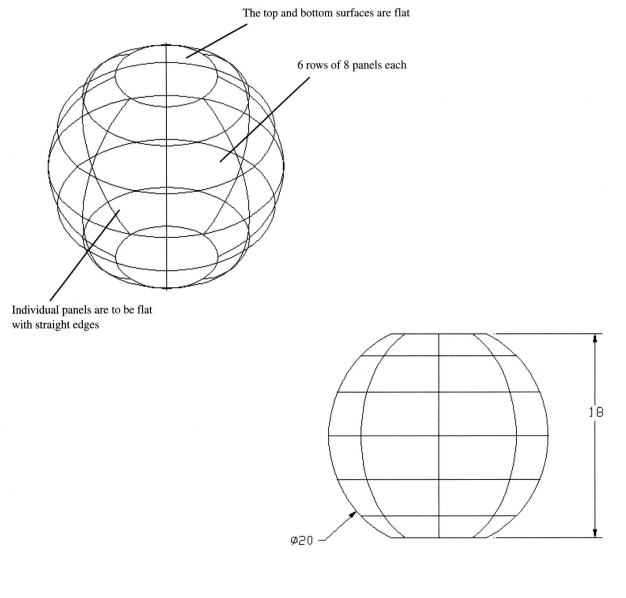

The top and bottom surfaces are flat

6 rows of 8 panels each

Individual panels are to be flat
with straight edges

18

⌀20

Appendix

PROMET is a suggested prototype drawing for use with metric units. The following values are recommended as default settings.

```
                 PROMET Settings
LIMITS:                              UNITS

    Lower left = 0.0000,0.0000          DECIMAL
    Upper right = 297,210
        (ZOOM ALL)                      Precision = 0.00

DRAW:
                                     HATCH:
    DTEXT = 5
                                        Pattern = ANSI31
SETTINGS
                                     SKETCH
    LTSCALE = 12
                                        Record Increment = 0.5
SETVAR
                                     DIM:
    DIMCEN = -2.0
                                        DIM VARS
DRAWING AIDS
                                           DIMASZ = 4
    GRIP = 10                              DIMEXE = 2
    SNAP = 5                               DIMEXO = 2
                                           DIMGAP = 2
LAYERS:                                    DIMTXT = 5

    Name        Color       Linetype

    CENTER      RED         Centerline
    HIDDEN      GREEN       Hidden
    DIM         BLUE        Continuous
    CONSTR      YELLOW      Continuous
```

American Standard Clearance Locational Fits

Nominal Size Range Inches Over — To	Class LC1 Limits of Clearance	Class LC1 Standard Limits Hole H6	Class LC1 Standard Limits Shaft h5	Class LC2 Limits of Clearance	Class LC2 Standard Limits Hole H7	Class LC2 Standard Limits Shaft h6	Class LC3 Limits of Clearance	Class LC3 Standard Limits Hole H8	Class LC3 Standard Limits Shaft h7	Class LC4 Limits of Clearance	Class LC4 Standard Limits Hole H10	Class LC4 Standard Limits Shaft h9
0 — 0.12	0	+0.25	0	0	+0.4	0	0	+0.6	0	0	+1.6	0
	0.45	0	-0.2	0.65	0	-0.25	1	0	-0.4	2.6	0	-1.0
0.12 — 0.24	0	+0.3	0	0	+0.5	0	0	+0.7	0	0	+1.8	0
	0.5	0	-0.2	0.8	0	-0.3	1.2	0	-0.5	3.0	0	-1.2
0.24 — 0.40	0	+0.4	0	0	+0.6	0	0	+0.9	0	0	+2.2	0
	0.65	0	-0.25	1.0	0	-0.4	1.5	0	-0.6	3.6	0	-1.4
0.40 — 0.71	0	+0.4	0	0	+0.7	0	0	+1.0	0	0	+2.8	0
	0.7	0	-0.3	1.1	0	-0.4	1.7	0	-0.7	4.4	0	-1.6
0.71 — 1.19	0	+0.5	0	0	+0.8	0	0	+1.2	0	0	+3.5	0
	0.9	0	-0.4	1.3	0	-0.5	2	0	-0.8	5.5	0	-2.0
1.19 — 1.97	0	+0.6	0	0	+1.0	0	0	+1.6	0	0	+4.0	0
	1.0	0	-0.4	1.6	0	-0.6	2.6	0	-1.0	6.5	0	-2.5

Figure A-2A

Nominal Size Range Inches Over — To	Class LC5 Limits of Clearance	Class LC5 Standard Limits Hole H7	Class LC5 Standard Limits Shaft g6	Class LC6 Limits of Clearance	Class LC6 Standard Limits Hole H9	Class LC6 Standard Limits Shaft f8	Class LC7 Limits of Clearance	Class LC7 Standard Limits Hole H10	Class LC7 Standard Limits Shaft e9	Class LC8 Limits of Clearance	Class LC8 Standard Limits Hole H10	Class LC8 Standard Limits Shaft d9
0 — 0.12	0.1	+0..4	-0.1	0.3	+1.0	-0.3	0.6	+1.6	-0.6	1.0	+1.6	-1.0
	0.75	0	-0.35	1.9	0	-0.9	3.2	0	-1.6	3.6	0	-2.0
0.12 — 0.24	0.15	+0.5	-0.15	0.4	+1.2	-0.4	0.8	+1.8	-0.8	1.2	+1.8	-1.2
	0.95	0	-0.45	2.3	0	-1.1	3.8	0	-2.0	4.2	0	-2.4
0.24 — 0.40	0.2	+0.6	-0.2	0.5	+1.4	-0.5	1.0	+2.2	-1.0	1.6	+2.2	-1.6
	1.2	0	-0.6	2.8	0	-1.4	4.6	0	-2.4	5.2	0	-3.0
0.40 — 0.71	0.25	+0.7	-0.25	0.6	+1.6	-0.6	1.2	+2.8	-1.2	2.0	+2.8	-2.0
	1.35	0	-0.65	3.2	0	-1.6	5.6	0	-2.8	6.4	0	-3.6
0.71 — 1.19	0.3	+0.8	-0.3	0.8	+2.0	-0.8	1.6	+3.5	-1.6	2.5	+3.5	-2.5
	1.6	0	-0.8	4.0	0	-2.0	7.1	0	-3.6	8.0	0	-4.5
1.19 — 1.97	0.4	+1.0	-0.4	1.0	+2.5	-1.0	2.0	+4.0	-2.0	3.0	+4.0	-3.0
	2.0	0	-1.0	5.1	0	-2.6	8.5	0	-4.5	9.5	0	-5.5

Figure A-2B

American Standard Running and Sliding Fits
(Hole Basis)

Nominal Size Range Inches Over — To	Class RC1 Limits of Clearance	Standard Limits Hole H5	Standard Limits Shaft g4	Class RC2 Limits of Clearance	Standard Limits Hole H6	Standard Limits Shaft g5	Class RC3 Limits of Clearance	Standard Limits Hole H7	Standard Limits Shaft f6	Class RC4 Limits of Clearance	Standard Limits Hole H8	Standard Limits Shaft f7
0 — 0.12	0.1 / 0.45	+0.2 / 0	−0.1 / −0.25	0.1 / 0.55	+0.25 / 0	−0.1 / −0.3	0.3 / 0.95	+0.4 / 0	−0.3 / −0.55	0.3 / 1.3	+0.6 / 0	−0.3 / −0.7
0.12 — 0.24	0.15 / 0.5	+0.2 / 0	−0.15 / −0.3	0.15 / 0.65	+0.3 / 0	−0.15 / −0.35	0.4 / 1.12	+0.5 / 0	−0.4 / −0.7	0.4 / 1.5	+0.7 / 0	−0.4 / −0.0
0.24 — 0.40	0.2 / 0.6	+0.25 / 0	−0.2 / −0.35	0.2 / 0.85	+0.4 / 0	−0.2 / −0.45	0.5 / 1.5	+0.6 / 0	−0.5 / −0.9	0.5 / 2.0	+0.9 / 0	−0.5 / −1.1
0.40 — 0.71	0.25 / 0.75	+0.3 / 0	−0.25 / −0.45	0.25 / 0.95	+0.4 / 0	−0.25 / −0.55	0.6 / 1.7	+0.7 / 0	−0.6 / −1.0	0.6 / 2.3	+1.0 / 0	−0.6 / −1.3
0.71 — 1.19	0.3 / 0.95	+0.4 / 0	−0.3 / −0.55	0.3 / 1.2	+0.5 / 0	−0.3 / −0.7	0.8 / 2.1	+0.8 / 0	−0.8 / −1.3	0.8 / 2.8	+1.2 / 0	−0.8 / −1.6
1.19 — 1.97	0.4 / 1.1	+0.4 / 0	−0.4 / −0.7	0.4 / 1.4	+0.6 / 0	−0.4 / −0.8	1.0 / 2.6	+1.0 / 0	−1.0 / −1.6	1.0 / 3.6	+1.6 / 0	−1.0 / −2.0

Figure A-3A

Nominal Size Range Inches Over — To	Class RC5 Limits of Clearance	Standard Limits Hole H8	Standard Limits Shaft e7	Class RC6 Limits of Clearance	Standard Limits Hole H9	Standard Limits Shaft e8	Class RC7 Limits of Clearance	Standard Limits Hole H9	Standard Limits Shaft d8	Class RC8 Limits of Clearance	Standard Limits Hole H10	Standard Limits Shaft c9
0 — 0.12	0.6 / 1.6	+0.6 / 0	−0.6 / −1.0	0.6 / 2.2	+1.0 / 0	−0.6 / −1.2	1.0 / 2.6	+1.0 / 0	−1.0 / −1.6	2.5 / 5.1	+1.6 / 0	−2.5 / −3.5
0.12 — 0.24	0.8 / 2.0	+0.7 / 0	−0.8 / −1.3	0.8 / 2.7	+1.2 / 0	−0.8 / −1.5	1.2 / 3.1	+1.2 / 0	−1.2 / −1.9	2.8 / 5.8	+1.8 / 0	−2.8 / −4.0
0.24 — 0.40	1.0 / 2.5	+0.9 / 0	−1.0 / −1.6	1.0 / 3.3	+1.4 / 0	−1.0 / −1.9	1.6 / 3.9	+1.4 / 0	−1.6 / −2.5	3.0 / 6.6	+2.2 / 0	−3.0 / −4.4
0.40 — 0.71	1.2 / 2.9	+1.0 / 0	−1.2 / −1.9	1.2 / 3.8	+1.6 / 0	−1.2 / −2.2	2.0 / 4.6	+1.6 / 0	−2.0 / −3.0	3.5 / 7.9	+2.8 / 0	−3.5 / −5.1
0.71 — 1.19	1.6 / 3.6	+1.2 / 0	−1.6 / −2.4	1.6 / 4.8	+2.0 / 0	−1.6 / −2.8	2.5 / 5.7	+2.0 / 0	2.5 / −3.7	4.5 / 10.0	+3.5 / 0	−4.5 / −6.5
1.19 — 1.97	2.0 / 4.6	+1.6 / 0	−2.0 / −3.0	2.0 / 6.1	+2.5 / 0	−2.0 / −3.6	3.0 / 7.1	+2.5 / 0	−3.0 / −4.6	5.0 / 11.5	+4.0 / 0	−5.0 / −7.5

Figure A-3B

American Standard Transition Locational Fits

Nominal Size Range Inches Over — To	Class LT1 Fit	Standard Limits Hole H7	Shaft js6	Class LT2 Fit	Standard Limits Hole H8	Shaft js7	Class LT3 Fit	Standard Limits Hole H7	Shaft k6
0 — 0.12	−0.10 +0.50	+0.4 0	+0.10 −0.10	−0.2 +0.8	+0.6 0	+0.2 −0.2			
0.12 — 0.24	−0.15 −0.65	+0.5 0	+0.15 −0.15	−0.25 +0.95	+0.7 0	+0.25 −0.25			
0.24 — 0.40	−0.2 +0.5	+0.6 0	+0.2 −0.2	−0.3 +1.2	+0.9 0	+0.3 −0.3	−0.5 +0.5	+0.6 0	+0.5 +0.1
0.40 — 0.71	−0.2 +0.9	+0.7 0	+0.2 −0.2	−0.35 +1.35	+1.0 0	+0.35 −0.35	−0.5 +0.6	+0.7 0	+0.5 +0.1
0.71 — 1.19	−0.25 +1.05	+0.8 0	+0.25 −0.25	−0.4 +1.6	+1.2 0	+0.4 −0.4	−0.6 +0.7	+0.8 0	+0.6 +0.1
1.19 — 1.97	−0.3 +1.3	+1.0 0	+0.3 −0.3	−0.5 +2.1	+1.6 0	+0.5 −0.5	+0.7 +0.1	+1.0 0	+0.7 +0.1

Figure A-4A

Nominal Size Range Inches Over — To	Class LT4 Fit	Standard Limits Hole H8	Shaft k7	Class LT5 Fit	Standard Limits Hole H7	Shaft n6	Class LT6 Fit	Standard Limits Hole H7	Shaft n7
0 — 0.12				−0.5 +0.15	+0.4 0	+0.5 +0.25	−0.65 +0.15	+0.4 0	+0.65 +0.25
0.12 — 0.24				−0.6 +0.2	+0.5 0	+0.6 +0.3	−0.8 +0.2	+0.5 0	+0.8 +0.3
0.24 — 0.40	−0.7 +0.8	+0.9 0	+0.7 +0.1	−0.8 +0.2	+0.6 0	+0.8 +0.4	−1.0 +0.2	+0.6 0	+1.0 +0.4
0.40 — 0.71	−0.8 +0.9	+1.0 0	+0.8 +0.1	−0.9 +0.2	+0.7 0	+0.9 +0.5	−1.2 +0.2	+0.7 0	+1.2 +0.5
0.71 — 1.19	−0.9 +1.1	+1.2 0	+0.9 +0.1	−1.1 +0.2	+0.8 0	+1.1 +0.6	−1.4 +0.2	+0.8 0	+1.4 +0.6
1.19 — 1.97	−1.1 +1.5	+1.6 0	+1.1 +0.1	−1.3 +0.3	+1.0 0	+1.3 +0.7	−1.7 +0.3	+1.0 0	+1.7 +0.7

Figure A-4B

American Standard Interference Locational Fits

Nominal Size Range Inches		Limits of Interference	Class LN1 Standard Limits		Limits of Interference	Class LN2 Standard Limits		Limits of Interference	Class LN3 Standard Limits	
Over	To		Hole H6	Shaft n5		Hole H7	Shaft p6		Hole H7	Shaft r6
0	0.12	0 0.45	+0.25 0	+0.45 +0.25	0 0.65	+0.4 0	+0.63 +0.4	0.1 0.75	+0.4 0	+0.75 +0.5
0.12	0.24	0 0.5	+0.3 0	+0.5 +0.3	0 0.8	+0.5 0	+0.8 +0.5	0.1 0.9	+0.5 0	+0.9 +0.6
0.24	0.40	0 0.65	+0.4 0	+0.65 +0.4	0 1.0	+0.6 0	+1.0 +0.6	0.2 1.2	+0.6 0	+1.2 +0.8
0.40	0.71	0 0.8	+0.4 0	+0.8 +0.4	0 1.1	+0.7 0	+1.1 +0.7	0.3 1.4	+0.7 0	+1.4 +1.0
0.71	1.19	0 1.0	+0.5 0	+1.0 +0.5	0 1.3	+0.8 0	+1.3 +0.8	0.4 1.7	+0.8 0	+1.7 +1.2
1.19	1.97	0 1.1	+0.6 0	+1.1 +0.6	0 1.6	+1.0 0	+1.6 +1.0	0.4 2.0	+1.0 0	+2.0 +1.4

Figure A-5

American Standard Force and Shrink Fits

Nominal Size Range Inches Over – To	Class FN 1 Limits of Interference	Class FN 1 Standard Limits Hole	Class FN 1 Standard Limits Shaft	Class FN 2 Limits of Interference	Class FN 2 Standard Limits Hole	Class FN 2 Standard Limits Shaft	Class FN 3 Limits of Interference	Class FN 3 Standard Limits Hole	Class FN 3 Standard Limits Shaft	Class FN 4 Limits of Interference	Class FN 4 Standard Limits Hole	Class FN 4 Standard Limits Shaft
0 – 0.12	0.05 / 0.5	+0.25 / 0	+0.5 / +0.3	0.2 / 0.85	+0.4 / 0	+0.85 / +0.6				0.3 / 0.95	+0.4 / 0	+0.95 / +0.7
0.12 – 0.24	0.1 / 0.6	+0.3 / 0	+0.6 / +0.4	0.2 / 1.0	+0.5 / 0	+1.0 / +0.7				0.4 / 1.2	+0.5 / 0	+1.2 / +0.9
0.24 – 0.40	0.1 / 0.75	+0.4 / 0	+0.75 / +0.5	0.4 / 1.4	+0.6 / 0	+1.4 / +1.0				0.6 / 1.6	+0.6 / 0	+1.6 / +1.2
0.40 – 0.56	0.1 / 0.8	+0.4 / 0	+0.8 / +0.5	0.5 / 1.6	+0.7 / 0	+1.6 / +1.2				0.7 / 1.8	+0.7 / 0	+1.8 / +1.4
0.56 – 0.71	0.2 / 0.9	+0.4 / 0	+0.9 / +0.6	0.5 / 1.6	+0.7 / 0	+1.6 / +1.2				0.7 / 1.8	+0.7 / 0	+1.8 / +1.4
0.71 – 0.95	0.2 / 1.1	+0.5 / 0	+1.1 / +0.7	0.6 / 1.9	+0.8 / 0	+1.9 / +1.4	0.8 / 2.1	+0.8 / 0	+2.1 / +1.6	0.8 / 2.1	+0.8 / 0	+2.1 / +1.6
0.95 – 1.19	0.3 / 1.2	+0.5 / 0	+1.2 / +0.8	0.6 / 1.9	+0.8 / 0	+1.9 / +1.4	1.0 / 2.6	+1.0 / 0	+2.6 / +2.0	1.0 / 2.3	+0.8 / 0	+2.1 / +1.8
1.19 – 1.58	0.3 / 1.3	+0.6 / 0	+1.3 / +0.9	0.8 / 2.4	+1.0 / 0	+2.4 / +1.8	1.2 / 2.8	+1.0 / 0	+2.8 / +2.2	1.5 / 3.1	+1.0 / 0	+3.1 / +2.5
1.58 – 1.97	0.4 / 1.4	+0.6 / 0	+1.4 / +1.0	0.8 / 2.4	+1.0 / 0	+2.4 / +1.8				1.8 / 3.4	+1.0 / 0	+3.4 / +2.8

Figure A-6

Preferred Clearance Fits — Cylindrical Fits (Hole Basis; ANSI B4.2)

Basic Size		Loose Running			Free Running			Close Running			Sliding			Locational Clear.		
		Hole H11	Shaft c11	Fit	Hole H9	Shaft d9	Fit	Hole H8	Shaft f7	Fit	Hole H7	Shaft g6	Fit	Hole H7	Shaft h6	Fit
4	Max	4.075	3.930	0.220	4.030	3.970	0.090	4.018	3.990	0.040	4.012	3.996	0.024	4.012	4.000	0.020
	Min	4.000	3.855	0.070	4.000	3.940	0.030	4.000	3.978	0.010	4.000	3.988	0.004	4.000	3.992	0.000
5	Max	5.075	4.930	0.220	5.030	4.970	0.090	5.018	4.990	0.040	5.012	4.996	0.024	5.012	5.000	0.020
	Min	5.000	4.855	0.070	5.000	4.940	0.030	5.000	4.978	0.010	5.000	4.988	0.004	5.000	4.992	0.000
6	Max	6.075	5.930	0.220	6.030	5.970	0.090	6.018	5.990	0.040	6.012	5.996	0.024	6.012	6.000	0.020
	Min	6.000	5.885	0.070	6.000	5.940	0.030	6.000	5.978	0.010	6.000	5.988	0.004	6.000	5.992	0.000
8	Max	8.090	7.920	0.260	8.036	7.960	0.112	8.022	7.987	0.050	8.015	7.995	0.029	8.015	8.000	0.024
	Min	8.000	7.830	0.080	8.000	7.924	0.040	8.000	7.972	0.013	8.000	7.986	0.005	8.000	7.991	0.000
10	Max	10.090	9.920	0.260	10.036	9.960	0.112	10.022	9.987	0.050	10.015	9.995	0.029	10.015	10.000	0.024
	Min	10.000	9.830	0.080	10.000	9.924	0.040	10.000	9.972	0.013	10.000	9.986	0.005	10.000	9.991	0.000
12	Max	12.112	11.905	0.315	12.043	11.950	0.136	12.027	11.984	0.061	12.018	11.994	0.035	12.018	12.000	0.029
	Min	12.000	11.795	0.095	12.000	11.907	0.050	12.000	11.966	0.016	12.000	11.983	0.006	12.000	11.989	0.000
16	Max	16.110	15.905	0.315	16.043	15.950	0.136	16.027	15.984	0.061	16.018	15.994	0.035	16.018	16.000	0.029
	Min	16.000	15.795	0.095	16.000	15.907	0.050	16.000	15.966	0.016	16.000	15.983	0.006	16.000	15.989	0.000
20	Max	20.130	19.890	0.370	20.052	19.935	0.169	20.033	19.980	0.074	20.021	19.993	0.041	20.021	20.000	0.034
	Min	20.000	19.760	0.110	20.000	19.883	0.065	20.000	19.959	0.020	20.000	19.980	0.007	20.000	19.987	0.000
25	Max	25.130	24.890	0.370	25.052	24.935	0.169	25.033	24.980	0.074	25.021	24.993	0.041	25.021	25.000	0.034
	Min	25.000	24.760	0.110	25.000	24.883	0.065	25.000	24.959	0.020	25.000	24.980	0.007	25.000	24.987	0.000
30	Max	30.130	29.890	0.370	30.052	29.935	0.169	30.033	29.980	0.074	30.021	29.993	0.041	30.021	30.000	0.034
	Min	30.000	29.760	0.110	30.000	29.883	0.065	30.000	29.959	0.020	30.000	29.980	0.007	30.000	29.987	0.000

Figure A-7

Preferred Transition and Interference Fits — Cylindrical Fits (Hole Basis; ANSI B4.2)

Basic Size		Locational Trans. Hole H7	Shaft k6	Fit	Locational Trans. Hole H7	Shaft n6	Fit	Locational Inter. Hole H7	Shaft p6	Fit	Medium Drive Hole H7	Shaft s6	Fit	Force Hole H7	Shaft u6	Fit
4	Max	4.012	4.009	0.011	4.012	4.016	0.004	4.012	4.020	0.000	4.012	4.027	-0.007	4.012	4.031	-0.011
	Min	4.000	4.001	-0.009	4.000	4.008	-0.016	4.000	4.012	-0.020	4.000	4.019	-0.027	4.000	4.023	-0.031
5	Max	5.012	5.009	0.011	5.012	5.016	0.004	5.012	5.020	0.000	5.012	5.027	-0.007	5.012	5.031	-0.011
	Min	5.000	5.001	-0.009	5.000	5.008	-0.016	5.000	5.012	-0.020	5.000	5.019	-0.027	5.000	5.023	-0.031
6	Max	6.012	6.009	0.011	6.012	6.016	0.004	6.012	6.020	0.000	6.012	6.027	-0.007	6.012	6.031	-0.011
	Min	6.000	6.001	-0.009	6.000	6.008	-0.016	6.000	6.012	-0.020	6.000	6.019	-0.027	6.000	6.023	-0.031
8	Max	8.015	8.010	0.014	8.015	8.019	0.005	8.015	8.024	0.000	8.015	8.032	-0.008	8.015	8.037	-0.013
	Min	8.000	8.001	-0.010	8.000	8.010	-0.019	8.000	8.015	-0.024	8.000	8.023	-0.032	8.000	8.028	-0.037
10	Max	10.015	10.010	0.014	10.015	10.019	0.005	10.015	10.024	0.000	10.015	10.032	-0.008	10.015	10.037	-0.013
	Min	10.000	10.001	-0.010	10.000	10.010	-0.019	10.000	10.015	-0.024	10.000	10.023	-0.032	10.000	10.028	-0.037
12	Max	12.018	12.012	0.017	12.018	12.023	0.006	12.018	12.029	0.000	12.018	12.039	-0.010	12.018	12.044	-0.015
	Min	12.000	12.001	-0.012	12.000	12.012	-0.023	12.000	12.018	-0.029	12.000	12.028	-0.039	12.000	12.033	-0.044
16	Max	16.018	16.012	0.017	16.018	16.023	0.006	16.018	16.029	0.000	16.018	16.039	-0.010	16.018	16.044	-0.015
	Min	16.000	16.001	-0.012	16.000	16.012	-0.023	16.000	16.018	-0.029	16.000	16.028	-0.039	16.000	16.033	-0.044
20	Max	20.021	20.015	0.019	20.021	20.028	0.006	20.021	20.035	-0.001	20.021	20.048	-0.014	20.021	20.054	-0.020
	Min	20.000	20.002	-0.015	20.000	20.015	-0.028	20.000	20.022	-0.035	20.000	20.035	-0.048	20.000	20.041	-0.054
25	Max	25.021	25.015	0.019	25.021	25.028	0.006	25.021	25.035	-0.001	25.021	25.048	-0.014	25.021	25.061	-0.027
	Min	25.000	25.002	-0.015	25.000	25.015	-0.028	25.000	25.022	-0.035	25.000	25.035	-0.048	25.000	25.048	-0.061
30	Max	30.021	30.015	0.019	30.021	30.028	0.006	30.021	30.035	-0.001	30.021	30.048	-0.014	30.021	30.061	-0.027
	Min	30.000	30.002	-0.015	30.000	30.015	-0.028	30.000	30.022	-0.035	30.000	30.035	-0.048	30.000	30.048	-0.061

Figure A-8

Preferred Clearance Fits — Cylindrical Fits
(Shaft Basis; ANSI B4.2)

Basic Size		Loose Running			Free Running			Close Running			Sliding			Locational Clear.		
		Hole C11	Shaft h11	Fit	Hole D9	Shaft h9	Fit	Hole F8	Shaft h7	Fit	Hole G7	Shaft h6	Fit	Hole H7	Shaft h6	Fit
4	Max	4.145	4.000	0.220	4.060	4.000	0.090	4.028	4.000	0.040	4.016	4.000	0.024	4.012	4.000	0.020
	Min	4.070	3.925	0.070	4.030	3.970	0.030	4.010	3.988	0.010	4.004	3.992	0.004	4.000	3.992	0.000
5	Max	5.145	5.000	0.220	5.060	5.000	0.090	5.028	5.000	0.040	5.016	5.000	0.024	5.012	5.000	0.020
	Min	5.070	4.925	0.070	5.030	4.970	0.030	5.010	4.988	0.010	5.004	4.992	0.004	5.000	4.992	0.000
6	Max	6.145	6.000	0.220	6.060	6.000	0.090	6.028	6.000	0.040	6.016	6.000	0.024	6.012	6.000	0.020
	Min	6.070	5.925	0.070	6.030	5.970	0.030	6.010	5.988	0.010	6.004	5.992	0.004	6.000	5.992	0.000
8	Max	8.170	8.000	0.260	8.076	8.000	0.112	8.035	8.000	0.050	8.020	8.000	0.029	8.015	8.000	0.024
	Min	8.080	7.910	0.080	8.040	7.964	0.040	8.013	7.985	0.013	8.005	7.991	0.005	8.000	7.991	0.000
10	Max	10.170	10.000	0.260	10.076	10.000	0.112	10.035	10.000	0.050	10.020	10.000	0.029	10.015	10.000	0.024
	Min	10.080	9.910	0.080	10.040	9.964	0.040	10.013	9.985	0.013	10.005	9.991	0.005	10.000	9.991	0.000
12	Max	12.205	12.000	0.315	12.093	12.000	0.136	12.043	12.000	0.061	12.024	12.000	0.035	12.018	12.000	0.029
	Min	12.095	11.890	0.095	12.050	11.957	0.050	12.016	11.982	0.016	12.006	11.989	0.006	12.000	11.989	0.000
16	Max	16.205	16.000	0.315	16.093	16.000	0.136	16.043	16.000	0.061	16.024	16.000	0.035	16.018	16.000	0.029
	Min	16.095	15.890	0.095	16.050	15.957	0.050	16.016	15.982	0.016	06.006	15.989	0.006	16.000	15.989	0.000
20	Max	20.240	20.000	0.370	20.117	20.000	0.169	20.053	20.000	0.074	20.028	20.000	0.041	20.021	20.000	0.034
	Min	20.110	19.870	0.110	20.065	19.948	0.065	20.020	19.979	0.020	20.007	19.987	0.007	20.000	19.987	0.000
25	Max	25.240	25.000	0.370	25.117	25.000	0.169	25.053	25.000	0.074	25.028	25.000	0.041	25.021	25.000	0.034
	Min	25.110	24.870	0.110	25.065	24.948	0.065	25.020	24.979	0.020	25.007	24.987	0.007	25.000	24.987	0.000
30	Max	30.240	30.000	0.370	30.117	30.000	0.169	30.053	30.000	0.074	30.028	30.000	0.041	30.021	30.000	0.034
	Min	30.110	29.870	0.110	30.065	29.948	0.065	30.020	29.979	0.020	30.007	29.987	0.007	30.000	29.987	0.000

Figure A-9

Preferred Transition and Interference Fits — Cylindrical Fits
(Shaft Basis; ANSI B4.2)

Basic Size		Locational Trans			Locational Trans.			Locational Inter.			Medium Drive			Force		
		Hole K7	Shaft h6	Fit	Hole N7	Shaft h6	Fit	Hole P7	Shaft h6	Fit	Hole S7	Shaft h6	Fit	Hole U7	Shaft h6	Fit
4	Max	4.003	4.000	0.011	3.996	4.000	0.004	3.992	4.000	0.000	3.985	4.000	-0.007	3.981	4.000	-0.011
	Min	3.991	3.992	-0.009	3.984	3.992	-0.016	3.980	3.992	-0.020	3.973	3.992	-0.027	3.969	3.992	-0.031
5	Max	5.003	5.000	0.011	4.996	5.000	0.004	4.992	5.000	0.000	4.985	5.000	-0.007	4.981	5.000	-0.011
	Min	4.991	4.992	-0.009	4.984	4.992	-0.016	4.980	4.992	-0.020	4.973	4.992	-0.027	4.969	4.992	-0.031
6	Max	6.003	6.000	0.011	5.996	6.000	0.004	5.992	6.000	0.000	5.985	6.000	-0.007	5.981	6.000	-0.011
	Min	5.991	5.992	-0.009	5.984	5.992	-0.016	5.980	5.992	-0.020	5.973	5.992	-0.027	5.969	5.992	-0.031
8	Max	8.005	8.000	0.014	7.996	8.000	0.005	7.991	8.000	0.000	7.983	8.000	-0.008	7.978	8.000	-0.013
	Min	7.990	7.991	-0.010	7.981	7.991	-0.019	7.976	7.991	-0.024	7.968	7.991	-0.032	7.963	7.991	-0.037
10	Max	10.005	10.000	0.014	9.996	10.000	0.005	9.991	10.000	0.000	9.983	10.000	-0.008	9.978	10.000	-0.013
	Min	9.990	9.991	-0.010	9.981	9.991	-0.019	9.976	9.991	-0.024	9.968	9.991	-0.032	9.963	9.991	-0.037
12	Max	12.006	12.000	0.017	11.995	12.000	0.006	11.989	12.000	0.000	11.979	12.000	-0.010	11.974	12.000	-0.015
	Min	11.988	11.989	-0.012	11.977	11.989	-0.023	11.971	11.989	-0.029	11.961	11.989	-0.039	11.956	11.989	-0.044
16	Max	16.006	16.000	0.017	15.995	16.000	0.006	15.989	16.000	0.000	15.979	16.000	-0.010	15.974	16.000	-0.015
	Min	15.988	15.989	-0.012	15.977	15.989	-0.023	15.971	15.989	-0.029	15.961	15.989	-0.039	15.956	15.989	-0.044
20	Max	20.006	20.000	0.019	19.993	20.000	0.006	19.986	20.000	-0.001	19.973	20.000	-0.014	19.967	20.000	-0.020
	Min	19.985	19.987	-0.015	19.972	19.987	-0.028	19.965	19.987	-0.035	19.952	19.987	-0.048	19.946	19.987	-0.054
25	Max	25.006	25.000	0.019	24.993	25.000	0.006	24.986	25.000	-0.001	24.973	25.000	-0.014	24.960	25.000	-0.027
	Min	24.985	24.987	-0.015	24.972	24.987	-0.028	24.965	24.987	-0.035	24.952	24.987	-0.048	24.939	24.987	-0.061
30	Max	30.006	30.000	0.019	29.993	30.000	0.006	29.986	30.000	-0.001	29.973	30.000	-0.014	29.960	30.000	-0.027
	Min	29.985	29.987	-0.015	29.972	29.987	-0.028	29.965	29.987	-0.035	29.952	29.987	-0.048	29.939	29.987	-0.061

Figure A-10

American National Standard Type A Plain Washers
(ANSI B18.22.1-1965, R1975)

Nominal Washer Size		Series	Inside Diameter			Outside Diameter			Thickness		
			Basic	Tolerance		Basic	Tolerance		Basic	Max.	Min.
				Plus	Minus		Plus	Minus			
#6	.138		.156	.008	.005	.375	.015	.005	.049	.065	.036
#8	.164		.188	.008	.005	.438	.015	.005	.049	.065	.036
#10	.190		.219	.008	.005	.500	.015	.005	.049	.065	.036
1/4	.250	N	.281	.015	.005	.625	.015	.005	.065	.080	.051
1/4	.250	W	.312	.015	.005	.734	.015	.007	.065	.080	.051
5/16	.312	N	.344	.015	.005	.688	.015	.007	.065	.080	.051
5/16	.312	W	.375	.015	.005	.875	.030	.007	.083	.104	.064
3/8	.375	N	.406	.015	.005	.812	.015	.007	.065	.080	.051
3/8	.375	W	.438	.015	.005	1.000	.030	.007	.083	.104	.064
7/16	.438	N	.469	.015	.005	.922	.015	.007	.065	.080	.051
7/16	.438	W	.500	.015	.005	1.250	.030	.007	.083	.104	.064
1/2	.500	N	.531	.015	.005	1.062	.030	.007	.095	.121	.074
1/2	.500	W	.562	.015	.005	1.375	.030	.007	.109	.132	.086
9/16	.562	N	.594	.015	.005	1.156	.030	.007	.095	.121	.074
9/16	.562	W	.625	.015	.005	1.469	.030	.007	.109	.132	.086
5/8	.625	N	.656	.030	.007	1.312	.030	.007	.095	.121	.074
5/8	.625	W	.688	.030	.007	1.750	.030	.007	.134	.160	.108
3/4	.750	N	.812	.030	.007	1.469	.030	.007	.134	.160	.108
3/4	.750	W	.812	.030	.007	2.000	.030	.007	.148	.177	.122
7/8	.875	N	.938	.030	.007	1.750	.030	.007	.134	.160	.108
7/8	.875	W	.938	.030	.007	2.250	.030	.007	.165	.192	.136
1	1.000	N	1.062	.030	.007	2.000	.030	.007	.134	.160	.108
1	1.000	W	1.062	.030	.007	2.500	.030	.007	.165	.192	.136
1 1/8	1.125	N	1.250	.030	.007	2.250	.030	.007	.134	.160	.108
1 1/8	1.125	W	1.250	.030	.007	2.750	.030	.007	.165	.192	.136
1 1/4	1.250	N	1.375	.030	.007	2.500	.030	.007	.165	.192	.136
1 1/4	1.250	W	1.375	.030	.007	3.000	.030	.007	.165	.192	.136
1 3/8	1.375	N	1.500	.030	.007	2.750	.030	.007	.165	.192	.136
1 3/8	1.375	W	1.500	.045	.010	3.250	.045	.010	.180	.213	.153
1 1/2	1.500	N	1.625	.030	.007	3.000	.030	.007	.165	.192	.136
1 1/2	1.500	W	1.625	.045	.010	3.500	.045	.010	.180	.213	.153
1 5/8	1.625		1.750	.045	.010	3.750	.045	.010	.180	.213	.153
1 3/4	1.750		1.875	.045	.010	4.000	.045	.010	.180	.213	.153
1 7/8	1.875		2.000	.045	.010	4.250	.045	.010	.180	.213	.153
2	2.000		2.125	.045	.010	4.500	.045	.010	.180	.213	.153
2 1/4	2.250		2.375	.045	.010	4.750	.045	.010	.220	.248	.193
2 1/2	2.500		2.625	.045	.010	5.000	.045	.010	.238	.280	.210
2 3/4	2.750		2.875	.065	.010	5.250	.065	.010	.259	.310	.228
3	3.000		3.125	.065	.010	5.500	.065	.010	.284	.327	.249

Figure A-11

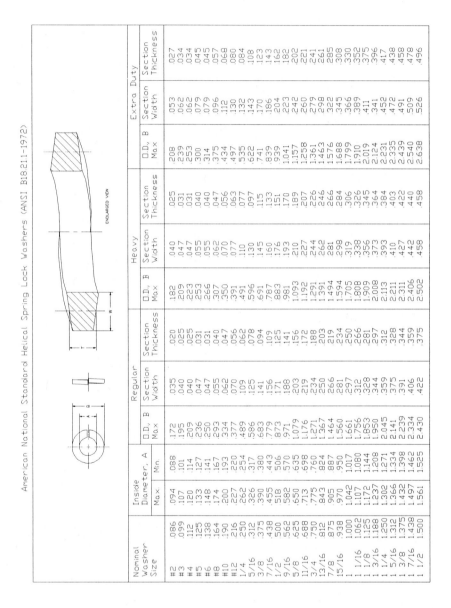

American National Standard Helical Spring Lock Washers (ANSI B18.21.1-1972)

Nominal Washer Size		Inside Diameter, A		Regular			Heavy			Extra Duty		
		Max	Min	O.D., B Max	Section Width	Section Thickness	O.D., B Max	Section Width	Section Thickness	O.D., B Max	Section Width	Section Thickness
#2	.086	.094	.088	.172	.035	.020	.182	.040	.025	.208	.053	.027
#3	.099	.107	.101	.195	.040	.025	.209	.047	.031	.239	.062	.034
#4	.112	.120	.114	.209	.040	.025	.223	.047	.031	.253	.062	.034
#5	.125	.133	.127	.236	.047	.031	.253	.055	.040	.300	.079	.045
#6	.138	.148	.141	.250	.047	.031	.266	.055	.040	.314	.079	.045
#8	.164	.174	.167	.293	.055	.040	.307	.062	.047	.375	.096	.057
#10	.190	.200	.193	.334	.062	.047	.350	.070	.056	.434	.112	.068
#12	.216	.227	.220	.377	.070	.056	.391	.077	.063	.497	.130	.080
1/4	.250	.262	.254	.489	.109	.062	.491	.110	.077	.535	.132	.084
5/16	.312	.326	.317	.586	.125	.078	.596	.130	.097	.622	.143	.108
3/8	.375	.390	.380	.683	.141	.094	.691	.145	.115	.741	.170	.123
7/16	.438	.455	.443	.779	.156	.109	.787	.160	.133	.839	.186	.143
1/2	.500	.518	.506	.873	.171	.125	.883	.176	.151	.939	.204	.162
9/16	.562	.582	.570	.971	.188	.141	.981	.193	.170	1.041	.223	.182
5/8	.625	.650	.635	1.079	.203	.156	1.093	.210	.189	1.157	.242	.202
11/16	.688	.713	.698	1.176	.219	.172	1.192	.227	.207	1.258	.260	.221
3/4	.750	.775	.760	1.271	.234	.188	1.291	.244	.226	1.361	.279	.241
13/16	.812	.843	.824	1.367	.250	.203	1.391	.262	.246	1.463	.298	.261
7/8	.875	.905	.887	1.464	.266	.219	1.494	.281	.266	1.576	.322	.285
15/16	.938	.970	.950	1.560	.281	.234	1.594	.298	.284	1.688	.345	.308
1	1.000	1.042	1.017	1.661	.297	.250	1.705	.306	.306	1.799	.366	.330
1 1/16	1.062	1.107	1.080	1.756	.312	.266	1.808	.319	.326	1.910	.389	.352
1 1/8	1.125	1.172	1.144	1.853	.328	.281	1.909	.338	.345	2.019	.411	.375
1 3/16	1.188	1.237	1.208	1.950	.344	.297	2.008	.356	.364	2.124	.341	.396
1 1/4	1.250	1.302	1.271	2.045	.359	.312	2.113	.373	.384	2.231	.452	.417
1 5/16	1.312	1.366	1.334	2.141	.375	.328	2.211	.393	.403	2.335	.472	.438
1 3/8	1.375	1.432	1.398	2.239	.391	.344	2.311	.410	.422	2.439	.491	.458
1 7/16	1.438	1.497	1.462	2.334	.406	.359	2.406	.427	.440	2.540	.509	.478
1 1/2	1.500	1.561	1.525	2.430	.422	.375	2.502	.458	.458	2.638	.526	.496

Figure A-12

American National Standard Internal–External Tooth Lock Washers
(ANSI B18.21.1-1972)

Size	A Inside Diameter Max.	A Inside Diameter Min.	B Outside Diameter Max.	B Outside Diameter Min.	C Thickness Max.	C Thickness Min.
#4	.123	.115	.475	.460	.021	.021
	.123	.115	.510	.495	.021	.017
			.610	.580		
#6	.150	.141	.510	.495	.028	.023
			.610	.580		
			.690	.670		
#8	.176	.168	.610	.580	.034	.028
			.690	.670		
			.760	.740		
#10	.204	.195	.610	.580	.034	.028
	.204	.195	.690	.670	.040	.032
			.760	.740		
			.900	.880		
#12	.231	.221	.690	.670	.040	.032
	.231	.221	.760	.725		
			.900	.880	.045	.037
			.985	.965		
1/4	.267	.256	.760	.725	.040	.032
	.267	.256	.900	.880		
			.985	.965	.045	.037
			1.070	1.045		

Size	A Inside Diameter Max.	A Inside Diameter Min.	B Outside Diameter Max.	B Outside Diameter Min.	C Thickness Max.	C Thickness Min.
5/16	.332	.320	.900	.865	.040	.032
	.332	.320	.985	.965	.045	.037
	.332	.320	1.070	1.045	.050	.042
			1.155	1.130		
3/8	.398	.384	.985	.965	.045	.037
	.398	.384	1.070	1.045	.050	.042
			1.155	1.130		
			1.260	1.220		
7/16	.464	.448	1.070	1.045	.050	.042
			1.155	1.130		
	.464	.448	1.260	1.220	.055	.047
			1.315	1.290		
1/2	.530	.512	1.260	1.220	.055	.047
	.530	.512	1.315	1.290		
	.530	.512	1.410	1.380	.060	.052
			1.620	1.590	.067	.059
9/16	.596	.576	1.315	1.290	.055	.047
	.596	.576	1.430	1.380	.060	.052
	.596	.576	1.620	1.590	.067	.059
			1.830	1.797		
5/8	.663	.640	1.410	1.380	.060	.052
	.663	.640	1.620	1.590	.067	.059
			1.830	1.797		
			1.975	1.935		

Figure A-13

British Standard Bright Metal Washers – Metric Series (BS 4320:1968)

Nominal Size of Bolt or Screw	Inside Diameter			Outside Diameter			Thickness					
							Form A (Normal Range)			Form B (Light Range)		
	Nom.	Max.	Min.	Nom.	Max.	Min.	Nom.	Max.	Min.	Nom.	Max.	Min.
M 1.0	1.1	1.25	1.1	2.5	2.5	2.3	.3	.4	.2			
M 1.2	1.3	1.45	1.3	3.0	3.0	2.8	.3	.4	.2			
M 1.4	1.5	1.65	1.5	3.0	3.0	2.8	.3	.4	.2			
M 1.6	1.7	1.85	1.7	4.0	4.0	3.7	.3	.4	.2			
M 2.0	2.2	2.35	2.2	5.0	5.0	4.7	.3	.4	.2			
M 2.2	2.4	2.55	2.4	5.0	5.0	4.7	.5	.6	.4			
M 2.5	2.7	2.85	2.7	6.5	6.5	6.2	.5	.6	.4			
M 3	3.2	3.4	3.2	7	7	6.7	.5	.6	.4			
M 3.5	3.7	3.9	3.7	7	7	6.7	.5	.6	.4			
M 4	4.3	4.5	4.3	9	9	8.7	.8	.9	.7			
M 4.5	4.8	5.0	4.8	9	9	8.7	.8	.9	.7			
M 5	5.3	5.5	5.3	10	10	9.7	1.0	1.1	.9			
M 6	6.4	6.7	6.4	12.5	12.5	12.1	1.6	1.8	1.4	.8	.9	.7
M 7	7.4	7.7	7.4	14	14	13.6	1.6	1.8	1.4	.8	.9	.7
M 8	8.4	8.7	8.4	17	17	16.6	1.6	1.8	1.4	1.0	1.1	.9
M 10	10.5	10.9	10.5	21	21	20.5	2.0	2.2	1.8	1.25	1.45	1.05
M 12	13.0	13.4	13.0	24	24	23.5	2.5	2.7	2.3	1.6	1.80	1.40
M 14	15.0	15.4	15.0	28	28	27.5	2.5	2.7	2.3	1.6	1.8	1.4
M 16	17.0	17.4	17.0	30	30	29.5	3.0	3.3	2.7	2.0	2.2	1.8
M 18	19.0	19.5	19.0	34	34	33.2	3.0	3.3	2.7	2.0	2.2	1.8
M 20	21	21.5	21	37	37	36.2	3.0	3.3	2.7	2.0	2.2	1.8
M 22	23	23.5	23	39	39	38.2	3.0	3.3	2.7	2.0	2.2	1.8
M 24	25	25.5	25	44	44	43.2	4.0	4.3	3.7	2.5	2.7	2.3
M 27	28	28.5	28	50	50	49.2	4.0	4.3	3.7	2.5	2.7	2.3
M 30	31	31.6	31	56	56	55.0	4.0	4.3	3.7	2.5	2.7	2.3
M 33	34	34.6	34	60	60	59.0	5.0	5.6	4.4	3.0	3.3	2.7
M 36	37	37..6	37	66	66	65.0	5.0	5.6	4.4	3.0	3.3	2.7
M 39	40	40.6	40	72	72	71.0	6.0	6.6	5.4	3.0	3.3	2.7

Figure A-14

American National Standard and Unified Square Bolts (ANSI B18.2.1-1972)

SQUARE BOLTS

Nominal Size or Basic Product Diameter		Body Diam., E	Width Across Flats, F			Width Across Corners, G		Height, H			Radius of Fillet, R
		Max.	Basic	Max.	Min.	Max.	Min.	Basic	Max.	Min.	Max.
1/4	.2500	.260	3/8	.375	.362	.530	.498	11/64	.188	.156	.03
5/16	.3125	.324	1/2	.500	.484	.707	.665	13/64	.220	.186	.03
3/8	.3750	.388	9/16	.562	.544	.795	.747	1/4	.268	.232	.03
7/16	.4375	.452	5/8	.625	.603	.884	.828	19/64	.316	.278	.03
1/2	.5000	.515	3/4	.750	.725	1.061	.995	21/64	.348	.308	.03
5/8	.6250	.642	15/16	.938	.906	1.326	1.244	37/64	.444	.400	.06
3/4	.7500	.768	1 1/8	1.125	1.088	1.591	1.494	1/2	.524	.476	.06
7/8	.8750	.895	1 5/16	1.312	1.269	1.856	1.742	19/32	.620	.568	.06
1	1.0000	1.022	1 1/2	1.500	1.450	2.121	1.991	21/32	.684	.628	.09
1 1/8	1.1250	1.149	1 11/16	1.688	1.631	2.386	2.239	3/4	.780	.720	.09
1 1/4	1.2500	1.277	1 7/8	1.875	1.812	2.652	2.489	27/32	.876	.812	.09
1 3/8	1.3750	1.404	2 1/16	2.062	1.994	2.917	2.738	29/32	.940	.872	.09
1 1/2	1.5000	1.531	2 1/4	2.250	2.175	3.182	2.986	1	1.036	.964	.09

Figure A-15

American National Standard and Unified Standard Hex Head Screws
(ANSI B18.2.1-1972)

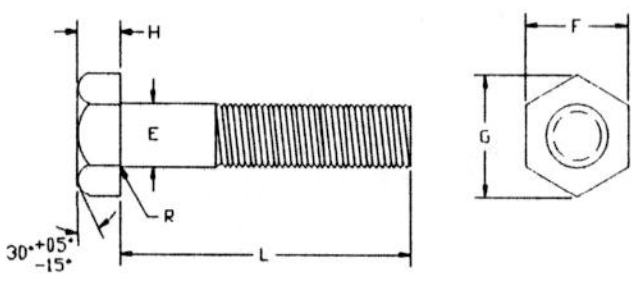

Nominal Size or Basic Diam.		Body Diam., E	Width Across Flats, F			Width Across Corners, G		Height, H			Radius of Fillet, R	
		Max.	Basic	Max.	Min.	Max.	Min.	Basic	Max.	Min.	Max.	Min.
HEX BOLTS												
1/4	.2500	.260	7/16	.438	.425	.505	.484	11/64	.188	.150	.03	.01
5/16	.3125	.324	1/2	.500	.484	.577	.552	7/32	.235	.195	.03	.01
3/8	.3750	.388	9/16	.562	.544	.650	.620	1/4	.268	.226	.03	.01
7/16	.4375	.452	5/8	.625	.603	.722	.687	19/64	.316	.272	.03	.01
1/2	.5000	.515	3/4	.750	.725	.866	.826	11/32	.364	.302	.03	.01
5/8	.6250	.642	15/16	.938	.906	1.083	1.033	27/64	.444	.378	.06	.02
3/4	.7500	.768	1 1/8	1.125	1.088	1.299	1.240	1/2	.524	.455	.06	.02
7/8	.8750	.895	1 5/16	1.312	1.269	1.516	1.447	37/64	.604	.531	.06	.02
1	1.0000	1.022	1 1/2	1.500	1.450	1.732	1.653	43/64	.700	.591	.09	.03
1 1/8	1.1250	1.149	1 11/16	1.688	1.631	1.949	1.859	3/4	.780	.658	.09	.03
1 1/4	1.2500	1.277	1 7/8	1.875	1.812	2.165	2.066	27/32	.876	.749	.09	.03
1 3/8	1.3750	1.404	2 1/16	2.062	1.994	2.382	2.273	29/32	.940	.810	.09	.03
1 1/2	1.5000	1.531	2 1/4	2.250	2.175	2.598	2.480	1	1.036	.902	.09	.03
1 3/4	1.7500	1.785	2 5/8	2.625	2.538	3.031	2.893	1 5/32	1.196	1.054	.12	.04
2	2.0000	2.039	3	3.000	2.900	3.464	3.306	1 11/32	1.388	1.175	.12	.04
2 1/4	2.2500	2.305	3 3/8	3.375	3.262	3.897	3.719	1 1/2	1.548	1.327	.19	.06
2 1/2	2.5000	2.559	3 3/4	3.750	3.625	4.330	4.133	1 21/32	1.708	1.479	.19	.06
2 3/4	2.7500	2.827	4 1/8	4.125	3.988	4.763	4.546	1 13/16	1.869	.1632	.19	.06
3	3.0000	3.081	4 1/2	4.500	4.350	5.196	4.959	2	2.060	1.815	.19	.06
3 1/4	3.2500	3.335	4 7/8	4.875	4.712	5.629	5.372	2 3/16	2.251	1.936	.19	.06
3 1/2	3.5000	3.589	5 1/4	5.250	5.075	6.062	5.786	2 5/16	2.380	2.057	.19	.06
3 3/4	3.7500	3.858	5 5/8	5.625	5.437	6.495	6.198	2 1/2	2.572	2.241	.19	.06
4	4.0000	4.111	6	6.000	5.800	6.982	6.612	2 11/16	2.764	2.424	.19	.06

Figure A-16

Coarse-Thread Series, UNC, UNRC, and NC — Basic Dimensions

Sizes	Basic Major Diam., D	Thds. per Inch, n	Basic Pitch Diam., E	Minor Diameter		Lead Angle at Basic P.D.		Area of Minor Diam. at D-2h	Tensile Stress Area
				Ext. Thds., Ks	Int. Thds., Kn	Deg.	Min.		
	Inches		Inches	Inches	Inches	Deg.	Min.	Sq. In.	Sq. In.
1 (.073)	.0730	64	.0629	.0538	.0561	4	31	.00218	.00263
2 (.086)	.0860	56	.0744	.0641	.0667	4	22	.00310	.00370
3 (.099)	.0990	48	.0855	.0734	.0764	4	26	.00406	.00487
4 (.112)	.1120	40	.0958	.0813	.0849	4	45	.00496	.00604
5 (.125)	.1250	40	.1088	.0943	.0979	4	11	.00672	.00796
6 (.138)	.1380	32	.1177	.0997	.1042	4	50	.00745	.00909
8 (.164)	1.640	32	.1437	.1257	.1302	3	58	.01196	.0140
10 (.190)	.1900	24	.1629	.1389	.1449	4	39	.01450	.0175
12 (.216)	.2160	24	.1889	.1649	.1709	4	1	.0206	.0242
1/4	.2500	20	.2175	.1887	.1959	4	11	.0269	.0318
5/16	.3125	18	.2764	.2443	.2524	3	40	.0454	.0524
3/8	.3750	16	.3344	.2983	.3073	3	24	.0678	.0775
7/16	.4375	14	.3911	.3499	.3602	3	20	.0933	.1063
1/2	.5000	13	.4500	.4056	.4167	3	7	.1257	.1419
9/16	.5625	12	.5084	.4603	.4723	2	59	.162	.182
5/8	.6250	11	.5660	.5135	.5266	2	56	.202	.226
3/4	.7500	10	.6850	.6273	.6417	2	40	.302	.334
7/8	.8750	9	.8028	.7387	.7547	2	31	.419	.462
1	1.0000	8	.9188	.8466	.8647	2	29	.551	.606
1 1/8	1.1250	7	1.032	.9497	.9704	2	31	.693	.763
1 1/4	1.2500	7	1.572	1.0747	1.0954	2	15	.890	.969
1 3/8	1.3750	6	1.2667	1.1705	1.1946	2	24	1.054	1.155
1 1/2	1.5000	6	1.3917	1.2955	1.3196	2	11	1.294	1.405

Figure A-17

Fine-Thread Series, UNC, UNRC, and NC — Basic Dimensions

Sizes	Basic Major Diam., D	Thds. per Inch, n	Basic Pitch Diam., E	Minor Diameter		Lead Angle at Basic P.D.		Area of Minor Diam. at D-2h	Tensile Stress Area
				Ext. Thds., Ks	Int. Thds., Kn	Deg.	Min.		
	Inches		Inches	Inches	Inches	Deg.	Min.	Sq. In.	Sq. In.
1 (.073)	.0730	72	.0640	.0560	.0580	3	57	.00237	.00278
2 (.086)	.860	64	.0759	.0668	.0691	3	45	.00339	.00394
3 (.099)	.990	56	.0874	.0771	.0797	3	43	.00451	.00523
4 (.112)	.1120	48	.0985	.0864	.0894	3	51	.00566	.00661
5 (.125)	.1250	44	.1102	.0971	.1004	3	45	.00716	.00830
6 (.138)	.1380	40	.1218	.1073	.1109	3	44	.00874	.01015
8 (.164)	.1640	36	.1460	.1299	.1339	3	28	.01285	.01474
10 (.190)	.1900	32	.1697	.1517	.1562	3	21	.0175	.0200
12 (.216)	.2160	28	.1928	.1722	.1773	3	22	.0226	.0258
1/4	.2500	28	.2268	.2062	.2113	2	52	.0326	.0364
5/16	.3125	24	.2854	.2614	.2674	2	40	.0524	.0580
3/8	.3750	24	.3479	.3239	.3299	2	11	.0809	.0878
7/16	.4375	20	.4050	.3762	.3834	2	15	.1090	.1187
1/2	.5000	20	.4675	.4387	.4459	1	57	.1486	.1599
9/16	.5625	18	.5264	.4943	.5024	1	55	.189	.203
5/8	.6250	18	.5889	.5568	.5649	1	43	.240	.256
3/4	.7500	16	.7094	.6733	.6823	1	36	.351	.373
7/8	.8750	14	.8286	.7874	.7977	1	34	.480	.509
1	1.0000	12	.9459	.8978	.9098	1	36	.625	.663
1 1/8	1.1250	12	1.0709	1.0228	1.0348	1	25	.812	.856
1 1/4	1.2500	12	1.1959	1.1478	1.1598	1	16	1.024	1.073
1 3/8	1.3750	12	1.3209	1.2728	1.2848	1	9	1.260	1.315
1 1/2	1.5000	12	1.4459	1.3978	1.4098	1	3	1.521	1.581

Figure A-18

American National Standard General-Purpose Acme Screw Thread Form—
Basic Dimensions (ANSI B1.5-1977)

Thds. per Inch	Pitch	Height of Thread (Basic)	Total Height of Thread	Thread Thickness (Basic)	Width of Flat	
					Crest of Internal Thread (Basic)	Root of Internal Thread
16	.06250	.03125	.0362	.03125	.0232	.0206
14	.07143	.03571	.0407	.03571	.0265	.0239
12	.08333	.04167	.0467	.04167	.0309	.0283
10	.10000	.05000	.0600	.05000	.0371	.0319
8	.12500	.06250	.0725	.06250	.0463	.0411
6	.16667	.08333	.0933	.08333	.0618	.0566
5	.20000	.10000	.1100	.10000	.0741	.0689
4	.25000	.12500	.1350	.12500	.0927	.0875
3	.33333	.16667	.1767	.16667	.1236	.1184
2 1/2	.40000	.20000	.2100	.20000	.1483	.1431
2	.50000	.25000	.2600	.25000	.1853	.1802
1 1/2	.66667	.33333	.3433	.33333	.2471	.2419
1 1/3	.75000	.37500	.3850	.37500	.2780	.2728
1	1.0000	.50000	.5100	.50000	.3707	.3655

Figure A-19

60-Degree Stub Threads

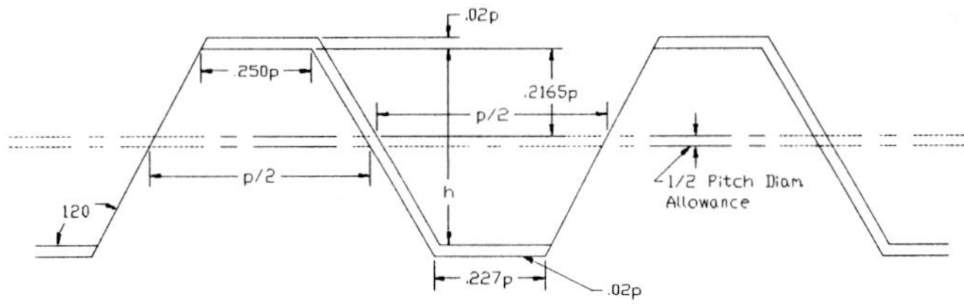

Threads per Inch	Pitch, Inch	Depth of Thread (Basic)	Total Depth of Thread	Thickness (Basic)	Width of Flat at Crest of Screw (Basic)	Width of Flat at Root of Screw
16	.06250	.0271	.0283	.0313	.0156	.0142
14	.07143	.0309	.0324	.0357	.0179	.0162
12	.08333	.0361	.0378	.0417	.0208	.0189
10	.10000	.0433	.0453	.0500	.0250	.0227
9	.11111	.0481	.0503	.0556	.0278	.0252
8	.12500	.0541	.0566	.0625	.0313	.0284
7	.14286	.0619	.0648	.0714	.0357	.0324
6	.16667	.0722	.0755	.0833	.0417	.0378
5	.20000	.0866	.0906	.1000	.0500	.0454
4	.25000	.1083	.1133	.1250	.0625	.0567

Figure A-20

American National Standard Slotted 100° Flat Countersunk
Head Machine Screws (ANSI B18.6.3-1972, R1977)

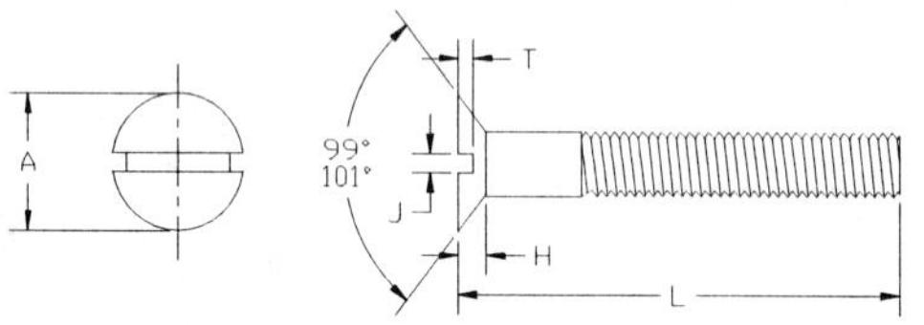

Nominal Size or Basic Screw Diam.		Head Diam., A		Head Height, H	Slot Width, J		Slot Depth, T	
		Max., Edge Sharp	Min., Edge Rounded or Flat	Ref.	Max.	Min.	Max.	Min.
0000	.0210	.043	.037	.009	.008	.005	.008	.004
000	.0340	.064	.058	.014	.012	.008	.011	.007
00	.0470	.093	.085	.020	.017	.010	.013	.008
0	.0600	.119	.096	.026	.023	.016	.013	.008
1	.0730	.146	.120	.031	.026	.019	.016	.010
2	.0860	.172	.143	.037	.031	.023	.019	.012
3	.0990	.199	.167	.043	.035	.027	.022	.014
4	.1120	.225	.191	.049	.039	.031	.024	.017
6	.1380	.279	.238	.060	.048	.039	.030	.022
8	.1640	.332	.285	.072	.054	.045	.036	.027
10	.1900	.385	.333	.083	.060	.050	.042	.031
1/4	.2500	.507	.442	.110	.075	.064	.055	.042
5/16	.3125	.635	.556	.138	.084	.072	.069	.053
3/8	.3750	.762	.670	.165	.094	.081	.083	.065

Figure A-21

American National Standard Slotted Truss Head Machine Screws
(ANSI B18.6.3-1972, R1977)

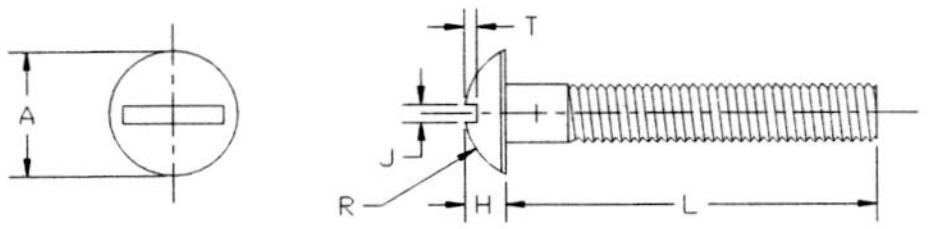

Nominal Size or Basic Screw Diam.		Head Diam, A		Head Height, H		Head Radius, R	Slot Width, J		Slot Depth, T	
		Max.	Min.	Max.	Min.	Max.	Max.	Min.	Max.	Min.
0000	.0210	.049	.043	.014	.010	.032	.009	.005	.009	.005
000	.0340	.077	.071	.022	.018	.051	.013	.009	.013	.009
00	.0470	.106	.098	.030	.024	.070	.017	.010	.018	.012
0	.0600	.131	.119	.037	.029	.087	.023	.016	.022	.014
1	.0730	.164	.149	.045	.037	.107	.026	.019	.027	.018
2	.0860	.194	.180	.053	.044	.129	.031	.023	.031	.022
3	.0990	.226	.211	.061	.051	.151	.035	.027	.036	.026
4	.1120	.257	.241	.069	.059	.169	.039	.031	.040	.030
5	.1250	.289	.272	.078	.066	.191	.043	.035	.045	.034
6	.1380	.321	.303	.086	.074	.211	.048	.039	.050	.037
8	.1640	.384	.364	.102	.088	.254	.054	.045	.058	.045
10	.1900	.448	.425	.118	.103	.283	.060	.050	.068	.053
12	.2160	.511	.487	.134	.118	.336	.067	.056	.077	.061
1/4	.2500	.573	.546	.150	.133	.375	.075	.064	.087	.070
5/16	.3125	.698	.666	.183	.162	.457	.084	.072	.106	.085
3/8	.3750	.823	.787	.215	.191	.538	.094	.081	.124	.100
7/16	.4375	.948	.907	.248	.221	.619	.094	.081	.142	.116
1/2	.5000	1.073	1.028	.280	.250	.701	.106	.091	.161	.131
9/16	.5625	1.198	1.149	.312	.279	.783	.118	.102	.179	.146
5/8	.6250	1.323	1.269	.345	.309	.863	.133	.116	.196	.162
3/4	.7500	1.573	1.511	.410	.368	1.024	.149	.131	.234	.182

Figure A-22

American National Standard Plain and Slotted Hexagon Head
Machine Screws (ANSI B18.6.3–1972, R1977)

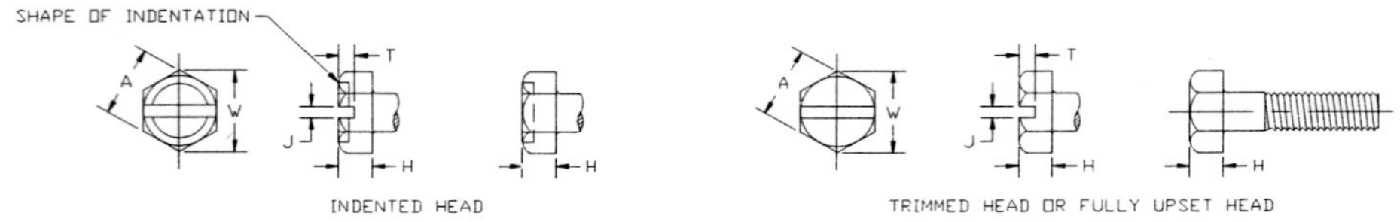

Nominal Size or Basic Screw Diam.	Regular Head				Large Head						Head Height H		Slot Width J		Slot Depth T	
	Width Across Flats A		Across Corn. W		Width Across Flats A		Across Corn. W									
	Max.	Min.	Min.		Max.	Min.	Max.	Min.			Max.	Min.	Max.	Min.	Max.	Min.
1	.0730	.125	.120	.134							.044	.036				
2	.0860	.125	.120	.134							.050	.040				
3	.0990	.188	.181	.202							.055	.044				
4	.1120	.188	.181	.202	.219	.213	.238				.060	.049	.039	.031	.036	.025
5	.1250	.188	.181	.202	.250	.244	.272				.070	.058	.043	.035	.042	.030
6	.1380	.250	.244	.272							.080		.048	.029	.046	.033
8	.1640	.250	.244	.272	.312	.305	.340				.093	.080	.054	.045	.066	.052
10	.1900	.312	.305	.340							.110	.096	.060	.050	.072	.057
12	.2160	.312	.305	.340	.375	.367	.409				.120	.105	.067	.056	.093	.077
1/4	.2500	.375	.367	.409	.438	.428	.477				.155	.139	.075	.064	.101	.083
5/16	.3125	.500	.489	.545							.190	.172	.084	.072	.122	.100
3/8	.3750	.562	.551	.614							.230	.208	.094	.081	.156	.131
											.295	.270				

Figure A-23

Slotted Round Head Machine Screws
(ANSI B18.6.3-1972, R1977 Appendix)

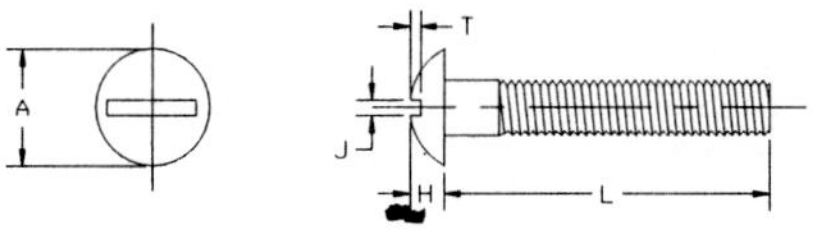

Nominal Size or Basic Screw Diam.		Head Diameter, A		Head Height, H		Slot Width, J		Slot Depth, T	
		Max.	Min.	Max.	Min.	Max.	Min.	Max.	Min.
0000	.0210	.041	.035	.022	.016	.008	.004	.017	.013
000	.0340	.062	.056	.031	.025	.012	.008	.018	.012
00	.0470	.089	.080	.045	.036	.017	.010	.026	.018
0	.0600	.113	.099	.053	.043	.023	.016	.039	.029
1	.0730	.138	.122	.061	.051	.026	.019	.044	.033
2	.0860	.162	.146	.069	.059	.031	.023	.048	.037
3	.0990	.187	.169	.078	.067	.035	.027	.053	.040
4	.1120	.211	.193	.086	.075	.039	.031	.058	.044
5	.1250	.236	.217	.095	.083	.043	.035	.063	.047
6	.1380	.260	.240	.103	.091	.048	.039	.068	.051
8	.1640	.309	.287	.120	.107	.054	.045	.077	.058
10	.1900	.359	.334	.137	.123	.060	.050	.087	.065
12	.2160	.408	.382	.153	.139	.067	.056	.096	.073
1/4	.2500	.472	.443	.175	.160	.075	.064	.109	.082
5/16	.3125	.590	.557	.216	.198	.084	.072	.132	.099
3/8	.3750	.708	.670	.256	.237	.094	.081	.155	.117
7/16	.4375	.750	.707	.328	.307	.094	.081	.196	.148
1/2	.5000	.813	.766	.355	.332	.106	.091	.211	.159
9/16	.5625	.938	.887	.410	.385	.118	.102	.242	.183
5/8	.6250	1.000	.944	.438	.411	.133	.116	.258	.195
3/4	.7500	1.250	1.185	.547	.516	.149	.131	.320	.242

Figure A-24

AMERICAN NATIONAL STANDARD SQUARE HEAD SET
SCREWS (ANSI B18.6.2)

Nominal Size of Basic Screw Diameter	Width Across Flats		Width Across Corners		Head Height		Neck Relief Diameter		Max Neck Relief Fillet Radius	Min Neck Relief Width	Min Head Radius
	Max.	Min.	Max.	Min.	Max.	Min.	Max.	Min.			
10	0.1900	0.188	0.180	0.265	0.247	0.148	0.134	0.145	0.140	0.027	0.083	0.48
1/4	0.2500	0.250	0.241	0.354	0.331	0.196	0.178	0.185	0.170	0.032	0.100	0.62
5/16	0.3125	0.312	0.302	0.442	0.415	0.245	0.224	0.240	0.225	0.036	0.111	0.78
3/8	0.3750	0.375	0.362	0.530	0.497	0.293	0.270	0.294	0.279	0.041	0.125	0.94
7/16	0.4375	0.438	0.423	0.619	0.581	0.341	0.315	0.345	0.330	0.046	0.143	1.09
1/2	0.5000	0.500	0.484	0.707	0.665	0.389	0.361	0.400	0.385	0.050	0.154	1.25
9/16	0.5625	0.562	0.545	0.795	0.748	0.437	0.407	0.454	0.439	0.054	0.167	1.41
5/8	0.6250	0.625	0.606	0.884	0.833	0.485	0.452	0.507	0.492	0.059	0.182	1.56
3/4	0.7500	0.750	0.729	1.060	1.001	0.582	0.544	0.620	0.605	0.065	0.200	1.88
7/8	0.8750	0.875	0.852	1.237	1.170	0.678	0.635	0.731	0.716	0.072	0.222	2.19
1	1.0000	1.000	0.974	1.414	1.337	0.774	0.726	0.838	0.823	0.081	0.250	2.50
1 1/8	1.1250	1.125	1.096	1.591	1.505	0.870	0.817	0.939	0.914	0.092	0.283	2.81
1 1/4	1.2500	1.250	1.219	1.768	1.674	0.966	0.908	1.064	1.039	0.092	0.283	3.12
1 3/8	1.3750	1.375	1.342	1.945	1.843	1.063	1.000	1.159	1.134	0.109	0.333	3.44
1 1/2	1.5000	1.500	1.464	2.121	2.010	1.159	1.091	1.284	1.259	0.109	0.333	3.75

Figure A-25

AMERICAN NATIONAL STANDARD SQUARE HEAD SET SCREWS (ANSI B18.6.2)

Nominal Size or Basic Screw Diameter		Cup and Flat Point Diameters		Dog and Half-Dog Point Diameters		Point Length				Oval Point Radius +0.031 −0.000	Cone Point Angle 90° ± 2° for these Nominal Lengths or Longer, 118° ± 2° for Shorter Screws
						Dog		Half-Dog			
		Max.	Min.	Max.	Min.	Max.	Min.	Max.	Min.		
10	0.1900	0.102	0.088	0.127	0.120	0.095	0.085	0.050	0.040	0.142	1/4
1/4	0.2500	0.132	0.118	0.156	0.149	0.130	0.120	0.068	0.058	0.188	5/16
5/16	0.3125	0.172	0.156	0.203	0.195	0.161	0.151	0.083	0.073	0.234	3/8
3/8	0.3750	0.212	0.194	0.250	0.241	0.193	0.183	0.099	0.089	0.281	7/16
7/16	0.4375	0.252	0.232	0.297	0.287	0.224	0.214	0.114	0.104	0.328	1/2
1/2	0.5000	0.291	0.270	0.344	0.334	0.255	0.245	0.130	0.120	0.375	9/16
9/16	0.5625	0.332	0.309	0.391	0.379	0.287	0.275	0.146	0.134	0.422	5/8
5/8	0.6250	0.371	0.347	0.469	0.456	0.321	0.305	0.164	0.148	0.469	3/4
3/4	0.7500	0.450	0.425	0.562	0.549	0.383	0.367	0.196	0.180	0.562	7/8
7/8	0.8750	0.530	0.502	0.656	0.642	0.446	0.430	0.227	0.221	0.656	1
1	1.0000	0.609	0.579	0.750	0.734	0.510	0.490	0.260	0.240	0.750	1 1/8
1 1/8	1.1250	0.689	0.655	0.844	0.826	0.572	0.552	0.291	0.271	0.844	1 1/4
1 1/4	1.2500	0.767	0.733	0.938	0.920	0.635	0.615	0.323	0.303	0.938	1 1/2
1 3/8	1.3750	0.848	0.808	1.031	1.011	0.698	0.678	0354	0.334	1.031	1 5/8
1 1/2	1.5000	0.926	0.886	1.125	1.105	0.760	0.740	0.385	0.365	1.125	1 3/4

Figure A-26

American National Standard Slotted Headless Set Screws
(ANSI B18.6.2)

Nominal Size or Basic Screw Diameter		Crown Radius Basic	Slot Width		Slot Depth		Cup and Flat Point Diameters		Dog Point Diameters		Point Length				Oval Point Radius Basic	Cone Point Angle 90°±2° for These Nominal Lengths or Longer, 118°±2° for Shorter
											Dog		Half Dog			
			Max.	Min.	Max.	Min.	Max.	Min.	Max.	Min.	Max.	Min.	Max.	Min.		
0	0.0600	0.060	0.014	0.0010	0.020	0.016	0.033	0.027	0.040	0.037	0.032	0.028	0.017	0.013	0.045	5/64
1	0.0730	0.073	0.016	0.012	0.020	0.016	0.040	0.033	0.049	0.045	0.040	0.036	0.021	0.017	0.055	3/32
2	0.0860	0.086	0.018	0.014	0.025	0.019	0.047	0.039	0.057	0.053	0.046	0.042	0.024	0.020	0.064	7/64
3	0.0990	0.099	0.020	0.016	0.028	0.022	0.054	0.045	0.066	0.062	0.052	0.048	0.027	0.023	0.074	1/8
4	0.1120	0.112	0.024	0.018	0.031	0.025	0.061	0.051	0.075	0.070	0.058	0.054	0.030	0.026	0.084	5/32
5	0.1250	0.125	0.026	0.020	0.036	0.026	0.067	0.057	0.083	0.078	0.063	0.057	0.033	0.027	0.094	3/16
6	0.1380	0.138	0.028	0.022	0.040	0.030	0.074	0.064	0.092	0.087	0.073	0.067	0.038	0.032	0.104	3/16
8	0.1640	0.164	0.032	0.026	0.046	0.036	0.087	0.076	0.109	0.103	0.083	0.077	0.043	0.037	0.123	1/4
10	0.1900	0.190	0.035	0.029	0.053	0.043	0.102	0.088	0.127	0.120	0.095	0.085	0.050	0.040	0.142	1/4
12	0.2160	0.216	0.042	0.035	0.061	0.051	0.115	0.101	0.144	0.137	0.115	0.105	0.060	0.050	0.162	5/16
1/4	0.2500	0.250	0.049	0.041	0.068	0.058	0.132	0.118	0.156	0.149	0.130	0.120	0.068	0.058	0.188	5/16
5/16	0.3125	0.312	0.055	0.047	0.083	0.073	0.172	0.156	0.203	0.195	0.161	0.151	0.083	0.073	0.234	3/8
3/8	0.3750	0.375	0.068	0.060	0.099	0.089	0.212	0.194	0.250	0.241	0.193	0.183	0.099	0.089	0.281	7/16
7/16	0.4375	0.438	0.076	0.068	0.114	0.104	0.252	0.232	0.297	0.287	0.224	0.214	0.114	0.104	0.328	1/2
1/2	0.5000	0.500	0.086	0.078	0.130	0.120	0.291	0.270	0.344	0.334	0.255	0.245	0.130	0.120	0.375	9/16
9/16	0.5625	0.562	0.096	0.088	0.146	0.136	0.332	0.309	0.391	0.379	0.287	0.275	0.146	0.134	0.422	5/8
5/8	0.6250	0.625	0.107	0.097	0.161	0.151	0.371	0.347	0.469	0.456	0.321	0.305	0.164	0.148	0.469	3/4
3/4	0.7500	0.750	0.134	0.124	0.193	0.183	0.450	0.425	0.562	0.549	0.383	0.367	0.196	0.180	0.562	7/8

Figure A-27

Lengths for Threaded Fasteners

DIAMETER   LENGTHS

	.250	.313	.375	.438	.500	.563	.625	.750	.875	1.000	1.250	1.500	1.750	2.000	2.500	3.000	3.500	4.000
5(.125)	●	●	●	●	●	●	●	●	●	●		●						
6(.138)	●	●	●	●	●	●	●	●	●	●	●	●		●				
8(.164)	●	●	●	●	●	●	●	●	●	●	●	●		●				
10(.190)	●	●	●	●	●	●	●	●	●	●	●	●	●	●				
12(.216)	●	●	●	●	●	●	●	●	●	●		●		●				
.250	●	●	●	●	●	●	●	●	●	●	●	●	●	●	●			
.313	●	●	●	●	●	●	●	●	●	●	●	●	●	●	●			
.375	●	●	●	●	●	●	●	●	●	●	●	●		●	●	●		
.438	●	●	●	●	●	●	●	●	●	●	●	●		●	●	●		
.500	●	●	●	●	●	●	●	●	●	●	●	●		●	●	●	●	●
.563			●	●	●	●	●	●	●	●		●		●	●	●	●	●
.625			●		●	●	●	●	●	●		●		●		●		●
.750						●	●	●	●	●		●		●		●	●	●
.875							●	●	●	●		●		●		●	●	●
1.000												●		●	●	●		●

Figure A-28

Lengths for Metric Threaded Fasteners

DIAMETER   LENGTHS

	4	5	8	10	12	16	20	24	30	36	40	45	50	60	70
1.6	●	●	●												
2	●	●	●												
2.5	●	●	●	●	●										
3		●	●	●	●										
4			●	●	●	●	●								
5			●	●	●	●	●	●							
6				●	●	●	●	●							
8					●	●	●	●	●	●	●				
10						●	●	●	●	●	●	●	●	●	
12						●	●	●	●	●	●	●	●	●	●
16							●	●	●	●	●	●	●	●	●
20								●	●	●	●	●	●	●	●
24									●	●	●	●	●	●	●
30										●	●	●	●	●	●

Figure A-29

American National Standard Square and Hexagon Machine Screw Nuts
(ANSI B18.6.3-1972, R1977)

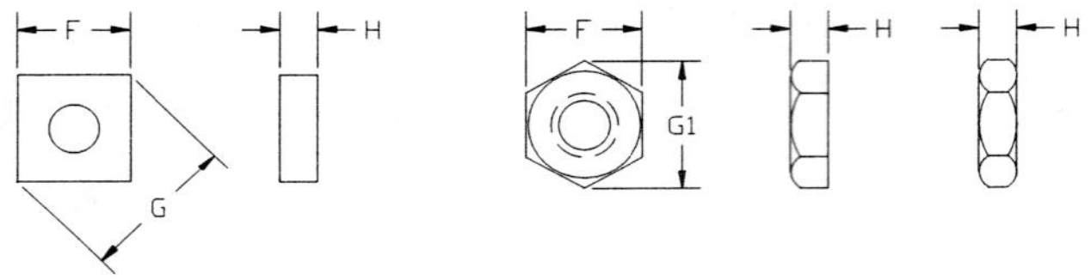

Nom. Size	Basic Diam.	Basic F	Max. F	Min. F	Max. G	Min. G	Max. G1	Min. G1	Max. H	Min. H
0	.0600	5/32	.156	.150	.221	.206	.180	.171	.050	.043
1	.0730	5/32	.156	.150	.221	.206	.180	.171	.050	.043
2	.0860	3/16	.188	.180	.265	.247	.217	.205	.066	.057
3	.0990	3/16	.188	.180	.265	.247	.217	.205	.066	.057
4	.1120	1/4	.250	.241	.354	.331	.289	.275	.098	.087
5	.1250	5/16	.312	.302	.442	.415	.361	.344	.114	.102
6	.1380	5/16	.312	.302	.442	.415	.361	.344	.114	.102
8	.1640	11/32	.344	.332	.486	.456	.397	.378	.130	.117
10	.1900	3/8	.375	.362	.530	.497	.433	.413	.130	.117
12	.2160	7/16	.438	.423	.619	.581	.505	.482	.161	.148
1/4	.2500	7/16	.438	.423	.619	.581	.505	.482	.193	.178
5/16	.3125	9/16	.562	.545	.795	.748	.650	.621	.225	.208
3/8	.3750	5/8	.625	.607	.884	.833	.722	.692	.257	.239

Figure A-30

STANDARD TWIST DRILL SIZES (inches)

SIZE	DIAMETER	SIZE	DIAMETER	SIZE	DIAMETER	SIZE	DIAMETER
40	.098	19	.166	C	.242	U	.368
39	.0995	18	.1695	D	.246	3/8	.375
38	.1015	11/64	.1719	1/4(E)	.250	V	.377
37	.104	17	.173	F	.257	W	.386
36	.1065	16	.177	G	.261	25/64	.3906
7/16	.1094	15	.180	17/64	.2656	X	.397
35	.110	14	.182	H	.266	Y	.404
34	.111	13	.185	I	.272	13/32	.4062
33	.113	3/16	.1875	J	.277	Z	.413
32	.116	12	.189	K	.281	27/64	.4219
31	.120	11	.191	9/32	.2812	7/16	.4375
1/8	.125	10	.1935	L	.290	29/64	.4531
30	.1285	9	.196	M	.295	15/32	.4688
29	.136	8	.199	19/64	.2969	31/64	.4844
28	.1405	7	.201	N	.302	1/2	.5000
9/64	.1406	13/64	.2031	5/16	.3125	9/16	.5625
27	.144	6	.204	O	.316	5/8	.625
26	.147	5	.2055	P	.323	11/16	.6875
25	.1495	4	.209	21/64	.3281	3/4	.750
24	.152	3	.213	Q	.332	13/16	.8125
23	.154	7/32	.2188	R	.339	7/8	.875
5/32	.1562	2	.221	11/32	.3438	15/16	.9375
22	.157	1	.228	S	.348		
21	.159	A	.234	T	.358		
20	.161	B	.238	23/64	.3594		

NOTES FOR TWIS DRILL SIZES - INCHES
1. This is only a partial list of standard drill sizes.
2. Whenever possible, specify hole sizes that correspond to standard drill sizes
3. Drill sizes are available in 1/64 increments between .5000 and 1.2500
4. Drill sizes are available in 1/32 increments between 1.2500 and 1.500

Figure A-31

Standard Twist Drill Sizes (Millimeters)

0.40	2.05	5.10	8.60	15.25	30.00
0.42	2.10	5.20	8.70	15.50	30.50
0.45	2.15	5.30	8.80	15.75	31.00
0.48	2.20	5.40	8.90	16.00	31.50
0.50	2.25	5.50	9.00	16.25	32.00
0.55	2.30	5.60	9.10	16.50	32.50
0.60	2.35	5.70	9.20	16.75	33.00
0.65	2.40	5.80	9.30	17.00	33.50
0.70	2.45	5.90	9.40	17.25	34.00
0.75	2.50	6.00	9.50	17.50	34.50
0.80	2.60	6.10	9.60	17.75	35.00
0.85	2.70	6.20	9.70	18.00	35.50
0.90	2.80	6.30	9.80	18.50	36.00
0.95	2.90	6.40	9.90	19.00	36.50
1.00	3.00	6.50	10.00	19.50	37.00
1.05	3.10	6.60	10.20	20.00	37.50
1.10	3.20	6.70	10.50	20.50	38.00
1.15	3.30	6.80	10.80	21.00	40.00
1.20	3.40	6.90	11.00	21.50	42.00
1.25	3.50	7.00	11.20	22.00	44.00
1.30	3.60	7.10	11.50	22.50	46.00
1.35	3.70	7.20	11.80	23.00	48.00
1.40	3.80	7.30	12.00	23.50	50.00
1.45	3.90	7.40	12.20	24.00	
1.50	4.00	7.50	12.50	24.50	
1.55	4.10	7.60	12.80	25.00	
1.60	4.20	7.70	13.00	25.50	
1.65	4.30	7.80	13.20	26.00	
1.70	4.40	7.90	13.50	26.50	
1.75	4.50	8.00	13.80	27.00	
1.80	4.60	8.10	14.00	27.50	
1.85	4.70	8.20	14.25	28.00	
1.90	4.80	8.30	14.50	28.50	
1.95	4.90	8.40	14.75	29.00	
2.00	5.00	8.50	15.00	29.50	

Figure A-32

Wire and Sheet Metal Gages

Gage	Thickness	Gage	Thickness
000 000	0.5800	18	0.0403
00 000	0.5165	19	0.0359
0 000	0.4600	20	0.0320
000	0.4096	21	0.0285
00	0.3648	22	0.0253
0	0.3249	23	0.0226
1	0.2893	24	0.0201
2	0.2576	25	0.0179
3	0.2294	26	0.0159
4	0.2043	27	0.0142
5	0.1819	28	0.0126
6	0.1620	29	0.0113
7	0.1443	30	0.0100
8	0.1285	31	0.0089
9	0.1144	32	0.0080
10	0.1019	33	0.0071
11	0.0907	34	0.0063
12	0.0808	35	0.0056
13	0.0720	36	0.0050
14	0.0641	37	0.0045
15	0.0571	38	0.0040
16	0.0508	39	0.0035
17	0.0453	40	0.0031

Figure A-33

Index